NOTORIOUS 92

Andrew E. Stoner

BLUE RIVER PRESS

Indianapolis, Indiana

Notorious 92, 3rd Edition
The Most Infamous Murders from Each of Indiana's 92 Counties
Copyright ©2007, 2009, 2017 by Andrew Stoner
All rights reserved

First edition published 2007

Published by **Blue River Press**
Indianapolis, Indiana
www.brpressbooks.com

Distributed by **Cardinal Publishers Group**
A Tom Doherty Company, Inc.
www.cardinalpub.com

ISBN: 978-1-68157-025-9

Author: Andrew Stoner
Editors: Dani McCormick, Morgan Sears
Cover Design: Phil Velikan

Printed in the United States of America

ACKNOWLEDGMENTS

This book would not have been possible without the outstanding work of journalists at Indiana newspapers, big and small, in all ninety-two counties. As the authors of the "first draft" of history, they have provided an outstanding record of these important criminal cases in our state's history.

In addition, police officers, firefighters and paramedics, prosecutors, defense attorneys, judges, and community members who have served as jurors are owed a great debt of gratitude for their part in ensuring justice is served in Indiana. Their service under sad circumstances is greatly admired and appreciated.

Several individuals were of particular help to this work, including: Javairya Ahmed, Joel Lyttle and Barry Nothstine, Indiana Department of Correction; John Clark, *Columbus Republic*; Kevin Corcoran and Barbara Hoffman, *Indianapolis Star*; Karen Davis, State of Indiana Public Access Counselor; William J. Dichtl, Ohio County Historical Museum, Rising Sun, Indiana; Donald Dunaway, Franklin County Historical Society, Brookville, Indiana; Alan January, Indiana State Archives; Craig Klugman and Andrea Cohn, *Fort Wayne Journal-Gazette*; *The Corydon Democrat*; Annette McMullen, Knox County Public Library, Vincennes, Indiana; Kevin Murley, Indiana State Clerk of the Courts Office; Darrol Pierson, Indiana State Library; David Remondini, Indiana Supreme Court; Rod Rowe, *Goshen News*; Julie Schlesselman, Whitewater Valley Community Library, Brookville, Indiana; Vince Sellers, Daviess County Museum, Jasper, Indiana; Shelley Williams, Margaret Cooper Public Library, Linton, Indiana; Fulton County Historical Society, Rochester, Indiana; and the Owen County Historical Society, Spencer, Indiana.

Special thanks to Mary Dieter, Randolph Scott, Scott Walters, Kathy Stolz, Karla Sneegas, Pam DiAgostino, Ian Hall, Lani Cohen, Stan Jackson, Mike Mulcahy, and Lou Bubala—for all of your support and story ideas.

For Chuck, Shelley, and Kirby.

INTRODUCTION

Booth Tarkington noted in his first novel, *The Gentleman from Indiana*, that "an Indiana town may lie asleep a long time, but there always comes a day when it wakes up…"

For many Indiana communities, that wake up has come in the sad realization that murder and incredible cruelty have not escaped the Hoosier ecology.

When considering murder and other violent deaths in Indiana, or any state, some sad truths become quickly known: People are often mean to one another and incredible violence cannot escape any community. According to U.S. crime statistics, in the last three decades, murders have continued to increase in our state—averaging just a tick over one murder every day—a rate of 5.8 murders for every 100,000 Indiana citizens. Despite that increase, Indiana's rank as having the nineteenth highest rate of murder in the nation is nearly equal to its rank in the 2010 census as the fifteenth most populous state.

Throughout history, the state has recorded some of the nation's most notorious crimes, and that distinction has held well into the nearly 200 years of statehood for Indiana. A legacy of law and order attitudes and values has provided swift and sure punishment for evildoers, but has not altogether prevented repeated offenses.

The state has produced or contributed two well-known killers in the nation's history—including ex-patriot Hoosiers Charles Manson and the Rev. Jim Jones—and even offered perhaps the most infamous victim of an alleged murder, Jimmy Hoffa the long-missing-and-presumed-dead former head of the Teamsters Union.

But it is the everyday, for lack of a better term, or more common cases of murder and violence in our communities that have provided some horrific context to the history of the state.

So why review some of the worst our state has to offer? Perhaps most importantly because of the reluctance of many to face the role violence has played in our history and our communities. If we pause to examine these portions of our history that we quickly work to put behind us, we see a commentary emerging about our lives, our families, and even our values. The truth is most people killed in Indiana are killed by someone they know or are related to.

Beyond these strong connections lies an even more difficult commentary to accept: alcohol and illicit drugs and the troubling intersection of sexual desire and violence contribute disproportionately to violence and the rivers of tears that flow from victims and their loved ones. Inexplicable acts have occurred on Hoosier soil that even in their review here offer little insight into the answer most needed: Why?

Children, the elderly, women, the poor, and seemingly all others who live at the margins of society including gay men and other marginalized minorities are at the center of this Indiana violence, but not exclusively. Without exception, some of our state's "best" communities and "best" families have produced some of our worst crimes.

There are the expected serial and spree killers here, the sexually violent men, the oppressive parents and reactive children of crippled families. And there are the cases that still cause us to shake our heads in sadness, or push us away in disgust and anger.

Consider what follows as a previously unexplored portion of Indiana history. Not the stuff of fourth-grade Indiana history lessons, for certain, but important nonetheless.

As we look at the means, motive, and opportunities killers have taken to destroy the lives of others, let us rededicate ourselves to preventing and eliminating such evil. The discussion can only benefit us and serve to awaken us from our long slumber of indifference.

We must not walk away without remembering the violence that has been perpetrated, and most especially, remembering the victims and their loved ones, and the law enforcement, courts, and correctional system left to deal with the aftermath of these acts.

—Andrew E. Stoner
Indianapolis, Indiana
June 2007

TABLE OF CONTENTS

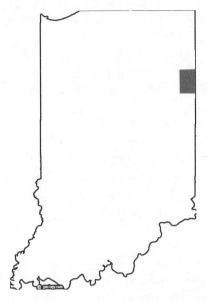

ADAMS COUNTY

VICTIM(S):
Cory R. Elson, 26

PERPETRATOR:
Mark L. Lichtenberger, 39

DATE OF DEATH(S):
April 3, 1999

A HIGH-POWERED AMBUSH

A routine traffic stop on a cool Saturday night, April 3, 1999, brought the debate on gun rights front and center to the normally peaceful streets of Decatur, Indiana, the county seat.

On that evening, Indiana State Trooper Cory R. Elson, twenty-six, attempted to stop a pickup truck driving along U.S. 27 with no working taillights. As Elson pulled the truck to a stop, the driver, Mark L. Lichtenberger, thirty-eight, stepped from the truck and began firing on Elson.

Elson, on the force for only four months at the time, was wearing his required body armor, but it was no match for the Norinko SKS semiautomatic weapon with an altered trigger assembly that Lichtenberger carried. As Lichtenberger blasted at least thirty rounds at the surprised Elson, the now fully-automatic assault weapon struck the rookie trooper in the head, legs, and the body armor meant to protect his chest and abdomen.

Lichtenberger, whom co-workers and friends described as a quiet man who believed in God and often quoted the Bible, began carrying weapons in his truck after having been stopped by police officers multiple times for various violations. Unknown to Elson, Lichtenberger had decided that the very next officer who stopped him would face his wrath.[1]

The weapon Lichtenberger carried with him was cheap and easy to access. It featured firepower far beyond what any hunter would need, or really beyond what any person would normally want in personal protection.

Its size and firepower were great, and when combined with Lichtenberger's violent thoughts, it was as lethal as could be.

Adding to its danger, Lichtenberger had altered the weapon by taping together two high-capacity magazines of bullets, allowing a quick switch to a second magazine of ammunition when the first one was expended.[2]

Following the senseless attack on Elson, a massive manhunt was undertaken throughout Adams County and neighboring counties of northeast Indiana. For hours, officers from the Indiana State Police, the Adams County Sheriff's Department, and the Decatur Police Department followed every lead they could. Lichtenberger, meanwhile, went about his regular life, even taking time to attend Easter Sunday morning worship services at the Decatur Missionary Church, as he did most weeks, but this time as he quietly sat in his regular church pew with his mother, Annabelle, he was just hours removed from having gunned down Elson.[3]

"It bothers me to think the man police say gunned down a state trooper for no apparent reason drove away from the crime scene, slept off the murder, and went to Sunday church like nothing happened," Decatur Police Chief Dick Noack said, summing up the feelings of aghast of many in the community.[4]

Although he had spent most of his life in and around Adams County, Lichtenberger was unknown to most residents. One of only ninety-eight graduates in the 1978 senior class of Adams Central High School, Lichtenberger made his living as a self-employed carpenter and self-proclaimed part-time pastor. What few knew, however, was he was a seething, ticking time bomb growing angrier by the day at law enforcement officers he thought were harassing him.

After he fired the thirty rounds at Elson, Lichtenberger drove off toward his family's home on the eastern edge of Adams County, near the Indiana-Ohio state line. Fortunately, off-duty Decatur Police Department Detective Eric Meyer and his young son were traveling by on North Thirteenth Street at about the same time. Meyer heard the shots, turned around, and investigated. It was then that he saw Lichtenberger's truck leaving the scene, and he followed briefly but gave up, fearing for the safety of his child in his vehicle. It was a good sighting—Lichtenberger was apprehended within twenty hours.

The trooper who lay dying on the street that evening had enjoyed a short but wonderful life. Just months into his new dream job as an Indiana State Trooper, he and his young wife, Amy, a Fort Wayne lawyer, were to close on their first home in Decatur on April 9. Instead, Elson's loved ones spent that day laying him to rest in a Hendricks County cemetery, near where he grew up in Brownsburg, Indiana. A graduate of Brownsburg High School, Elson had also completed a bachelor's degree in criminal justice from Indiana

University at Indianapolis, and graduated the Indiana Law Enforcement Training Academy.

"Cory was a wonderful person whose life cannot be summed up in one statement," Amy said in the days following his death. "He spent each day trying to make this world a little better for all of us, and through his efforts, he has touched so many lives."[5]

Lichtenberger never denied his responsibility for the shooting, telling the initial officers who arrested him that he was responsible for the attack.[6]

Months of legal wrangling continued, with Adams County Prosecutor Christopher Harvey opting against pursuing the death penalty against Lichtenberger when the defendant agreed to a deal that sentenced him to life in prison, with no chance of parole, plus twenty years. The judge also fined Lichtenberger $20,000—a sum no one will ever see. The plea agreement meant that four additional charges related to firearms violations were dropped.

During a plea hearing in Adams Circuit Court, Lichtenberger admitted in court that he was the one who shot at Elson's car, but "not necessarily him, but the person in the vehicle."[7]

He hesitated, however, before accepting the plea agreement. He said "my deep inner thought is not to go with this plea" but that his attorneys told him that "I could not use religious beliefs to try and save myself. The State of Indiana doesn't allow a religious defense. I understand [the plea]. There's no appeal. It's over."[8]

A month later, Lichtenberger was back in court to hear his sentence in a dramatic hearing that pitted the heartbroken family and friends of the slain young trooper against the grieving kin of the defendant, struggling to understand his horrible act.

"I don't presume to understand the sorrow the Elson family has experienced, but I fully understand the sorrow my family has experienced," Leah Lichtenberger said, in praising her brother as a "law-abiding, upstanding and fair-minded member of the community."[9]

Most of the attention, however, focused on a composed and impressive Amy Elson, who said the death of her husband had robbed her of the person who was the purpose of her life. She said Cory's "savage murder" had ended not just his life, "but also his dreams and his unlimited potential."[10]

She said she and her family were sickened and offended by Lichtenberger's attempts to use his religious beliefs to defend his actions, calling them a "mockery of Christianity."

Special Judge Steve David from Boone Circuit Court (presiding over the Adams County proceedings) agreed with the Elson family and called

Lichtenberger "a coward and a murderer. Forever after, in this community, the name 'Lichtenberger' will be associated with the murder of Trooper Elson."[11]

As Lichtenberger, just days shy of his fortieth birthday, was led from the Adams County Courthouse to begin his life behind bars, a flank of police officers silently lined both sides of the sidewalk as the killer of one of their own was led away forever.

Endnotes

1. *Decatur Daily Democrat*, April 5, 1999.
2. Ibid.
3. *Decatur Daily Democrat*, April 9, 1999.
4. Ibid.
5. *Decatur Daily Democrat*, April 5, 1999.
6. *Decatur Daily Democrat*, April 7, 1999.
7. *Decatur Daily Democrat*, June 15, 2000.
8. Ibid.
9. *Decatur Daily Democrat*, July 11, 2000.
10. Ibid.
11. Ibid.

ALLEN COUNTY

VICTIM(S):
Daniel Osborne, 35;
Jane Osborne, 34
Benjamin Osborne, 11

PERPETRATOR(S):
None convicted

DATE OF DEATH(S):
September 17, 1983

A DEADLY INVASION

Lust and greed lie at the base of one of the most horrible crimes ever in the state's second most populous county, Allen County, and the state's second largest city, Fort Wayne.

Perhaps most troubling of all is the entirely random nature of the case that unfolded during the warm fall weekend of September 17, 1983. It was then that three members of a young Fort Wayne family were brutally beaten to death in their home, while a two-year-old daughter survived. The Osborne family had just moved to Fort Wayne five months earlier when Daniel Osborne, thirty-five, accepted a new position as the editorial page editor of the city's afternoon daily, the *News-Sentinel*.

The Osbornes chose a home in the older part of the city, on the south side, at 4035 South Harrison Boulevard. The home sat in a neighborhood of well-maintained mid-century homes and boulevard streets that reflected an earlier era in this city. The random and vicious nature of the attack on the Osborne family, however, would transform the south-side neighborhood forever and signal the beginning of the exodus of professional families who fled to suburban homes in the years and decades that followed.

The terror faced by the Osborne family was not discovered until two days later on Monday morning, September 19, 1983, when Daniel did not show up for his regular shift at the newspaper. Concerned co-workers went to the home and found it locked up tight—but peering into a downstairs window they could see the slain body of Daniel's wife, Jane Osborne, thirty-four, lying on the floor.[1]

Upstairs, even more horror awaited responding police officers who located the body of Daniel's young son, Benjamin Osborne, eleven, crouched inside a sleeping bag at the foot of his parents' bed. Daniel and the family dog were both beaten to death in the bed, while the lone survivor, two-year-old daughter Caroline, wandered the house aimlessly and bloodied. She told responding police officers that "mommy and daddy are sleeping."[2]

As the investigation unfolded, ugly details came to surface. Both Mrs. Osborne and Caroline had been sexually assaulted, and it appeared Mrs. Osborne had been chased and attacked throughout the first and second floors of the home as she tried to escape her attacker.

Benjamin was the last member of the family seen alive, mowing the family's lawn about 7 p.m. Friday evening. Police were unsure why he was sleeping in his parents' room, but given that the home was new to the family and it was Friday night, his parents may have granted his request to stay in their room.

Mrs. Osborne reportedly spoke to a friend by phone at about 9:30 p.m. Friday evening and revealed nothing was wrong. The violence that would end her life had yet to be set upon her.

It wasn't until four months later, in January 1984, that a massive, high-profile investigation offered the big break that Fort Wayne Police Department detectives needed as they arrested Calvin Perry, III, an eighteen-year-old from the Osbornes' neighborhood. He was the prime suspect in another attack on a seventy-four-year-old woman in her south-side home.

Under questioning for that crime, he confessed he had committed the crimes at the Osborne home late that Friday night and randomly selected the home for a break-in because he saw the lights on and longed for a confrontation. Perry used a baseball bat and a clock radio he found in the home to bludgeon his victims to death.[3]

No trial could be held, however, and the case came to an abrupt end just days later on January 17, 1984, when Perry was found hanging from a noose investigators said he fashioned from the fabric cover on the mattress in his cell. A note reading, "I haven't killed nobody," was found, but little else. A ten-month investigation by the U.S. Justice Department ruled Perry's death a suicide involving no foul play.[4]

Local civil rights activists remained unconvinced. Perry, who was black, was found hanging "hammock style" in his cell with his feet tied to the jail cell bed and his neck tied to the bars. A local coroner said a person could hang himself that way, but many others remained skeptical.[5]

For her part, Caroline Osborne told the *Fort Wayne Journal-Gazette* in a 2003 article on the twentieth anniversary of the attacks that she had no memories of what had happened to her or her family. "I was so young that I don't remember," she said.

Living out of state with extended relatives, Caroline has asked questions over the years about the death of her family and talked to a therapist when she was an adolescent. "I do wish I could have known my mother," she said. "I wish I could have known my father and my brother."[6]

She's never returned to Fort Wayne but has researched the sad case through online newspaper archives. She thinks she will never visit Fort Wayne. If she did, she'd find the Harrison Boulevard area greatly changed.[7]

Perry was eventually linked to a dozen other break-ins, including six rapes on the south side, though many remained convinced someone carried out an ultimate punishment on Perry inside the Allen County Jail.

Endnotes

1. *Fort Wayne News-Sentinel*, Sept. 19, 1983.
2. *Fort Wayne News-Sentinel*, Sept. 20, 1983.
3. *Fort Wayne Journal-Gazette*, Jan. 14, 1984.
4. Associated Press, Jan. 18, 1984; Associated Press, Oct. 14, 1984.
5. *Fort Wayne News-Sentinel*, Jan. 18, 1984; *New York Times*, Jan. 21, 1984; Associated Press, Oct. 14, 1984.
6. *Fort Wayne Journal-Gazette*, Sept. 14, 2003.
7. Ibid.

BARTHOLOMEW COUNTY

VICTIM(S):
Jamie Engelking, 21;
Amanda Davis, 12;
Jessica Brown, 2;
Brandon Engelking, Jr., 1

PERPETRATOR(S):
Robert Bassett, Jr., 35

DATE OF DEATH(S):
August 15-16, 1998

TAKING ADVANTAGE OF JAMIE

Twenty-one-year-old Jamie Engelking was a lot like other young women who become young mothers—she wanted a normal family, a nest for her children, and a man in her life.

In fact, it was Jamie's desire for her husband, the father of the youngest of her two children, to be with her that caused her to be swindled out of nearly $25,000 in the last months of her life. A trio of "friends" had convinced Jamie that if she sold her house and took out an additional personal loan, she could afford to pay a Jennings County lawyer to work on getting her husband, Brandon Engelking, Sr., released from the Plainfield Correctional Center. Brandon was housed there on burglary and auto theft charges. Jamie sold the house in 1998 and turned over the proceeds to her "friends," which eventually led nowhere but to the realization that she'd been ripped off and there was no lawyer to help.

The weeks leading up to Jamie's death were ones of change. During one of the last weekends of August 1998, she began moving into a new apartment while trying to hold on to her second-shift, hourly-wage job at R.R. Donnelly in Seymour, Indiana. Family and friends helped care for her kids, Jessica Brown, two, and Brandon Engelking, Jr., one. One of those who helped watch over Jamie's kids was a mature twelve-year-old family friend, Amanda Davis, who was as much Jamie's friend as many adults were.

It was during the weekend of August 15-16 that Jamie announced she was going on a quick camping trip in southern Bartholomew County, to an area known as Azalia Bottoms along the east fork of the White River just outside tiny Waynesville, Indiana. The camping trip seemed a bit abrupt to some, especially since Jamie had not finished moving all of her belongings into her new apartment. Regardless, she packed up the kids and asked Amanda to come along. It's unknown how far into the camping trip the group got— Jamie and the kids were last seen about 5:30 p.m. Saturday evening, August 15 riding in a two-tone brown pick-up truck driven by a white male with shoulder-length brown hair.

Some concern rose when the four did not return as expected on Sunday afternoon, and that concern grew ever greater when Jamie missed a child custody hearing on Tuesday in Jackson Circuit Court, something she would never do.

Detectives from the Seymour Police Department, the sheriff's departments in both Jackson and Bartholomew counties, and the Indiana State Police conducted an extensive search. A month into the search and following a hunch by two investigators, Bartholomew County Sheriff's Captain Keith Foster and Detective Todd Downs, the officers took all-terrain vehicles on a quick ride along the river. It led to the grisly discovery of a bone and a baby's diaper along the river's edge on Thursday morning, September 17. The officers followed a growing stench in the area to four shallow graves. A forensic investigation led by the Bartholomew County Coroner and anthropologists from the University of Indianapolis revealed the truth: The graves contained the bodies of Jamie Engelking, Amanda Davis, Jessica Brown, and Brandon Engelking, Jr. All four had been murdered.

The intense summer heat had already begun to quickly decompose the bodies. Small red flags were planted in the sandy ground to mark pieces of evidence, body matter, or bone found. The graves were slightly disturbed by animals in the nearly four weeks since the group went missing. Autopsies were difficult to conduct since the bodies had been reduced to mostly skeletal remains by the time they were found. Pathologists did determine that two-year-old Jessica died from a stab wound to the head and had a broken arm and shoulder, while one-year-old Brandon suffered a fatal fracture to the back of his skull. Their mother, Jamie, died from multiple stab wounds to the back that pierced her spin and ribs, while twelve-year-old Amanda Davis suffered a slashed throat and spinal cord.

Police quickly narrowed in on Robert Bassett, Jr., thirty-five, of Rosstown, Indiana, who had once shared a prison cell with Jamie's husband at Pendleton.

Bassett's brown pick-up truck was impounded and searched, although police stopped short of publicly naming him a suspect. Bassett did have a troubled past—he served consecutive sentences for two counts of child molestation and was held at the Plainfield Correctional Center from June 12, 1987 until May 3, 1998, just three months before Jamie and the children were found dead. He previously pled guilty to the rape of a sixteen-year-old girl when he was just nineteen years old, and while on probation from that charge, he was accused of the rape, criminal confinement, and battery of the woman he lived with. A hung jury ended his trial on those charges.

Jamie had mentioned to family and friends that she had met a new guy, Bob, and was dating him despite still being married to her incarcerated husband. In fact, Jamie's telephone conversation during the early morning hours of the day she left for the camping trip with a "Bob" was overheard by victim Amanda Davis's mother, Kim Galbraith. Police review of phone records from Galbraith's home indicated that call (and many other calls from Jamie's home) went to Bassett's home in Bartholomew County.

It took two years of work, but answers finally began to fall into place. As he was led to the Bartholomew County Jail in Columbus on July 6, 2000 to face the quadruple murder charges pending against him, Bassett pulled his T-shirt over his face and hid from news cameras.[1]

A lynchpin to the state's case would prove essential in the months to come. Bassett's alibi that he stayed home throughout the night of August 15, 1998 playing video games with his nephew Jessie Bassett fell apart immediately. Jessie, after initially lying in a vain attempt to cover for his uncle, eventually told police and testified in court that his uncle left the Bassett home between midnight and 1 a.m. during the overnight hours of August 15-16, 1998 and did not return until the next day—leaving him plenty of time to kill and bury the four victims.

Police also enlisted the help of the FBI in analyzing and comparing soil from the scene of the shallow graves to that of soil found on shovels at Bassett's home. Fibers recovered at the murder and burial site also matched those of a seat cushion cover in Bassett's pick-up truck.

Finally, police developed what they always believed was at least part of a motive for the crime. In the trash can in Jamie Engelking's apartment was an unfinished letter to "Bob" that indicated she might be pregnant with his child. Further, medical records indicated that Jamie had taken her daughter, Jessica, to a pediatrician on August 6, 1998 (just before the camping trip) to determine whether she had been sexually molested.

Given Bassett's past for sexual molestation, he was not permitted to have a female friend with small children present—and a pregnant Jamie would make it impossible to deny a relationship with her, a violation of his parole that would send him back to prison. Jamie may have confronted Bassett in the closing weeks of her life with her suspicions about Jessica's possible molestation. Police interviewed Jamie's aunt who told them Jamie said Bassett would kill her if she revealed their relationship to anyone.

Regardless, little conclusive physical evidence linked Bassett to the killings, and a weapon was never recovered. Pathologists said marks on the victims' bones indicated a knife or some other blunt, sharp object was used in the attacks.

Bassett's first trial began in July 2001 and included testimony from Jamie's still-incarcerated husband, Brandon Engelking, Sr., who said Jamie told him Bassett had raped her and threatened to kill her and the children.

Bassett testified as well, denying he killed Jamie and saying he had met Jamie only one time to receive $100 from her as a repayment of a loan he had made her husband in prison. He admitted they had talked many times subsequent to that on the phone, but that he had never been in her company since. His claim of playing Nintendo video games all night with a nephew, the same night Jamie and the children went missing, was contradicted by the earlier testimony from his nephew who did not verify his story.

Prosecutors were able to get Bassett to admit on the stand that although he considered Jamie his friend, he never again called or checked into her whereabouts after August 16, 1998, when it was reported to him by her family members that she was missing.

The eight-woman, four-man jury returned a guilty verdict against Bassett on July 26, 2001 on all four counts. He later was sentenced to life in prison, but in 2003, the Indiana Supreme Court overturned his conviction, ruling that some evidence and testimony in his original trial were presented improperly.

Prosecutors tried again, this time with the trial moved further east to Dearborn County in Lawrenceburg, Indiana. Testimony in the second trial closely mirrored the first; however, investigators did focus on a photograph of Bassett found under the mattress of Jamie's bed in her apartment, and a mix of cigarette butts found at her home and the murder scene that may have linked Bassett to both locations. On May 22, 2006, jurors again announced Bassett guilty on all four counts.

In July 2006, Dearborn Circuit Court Judge James Humphrey sentenced Bassett to life in prison without the possibility of parole. Bassett, who has continually denied any involvement in the four deaths, plans another appeal.

Endnotes
1. *Columbus Republic*, July 7, 2000.

BENTON COUNTY

VICTIM(S):
John W. Barce, 73

PERPETRATOR(S):
Lloyd D. Lichti, 63

DATE OF DEATH(S):
August 1, 2001

REVENGE DELAYED, BUT NOT DENIED

When Lloyd Lichti's father, Herv, died in 1980, Lloyd believe he was entitled to $40,000 from his father's estate and the sale of his Jasper County farm. When he got nothing, Lloyd began to seethe in anger and began looking for someone to blame.

Herv Lichti had left his entire estate to his new wife, Ella Lichti, and Lloyd got nothing. Lloyd, a struggling independent mortgage broker from West Lafayette, believed his stepmother Ella had conspired with her attorney to cut him and his two older brothers out of their share of the money. As the years went by, Lloyd's anger at the situation grew almost as fast as his own personal debt and the realization that his mortgage business was broke.

Lloyd continued to press for a portion of the estate from his father's widow, prompting her attorney, John W. Barce of Fowler, Indiana, to step in in 1995. Barce, the former Benton County prosecutor and the proud father of two sons who also became county prosecutors in Benton and Newton counties, had settled into a comfortable private practice. He was used to handling estate issues, and drafted what seemed to be a routine letter to Lloyd Lichti on behalf of his client. The letter said, "Mrs. Lichti is under no legal obligation to you. Mrs. Lichti is not in a financial position to make further money advances to you, and has made her own arrangements for handling her further financial disbursements."[1]

It was an answer Lloyd was unwilling to accept.

Later in the fall of 2000, Lichti began telephoning Barce's office using the name of "Martin Price" and requesting a meeting. Lloyd left Barce waiting at two meetings where he failed to show. He called again in July 2001, asking for another meeting. Barce agreed to meet "Martin Price" at the Radisson Hotel in Lafayette and told his staff he planned to bill the man for the missed meetings if he missed for a third time.

Barce showed up for the 9 a.m. meeting on August 1 at the Radisson and was never seen alive again. Witnesses would later say they saw Barce leaving the hotel with a man fitting Lichti's description.

Later that day, Barce's wife, Patricia, received a startling telephone call with what she believed to be a tape-recorded message from her husband saying, "We have a problem. We have a serious problem."[2]

Mrs. Barce said she was instructed by a man calling himself "Chicago" to get $100,000 in $100 bills and take them to the Payless Supermarket in nearby West Lafayette and wait for more instructions via the pay phone outside the store. Mrs. Barce reported that her husband's voice did not respond to her questions, causing her to believe he had been recorded earlier.

What Mrs. Barce did not know was that after the money demand was made, Lichti had decided to release John Barce back at the Radisson. Lichti would later claim that while en route to abandon his plan, Barce suddenly died while bound inside a van. Lichti said he panicked and drove off Soldiers Home Road in Tippecanoe County (near his home) and dumped the well-known attorney's body in a grassy field. It would lie there decomposing until discovered many weeks later on September 16, 2001.

It's believed Barce died of a heart attack during the excitement of being abducted, bound, and driven around in Lichti's van. A doctor would later testify that Barce suffered two previous heart attacks and took two blood pressure medications daily.[3]

Even though John Barce had died, and Lichti claimed later that he had given up his plan to extort money from the Barce family, the calls from "Chicago" to the grandmotherly Patricia Barce continued. An August 23, 2001 typed letter to the family claimed Barce was still alive and demanded $200,000 in cash to be left at a Taco Bell restaurant. No abductor ever showed at the cash drop.

The calls continued even after Barce's body was found in mid-September, still demanding money in exchange for the return of personal items taken from Barce's body, or alleged information about his abductors. In total, five separate calls from "Chicago" to Mrs. Barce's Fowler home were tape recorded by the FBI. In one, a deal was struck to leave $2,000 in a park near Purdue University in exchange for John Barce's prosecutor's badge and checkbook. The drop was made on November 3, 2001, under secret surveillance, but no one ever claimed it. Ironically, police spotted Lichti in the park the same day as the money drop but failed at that point to make a connection between him and the Barce case.

During the calls, Mrs. Barce remained calm and negotiated with the caller regarding his demands. In one, she expressed her concern for her husband's abductor, urging him to come forward, and said, "I want you to know I really am concerned about your safety and we're praying for you."[4]

On January 2, 2002, a full five months after Barce had been abducted and more than three months since his body had been found, the family received yet another call asking for money. This time, the call was traced to a telephone at the Creative Arts building on the Purdue University campus. State Police and Purdue University Police officers made it to the phone in time to see Lichti still on the line. When he hung up the phone, they detained him and took him in for questioning.

During questioning, Lichti initially told a hard-to-believe tale of a band of kidnappers who had used him to get Barce. He later recanted and told detectives that he had acted alone in abducting the former prosecutor and had done it to get back at Barce for how he handled the estate, cutting him and his brothers out. A third time through, Lichti withdrew that version and went back to his tale of describing outside abductors who used Lichti to nab Barce.[5]

Lichti stood trial for two counts of the kidnapping, criminal confinement, robbery, theft, and felony murder of Barce in March 2004 in Tippecanoe County, where it is believed Barce actually succumbed. At trial, prosecutors had a solid case—including a pre-paid calling card used by the "Chicago" caller to make demands of Mrs. Barce (and in Lichti's possession when he was first detained by police) and envelopes and handwriting samples in Lichti's houses that forensically matched those containing ransom demands.

Sequestered jurors listened to five days of testimony and deliberated about eleven hours over two days before returning guilty verdicts on all seven charges pending against Lichti. Jurors reported they struggled over the robbery and felony murder counts; however, Indiana law states that a person is guilty of murder if they cause, even unintentionally, the death of another person while committing a felony. Jurors believed that the stress Barce was placed under, combined with high temperatures (above 90 degrees) and high humidity that August day, led to his death.

Ironically, Ella Lichti, the stepmother Lloyd believed conspired to keep him from his share of his father's money, died of natural causes at age ninety on August 7, 2001—just six days after Barce was abducted and died. Police determined that Mrs. Lichti's death in Florida was unrelated to the Barce case.

Lichti was sentenced to fifty-five years for felony murder and another four years for the robbery charge, and transported to the Indiana State Prison at Michigan City. His May 2005 appeal to the Indiana Court of Appeals was unsuccessful. He will not be eligible for parole before 2029, when he will be 87 years old.

Endnotes

1. *Lafayette Journal & Courier*, March 2, 2004.
2. Ibid.
3. *Lafayette Journal & Courier*, March 3, 2004.
4. Ibid.
5. *Lafayette Journal & Courier*, Jan. 4, 2002.

BLACKFORD COUNTY

VICTIM(S):
Gerald L. Uptegraft, 42

PERPETRATOR(S):
Rollie A. Cook, 36

DATE OF DEATH(S):
June 22, 1949

A MOTHER'S LAMENT; A SON'S DOWNFALL

Iva Cook declared she was "glad it was all over" and that her son Rollie's downfall had been his own fault because of his obsession with "liquor and affairs with women."

Thirty-six-year-old "Big Rollie," as he was known, met his demise on Monday, June 20, 1949, in a deadly shootout with Blackford County Sheriff Gerald L. Uptegraft and other officers after terrorizing his mother and neighbors over the lost love of an eighteen-year-old girl. Who knows if the death of his father, Alonzo Cook, just three weeks earlier was a contributing factor, but investigators believe Rollie became increasingly agitated as he drank a bottle of wine inside his mother's Hartford City home at 620 West Fulton Street. At that time, he told his mother he was going to walk down the street and kill Betty Monroe, the eighteen-year-old daughter of neighbors Mr. and Mrs. Raymond Monroe. He also threatened to then kill Blackford County Prosecutor Alfred Hollander before killing himself so he could "go to hell," his mother said.

Concerned about his continued rants and threats, Mrs. Cook went downtown to the Blackford County Jail to report her son's actions to police. Sheriff Uptegraft tried to "dismiss her from her worries and ... forget about his troubles."[1] Mrs. Cook said her son would listen to the sheriff and be peaceful but would resent other officers coming along or trying to arrest him.

Sheriff Uptegraft left the jail just before 7 p.m. to go to the Cook home to try to calm Rollie. Once there, he found Rollie in the living room holding a .22 caliber Mossburg automatic rifle, leveled at the officer during the entire time of their conversation. Uptegraft remained calm, talking gently to Rollie and asking him to calm down.

"It was reported that as [Rollie] Cook talked about grievances relating to his anger toward members of the Monroe family, and particularly toward the Monroe daughter, Betty, he became more disturbed and restless," the *Hartford City News-Times* reported. At one point, Rollie stepped outside briefly, allowing Sheriff Uptegraft to call for assistance from other officers.

One deputy sheriff, one Hartford City patrolman, and Hartford City Police Chief John Landis responded to Uptegraft's call. As the officers attempted to enter the home, Rollie began firing his weapon, capable of shooting twelve rounds before reloading. Although the shooting was fast and furious, Sheriff Uptegraft and the other officers got off rounds in return fire. By now, Cook "had gone totally berserk ... he leveled the gun at the sheriff, the shot striking the officer in the side. Cook then switched the weapon to the other officers, with one shot striking Landis."[2]

Although critically wounded, Sheriff Uptegraft remained on his feet until the officers' shots silenced Cook. In the melee, Chief Landis was struck with a bullet. The remaining two officers rushed the sheriff to an ambulance for transport to the Blackford County Hospital, and loaded Chief Landis into a squad car for treatment as well. In the end, the sheriff's wounds were fatal with the officer finally expiring at 9:30 a.m. on Wednesday, June 22, 1949. Chief Landis, struck in one leg by a bullet, recovered from his wounds.

The hours leading up to the shootout that broke the normal quiet of the Hartford City neighborhood foretold the violence to come. Mrs. Cook said her son brooded for hours over the latest broken romance in his life. Married four times previous, and the father of seven children by two of his previous wives, Rollie had developed an infatuation with Betty Monroe. Mrs. Cook said she sought to dissuade his interest in the eighteen-year-old because of the difference in their ages.

There was no dissuading Rollie. He had become obsessed with Betty, visiting the Hartford County Prosecutor's Office earlier in the week asking them to file charges against her and her family for breach of promise. He also nailed a small sign to a tree in the yards separating the Cook and Monroe homes warning the Monroe family to keep out of sight or risk being shot.

The gun used in the incident was borrowed by Rollie from another neighbor on the pretext of going crow hunting. When the neighbor later attempted to retrieve the gun, Rollie shot at his feet. He did similarly to a third neighbor who, when questioned, said he did not know where the Monroe family was at the time. Unknown to Rollie, Mrs. Cook had already used her car to spirit the Monroe family away from the area earlier in the afternoon before Rollie could see them.

"I knew death was in his eyes," Mrs. Cook said. "But all the pleading I could do did not stop him. He was wild and I knew it would be someone's life or his own."[3]

Investigators believed the shootout was planned. Officers found a note in the house written by Rollie that said, "Before the night is over, I will kill Betty and I ain't fooling. I love her so much and no other mother fucker will get her and that will settle a lot of trouble in this end of town. I am old enough to die anyhow. Tell Gerald's [Uptegraft] wife I loved Gerald, he is a good man, but not to try and take me alive. I was in the army too long. I got a gun now that can really talk now."[4]

Another note, apparently addressed to his mother, attempted to explain his actions. "Mom, now you don't know where I am, but I am going to kill Betty, and I ain't fooling. She has made an ass out of enough people. And the prosecutor won't do anything, so I am going to take him with me. Big Rollie."[5]

An autopsy showed that the officers' shots struck Rollie Cook five times—in the hand, shoulder, neck, and twice in the chest. The county coroner quickly ruled the death a "justifiable homicide" and noted Cook's coveralls contained two concealed knives as well.

A World War II veteran, reports indicated he suffered "shell shock" from intense fighting he witnessed in Luxemburg, France, and Czechoslovakia. He received a general discharge due to his mental state in February 1946. His mental state never much improved after the war, Mrs. Cook said, and neighbors reported he had grown increasingly agitated over the days leading up to the shooting.

Sheriff Uptegraft was buried two days later. A Purple Heart recipient, Uptegraft was a navy veteran of World War II, where he served in the Pacific theatre. Seriously injured in a 1945 Japanese attack, Uptegraft had suffered first-, second-, and third-degree burns in the battle and took several months to recover before coming home to Indiana. He won re-election to a second term as sheriff in the November 1948 election until his life was cut short by a madman.

Endnotes
1. *Hartford City News-Times*, June 21, 1949.
2. Ibid.
3. Ibid.
4. Ibid.
5. Ibid.

BOONE COUNTY

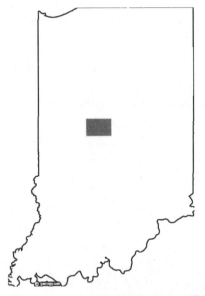

VICTIM(S):
Rev. William H. Radcliffe, 39

PERPETRATOR(S):
Gerald Wayne Bivens, 41

DATE OF DEATH(S):
January 17, 1991

A PASTOR MAKES HIS FINAL CALL

The Reverend William H. Radcliffe had already resigned as pastor of the Badger Grove Community Church in Brookston, Indiana, on January 16, 1991, but he kept his word and went to visit a church member scheduled for surgery at an Indianapolis hospital. He didn't have to go; he was no longer the pastor. But it was a commitment he made, and he wanted to be of pastoral service wherever he could.

It was during his return to his Boone County home that his life would come to a violent and tragic end. His path would cross with someone he likely had met before, but whether he recognized the man or not, it didn't matter. A killer was in his presence, and Rev. Radcliffe would not make it home to his family.

As he drove north on I-65 that Wednesday night, Radcliffe's 1985 Chevrolet overheated and stopped running. Radcliffe called his wife, Karen, at about 11:45 p.m. from a state highway rest stop, about seven miles north of Lebanon. He told her he was having car trouble but would be on his way shortly, after filling some water bottles to cool off the radiator.

A short time later, at 12:06 a.m., Radcliffe was found by a trucker crumpled on the floor of the men's room, clinging to life. He had been shot execution style in the back of the head in a toilet stall. He was rushed by ambulance back to the same hospital he had just left, Methodist Hospital in Indianapolis. His wallet, credit cards, and car keys were all missing, although his car remained on the scene.

Despite the best efforts to save him, Radcliffe died two hours later.

The robbery and shooting of Rev. Radcliffe was the last in a violent series of crimes that evening. Earlier, at around 9:30 p.m., a group of men stole items from the Lazarus Department Store in Lafayette. A short time later, around 10:30 p.m., the Dollar Inn near I-65 in Lafayette was robbed at gunpoint. A closed gas station across the street was also burglarized. Thirty minutes later, the Holiday Inn at I-65 and State Road 39 in Lebanon was robbed. Bullets fired into a wall at the armed robbery, likely from a .38 caliber weapon, matched the one that entered and exited Rev. Radcliffe's head.

As disturbing as Radcliffe's slaying had been, the Holiday Inn robbery proved equally troubling. A hotel guest from Michigan was robbed at gunpoint and tied up, and worked for three hours to free himself and call police. The man had been swimming in the hotel's pool when confronted by the men and forced back to his room. The hotel employees at the Dollar Inn were also tied up in the robbery there.

Boone County Sheriff Ern Hudson and other area investigators acted quickly and were able to release a composite drawing of one of the suspects, a white male, the very next day. A van stolen from the Holiday Inn guest was also quickly recovered by Lebanon Police. But arrests would be longer in coming.

On February 20, Hudson and sheriff's deputies picked up Gerald Wayne Bivens, a thirty-one-year-old man from Indianapolis, who had been in trouble before. At the time of detaining him, Bivens was viewed as only an informant providing police with information about the Radcliffe murder. He had already given police the names of two men he said were responsible for the murder. It was in the role of informant that Bivens was leading police to a home on the south side of Indianapolis on March 27. Hudson had agreed to remove Bivens' handcuffs and wear a wire, while pretending to be Bivens' uncle in an attempt to gain more information about the murder. Moments after removing the cuffs, however, Bivens struck the sheriff over the head with a blunt object and fled on foot. He was arrested a short time later at a Beech Grove home.

Shortly thereafter, detectives obtained an incriminating statement from Bivens' wife, Patricia, detailing the activities of Bivens and his friends the night of the murder and robberies. Police charged Bivens on April 11 with Rev. Radcliffe's murder, the robberies, vehicle theft, and perjury. Eventually, Bivens began implicating himself in statements to police and at one point led them to a .38 caliber gun, which officers recovered from Wildcat Creek in Tippecanoe County.

The dominoes started to fall quickly: On April 12, police arrested one of Bivens' co-conspirators, Ronald L. Chambers, thirty, of Lafayette, and also charged him with murder, robbery, and vehicle theft. A third man, Scott "Red

Dog" Weyls, thirty-three, of Lebanon, was nabbed two days earlier on similar charges by police in Fountain County, and gave a statement implicating himself, Bivens, and Chambers.

Weyls' statement also provided the first idea of a possible motive for killing Rev. Radcliffe. Weyls quoted Bivens as saying he killed him "to see what it felt like to kill someone," but trial testimony would later reveal that Bivens was worried Rev. Radcliffe had recognized him. Bivens had previously been treated for alcohol and drug addiction problems at New Directions, a court referral agency in Lafayette. Rev. Radcliffe had just started work there as a counselor/director.

Bivens, who at first hoped to just serve as a police informant to try to elude being implicated in the crime, told a reporter he first started feeding police information about the crimes because his conscience bothered him. "It had been bothering me, it still bothers me," Bivens said. "I woke up many nights with nightmares."[1]

Because much of the information he provided police was false, perjury charges were also added. An Indianapolis man and a Bloomington man, in fact, were held for about forty-eight hours for possible involvement in the case on the basis of information Bivens provided to police.

Bivens was convicted on March 7, 1992, for murder, robbery, criminal confinement, auto theft, and two additional counts of theft. On June 5, 1992, he was sentenced to death by Boone County Superior Court Special Judge Thomas Milligan for the murder and robbery of Rev. Radcliffe. In late 1994, Bivens announced he would waive further appeals of his conviction but changed his mind and pursued additional appeals to the U.S. Supreme Court in 1996, and the Indiana Supreme Court in 2000.

Life on Indiana's Death Row had not been easy for Bivens. Indiana Corrections officials reported he had been involved in at least nineteen of the more than sixty serious offenses reported on Death Row in a ten-year period, including a violent attack on a guard that meant he had to be locked down in his cell twenty-two hours a day.

Declaring he was tired of life in prison, citing what he said was abusive treatment from prison officials and displeasure with his lawyers, Bivens said he would pursue no further appeals. "It's the only way I can escape them and the abuse … it's constant, that and the frustration with the attorneys. It comes back to haunt you, taking someone's life," he said in the final days before his execution.[2]

He still had little in the way of a meaningful explanation for taking Rev. Radcliffe's life, other than saying he thought he saw a "fat wallet" in the man's pocket and was worried that he would recognize him. In the end, robbing Rev. Radcliffe only netted the men $18.

Bivens was executed by lethal injection at the Indiana State Prison in Michigan City on March 14, 2001.

Weyls was sentenced on the robbery charges and auto theft charges in Boone County in August 1991 and received a lesser sentence after it was learned Bivens was the triggerman. Chambers was convicted on various robbery charges in both Tippecanoe and Boone counties in December 1991 and January 1992, respectively. He was rearrested and convicted of criminal recklessness charges in 2006 in Marion County.

Rev. Radcliffe's wife, Karen, offered a brief written statement at the time of Bivens' execution saying, "Although I may have been able to forgive the men involved, forgiveness does not mean that it's OK. Neither does it imply a memory loss, as in forgive and forget."[3]

Endnotes

1. *Lebanon Reporter*, April 15, 1991.
2. *Lafayette Journal & Courier*, March 9, 2001.
3. *Lafayette Journal & Courier*, March 12, 2001.

BROWN COUNTY

VICTIM(S):
Clarence Roberts, 62;
Geneva Roberts, 59;
"John Doe," unknown white male,
60-65 years of age

PERPETRATOR(S):
Clarence Roberts, 62

DATE OF DEATH(S):
November 18, 1970 and
November 30, 1980

THE TWO DEATHS OF CLARENCE ROBERTS

In his time, Clarence Roberts had established himself as a trustworthy and respected member of the Nashville, Indiana, area, so much so he was elected sheriff of Brown County and served as a director of the Nashville State Bank.

After finishing his term as sheriff, Clarence and his brother Carson Roberts started the Roberts Brothers Lumber Company of Nashville, and also owned an apartment building in Nashville. At the same time, another brother, Warren Roberts, was serving a term as Brown County sheriff.

Unknown to most, however, was that Clarence Roberts was in big trouble financially. His debt far outweighed his assets, and civil court cases and judgments were already pending against him in the Brown County courts. His debts also stretched into Fulton County in northern Indiana where Clarence had grain mill and lumber company properties in Akron, Claypool, and Mentone, Indiana.

The Farmers State Bank of Mentone won a $45,000 judgment against Clarence; the Irwin Union Bank & Trust Company of Columbus said Clarence owed them more than $9,000; while the First State Bank of Morgantown reported it held a defaulted $25,000 mortgage on Clarence's home. The

Nashville State Bank, where Clarence had once served as a director, confirmed Clarence owed the bank money but declined to say how much.

Adding to the worries, a half-dozen lumber company and wholesale suppliers also held unpaid bills from Clarence ranging from as little as $900 to as much as $12,000.

Clarence may have been looking for a way out.

It was during this time that he purchased just under $1 million in life insurance on himself.

Then on November 18, 1970, a fire was reported on the Roberts' property located about three miles north of Nashville along Indiana Route 135, near Grandma Barnes Road. The fire was contained to a garage but destroyed the structure, and firefighters sifting through the rubble found the charred remains of a man.

Investigators initially referred to the burned body as a "mystery man, 60-65 years old, balding white hair and about 5' 8" in height."[1]

State Police Detective Donal Kuster said, "We have no idea of this man's identity, but we have at least 12 witnesses who say they saw him with [Clarence] Roberts."[2]

Kuster said witnesses described seeing Clarence stopping to assist an obviously intoxicated man on Friday, November 17. The man had been asked to leave a Nashville liquor store, and then fell on a sidewalk outside. Another witness reported seeing the two men drive off together in Clarence's 1969 Oldsmobile before an ambulance summoned for the man could arrive.

One witness even reported speaking to Clarence directly, suggesting that if he intended to take him to the hospital, it would be easier if he drove his car over to where the man was, rather than having the man walk. Clarence complied, and the two left the scene.

It would not be the last sighting of Clarence, but it would prove to be the last clue in a never-ended mystery into the identity of the man who stumbled and fell and whom witnesses believed the former sheriff assisted that day.

At 6:15 p.m. on Saturday, November 18, as volunteer firefighters were summoned to the Roberts' property to put out the garage fire, they encountered a stubborn blaze and were able to save a pick-up truck from the blaze, but Clarence's 1969 Olds was destroyed.

The garage, a fifty-by-twenty-foot structure had a small addition built onto it, and that is where firefighters found the body of the man, lying on his back, with a 16-gauge shotgun stretched across his chest and a 33rd degree Mason ring with the name "Clarence Roberts" inscribed inside the band near the body.

Detective Kuster was dubious that the body was that of Clarence from the start. During the autopsy, medical examiners reported the body had only one tooth remaining. Clarence wore a partial denture but still had many of his own teeth, his wife told police. Death was ruled due to carbon monoxide poisoning from the fire, but pathologists believe the victim (who only had one kidney) was dead *before* the fire was set. (Clarence's wife, Geneva, said her husband had never undergone surgery.)

Although an exact identity had not been made on the man's body, Clarence's wife and sons conducted a funeral for him, and the remains were buried on November 21, 1970, in Nashville's Memorial Park Cemetery under the name "Clarence Roberts."

Joining Kuster in initially doubting the body to be that of Clarence, however, was even Clarence's brother, Brown County Sheriff Warren Roberts.

"While the search continues for the mystery man, ambiguity of rumor and fact have set the normal quiet winter of this summer tourist mecca to humming with speculation on the puzzling circumstances surrounding the Nov. 18 fire which burned a man's body beyond recognition," the *Bloomington Herald-Telephone* reported on the mood in Brown County.[3]

Because the Mason's ring was found, Clarence's wife, Geneva, and her sons, Bernard, Forrest, and Loren Roberts, were convinced the body found in the burned garage was that of their loved one.

"He loved that ring, and all that it stood for. I just can't believe he would take it off for any reason," she told the *Bloomington Herald-Telephone*.[4]

She did question why the ring was found near the body and not on his left hand as it normally was worn. Investigators reported that both hands of the man's body had been burned off in the intense blaze.

Mrs. Roberts and her sons were not home at the time of the fire, and came home to find firefighters already there. The state fire marshal eventually declared the fire arson.

On December 8, 1970, Indiana State Police announced that blood samples taken from the corpse during the autopsy revealed a blood type of AB, and "from blood samples we have taken from all members of Clarence Roberts' family, we have determined Roberts cannot have AB blood."[5]

Despite such news, Geneva Roberts remained convinced her husband had died in the fire. "He wasn't a coward about anything," she said, acknowledging his financial troubles, but dubbing them "not that bad."[6]

"I am so certain it was him," she said. "They found his ring in the fire. He thought more of that ring than most anything. By that ring being there, I am satisfied it was him. The ring itself is evidence enough for me."[7]

A wedding ring Clarence had worn for the more than thirty years he was married to Geneva was not found on the scene, however.

On December 21, 1970, the body buried by the Roberts' family earlier was exhumed and sent to Indianapolis for additional testing, which again failed to prove it was Clarence. As the months rolled into years, the police investigation of the fire and death grew to folklore proportions.

In 1972, one investigator indicated that the "mystery man" killed in the fire may have been John Kupse of Brown County. However, Kupse was later found alive and well in 1974.

In December 1975, a Brown County grand jury indicted Clarence Roberts for kidnapping and murder for the still unidentified man's body found after the fire. The warrant would remain unserved, as police said they could not find any trace of Clarence.

Three years later, a Bloomington man came forward to say he saw Clarence Roberts eating at a restaurant in Mexico in 1975. Other sightings would be reported through the years, including some from near Mentone, Indiana, in Fulton County where some of Clarence's now-defunct businesses were.

On May 2, 1979, Special Judge James Dixon ruled against Geneva in her pending lawsuit against insurance companies who had refused to pay out on the life insurance policies on Clarence's life because of the remaining questions about whether he was dead. Judge Dixon ruled there was insufficient evidence to believe Clarence in fact was dead.

Geneva needed the money. Basically destitute after the 1970 fire, she took work baking pies at the Nashville House bed and breakfast, and lived alone in an older trailer home on land six miles south of Nashville along Indiana 135.

Just a month after losing her appeal of Dixon's ruling at the Indiana Court of Appeals, a fire and explosion were reported at her trailer home at about midnight, November 30, 1980. When firefighters doused the flames, they found two bodies in the charred remains. Police immediately identified one of the victims as fifty-nine-year-old Geneva. A male victim found was believed to be Clarence. Both died of smoke inhalation. The fire was ruled caused by arson, started by an unknown third party using an accelerant.

Former Brown County Coroner Earl Bond, who had removed what he initially believed to be Clarence's body from the original 1970 fire scene, said upon learning of Geneva's 1980 death: "I've agonized the last 10 years, spent 10 years laying awake at night wondering if I did the right thing for Geneva." Bond said Geneva was "a fine lady who was totally innocent" of any wrongdoing.[8]

Clarence and Geneva's son Forrest Roberts still doubted the man's body was that of his father when asked about it in the days following the 1980 fire. He said his family would pay for the funeral and burial of Geneva, but did not plan to claim the man's body—now identified by police as that of Clarence Roberts.

Finally, on December 4, 1980, respected criminal pathologist Dr. John Pless, bone and forensic specialist Dr. Clyde Snow, and a dentist, Dr. Clay Stuckey, addressed a packed news conference in Indianapolis where they declared the identities of the two victims found in the 1980 fire to be those of Geneva *and* Clarence Roberts.

Pless said Clarence's identity was confirmed by comparing x-rays of the dead man's body to x-rays taken of Clarence years before at Bloomington Hospital and Bartholomew County Hospital. Dental records were also matched. Pless told reporters there was "no margin for error" in confirming Clarence's identity, along with that of his wife.[9]

Dr. Snow assisted in the case because of the questions that were raised in the previous decade over Clarence's alleged "first death." Snow, a physical anthropologist, had gained notice in the months prior to his work on the Clarence Roberts case by helping Illinois officials identify the remains of thirty-three young men and boys attributed to Chicago-area serial killer John Wayne Gacy.

Brown County officials were left with the task of burying the second body now positively identified as Clarence since his sons refused to claim it. Geneva Roberts' remains were cremated and buried at an undisclosed location, her sons told the sheriff.

NBC's *Unsolved Mysteries* took up the Clarence Roberts case during a 1988 national telecast, and one local author attempted a novel based on the case.

The man first killed in 1970, whom police say remains unidentified, remains buried under the name "Clarence Roberts" because that's the way Clarence's family wants it.

Endnotes

1. *Bloomington Herald-Telephone*, Dec. 2, 1970.
2. Ibid.
3. *Bloomington Herald-Telephone*, Dec. 3, 1970.
4. *Bloomington Herald-Telephone*, Dec. 6, 1970.
5. *Bloomington Herald-Telephone*, Dec. 8, 1970.
6. Ibid.
7. Ibid.
8. *Bloomington Herald-Telephone*, Dec. 1, 1980.
9. *Bloomington Herald-Telephone*, Dec. 4, 1980.

CARROLL COUNTY

VICTIM(S):
Todd Burman, 28

PERPETRATOR(S):
Jack Lenon, 66

DATE OF DEATH(S):
July 29, 1993

GUNNED DOWN IN THE PRIME OF LIFE

When Indiana State Trooper Todd Burman, twenty-eight, was shot and killed in the line of duty on Thursday, July 29, 1993, his death hit as close to home as if any Carroll County officer had been killed.

Carroll County Sheriff Lee Hoard said, "He was an Indiana State Police officer, but he was accepted like he was a Carroll County officer. He was one of the team members."[1]

Burman's death, the second ISP officer to be gunned down in a five-month period of 1993, sent shock waves from Carroll County across the state. Master Trooper Michael E. Greene, forty-three, of Thorntown, Indiana, was shot to death February 5, 1993, as he attempted to make a traffic stop along Interstate 65 near Indianapolis.

Burman was shot while trying to assist other officers in arresting sixty-six-year-old Jack Lenon of Camden, Indiana, at his home. Lenon would also die that evening, but not from a gunshot wound, and not before killing Burman. Lenon was pronounced dead moments after gunning down Burman with a .30-30 caliber rifle. The coroner ruled he suffered a massive heart attack brought on by the terror he created.

The incident began about 10:30 p.m. when Lenon complained to Camden Town Marshal Steve Jones that he was writing too many traffic tickets near his home. The agitated Lenon also demanded that the town marshal cut some tall grass at an intersection near his home.

As Jones and Lenon's discussion of the matter grew heated, Jones decided to place Lenon under arrest for disorderly conduct. But instead of submitting to the arrest, Lenon fled to his home with Jones in pursuit. Burman joined Jones at Lenon's home along with a deputy from the Carroll County Sheriff's Department and an officer from the Flora Police Department.

At first, it seemed Lenon would submit peacefully, coming out on his porch to talk to the officers. When Burman told him he was under arrest, however, he fled back inside. Burman led the pursuit into the home where he encountered Lenon's wife, seventy-year-old Donna Belle Lenon. The trooper told Mrs. Lenon her husband was under arrest, but as he started toward an interior hall in the home to find the man, a deafening shot rang out from the .30-30 rifle.

The power of the blast was enough to pierce the bulletproof vest Burman wore, and the bullet entered his chest. As Lenon attempted to reload, Sheriff's Deputy Mark Back wrestled with him and was able to knock the .30-30 away. Flora Patrol Officer Clyde Knight assisted in handcuffing the now-subdued Lenon, who immediately fell limp and died instantly.

At the same time, Burman lay dying in the crowded hallway of the small home. He was immediately rushed to a Lafayette hospital, where he was pronounced dead on arrival.

"The Thursday slaying … has dealt a serious blow to the morale of the [Indiana State Police] department's officers, some of whom are still troubled by the killing of a trooper in February," the *Indianapolis Star* reported.[2]

Although he had no criminal history, Camden area residents reported Lenon was often "temperamental" and became irate when stray pets or children ventured onto his property. The arrival of the police at his home, neighbors believed, was more than he could stand.

Trooper Burman, who joined the department just under three years earlier on December 9, 1990, was the son of a cop. His father, Gerald Burman, served for many years as a deputy sheriff in nearby Newton County. A single man, Todd Burman's career in law enforcement was just getting started.

"He was a really well-rounded trooper who did everything well," said ISP detective Jerry Janke. "He was always willing to help someone out, whether it was the public or another agency."[3]

Lieutenant Richard M. Reece, at that time the district commander of the Redkey ISP Post in northwest Indiana, said Burman's death was a heavy blow for officers. "We weren't healed from losing Mike Greene … our sorrow now is just compounded."[4]

Hundreds of mourners, including Governor Evan Bayh, poured into the gymnasium of South Newton High School on August 1, 1993, to offer their final respects to Todd Burman. As taps rang out and officers quietly strolled by his casket, all hoped they would never see such a sad sight again.

Endnotes

1. Associated Press, Aug. 1, 1993.
2. *Indianapolis Star*, July 31, 1993.
3. Associated Press, July 31, 1993.
4. Ibid.

CASS COUNTY

VICTIM(S):
Paul Minneman, 33

PERPETRATOR(S):
Rhuel James Dalhover, 41;
Alfred James Brady, 27;
Clarence L. Schaffer, Jr., 21

DATE OF DEATH(S):
May 27, 1937

A GANG TO MAKE JOHN DILLINGER 'LOOK LIKE A PIKER'

The Federal Bureau of Investigation lists among its historic cases the work of the Brady Gang, "three human vultures [that] ... formed a coalition for the purpose of engaging in criminal activities which later were to make them the objects of one of the greatest manhunts in the history of American crime."[1]

Their vulturous purposes would cross many Indiana counties in the 1930s, but turned deadly in Marion County in 1936, and again in 1937 in northwest Cass County, Indiana, just outside Royal Center, Indiana.

The FBI labeled "the depredations of this gang of desperadoes" as rivaling those of the most bloodthirsty characters in American criminal history. The Brady Gang, though far less famous than the John Dillinger Gang operating in the same part of middle America in the 1930s, gloated their desperate acts "would make Dillinger look like a piker."

Credited with at least 150 holdups and robberies, and at least four murders, including the deaths of three law enforcement officers between 1935 and 1937, one of the gang's leaders, Rhuel James Dalhover of Madison, Indiana, would pay for his crime in Indiana's electric chair.

The gang's namesake, Alfred James Brady, was born in Kentland, Indiana, and was in trouble with the law as early as his late teens. Dalhover was also arrested numerous times as a youth (along with his brother John) and met Brady during the early part of 1935 in Jefferson County, Indiana. Dalhover

31

had just returned from his most recent sixty-day sentence at the Indiana State Farm at Greencastle when Brady convinced him to help rob a "moving picture theatre" at Crothersville, Indiana, and later a grocery store at Sellersburg, Indiana.

In October 1935, the Brady Gang gained its final member when Clarence Lee Schaffer, Jr. of Indianapolis joined the two villains and helped in the robberies of stores, theatres, gas stations, and other businesses across Indiana, Illinois, Ohio, and Wisconsin.

Interestingly, as the intensity of the investigations picked up to find them, eventually pulling in the agents from the FBI, the gang decided to centralize their efforts hundreds of miles east in Baltimore, Maryland, and limit their criminal activities to the state they knew best: Indiana. In Baltimore, the men carried on seemingly normal lives with common law wives and little criminal activity.

On May 23, 1937, the gang left Baltimore and headed west in a stolen Ford Roadster to Sheldon, Illinois, where they planned to rob the bank there. Unknown to them until they arrived, the bank had failed and was closed. The gang then set their sights on the Goodland State Bank at Goodland, Indiana, in Newton County. That bank was robbed on May 25, 1937, for a total of $2,528.

As they made their escape from Newton County, they fled east to Cass County and at about 11 a.m. spotted an Indiana State Police car driven by Trooper Paul S. Minneman at a quiet crossroads just outside Royal Center.

Minneman and Cass County Sheriff's Deputy Elmer Craig, forty-five, had been at the courthouse in Logansport when the call came in alerting all area police that the bank at Goodland had been robbed. Minneman and Craig jumped in the trooper's car and headed to northwest Cass County, and encountered a maroon automobile two miles west of the Caley Church. As the officers investigated further, "the maroon color auto was brought to a sudden halt and the point of a machine gun was stuck from behind the windshield and a rain of bullets pierced the air above the officer's head. The bandit then hurriedly backed his machine to the crossroads, and headed west," the *Logansport Pharos Tribune* reported.[2]

The officers gave chase in their car but lost the vehicle shortly, and came upon the Caley Church crossroads. As they entered the intersection, a machine gun again rang out, this time the shots coming from behind the small country church.

"The volley of bullets blasted the driver [Minneman] from the machine, as the car glided on westward. Craig remained in the auto, a hole through his foot. As the bullet-riddled police car crashed to the side of the road in front of the Caley Church, Craig climbed from the auto with the gun in his hand," the *Pharos Tribune* relayed.

"By that time, the gang had again sprinkled the fallen state trooper with a round of bullets as he lay in a mud puddle, apparently dead," the report continued.[3]

Craig was unable to return fire. As he lifted his gun to fire, the machine gun pellets struck his hand, knocking the weapon from him.

Craig later told investigators he heard the machine gun shooter ask, "Shall I let him have it?" to which his companion replied, "No" and pointed to Minneman's body and said, "That son of a bitch is dead and this son of a bitch will die."[4]

Their evil deed done, the trio scooped up Minneman's and Craig's guns, and jumped back in their car and continued fleeing east.[5]

The shooting had interrupted piano lessons for both eleven-year-old Eva Dell and eight-year-old Paul Lind going on just a short distance away inside the Lind farmhouse. Their piano teacher, Clayton Heiny, drove to the scene and found Craig standing in the road, spattered with blood, and Minneman nearby, mortally wounded.

Minneman told the farmer he believed he was dying and asked him to drive him to St. Joseph Hospital in Logansport, about twenty miles away. Heiny and Craig loaded the wounded trooper into the car and raced for help.

At the hospital, doctors discovered that Minneman had suffered at least twelve separate gunshot wounds, including ones that badly tore his liver, punctured one of his lungs, shattered bones, and caused severe internal bleeding.

Craig's injuries were less serious, though his foot injury was painful.

Meanwhile, local authorities "ordered the road blockade system inaugurated during the two-year search for the original Dillinger terrorists, thrown up in all the surrounding counties in the search for the bandits," the *Pharos Tribune* reported.[6]

The roadblock system, used by state and local police, consisted of portable roadblocks using sandbags as road obstructions across highways.

Two airplanes were also employed in the search for the shooters.

The description of the getaway car from witnesses at the Goodland heist confirmed this was the Brady Gang—the stolen license plate on the car being the same one used in a robbery of the Farmland State Bank just a month earlier.

The Goodland State Bank president, Lyle Constable, told police that one of the bandits, believed to be Dalhover, said to him as he exited the bank: "If you see a state detective named Winn, give him my regards."[7]

ISP Detective Donald Winn was from Madison, Indiana, and well-familiar with Dalhover's criminal history.

Winn was just one of many detectives hungry to get their hands on Dalhover and the rest of the Brady Gang. The gang was deeply resented among law enforcement officers already (before the Royal Center shooting) for the murder of Indianapolis Police Sergeant Richard Rivers in April 1936.

The Brady Gang trio had been arrested and jailed for killing Rivers but escaped the Hancock County Jail at Greenfield months later by beating the sheriff over the head with a lead pipe.

As doctors pumped multiple blood transfusions into the wounded Trooper Minneman, State Police Superintendent Don F. Stiver of Indianapolis visited him in his hospital room. Minneman reportedly apologized to the superintendent for disobeying orders by venturing out on his own to try to locate the robbers.

By Thursday, May 27, the *Pharos Tribune* reported the sad news that Minneman's bride of only five months, Margaret, his parents, and sisters had all gathered at his bedside as "all hopes for recovery of the wounded patrolman were abandoned." He finally succumbed to his injuries at 6:50 p.m. that day.[8]

As news of Minneman's death was broadcast over police radios, "officers issued a new order to 'shoot to kill' to those aiding in the hunt for the killers."[9]

Minneman was laid to rest on Monday, May 31, following services at St. Vincent de Paul Church. Local reports indicated as many as 2,000 people attended, or were in the community lining the street as the funeral passed by.

The *Pharos Tribune* noted, "Paul Minneman is in his grave, but is not forgotten. Nor will the atrocious crime that cost his life be forgotten by his fellow state policemen, for today they take up the trail which they vow will end in the early elimination of the Brady gang of murderers."[10]

Indiana Governor M. Clifford Townsend said he had decided against offering a reward for the capture of the Brady Gang, saying, "Our state police and local law enforcement officers are loyal and fearless and need no extra enticement to track down these criminals."[11]

By this time, unknown to Indiana authorities, the Brady Gang was already back home in Baltimore, Maryland, telling their wives they had just returned from a business trip to Maine. The trio purchased a boat and a new car, and settled into a quiet life until August when their money began to run out.

On August 23, 1937, they returned to the Midwest and robbed the Peoples Exchange Bank at Thorp, Wisconsin. The heist netted a tidy $7,000.

The FBI finally picked up their trail on September 21, 1937, as they journeyed to Bangor, Maine, to purchase more guns. They had heard a sporting goods store owner there would sell large amounts of weapons and ammunition with no questions asked. With the sale arranged, the gang went to the store on both October 5 and 11, 1937, to retrieve their purchases—including a submachine gun.

A store employee tipped off local police and the FBI, and surveillance was set up on the store for the Brady Gang's planned return visit. At about 8:30 a.m. on October 12, 1937, Dalhover entered the store, Schaffer stood guard outside, and Brady waited in the back seat of a Buick bearing Ohio license plates.

An undercover agent inside the store immediately detained Dalhover, but as they did so, Schaffer saw what was happening and began firing at the officer through the front window of the store. Agents inside the store returned fire and killed Schaffer on the spot.

Brady, still inside the car, was surrounded and told to get out of the car. Telling officers that he would not resist, it was one final lie for the Hoosier killer. He pulled a gun from his jacket as he exited the car, and officers returned fire, killing him on the spot as well.

Police recovered from Brady's dead hand the .38 caliber handgun he had taken from Trooper Minneman's wounded body in Indiana.

Dalhover was returned to Indiana and convicted of Minneman's murder. He was electrocuted in Indiana's electric chair at the state prison in Michigan City on November 18, 1938.

Endnotes
1. FBI History, Famous Cases, Web site.
2. *Logansport Pharos Tribune*, May 25, 1937.
3. Ibid.
4. Ibid.
5. *Logansport Press*, May 26, 1937.
6. *Logansport Pharos Tribune*, May 25, 1937.
7. Ibid.
8. *Logansport Pharos Tribune*, May 27, 1937.
9. Ibid.
10. *Logansport Pharos Tribune*, June 1, 1937.
11. *Logansport Press*, May 28, 1937.

CLARK COUNTY

VICTIM(S):
Christian "Christie" Melcher, 23;
Jaiden Melcher, 11 months

PERPETRATOR(S):
Zachariah "Zack" Melcher, 27

DATE OF DEATH(S):
April 16, 2005

A NEW LAW TO PROTECT VICTIMS' FAMILIES

Some crimes are so awful, they not only reveal the capacity of people to be cruel and evil to one another, they also reveal serious problems with existing law that need to be corrected.

The murders of Christie Melcher, a twenty-three-year-old mom (eight months' pregnant with another child), and her eleven-month-old son, Jaiden, in April 2005 were just such a case.

After they were murdered, their murderer (Christie's husband and Jaiden's father) refused, as next of kin, to immediately release their bodies for burial.

The capture of twenty-seven-year-old Zachariah Melcher for the murders on the same day the bodies were found was rather straightforward.

It was one of the last simple things that would occur in a case that shocked Clark County residents.

On Saturday, April 23, 2005, Jeffersonville police responded to the Melcher apartment on East Maple Street after a downstairs neighbor reported finding two bodies as she investigated a foul odor in the apartment.

What the neighbor and police found were Christie's and Jaiden's bodies, both stuffed into a thirty-six-inch-by-twenty-inch plastic Rubermaid container. Several bottles of ammonia, cleaning solutions, and air freshener were also found in the home in a fruitless attempt to mask the smell of the decomposing bodies.

Homicide investigators later determined the two were murdered one week earlier, on Saturday, April 16. Police reports showed that officers had visited the Melcher apartment on Thursday, April 21, after Christie's parents reported her missing, but did not notice anything out of the ordinary.

Zachariah was picked up a few hours later at a friend's house—held initially on a charge of failure to appear. He had served time before, five years of a twenty-year sentence for a 1997 Floyd County conviction for robbery, criminal confinement, burglary, battery, and theft. He was given early release in 2002.

The 1997 conviction was a plea agreement for twelve separate incidents in which Zachariah allegedly attacked, robbed, and confined several people between April and August of that year.

In 2002, he asked for and was granted an early release despite a report by the Floyd County Adult Probation Office that said he showed "a lack of reasoning skills and anger management" and that he was a "high to medium risk" to commit more crimes.[1]

In making his request for early release, he wrote to the court that "I need this chance to make things up to my uncle whom I hurt physically as well as emotionally by my crimes. I need the chance to prove to myself, my family and the court that I am better than my terrible actions have shown in the past."[2]

On October 2, 2004, he married Christie during a ceremony at the New Hope Church in Shelbyville, Kentucky. Christie was six weeks pregnant with Jaiden at the time.

There were problems almost immediately.

Christie's family said Zachariah began expressing serious reservations about being married to her just two weeks into the marriage, and a month later was openly engaging in a sexual relationship with another woman.

"I knew Zack was making a lot of bad choices, and Christie and the babies deserved better," said Linda Young, Christie's mom.[3]

Young added, "I begged her and begged her and begged her to leave him. And she said, 'Momma, if I can forgive him, then you should.'"[4]

The official court "forgiveness" he had been given with an early release was not working, however. Zachariah continued to struggle to follow the rules outside of prison.

Child welfare officials had been called at least once when family members questioned how Zachariah was caring for his wife and son.

Just before the murders, Floyd County Prosecutor Keith Henderson filed a petition to revoke his probation and send him back to prison. He was scheduled for a hearing on that matter just two days after Christie was last seen alive. He did not show up for the hearing.

An autopsy showed that Christie, eight months pregnant with a second child at the time, had been manually strangled to death. Her eleven-month-old son Jaiden had been smothered.

Under police questioning, Zachariah confessed to the murders, saying he used a plastic bag from the kitchen to smother the little boy.

He told investigators he was not sure why he had killed his family, and had done so after they had been out for pizza at a Louisville, Kentucky, restaurant. He told detectives that "he started the killings precisely at 6:59 a.m., and 32 seconds," the *Louisville Courier-Journal* reported.[4]

In court, he told the judge he wanted no lawyer, and wanted the death penalty. Even members of his own family wanted him to die.

"If he wants the death penalty, he deserves it," said Zachariah's brother Jason. "He killed my nephew and my sister-in-law."[6]

In the days following the discovery of the bodies, Zachariah began making it difficult for Christie's family to go forward with funeral arrangements. Christie's family finally relented to repeated requests and sent a family friend to meet with Zachariah at the Clark County Jail in exchange for giving the okay for releasing the bodies for burial.

The family friend, Laura Cambron, met with Zachariah for about two hours and afterward expressed the family's frustration when she said state law should be changed "so that ... families do not have to get permission from a killer to bury their children."[7]

In August 2006, Zachariah entered a guilty plea to killing his pregnant wife and son, and was sentenced to sixty-five years in prison, without the possibility of parole.

At the hearing, he told Clark County Circuit Court Judge Daniel Donahue, "I placed my hands around [Christie's] neck and strangled her until she died."

Clark County Prosecutor Steven Stewart read a statement from Christie's mom, Linda Young, causing the prosecutor to momentarily lose his composure. "My family is not just another statistic. They were someone's children, someone's grandchildren," the statement said.[8]

Zachariah sat silent when Judge Donahue asked him if he wished to make a final statement.

Just four weeks later, Linda Young appeared at the Indiana Statehouse in Indianapolis to urge a legislative study committee to take up a change in state law regarding control of bodies when the murder suspect is the next of kin.

"I'm hoping to help future families to not have to go through what we had to go through," Young said. "I'm asking you to put yourself in my shoes. I'm asking you what would you do if it were your daughter?"[9]

State Senator Connie Sipes of New Albany vowed to sponsor a bill to address this problem, as well as state laws that prohibited autopsy findings being released only to spouses and not parents of married children.

Sipes' bill, Senate Enrolled Act 271, was passed during the 2007 session of the Indiana General Assembly, by a vote of 46-0 in the State Senate and later in the Indiana House of Representatives by a vote of 93-0. It was signed into law by Governor Mitch Daniels in May 2007.

Endnotes

1. *Louisville* (Ky.) *Courier-Journal,* April 23, 2005.
2. *Louisville* (Ky.) *Courier-Journal,* April 24, 2005.
3. *Louisville* (Ky.) *Courier-Journal,* May 27, 2005.
4. Ibid.
5. *Louisville* (Ky.) *Courier-Journal,* April 24, 2005.
6. *Louisville* (Ky.) *Courier-Journal,* April 27, 2005.
7. Ibid.
8. *Louisville* (Ky.) *Courier-Journal,* Aug. 4, 2006.
9. *Louisville* (Ky.) *Courier-Journal,* Aug. 31, 2006.

CLAY COUNTY

VICTIM(S):
Perry Haviland, 73

PERPETRATOR(S):
James Corder, 25

DATE OF DEATH(S):
September 17, 1967

A QUIET JOB IN RETIREMENT TURNS DEADLY

Perry Haviland retired from a career as a coal miner. He took on a new and interesting job as the night town marshal in tiny Clay City, Indiana, in southern Clay County. Being a coal miner was dangerous work. Being a town marshal would prove to be deadly.

Four years into his job, Haviland, seventy-three, had proven to be a conscientious officer who helped keep the peace in the almost-always-peaceful town. Assigned the overnight watch for the tiny community, Haviland's job came with a badge, gun, nightstick, and flashlight but no uniform.

His retirement job would come to an end during the early morning hours of Sunday, September 17, 1967, as Haviland met up with prison parolee James Corder, twenty-five, from Patricksburg, Indiana, in adjacent Owen County.

It was Haviland's conscientiousness, however, that helped track down his killer.

Haviland was on walking patrol in the business district of Clay City when he stumbled upon a burglary at Easley's Pharmacy. While walking the alley behind the store, Haviland noticed a broken pane in the rear window of the store and soon encountered Corder as he emerged from the store (his total take: $10 in coins).

As Haviland attempted to make his arrest, Corder was having none of that. A brutal fight ensued with Haviland suffering crushing blows to the head. At some point, his .357 sidearm was wrestled away from him, and Corder allegedly shot Haviland three times. The first shot hit him in the right shoulder. A second shot entered Haviland's spinal cord through his arm, causing him to fall. The third shot was likely made as he lay on the ground dying, piercing his abdomen. He bled to death on the spot, the coroner saying if the gunshot wounds had not killed him, the beating (likely with a flashlight) would have.

A local resident, Wesley Funkhouser, who rented a small room at the rear of the Crist Jewelry Store next to the pharmacy, reported he heard a scuffle at about 3:40 a.m. When he went to the alley to investigate, he saw a white station wagon parked behind the jewelry store and saw a man lying on the ground, another man standing over him.

Funkhouser said the man standing over the wounded man said, "This guy's been hurt," and Funkhouser ran to get the day marshal, Joe Moore.

When they returned, they found Haviland dead, the white station wagon and the other man gone.

A search of Haviland's pockets produced a promising lead. In his pocket, the night marshal had a small spiral tablet where he'd written a note at 3:30 a.m. about a strange car parked near the town square. Haviland had even written down the license plate number, which when checked, came back registered to Corder.

When police went to Corder's Patricksburg home in Owen County, his mother, Mrs. Ruth Smoot, reported that her son had come home about 4:30 a.m. and told her he had killed a policeman. She believed him—his clothing was blood-stained, and he quickly changed his clothes before packing a bag and calling someone to ask him or her to take him to the bus station in Terre Haute.

Police later questioned Lawrence L. Hutchinson, a twenty-six-year-old friend of Corder's from Spencer, Indiana. Hutchinson said that he and Corder had been drinking earlier on Saturday night until about 2 a.m. Sunday morning. He said Corder found him again around 5 a.m. that day and asked him to take him to the bus station in Terre Haute, but that he refused his friend. Under intense questioning that proved a costly delay, Hutchinson finally admitted that he had given his friend a ride to Terre Haute and that he boarded a 6 a.m. bus headed west.

Despite the excellent clue the slain officer Haviland had left, the delay meant investigators remained a step behind Corder.

Police later learned he called a cousin about 3:30 p.m. Sunday afternoon to inquire about whether his mother was all right and whether the police were looking for him.

Days later, Corder called his sister from a phone in Tulsa, Oklahoma, asking her for money. His sister, Mrs. Gary Wallace of El Paso, Texas, urged him to turn himself in.

Despite her pleas, an intense manhunt raged on, the FBI joining with Indiana authorities in distributing Corder's picture, which was picked up by Associated Press and United Press International news services for newspapers across the Midwest and West.

With no money and his picture appearing now seemingly everywhere, his sister successfully talked Corder into turning himself in to police in El Paso, Texas. He was detained on the same day family and friends gathered back in Indiana to bury Haviland.

Clay County Sheriff Glenn A. Van Horn declared that although Corder's surrender had "ended one of the biggest searches ever conducted by the county, state and federal officials ... Corder was barely ahead of the law and it would only be a matter of time until he was caught."[1]

Corder's return to jail came less than six months after he had been released on parole on a two- to five-year sentence for burglary in Marion County, for which he was originally sentenced in August 1965.

Haviland's wife and four adult children and his many friends mourned his passing. His death reminded many that even in a small Clay County town, law enforcement can be dangerous.

Upon return to Clay County, Corder made matters easier by pleading guilty to a charge of murder and was sentenced to life in prison on October 30, 1967. Generally regarded as a good prisoner, Corder was finally released on February 28, 1994, having served more than twenty-five years for his crime.

Endnotes
1. *Brazil Daily Times*, Sept. 20, 1967.

CLINTON COUNTY

VICTIM(S):
Anna Marie Arguello, 3

PERPETRATOR(S):
Anita Marie Vega, 51

DATE OF DEATH(S):
Unknown date, 1969 or 1970

A FAMILY'S SECRET COMES UNFURLED

Margarita Booth stayed home from school one day in either 1969 or 1970—her memory was cloudy over the exact date—and witnessed a horrible event that frightened the little nine- or ten-year-old girl into a silence that lasted two decades.

Finally in 1993, she approached an Indiana State Police detective with an incredible story that, if true, meant not only had a small child suffered a brutal death twenty years before, but also that nothing had ever been done about it.

Margarita, now thirty-three years old, told the detective about the day she stayed home from school and her mother, Anita Marie Vega of Frankfort, Indiana, ordered her to participate in punishing her younger three-year-old sister, Anna, for once again wetting the bed.

Margarita's statement would lead to a Clinton County grand jury being called, and the house of lies that had surrounded Anita Vega—a woman now in her fifties—began to crumble.

Clinton County Prosecutor Louis D. Evans charged Vega with involuntary manslaughter on October 5, 1993, and also held her daughter, Guadalupe Thomas, thirty-one, also of Frankfort, on three charges of perjury for her alleged lies to investigators on behalf of her mother.

Evans said, "She subjected [Anna] to physical punishment which resulted in the child's death. The death came through the course of inflicting punishment."[1]

Evans said only family members knew about Anna's death, or even her life. No funeral was ever conducted, and a mystery surrounds where he body was buried. One family member said he or she believed Anna was buried along a railroad track in a rural area of Clinton County. Another reported she was buried on top of another rave in Bunnell Cemetery in Frankfort—but an exhumation of the site revealed nothing.

Investigators did locate a birth certificate from Muskegon County, Michigan, where the Vega family had lived prior to moving to Frankfort. It listed Anna's date of birth at September 12, 1967, making her at least three but possibly four years old when she died.

How could no one notice that a small girl had disappeared?

Prosecutors believed it was because the Vega family was very private when they moved to Frankfort, possibly to conceal the fact that the patriarch of the family, Luis Vega, was reportedly in the U.S. from Mexico illegally. Vega was not Anna's father, however, and investigators believe Martinez Arguello, one of Mrs. Vega's previous husbands, fathered her. He was believed to be dead at the time charges were brought against Anita Vega, Evans told reporters.

As expected, Margarita was the "star witness" at Anita's trial conducted in July 1994 at the Clinton County Courthouse in Frankfort. She testified that her mother ordered her to fill the bathtub in their Seventh Street home with cold water that winter day in either 1969 or 1970—the exact date long lost to faded memory and pain.

"While I was running the water, she went in and started beating on Anna," Margarita told jurors. Blood ran from Anna's nose and mouth from the slaps her mother inflicted, Margarita testified.

She said her mother continued to slap the small child as she forced her to sit in the cold tub, even though Anna attempted to fight being placed in the water. "[Anna] shook her head no, because she knew it was cold water," Margarita testified. "She told her to get in or she'd beat her some more, but Anna Marie kept shaking her head no. I said [to Anna], 'Please, please get into the tub.'"[2]

Margarita testified that her mother finally succeeded in getting the much smaller Anna into the water, and then held her head under the water until the child went weak and stopped fighting. Margarita said her mother ordered her to keep a shower head spewing cold water onto the lifeless form of her young sister.

This punishment went on for a long time. Margarita testified it was not until her other siblings returned home from school that her mother told her to go check on Anna in the tub. There she found Anna face down in the water.

Margarita said she pulled Anna from the water and tried to mimic rescue efforts she had seen on TV or in movies and succeeded in pushing some water out of her body. "Water started coming out of her nose and mouth. I was scared—I thought she was dead because she wasn't moving or doing anything, and she was ice cold," Margarita said.[3]

Alarmed, Margarita said she went into the living room to tell her mother she thought Anna Was dead. Her mother ordered her to bring the girl's body to the living room floor, but quickly changed her mind and told her to leave her on an enclosed, unheated back porch. Margarita did what she was told but stopped to wrap her sister's lifeless body in an old army blanket.

Another sister, Guadalupe Thomas, who originally lied to investigators and faced perjury charges because of it, at trial confirmed parts of Margarita's story under separate questioning before jurors. She said she had witnessed her mother rubbing Anna's back as she was wrapped in a blanket on the back porch, but her youngster sister didn't stir.

"There was a blue color to [Anna], like she was cold," Guadalupe testified, while also confirming that her mother had used the cold water punishment before after one of them had wet the bed.

Margarita testified that Vega seemed to know what had happened. Returning from rubbing Anna's back, she grabbed the front collar of Margarita's shirt. "She told me, 'If you ever tell anyone, I'll kill you. And you've seen me do it, so you know I can,'" Margarita testified.[4]

Vega apparently waited until her new husband, Luis Vega, arrived home from work late that evening before acting again. Margarita testified that she saw her father carry a crate out of the house that had pieces of the old army blanket Anna had been wrapped in sticking out between the slats.

"I looked at the box … and I got scared because I knew I had covered Anna Marie with that army blanket. I don't know how I knew, but I knew she was in that box," Margarita said.[5]

Sometime later, Luis Vega returned to the home, only to be chastised by Anita Vega for taking so long. Margarita said Luis defended himself by saying that it was not easy digging a grave in the frozen Indiana ground.

Luis was never charged with a crime—he too died before Anita was charged, murdered in Mexico in the 1980s, family members said.

At trial, investigators introduced an initial statement Anita Vega gave at first denying any knowledge of Anna having ever been born. When shown the birth certificate, she attempted to lie and say Martinez Arguello had had an affair with another woman and lied on the birth certificate. When pressed further, she admitted having delivered Anna in 1967, and that she had died of natural causes following a bath.

Although defense attorneys strenuously attacked Margarita for her story and for waiting for so long to come forward, police had the added benefit of having secretly recorded a conversation between Margarita and her sister, Guadalupe, which confirmed some of the details of Anna's punishment that Margarita could not recall.

Margarita and her family had fallen out of contact for about five years at the time she came forward with her repressed memories, and defense attorneys tried to paint a picture of her just wanting to get revenge on a family she was angry with.

Anita Vega's defense attorney, Michael Troemel, also attacked the testimony of Guadalupe, saying prosecutors had cut a deal with her to "say something about her mother" in exchange for a plea agreement on the perjury charges.[6]

Guadalupe denied that claim and told jurors she had initially lied to investigators because "I loved my mother."[7]

In the end, the jury took less than an hour to determine Anita Vega's fate, convicting her more than two decades after the fact for the death of her daughter, Anna Marie.

Other members of the Vega family were angry at the outcome and attacked Margarita for coming forward with her version of events.

A younger sister, Mary Fricke, who would have been an infant at the time Anna died, told reporters, "I hope my ex-sister is happy. I feel sorry for her—I think she's mentally ill."[8]

In discussing Anna, Fricke said, "We knew she existed, and we knew she had died. But we're the type of kids who don't always ask questions."[9]

Fricke said she was not angry, however, at Guadalupe for her testimony. "Lupe was scared, she said what they wanted her to say because she wanted to stay out of trouble. She had three kids of her own," Fricke said.[10]

Guadalupe pled guilty to a single count of perjury for lying to the grand jury and agreed to testify against her mother. For her part, after the verdict was read, Anita Vega tearfully hugged friends and family before being led from the courtroom. She said to no one in particular, "I don't hold any grudges."[11]

A month later she was sentenced to serve at least one year and no more than ten years for the involuntary manslaughter charge, using sentencing guidelines that were in place in 1969-70 when the crime is alleged to have occurred. Evans objected to such a light sentence, but the judge said he was bound by laws in place at the time of the crime.

An October 1995 appeal by Vega of her conviction was turned down by the Indiana Court of Appeals. She completed her prison sentence with credit for good behavior and was discharged from the Indiana Department of Correction on July 28, 1999.

Endnotes

1. *Frankfort Times*, Oct. 5, 1993.
2. *Frankfort Times*, July 28, 1994.
3. Ibid.
4. Ibid.
5. Ibid.
6. Ibid.
7. Ibid.
8. *Frankfort Times*, July 29, 1994.
9. Ibid.
10. Ibid.
11. Ibid.

CRAWFORD COUNTY

VICTIM(S):
Thomas Vandiver, 30;
Beatrice Vandiver, 44;
Wanda Johnson, 17

PERPETRATOR(S):
None ever arrested.

DATE OF DEATH(S):
Unknown date,
approximately January 7, 1949

A FAMILY GOES MISSING AND A MYSTERY IS BORN

The fate of Thomas and Beatrice Vandiver, and her seventeen-year-old daughter Wanda, has never been discovered, and in the nearly six decades since they were last seen, their story has become one of legend in Crawford County.

The Vandiver family of three lived on a farm near Mifflin, Indiana, and were last seen by their "friend" William D. Messamore, thirty-two, on Friday, January 7, 1949. He did not report them missing, however, until twelve days later on January 19, 1949.[1]

Messamore told police he saw the three before he left for a day trip to nearby Louisville, Kentucky, and that they were not at home when he returned later that evening.[2]

The land on which the Vandivers and Messamore lived was owned by Messamore's mother, Dashie Colgate. "Messamore was a character about whose pursuits little was known, and who was in and out of the area every whipstitch," a Crawford County history book recounts.[3]

Police reported that as far as they could tell, most of the family's belongings were left behind at the farm and they could come up with no reason why the Vandivers would pull up so quickly.

"Several theories have been advanced to account for their absence," the *Corydon Democrat* reported. "Most popular of which around Crawford

County leans to a suspicion of foul play. Other theories advance the belief that the family suddenly pulled up stakes and left for parts unknown."[4]

Crawford County Sheriff Marcus O. Lane assembled a posse of eighty men and spent days searching the area in and around the farm in a fruitless effort to find the family. The search included "the maze of sandstone caves and sinkholes with which the countryside abounded."[5]

Messamore was arrested on February 12, 1949, in Louisville, Kentucky, on an outstanding warrant from Crawford County on a charge of dog stealing. While not the most serious crime ever reported in the county, Crawford County officials were desperate to keep their hands on Messamore, whom they now considered their prime suspect in the disappearance of the Vandivers.[6]

"The charge alleges Messamore stole a large Blue Tick male dog from Ermal Hughes of English, Indiana on December 5, 1947," the *Corydon Democrat* reported in a breathless front page account of a dog theft that allegedly occurred two years before. "The dog was valued at $30."[7]

The report went on to explain that Messamore was wanted for further questioning in the Vandiver case. He also was in trouble with Kentucky authorities, the *Democrat* reported, for failing to report to his parole officer.[8] Messamore, on parole for his conviction for a 1933 robbery, served time in Kentucky's Eddyville Prison from 1938 to 1947.[9]

While under arrest and held in jail, Messamore was unforthcoming on any details about what may have happened to the Vandivers, but he did confess to a bank robbery. Crawford County Prosecutor Eugene E. Feller "persuaded Messamore to confess to the bank robbery after Messamore had let something slip about where he had obtained a large sum of money said to have belonged to him at the time of his arrest," the *Corydon Democrat* said.[10]

Federal authorities charged Messamore with robbing a Kevil, Kentucky, bank in August 1948 following his confession and said it included details of stealing a car he took for a test drive in Paducah, Kentucky, and then using it to hold up the bank at Kevil—a job that brought him about $19,000.[11]

Messamore implicated Thomas Vandiver in the planning and execution of the bank robbery, saying Vandiver received about $7,000 of the take for his part in the job. Messamore said that once paid, Vandiver and family disappeared, and he "professed to be as much puzzled by the whereabouts of the Vandiver trio as authorities."[12]

Local officials, however, were skeptical of his tale of Thomas Vandiver's involvement in the case and assured federal authorities they were going to hold on to Messamore until they could learn more.

Their plans to keep a tight lid on Messamore included transferring him to the larger, more secure Harrison County Jail at nearby Corydon. Their plans were thwarted, however, just before 1 a.m. on Monday, March 14, 1949, when the suspect "engineered a dramatic escape from the Harrison County Jail by leaping from a second story bathroom window."[13]

Before escaping, Messamore successfully locked Harrison County Sheriff Walter Baxley and his deputy Clarence Klee in another cell. Sheriff Baxley and Klee were "taken in" by Messamore's repeated requests to change his clothes. When they opened his cell, he tricked the two officers, locked them in his cell, and jumped twenty-five feet to an alley below from the bathroom window.[14] Klee was able to fire one shot at Messamore, but missed. Corydon resident Claude Stonecipher brought in his acetylene torch to cut through the cell bars to free the two men.

Messamore remained at large only twenty-two hours before he was captured in Brandenburg, Kentucky, and returned to Corydon under heavy guard. News photographers captured a smiling Messamore as he was led by federal marshals from the city jail in Brandenburg to the federal courthouse to face additional charges.[15]

Later convicted of the Kentucky bank robbery, Messamore received a new twenty-five-year sentence in the federal penitentiary at Leavenworth, Kansas, and served out the remainder of his sentence at the Kentucky State Prison. He had three additional years added to his sentence for the Corydon jail break. He won release from prison in the 1970s.[16]

Clues to the Vandivers' disappearance grew harder to find when the farmhouse they had lived in burned on April 13, 1949.

In the 1950s, Crawford County Sheriff Harvey Jones and a state police investigator discovered a sandstone cliff in the county that they believed could have been created by a dynamite blast in order to cover the bodies. No bodies were ever unearthed there, however.[17]

Local officials thought they might have a break in the case, finally, on March 3, 1983, when new landowners of the Messamore land reported finding a skeleton on their property. A review from forensic experts from Indiana University confirmed the remains were those of a Native American, and not any of the Vandivers.[18]

In 1983, Crawford County Sheriff Pete Eastridge also reported receiving a postcard with a Kentucky postmark and a map saying, "south of Eckerty of great interest to you." Eckerty was a tiny settlement located about nine miles west of English, near the present-day Interstate 64.

The proximity of Eckerty to the interstate has fueled long-term rumors that the bodies of the Vandivers were buried under construction for the major east-west thoroughfare stretching across southern Indiana.[19]

Sheriff Eastridge said he questioned Messamore at his home in Louisville, Kentucky, in March 1983 and that the man "talked freely, but sometimes in poetic terms." The sheriff said Messamore maintained his silence about the possible whereabouts of the Vandivers.[20]

Endnotes

1. *Louisville* (Ky.) *Courier-Journal*, March 15, 1949.
2. *Corydon Democrat*, Jan. 26, 1949.
3. Jones, H.O. "Whitey," *A Twentieth Century History of Crawford County, Indiana (1984)*, Book Crafters, Inc.: Chelsea, Mich., page 53.
4. *Corydon Democrat*, Jan. 26, 1949.
5. Jones, pages 53-54.
6. *Corydon Democrat*, Feb. 16, 1949.
7. Ibid.
8. Ibid.
9. Ibid.
10. *Corydon Democrat*, March 2, 1949.
11. Ibid.
12. Ibid.
13. *Corydon Democrat*, March 16, 1949.
14. *Louisville* (Ky.) *Courier-Journal*, March 15, 1949.
15. *Corydon Democrat*, March 16, 1949.
16. Jones, pages 54-55.
17. Ibid., page 56.
18. Ibid., page 55.
19. Ibid., page 55.
20. Ibid., pages 55-56.

DAVIESS COUNTY

VICTIM(S):
Marlin Ray Knepp, 26;
Jeremiah J. Miller, 18;
Paula J. Cook, 36;
Larry Sams, 48

PERPETRATOR(S):
Steven A. Hale, 22;
Chalk A. Wessell, 19

DATE OF DEATH(S):
April 1, 1998

TWO 'APRIL FOOLS' ON A KILLING SPREE

Steven Hale and Chalk Wessell started April Fool's Day 1998 as they had every day for a week—getting high on crank, cocaine, and alcohol. They finished the day with a two-state killing spree that left four people and Wessell dead.

There has never been a good excuse for what twenty-two-year-old Hale and nineteen-year-old Wessell did. Perhaps the massive amount of drugs and alcohol they consumed in the six days prior to the acts give some sort of reason for their acts, but it certainly gives no excuse.

The two men killed their friend, eighteen-year-old Jeremiah Miller of Montgomery, Indiana, as he sat in his red pick-up truck along a county road near Cannelburg, Indiana. Miller had agreed to give Hale and Wessell a ride as early as 4 a.m. that Wednesday morning and left the house without telling his mother—leaving her only a note saying that he was giving some friends a ride.

He was dead by 9 a.m.

His family said he was working on getting his act together. Released just the week before from jail on a burglary charge, he had attended church the Sunday before with his mom.

"He said he knew he had a long road ahead of him, but he was a lot stronger and he was ready to get on with changing his life," his mom, Karla Miller, said.

Mrs. Miller was convinced her son needed to hang out with a better set of friends. "He just got caught up with the wrong people. But I knew my son, my son was a good kid who loved his family and was on the right track."[1]

One of the friends she wanted him to stay away from was Wessell, a troubled teen from Loogootee. A self-described admirer and follower of mass murderer Charles Manson, Wessell was no stranger to law enforcement, even as a juvenile. As day broke that Wednesday morning, Wessell was wanted on warrants charging him with illegally carrying handguns.

By 1 p.m. that day, Daviess County police, unaccustomed to investigating *any* murders, now had a *second* one on their hands.

Neighbors had found the body of a young Amish farmer, twenty-six-year-old Marlin Knepp of Loogootee. Investigators believe Knepp was shot as he stopped his tractor to talk to Hale and Wessell in their car.

Knepp was en route from his farm to a sawmill to pick up wood shavings, and was known to be friendly about giving directions or helping others. The young Amish man worked on a 200-acre Daviess County farm with his family.

"He was very obedient and submissive to his parents," a Knepp family friend told a reporter. "He was very devoted to his church life—that was his life."[2]

Less than two hours later and further northeast in Daviess County, near Odon, Indiana, and the Crane Naval Surface Warfare Center, Pamela J. Cook, a thirty-six-year-old mom of four children was about to also cross paths with Hale and Wessell.

Cook was home with her eight-year-old child that Wednesday afternoon, her husband having gone south to the Ohio River for a day of fishing. Her 1974 Chevy Camaro T-top likely drew the attention of Hale and Wessell. They saw the car; they took it. But not before shooting Cook dead on her front porch.

Hale and Wessell continued on from Cook's home, heading west across the Wabash River into Illinois as twilight approached. In Albion, Illinois, about eighty-five miles from their homes in Loogootee, a stop at a local convenience store by Hale and Wessell stirred the suspicion of the store manager, causing the two killers to go hunting for a new car. Their hunt led them to the farmhouse of David Chalcraft.

Chalcraft was just a short distance away from his home at the time, finishing dinner at the nearby home of his parents. As he left, his friend Larry Sams, forty-eight, stopped by to say hello. As they talked, they noticed in the distance that a strange car had entered Chalcraft's driveway. The two men went to investigate, in time to see the green Chevy Camaro making a U-turn and coming back down the farm lane.

Both the Camaro and Chalcraft's pick-up truck stopped in the narrow farm lane, face to face. A steep embankment on either side of the lane meant someone would have to back up for the other vehicle to pass.

Given it was Chalcraft's property and these were strangers, he was not in a mood to move.

Chalcraft exited his pick-up truck and approached the driver of the Camaro to find out what he was doing on his land. As he leaned forward to speak to the driver, Wessell reached out from behind the wheel and shot him at point-blank range. The bullet passed through Chalcraft's neck, and he fell to the ground and down the steep embankment along the lane. He remained still, hoping to fool the shooter into thinking he was dead. It worked. But as he lay there motionless, he heard Hale approach the still-idling pick-up truck where Sams remained seated, and Hale shot him in the face, between the eyes.

An autopsy would show Sams suffered a straight-on gunshot wound to the eye, five wounds in total to his head, one to his chest, and one in his back, as Hale and Wessell fired multiple shots into the cab of the truck.

As Chalcraft continued to lay motionless in the ditch, he heard one of the shooters back the Camaro up to near the house, while the other drove the pick-up in the same direction, clearing the lane.

As the vehicles moved away, Chalcraft jumped up and ran in the darkness to his barn and retrieved his shotgun there. When he emerged, he saw Hale and Wessell driving the Camaro slowly down the farm lane (presumably looking for Chalcraft to finish him off). Chalcraft took his pick-up truck and drove it back in their direction, and Hale and Wessell fled at the sight of the truck now moving again and a shotgun pointed in their direction.

Chalcraft drove his injured self and his dying friend back to his parents' house to call the sheriff. A massive manhunt that stretched into the early morning hours of April 2 finally produced the Camaro abandoned in a cemetery.

As the officers closed in on Hale and Wessell hiding in a field near the cemetery, they heard a gunshot.

They found Hale unarmed and arrested him. They also found Wessell dead from a gunshot wound to the head.

Illinois State Police ruled Wessell's death a suicide, but an Edwards County, Illinois, coroner's jury ruled June 24, 1998, that Wessell was the victim of a homicide—presumably committed by Hale.

As his nose bled from massive cocaine use, Hale gave Illinois and Indiana detectives a taped statement in which he said killing his friend Jeremiah Miller earlier in the day was "pointless" but killing Marlin Knepp was "necessary." Hale painted a picture of a domineering Wessell who demanded Hale kill someone to prove himself equal in their crimes. Paula Cook had died for the same reason Larry Sams died—to facilitate stealing a vehicle.

Hale's version of the attack on Chalcraft and Sams indicated that Sams was shot after he "rushed them." Evidence at the scene and Chalcraft's account, however, did not support that claim.

Illinois authorities held Hale for trial, and he was convicted of first-degree murder in Edwards County, Illinois, on June 15, 1999. The jury decided not to impose the death penalty. On July 15, Edwards County Circuit Court Judge Terry Gamber imposed a life sentence without the possibility of parole for Hale.

Added to the life sentence were convictions for armed violence, aggravated battery with a firearm, and aggravated vehicle hijacking. Another thirty years was added to his sentence for those crimes.

In March 2000, Hale pled guilty to killing the three Hoosiers in Daviess County Circuit Court after a judge ruled his taped confession could be used against him at trial in Indiana. In his plea, he admitted that he and Wessell shot and killed Miller, Knepp, and Cook during a drug-induced shooting spree.

In August 2000, Hale was sentenced to another sixty-five-year sentence for the three slayings in Indiana. He'll never serve a day in an Indiana prison, however, because his life sentence without parole in Illinois means he's staying put across the river.

Endnotes

1. *Indianapolis Star*, April 3, 1998.
2. Ibid.

DEARBORN COUNTY

VICTIM(S):
Johnston Agrue, 60;
Nina Agrue, 60;
Leo Agrue, 33;
William Agrue, 22;
Mary Elizabeth Breedon, 12

PERPETRATOR(S):
Virginius "Dink" Carter, 33

DATE OF DEATH(S):
May 16, 1941

A KILLER OF A SON-IN-LAW NAMED "DINK"

On Friday evening, May 16, 1941, Virginius "Dink" Carter was welcome for dinner at his in-laws' home near Aurora, Indiana—his mother-in-law had even made a place for him at her dining room table.

It was a dinner no one would ever eat. Dink chose that spring day to kill most of his in-laws in a senseless attack that reflected the aimless life of Dink himself.

Dink confessed to Dearborn County Sheriff William Winegard four days after the brutal mass killing that he had shot his brothers-in-law, thirty-three-year-old William Agrue and twenty-two-year-old Leo Agrue, and their sixty-year-old father, Johnston, "because they hated me and because I was afraid."[1]

Killing his mother-in-law, Nina Agrue, sixty, and her granddaughter Mary Elizabeth Breedon, twelve, was presumably to eliminate any witnesses to his crimes. Sadly, Mrs. Agrue didn't know Dink had slain her sons and her husband.

"Without any emotion, the stocky, bald Auroran recounted how he left the body of an innocent 12-year-old girl lay asprawl at the entrance to a barn where she fled hoping for safety," the *Lawrenceburg Press* reported. "Mary Elizabeth fell face down, as all the bodies were found, her little hands clutching dirt and straw as she dragged her form on the ground before death gripped her."[2]

The account continued, "Her body saturated in blood, Carter left her dying as he smelled the sickening lethal fumes of the shot gun."[3]

Dink told the sheriff he killed William and Leo first, and then shot their father, Johnston, as he returned home from work walking down a dirt path to his home. Their killings came after many years of differences between the men.

Dink said he arrived on the Agrue farm at about noon that day, asking where the men were. Mrs. Agrue said "they were up on the hill planting corn. I walked up on the hill. I walked up where the boys was and I said 'Hello' to Leo and I asked Leo what he was doing. He said, 'By God, ain't doing much of nothin'.'"[4]

Investigators later learned that Dink and the Agrue boys had exchanged words, including some that irritated or ridiculed Dink. The Agrue boys were everything Dink wasn't—hardworking, honest, and dependable. Both brothers had been notified they were to be called up for the draft as the likelihood of World War II became more and more evident in 1941. Dink, his mental and criminal problems persisting, was not draft eligible.

For his part, Dink said Leo's younger brother William, who was holding a gun, lowered it and "I ran underneath the gun and threw the gun in the air and I hit him with my fist and took the gun away from him, whirled around and shot him."[5]

After shooting William, Leo began to flee, and Dink said he shot him in the back. Following the shooting, Dink returned to Mrs. Agrue's kitchen and acted like nothing was wrong, pretending he had not heard any shots. He stayed there until almost 3 p.m. when his father-in-law, Johnston Agrue, was due home from his job at the Jefferson Ordinance Proving Ground at Madison, Indiana.

Dink said, "I walked up to the creek with the gun and I met Mr. Agrue coming down the hill and I shot him twice. I came on back to the house and Mrs. Agrue asked me what was the matter, and I said 'Nothing' [and] she whirled around to me and I shot her. I picked up the gun and started to the door and I told the little girl to come with me, to go with me. She got to the barn and went to screaming and said she wasn't going and I shot her."[6]

Before he left, he allegedly stole a payroll check from Johnston Agrue's body. Dink then hid the shotgun in a hollow tree log about a half mile from the farmhouse and returned home to his wife Leona, saying nothing about slaying her family.

Leo Agrue was the twin of Dink's wife Leona. Leona was devoted to Dink despite the fact her family did not like him. She also loved Dink despite the fact that he had once been married to her older sister, Mary. Dink and Leona's marriage had produced a child, as did his previous marriage to Mary.

Johnston Agrue was unhappy that Leona had chosen to "marry" Dink. Testimony at the trial would reveal why—no official divorce had ever been granted between Dink and the first Agrue daughter he married, Mary. Mary told investigators her father and her brothers made her marry Dink after she had run off with him and was living with him for a short time "without the benefit of marriage."

It was not a happy marriage—as Dink was known to sneak out of the house to go have sex with his wife's younger sister, Leona. Dink was also suspected of stealing a shotgun and other valuables from the Agrues.

Neighbors discovered the Agrues' team of horses grazing on a hillside without a harness and attempted to return them to the farm, when they found the bodies. Dink was arrested one day later, on Sunday, but did not confess until Sheriff Winegard convinced him to do so.

The Agrue family were "hard working, honest people, respected and liked, according to neighbors. The farm where they lived [for 28 years] ... was very well kept, gave mute evidence of the thrift and tidiness of the tenants," the *Lawrenceburg Register* reported.

A combined and private funeral service was conducted for the five family members, and they were buried at Riverview Cemetery near Aurora, adjacent to their farm land.[7]

Dink was indicted on five counts of first-degree murder and held without bond. The Dearborn County Circuit Court was jam packed with spectators as his trial got underway in October 1941. During the trial, Dink made headlines away from the courthouse when it was revealed sheriff's deputies found a rope and a B&O Railroad schedule in his cell assumed to be part of a plan by Dink to escape the jail.

Dink told Sheriff Winegard he would not give up trying to escape—that he preferred being shot while trying to do so to a seat in Indiana's electric chair.

Dink's defense attorney attempted to convince jurors that the confession had been gained by pressuring the defendant during fifty or sixty hours of questioning. "Carter is an illiterate, and has had no education, can hardly read or write and cannot sign his name twice alike," attorney William M. Dean said.[8]

During his closing argument, twenty-seven-year-old Dearborn County Prosecutor Lester G. Baker drew a sad picture for jurors, and drew sobs and weeping from Dink's wife Leona as she sat behind the defense table.

"We can understand why [Leona] sticks to her husband. I suspect he is all she has left," Baker said. "Her sisters have no enmity or bitterness for her. They simply can't understand why she would forsake the memory of her father and mother to cling to a man who murdered them. But the sisters have compassion, they will take her back into their hearts."[9]

Baker pleaded with jurors to find him guilty and recommend a death sentence. "If this man does not deserve death, then what kind of crime could the Devil think up in his fiendish mind that would deserve the death penalty?" Baker asked.[10]

Dean was equally impassioned in his closing remarks. He reminded jurors that Leona Carter had stood by her husband in sickness and in health, and for better or for worse, even as the couple struggled to support their young family because no one in Dearborn County wanted to hire a woman married to Dink Carter.

"I now surrender all to your hands," Dean said, "confident that you, looking to your God, will deal with this man as you or I might wish others to deal with us under different circumstances."[11]

Jurors listened to the young prosecutor and convicted Dink and recommended a sentence of death. Dink's death sentence would be the first in Dearborn County in more than a century—the last person sentenced to die being Amasa Fuller of Lawrenceburg who was hung on the courthouse grounds on March 8, 1820, on a charge of murder.

As the verdict was read, Dink's wife Leona "rushed to her husband, threw her arms around him and sobbed and cried frantically. She was followed by Tom Carter, 74-year-old father of Dink. The old man repeated, over and over, 'I'll take care of them Dink. You don't need to worry. I'll take care of the babies. I'll do the best I can.'"[12]

As his son was removed from the courtroom, Tom Carter said to no one in particular, "I ain't done nothing. I've always been good to everybody, why does my son have to go this way? I don't believe in killing anybody."[13]

Dean continued to plead Dink's case, filing a petition for a new trial that was denied in February 1942. Pleas to the governor to save Dink's life went unanswered.

Dink Carter was electrocuted in the state's electric chair at the state prison in Michigan City at 12:13 a.m. on February 10, 1942. He was buried in a private ceremony conducted by his wife at the Riverview Cemetery near Aurora, Indiana—only about 100 yards away from where he had shot and killed the Agrue brothers.

The *Lawrenceburg Press* reported that the state prison sent the Dearborn County sheriff a bill for $50—the cost of the electrocution.

Endnotes

1. *Lawrenceburg Press*, May 23, 1941.
2. Ibid.
3. Ibid.
4. "Confession of Carter," *Lawrenceburg Register*, May 22, 1941.
5. Ibid.
6. Ibid.
7. *Lawrenceburg Register*, May 22, 1941.
8. *Lawrenceburg Press*, Oct. 17, 1941.
9. *Lawrenceburg Press*, Oct. 24, 1941.
10. *Lawrenceburg Register*, Oct. 23, 1941.
11. *Lawrenceburg Press*, Oct. 24, 1941.
12. *Lawrenceburg Register*, Oct. 23, 1941.
13. Ibid.

DECATUR COUNTY

VICTIM(S):
Anthony M. Bunch, 3

PERPETRATOR(S):
None

DATE OF DEATH(S):
June 30, 1995

A YOUNG MOTHER FINDS FREEDOM
AND VINDICATION

A lot has changed since a pregnant Kristine "Kristi" M. Bunch, then just twenty-one-years-old, was led in and out of the Decatur County Courthouse in Greensburg, charged with the arson-related murder of her three-year-old son, Anthony M. Bunch.

Just after the early morning fire on June 30, 1995, investigators settled early on the idea that Kristi had set the deadly fire as a means of escaping the challenges of being a single mom to an active boy (and pregnant with her second child).

Her sentencing appearance in the Greensburg courthouse, more famous for the tree that grows from its clock tower than for any major trials that have occurred there, was the last most locals ever thought of her. Sentenced to sixty years in prison, people in Decatur County are like most places across the nation – if arrested by police, convicted in a court trial, and sentenced by a judge – most believe a person is guilty.

While the story might have ended there, a small group of people never believed Kristi could do such a thing and undertook a determined and extraordinary journey to win not only Kristi's freedom from prison, but also vindication of her name.

The process revealed startling and sad aspects of the criminal justice system—and it didn't convince everyone of Kristi's innocence. Ultimately, however, it did convince those with the power to set her free and she walked away from the Indiana Women's Prison on August 22, 2012, unlikely to ever face charges again. On that day, she had given up seventeen years and forty-seven days of her life.

Her release followed a ruling by the Indiana Court of Appeals that prosecutors were negligent in failing to provide Bunch's defense attorneys with lab reports that would have supported her claims of innocence.[1] The Indiana Supreme Court declined to take up the matter further, and in December 2012, the Decatur County Prosecutor's Office announced it was dismissing all murder charges against Bunch (although they could be refiled again later if new and more reliable evidence were to be produced).[2]

As she left prison, Kristi said to a small group of reporters, "I want to take my shoes off and go running and stick my feet in the water and do everything I haven't been able to do" (including getting to know her second son, Trenton, who has been raised by her mother in the years she has been in prison).[3]

Her release was a nationwide story – the Associated Press distributing a photo of Kristi admiring her new high heels as she carried her former state-issued Department of Correction shoes and clothing in a plastic bag. Met by her mother, Susan Hubbard, and others who never stopped believing, tears flowed outside the reach of the prison as Kristi began to consider life as a free woman.[4]

In the years since leaving prison, she has left rural Decatur County—a community where judgmental, peering looks persist for some. A lot has changed there since Kristi was arrested and later convicted. A giant Honda plant has arrived on the edges of the county seat of Greensburg bringing literally thousands of new workers and residents to the area. But some things never changed – the tree still grows in the courthouse tower, and old-timers still believed Kristi was a killer.

Kristi has had to endure the doubters all along, but remained optimistic. "I haven't been by myself," she said. "I had a family that stood by me. I had people that believed in me and stepped up. And you can't receive blessings like that and be bitter."[5]

One of her first moves after winning her freedom was to visit the grave of her son Anthony in a quiet Bartholomew County cemetery. While in jail, Kristi earned undergraduate degrees in English and anthropology through a special prison program with Ball State University, and converted to Catholicism.

"I wrote hundreds of letters," Kristi told a panel of attorneys and others who help the wrongfully convicted. "I kept pushing forward. I took classes, got degrees. The [prison] superintendent encouraged me to do research in the law library, so I was there every day. I wanted out [of prison] more than anything in the world. So many people believed in me, I just couldn't not get what I wanted."[6]

Today, Kristi's life is about helping others wrongly accused. She is employed by Northwestern University in Chicago and gives back to the Center for Wrongful Conviction, who took up her case and believed along with a small handful of others that she was not a murderer.[7]

A college degree earned behind bars and a voracious appetite for reading about advances in arson fire investigations and innocence projects across the nation proved to be important steps on Kristi's road back to freedom. Tenacious digging helped her and attorneys from the Center for Wrongful Conviction to uncover allegedly altered and withheld arson investigation documents. Those documents pointed away from the original theory that Kristi had set her own trailer on fire with her young son trapped inside. Instead, it found that accelerants originally claimed to be present at the scene were not there.[8]

Claims of an alleged confession Kristi gave police further eroded the state's case for her conviction—more careful examination revealed that the distraught mother was no match to homicide investigators who spent hours drilling her about the details of the fire.

While in prison, Kristi found few supporters beyond her immediate family and said, "I would just cry until I couldn't cry anymore. If I hadn't woken up on any of those days, I wouldn't have cared."[9]

Kristi's brother, Michael, ignored the judgment of locals around Decatur County and maintained his belief in Kristi's innocence. He suggested that the sensational national headlines generated by the Susan Smith case in South Carolina (a young mother convicted of pushing her minivan into a lake and drowning her young sons) in the days before Kristi's Greensburg trial were not helpful.

Kristi is seeking her own justice. Limited in what she can do in terms of suing the State of Indiana or Decatur County for her conviction, she is suing the Indiana State Fire Marshall's Office and the Bureau of Alcohol, Tobacco, Firearms, and Explosives for their alleged missteps in investigating the fire. Bunch and her attorneys hope her story and lawsuit will bring vindication to both her and perhaps other wrongfully accused persons convicted on less-than-rock-solid arson investigations.[10]

"The prosecution of Kristine is a tale of mistakes, missing information and suppressed evidence," said Jane Raley, co-legal director of the Center for Wrongful Conviction at Northwestern University. "We were struck by the fact that Kristine had no prior [criminal] record at all, no history of mental illness, no witnesses or motive and had never confessed. The trailer [where the fire occurred] was uninsured."[11]

The long search for justice has caused many to think again about fire science, and about the need to focus on problematic prosecutions that may result in wrongful convictions such as the one that took almost two decades of Kristi's life.

Endnotes

1. *Greensburg Daily News*, Aug. 22, 2012
2. *Indianapolis Monthly*, Jan. 16, 2014
3. *Greensburg Daily News*, Aug. 22, 2012
4. *Indianapolis Star*, Aug. 23, 2012; Associated Press, Aug. 23, 2012
5. *Indianapolis Star*, Aug. 23, 2012
6. *Lake County Journal* [Grayslake, Ill.], April 17, 2014
7. *Indianapolis Monthly*, Jan. 16, 2014
8. *Indianapolis Star*, Jan. 19, 2016; ABC News *"20/20,"* May 5, 2010; *Time* magazine, June 7, 2016.
9. WTHR-TV, Indianapolis, April 6, 2015
10. *Greensburg Daily News*, Feb. 10, 2015
11. *Lake County Journal* [Grayslake, Ill.], April 17, 2014

DeKALB COUNTY

VICTIM(S):
Juan "Poncho" Placencia, 77

PERPETRATOR(S):
David Leon Woods, 19;
Gregory Joe Slone, 19;
Patrick C. Sweet, 19

DATE OF DEATH(S):
April 7, 1984

'THEY BURIED A GOOD GUY TUESDAY'

The citizens of Garrett, Indiana, know a lot about each other and tend to keep track of what is happening to one another. And everyone in town knew that when Juan "Poncho" Placencia was murdered, something was terribly wrong.

Placencia, also known as the "The Vegetable Man" for his long-time practice of selling vegetables from a roadside stand, was stabbed to death on Saturday morning, April 7, 1984, as he was ambushed at the front door of his wood-frame home at 316 S. Lee Street in Garrett.

A Mexican native, Placencia had come to Garrett four decades ago and grew most of the vegetables that he sold each summer. He had known a peaceful life in America, a country he loved. That all ended early one April morning.

Investigators alleged nineteen-year-old David Leon Woods led two of his friends to Placencia's house to steal his television. Woods's mother reportedly had dated Placencia, and so David knew what valuables existed inside his home.

When they knocked at the front door around four a.m., Placencia answered and was quickly pushed back and stabbed numerous times. Stumbling to a chair nearby, Placencia was helpless to stop the robbery. One of Woods's friends, nineteen-year-old Gregory Joe Slone, entered the home with him, while a third, Patrick C. Sweet, also nineteen, waited outside as a lookout. The trio fled with the TV and about $130 in cash. They later sold the TV for $20.

Woods would claim in appeals of his later conviction for the crime that he had only intended to scare the elderly man with the knife, but his story did not match the facts. Placencia suffered twenty-one stab wounds to the face, neck, and torso, including at least three stab wounds that pierced his heart in a furious and deadly assault. He suffered separate stab wounds to the head that pierced his skull and brain.

After the attack and robbery, investigators learned the youths threw the murder weapon into Little Cedar Creek about six miles southeast of Garrett, washed Placencia's blood from their bodies and clothing, and returned home, acting as if nothing was wrong.

Woods, however, had to carry out the next part of the plan. The young men thought that police would be unlikely to suspect them of the crime if they were the ones to report it, so around 9:45 a.m. that day, Woods returned to Placencia's house on the ruse of a visit. Finding the body, he called police and acted as if he had stumbled upon someone else's crime. The first Garrett Police Department officers to arrive reported finding Woods on the front porch of the home crying over finding his "friend" dead.

While police were still at the scene questioning Woods, his mother, Mary Lou Pilkinton, arrived and told police she thought her son was somehow involved in the murder. She consented to a search of her home where police found a knife sheath, bloody socks worn by Woods, and a bloodstained towel. As evidence mounted, Woods quickly confessed and implicated the other two suspects, Slone and Sweet. All entered pleas of not guilty.

DeKalb County Prosecutor Paul R. Cherry filed a motion to seek the death penalty against Woods for his action. The trial was moved to Boone County, because of intense publicity for the case in northeast Indiana, and was conducted over nine days in February and March 1985. Found guilty of murder and robbery, Wood was sentenced to death by Boone County Superior Court Judge Donald R. Peyton on March 28, 1985.

Woods continued to file multiple appeals of his conviction, including challenging the damaging search police had made of his mother's home to find evidence. He also raised concerns about his statements to police because of drowsiness he suffered from prescription medications he took for depression. Lurid details of a troubled transient childhood were also introduced during appeals as a means of helping explain Woods's alleged actions.

Slone was found guilty on charges of aiding a murder and was sentenced to sixty years in prison on April 2, 1985. He was released from prison on September 18, 2011, after serving twenty-six years.

Sweet's case was venued to Marshall County and charges were later reduced because it was determined he had not entered Placencia's home or participated in the murder-robbery at the same level as the other defendants. He pled guilty to a lesser charge of aiding a burglary on November 16, 1984, was sentenced to ten years in prison, and was released early with credit for good behavior.[1]

Woods's appeal of his death sentence came to an end in 2007, and on his last day, he told a prison spokesman to say, "I want Juan's family to know I am truly sorry and I do have remorse."[2]

Placencia's son David from Bakersfield, California, replied, "I'm not one to forgive."[3]

At 12:35 a.m. on May 4, 2007, Woods was executed by lethal injection at the Indiana State Prison in Michigan City. His execution was the first one conducted in Indiana under a new law that allowed members of the victim's family to be present. Five of Juan Placencia's children were present as Woods expired.

As Placencia was laid to rest in 1984, the *Auburn Evening Star* reported on the reaction of Garrett residents: "They called him Poncho, a friend explained, because Poncho in Spanish means good guy . . . people considered him a good guy. They buried a good guy Tuesday. That is the man everybody in Garrett knew, the man who whistled while he worked, the father of thirteen children—a good guy, Juan J. *Vaya con Dios.*"[4]

Endnotes

1. Marshall County Clerk's Office, Plymouth, Ind.
2. Associated Press, May 4, 2007.
3. Ibid.
4. *Auburn Evening Star*, April 11, 1984.

DELAWARE COUNTY

VICTIM(S):
Ethan Dixon, 16;
Kimberly S. Dowell, 15

PERPETRATOR(S):
Unknown

DATE OF DEATH(S):
September 28, 1985

KILLINGS REMIND A COMMUNITY OF 'SON OF SAM'

Less than a decade after New York City authorities captured serial killer David Berkowitz, who became known as the "Son of Sam" killer, an eerily similar attack occurred in Muncie, Indiana, that has never been solved.

The modus operandi of the September 28, 1985, assault on two Muncie teenagers rang familiar to anyone who followed Berkowitz's reign of terror that took six lives between 1975 and 1977 in New York City. Berkowitz would prey on young couples sitting in cars after dark and shoot them dead on the spot.

On this Saturday night in Muncie, the two teens were inexplicably gunned down as they sat inside a two-door Volkswagen hatchback inside West Side Park.

They were popular, well-known students, the kinds of kids "who do not get into difficulties at school. They were good students," their principal, Owen Lemna, said.[1]

Their bodies were discovered by Muncie Police Patrol Officer Terry Winters at 11:50 p.m. as he walked his police dog in the park and inquired about the parked car.

In the driver's seat was sixteen-year-old Ethan Dixon, a popular and handsome student at Muncie North High School. In the passenger's seat was his friend, fifteen-year-old Kimberly Dowell, a beautiful young blonde girl and a classmate at North High.

Delaware County Coroner Glen Scroggins said both Ethan and Kimberly were in reclined positions on their seats, but both were fully clothed. A sleeping bag had been placed over both seats and was found under the victims. A tape player was set up in the back of the hatchback as well.

The car was parked at the end of a dead-end road at the far west end of the park, overlooking the White River. The car's engine was running when police found the bodies, and the driver's side window was rolled down, but the passenger's side window had been shot out.

A witness elsewhere in the park around midnight that fall evening said he heard three shots and saw a dark car leaving the area.

Scroggins ruled that Dixon suffered a single gunshot wound to the left side of his chest, while Dowell died of a single gunshot wound to her left temple. He estimated their deaths occurred at about 11 p.m.

The gunshots were fired "at a relatively close range, within a few feet of the car," Scroggins told the *Muncie Star-Press*. At least three shots were fired, with only two striking the victims. A .38 caliber weapon was used.[2]

"There is no evidence of a motive," Scroggins said, discounting that robbery could have been a motive. No alcohol or drugs were found in the car or on Dixon or Dowell's bodies.[3]

However, police did recover an empty gun holster from under Dixon's seat and a small pocketknife was found on the car's dashboard. Given that no gun was found in the car, investigators ruled out a murder-suicide for the couple.

Police learned that the young couple left Dowell's home on Euclid Avenue in Muncie at about 9 p.m. that evening. The shooting took place in a popular city park less than two miles from her home. She was due home from her date with Dixon at 11 p.m.

The two youths' deaths shocked students, faculty, and parents at Muncie North High School, and the entire community.

Dixon had been elected president of the junior class. Dowell was a junior varsity cheerleader and the sophomore class representative on the Homecoming Court that fall.

"Ethan was on the debate team as a sophomore last year, and that team finished fifth in the state," said Principal Lemna. "He was very popular and very bright. He was popular with students and faculty alike."[4]

About 1,000 students, parents, and community members assembled for the funerals for Dixon and Powell conducted on Tuesday, October 1.

"If God exists, why did He permit such a thing to happen?" the Reverend William Grady of St. Mary's Catholic Church asked. He said there was no easy answer.

"God is no more pleased with this act than you or I are pleased with this act," he added. "[But] it is the risk that God was willing to run if He were to create a human being."[5]

The homicide investigation focused on who was in the park that Saturday night. Muncie police determined eleven cars, including the one driven by Dixon, were in the park around 11 p.m. that evening. Of those, all but two could be accounted for, and those two were reported as being near Dixon's car at one point.

"One of them has got to be a damn good witness, and the other one is a suspect," Muncie's Deputy Police Chief Marvin Campbell told reporters.[6]

Campbell said a motive still eluded police as did any witnesses who had actually seen the couple together between 9:30 and 11 p.m. that evening. A police search of the water and riverbanks inside the park also produced no evidence.

As the days wore on, Muncie Mayor James P. Carrey and his wife, Marilyn, personally donated $5,000 to start a reward fund for information leading to the killer. The fund grew to more than $10,000 with other community contributions.

"We needed to let people know how we feel about this," Mayor Carey said. "It's a unique situation because we know these people, and we will offer the reward to anyone who can provide information leading to the arrest and conviction of those involved."[7]

A few days later, hopes were raised when police reported they had interviewed one of the men seen in a car near Dixon's that evening. Known to Dixon, police said the man was a possible suspect but had not provided very much new information. He was not arrested.

Hopes faded, however, as sixteen-hour days rolled into weeks and no arrest was imminent. Further dashing hopes, no fingerprints of a suspect could be found anywhere on Dixon's car.

"We have nothing new," Muncie Detective Lieutenant David Nicholson told the *Star-Press*. "There is a lack of clues. You have almost nothing solid to go on in something like this. It would be great if someone would just walk in and confess, but it's not that easy."[8]

Nicholson said eyewitness accounts were a struggle for police to work through. "I have a problem with some of the accounts by witnesses," he said. "Some are so exact. They say they saw this color car or this make. They're almost too sure. It just doesn't figure."[9]

In the following days, police issued a sketch of a possible suspect or witness in the case. Campbell said the man was believed to have been the driver of a black 1972-75 Chevrolet Monte Carlo and was seen near the victims shortly before the shooting.

Police said the car was "jacked up, [with] wide tires on the back, with chrome mag wheels," Campbell said.[10]

From there, the trail went cold. And it remained so.

Two decades later in 2005, many Muncie residents had long forgotten about the case, or never even heard of it.

The *Star-Press* included the brutal slaying of Dixon and Dowell in a news story about unsolved murder cases in the Delaware County area. They noted that Muncie police had interviewed more than 100 witnesses in the case, but "the investigation just never did produce any solid physical evidence of any kind," said George Wilson, a retired Muncie police detective.[11]

Wilson said he remains troubled about the case.

"It's a disturbing case, I can say that," he said. "That was one that visibly took a toll on the [police] department. It's not just the time and effort involved. You are concerned about the victim's families and the victims themselves."[12]

Endnotes

1. *Muncie Star-Press*, Sept. 30, 1985.
2. Ibid.
3. Ibid.
4. Ibid.
5. *Muncie Star-Press*, Oct. 2, 1985.
6. *Muncie Star-Press*, Oct. 3, 1985.
7. *Muncie Star-Press*, Oct. 4, 1985.
8. *Muncie Star-Press*, Oct. 6, 1985.
9. *Muncie Star-Press*, Oct. 8, 1985.
10. Ibid.
11. *Muncie Star-Press*, Oct. 1, 2005.
12. Ibid.

DUBOIS COUNTY

VICTIM(S):
Sean Tilk, 12;
Jarod William Ritzert, 6;
Brandi Marie Ritzert, 3;
John M. Ritzert, 30

PERPETRATOR(S):
John M. Ritzert, 30

DATE OF DEATH(S):
July 10, 1998

A BROKEN-HEARTED FATHER BREAKS THE EARLY MORNING SILENCE

John Ritzert was a quiet, shy man who worked as a union bricklayer and deeply loved his family and did all he could to support them.

His love for them, however, could not overcome his grief and anger over his wife Theresa's decision to divorce him. Their divorce, granted on June 30, 1998, ended seven years of marriage, and John was struggling to accept the end of his family.

Living back home with his parents in Evansville, John finally snapped and showed up at the family's well-kept home on Kluemper Road in Jasper just before dawn on Friday morning, July 10, 1998.

Before he entered the home he had lived in for four years with Theresa, thirty-two, and their three children, he cut the phone line. He then proceeded to kill his family. Only Theresa would escape, running frantically from the home to try to get help from a neighbor.

The help was too late—John shot and killed twelve-year-old Sean, six-year-old Jarod, and three-year-old Brandi as they slept in their beds. John shot himself in Sean's basement bedroom after killing his stepson.

Theresa told investigators John had broken a window in a back door to gain entry, and she confronted him in a hallway. She said he pleaded to see his children and professed how much he missed his family. Her attempts to calm him were not working.

As she ran next door to call police, she could hear the shots ringing out from inside her home.

The violence that took four lives was something unheard of in Jasper. "The neighborhood on Kluemper Road is a storybook ideal from middle America with children playing on well-kept lawns, and bicycles plying the paved road," the *Jasper Herald* reported.[1]

Except for one other case, the last murder in the town was in 1854.

Jasper police, the Dubois County Sheriff's Department, and the Indiana State Police all responded to Theresa's call for help, initially surrounding the house, unsure if John was still alive or dead.

"It's always shocking," Jasper Police Chief Rick Gunselman said. "I've been [an officer] for 20 years. I've seen [other] incidents … it's still shocking."[2]

Theresa had first sought a divorce from John in April 1998 listing an "irretrievable breakdown of the marriage." Case files at the Dubois County Courthouse showed no restraining orders had been sought by either Theresa or John, although police records show a 911 call was placed on June 28 when Theresa said John physically assaulted her at their home during an argument over items, including golf clubs that he wanted to remove from the house.

The divorce order said John was to have "liberal visitation at all times agreed upon by the parties." It also specified that Theresa would keep the house and a Ford Explorer, while John got a Dodge Dakota pick-up truck.[3]

Chief Gunselman was sure Theresa had saved her own life by fleeing. "John Ritzert was so focused on the children, he probably wasn't even aware that she left."[4]

John's actions shocked everyone who knew him.

An active member of Bricklayers Local No. 4, co-workers described him as quiet, shy, and hardworking. "He was a very good employee," said Jerry Paul, a representative of the union. "He was very well liked among bricklayers and contractors. He had an excellent work record."[5]

John's retired parents, with whom he had returned to live after the divorce, were equally shocked. "My boy was a hard working boy, and he done everything he could for his family. He loved those kids dearly … He just loved them too much maybe," said John's father, William Ritzert of Evansville.[6]

A combined funeral mass was conducted for Sean, Jarod, and Brandi at St. Peter Celestine Catholic Church in Jasper, and they were buried in the church yard cemetery.

Theresa Ritzert wrote a statement published by the *Jasper Herald* the day after the killings.

"I know everyone is wanting a statement from me," she wrote. "Most important, all the love and prayers sent to my children, my family and myself are felt and truly appreciated."

She said, "Death is always an unbelievable loss in any situation. However, there are a small number of people who can truly understand my emotions. All three of my beloved children were taken from me under such horrible circumstances. Witnessing and being completely helpless to save my children will be a vision placed in my mind forever."[7]

Theresa said that "no one will ever know why an individual can just 'snap' and take his children's lives. I know John was hurting because of the divorce, even though it was a mutual agreement. One of the few things John said to me in the house was, 'I have to take back my kids and my house.'"[8]

"I will eventually pick up the remaining pieces of my life and live on," Theresa wrote. "My children would want me to cherish their memories ... all I ask is to try to understand my pain, which is greater than words. In that understanding, please let me grieve and mourn."[9]

She offered broken-hearted advice in closing her note to the community, "Always cherish your family and friends and each minute you have with them ... the love you exchange between family, friends and the Lord should be all important."[10]

Endnotes

1. *Jasper Herald*, July 10, 1998.
2. Ibid.
3. *Jasper Herald*, July 10, 1998; *Evansville Courier*, July 11, 1998.
4. *Jasper Herald*, July 11, 1998.
5. Ibid.
6. Associated Press, July 11, 1998.
7. *Jasper Herald*, July 11, 1998.
8. Ibid.
9. Ibid.
10. Ibid.

ELKHART COUNTY

VICTIM(S):
David E. Rock, 26

PERPETRATOR(S):
Shirley M. Rock, 24

DATE OF DEATH(S):
May 25, 1972

A WOMAN WHO DIDN'T BELIEVE IN DIVORCE

Shirley Rock told a police detective that because of her religion, she didn't believe in divorce.

She felt this way despite the fact that she was carrying on an extramarital affair and had just admitted to systematically poisoning her young husband, David, to death.

At the time, Shirley was a twenty-four-year-old Sunday school teacher from a respected family in tiny New Paris, Indiana, where she also led the children's and young adult choirs at the Union Center Church of the Brethren.

She agreed to be questioned by detectives multiple times in the early days of June 1972 following David's unexpected death. David, twenty-six, had died May 25, 1972, at Elkhart General Hospital after a brief illness that mystified doctors.

Before arriving at the Elkhart County Sheriff's Department in Goshen for what would be her final interview with detectives, Shirley dropped off her eight-year-old sister at home. She and her sister had just attended a Walt Disney Production at the University of Notre Dame.

As police questioned Shirley, they determined they had enough information to hold her on a preliminary charge of murder. Then-deputy Elkhart County Prosecutor Michael Cosentino (who would later be elected to multiple terms of his own as county prosecutor) presented evidence against Shirley to a grand jury, who promptly indicted her for first-degree murder on

June 14, 1972. The panel deliberated less than two hours and only heard from two witnesses, Elkhart County and Indiana State Police detectives.

Cosentino told reporters the mystery over David's unexpected death was over: Laboratory tests confirmed he died of massive arsenic poisoning.

The indictment read that Shirley murdered her husband by "giving and feeding arsenic to him." Her statements to police would indicate she first tried to feed him rat poison on April 29 in a drink of scotch and water. When that made David ill, he blamed it on the scotch and switched to his favorite drink, 7-Up.[1]

Cosentino's boss, Elkhart County Prosecutor C. Whitney Slabaugh, told reporters that Shirley had admitted during questioning that she used rat poison on David by spiking her husband's drinks. She targeted especially his favorite, 7-Up, laced with an arsenic-based rat poison known as "Fatsco." She did so on May 2, 6, and finally on May 20, just five days before he died. On her previous attempts, she had just made David violently ill, rendering him unable to work for days at a time.

An autopsy report from County Coroner Dr. Frederick Bigler confirmed that arsenic was the contributing factor to David's death. He died just three days after being admitted to the hospital to undergo a scheduled tonsillectomy, but had been ill for at least a month before that.

The doctors treating him for the tonsillectomy could not figure out why David was so sick and could not recover. A "Reinsch test" ordered on the day before he died indicated the presence of toxins in his system. When he died less than twenty-four hours later, the doctors asked for the autopsy.

Shirley, meanwhile, was complaining that Coroner Bigler had not signed David's death certificate and was holding up settling life insurance payments she was due.

Shirley's attorney Robert J. Helper entered a plea of not guilty by reason of insanity on her behalf in September 1972 after she had been incarcerated without bond for three months. He asked the court that she be examined to determine her competency to assist in her defense. Physicians who examined her said she was competent to stand trial.

Although headed to trial, Shirley's attorneys knew her case would be a tough one to win anywhere in Indiana, let alone conservative Elkhart County.

On September 22, it was announced that Shirley was ready to withdraw her not guilty by reason of insanity plea and instead plead guilty to a charge of second-degree murder. Helper convinced the court to accept psychiatric testimony about Shirley at her sentencing hearing for the plea in an attempt to mitigate the evidence against her.

During Shirley's sentencing hearing on October 3, 1972, prosecutors presented evidence that Shirley had planned David's death for an extended period. During her lunch hours from her job as a secretary in Syracuse, Indiana, Shirley had gone to the local library and checked out several books, including one titled *To Kill With Kindness*.

Dr. Robert Yuhn, a psychiatrist, told the court he examined Shirley on three separate occasions and that her incompatibility with David, both sexually and in terms of day-to-day living, drove her to kill her husband. She was, Dr. Yuhn testified, "tortured between religious conscience and emotional need."[2]

Dr. Yuhn said Shirley was a "confused, immature individual" with a strong religious background.

He noted that her marriage with David had never been consummated sexually and said she "was humiliated and suffered great emotional distress because of certain unnatural acts she was made to perform with her husband, acts which were particularly abhorrent to her because of her deep religious feelings," the *South Bend Tribune* reported.[3]

The couple had married in July 1967, just before David was drafted into the U.S. Army and was sent to a base in Washington. He was never called up to Vietnam.

During the time David was away in the army, Shirley met a man who was to become her lover. Police said her lover was never aware of Shirley's intentions to kill David once he returned to Elkhart County after 1970. After he returned from military duty, David took a good job as a cost accountant for Keene Products in Middlebury.

At the sentencing hearing, prosecutors noted that the May 1972 murder was just the latest attempt on David's life. Shirley had admitted two previous attempts to kill her husband with poison that had failed, prompting her to seek out the library book for additional information on how to kill someone.

Prosecutors said Shirley wanted out of her marriage to be with her lover but did not believe in divorce because of her religious views.

Shirley had used at least two three-quarter ounce bottles of "Fatsco" rat poison purchased at a Nappanee drug store to kill her husband. Each bottle contained 2 percent arsenic. She admitted first using the rat poison in April, and continued to spike his drinks—so strongly that David had to call in sick for work repeatedly.

Detectives and friends said David Rock was "an ordinary guy with ordinary problems" who had been a good student at New Paris High School, where he graduated in 1963. His parents were well-known in the county, as were Shirley's.

Shirley had been an active student in high school as well, serving as a varsity cheerleader and "sweetheart" of the local FFA chapter. At the time of her arrest, in addition to her volunteer duties at the church, Shirley had been elected president of the local Public Service Club.

Defense attorney Helper asked the court for leniency in its sentencing, noting that "his client expected and wanted to be punished ... [but] that she had been subjected to anxieties and degradation instead of receiving the affection she needed. He said the great tragedy of her life was that because of the circumstances of her marriage, she was not able to attain fulfillment as a woman," the *South Bend Tribune* reported.[4]

Prosecutor Slabaugh said he opposed a lighter sentence since the state had already accepted a lesser charge of second-degree murder.

Elkhart Superior Court I Judge Charles E. Hughes asked Shirley if she had any statement before he rendered his sentence. She uttered a quiet, "No, your honor."[5]

Judge Hughes said the argument about Shirley's religious beliefs was "paradoxical" and "a self-contradiction based on a false premise," reminding those attending the hearing that the Bible also offers a commandment: "Thou shalt not kill."

The judge acknowledged what he called "an impossible domestic situation" but said Shirley had ample opportunities to consider her actions over a period of time and was not acting in the heat of the moment. He said he could find nothing in the facts presented to indicate Shirley deserved any great compassion—including efforts by Shirley to buy more poison when her first bottle of "Fatsco" ran out.[6]

With that, he sentenced her to life in prison.

"Mrs. Rock's parents and her late husband's parents were present along with friends and relatives when the sentence was passed in the tension-packed courtroom," the *Goshen News* reported. "Wearing a slack suit and remaining poised, Mrs. Rock stood for sentencing ... and seemed to show 'relief' after the sentencing was over. Mrs. Rock was able to say goodbye to relatives and friends, many of whom were in tears."[7]

Shirley was immediately transferred to the Indiana Women's Prison in Indianapolis and began using her maiden name, Shirley Etsinger.

She filed a petition for "post conviction relief" in October 1977, which was denied, and another appeal to the Indiana Supreme Court in May 1979, which also failed.

Shirley petitioned for her freedom from jail each year from 1982 to 1985. In June 1985, the Indiana Parole Board voted to recommend clemency for Shirley, but that vote was later invalidated because the vote was taken in a meeting that was not held in public.

The board met again, this time in public, and one board member changed his vote and Shirley was denied clemency on a 3-2 vote.

Shirley kept trying for clemency and in a 1986 hearing before the parole board told them, "I'm sorry about what happened, but there isn't anything that I can do about it now. I can't go back and undo the wrong that was done. If I could, I would."[8]

At that hearing, Shirley reminded the board that she now had served more time than any other female offender currently in the Indiana prison sentence. "When I came in here, there were 13 other 'lifers,'" she said. "All of those are gone except for me. So I'm number one as far as women are concerned in the state of Indiana."[9]

She would have to remain in prison a little while longer.

In June 1988, the parole board again took up the issue of her clemency, this time voting 3-1 to recommend that Governor Robert D. Orr release her.

At that hearing, board members said they were impressed that she had finally directly admitted her guilt in David's death.

"I've had much, much time to think and there is much remorse about the rash solution I took to my martial problems," a now forty-year-old Shirley told the board. "If I could, I would go back 16 years and bring my husband back. But I can't undo what I did. Yes, I killed him."[10]

Shirley's father, Mervin E. Etsinger of New Paris, said he was pleased with the vote. "This is the best news we've had for 16 years," he said. "We've had a lot of disappointments. Shirley just wants to start over and get on with her life."[11]

David's father, Eugene J. Rock also of New Paris, said he felt no bitterness toward Shirley but felt she should serve at least twenty years of her sentence. "When you lose your son, it leaves quite a void. Anybody who says you get over it, they're wrong," he said.[12]

Mr. Rock's wishes would come true. Shirley would not win release until she was paroled on December 13, 1995—having served just over twenty-three years of her life sentence. She was forty-eight at the time of her release and slipped into anonymity.

Endnotes

1. *Elkhart Truth*, Sept. 22, 1972; *Indianapolis Star*, June 8, 1988.
2. *Elkhart Truth*, Oct. 4, 1972.
3. *South Bend Tribune*, Oct. 4, 1972.
4. Ibid.
5. *Goshen News*, Oct. 4, 1972.

6. *Elkhart Truth*, Oct. 4, 1972.
7. *Goshen News*, Oct. 4, 1972.
8. *Indianapolis Star*, June 11, 1986.
9. Ibid.
10. *Indianapolis Star*, June 8, 1988.
11. Ibid.
12. Ibid.

FAYETTE COUNTY

VICTIM(S):
Howard Kelley, 61;
George Wolfe, 53

PERPETRATOR(S):
George Wolfe, 53

DATE OF DEATH(S):
July 22, 1934

A POLICE OFFICER PAYS A HEAVY PRICE

On Monday, July 23, 1934, the day the nation's newspapers carried the startling news that the country's most-wanted man, Hoosier John Dillinger, had been killed in a Chicago shootout with federal agents, Fayette County residents were reading about a deadly shootout in their own community.

The *Connersville News-Examiner* ran blaring headlines that read, "Gunman Slain; Wounds Officer," which had nothing to do with Dillinger's case. A smaller headline next to Dillinger's photo said, "Dillinger Killed by U.S. Men at Chicago."

The Connersville gun battle involved fifty-three-year-old George Wolfe who police caught in the act of siphoning gasoline from a car parked on West Tenth Street early Sunday morning, July 22.

As Officers Howard Kelley and Lawrence Poe approached Wolfe, he began to run, but they soon caught him. A quick search of Wolfe revealed no weapon. However, Wolfe had concealed a .38 caliber revolver on his waist, and Wolfe broke free from Kelley's grasp and fired at him, seriously wounding the officer.

Poe, who had initially turned to go get his police cruiser to detain Wolfe, pulled his revolver and fired seven shots at Wolfe as he ran from West Tenth Street to Sycamore Street. As other officers arrived, Poe loaded the wounded Kelley into the police cruiser and rushed him to the Fayette Memorial Hospital.

Wolfe, though gravely injured from a wound to an artery in his left thigh, was reported alive by the back-up officers responding and was taken to the hospital but was pronounced dead on arrival.

X-rays showed the bullet that entered Kelley was lodged in his face about an inch above his mouth. It could not be removed.

Poe told fellow officers that he and Kelley were making their final rounds on patrol early Sunday morning when they spotted Wolfe filling one gasoline can from the tank of the car, with another can sitting nearby.

The investigation showed Wolfe had an established criminal history. In 1912, he was sentenced to serve ten to twenty years for burglary but was later paroled by the governor. Six years later in 1918, he was again sentenced to ten to twenty years for robbing a Beech Grove, Indiana bank. Paroled and discharged in 1929, he was given a sixty-day sentence in July 1931 on a liquor-related charge in Rush County.

Relatives said Wolfe had come to Connersville just three years before and was employed at a local factory as a laborer. Others in town said Wolfe occasionally bragged about his criminal exploits, including claiming he had killed his first wife—apparently a big lie.

At the time he was killed by police, Wolfe was married and the father of three sons from his first marriage. One of his sons told police he had worried that his father's habit of stealing gasoline from others' cars would one day get him shot by someone.

His son Herbert Wolfe hosted his father's funeral in his home, and Wolfe was buried in East Hill Cemetery in Rushville.

On the same day, the *News-Examiner* reported that Kelley was listed in "fair condition" at the hospital and was "doing as well as could be expected."[1] He could not return to duty as a police officer until January 1935.

His condition would worsen, and he would struggle for many years with terrible headaches and other ailments related to the shooting. On November 9, 1937, the *News-Examiner* carried the sad news that Kelley was dead, the victim of a self-inflicted gunshot wound from his city-issued .38 caliber sidearm. He had never returned to work from his lunch break that Tuesday midday.

Fayette County Coroner D.G. Pugh said Kelley died of a single gunshot wound, the bullet traveling through his head, out a window of his home at 211 West Twelfth Street in Connersville, and landing on the floor of the home next door.

"Ill health ... is believed to have been the motive for the suicide," the *News-Examiner* reported. "Although he seldom complained, Kelley had told fellow officers ... this morning that his head was aching so badly that he 'would just as soon be dead.'"[2]

The report added that since he had been shot in 1934 "he had never been free from pain … although he was always in good spirits and ready to joke with his fellow officers."[3]

Police officers from across Indiana attended his funeral at the First Baptist Church in Connersville two days later. He was laid to his final rest in Dale Cemetery.

Endnotes

1. *Connersville News-Examiner*, July 24, 1934.
2. *Connersville News-Examiner*, Nov. 9, 1937.
3. Ibid.

FLOYD COUNTY

VICTIM(S):
Kimberly S. Camm, 36;
Jill Catherine Camm, 5

PERPETRATOR(S):
Charles D. Boney, 35

DATE OF DEATH(S):
September 28, 2000

A LONG SEARCH FOR JUSTICE

The brutal murder of Kimberly Camm and her two beautiful children, Bradley and Jill, drew national attention to the tiny Floyd County bedroom community of Georgetown, Indiana.

Four trials were held and two men were eventually charged, but in the end, only one man would be imprisoned and the other released after a sensational trial and incredible path to freedom.

The undisputed facts are that Kimberly and her children were found shot to death in the garage of their home at 7534 Lockhart Road on Thursday, September 20, 2000. Investigators believed Bradley and Jill were both shot while still seated inside their mother's Ford Bronco (although Bradley's body was removed from the SUV after he was shot), while Kimberly's body was on the garage floor beside the bloody vehicle.

David Camm, Kimberly's husband and the father of the two young children, reported the incident to the State Police Post (not the local 911 Center) at about 9:30 p.m. that evening as he returned from a pick-up basketball game at a local church gym.

A former Indiana State Police trooper, David was almost inconsolable, initial officers who responded to the scene reported. "It was the most emotional crime scene I've been to in twenty years," said Floyd County Prosecutor Stan Faith.[1]

David quickly fell upon his large, well-known, and respected extended family, as well as members of the Georgetown Community Church, where David's uncle Leland Lockhart served as pastor, for support.

David's family had also been there when he had become disillusioned with his career as a police officer and quit after a decade of service in May 2000. Another of David's uncles, Stan Lockhart, hired David as a manager for the basement waterproofing division of his company, United Dynamics, Inc., of Jeffersonville.

Kimberly Camm, who worked as a senior accountant across the river for Aegon Insurance Group in Louisville, Kentucky, was a devoted working mom. She had spent this Thursday evening with her children as she usually did, coming home from work and taking her kids to swim practice. She seemingly had just returned home with the children from their activities when the attack occurred inside the garage.

The Camm children were described as beautiful, obedient and bright kids who won the hearts of everyone who met them. Bradley, a second-grade student at Graceland Christian School, was more reserved than his younger sister, Jill, who was in kindergarten at the same private school. Family members described little Jill as a tomboy, her great uncle Sam Lockhart telling one reporter that she and her father had a tackling game they loved to play.

"She was always hounding him, 'Dad, let's go play,'" he said.[2]

Questions about the relationship between David and his young daughter would be raised later, but for now, everyone folded in around David to try and comfort him in the midst of a tremendous loss.

"David is experiencing a loss that cannot be explained, that cannot be put into words," Sam Lockhart said.[3]

David finally appeared before a pack of curious reporters on October 1, after attending Sunday morning services at the Georgetown church. With his sister at his side and his family standing behind him, he called for the person responsible for killing his family to come forward.

"If they have any decency, they'll turn themselves in," he said. "You can't live with the guilt."[4]

During the worship service that morning, about forty members of the church had come forward to "lay hands" on David as he knelt at the church's alter.

He added to reporters in a choked voice, "I want my family back. I want my babies back. I want my wife back."[5]

A combined funeral for all three victims was planned for Monday, October 2, at Graceland Baptist Church.

David Camm would not be in attendance.

The Monday morning newspaper headlines carried the startling news of why: Police had arrested David and charged him with killing his family.

State troopers detained David just hours after his public statements outside of the church, and they remained initially tight-lipped about what evidence was found to link David to the killings.

A probable cause affidavit filed by prosecutors gave more details. Police indicated there were traces of blood found on David's T-shirt and that the autopsy had revealed evidence that five-year-old Jill had been sexually abused.

Investigators also disclosed that the murder scene in the Camm family's garage had been partially cleaned by someone, with bleach used on the floor and thrown off a back deck of the house.

The affidavit said Jill and Kimberly had died of gunshot wounds to the head from a .38 caliber weapon, and that Bradley had been shot in the chest.

Although under arrest, police secreted David into the Graceland Baptist Church shortly after arresting him on Sunday evening so he could see the bodies of his family resting there for funeral services scheduled the following morning.

The church's pastor, who was present when a handcuffed David was brought into the church's sanctuary to view the caskets containing the bodies, said David turned to him and said, "I didn't do it."[6]

During an initial hearing in Floyd County Superior Court, David (now represented by a lawyer) would begin a vigorous defense that would stretch on for years to come. At the center of the defense was David's repeated claim that he had not killed his family or had anything to do with their murders. David's attorneys said the state lacked enough evidence to hold his client on multiple charges. Prosecutor Faith vehemently disagreed, saying that the standard of proof to hold David "is that, based on evidence, a reasonable man will believe a crime has been committed and a certain person committed the crime."[7]

Faith pointed to evidence collected so far that he said indicated "high velocity blood mist" on David's T-shirt, "recent tear(s) in Jill's vaginal area consistent with intercourse," witness statements from David's basketball chums who said he had left the gym for a short period of time the evening of the murders, a statement from a neighbor who reported hearing three "distinct" sounds that could have been gunshots between 9:15 and 9:30 p.m., blood in the garage "thinned out" by water and bleach, and a wet mop found in the family's utility room carrying a strong odor of bleach.

More damning circumstantial evidence would eventually emerge—David and Kimberly had less than a "perfect marriage." David had moved out of the family's home in 1992 for a short time to live with a girlfriend. In addition, multiple females came forward to report alleged lecherous behavior by David during his decade-long tenure as a state trooper.

Further, Faith pointed out that David had a lot to gain financially from the death of his family with large insurance policies in place, one purchased just two months before the murders.

David continued to proclaim his innocence, his family standing firmly behind him, but Kimberly's family eventually breaking with David amidst growing doubts about whether he had played a role in the murders.

In January 2002, the case finally came to trial, but not before national attention was focused on the case by a variety of newspapers and TV stations, including repeated hour-long programs devoted to the case by primetime CBS News program *48 Hours.*

At trial, forensic experts testified that eight droplets of blood were found on David's T-shirt and were a match for Jill's DNA. One microscopic drop of blood on David's shoe was also confirmed to match Kimberly's DNA, the jury was told. In total, Faith called eighty-four witnesses to build his case against David Camm.

David's defense attorneys countered the blood splatter evidence presented and questioned repeatedly the expertise and conclusions of the state's witnesses.

Not helping David's case, however, was the testimony of some of the men who had played basketball with him that evening at the nearby gym. Some testified that David had never left the gym during the entire evening, others were unsure, and still others said he had left the building.

To top off his case, Faith brought forth a parade of women who testified to either having engaged in sexual activity with David Camm in the years prior to the murders, or having experienced sexual advances from him during his work as a state trooper. One co-worker, a police dispatcher, also testified that David was highly flirtatious and solicitous with women at the state police post.

A family friend also testified that Jill Camm had complained about soreness in her vaginal area—testimony meant to buttress suggested, but not proven, charges that David Camm had molested his own daughter.

The initial trial for David Camm stretched on for more than two months, with the defense waiting until March 7, 2002 to call David to testify on his own behalf. He gave a heartbreaking account of finding the bodies of his family in the garage and told of how he had lifted Bradley's body from the Bronco in a fruitless attempt to perform CPR on him.

Prosecutor Faith vigorously cross-examined David, including questioning him about alleged sexual improprieties in his past, and the quality of his marriage. David's defense attorney Michael McDaniel was not impressed and blurted out to the court that the state was attempting to "smear David. The State is attempting just one more incident of 'We ain't got much of a case, so let's just hammer David on behaving badly.'"[8]

Final arguments were heard on March 14, 2002, and jurors began to pore over more than 400 exhibits and testimony from more than 100 total witnesses over the previous nine weeks. Sixteen hours of deliberations on the first day produced no verdict. As jurors worked, David gave an exclusive jailhouse interview to CBS News.

Another full day of deliberations followed until, just before midnight on Sunday, March 17, jurors sent a note to the judge saying they had reached a decision. Jurors would later tell reporters that deliberations had been intense and angry at times with significant hostilities exchanged between the twelve.

The verdict: Guilty on all three counts.

David was returned to the Floyd County Jail to await sentencing, which took place on April 11. Judge Richard Striegel heard testimony from members of Kimberly's family, asking for the maximum sentence allowed—195 years total for all three murders.

David himself spoke, telling those who believed he was guilty, "You may have gotten your wish and had me imprisoned in my body, but I will always remain free on the inside . . . Regardless of where I am, but I will always in good conscience, conscience knowing that Kim, Brad, and Jill are walking this walk with me, because they know I am innocent . . . ."[9]

Judge Striegel said the evidence had convinced him that David was "a cold and unmerciful" person who deserved the maximum sentence allowed, which he then entered: 195 years.

David was transferred to the Wabash Valley Correctional Facility at Carlisle, Indiana, and although he was reported to be a "model prisoner," his past as a police officer required correctional officials to handle him carefully.

He would not remain in that Wabash Valley cell, however.

On August 10, 2004, the Indiana Court of Appeals shocked state and national observers of the trial when it reversed the three murder convictions against David. The court ruled unanimously that Judge Striegel had erred in allowing testimony about David's alleged extramarital affairs and that this information served to prejudice jurors against him.

The State of Indiana immediately appealed the ruling to the Indiana Supreme Court, which later back the lower appeals court ruling. As a result, David Camm was released from prison on bond in January 2005 as Floyd County officials scurried to refile charges against him for a second trial.

The second trial would be moved far from Floyd County and the ubiquitous eye of the Louisville, Kentucky TV audience on both sides of the Ohio River. In tiny Boonville, Indiana, the Warrick Superior Court would take up the second attempt to convict David Camm.

A new twist would provide even more shocking developments as Floyd County and Indiana State Police investigators announced on March 5, 2005 that they had arrested a second suspect in the Camm family murders.

Police said they were holding a thirty-five-year-old ex-con from Louisville named Charles D. Boney. Boney had admitted under questioning that he had met David twice in 2000 while playing basketball and that David had talked to him about Jesus—but also about a plan to kill his family. Boney said he had given David the gun used to kill his family, but stopped short of implicating himself in the actual murders.

Prosecutors immediately added conspiracy to commit murder charges against David and had him arrested yet again.

The evidence used in charging Boney for his part in the case was familiar—investigators said they had a sweatshirt found at the scene of the murders linked to Boney, and that Boney had drawn an accurate map of the murder scene in the garage.

Boney was tried separately on murder and conspiracy charges in January 2006 and convicted in Floyd Circuit Court. He was originally sentenced to 225 years in prison. Boney filed multiple appeals to his conviction, alleging juror misconduct among other things. His conviction was affirmed by Indiana's appellate courts, but his sentence was modified to sixty-five years on each of three counts of murder, and one count of conspiracy to commit murder. He will die in prison, pending any further appeals, as his earliest release date won't come until he is 148 years old.

At nearly the same time, David Camm's second trial was underway in Boonville in January 2006, this time without evidence presented of David's alleged philandering. Instead, new Floyd County Prosecutor Keith Henderson introduced a new possible motive for the crime—that David was trying to cover up the alleged sexual molestation of his five-year-old daughter.

Boney did not testify in the Boonville trial for David, but evidence was presented from his prior trial that he had conspired with Camm to kill his family. Jurors found Camm guilty a second time in March 2006, and Warrick County Judge Robert Aylsworth sentenced him to life in prison without the possibility of parole.

Another appeal was filed, and remarkably, in June 2009 Camm was successful again as the Indiana Supreme Court ruled 4-1 to overturn his second conviction, ruling that information about the alleged molestation of his daughter was improperly presented at trial without competent evidence to support the claim. They ordered a new trial.

Camm's third and final trial was moved to the Boone County Courthouse in Lebanon, just outside of Indianapolis, and featured two new aspects: enhanced DNA evidence from both the state and the defense, and the less-than-credible testimony of Charles Boney about David's alleged role in the crime.

The third time was the charm, at least for David Camm, as on January 24, 2013, the jury found him not guilty on all charges and he walked free—fully free—for the first time since 2000.

Subsequent to his release, Camm was sued by Kimberly's parents, Frank and Janice Renn, in a wrongful death suit, but they later dropped the case and focused instead on efforts to keep David from collecting an estimated $625,000 in insurance proceeds from his wife's death.

About a year after his acquittal, Camm met privately with the Boone County jurors who set him free. He also initiated a suit against Floyd County for damages related to his thirteen years of imprisonment. He also sued Boney for the wrongful death of his family. Since his release, he has returned to Floyd County to live, engaged in public speaking, and joined various innocence projects around the country working to free persons who believe they are wrongly incarcerated.

Endnotes

1. *Louisville Courier-Journal*, Sept. 30, 2000
2. *Louisville Courier-Journal*, Oct. 1, 2000
3. Ibid.
4. *Louisville Courier-Journal*, Oct. 2, 2000
5. Ibid.
6. *Louisville Courier-Journal*, Oct. 3, 2000
7. Ibid.
8. Glatt, John. (2005). *One Deadly Night*. St. Martin's Press: New York (p. 302).
9. Glatt, John. (2005). *One Deadly Night*. St. Martin's Press: New York (p. 321-322).

FOUNTAIN COUNTY

VICTIM(S):
Vida Mae Foxworthy, 54

PERPETRATOR(S):
Thomas Harold Johnston, 52

DATE OF DEATH(S):
May 4, 1957

A TRAVELING SALESMAN KILLS THE HOTEL MAID

By all accounts, traveling salesman Thomas Harold Johnston, fifty-two, was not much of a success. In financial straits brought on by the lack of sales, and seemingly unable to go home as a failure, he took drastic measures on Saturday, May 4, 1957, as a guest of the Hotel Attica in Fountain County.

On that day, Attica police responded to a 2:45 p.m. call when Johnston asked the front desk, and moments later, the hotel bar for a doctor or an ambulance.

Responding officers found the hotel's maid, fifty-four-year-old Vida Mae Foxworthy, lying face down on the bed in Room 21, dead from multiple shotgun blasts. A blanket had been pulled over her but failed to cover the macabre scene of the top of Mrs. Foxworthy's skull blown off from the blast and splattering the room with blood.[1]

Nearby sat Johnston, suffering a shotgun wound to the inside of his mouth that had blown a grotesque hole in the side of his face. Smoke and powder burns on his face indicated he had been shot at close range. Police immediately suspected a murder and an attempt at suicide.

Attica Police Officer Tom Turner would later confirm that responding officers found the door to the second-floor hotel room partially blocked but were able to open it with a pass-key and force.[2]

Johnston immediately told officers that Mrs. Foxworthy had shot him, and a 12-gauge shotgun was recovered from the room. Johnston couldn't say much, however, as his face wound made speaking almost impossible and he passed out as he was being placed on an ambulance gurney, Turner said.[3]

Mrs. Foxworthy, married for thirty years to Roy Foxworthy of Attica at the time of the attack, was the mother of two grown sons and a soft-spoken woman.

Fountain County Coroner Charles Fishero said the shotgun blasts had severed the left hand of Mrs. Foxworthy at the wrist as she put up her hands to defend herself. Shotgun "wadding" was taken from her head, chest, and arm and from a wall over the bed.

A Fountain County grand jury indicted Johnston on a charge of murder on May 17, 1957. His trial got underway in October 1957.[4]

Fountain County Prosecutor Karl Overbeck said he would prove that Johnston was not legally drunk at the time of the attack and that there had been no evidence found of a sexual encounter between the defendant and the deceased.

Overbeck scoffed at Johnston's repeated claims that Mrs. Foxworthy shot herself moments after shooting him, given that she knew nothing of firearms and that Johnston's wound was inflicted at close range, from inside his mouth.

Overbeck suggested robbery was the actual motive. Mrs. Foxworthy's purse was found on the dresser in Johnston's room—something she normally safely stored away in a storage closet she used for her cleaning supplies. The prosecutor noted that on the day of the shooting, Mrs. Foxworthy had just been paid and Johnston had just become two weeks past due on his bill for the hotel.[5]

Prosecutors called a series of Johnston's relatives who confirmed he picked up the shotgun and fifteen shells from their home at Independence, Indiana, on Friday, May 3, and that he was well acquainted with firing a shotgun. Those same relatives reported Johnston had not been a regular visitor at their home, and his unannounced visit on that day surprised them.[6]

Johnston took the stand in his own defense and said Mrs. Foxworthy had visited his room at 7:45 a.m. on Saturday, May 4, and had kissed him and removed her underwear during a twenty-minute visit in his room.[7]

He said she left but returned moments later and invited him to join her in cleaning rooms on the second and third floors of the hotel. Johnston said he placed beer on the maid's cleaning cart, and the two drank together in a vacant room on the third floor at about 10 a.m.[8]

Johnston then said Mrs. Foxworthy left again, but returned at about 1:30 p.m. and began expressing an interest in his shotgun, propped up against the wall of the room, and asked to be shown how to use it.

"They talked about their mutual affection, the accused testified," according to an account in the *Fountain-Warren Democrat.* "He told her he was going to leave town on Monday to go to Fort Wayne to get some work done. He had not left before because she had asked him not to, he said."[9]

As she now handled the shotgun, Johnston testified, Mrs. Foxworthy asked him if he trusted her. "I certainly do," he said he replied, and moments later she fired the gun, striking him in the face.[10]

A brutal cross-examination lasted more than an hour, with Johnston sticking to his story or offering a pat "I don't remember" when he couldn't answer.[11]

Prosecutors were able to get Johnston to admit he had been married and divorced twice, and that his license to sell insurance in the state of Indiana had been revoked. He had since turned to selling advertising novelty clocks.

Jurors took only three hours to convict Johnston following a fifteen-day trial. He showed no emotion as the verdict was read—nor when he learned that the jury had recommended he be executed for his crime.[12]

His death sentence would be the first ever in Fountain County.[13]

Johnston appealed his conviction and his sentence, and in December 1958 won a third stay of execution from the Indiana Supreme Court as his appeal went forward.[14]

On December 23, 1958, the Indiana Supreme Court set aside Johnston's conviction and sentence and ordered a new trial. The Supreme Court said "misconduct prejudicial to the defendant" by one juror, Alice Leoma Harvey, meant his first trial was unfair.[15]

Mrs. Harvey, during jury selection, had failed to disclose that she was a second cousin of the victim, Mrs. Foxworthy. The high court said failure to disclose such a relationship was unacceptable, even in civil cases, and that "this rule certainly should apply with intensified force when a man's life is at stake."[16]

Following the high court's ruling, Fountain County Circuit Court Judge Roy C. Fenters ordered Johnston returned to Fountain County from the Indiana State Prison so a new trial could be conducted.[17]

In April 1959, Judge Fenters approved a motion by Johnston's attorneys to move his case to Vermillion County on a change of venue.[18]

A new trial for Johnston began at Newport, Indiana, on October 8, 1959, and included most of the same witnesses as the first trial, except Johnston, who did not testify in the second trial. The outcome was also the same as jurors voted to convict Johnston on October 21, 1959, and set his penalty at life imprisonment.[19]

Endnotes

1. *Fountain-Warren Democrat*, May 10, 1957.
2. *Fountain-Warren Democrat*, Oct. 18, 1957.
3. Ibid.
4. *Fountain-Warren Democrat*, May 17, 1957.
5. *Fountain-Warren Democrat*, Oct. 18, 1957.
6. *Fountain-Warren Democrat*, Oct. 23, 1957.
7. Ibid.
8. Ibid.
9. Ibid.
10. Ibid.
11. Ibid.
12. *Fountain-Warren Democrat*, Nov. 1, 1957.
13. Ibid.
14. *Covington Republican*, Dec. 11, 1958.
15. *Fountain-Warren Democrat*, Dec. 26, 1958.
16. Ibid.
17. *Fountain-Warren Democrat*, Jan. 23, 1959.
18. *Fountain-Warren Democrat*, April 10, 1959.
19. *Fountain-Warren Democrat*, Oct. 22, 1959.

FRANKLIN COUNTY

VICTIM(S):
Harry A. Miller, 59

PERPETRATOR(S):
Heber "Jimmy" L. Hicks, 36;
William A. Kuhlman, 27;
John J. Poholsky, 35;
Frank Gore Williams, 40

DATE OF DEATH(S):
June 11, 1936

'THE HEAD AND HANDS CASE'

Harry Miller, a retired fire captain from the Cincinnati Fire Department, liked to convince others he had made a fortune in the stock market and other investments. The level of his financial success was subject to debate—after his death. Before his grisly death, he had apparently convinced many, including his killers, that he was a wealthy man and they wanted his money.

Captain Miller's murder was headline news across Indiana, Ohio, and Kentucky in the hot summer of 1936, and quickly gained fame as "the head and hands case" for the gruesome discovery of Miller's severed hands and head in two separate locations.

Captain Miller was last seen alive late on Thursday, June 11, 1936, at the Harrison Dog Track not far from his summer home near New Trenton, Indiana, about eleven miles southeast of Brookville near the Franklin-Dearborn county line.

In the days following, Captain Miller's eccentric sister Flora Miller of Cincinnati reported receiving a postcard signed with her brother's name. Some thought the signature looked like Harry's; others did not.

On Friday, June 19, about thirty miles south of the Ohio River at Eminence, Kentucky, police announced the body of an unidentified white male had been found stuffed in a culvert. The man's head and hands had been severed. He weighed about 250 pounds, matching Captain Miller's stout figure.

Captain Miller's family and friends were beginning to worry this could be his body, despite the postcard received earlier. Their worries were founded in the fact that clothing left on the body matched that of Captain Miller's.

Flora, sixty-six, was seemingly worried about her brother but also seemed to enjoy the attention of reporters. She told reporters, "If the police don't clear this case up in a few days, I'll bust this thing wide open myself."[1]

On Sunday, June 28, 1936, police got another big break.

Three young men swimming in a lake near Carrollton, Kentucky, east of Madison, Indiana, on the Kentucky side of the Ohio River, were attracted to a large school of fish gathering in the water near a box submerged in two feet of water. As they lifted the box from the water, at least one human hand was exposed from inside. Police were immediately called and quickly determined that the box contained two male hands and a man's severed head.

The head and hands had been encased in a cardboard box measuring fourteen by twenty-eight inches, which was then lined with cement. Although lime had been used inside the box in an attempt to speed up decomposition (and thus thwart identification), the killers used "slack lime" instead of "quicklime"—the "slack lime" acting almost as a preservative for the head. Water decomposition of the hands, however, made fingerprinting to assist in identification impossible.

Carroll County, Kentucky, Sheriff Walton Banks said the head suffered a gunshot wound, and "the head was cut from the body near the top of the man's neck, and each hand was smoothly amputated at the wrist."[2]

A local doctor examined the head and declared the victim had received excellent dental care throughout his life, including a bridge and many fillings. He estimated the man's age at between fifty-five and sixty years of age.

Sheriff Banks said he believed the head and hands matched the torso found earlier at the town of Eminence, Kentucky.

Eventually, friends of Captain Miller from Indiana and Ohio, and his sister Flora, identified the head as being that of the "Cap."

Days later on Friday, July 3, 1936, headlines across three states bore the startling news that Captain Miller's sister Flora and her chauffer Heber L. Hicks had been arrested and charged with the slaying. The suspects were held "somewhere in Indiana," reporters learned, although their exact location was not disclosed as Kentucky officials were attempting to arrest the duo as well. A short tug-of-war took place between Indiana and Kentucky officials until it was determined Captain Miller had been killed in Indiana and only his body parts dumped in Kentucky.

Hicks was familiar with the criminal justice system. He had been convicted of the murder of a young widow at Clay, Kentucky, in 1918, but had won parole after serving only eleven years. He also had 1932 and 1933 arrests on liquor and robbery charges. Despite that, he had gained employment and trust from Flora Miller and, by doing so, gained access to her wealthy brother, Captain Miller. Captain Miller was said to hate Hicks and wanted him away from his sister.

As Hicks and Flora Miller were shuttled around Indiana, moving between six jails in Brookville, Indianapolis, and other locations not disclosed, Indiana State Police investigators continued to question them, led by Captain Matt Leach. Both also underwent lie detector tests.

Finally on Sunday, July 7, four days after their arrest and after more than twenty hours of continuous questioning at the ISP Post at Seymour, Indiana, Hicks confessed that he had "instigated" the murder of Captain Miller. He did so after meeting privately with Flora, and then exonerated her as having no part in the crime, or the plan to commit it.

Upon her release, Flora told reporters that she had no idea Hicks had any part in the murder and said she had tried "to keep still, say nothing and keep my trap shut until I had all the dope, then move into action."[3]

She said she had no complaints about how police had treated her—again seeming to enjoy the attention the case brought her—and said "everyone of them [the police] were perfect gentlemen."[4]

In his confession, Hicks said, "I figured that if [Captain Miller] was out of the way, that Miss Flora Miller would receive the estate and that I indirectly would benefit by it, because of the fact that I was employed by Miss Miller."[5]

Hicks said he had planned the killing for about six weeks and had paid three other men, all seasoned convicts. He named the men as John J. Poholsky, William Kuhlman, and Frank G. Williams—each receiving a starting fee of $30. Hicks had promised the men they ultimately would receive more than $5,500 in cash and stocks from Miller's accounts, and said he was going to the movies during the attack in order to establish an alibi for himself. He told the men to take Captain Miller's body at least 400 miles away from his Franklin County home—but had not told them to dismember the body.

"... they told me that the lick was first struck in the kitchen with the metal pipe. And after several licks the man went down on his front porch, and in the scuffle, someone went into the screen [door]. There was blood on the porch and they mopped that up with water," Hicks said in describing the attack.[6]

Hicks said the men told him they loaded Miller's unconscious body into the trunk of their Ford V-8 and set off for Kentucky. The three killers told him that Kuhlman fired the shots that killed their victim as he awakened in the trunk as they approached the Ohio River ferry at Madison, Indiana. Poholsky dismembered the body later in Kentucky.

After Hicks' confession was revealed, Kentucky authorities released to their Indiana counterparts a large amount of evidence they had collected in the case.

Franklin County Special Prosecutor Charles A. Lowe and Deputy Attorney General J. Edward Barce would try the state's case against Hicks. The judge ruled that live radio broadcasts from the courtroom inside the Franklin County Courthouse would not be allowed, despite requests from Indianapolis and Cincinnati reporters.

Hicks' trial was to go forward with the other three defendants still at large until finally in November 1936 police lucked out and picked up Poholsky as he worked a corn husking job in Warren, Ohio. Hicks' trial opened December 10, 1936, and the state opened its case with a bang by calling Poholsky as its first witness. Poholsky promptly implicated Hicks in not only planning the murder but carrying it out as well.

"Seldom has a courtroom heard a story of such shocking brutality—a story in which Poholsky made no effort to spare himself," the *Cincinnati Enquirer* reported. "Each time as he repeated—three or four times during his testimony—the matter-of-fact statement, 'I cut off his head and hands,' a gasp went up from the spectators."[7]

Poholsky said all four of the men were guilty and "I expect to be tried. I am not afraid of the electric chair."[8]

He said that after the men beat Captain Miller, Hicks gave them a mop, bath towel, and a sweater to clean blood off the front porch of the home. The three men then left with Captain Miller's body in their trunk, and Hicks stayed behind at the New Trenton home to clean up further evidence.

Poholsky said that as the group drove toward the ferry at Madison, Indiana, to cross into Kentucky, they heard Miller becoming conscious in the trunk. It was at that time that Kuhlman shot and killed him—in Indiana.

A plan to bury Captain Miller's body near Carrollton, Kentucky, was abandoned, Poholsky told the court, because they grew tired of digging in the hard, rocky soil. Instead, "we took the man out of the car and I cut off his head and hands," Poholsky said. He added, "blood gushed out" as the head was severed.[9]

As shocking as Poholsky's testimony had been to the start of the trial, events outside the courtroom on Friday, December 11, 1936, would match that excitement. Police in Portland, Oregon, announced they had arrested the alleged triggerman, Kuhlman, as he attempted to rob a theatre there. Kuhlman told Oregon detectives that Hicks had paid him $5,100 so far for the killing, but he never received any more because Hicks was arrested. He said the plot was intended to indicate Miller had left town on a trip, while Hicks led the men in raiding his assets.

Kuhlman said he "read about [Hicks' arrest] in Cleveland, so I blew."[10] He added, "The only connection I had with the job was that I was supposed to shoot the fellow. When the others involved started to mutilate him, I objected but I was in too deep then, so I walked down the road while the body was cut up."[11]

Back at Hicks' trial, which continued in Brookville, his attorneys unsuccessfully argued that Hicks' confession should not be admitted because police had used illegal tactics to obtain it. Franklin County Judge Roscoe C. O'Byrne disagreed and ruled the jury would hear Hicks' confession.

Things got worse for Hicks when prosecutors announced they would present Kuhlman as a last-minute witness, having successfully extradited and transported him back to Indiana from Oregon.

"He is just as guilty as I am," Kuhlman declared from the witness stand as Hicks sank in his seat.[12]

Kuhlman dramatically added, "I've seen all I want to see. I've done everything I want to do, and I'm ready to go to the electric chair. I'm glad this damn thing is off my mind."[13]

As the state rested its case on Wednesday, December 16, another out-of-court development brought big headlines—police in San Francisco, California, arrested the fourth and last suspect in Captain Miller's death: Frank Gore Williams. Williams was picked up at a San Francisco department store where he had gained a job as a clerk and, under questioning, gave a complete confession that matched ones already given by Poholsky and Kuhlman.

Hicks had no choice—he would have to testify on his own behalf to try to counter the damning testimony offered by Poholsky and Kuhlman.

He told jurors that Flora Miller had promised him outstanding legal defense if he took the rap for hiring the murderers "and that she would place $25,000 in my mother's name which I could get when I finished serving the light sentence the Indiana police promised to give me if I confessed."[14] He said Poholsky and Kuhlman only named him as a participant because they were bitter because he had given their names to police.

His testimony could not save him—jurors voted to convict him of premeditated murder, but did not find against him on charges of robbery or burglary. Judge O'Byrne immediately took up the issue of sentencing and asked Hicks if he had anything to say first.

Hicks remained calm, having just heard the guilty verdict, and said, "I have violated no law in the state of Indiana."[15]

With that, Judge O'Byrne sentenced Hicks to death in Indiana's electric chair.

On February 3, 1937, Poholsky, Kuhlman, and Williams all appeared before Judge O'Byrne, prepared to enter guilty pleas to the same murder indictment to which Hicks had been convicted; however, a trial would still have to be conducted to determine the sentence for Kuhlman, who did not want to be sentenced by the judge.

On February 15, 1937, a special jury began hearing evidence against Kuhlman and ruled on February 18 that Kuhlman should be executed for his crimes. On February 25, Judge O'Byrne sentenced Poholsky and Williams to be executed as well.

Poholsky and Kuhlman took their sentences without comment, but Williams told the court, "I was involved in killing a good man and deserve the punishment."[16]

On June 10, 1937, Poholsky, Kuhlman, and Williams were all executed in the electric chair at the state prison in Michigan City. It was the first time in Indiana history that three men had been executed on the same day.

Hicks continued to win stays to his scheduled execution from the Indiana Supreme Court as his appeal, based on the admissibility of his confession, was completely reviewed. When the U.S. Supreme Court refused to hear Hicks' case, and Governor M. Clifford Townsend refused to intervene with a clemency order, Hicks' execution finally went forward on May 6, 1938.

Endnotes
1. *Cincinnati* (Ohio) *Enquirer*, July 2, 1936.
2. *Cincinnati* (Ohio) *Enquirer*, June 29, 1936.
3. *Cincinnati* (Ohio) *Enquirer*, July 8, 1936.
4. Ibid.
5. *Cincinnati* (Ohio) *Enquirer*, July 8, 1936.
6. Ibid.

7. *Cincinnati* (Ohio) *Enquirer,* Dec. 10, 1936.
8. Ibid.
9. Ibid.
10. *Cincinnati* (Ohio) *Enquirer,* Dec. 12, 1936.
11. *Cincinnati* (Ohio) *Enquirer,* Dec. 13, 1936.
12. *Cincinnati* (Ohio) *Enquirer,* Dec. 15, 1936.
13. Ibid.
14. *Cincinnati* (Ohio) *Enquirer,* Dec. 18, 1936.
15. *Cincinnati* (Ohio) *Enquirer,* Dec. 22, 1936.
16. *Brookville American*, Feb. 25, 1937.

FULTON COUNTY

VICTIM(S):
Mary Singer, 48;
Alonzo Singer, 23;
Charles Clark, 68

PERPETRATOR(S):
Charles Clark, 68

DATE OF DEATH(S):
March 3, 1935

AN OLD MAN FALLS INTO DARKNESS

Charles Clark and his common-law wife, Mary Singer, led a life punctuated by poverty and loss.

Two years before they began living together (an uncommon practice in 1930s Indiana), Clark's wife died after a long illness.

In early March 1935, his beloved dog also died. The loss of Clark's dog proved to be one loss too many.

Suspecting Mary or her son Alonzo had something to do with the dog's death, Clark took an ax and murdered both of them as they slept in the rural Fulton County home they shared with Clark.

Police only discovered Clark's sickening acts after he swallowed carbolic acid and took his secrets to his grave.

The bodies of Mary, forty-eight, and Alonzo Singer, twenty-three, were found by police on Tuesday, March 5, 1935, although authorities believe they were killed sometime on Sunday, March 3.

Fulton County Sheriff Boyd Peterson went to the ramshackle home of Clark and Singer after Howard County authorities notified him that Clark had killed himself in a home there.

The *Rochester News-Sentinel's* account captured the startling nature of the crime: "A farm woman and her son were found hacked to death by an ax in their single room farm house, five miles northwest of Rochester in the Burton neighborhood late Tuesday afternoon."[1]

The "farm house" the common-law family lived in reflected their struggle. Measuring only twelve by fifteen feet, the one-room structure sat on a cement foundation insulated from the cold winter winds on the outside with bales of straw and hay.

Fulton County sheriff's deputies "broke in the only door to the shack and found the bodies of Mrs. Singer and her son lying within the bed and covered with a number of comforters ... decomposition had begun," the *News-Sentinel* reported.[2]

The detailed newspaper account told readers that a blood-soaked ax was also found beneath the bed in the "small room spattered with blood. Bloody handprints were on the table in the room which also held four loaves of bread which had probably been baked a few hours before the murder. Crimson hand prints of a man could be found here and there on the clothing of the bed, while spots of blood were on the few pieces of furniture in the room ..."[3]

The coroner ruled that Mrs. Singer and her son were both struck with a blunt object as they slept, as both were still clad in their nightclothes. An ax was then used on both victims, particularly to the victims' heads, almost severing their skulls in the brutal attack.

The *News-Sentinel* reported that Alonzo held a death grip on a large flashlight, while Mary's hands were outstretched in front of her as if trying to defend herself from a blow.

A motive for the attack was developed by talking to neighbors who said Clark loved his little black dog more than anything in the world and that he had become deeply depressed when the dog disappeared two weeks before.

Police believe Clark particularly suspected Alonzo of killing the dog, with news reports describing Alonzo as "subnormal mentally."[4]

Neighbors reported at least one quarrel between Clark and Alonzo, with Clark allegedly saying, "If I find that dog's body, it will be too bad for you."

Clark apparently did find the dog's body, spent hours praying over it hoping for its recovery, and when that failed, buried the dog in a small thicket near his home on Sunday afternoon. Sometime after that, he set about killing Mary and Alonzo.

By Tuesday morning, no one had seen Mary and Alonzo for a few days, but Clark told a neighbor they were away visiting relatives in Kokomo. That day, he also sold some pigs and chickens to a neighboring farmer, who gave him a ride into Rochester.

While in Rochester, Clark visited the Blue Drug Store downtown, where he reportedly bought a bottle of carbolic acid. He then purchased flour and sugar for his chauffeur, as well as some gasoline.

It is believed he then hitchhiked his way to Kokomo, about forty-three miles south of Rochester.

Clark made it to his daughter's home at 814 West Foster Street in Kokomo, but not before visiting his landlord and paying to fix a tire on his nephew's car so he could get a ride to his daughter Hazel Christy's home. Finding her not at home, he asked his nephew to take him to his daughter Mable Burton's home on Foster Street.

Mable told authorities he was acting weird and brought a suitcase into the house saying it contained silverware, rings, and other belongings of his deceased wife. Mable could see that he was troubled and asked if he was in trouble. She told police he said "nothing much" and then retired to the bathroom.

A short time later, Mable heard groans from the bathroom and found him collapsed and dead on the floor from having consumed the acid.

Mable notified authorities about her father's suicide, and the ugly details emerged.

Clark provided no details about what he had done or whether the dog's death had been the reason. His daughters reported he had been despondent since the death of his wife (and their mother). Since that time, he had lived on and off with Mary Singer, although he was twenty years her senior, and no record of a marriage between the two was ever located.

Mrs. Singer, a widow who gained her property at her husband's death, had another son who was serving a lengthy sentence at the Pendleton Reformatory. It is unclear if she had much contact with a married daughter living further south at Peru, Indiana.

Mary and Alonzo were buried immediately because of the state of decomposition. Clark's family buried him in a separate cemetery.

Endnotes

1. *Rochester News-Sentinel,* March 6, 1935.
2. Ibid.
3. Ibid.
4. Ibid.

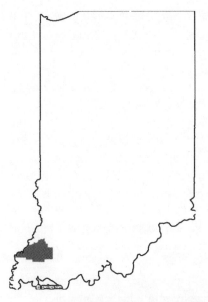

GIBSON COUNTY

VICTIM(S):
Nora Kifer, 18

PERPETRATOR(S):
Joseph D. Keith, 40

DATE OF DEATH(S):
April 3, 1900

A DESPERATE MAN SILENCES HIS LOVER, PERMANENTLY

On May 23, 1900, two men en route home from Evansville, Indiana, were startled to find the mostly nude body of a young woman floating in Pigeon Creek, near the confluence of three Indiana counties: Gibson, Warrick, and Vanderburgh.

The body was soon identified as that of eighteen-year-old Nora Kifer of the tiny Warrick County village of Elberfeld, Indiana. She had been missing since she was last seen leaving her parents' home on April 3, 1900.

Investigators worked quickly to try to provide answers to "a most atrocious case and one of the most cold-blooded crimes ever committed in southern Indiana," as the *Princeton Daily Clarion* described it.[1]

A heavy stone was tied by a cord to the young woman's neck in an unsuccessful effort to keep her body from reaching the surface of the water. An examination of the body showed she had suffered numerous blunt force injuries to the head from an unknown object. The coroner reported her head was crushed on both sides and the upper jaw was broken. Despite the severe decomposition, her body was in rather good shape for having been dead for so many weeks. This view buttressed the suspicion that Nora's body had originally been dumped in a well at Elberfeld and then later moved to Pigeon Creek.[2]

Nora's father, Zachariah T. Kifer, traveled to an Evansville mortuary to identify his daughter's body. He had last seen her alive walking away from his home near a tow path leading to a bridge that crossed the creek she was found floating in.

Just a day later, police arrested Joseph D. Keith, described as "a well-to-do farmer and real estate dealer."

The *Princeton Daily Clarion* covered the case closely as it was moved to the Gibson County Courthouse there. The *Daily Clarion* told its readers, "There were many circumstances which formed a strong chain of evidence indicating [Keith's] guilt. It was known around Elberfeld that Keith had been intimate with the girl and had been threatened with a seduction suit, although himself a man of family."[4]

Keith was known to be "of very penurious disposition." The reporter added, "It was not put above him to do away with the girl rather than to pay her any money."[5]

Investigators said a letter sent to Nora's mother six weeks before her body was found purported to place the young woman in Chicago on a previously unannounced trip. If the letter was meant to fool Nora's parents who worried terribly about her whereabouts, it didn't work. Written in red ink, the note read: "Dear mother, I start this evening for Chicago with a friend on a trip. I may be gone three months and might six. Do not be uneasy about me. From your daughter, Lora."[6]

That it was signed "Lora," rather than "Nora," tipped off Kifer's parents that it may have been written by the only person they knew who had ever called their daughter "Lora": Joseph Keith.[7]

Further pointing to Keith was the fact that his sixteen-year-old son, Jesse, told police he had taken a note from his father to Nora (as he had before) on the afternoon of April 3, 1900, that said he wanted her to meet him on a bridge over Pigeon Creek. April 3, 1900, was the last time Nora was ever seen alive.

Keith's buggy was seized by investigators the day after he was arrested; it was found to be freshly painted despite the winter snow. A rug on the base of the buggy was confiscated and later determined to be carrying a great deal of blood. Keith told police it was blood from meat he had purchased from a local butcher. Investigators believed it was Nora's blood.

Keith, despite being a respected local businessman, did not seem to help himself when he at first told detectives that he had hired a "peddler" from outside of the area to take Nora out of the area and abandon her. He later confessed under questioning that that story was not true.

The trial for Keith opened on January 1, 1901, at Princeton. An early witness was Nora's father, Zachariah, who insisted the body he had seen at the mortuary was that of his daughter. Nora's mother, Mary Kifer, also testified about the clothing that Nora wore the last day she was seen, some of which was recovered with her body, including a new corset still on her bloated, ·decomposing body.

Mary Kifer said that Joseph Keith had never visited their home before November 1899. After that, she said he always came to their house on some sort of business, but his visits became more and more frequent, several times a week, and he always asked for or about "Lora," the name he called Nora. On his last visit on April 2, 1900, Mary Kifer said they discussed the fact that Nora was preparing to marry a young man she had been dating.

Other witnesses called confirmed that Keith had paid a boarding house bill and other expenses Nora had run up during a few brief stays in Evansville.

In the weeks Nora was missing, rumors apparently grew about Keith's alleged involvement, and Keith was actively seeking to stop the rumors. Willie Butcher of Warrick County testified that Keith confronted him twice about alleged rumors he was spreading placing Nora and Keith together on the bridge over the creek.

"He said there was a right smart of talk around about me telling that and said he wanted it bluffed down or it would cause him trouble," Butcher said. "[I] talked to him again about a week before he was arrested ... the conversation was like the other one. He told me he was about to get in trouble about this with old man Kifer ... said he wanted the talk bluffed down."[8]

Butcher also said Keith alleged Nora was in Evansville at "a sporting house" and that "she'd been lying on him and that she was going to bring a suit against him."[9]

Joey Duffy, a friend of Joseph Keith's son Jesse, said he talked to Joseph Keith on May 20, 1900, three days before Nora's body was found.

"He asked me if I heard anything about him and Nora Kifer. Replied that I had heard some. Joseph said it was all a lie, and said he'd make someone pay for it," Duffy testified.[10]

He added that Keith told him, "If [Nora] had lied about people around Evansville like she has done around Elberfeld, she's liable to be killed and thrown in the river."[11]

Lucy Greer, a local resident, testified she saw Nora on the bridge near sundown on April 3, 1900, and that she was pacing back and forth there as if waiting for someone to arrive.

Prosecutors also called Phillip Skora, an Evansville jeweler and pawnbroker, who said he sold Keith a $3 gold ring in the early spring of 1900 and that Keith had asked him to tell the young woman with him (who was later identified as Nora) that the ring cost $10.

Skora said Keith told him "he was having some trouble with the girl …
and he wanted her to think that he thought a great deal of her in buying a $10
ring." Skora said he refused to lie to the woman and said nothing.[12]

Harry Voges, the night desk clerk at the Hotel Richmond in Downtown
Evansville, was also subpoenaed and testified that Keith and a young woman
he later learned was Nora had registered at his hotel on December 13, 1899,
as "J. Smith and wife, Princeton, Indiana." He said the couple stayed in
room 18 of the hotel for two days. Prosecutors presented the hotel register as
evidence as well.

Sixteen-year-old Jesse Keith was called to testify against his father as
well.

"I took a note to Nora, papa gave it to me when I was at school [and]
Papa called me out," he said. "He wrote on a piece of paper he got out of his
pocket, using lead pencil. He told me to take it to Kifer's and give it to Nora.
Told me to give it to no one else."[13]

Jesse said he did as he was told and after delivering the note, did not
return to school.[14]

Jesse reluctantly admitted he had read the note before delivering it to
Nora. He said it read, "Nora, meet me at the barn about dark."

Prosecutors pressed Jesse, asking if the note actually said "bridge" instead
of "barn."

"I thought it said 'barn,' but I couldn't make out the word. That's all
I remember about the note. It might have said, 'I want to see you on some
business,'" Jesse replied.[15]

The *Daily Clarion* reported that one of "the most pathetic and the most
sensational scenes of the trial occurred when Zachariah Kifer was recalled to
the stand." Nora's father wept bitterly as he retold the fact that he had talked to
Joseph Keith on May 13, 1900, a little over a month after Nora had disappeared.
He said Keith volunteered at one point in the conversation, "I understand you
got another letter from Nora."[16]

Mr. Kifer said he told Keith, "I replied that I had not and never had got
a letter from her since she went away. Joe told me he heard it talked that way
around the neighborhood."[17]

Mr. Kifer said Keith continued telling him that he had heard his daughter,
Nora, planned to sue him for $1,500 on a charge of seduction.

"I asked him if he had had anything to do with the girl, and he had
said he had not," Mr. Kifer said. "Then he told me my daughter was of loose
character, that the boys of the neighborhood were running around with her;
that they would go to her window at night, peck on the glass, and crawl into
the house when she raised the window."[18]

News reports indicated that "at this point, Mr. Kifer broke down completely, sobbing like a heart-broken child and using a large red handkerchief freely."[19]

Rebecca Hardin, Joseph Keith's aunt, admitted she had ill feelings for her nephew in her testimony about a visit she had with him in jail in which he said, "[Nora] broke my peace at home, she was getting away with all my money and something had to be done!"[20]

Hardin said she told her nephew that "he ought to acknowledge to the court if he was guilty and he didn't reply."[21]

Keith's defense consisted almost entirely of a series of character witnesses, local officials, and others who had real estate and other business dealings with him. All testified that, to their knowledge, he was an upright and responsible citizen. Keith's wife of seventeen years, Jennie Keith, also testified and said her husband had never been away from their home overnight and was never involved with another woman. She denied earlier statements she made to a coroner's inquest that her husband had been away from their home on the evening of April 3, 1900, and did not return until after the rest of the family had retired for the night.[22]

On Monday, January 7, 1901, Keith took the stand in his own defense and admitted he had been in Evansville with Nora but denied any sexual involvement with the woman. He attempted to show he had taken her to a boarding house in Evansville in order to help her out but that the boarding house operators later tried to sue him because Nora had caused trouble there, he said.[23]

"I went to [the boarding house] to see about the matter. I told [the operator] that I thought she was putting up a scheme to get a little money," Keith testified. He admitted he then paid a total of $150 to settle the complaint.[24]

He denied telling Nora's father that she was planning on suing him for seduction but did say he had heard rumors about himself and Nora in the area that concerned him greatly.

Although prosecutors had presented a highly circumstantial case, jurors found Keith guilty of murder on January 11, 1901, and fixed his sentence at death.

As he was being led back to the jail, Keith told a reporter from the *Daily Clarion*, "I am not surprised at the verdict, but I am innocent or I could never endure the ordeal in this way. I am confident I will yet vindicate myself."[25]

Keith and his lawyers were back in court a few weeks later arguing for a new trial alleging misconduct by three jurors who allegedly formed and expressed opinions about his guilt before the trial was concluded. Each of the three jurors was called, and each denied saying that Keith should be hung for his crimes prior to jury deliberations.

Keith himself testified for more than forty minutes starting off with, "I am absolutely innocent of the crime charged against me."[26]

Keith was able to get out before he began to sob, "Honorable judge, is it possible that any man in my hearing would believe that I would willfully destroy my peaceful and happy home by killing a girl against whom I had no malice, and thereby destroying the hopes of ever meeting my dear old mother in Heaven?"[27]

After two days of testimony on the appeal, Gibson County Circuit Court Judge Oscar M. Welborn overruled the appeal citing no known reason for witnesses, including members of Keith's family, to lie against him, and the fact that Keith had given incriminating statements or at least partial confessions to detectives. He said Keith's execution should go forward.

Keith's wife, Jennie, did not give up on her husband and continued to circulate petitions and write letters on his behalf. His attorneys petitioned the Indiana Supreme Court on his behalf, but the high court did not act on the case.

"Unless the unforeseen happens, Keith will meet his death on the scaffold shortly after midnight Thursday night," the *Evansville Courier* reported.[28]

The *Courier* also reported, "It is believed Mrs. Keith is at her home near Elberfeld and that she has abandoned hope of asking the governor to save the life of her husband. The wife of the condemned man has spent her fortune trying to save him from the gallows and is not able to go to Michigan City to bid her loved one a last farewell."[29]

Keith was hung on the gallows at the Indiana State Prison in Michigan City on November 15, 1901.

Endnotes

1. *Princeton Daily Clarion*, Jan. 1, 1901.
2. *Princeton Daily Clarion*, Jan. 6, 1901.
3. *Princeton Daily Clarion*, Jan. 1, 1901.
4. Ibid.
5. Ibid.
6. *Princeton Daily Clarion*, Jan. 4, 1901.
7. *Princeton Daily Clarion*, Jan. 1, 1901.
8. *Princeton Daily Clarion*, Jan. 3, 1901.
9. Ibid.
10. Ibid.
11. Ibid.
12. Ibid.
13. *Princeton Daily Clarion*, Jan. 4, 1901.
14. Ibid.

15. Ibid.
16. Ibid.
17. Ibid.
18. Ibid.
19. Ibid.
20. *Princeton Daily Clarion*, Jan. 5, 1901.
21. Ibid.
22. *Princeton Daily Clarion*, Jan. 8, 1901.
23. Ibid.
24. Ibid.
25. *Princeton Daily Clarion*, Jan. 11, 1901.
26. *Princeton Daily Clarion*, Jan. 12, 1901.
27. Ibid.
28. *Evansville Courier*, Nov. 13, 1901.
29. Ibid.

GRANT COUNTY

VICTIM(S):
Wayne Salyers, Sr., 37

PERPETRATOR(S):
Wayne Salyers, Jr., 10

DATE OF DEATH(S):
August 25, 2000

WHEN A BOY KILLS HIS FATHER

Fairmount, Indiana, is famous for having produced the ultimate rebel—actor James Dean, who turned simmering discontent with his parents and other adults into an art form.

But another son of Fairmount, Wayne Salyers, Jr., would commit an act that would cause Dean's cinematic rebellion to pale.

At just ten years of age, Wayne Jr. took his father's .44 caliber handgun and shot him to death on a Friday night in August 2000. There would be disagreement about why Wayne had taken such a turn, and even deeper disbelief that a child so young could act so violently.

The story unfolded just after eight p.m. on Friday, August 25, when a 911 call came in asking for help at the Salyers' home at 609 N. Buckeye Street. Someone had been shot and the police were needed immediately.

The Fairmount town marshal and ambulance personnel found thirty-seven-year-old Wayne Salyers Sr., patriarch of the small four-member family, lying face down on the kitchen floor, a mortal gunshot wound to the upper right side of his chest. He was dead where he lay.

"This is going to be treated as a non-accidental shooting," said James Luttrell, Jr., chief deputy prosecutor for Grant County.[1]

Angela Salyers stayed with her husband as he died, but her young son Wayne Jr. walked away from the house after the shot was fired. He was picked up by Fairmount Town Marshal Brian Reneau a short time later as we walked along Indiana State Route 9.

Under questioning that stretched into the early morning hours of Saturday, Wayne Jr. initially denied knowing how his father was shot. Under further questioning, however, he admitted that he had a gun in his hand "and then it went off 'cause [my dad] pulled and my finger was . . . on the trigger, and he pulled and it went off."[2]

Later, in a second interview, Wayne Jr. told a version of the story investigators believed most closely matched the truth.

"[My parents] had a little sheet covering their [bedroom] door and I snuck inside of it without making it move and I stood up on my dad's guitar cases and pulled [a gun] out of a holster," Wayne Jr. told detectives. "And then, like the first time I got [the gun], I said, 'I can't do this,' and then I put it back up and then I said, 'But I have to 'cause I'm tired of getting whipped.'"[3]

Wayne Jr. then told detectives he called his father to his room, his father immediately recognizing that the boy was holding a .44, but not before the shot was fired. Wayne Sr., wounded, apparently grabbed the gun from Wayne Jr. after he shot and staggered from the room and collapsed on the kitchen floor.

"And there was still blood spillin' out of his mouth and I just took off," Wayne Jr. said.[4]

Wayne Jr. told the detectives that after he fled he had wished he had shot himself instead of his father and admitted that he had cut himself in the past with sharp knives.

On August 28, 2000, Grant County prosecutors charged Wayne Jr. with voluntary manslaughter with a deadly weapon, a Class A felony, and in December 2000, they added a murder charge. The charges were filed in Grant County's juvenile court, normally shielded from public and media scrutiny, but in this case, the community and the media already knew who the suspect was.

"This is a tragedy that has to be dealt with carefully," said Deputy Prosecutor Luttrell. "The charge speaks for itself . . . it's the appropriate charge given the circumstances."[5]

Investigators said Wayne Jr. had reportedly undergone gun safety training and that the boy's mother told them that the family's guns were kept in a locked cabinet in the parents' bedroom. Several long hunting rifles were found, along with the .44 believed to be used in the shooting.

An immediate issue before the court was whether statements Wayne Jr. had made to the police in the presence of his mother were properly obtained and could be used against him. Angela Salyers had urged her son to "tell the truth" when questioned by police.[6]

Grant County Juvenile Court Referee James McKown later ruled that the boy's statements could be used in prosecuting the case against him.

By April 2001, eight months after the shooting, prosecutors and attorneys representing Wayne Jr. had come to an agreement that the young boy, now eleven years old, would plead guilty to shooting his father. In exchange, prosecutors agreed to drop the murder charge and let the voluntary manslaughter charge stand. They also agreed that Wayne Jr. would receive mental health treatment in a facility other than one operated by the Indiana Department of Correction.

His defense attorneys reasoned that they could try to argue that Wayne Jr. had responded in the only way he knew due to repeated episodes of physical abuse, but that if he were found guilty, he may not receive the mental health treatment and counseling he needed.

On April 12, 2001, Wayne Jr. appeared before McKown to answer the charges. He told the court, "I got abused and I felt [shooting my father] was the only way to get out of it."[7]

The state agreed there was evidence of abuse and signed a statement that said "the State of Indiana acknowledges that Wayne Jr., a ten-year-old child, was the victim of repeated physical and psychological abuse at the hands of his father, Wayne Salyers Sr."[8]

As Wayne Jr. answered McKown's questions, his mother, Angela, wept in the audience. The boy explained that his mother and sister were watching TV and his father was on the computer when he called him into his bedroom and subsequently shot him.

He admitted firing the gun at his father. After being shot, "he came forward, got the gun [from me], then fell down," Wayne Jr. said.[9]

McKown ordered the boy held in a treatment facility, a sentence that he planned to review every six months. The boy could be treated for up to ten years, until he was twenty-one years old, but most observers did not believe he would be held that long.

The ten years of treatment would match the ten years of life he had lived so far, most of it, by all accounts, in an abusive setting with a hard-to-please and demanding father.

It was not as if Wayne Jr. had not reached out for help before he shot his father. He did.

Earlier in 2000, he wrote a note to his school counselor in which he said, "I am writing this note because I need to tell you something very important and it is about my dad. My dad abuses me and my mom and my sister. He abused me with leather belts, boards and two-by-fours. Please contact me as soon as you can. Sincerely, Wayne Salyers."[10]

The school counselor, Donna Hull, did follow-up, but only to find Wayne Jr. wanted to take his note back. "I didn't push the issue when he said he changed his mind and he didn't want to come in," Hull told investigators.[11]

Following up with the boy and his family was complicated by the fact that Wayne Salyers Sr. had contacted school officials in March 1999 and demanded that he be notified if he son sought any counseling at school.

The boy's elementary school principal, Lynn Wilson, told reporters about one time that she told Wayne Jr. she was going to have to call his parents about his behavior at school. "He ended up on the floor, holding onto my ankle, begging me not to call his father," Wilson said.[12]

Court records showed Child Protective Services reviewed one incident in which Wayne Jr. came to school with a severe limp, saying his father had stabbed him in the foot with a fork. The investigation, however, showed the allegation could not be substantiated.[13]

"What we have here was a boy that was crying out for help, and didn't get that help," said attorney Paul Mones of Oregon, who assisting in defending Wayne Jr.[14]

His other attorney, Martin Lake, echoed that sentiment. "His mother didn't help him, his school didn't help him, and [Child Protective Services] didn't help him," he said.[15]

Wayne Sr.'s friends and some of his family members cast doubts on the claims of abuse at his hand. His sister, Nancy Elswick told the Indianapolis Star that "he was a very good brother. He was a good man, as far as I could tell."[16]

Wayne Jr. showed some outward signs of abuse even on the day he was arrested for shooting his father. Investigators reported that he had bruising and red marks on his buttocks from a spanking he had endured earlier that day. Other relatives estimated Wayne Jr. was spanked by his father at least twice a week, every week.

Angela Salyers's married life had documented some instances of abuse as well. An earlier investigation had looked into an incident at the home when Wayne Sr. allegedly burned his wife's clothing and broke her car's windshield with his fists. At that time, police recorded Angela as saying, "If he ever smelled cigarette smoke on my face, on my breath, it was just hell to pay. He would throw something at me or hit me on the head."[17]

A psychologist who examined Wayne Jr. after the shooting concluded that the boy believed he was out of options when it came to dealing with his father. "The only alternate he saw was an endless series of abusive events occurring into the future," said Richard Lawlor, a court-order psychologist.[18]

After his sentencing, Wayne Jr. talked to reporter Abigail Johnson of the *Marion Chronicle-Tribune* and gave a glimpse of his life in the Salyers home.

The boy's sense of "fun" included an embarrassing tale of his father violently smashing birthday cake in his face at a restaurant as the family celebrated his ninth birthday. "We all got in a food fight," Wayne Jr. reported with an awkward smile.[19]

Wayne Jr. recalled cleaning the cake and frosting off his face and out of his hair, and the family eventually being asked to leave the restaurant by the manager because of the incident.

He also recalled that on his seventh birthday he wasn't allowed to celebrate because he was still serving a punishment for spray painting on a neighbor's garage door.

He told of his life in the juvenile detention center as the adult experts figured out what to do with him. He said from his room at the center he was able to see a family outside in their back yard, and of having troubling sleeping because of the attention deficit disorder drugs he had been prescribed.

Time in detention had given him time to think about his life so far.

He told *Indianapolis Star* reporter Rob Schneider, "It seemed whether I took the straight path or the crooked path, I always got into trouble."[20]

Because the case was handled by juvenile courts, records about the adjudication of the charges against the young Salyers boy are sealed. However, media reports indicate he pled guilty to the involuntary manslaughter charge in 2001. Mixed in with reports of the honor roll from local schools in the *Anderson Herald-Bulletin* was notice that Wayne Jr. was to be sent to the George Junior Republic juvenile treatment center in Grove City, Pennsylvania, at least until his twenty-first birthday, which he reached in 2011.[21]

Endnotes

1. *Marion Chronicle-Tribune*, Aug. 27, 2000
2. *Marion Chronicle-Tribune*, Jan. 17, 2001
3. *Marion Chronicle-Tribune*, Jan. 17, 2001
4. *Marion Chronicle-Tribune*, Jan. 17, 2001
5. *Marion Chronicle-Tribune*, Aug. 29, 2000
6. *Marion Chronicle-Tribune*, Nov. 1, 2001
7. *Marion Chronicle-Tribune*, April 13, 2001
8. *Marion Chronicle-Tribune*, April 13, 2001
9. *Marion Chronicle-Tribune*, April 13, 2001
10. *Indianapolis Star*, April 26, 2001
11. *Indianapolis Star*, April 26, 2001
12. *Indianapolis Star*, April 26, 2001
13. *Indianapolis Star*, April 26, 2001
14. *Indianapolis Star*, April 26, 2001
15. *Marion Chronicle-Tribune*, April 26, 2001
16. *Indianapolis Star*, April 26, 2001
17. *Indianapolis Star*, April 26, 2001
18. *Indianapolis Star*, April 26, 2001

19. *Marion Chronicle-Tribune*, April 26, 2001
20. *Indianapolis Star*, April 26, 2001
21. *Anderson Herald-Bulletin*, May 9, 2001

GREENE COUNTY

VICTIM(S):
Pam Foddrill, 44

PERPETRATOR(S):
Roger L. Long, 47;
John A. Redman, 42;
Jerry E. Russell, 37;
Wanda Sue Hubbell, 37;
Plynia "Pixie" Fowler, 35

DATE OF DEATH(S):
Sometime after August 18, 1995

A GROUP OF SCOUNDRELS ABDUCT 'A PERFECT VICTIM'

Although she was forty-four years old, Pam Foddrill had the mental capacity of a young girl and stayed close to her aging mother at their Linton, Indiana home.

Her mom, eighty-one-year-old Irene Foddrill, kept a close watch on Pam but allowed her to make the three- to five-minute walk down the block to the IGA Grocery Store in Linton. That's what she allowed on Friday morning, August 18, 1995.

After twenty minutes had passed and Pam still had not returned, Irene began to worry and to search for her daughter. She would never find her. And she would wait for four months before she knew the horrible truth about what had happened to Pam.

Pam, who was attractive and acted child-like, apparently had attracted the attention of a roving band of three men and their girlfriends—all of whom had already rolled up depressing records of arrests for child molestation, assault, and other offenses.

After luring Pam up to a minivan, police later determined that Roger Leon Long, forty-seven, and John A. Redman, forty-two, used a stun gun to subdue Pam and force her into the van. An eyewitness, who saw Pam leaving the IGA

118

store, said he or she saw a woman being shoved into a white van but thought it was just teenagers playing around and did not immediately report the incident.

Initially, police had little to go on. Tracking dogs picked up Pam's scent near the grocery store and then lost it. Family members quickly grew weary in their own search for Pam—Irene not able to stand for great lengths of time, or to walk any distance. Soon more than 100 volunteers were assembled to help search for Pam across rural Greene County.

The search produced nothing.

"She would not have gone anywhere else on her own unless someone stopped her and said they needed help," said Pam's sister, Anita Bowersock. "She would take time to help anyone."[1]

Bowersock said, "We are afraid that if she is still alive, that she is wondering why we don't come and get her and bring her home."[2]

It was a well-founded fear. Pam was alive and was suffering a degrading, painful torture that would lead to her death.

Just across town in the squalid home of Jerry Russell, thirty-seven, Pam was being held bounded by electrical cord and gagged with a dirty rag in her mouth, stuffed away in a stifling attic of the house.

Wanda Sue Hubbell, thirty-seven, would later tell police that Long, Russell, and Redman had attempted to abduct Pam twice before on August 14 and 15, attempts she had assisted with. She claimed that while she was out of the state attending a family funeral, the men finally succeeded in nabbing Pam on August 18. Hubbell said she saw Pam alive as late as August 26—just over a week after she had been abducted.

Hubbell said Long and Redman had forcible sex with Pam, both at the same time—something that Pam, weighing just under 100 pounds, was unable to stop. She was frightened and tried to resist, Hubbell said, but "she wasn't big enough to put up too much of a resistance."[3]

The men, in meth-induced states, could sustain sexual assaults on Pam for three to four hours at a time, several days in a row, Hubbell said. The men did try to force feed some food to Pam during her confinement, and attempted to bathe her, and eventually allowed her to use a bucket as a toilet since Russell's home had no running water.

After days of torture and abuse, Pam had given up. She did not resist the final sexual assaults committed on her by Long and Redman, only opening and closing her eyes, as the two men had their way with her. Russell stood by and masturbated over her tortured body, Hubbell said.

Hubbell said the men grew disinterested and eventually angry with the listless Pam and decided it was time to kill her. She said the men took turns punching her in the face, head, and back with their fists and a baseball bat, and then stabbed her multiple times in her abdomen with a butcher knife. Now dead, they loaded Pam's body into a van and put her in a shed on Redman's property, also in Greene County.

Concerned about the growing smell of Pam's decomposing body in the shed, the men made another decision—to wrap Pam in a blue sleeping bag and drive about fifty miles west, across the Wabash River, to dump her body along a rural road near Russellville, Illinois. It was there Pam's badly decomposed body was found months later on December 2, 1995.

"We didn't have any hopes that she was alive. It was a relief," said one of Pam's older sisters, Darla Mifflin. "We were very close. I won't be able to do anything without thinking of how I used to do things with her."[3]

Solving the case of who killed Pam would take more work. Police initially thought a traveling salesman who was in Linton at the time of Pam's disappearance may be a suspect, but were able to clear him.

Two more years would slowly pass with no more leads in the case until October 1997 when Roger Long, a Bedford resident, began shooting off his mouth to inmates at the Lawrence County Jail in Bedford (where he was serving time for a probation violation). It was a critical mistake—he was just hours removed from being released from the jail when Greene County Prosecutor Scott Callahan swooped in with murder charges for Long.

After Long began implicating himself while bragging about having abducted Pam, police were making progress on other fronts. Long's sister confirmed that she had loaned him her white 1980 Chevrolet van at the time of Pam's abduction. Long's sister also told police she had found a box containing photographs of various nude women, including ones she thought were of Pam, bloody and possibly dead.

For some reason, Long agreed to take a polygraph test for authorities regarding Pam's disappearance—and failed badly.

Described as a frequent drifter in both Bedford and Linton, neighbors back in Bedford said Long was "a strange guy" who walked the neighborhood wearing a long black coat and playing a guitar. He used to live in a camper parked behind his sister's house "but would sleep anywhere he could find a place to sleep," another neighbor said, also confirming Long also ventured to nearby Linton often to visit a girlfriend he had there.[4]

As investigators worked their case on Long, John Redman's ex-wife Plynia "Pixie" Fowler, thirty-five, came forward in May 1998 and gave information implicating Redman and others in the crime. She also led them to a shed on their property where forensic investigators gathered hair, blood and tissue samples belonging to Pam. Redman, at the time, was serving a sentence for child molestation at the Putnamville Correctional Center, and was subjected to blood, hair and saliva DNA tests, and fingerprinting.

His ex-wife gave investigators even more detail—she was the one who had talked Pam into coming near their van. Once Pam reluctantly did so, Redman and Long pulled her inside. She said her ex-husband threatened to kill her and her son if she ever told what had occurred, and had invited her to participate in sex with Pam and the other men.

She also reported seeing Redman cleaning red stains off the floor of his shed with water and bleach, and said things had "got out of hand" with Pam and she had to be killed. Redman soon had murder charges added as he sat in a cell at Putnamville.

Police later charged Fowler with criminal confinement, perjury, and aiding in felony murder because she failed to fully disclose her role in the abduction of Pam, including assuring the easily confused Pam that she would be all right if she got into the van with the men.

On October 20 and 22, 1998, the house of cards constructed by the final members of this group of scoundrels collapsed for good, as Russell and Hubbell were both arrested and held on murder, rape and conspiracy charges. Hubbell implicated Russell in the attack on Pam—and implicated herself as having engaged in nonconsensual sex with Pam as well.

By January 1999, new Greene County Prosecutor David N. Powell had reached a plea agreement with Hubbell, who would provide damning testimony against the men in exchange for a lesser sentence.

On January 27, 1999, Hubbell was sentenced to twenty years in prison for her participation in planning the abduction, rape and murder of Pam. "Although you had the opportunity to take actions which would have resulted in the life of Pamela Foddrill being spared, you did not do that," Greene County Superior Court Judge David Holt said.[5] She was released from prison on January 5, 2016 after serving just under seventeen years.

Long's trial got underway in April 1999 at the Greene County Courthouse at Bloomfield. Long's attorneys argued that he was not involved in the case, never knew Pam, and was only being implicated by others who wanted to escape responsibility.

Hubbell's testimony stole the show as she graphically described the horror of the last days of Pam's life. Pam's mother, Irene, and her sisters all eventually left the courtroom, unable to sit through the disgusting details of what Pam endured.

Veteran FBI Special Agent Gary Dunn testified about the difficulty investigators faced as each of the participants wove complicated lies and stories to try to cover their actions. "These people we were dealing with, it was very difficult to secure a firm answer from a lot of them," Dunn said.[6]

As Long's trial continued, Redman's ex-wife "Pixie" Fowler prepared to enter a guilty plea to a charge of criminal confinement in exchange for a fourteen-year prison sentence. The perjury and aiding in murder charges were dropped as part of the deal. She was released from prison on February 9, 2003.

Long declined to testify in his own defense. "I'm not going to testify because I don't have to prove myself," Long said in court. "I know the truth."[7]

Jurors deliberated less than three hours before finding Long guilty on all charges and recommended that he be sentenced to prison without the possibility of parole. Judge Holt sentenced Long to life in prison, plus an additional 120 years.

Redman's case went forward with a jury from Dubois County in June 1999 and produced the same outcome: guilty on all charges. Judge Holt offered the same sentence, sending Redman to prison to life, plus 120 years.

Jerry E. Russell's trial was delayed until October 1999 and included jurors selected from Putnam County. A fourteen-day trial followed with Russell vigorously denying any guilt. His family insisted he was being framed for the crime.

Russell himself claimed a jailhouse conversion, saying he had earned "ordination" as a "pastor" from the Universal Life Church in Modesto, California—a Web-site offering "free online ordinations."[8]

Judge Holt again offered a life sentence plus 120 years. He noted that although evidence did not show Russell had swung the bat or knife that killed Pam, "you provided your house as the major place where she was held, the place where she was killed. And this was not an event that occurred one afternoon."[9]

He added, "People don't treat pets the way Pam Foddrill was treated. The horror of having someone confined in such a miserable, filthy, hot attic is, I think, unfathomable."[10]

The FBI later honored fifty agents and local law enforcement officials for their dogged determination to solve Pam's case—performances "in the highest tradition of effective law enforcement."

Greene County Detective Dan Conley said it best: "I can't bring Pam back, but I made a promise to her mother on the day they found [her] body that we would not stop until the case was solved."[11]

Endnotes

1. *Bloomington Herald-Times*, Aug. 22, 1995.
2. Ibid.
3. *Bloomington Herald-Times*, April 13, 1999.
4. *Linton Daily Citizen*, Dec. 5, 1995.
5. *Bloomington Herald-Times*, Oct. 12, 1997.
6. *Bloomington Herald-Times*, Jan. 28, 1999.
7. *Bloomington Herald-Times*, April 13, 1999.
8. *Bloomington Herald-Times*, April 15, 1999.
9. *Terre Haute Tribune-Star*, Nov. 13, 1999.
10. Ibid.
11. Ibid.
12. *Bloomington Herald-Times*, Dec. 4, 1999.

HAMILTON COUNTY

VICTIM(S):
Remains of eight men reported missing between May 1993 and March 1995. All remains found on the Baumeister property near Westfield, Indiana. Remains of three other male victims and bone fragments from as many as eight other victims also found on the property could not be identified. The remains of nine other men found between June 1980 and September 1990 in various locations in central Indiana and western Ohio attributed to Baumeister.

DATE OF DEATH(S):
Various dates, 1980-1999

PERPETRATOR:
Herbert R. Baumeister, 49

THE TWO LIVES OF HERB BAUMEISTER

Before dawn on July 4, 1996, Juliana Baumeister's divorce attorney Bill Wendling, Jr., drove slowly down the winding lane to her million-dollar Fox Hollow Farm estate to bring the news that her husband, Herbert Baumeister, was dead.

Herb had died of a self-inflicted gunshot wound to the forehead from a .357 Magnum revolver. His body lay next to his car at a beach parking area inside the Pinery Provincial Park in Grand Bend, Ontario, Canada—about ninety miles northeast of Detroit, Michigan. A four-page suicide note accompanied Herb's body.

His death was the last one in a series of as many as twenty-seven deaths that would be assigned to the forty-nine-year-old husband, father of three, and Westfield businessman. His death would also reveal the twisted double life Herb had led for years.

In the days leading up to Herb's suicide, his Westfield estate along West 156th Street had been turned into a massive crime scene with media from across the state and nation lined up at the end of the driveway waiting for the latest updates on human remains being unearthed there.

The final tally would reveal the bone specimens of at least nineteen different individuals—only eleven of whom were ever identified through DNA testing, matching missing men with their grieving families.

It seemed Herb had left Julie to answer for the other part of his life that she said she never knew.

"Do I feel sorry for myself? Yes," Juliana told the *Indianapolis Star.* "I didn't deserve this, my kids didn't deserve this and the people who died didn't deserve this. How do you explain this to your kids?"[1]

There really was no explanation. Juliana had been married to a man for twenty-four years but only knew a part of him.

The part she did not know was revealed to her, it seems, for the first time in November 1995 when Detective Mary Wilson of the Indianapolis Police Department approached Juliana at her north-side Indianapolis Sav-A-Lot Thrift Store to discuss the case of a missing man last seen with Herb. Wilson told Juliana that police needed permission to enter the property at her Fox Hollow Farm in order to search for possible clues to the man's whereabouts.

"I don't know of a word or collection of words to describe the degree of shock I felt," Juliana told the *Star.* "I can remember barely having enough strength to get to my car [after talking to Wilson]."[2]

Wilson's request sent Juliana immediately to her husband, Herb, who ran the couple's other Sav-A-Lot store on West Washington Street in Indianapolis. Herb reassured her that there was nothing to worry about and that she had done the right thing in denying police entry to their eighteen-acre property.

It was the same kind of reassurance Herb had given her in the summer of 1994 when the couple's teenage son, Erich, reported finding a human skeleton and skull just off the cement patio in the overgrown weeds behind their home. Herb explained the bones were the remnants of a cadaver model belonging to his late father, a physician.

For Juliana and Herb, however, this was just the latest struggle. The Sav-A-Lot Thrift Stores were teetering on collapse. The couple had borrowed $4,000 from Herb's mother in 1988 to start the first store, which quickly generated a second store. Selling used clothing and other secondhand items, the stores were designed to benefit the Children's Bureau of Indianapolis.

By 1994, however, the financial struggles involved in keeping the stores open were getting quite real. Complicating matters was a huge monthly land contract payment on the Fox Hollow Farm property that was valued at more than $1 million.

During this period, Juliana would sometimes escape to the Lake Wawasee condominium belonging to Herb's parents. Herb would escape by increasing his drinking, frequently traveling between Indianapolis and Columbus, Ohio, (presumably to buy used goods for their stores), and staying out all night.

In fact, Juliana would later tell reporters and others that the couple had only consummated their marriage six times in the quarter century they were together. "Julie later admitted that she and Herb had engaged in sex only six times in the 25 years they were married," said private detective Virgil Vandagriff, hired by one of the victims' families.[3] The Baumeister union had resulted in Juliana giving birth in 1979, 1981, and 1984 to their three children—Marie, Erich, and Emily, respectively.

On January 4, 1996, Juliana took matters into her own hands and hired Wendling, subsequently filing for divorce in Hamilton County Superior Court. She cited Herb's "serious emotional instability" (based on increased drinking and threats of suicide) and the "serious financial jeopardy" the couple faced from their failing stores and their huge house payment. A March 1996 suit against their stores listed more than $167,000 in past-due rent, property taxes, and utility payments owed on just one of their two stores.

In spite of telling the court her marriage was "irretrievably broken," Juliana relented and let Herb return to their home later in January 1996. The reconciliation would not last, however, and Herb moved out again. It was not the first indication of marital strife; the couple had followed a similar pattern in 1991 when Herb had filed for divorce, but the couple reconciled.

This time, no lasting reconciliation would be possible. Juliana told Wendling in a private meeting in June 1996 about her son, Erich, finding the skull and other bones in their back yard. Balancing the requirement of attorney-client privilege and the need to assist law enforcement, Wendling was put in a difficult position. Detective Wilson would later tell A&E TV's *Investigative Reports* that she could tell by the manner in which Wendling spoke to her that she should not give up on investigating Herb Baumeister.[4]

The arguments between Juliana and Herb grew as fast as their debts, and in June 1996, Juliana had reached her limit. Herb had unilaterally decided to enroll his three children in the prestigious—and expensive—Culver Military Academies in northern Indiana. He had also taken off with her son, Erich, and she wanted him back.

On June 23, 1996, Wendling informed Detective Wilson that Juliana wanted to talk to her. Wilson and detectives from the Hamilton County

Sheriff's Department went to the Baumeister home on Tuesday, June 25, and were shocked at what they saw inside. Despite the million-dollar façade, an indoor swimming pool, and the horse fences surrounding the property, the interior of the home was in disarray. A dusty Christmas tree was still standing, fully decorated, in the home's living room six months after the holidays.

Juliana told detectives about her son Erich's encounter with the skull and other bones in the back yard. She then took the officers to the area where Erich said he had found the bones. Despite the heavy weed cover on the ground, detectives made a startling discovery: Dozens and dozens of human bones were scattered out around the area beneath their feet.

Samples of the bones were collected and immediately taken to Dr. Jay Nawrocki, a forensic anthropologist at the University of Indianapolis. Nawrocki blew a hole through Herb's earlier claim that the bones had come from a cadaver model. Nawrocki said the bones were human.

Eventually the remains of these missing men would be identified in Herb's "killing field" behind his house: Johnny Bayer, twenty; Jeff A. Jones, unknown age; Richard D. Hamilton, unknown age; Manuel Resendez, thirty-one; Steven S. Hale, twenty-six; Allen W. Broussard, twenty-eight; Roger A. Goodlet, thirty-three; and Michael Kiern, forty-six. Remains of three other men found were never identified, and bone fragments suggested as many as eight other victims were present, but could not be identified.

The discovery was big news in Indianapolis and across the state.

"It's disturbing," Hamilton County Prosecutor Sonia Leerkamp told reporters. "The more [bodies] they think there could be, the more disturbing it becomes."[5]

Little was initially known about the bones because they had been scattered over such a large area. Some were carried off by animals in the woods. Others had been burned on a small burn pile just seventy-five feet from the lower level back door of the Baumeister home. Hamilton County Coroner Joe Roberts led the probe for bones with assistance from Nawrocki and dozens of others.

As more and more news leaked out of the Fox Hollow Farm estate, Herb Baumeister was nowhere to be found. Juliana and her two daughters were huddled inside their home, trying to ignore the anthropological dig going on all around them. Herb had taken his son, Erich, who was fifteen, with him to the lake condo at Wawasee.

Detectives would later retrieve Erich from his father and return him to his mother, but Hamilton County authorities did not believe they had enough information to arrest or detain Herb. They let him go. No one would ever talk to him again.

An investigation showed Herb traveled almost immediately to Saugatuck, Michigan, and then east across Michigan and entered Ontario, Canada, via the bridge at Port Huron, Michigan. Herb's brother, Brad, had wired money to him in Michigan twice. He was found dead on Wednesday, July 3, 1996.

Fourth of July newspapers across the state and TV news reports peppered with announcements about fireworks displays also carried the news of Herb's death. Prosecutor Leerkamp said police had intended to question Herb but had not been able to find him since they picked up his son in Kosciusko County.

Wendling told reporters that Juliana "was shocked and upset, and so were the kids" at the news of Herb's death and that they were "coping and trying to get by."[6]

Herb's suicide note said he was upset about the failure of his marriage and his business but made no mention whatsoever of the ongoing discovery of human remains on his property. He ended his note by saying he was going to eat a peanut butter sandwich and "go to sleep."[7]

Authorities eventually identified remains from at least eleven men on the Fox Hollow Farm estate, though Nawrocki said bone specimens indicated as many as nineteen bodies may have been dismembered there.

In November 1997, the A&E Television Network ran an hour-long *Investigative Report* on the Baumeister case that included an interview with Mark Goodyear of Indianapolis who said he had survived a near-death encounter with Herb in earlier years.

Goodyear reported that Herb had propositioned him for sex at an Indianapolis gay bar and that the two men had left together for Herb's Hamilton County home. Once there, Goodyear said Herb asked him to engage in a form of auto-erotica asphyxiation in his indoor pool.

Goodyear's story would match how police believe all of the victims died—by a form of strangulation. The involvement of the pool would also match the characteristics of nine other unsolved murders investigated between 1980 and 1990 of men with ties to the gay community.

In each of those cases, the men's bodies were dumped either in or near small waterways in Indiana and Ohio. The first victim found, fifteen-year-old Michael Petrie, was dumped in a Hamilton County ditch in June 1980. The last victim, thirty-two-year-old Clay R. Boatman, was found in Preble County, Ohio, (just across the Indiana state line) in August 1990—just before Herb and Juliana moved into their new Fox Hollow Farm estate.

In April 1998, law enforcement officials from Hancock and Shelby Counties in Indiana and from Darke and Preble Counties in Ohio said they believed Herb had killed the nine additional victims. All found between June 1980 and September 1990, police said Baumeister was responsible for the deaths of Petrie; Boatman; Maurice A. Taylor, twenty-two; Michael A. Riley, twenty-two; Eric A. Roetiger, seventeen; Michael A. Glenn, twenty-six; James B. Robbins, twenty-one; Steven L. Elliott, twenty-six; and Thomas R. Clevenger, Jr., seventeen.

Hancock County Sheriff Jim Bradbury said the strongest link between Herb and the victims was the disappearance and murder of twenty-two-year-old Michael A. Riley of Indianapolis whose body was found partially submerged in a ditch southeast of Greenfield, Indiana, on June 5, 1983. He had been strangled. Witnesses identified a photograph of Herb Baumeister as the man they saw Riley with at the Vogue nightclub in Broad Ripple before he disappeared.

Sheriff Bradbury said, "They were all found in a small body of water. They were all dumped over a concrete culvert out in rural areas of the county that just wasn't your everyday traveled parts of the county. All were partially nude. All were white males. They all had ties to the gay community in one way or another."[8]

The experience of Rose Dewey of Noblesville was typical. Police turned over one rib bone belonging to her missing son, twenty-year-old Johnny Bayer, whom she last saw on May 28, 1993, as he left for his job at a McDonald's Restaurant in Carmel. She waited five years for his remains to be returned by investigators and buried the single bone recovered from his body in a grave at Calvary Cemetery in Indianapolis.

"Herb Baumeister took the normal things away from us," Dewey said. "He left us with a lot of unanswered questions."[9]

Testing on the remains of eleven of the victims found on the Baumeister property were inconclusive as to how they died because the bodies had been cut into so many pieces and the bones scattered over such a large area. Burning of other bones made cause-of-death determinations impossible.

Bones found in July 2000 at Lake Wawasee in Kosciusko County where Herb was known to vacation were later ruled to be ancient bones of a Native American and not related to the Baumeister case.

Endnotes

1. *Indianapolis Star*, Nov. 25, 1996.
2. Ibid.
3. "Herb Baumeister: Skeletons Beyond the Closet," www.crimelibrary.com, CourtTV.
4. "The Secret Life of a Serial Killer," Investigative Reports with Bill Kurtis, A&E TV Network. VHS Release Date: Feb. 10, 2000, A&E Home Video.

5. *Indianapolis News*, June 29, 1996.
6. *Indianapolis Star*, July 5, 1996.
7. *Indianapolis News*, July 6, 1996.
8. *Indianapolis Star*, April 28, 1998.
9. *Indianapolis Star*, June 16, 1999.

HANCOCK COUNTY

VICTIM(S):
Margaret "Peggy Sue" Altes, 11

PERPETRATOR(S):
Jerry E. Watkins conviction for murder overturned.
Jerry M. McCormick and Kenny Munson murder charges dropped, convicted of rape.
Murder charges against two other defendants also dropped.

DATE OF DEATH(S):
November 12, 1984

A TANGLED WEB ON THE PATH TO JUSTICE

Peggy Sue Altes's mother and aunt left their eastside Indianapolis home on the evening of Monday, November 12, 1984, to attend a nearby religious revival meeting. When they left, Peggy Sue was waiting at home for the arrival of two friends who were coming over to visit.

Five days later, hunters found her naked body dumped in a field in southeastern Hancock County along Jacobi Road, about a mile south of Philadelphia, Indiana.

She had suffered a stab wound to her neck and superficial knife wounds to her head. She had also been raped.

An early winter snow blanketed the farm field and hampered the search for evidence to determine what had happened to her, although tire ruts in the mud indicated that a vehicle had driven back from the road about 300 feet before dumping the body. The snow was just the latest roadblock in what would be a long and complicated journey to the truth about who killed Peggy Sue.

The eleven-year-old girl lived with her mother and her older sister in the 400 block of St. Peter Street on the near eastside of Indianapolis. Her sister had run away seventeen times between April 1983 and June 1984, an

Indianapolis Police detective said, and so when Peggy Sue turned up missing, some were not alarmed.

Her family blamed police for reacting slowly. Her brother, James Altes, told the *Indianapolis Star,* "They haven't done all they could do."[1]

Police initially followed up on a lead that Peggy Sue was playing at a neighborhood playground known as Porter Park near the Lane Bryant Distribution Center along Southeastern Avenue. Family members posted signs on the near eastside that carried a picture of Peggy Sue and begged for help finding her.

The case took a weird turn the day after Peggy Sue's body was recovered as police investigated the apparent suicide of her cousin, twenty-four-year-old Franklin Altes, who was found dead about 9 a.m. on Sunday, November 18, in a running car in the garage of his parents' Indianapolis home. Police never discovered any connection between the man taking his own life and Peggy Sue's murder.

But that did not stop investigators from looking closely at Peggy Sue's family, especially the adult men in her life. That focus turned almost exclusively on Jerry E. Watkins, who was twenty-eight years old in 1984. Watkins was married to Peggy Sue's sister, Janice, at the time of her disappearance. He even served as a pallbearer at her funeral.

Even though he passed a polygraph test, investigators built their case against Watkins and eventually charged him with her murder in March 1986. He was convicted of her rape and murder in September 1986 in Hancock County Superior Court, although he testified he had nothing to do with her death. Damaging his claims, however, was his guilty plea to having molested her two months before her death. Watkins served five months in prison on the molestation conviction before being charged with killing Peggy Sue.

At the murder trial, blood tests taken were inconclusive as to whether Watkins had raped the girl before her death, and DNA testing was still years into the future. He was sentenced to sixty years in prison in January 1987. Peggy Sue's sister, Janice, later divorced Watkins.

Most people accepted that the case was closed—everyone accept Jerry Watkins and anyone who would listen to him. In 1997, Watkins lost his appeal before the Indiana Court of Appeals and turned instead to the U.S. District Court in Indianapolis, acting as his own lawyer.

U.S. District Judge David F. Hamilton appointed Indianapolis attorney Joseph Cleary to represent Watkins. As Cleary dug into the case, he began to find several troubling things: evidence police and prosecutors had not turned over to Watkins' defense attorneys, polygraph test results of other suspects who had failed or were untruthful, and other mitigating evidence in Watkins' favor.

Cleary said he immediately saw how fortunate Watkins had been in avoiding a death sentence.

Judge Hamilton agreed, offering an April 2000 ruling that shocked everyone: He overturned Watkins' conviction and ordered him released from prison—after having served fourteen of his original sixty-year sentence in prison.

Hamilton said police and prosecutors had failed to turn over key evidence to Watkins' defense lawyers and that newly processed DNA evidence cleared him of the rape of Peggy Sue. He cited an eyewitness report of Peggy Sue entering a black sports car at the time she was abducted and when Watkins was at work and could not have been present.

The ruling would make statewide headlines. It was the first time genetic test results had been used as a factor in overturning a murder conviction in Indiana history.

"With the addition of the DNA evidence … this court is confident that no reasonable juror would find Watkins guilty of murdering Peggy Sue Altes," Judge Hamilton wrote in his sixty-seven-page ruling. "In short, in the American criminal justice system, no one should be sentenced to sixty days in prison, let alone sixty years, on the theory and evidence the state relies upon in this case to keep Jerry Watkins in prison."[2]

Peggy Sue's family could not believe what they were hearing and reacted angrily to the news that Watkins may be set free. "If you want a pervert out on the street, that's what you're going to get," said Peggy Sue's mother, Myrlene Altes. "I'm angry because this guy is dangerous."[3]

Attorneys for the state were shocked as well. They had argued in the federal appeal that Watkins could still have murdered Peggy Sue, even if the DNA evidence now showed he did not rape her. Hamilton threw out that claim, however, because prosecutors had relied heavily on Watkins' admitted earlier molestation of the young girl during the trial to convict him and convince jurors that he had raped *and* murdered her.

On July 21, 2000, Watkins, now forty-three years old, finished an early-morning shift in the boiler room at the Pendleton Reformatory in Madison County and was released later that day. He carried with him a box holding the transcripts of his court cases and his Bible. The Indiana Department of Correction gave Watkins the standard parting sum of seventy-five dollars, plus any earnings he had made in prison. He immediately went to his mother's home in Acton, Indiana, where he planned to help his aging mother who was confined to a wheelchair.

His freedom wouldn't last. Four days later, Hancock County Judge Richard Payne ordered Watkins arrested again on the original murder charges from 1986 and held at the Hancock County Jail at Greenfield. It would be a short stay. Deciding they now did not have enough evidence to keep Watkins on a murder charge, Hancock County Prosecutor Terry Snow later dropped the charges, and Watkins was released for a second and final time on July 31, 2000. He later won a civil judgment against Hancock County and Indianapolis officials for $475,000 in damages.

Snow said, "It is exceedingly difficult to resurrect a sixteen-year-old murder case and go forward." He said investigators, however, were not giving up. "Someone murdered Peggy Sue. I hope we can find and charge that person."[4]

Those longing for justice in Peggy Sue's case would have to wait.

In August 2001, police arrested thirty-nine-year-old Joseph M. McCormick of Indianapolis and charged him with the rape and murder of the girl. McCormick's arrest came about based primarily on the statements of Kenny Munson, also thirty-nine. He said he witnessed as many as five men raping Peggy Sue and then watched McCormick restrain her as another man stabbed her.

Munson had been identified as a possible witness shortly after the murder in 1984 but was uncooperative with detectives in the early stages. Police then pursued leads culminating in the arrest and conviction of Watkins instead.

"I knew Watkins could not have killed the little girl, because I knew who killed the little girl," Munson told the court.[5]

Munson testified at a September 2001 bond hearing for McCormick that he was in a van where Peggy Sue sat bound on a milk crate between the two front seats after she was abducted. He said he witnessed McCormick rape her both in an alley in Indianapolis but also later in a park in Hancock County.

DNA testing provided additional evidence—it conclusively linked McCormick to a sexual assault on the young girl just before her death. In March 2003, he agreed to a plea agreement on charges he sexually molested Peggy Sue in exchange for murder charges being dropped and agreeing to assist prosecutors in finding the other suspects. He was sentenced to twenty years, with fourteen years suspended.

On March 18, 2003, police made three new arrests in Peggy Sue's murder—including their previous witness against McCormick, Kenny W. Munson; his brother, forty-four-year-old Hugh P. Munson III of Keystone Heights, Florida; and forty-six-year-old William L. "Billy" Beever of Danville, Indiana. All of the men were in their twenties when Peggy Sue was attacked two decades before.

Hancock County Sheriff Nick Gulling said, "I think we now have a pretty good idea what happened in that cornfield. I hope this is the end of this."[6]

Kenny Munson called a reporter from the *Indianapolis Star* from his jail cell to declare, "I didn't kill nobody. I had nothing to do with this, and my brother didn't either. I did not kill that little girl."[7]

Beever told reporters as he was led into the Hancock County Jail, "I don't know nothing about it. They've tried to do this before, and I don't know what they're looking for out of me."[8]

Hugh Munson, a married father of three, working as a mechanic in Florida, was fighting his extradition to Indiana, also claiming he was innocent. He would eventually be cleared of all charges in June 2003 after DNA tests, polygraph tests (which he passed), and recanted statements from his brother who previously implicated him in the crime.

Kenny Munson would eventually plead guilty to lesser charges of conspiracy to commit battery resulting in serious bodily injury to a child. He received a six-year sentence.

Another twist came in April 2004 when prosecutors dismissed charges against Beever, saying they needed more time to investigate the alleged crime. They reserved the right to file the charges again later.

Beever was released from the Hendricks County Jail and transferred to the Marion County Jail, where he was held on three charges related to the molestation of his nephew. Beever was found guilty on two counts and sentenced in September 2005 to separate terms of sixty-nine and forty years in prison. Given his prior convictions for drunk driving and burglary, he is not eligible for parole before 2023.

A final twist came in July 2006—almost twenty-two years after Peggy Sue was abducted, raped, and murdered. Police searched property on the south side of Indianapolis for Peggy Sue's clothing that a prison tipster said he helped bury behind a barn there shortly after her murder. Materials collected at the scene were subjected to DNA testing, but no further arrests occurred in the case.

Endnotes

1. *Indianapolis Star*, Nov. 19, 1984.
2. *Indianapolis Star*, April 26, 2000.
3. Ibid.
4. *Indianapolis Star*, Aug. 1, 2000.
5. *Indianapolis Star*, Sept. 29, 2001.
6. *Indianapolis Star*, March 20, 2003.
7. Ibid.
8. WRTV-TV, Channel 6, Indianapolis, March 18, 2003.

HARRISON COUNTY

VICTIM(S):
Hobert A. Pittman, Sr., 59;
Myrtle L. Satterfield, 80

PERPETRATOR(S):
Hobert A. Pittman, Jr., 23;
John M. Naylor, 22

DATE OF DEATH(S):
June 12, 2004

A MURDER IN THE FAMILY

From the outset, police said it was not precisely clear why fifty-nine-year-old Hobert A. Pittman, Sr., and his eighty-year-old wheelchair-bound mother-in-law, Myrtle L. Satterfield, were shot to death on the rainy Saturday afternoon of June 12, 2004.

The motive may have been a mystery, but the suspects were not.

Police quickly focused in on Pittman's twenty-three-year-old son, Hobert "Albert" Pittman, and his twenty-two-year-old friend, John M. Naylor, as likely suspects. They had good reason to suspect the two men who became friends while serving stints at the Harrison County Jail: A third victim, fifty-five-year-old Linda K. Pittman, the elder Hobert's wife, had survived the ambush-style slaying.

It was Linda who had driven her bullet-ridden van through a locked gate at her home where the ambush occurred back to the parking lot of the Riverbottom Inn in Mauckport, Indiana—a tiny river town at the bottom edge of Harrison County along the Ohio River. As she made her way, driving as best she could though shot and bleeding profusely, she caught the attention of two Harrison County men departing on a fishing trip.

One of the men, Darryl Mosier, said Linda cried out, "My stepson shot me and my family!"[1]

Pittman was rushed to University Hospital across the river in Louisville, Kentucky, and was listed in serious condition. She would recover and identify her wayward stepson as one of two men who stood at the front of her van and fired repeated shots through the windshield and side window.

The shots not only struck the driver, Linda, but struck the eighty-year-old woman, who was wheelchair bound after having both of her legs amputated years before. If ever there was a defenseless victim, Linda's mother, Myrtle, was it.

Linda and Myrtle were just returning home from Myrtle's home near Marengo, Indiana, where Linda and Hobert had done some yard work and other chores about the older woman's home. Hobert had gone ahead of the two women in another vehicle. Unknown to them, he was already dead, having been ambushed in the driveway of his Walnut Street home; his body was shoved under a nearby tarp. He'd suffered a violent gunshot wound that went all the way through his head, from his face to the back of his skull.

Linda had only survived the attack by slumping in her driver's seat and pretending to be dead while the two assailants fled in a Ford Explorer. Moments later, at the Riverbottom Inn where she sought help, Mosier said Linda cried out again and pointed out that the suspects' Ford Explorer was approaching the area on State Road 11. Once spotted, the men in the Explorer did an abrupt U-turn and fled in the other direction, Mosier said.

Mosier followed the Explorer while his fishing buddy, Matt Stanley, stayed behind to tend to the injured woman. Myrtle was already dead in her wheelchair in the back of the van.

Mosier said he witnessed the men under the State Road 135 bridge moving items from the Explorer into a Plymouth Horizon car and then fleeing south across the Ohio River on the SR 135 bridge.

Harrison County authorities launched a massive manhunt—a rarity in the peaceful county on the river best known as home of Indiana's first state capital, Corydon, Indiana. The search expanded far beyond Indiana, and on Monday, June 13, 2004, police in Daytona Beach, Florida, arrested both the younger Pittman and Naylor as they drove the Plymouth (registered to Naylor's father) and charged both with two counts of murder and one count of attempted murder and other charges. Police in Florida had been tipped off to their whereabouts after Albert contacted his mother, Eva Mullin, in Indiana, and the phone call was traced.

Two years later, Albert stood trial at the Harrison County Courthouse in Corydon. Harrison County Sheriff's Captain Bruce LaHue told jurors about being the first to respond to the Riverbottom Inn and finding Linda seriously injured and Myrtle dead.

"[Linda] had several visible bullet wounds," Captain LaHue said. "There was a lot of blood. The blood was coming down the running board [of the van] and onto the ground."[2]

LaHue said the older woman was "slumped forward" in her wheelchair and was obviously dead. He said Linda kept insisting someone go back to the Pittman's home and check on Hobert.

Harrison County Chief Deputy Prosecutor John Colin said the best guess on a motive was burglary. Albert led Naylor to his father's house where they stole guns and ammunition from a cabinet, along with the keys to his father's Ford Explorer. Apparently not content to leave it at that, the two waited for the family to return in two separate vehicles and ambushed both, Colin said.

Albert's defense was that no DNA evidence linked him to the crimes and that Naylor had admitted to police that he shot the victims but had not implicated Albert.

Jurors didn't buy the defense and deliberated just an hour before returning a guilty verdict against Albert on June 26, 2006. Albert showed no response to the verdict, but his mother Eva sobbed loudly. In August 2006, Harrison County Superior Court Judge Roger Davis sentenced Albert to two consecutive life terms in prison, plus another seventy-three years.

Naylor's trial did not start until January 2007 and included heart-wrenching testimony from Mosier and Stanley who described Linda's desperate efforts to get help to save herself and her mother. Defense attorneys for Naylor attempted to make an issue of the fact that Mosier now lived in Hobert and Linda Pittman's home.

Linda Pittman was again called as a witness and told jurors, "I sat there acting like I was dead. I figured that was the only way to stay alive." She also described how she had put up her hands in a useless attempt to try and shield herself and her mother from being shot. Doing so cost her a thumb, as one of the shotgun pellets blew the digit off her hand.[3]

She added that after she was shot, "I started praying and it seemed like I gave them enough time to get away."[4]

She testified that she "knew something was wrong" with her husband, Hobert, when he did not emerge from the house to try and help the two women as they were being attacked. Adding to the sad news that Hobert was dead, he was killed on the couple's thirteenth wedding anniversary.

A Harrison County Jail officer, Brian E. Wininger, testified that Naylor told him at the jail, "I'm guilty of killing those two people; I'm about to go crazy for what I've done."[5]

As the trial wound down, jurors visited the scene of the shooting at the Pittman home and the Riverbottom Inn where Linda had sought help.

Naylor's defense seemed to rest on assertions by his attorneys that he was in fear of Albert, was a naïve young man from having been "home schooled," and did whatever the more assertive Albert told him to do. The only witness called by his lawyers was his father, Dennis, who testified that his son had grown depressed and despondent since his arrest.

In a split decision, jurors returned a guilty verdict against Naylor on February 9, 2007, for the murder of Myrtle Satterfield but acquitted him of the murder of Hobert Pittman.

Harrison County Prosecutor Dennis Byrd agreed with a request from Naylor's attorneys to allow Judge Davis to determine his sentence without a recommendation from the jury members (given the jurors' split decision). On March 2, 2007, Judge Davis sentenced Naylor to 120½ years in prison for the murder of Myrtle and the attempted murder of her daughter, Linda Pittman.

Linda Pittman, who had to bury her husband and her mother at the same time, said, "I'm just thankful it's done and over with. I'm going to get on with my life and try to get some sense of normalcy."[6]

Endnotes

1. *Louisville Courier-Journal*, Jan. 30, 2007.
2. *Louisville Courier-Journal*, June 16, 2006.
3. *Corydon Democrat*, Feb. 7, 2007.
4. *Louisville Courier-Journal*, Feb. 7, 2007.
5. *Corydon Democrat*, Feb. 14, 2007.
6. *Corydon Democrat*, March 7, 2007.

HENDRICKS COUNTY

VICTIM(S):
Rev. Roland Phillips, Jr., 36

PERPETRATOR(S):
Elizabeth Mayberry, 36

DATE OF DEATH(S):
September 19, 1993

A MURDER TO END MORNING WORSHIP

The Reverend Roland Phillips, Jr., decided to finish his sermon on forgiveness during morning worship on Sunday, September 19, 1993, at the North Salem United Methodist Church, even though he could see his former girlfriend, Elizabeth Mayberry, standing in the center aisle of the church.

Phillips finished his sermon and announced the closing hymn, and the church organist began playing the hymn's introduction. It was then that Mayberry took a few more steps forward toward the altar and pulled a .38-caliber handgun from her purse and fired four shots at the minister. He died on the floor behind the pulpit, asking for his thirteen-year-old daughter, Rachel, to come to his side before he expired.

Church members wrestled the gun away from Mayberry and detained her until police and paramedics arrived. It was too late to save Rev. Phillips.

Choir member Irene Wyeth, a member of the congregation in the tiny western Hendricks County settlement of North Salem for forty-eight years, would later say she worried that Mayberry had a gun in her purse but was unsure if that was the outline she was seeing on the handbag. Wyeth said she was unsure whether to yell, "Gun!" or throw a hymnal to get attention.

"I was quite uneasy; you are always reading about shootings," Wyeth said. "I saw her there and hoped my gut feelings were wrong."[1]

As many as thirty church members witnessed the shooting—a shocking and unheard of end to a peaceful church service on a sunny fall morning. Tim

Fretz, another church member, said he noticed Mayberry's entrance because she came late and stood in the aisle during the sermon.

"She had a definite look of determination—anger—on her face," he said.[2]

Another church member, June Ward, who was seated in the choir facing the congregation, said she became quite nervous when Mayberry began coming up the center aisle. "I thought there might be a scene of some sort. I gave a sigh of relief when we stood up to sing. There wasn't going to be a scene and Ron [Rev. Phillips] was going to talk to her."[3]

Choir member Rebecca Compton said she saw the gun. "I realized it was a gun. Then I saw the silver part come out [of her purse] ... she started firing the gun. A fear that went through me was so intense I would have willed myself somewhere else if I could have."[4]

Ward said she jumped up from her seat to go to the pastor, but "by the time I got there, she had already shot Ron. He looked at her in surprise, his knees buckled, and he fell backwards."[5]

Compton said Mayberry began yelling, "You raped me! You raped me!" as men in the congregation wrestled her to the floor.

Ward sat on Mayberry's body so that she could not get away and told her, "Don't even think about moving."[6]

Rev. Phillips looked at Mayberry and uttered what would be some of his last words, "I didn't do it."[7]

The investigation would reveal Mayberry had grown disillusioned and angry with not only Rev. Phillips, whom she had dated for a few months in 1992, but also the United Methodist Church. The church had initially suspended Phillips from preaching and delayed his ordination after Mayberry made allegations of improper sexual conduct—but had later reinstated him, infuriating Mayberry—who, until then, had been a devoted member of a United Methodist Church in her hometown of Bloomington, Indiana.

Mayberry was questioned by Hendricks County sheriff's detectives and freely admitted she had purchased a gun for $240 in August for the intention of first killing Rev. Phillips and then herself. Police charged Mayberry with murder, and she was held without bond at the Hendricks County Jail at Danville.

Her attorney, Ron Chapman, notified the Hendricks County Superior Court in October that he intended to enter a plea of not guilty by reason of insanity for Mayberry. Indiana law allows that a person is not responsible for illegal or wrongful conduct if "as a result of mental disease or defect, [she] was unable to appreciate the wrongfulness of the conduct."[8]

Mayberry, a single woman who had never been married, had been going downhill for months, friends and coworkers said. She had been a trusted graphic artist at the *Bloomington Herald-Times* in Monroe County for a decade. In the days before shooting Phillips, she had left a last will and testament on her work computer at the newspaper.

Mayberry met Phillips in June 1992 at a singles seminar sponsored by the church at McCormick's Creek State Park. After they started dating, she engaged in her first sexual relationship with any man, although she was thirty-six years old. In December 1992, Phillips, a divorced father of one, told her he wanted to end the relationship. Shortly after, she filed sexual misconduct charges against him, claiming they had engaged in sexual acts prohibited for unmarried pastors.

In March 1993, United Methodist Church officials met and decided not to ordain Phillips, who was still completing work as a "student pastor." Members of the North Salem Church, however, asked denominational leaders to reconsider. Following the pastor's submission to personal counseling, the denomination reversed its decision and allowed the ordination to go forward.

Mayberry was angry. She told detectives, "It just built up to where I couldn't stand it anymore. I had this incredible anger that went into a depression."[9]

She withdrew her membership from First United Methodist Church in Bloomington and began writing notes and letters to God saying, "I never would have trusted Ron if he hadn't been a minister. Without my belief in [God], I would have seen through his tricks."[10]

Her attorney said her writings revealed that she had been driven to insanity—first losing the man she had given her body to and believed would someday be her husband and then losing faith in her church.

After learning Phillips would be ordained in a letter from the denomination, coworkers said Mayberry's weight dropped from about 145 to 90 pounds and that she donned headphones at work and refused to talk to anyone.

In July 1993, Mayberry submitted to four counseling sessions with Penny O'Conner, a peer counselor at the Center for Women's Ministries in Bloomington.

"She was, I think, devastated by what she considered an abusive relationship with her minister and the way the church had handled the crisis," O'Connor said. "She felt lost, betrayed by the church, and by, I think, the reverend ... She felt like God did not exist anymore."[11]

Mayberry's trial got underway in June 1994 in Hendricks County Superior Court with unsuccessful efforts by Chapman to block her statement to investigators.

In that statement, she told a detective, "He can't do that to me and walk away like he did. Everybody just told me to forget it and go on. And I just couldn't because then that means nothing means anything ... he took too much. He took God, and he took my respect and everything that made me me; he took it away."[12]

The case quickly moved into conflicting testimonies by court-appointed psychiatrists who had examined Mayberry. One said they believed she was sane and could appreciate and understand the severity and wrongfulness of her actions. Another said she was not sane and noted she showed no normal remorse for the shooting.

One psychiatrist, Dr. David Crane, told the court he believed she was insane and that Mayberry insisted her actions were "a right thing, a good thing" that solved a problem.[13]

A friend reported Mayberry had become sarcastic, angry, and withdrawn after learning Rev. Phillips was going to be ordained. In resigning from her home church, she wrote her pastor, "I will not belong to an organization which would allow a man who would rape a woman [to] continue to lead and counsel the spiritual lives of others."[14]

On Monday, June 20, 1994, Mayberry took the stand in her own defense and said she had intended to kill herself in front of the North Salem congregation and Phillips.

"I wanted him to see what he'd done to me," Mayberry said. "I knew if he saw me die, he'd know in his heart that he did it."[15]

She said she wrestled with the idea of killing Rev. Phillips as well, but determined, "No, I had to die." She denied ever having decided to kill Phillips—and would have killed herself with the two remaining bullets in her gun had church members not stopped her.[16]

"I was really looking forward to peace, that things would stop," she said.[17]

Jurors deliberated over two days before declaring on June 22, 1994, that Mayberry was guilty of killing Rev. Phillips and of being mentally ill. None of them believed she was entitled to a "not guilty by reason of insanity" verdict. As the guilty verdict was read, she showed no emotion.

One juror, Frank Moses, told reporters that he had sympathy for Mayberry but that he believed "the act was cold-blooded, calculated, and premeditated, and she should be held accountable."[18]

He added, "Insanity was never really an issue. It was unanimous. She knew what she was doing was wrong."[19]

On July 19, 1994, Hendricks County Superior Court Judge Mary Lee Conner sentenced Mayberry to a sixty-year prison term.

Mayberry told Judge Conner, "I wish it was within my power to let them shoot me dead to take away the pain. I needed to die. I still need to die. I find comfort in knowing that death is eventual."[20]

Mayberry was ordered confined to the Indiana Women's Prison in Indianapolis. Her sentence was later reduced to forty years and she won release on September 27, 2011, after serving seventeen years in prison.

Rev. Phillips' ex-wife, Rev. Sarah Chandler, has taken custody of the couple's daughter, Rachel (who witnessed her father's murder). "We talk about her dad a lot," Chandler said. "But we talk about it in a normal way and try to not make it some horrendous moment in life, although it is."

She added, "There's no monsters in this story. There's nothing but losers here."[21]

Endnotes

1. *Bloomington Herald-Times*, June 15, 1994.
2. Ibid.
3. Ibid.
4. Ibid.
5. Ibid.
6. Ibid.
7. Ibid.
8. *Bloomington Herald-Times*, Oct. 15, 1993.
9. *Bloomington Herald-Times*, June 15, 1994.
10. Ibid.
11. *Bloomington Herald-Times*, June 16, 1994.
12. *Bloomington Herald-Times*, June 17, 1994.
13. *Bloomington Herald-Times*, June 18, 1994.
14. Ibid.
15. *Bloomington Herald-Times*, June 21, 1994.
16. Ibid.
17. Ibid.
18. *Bloomington Herald-Times*, June 23, 1994.
19. Ibid.
20. *Indianapolis Star*, July 20, 1994.
21. *Bloomington Herald-Times*, Feb. 25, 1994.

HENRY COUNTY

VICTIM(S):
Jessica Nicole Robinson, 4;
Ashley Joy Robinson, 2;
Jason Michael Robinson, 20 months

PERPETRATOR(S):
Amy J. Bostick Robinson, 23

DATE OF DEATH(S):
March 16, 1998

A YOUNG MOTHER NOT READY TO GROW UP

At age twenty-three, Amy Bostick Robinson was already the mother of three children and virtually tied down to her life as mother and provider.

She told others she hated being a mother. She also hated her husband, Jason Robinson.

Her life was full of roles she was unwilling to accept. To accept what people expected of her as a wife and mother meant growing up and becoming an adult. By 1998, Amy was just not ready to do so.

Instead, she chose a sickening and incredible means of changing her life—she burned her three children to death inside her New Castle, Indiana home.

Firefighters were called to Amy's home at 612 N. 12th St. just after 1 a.m. on Monday, March 16, 1998, and found flames pouring from the front windows of the rental property. Amy and her seventeen-year-old male friend were outside of the house alerting firefighters to the fact that Amy's three children, four-year-old Jessica, two-year-old Ashley, and twenty-month-old Jason were still inside.

Although the first police officer arrived within fifteen seconds of Amy's 911 call, and firefighters were less than a minute from arrival, they were too late.

"We went initially without a hose in an attempt to rescue the children," New Castle Fire Chief Ron Rigney said. "If there's entrapment, they're going to try and go in. But the heat was too intense."[1]

145

Local and state fire investigators poured over the smoldering shell of the house and pinpointed the start of the fire to a location along a closet and wall adjoining the front bedroom where all three children's bodies were found. All three had died of smoke inhalation, although each of their bodies suffered massive thermal or fourth-degree burns.All three had died while sleeping in their street clothes, the pathologist reported, and were frozen in a "pugilist's pose" with their fists clenched in front of them indicating their last final struggle to breathe.

As investigators probed deeper and deeper into the rubble, one fact became clear: The fire was set intentionally, and they believed they knew who did it.

Prosecutors charged Amy with three counts of murder, one count of arson, and one count of sexual misconduct with a minor for what was now revealed to be a sexual relationship with the teenage boy at her home the day of the fire.

Amy's trial opened in September 1999 before a packed courtroom in Henry Circuit Court.

Henry County Prosecutor Kit Crane said the evidence would show that Bostick, who divorced her estranged husband, Jason Robinson, before going to trial, had begun a sexual relationship with a New Castle boy, Jacob Gulley, when he was just fifteen years old. That relationship continued until the time of the fire that killed the three children.

Crane said the state would also prove the fire was intentionally set—and set by Amy Bostick. To prove it, he immediately began calling a series of witnesses related to the fire investigation, from the very first firefighters to arrive on the scene to trained arson investigators from the state fire marshal's office.

A paramedic who treated Amy for a minor cut on her hand (that did not require stitches) reported that her vital signs were all normal as firefighters worked to rescue her children and put out the fire. The paramedic also reported there were no signs of burns, soot, or ash on Amy's body or clothing, although she insisted she had tried to rescue her kids.

Jacob Gulley, however, did have soot and ash on his hands, arms, and clothing and was highly agitated, yelling for firefighters to get inside the house, pointing out which room housed the children, and pleading with them to save the three children. Gulley even took off his shirt at one point and attempted to break in the window to the children's burning bedroom in a last-ditch effort to save them.

Under questioning at the scene, Amy admitted that it was her practice to lock the children into the bedroom at night.

Jason Robinson's parents, Paul and Mable Porter, testified that they had witnessed the children's bedroom door locked from the outside many times.

"At first, it was just tied, then there was a padlock," Paul Porter told the jury, describing his daughter-in-law as "strange."[2]

Mr. Porter said Amy had said she was using the lock on the door because her oldest daughter, Jessica, would let her father, Jason, into the house—something Amy wanted to prevent.

Mrs. Porter testified that she and her husband often took the three youngsters to their home because of their concern about how poorly Amy provided for them. She also said Amy had asked her more than once if she would like to take the children on a more permanent basis because "she was tired of them."

"We had the kids nearly every weekend," Mrs. Porter said.[3]

In fact, just hours before the children perished in the blaze, they had been taken back to their mother's house by the Porters after having spent most of the weekend with their grandparents.

Mrs. Porter would learn her grandchildren were dead the next morning when Amy called her and said, "The children are dead—burned up."[4]

Jacob Gulley's sister, Starri Gulley (who was also a neighbor to Amy), told the court that she had heard her complain about having to care for her children. "She was saying all this stuff, that she wanted to move and get away from everything," Starri Gulley testified.[5]

She said Amy's parenting skills continued to deteriorate after her husband, Jason, moved out. "It just started getting worse," she said. "She wouldn't take them to the bathroom or change the little one's diapers."[6]

A great aunt testified that after Jason moved out, Amy began to scream at the children more frequently and keep them locked in their bedroom. "Everything kind of changed," Jane Cridge testified. "She didn't do anything with [the kids]. It was all Jake [Gulley]."[7]

Amy's friend, Erin Casteel, testified that Amy told her that the children "were holding her back from starting a new life with Jake [Gulley]."[8]

Arson investigators testified they found the remnants of a belt used to keep the children's bedroom door closed, a can of varnish remover, and paint, as well as an empty gas can inside the home.

New Castle Fire Department investigator Chris McCartt told the court, "I believe this was an incendiary fire … a fire that was intentionally set."[9]

McCartt said an area in a closet of the children's bedroom was determined to be the point of origin. He said "pour patterns" for a flammable liquid were also detected on the floor of the bedroom and the adjacent living room—the exit route from the bedroom.

A fire investigator from the U.S. Bureau of Alcohol, Tobacco, and Firearms (ATF) also testified that it was his opinion the fire was intentionally set. However, the ATF agent confirmed that no flammable liquids were detected on the flooring or carpeting taken from the home.

Prosecutors then played all or portions of five separate videotaped statements Amy gave to police in the days after the fire. On one of them, she said, "I don't know how the fire was started. I know it was not me. I would never, ever do that."[10]

She added, "If somebody set that fire, I want to know who. But I didn't do it. I would never do that to my children."[11]

In her statements, Amy denied ever having said she wanted to give up her kids and said she was doing all she could to provide for them. She explained that locking the children in their room at night was to keep them from wandering around or getting into mischief.

Amy also tried to take credit in her statement for busting out the window of the children's bedroom in an effort to try and save them—however, firefighters and police officers on the scene had witnessed Gulley do that, not Amy.

Initially denying a sexual relationship existed between her and the teenage boy, Amy eventually admitted it and said the two were asleep in her bed when she smelled smoke inside the house.

Her feelings for Gulley must not have been deep—in a third taped statement to police when they asked who might want to burn her house, she pointed the finger at Gulley.

New Castle Police detective Terry Haynes, who conducted the interviews with Amy, said, "During the time I sat with her, my main observation was she didn't seem too upset. During this time, she just didn't seem to be too distraught."[12]

An ATF agent in town assisting New Castle investigators offered the trial's bombshell. He testified that he overheard Amy talking to her father in an office at the New Castle Police Department. He reported hearing her say, "They got me. I admitted I did it. But I can't remember the details."[13]

Finally, Jason Robinson testified about a troubled five-year relationship between him and Amy, even though the marriage had produced three children in succession. He admitted he disliked Gulley, a neighbor who spent a lot of time at the young couple's home. He admitted saying he would burn down Amy's house at the time she asked him to move out but denied he had set the fire or set a smaller fire a week earlier that damaged Amy's car. Jason told jurors that Amy promised to make his life "a living hell" just prior to the house fire.

During a pathologist's testimony that followed, Amy refused to come into the courtroom, telling the judge she was exercising her constitutional right not to sit through the gruesome testimony.

Defense Attorney David Whitton started his case by trying to demonstrate that Amy's mental state was not stable and that any "confession" she gave to investigators was coerced. A psychiatrist testified about how a person like Amy was susceptible to a coerced confession. Dr. Hanus Grosz, a physician specializing in psychiatry and neurology, told the court that he administered a "compliance test" to Amy and that she scored very low, indicating a high amount of willingness to comply or adapt to requests of others.

Jurors finally began deliberations on Tuesday, September 29, and worked a little over six hours before returning a verdict of guilty on all charges. The jury could not come to a consensus, however, on how to fix Amy's sentence, leaving it to Henry County Superior Court Judge Michael Peyton to decide.

In October 1999, Judge Peyton sentenced Amy to three life sentences without the chance of parole. That sentence was later overturned by the U.S. Supreme Court which ruled that juries, not judges, should determine sentences in cases carrying possible life terms or capital punishment.

Judge Peyton entered a new sentence against Amy in July 2003, ordering her to serve 210 years in prison for the three murders, the arson, and the sexual misconduct with a minor. She won't be eligible for parole before 2099.

Endnotes

1. *New Castle Courier-Times*, March 16, 1998.
2. *New Castle Courier-Times*, Sept. 11, 1999.
3. Ibid.
4. Ibid.
5. *New Castle Courier-Times*, Sept. 20, 1999.
6. Ibid.
7. *New Castle Courier-Times*, Sept. 21, 1999.
8. *New Castle Courier-Times*, Sept. 22, 1999.
9. *New Castle Courier-Times*, Sept. 13, 1999.
10. *New Castle Courier-Times*, Sept. 14, 1999.
11. Ibid.
12. Ibid.
13. *New Castle Courier-Times*, Sept. 22, 1999.

HOWARD COUNTY

VICTIM(S):
Robert D. Gray, Sr., 42

PERPETRATOR(S):
Robert D. Gray, Sr., 42

DATE OF DEATH(S):
April 14, 1987

A DEADLY DETERMINATION

On the day he died, and nearly killed a dozen others, Robert D. Gray, Sr., mailed a letter to his mother, Betty, thanking her for her help and guidance. He said, "Mom, this is going to be short. I love you … I'm sorry, but I couldn't see the rest of my life in prison. Why they want me so bad, I don't know. I've been trying to be good for the last few years."[1]

His attempts at "being good," however, had not kept him from allegedly selling narcotics to coworkers and others, including an undercover police officer. A twenty-two-year employee of the Chrysler transmission plant in Kokomo, Gray was on trial during the rainy first days of April 1987. Soon, everything would change.

"He just couldn't [go to prison]," Gray's mother Betty McKinley of Marion would tell reporters later. How else could she explain what he had done?

On Tuesday, April 14, 1987, Gray appeared in Howard Circuit Court at the Howard County Courthouse to answer to several drug-related charges. He had allegedly sold LSD and faced a possible maximum sentence of forty years in prison.

It was just his latest run-in with the law. His record was peppered with prior arrests dating back into the 1970s.

When Gray returned to the courthouse for the afternoon session, he was still carrying a hard plastic briefcase he had brought with him to the morning session. Howard County Sheriff John D. Beatty, suspicious of Gray's intentions, had already decided to search the briefcase.

Gray's defense attorney, Charles H. Scruggs, would later say Gray "... had the briefcase all morning during the trial and that's not uncommon for clients to bring briefcases to court and you wouldn't necessarily be suspicious of that."[2]

Scruggs and the sheriff *did* have reason to be suspicious, however. Gray had told his attorney earlier that he planned to kill himself. Gray was "a likeable man" but one who "had been in the drug culture for so long, I think he ceased being a person," Scruggs would later say.[3]

Even more troubling, there were no metal or weapon detectors in the Howard County Courthouse—allowing a defendant to enter the building undeterred.

As Gray and Scruggs awaited the start of the afternoon session, Sheriff Beatty asked Gray to come with him to his third-floor office in the courthouse, just down the hallway from the Howard Circuit Court courtroom of Judge R. Alan Brubaker.

Gray initially objected, saying he wanted to have his briefcase opened and inspected in the courtroom. When Sheriff Beatty refused, Gray complied, and he and Scruggs went with the sheriff to his adjacent office.

Once inside the small office, Scruggs told reporters that Sheriff Beatty confronted Gray about the contents of the briefcase. Gray claimed he did not have the key to open it.

The sheriff persisted and asked whether he had a pistol in the briefcase. Gray denied that, Scruggs said, but "then the sheriff said, 'Is it a bomb?' [Gray] said yes."[4]

Scruggs then said that Gray turned to him and said he wished police informant James Wicks was present. He asked his attorney, "Do you want to get out?"

Police believe Gray intended for the explosive to kill or injure Wicks whom Gray believed was going to testify against him during the trial. Unknown to Gray, however, prosecutors had already decided not to call Wicks as a witness in the trial.

As the sheriff questioned him, Gray held on to the briefcase tightly. It now rested on the chair between his legs. It was at this moment that Scruggs and the sheriff noticed a small toggle switch near the handle of the briefcase.

"I just had time to turn, but I didn't have time to take a step or anything, and he said, 'We might as well all go now,' and detonated the bomb," Scruggs said.[5]

The blast rocked the courthouse, throwing Scruggs through a closed door and onto the floor in the next room and resulting in serious injuries. The forty-one-year-old sheriff was critically wounded as well, suffering a head wound and severe burns over 40 percent of his body. Beatty's wounds included metal fragments imbedded in his torso, arms, and legs, and were initially thought to be life-threatening as he was standing directly over Gray at the time he detonated the bomb.

Light fixtures, plaster, and windows all crashed in around the hallway outside the courtroom. Judge Brubaker hurriedly ordered jurors down the hall into a small holding room and asked them to get under large tables there.

In the hallway between the sheriff's office and the courtroom, several other persons in the courthouse were injured. In all, fifteen people suffered injuries that day.

While Sheriff Beatty and Scruggs were the most seriously injured, Indiana State Police trooper Joe Coate, Kokomo Police officer Jack Adams, and Howard County Sheriff's detective Don Howard, who were standing outside the sheriff's office when the blast occurred, also suffered injuries serious enough to require hospitalization.

Gray was killed instantly.

Kokomo Tribune reporter Ann Taylor, who was seated outside Sheriff Beatty's office waiting to speak to him about other cases, was uninjured but witnessed the force of the blast.

"The sound was incredible, like nothing I had ever heard," she wrote in her first-person account the next day. "But after the initial boom, there was no noise or movement. Silence was more frightening than the explosive noise itself. Instinctively, I somehow had curled my head into my lap … my body felt almost numb."[6]

Later that day, Howard County Prosecutor James Andrews lamented the lack of security measures allowing officials to search defendants entering the courthouse facing long sentences. "We have no security in the courthouse," Andrews said. "We do not have any security to search defendants, any metal detecting devices."[7]

An intensive investigation by local, state, and federal officials followed and revealed Gray's briefcase had contained three powerful metal pipe bombs. While the briefcase itself was plastic, authorities indicated the bombs were metal pipes, 1½ inches in diameter, and eight to ten inches long. Each was filled with an undetermined type of explosive material and metal ball bearings, to increase their lethalness.

Investigators from the U.S. Bureau of Alcohol, Tobacco, and Firearms said the device was electronically operated with a small battery and toggle switch on the outside of the briefcase. Gray only had to flip the switch to make it explode. They found no timing device. The bomb probably cost less than $20 to make, investigators believed. Police also found what remained of a .38-caliber handgun and ammunition in Gray's now-destroyed briefcase.

Subsequent searches of Gray's home, car, and locker at the Chrysler plant turned up no other explosive devices, but they did find a fourteen-foot long boa constrictor in a tank in his home.

It was not the first time, however, Gray had been involved in a bombing. In 1984, Gray was a suspect in a pipe bombing that blew up his former girlfriend's car in Marion, Indiana, but was never arrested because witnesses were afraid to testify against him.

Gray's body was removed from the Howard County Courthouse during the early morning hours of the next day. The cause of death was blunt force injuries. The divorced father of two avoided prison but could not avoid death.

Years of discussion followed about how to properly equip the Howard County Courthouse with security devices. Finally, almost two decades later, in October 2006, county officials announced they would use a special grant from the Indiana Department of Homeland Security to buy an X-ray machine, tables, and metal detectors for public entrances of the facility.

Sheriff Beatty recovered from his wounds, completed his term, and died in 1999.

Endnotes

1. *Kokomo Tribune*, April 15, 1987.
2. *Kokomo Tribune*, April 16, 1987.
3. *Indianapolis News*, April 16, 1987.
4. *Kokomo Tribune*, April 16, 1987.
5. Ibid.
6. *Kokomo Tribune*, April 15, 1987.
7. Ibid.

HUNTINGTON COUNTY

VICTIM(S):
Eldon T. Anson, 57

PERPETRATOR(S):
Jarrod M. Wall, 17;
Erick V. Esch, 17;
John J. Velasquez, 17

DATE OF DEATH(S):
February 7, 1989

A SEASON OF FAME AND NOTORIETY

As winter gave way to spring in early 1989, the people of Huntington County were understandably excited about events happening around them.

One of their own, Dan Quayle, had just been inaugurated as the forty-fourth vice president of the United States—the Huntington North High School marching band making an appearance in the presidential inaugural parade in Washington, D.C. It was a happy distinction few small towns anywhere could claim.

Of even more local interest, the Huntington North High School girls' basketball team qualified for the first time for the state final four in Indianapolis that spring. The Vikings would lose an early round game and not make the championship game—a small disappointment compared to what was around the corner in this Northern Indiana community.

Around 3:30 a.m. on Saturday, February 4, 1989, Huntington County sheriff's deputies were called to the home of fifty-seven-year-old Eldon T. Anson, which was located along U.S. 24, just east of Huntington. There, they found Anson lying face up on the snowy ground, suffering from deep lacerations to the head and fingers and multiple gunshot wounds.

Anson's tenant, John Burris, had called police when he found his landlord in the snow. Anson was rushed to Lutheran Hospital in Fort Wayne where he remained in critical condition before and after emergency surgery.

Huntington County Sheriff Thais Wilhelm said she had few clues to go on, but did know that Anson had been lying near the lane leading to his home for several hours before being discovered by Burris who was returning home from a night on the town.

Police initially suspected a motive of robbery, given that Anson enjoyed restoring, trading, and selling classic cars that he kept in his large barn or parked along the lane leading to his home. U.S. 24 was a heavily traveled route between Huntington and nearby Fort Wayne, and many people could see some wonderful old cars for sale on Anson's land.

However, police found no signs of a forced entry or robbery, and they quickly ruled Burris out as a suspect. "Everything looks pretty normal," said Huntington County Sheriff's Department detective Kent Farthing. "This is a pretty thin one here. We've got a lot of work ahead of us."[1]

Three days later on February 7, 1989, Anson finally succumbed to his injuries and died at Lutheran Hospital without ever regaining consciousness or being able to help police locate his attacker(s). At that moment, his case went from a brutal assault and battery to a rare care of murder in this quiet community.

State Police forensic experts poured over the limited physical evidence available at the scene, including Anson's body and a blood smear on one of his classic cars. The only fingerprints on the cars belonged to Anson.

Detectives began to feel discouraged a month into their investigation. They had few solid leads.

Finally, late in the afternoon of Wednesday, March 8, 1989, Huntington County Prosecutor John Branham received a phone call that would blow the case wide open.

The call came from a parent of a Huntington North High School student who claimed to have knowledge of who killed Anson. Branham immediately rushed to the student's home and met with the student and his parents as he laid out an incredible tale.

The youth told Branham that a fellow classmate, seventeen-year-old John J. Velasquez, had implicated himself and Jarrod M. Wall, another seventeen-year-old, in an attempted robbery of Anson's home. The youth's story included a key fact not previously known publicly—Anson had been shot multiple times by a .22-caliber weapon.

In fact, Anson had suffered six separate head wounds from the small caliber weapon. News reports, however, were purposefully vague, referring only to the lacerations Anson suffered in the attack.

Branham quickly notified Detective Farthing and State Police Detective Jim Waters (who had joined the investigation), and obtained a full statement from the boy.

By the end of the next day, Branham and police had obtained a search warrant for the Velasquez family home on North Rangeline Road. They also took John, accompanied by his parents, in for questioning.

Velasquez told detectives about a plan to rob Anson based on a rumor that he had a large safe in his home containing cash and guns—a rumor eerily similar to the one at the center of famed author Truman Capote's epic true-crime thriller In Cold Blood. Velasquez claimed, however, that he had not participated in the robbery or the attack on Anson as his mother had required him to stay home on the night of the attack to babysit for his two younger sisters.

Velasquez claimed that Wall and Erick V. Esch, another seventeen-year-old classmate, had visited him at his home before and after going to Anson's home, but that he did not know the full nature of what they had done until he read about the attack in the newspaper a few days later.

Police were skeptical about Velasquez's story since it heavily implicated Wall and Esch, but not himself. It also didn't match the gloating version he had told his classmate in which he was a major player in the crime. It was his gloating that had caused the whole ugly secret to be exposed.

Under further questioning, Velasquez admitted that he had lied to his classmate to try and impress him and that he and Wall had hatched up the plan to rob Anson. He also admitted that he had assisted Wall in burglarizing the home of a Huntington County Sheriff's deputy a few weeks after the Anson attack. Stolen from the deputy's home was a 9-millimeter semi-automatic handgun.

Wall was a good-looking teenager, a standout on the track team at the high school, and an honor-roll student. He had been elected class president as a freshman and a sophomore. A member of the 4-H Sheep Club, he was active in his local Youth for Christ chapter and served as a volunteer Sunday school teacher at church. He was also the son of two well-known residents; his father was a teacher in the local schools, and his mother a local bank employee.

Esch, a highly athletic but less popular teen than Wall, had only lived in the community for one year. It had been a good year; he made his mark as a slot back receiver for the Vikings football team in the fall 1988 season. Living now with his father, it appeared he had begun to put his petty juvenile record (unknown to most adults in Huntington) behind him.

Branham and Farthing had enough to arrest Velasquez on various charges and then set about obtaining arrest warrants for Wall and Esch. Both were asleep in their beds before dawn on Friday, March 10, when arrest warrants were served for Wall at his parent's home on Huntington County Road 400 East. Esch was picked up at his father's apartment on West Maple Grove Road. Both were booked at the county jail.

Prosecutor Branham was tight-lipped with the local Huntington and Fort

Wayne media who had jumped on the story. The Friday afternoon edition of the Huntington *Herald-Press* carried the large headline, "Two Teems Charged in Anson Slaying," and featured a photo of a smiling Wall from his high school yearbook and a picture of Esch in his football uniform.

The next day, Branham acknowledged that a third suspect, the so-far publicly unnamed Velasquez, was being held on a juvenile charge related to the case. Branham told reporters he had "a pretty good notion" of who wielded the murder weapons on Anson and for the first time acknowledged there may have been more than one weapon used.[2]

Branham expressed what many in the community were feeling when he described the arrests as "a real tragedy for the Huntington community and local school system."[3]

The Herald-Press editorialized about its sense of "shock" over the arrests in the case but asked community members to remain calm and avoid spreading rumors. "The people of Huntington are owed as clear and thorough an explanation of this tragedy as authorities can provide, but the people are going to have to be patient," editor Michael V. Perkins wrote.[4]

On Monday, March 13, Wall and Esch were marched into the Huntington County Courthouse to be arraigned on charges of murder and robbery. Both were ordered to be held without bond: Wall at the Wabash County Jail, and Esch at the Whitley County Jail.

The probable cause affidavit used to secure the arrests of Wall and Esch revealed for the first time that Anson's head had been slashed numerous times with an ax, causing deep lacerations to his skull. It also revealed that Anson had suffered six non-fatal shots to the head from the .22-caliber gun that police now knew Wall had stolen from his father.

At least one motive for the brutal assault emerged: a botched attempt to rob Anson by inexperienced, but deadly, young men. Wall's attempts to shoot Anson to death had failed, so he returned and began slashing Anson over the head with a hatchet.

The next day, prosecutors formally charged Velasquez with conspiring to commit murder. He was waived from juvenile court to adult court and ordered to be held at a juvenile detention facility in Allen County. Known as "The Fly" for his participation in a local break-dancing group, Velasquez had befriended Wall while both were members of the track team at the high school.

Now that the suspects were in custody, the legal process would take its course. But not before Wall surprised most of the community by revealing he had actually harbored an altogether different motive for the attack on Anson than most people had heard.

While Esch and Velasquez told police the attack was all about robbing Anson of money and guns, Wall said he had another motive.

In a lengthy letter written from his cell to his classmates at Huntington North High School, Wall told of his growing anger and resentment over the fact that a favorite uncle had contracted HIV, the virus that causes AIDS.

Wall said he believed unfounded rumors around town that Anson might be gay or was a drug dealer who kept a large amount of money in a safe. Wall said he believed the rumors and thought Anson was someone who took advantage of others; he thought such a person was also to blame for his uncle's HIV status.

What Wall did not reveal at that time, but testified to later in court, was the he himself had started a gay relationship with an unnamed local man that he maintained throughout his years in middle school and high school, fueling speculation that self-loathing and latent homosexual feelings had caused Wall to target Anson—someone he believed was gay.

Wall advised his classmates to "learn from my mistake" and "don't ruin your life."

By August, Wall and his attorneys were ready to discuss a plea agreement as statements from Esch and Velasquez sealed the case against him as the ringleader in the murder of Eldon Anson.

On September 5, all three young men were escorted into Huntington Circuit Court for a plea and sentencing hearing for Esch. Oddly, a large photograph on the front page of the *Herald-Press* showed Wall smiling widely, seemingly glad to again be in the company of his more subdued co-conspirators, whose faces bore more serious expressions.

During the hearing, Esch made a tearful apology for his role in the awful crime. "I want to apologize to the Eldon Anson family for any part that I played in this . . . I hope they don't hold any grudges."

Anson's daughter, Cindy Morris, spoke up from the audience and said softly, "You're forgiven."[5]

The court also heard a psychiatric evaluation of Esch from his earlier run-ins with the law in Marion County that indicated he had the potential to develop a personality disorder and had "weak social and moral values," was "highly reactive to peers," and that "further misconduct is likely."[6]

Esch's father and others testified about his good traits, asking the judge for leniency.

Huntington County Circuit Court Judge Mark McIntosh was in no mood for leniency. He sentenced Esch to the maximum sentence allowed—twenty years for burglary and eight years for assisting a criminal, the charges to which Esch had agreed to plead guilty. The twenty-eight years were to be served consecutively, McIntosh ruled.

A little over a week later, on September 12, John Velasquez entered the same courtroom to hear his fate for pleading guilty to burglary and conspiracy to commit burglary charges. McIntosh was again strict, sentencing Velasquez to twenty years for the burglary of the sheriff deputy's home and another ten years for conspiring to rob Anson. The thirty year total was to be served consecutively, McIntosh ruled.

As in the Esch sentencing hearing, Velasquez and his attorneys cast Wall as the mastermind of the crimes and the leader of their small band.

The suspects convicted in this case, Detective Farthing said, ". . . are not what we usually deal with, and that makes it a little harder . . . We tend to think that things like this can't be done by the young . . . even though we see all around us that they do."[7]

Wall faced sentencing later in September after also agreeing to plead guilty but mentally ill to a felony charge of murder, and avoiding a trial. During his sentencing, Dr. Jack A. Morgenstern, a child psychologist who examined Wall, said the young man killed Anson because of delusional thoughts. "He decided this man was evil and deserved to die, then slew him," Morgenstern said.[8]

Judge McIntosh read from Wall's own statement when deciding on the sentence. Wall had written that Anson was "bleeding and staggering around; then he fell, after being shot between one and six times."[9]

"I remember being very mad at this moment because he wasn't dead," Wall wrote.[10]

As Anson put up his hands to defend himself against the attack, Wall swung the hatchet wildly cutting off the fingers of his victim's hands before landing blows to the older man's head.

Wall wrote that he began thinking about splitting wood with his father and hit Anson repeatedly over the head with the ax.

Wall showed no reaction as the judge read out loud the gruesome details of the attack. It rang eerily similar to how Wall had reacted on the morning after he brutally attacked Anson. Returning home after the attack, Wall got up on Saturday morning as usual and went to work his regular morning shift at the McDonald's restaurant in Huntington.

The judge declared, despite witnesses who told of Wall's good activities at school and in the church, "The court believes there is no remorse. [Wall] is in fear of imprisonment, not in remorse for the death of Eldon Anson."[11]

The judge then gave Wall the maximum sentence allowed—sixty years in prison.

In March 1992, Judge McIntosh suspended the balance of the sentence against Erick Esch, now a twenty-eight-year-old man, and ordered him placed on probation. In January 1996, Grant County Special Judge Thomas Wright reduced John Valesquez's sentence from thirty years to sixteen, allowing him to be released on probation in 1997 after serving eight years.

Jarrod Wall also attempted to appeal his sentence, unsuccessfully. In March 2001, Wall asked Judge McIntosh to cut his sentence in half, saying his growing knowledge of his own homosexuality at the age of twelve and the knowledge that his uncle was gay caused him to project "self-hatred" onto the victim, Eldon Anson.

In August 2001, McIntosh ruled against Wall's request, although he acknowledged that the now thirty-year-old man had made good progress behind bars. A separate direct appeal to the Indiana Supreme Court also failed. Wall remained incarcerated at the Pendleton Correctional Facility Wall until he won parole on March 11, 2016 after serving twenty-six and one-half years behind bars.

Endnotes

1. *Huntington Herald-Press*, Feb. 6, 1989.
2. *Huntington Herald-Press*, March 12, 1989.
3. Ibid.
4. Ibid.
5. *Huntington Herald-Press*, Sept. 6, 1989.
6. Ibid.
7. *Fort Wayne Journal-Gazette*, March 11, 1989.
8. *Huntington Herald-Press*, Sept. 18, 1989.
9. *Huntington Herald-Press*, Sept. 19, 1989.
10. Ibid.
11. Ibid.

JACKSON COUNTY

VICTIM(S):
Katlyn "Katie" Collman, 10

PERPETRATOR(S):
Anthony Ray Stockelman, 39

DATE OF DEATH(S):
January 25, 2005

KATIE'S KILLER FACES REVENGE

Five months into his life sentence for the rape and murder of ten-year-old Katie Collman, Anthony Ray Stockelman was forcibly given a permanent tattoo that will forever mark him as a child molester and killer.

In September 2006, a Web site blog, known as "Lost in Lima, Ohio," posted a close-up photo of Stockelman's forehead bearing the words "Katie's Revenge" scratched into his skin. Two prison guards at the Wabash Valley Correctional Center near Carlisle, Indiana, were accused of turning the photo over to the Web site for the entire world to see.

"If I had to guess, I'd say it's a statement from the inmates," Katie's father, John Neace, said when told of the tattoo.[1]

The DOC immediately placed Stockelman in protective custody away from the general prison population after the tattoo was discovered. He had to be held in similar isolation at the Jackson County Jail in Brownstown, Indiana, as he awaited trial for Katie's murder.

"People accused of crimes against children face what they call 'jailhouse justice,' so we've kept [Stockelman] pretty well isolated for his own protection," said Jackson County Jail Commander Marc Lahrman.[2]

The forcible assault on Stockelman was the latest twist in an incredible search for the truth to what happened to Katie. She disappeared while walking home from the Dollar General store in Crothersville, Indiana, at about 4 p.m. on Tuesday, January 25, 2005. A clerk at the store said Katie purchased toilet paper and had talked to a friend about a block away before she was seen moments later riding inside a truck driven by a male subject.

The fourth-grade girl "always had a smile on her face," said Terry Goodin, superintendent of Crothersville Community Schools. His twin brother, State Police Sergeant Jerry Goodin, led the police search for Katie.[3]

At the time of her disappearance, Neace, Katie's father, and her mother, Angie Collman, issued a heartfelt plea: "Please do not harm [Katie]. We ask that you just drop her off anywhere so that she may return to a family and community that loves her very much and misses her dearly."[4]

Police issued a composite sketch of a man believed to have taken Katie into his Ford F-150 pickup the day before the search for her would come to an end. An Indiana State Police trooper on routine patrol found Katie's body in a small stream in rural Jackson County on Sunday, January 30, just five days after she went missing.

Her body was found about a quarter of a mile from Interstate 65 and about five miles north of Seymour, Indiana. Katie's murder would hit her family and the community hard. It was the first murder in Crothersville, a community of about 1,500 citizens, in a quarter century.

On February 4, 2005, investigators thought they had a big break in the case with the arrest of twenty-year-old Charles J. Hickman of Crothersville on preliminary charges of murder, felony murder, and criminal confinement. Under questioning about Katie's disappearance, police said Hickman confessed to the crime.

Investigators were not convinced, however, that Hickman was the only one responsible for the girl's death. "If there are other people involved, then we are going to seek those other people out," Sergeant Goodin said.[5]

In the charges against Hickman, Jackson County Prosecutor Steve Pierson alleged that Hickman killed Katie to keep her quiet after she accidentally witnessed a methamphetamine operation in her neighborhood. Pierson said Hickman had admitted picking up Katie in his truck, tying her hands behind her back, and planned to take her to a rural area when the girl attempted to flee, tripped, and fell into the creek and drowned. The prosecutor alleged that Hickman had watched Katie struggle in the water "for about twenty minutes until she finally lay still in the water."[6]

"They decided to scare her with the hope that she would be intimidated enough to keep her observations to herself," FBI agent James Kouns wrote in a supporting document for Hickman's arrest.[7]

The "meth" or "crank" angle would make sense in any rural part of Indiana. Methamphetamine operations had exploded across the state in the decade prior to 2005, with more than 1,500 homemade labs dismantled by police in 2004 alone.

As investigators moved forward with building their case against Hickman, DNA evidence returned from Katie's autopsy confirmed she had been sexually molested prior to her death. The twist, however, was that the DNA did not match the "confessed" killer, Charles Hickman.

The DNA, it turns out, matched one collected in a recent sample from Stockelman. Stockelman was arrested April 7, 2005, and charged with sexual molestation while investigators tried to sort out the case. Stockelman had been a "person of interest" in the early going of the investigation, police said, but when Hickman stepped forward and confessed, the probe focused in his direction.

Then on May 20, 2005, the case took another startling turn as Pierson announced that Stockelman was now being charged with Katie's murder and that murder charges against Hickman were being dropped. Pierson also revealed new evidence that led him to conclude Stockelman, who professed his innocence, was the killer. A cigarette butt left at the scene of Katie's murder contained DNA that matched his as did the semen recovered from Katie's body. The cigarette butt was from an uncommon brand as well, known as Roger Light 100s, the kind smoked by Stockelman.

Pierson told reporters, "It now appears that the alleged sighting of a meth lab by Katie was more false information." He said he had no idea why Hickman would have falsely confessed to a crime he did not commit, but added, "I don't think the science in [this] case lies. I think the police have to follow what the facts are and not speculate as to why people say what they say sometimes."[8]

Stockelman was held without bond at the Jackson County Jail and had an additional charge of possessing a deadly weapon added in January 2006 after jailers found him armed with a toothbrush sharpened into a shank. Stockelman had allegedly told a fellow inmate he planned to kill a jail guard and Prosecutor Pierson.

His denials notwithstanding, a mountain of DNA evidence tying Stockelman to Katie's rape and murder began to build. On March 23, 2006, he decided to enter a guilty plea to the molestation and murder of Katie, rather than face a trial and risk the possibility of a death sentence. As he was led into the Jackson County Courthouse, Stockelman appeared roughshod with a heavy beard and unkempt long hair.

His once supportive wife, Tabitha Stockelman, shouted to him as he walked across the courthouse lawn, "Why'd you do it, Tony?"[9]

In the courtroom, Stockelman acknowledged to Jackson County Circuit Court Judge William E. Vance that he understood his plea would mean that he was waiving his rights to a later appeal.

During his plea hearing, Stockelman's wife, Tabitha, revealed her change of heart—she now believed her husband had killed the girl. She said on the night Katie disappeared, Stockelman was insistent that the family sit down to eat a family dinner, "While I still have the chance," she quoted him as saying. It was an unusual move—Stockelman normally ate his meals in front of the TV alone.[10]

Tabitha also told the court her husband wanted to drive by the area where Katie's body was found. She said, "He kept saying and saying that they were going to pin Katie Collman on him."[11]

Katie's mother, Angie Collman, also testified that the young girl was always eager to help and excited about going to the Dollar Store on an errand for her mother. She left just after 3 p.m. that day, but by 4:30 p.m., the family was convinced something was terribly wrong. Katie's father, John, was still too emotional to testify.

On April 20, 2006, Judge Vance sentenced Stockelman to life in prison without the possibility of parole.

In May 2006, Stockelman told WISH-TV in Indianapolis that he did not remember molesting or killing Katie and implicated Hickman in the assault.

"I was still in the truck, and when I looked around [Hickman] pushed her in and I jumped out of the truck and asked him what he was doing," Stockelman told WISH-TV. "… About that time, I was trying to sober up and didn't know what was going on."[12]

Stockelman saved his "best" for last—angering almost anyone who heard him by blaming Katie's parents for letting her go to the store alone. "To let a ten-year-old girl take off more than two blocks away from home, that shouldn't happen," Stockelman said. "I don't even let my fourteen-year-old boy go to the store by himself."[13]

Katie's father told reporters later that Stockelman's remark "… confirms that he's a stinking idiot."[14]

Stockelman pursued an unsuccessful appeal of his sentence, despite acknowledging in court that he was giving up that right. His attorney said the judge's sentence was inappropriate "given the nature of the offense and the character of the offender."[15]

Officials at the Wabash Valley Correctional Center eventually charged twenty-two-year-old Jared Harris, Katie's cousin, who was also serving a sentence at the facility, with forcibly tattooing Stockelman's head.

"I told him that if he would allow me to place this tattoo on his forehead … everything would be taken care of and he wouldn't have to worry about any future attacks," Harris told a Bartholomew County judge in December 2006.[16]

Endnotes

1. Associated Press, Sept. 29, 2006.
2. *Seymour Tribune*, Sept. 29, 2006.
3. Associated Press, Jan. 31, 2005.
4. Associated Press, Jan. 30, 2005.
5. Associated Press, Feb. 4, 2005.
6. Associated Press, March 24, 2005.
7. Associated Press, Feb. 5, 2005.
8. Associated Press, May 21, 2005.
9. Associated Press, March 25, 2006.
10. *Seymour Tribune*, March 24, 2006.
11. *Seymour Tribune*, March 24, 2006.
12. WISH-TV, Channel 8, Indianapolis, May 26, 2006.
13. Ibid.
14. Ibid.
15. Associated Press, undated article.
16. Associated Press, Dec. 8, 2006.

JASPER COUNTY

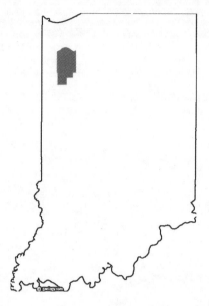

VICTIM(S):
Bradley Lonadier, 3

PERPETRATOR(S):
Larry Lonadier, 25;
Lucy Lonadier, 25;
Steven Ray Jackson, 25

DATE OF DEATH(S):
August 6, 1982

'DO AS I SAY, NOT AS I DO'

Twenty-five-year-old Steven Ray Jackson considered himself a chosen prophet of God, a man who claimed authority over demonic spirits and demanded absolute devotion from the followers of his teachings.

Leader of the Community Covenant Fellowship of DeMotte, Indiana, in northern Jasper County, Jackson declared himself "Moses" of the fellowship.[1]

His strict rules were apparently ones only others were expected to follow. Jackson did what he pleased.

Jackson's demands of the eight adult members of the CCF included requirements that pregnant women fast and children be beaten into submission. One of those children, three-year-old Bradley Lonadier, was punished severely by his parents at Jackson's instruction—so severely that he lived in a comatose state for four days before dying from an intracranial hemorrhage on August 6, 1982, just a month shy of his fourth birthday.

Bradley's young parents, Larry and Lucy Lonadier, both twenty-five, would admit they had severely punished the boy not only on the day he fell unconscious but in the past as well. They told authorities they were simply following the demands and teachings of their spiritual leader, Steven Ray Jackson.

Larry and Lucy Lonadier agreed to plead guilty to manslaughter charges and five additional charges on the eve of Jackson's trial in November 1982.

In exchange for their pleas, prosecutors required they provide testimony and evidence against Jackson. Jackson faced involuntary manslaughter and child neglect charges of his own.

In court, Larry admitted he beat little Bradley. "I was pushing my son down," Lonadier said, "and making him get back up and then doing the same thing again."[2]

Larry said Bradley fell unconscious around 8 a.m. on August 2, 1982, but that "it was probably two that afternoon before we took him to the hospital."[3]

During the seven-hour delay in taking Bradley to St. Anthony's Medical Center at Crown Point, members of the commune prayed over his unconscious body. When they finally did take him to the hospital, he was found unresponsive with bruises on his face and neck. He was immediately placed on life support.

Investigators worked hard to hold the Lonadiers and Jackson responsible for their role in Bradley's death. Jackson's trial drew heavy interest in the community and opened with a bang.

Larry Lonadier's brother, David, who at one time was also a member of the Community Covenant Fellowship, testified via deposition that Jackson considered himself "a latter-day prophet. 'I am your Moses,'" David's statement quoted Jackson as saying.

David Lonadier said Jackson believed heavily in male supremacy over women, vigorous discipline of rule-breakers, and "his own Godly insight."

David Lonadier said Jackson had told him, "Man, your whole family's out of control ... your wife is unsubmissive."[4]

Jackson felt so strongly about child discipline that he ordered Larry and Lucy Lonadier to disciple their two-week-old daughter, Bradley's younger sister.

For his punishment, Bradley would be taken to the basement of the Lonadier home. His uncle, David Lonadier, told the court, "I could hear him yelling. They taught him to scream, 'Help me Jesus!' while he was being spanked ... [the paddle] had bloodstains on it after a beating."[5]

Apparently, Jackson had come to the conclusion that any crying or fussiness by a baby or child was a sign of rebellion.

Larry Lonadier's father, Morris, also testified, telling the jury that his son and daughter-in-law began to drift away from their blood relatives after 1980 when they met Jackson.

"I could not get anywhere with Larry," Morris Lonadier testified. "I could not get him to listen to me."[6]

Morris said a once-close relationship with his son, his wife, and his children continued to grow cold up until the time of Bradley's funeral in August 1982.

Neighbors and family members attempted to do what they could. Child welfare officials had been investigating the Lonadiers and their treatment of not only Bradley but also their ten-month-old daughter, Christen.

A hearing was conducted in July 1982 in Jasper Circuit Court to determine whether to remove Bradley and Christen from their parents' custody. At that time, the court ruled there was insufficient evidence to support such a move.

It was a ruling many would later regret, but few blamed the judge, prosecutors, or child welfare officials. Each of them believed they did what they could to prevent a tragedy.

Their efforts, however, were not enough.

"I couldn't believe it," Morris Lonadier said, describing his son and daughter-in-law's behavior at the funeral for Bradley. "The lack of feelings, the lack of compassion, the lack of grief that they showed. I sat right by my son at my grandson's funeral. He made no effort or sign of recognition at all."[7]

Lynne Lonadier, an aunt to young Bradley, had also lived at the CCF commune on Potomac Drive in DeMotte for a short time. She quoted Jackson as saying it was scriptural to kill rebellious children.

"Steve Jackson told us that children need to be under submission to their parents … no matter what it takes or how long you have to beat them," Lucy Lonadier told the court. "He said that in the Old Testament, they used to beat their children and sometimes kill them."[8]

Testimony from the Lonadier family was meant to demonstrate the depth and level of control Jackson had obtained over the young couple and others who joined the sect.

The testimony was also key to demonstrating that not only did Jackson encourage beating Bradley for what he perceived to be rebellious behavior but that he also had beaten the child.

Lynn Lonadier said she heard the belt striking young Bradley's buttocks in the basement below and heard Jackson yelling at the boy, "Turn around, put your hands on the bed, and stop crying."[9]

The beatings were not "over and done" events but instead, were drawn-out, lengthy ordeals. Lynn Lonadier said a beating could last for as little as thirty minutes or as long as three hours.

Following the three-hour spanking, Lynn Lonadier said she witnessed Bradley with a black eye and said that he was unable to sit or lie down because of the wounds on his buttocks and the back of his legs.

Other punishments for Bradley included binding and gagging the boy and making him stay under a bathroom sink vanity for hours at a time. The boy was also repeatedly tied down to his bed and had tape placed across his mouth for hours at a time.

Jackson may have believed Bradley was possessed by demonic spirits, something he apparently told the boy on more than one occasion. Bradley himself once told his mother, "Mommy, I'm sad. I think the devil's trying to get me."[10]

Jackson ruled the commune with absolute force. The families that lived there had their outside activities strictly monitored, and the fifteen to twenty individuals who lived there had to ask for Jackson's permission before being allowed to leave on their own.

"If Steve Jackson said no, you just didn't go," Lynn Lonadier said.[11]

Lynn Lonadier also testified that Jackson frequently broke his own rules, including attending R-rated films and coming back to the commune and making crude remarks about the breasts of some of the women in the films he had seen.

"He was a hypocrite," she said.[12]

He also was a lecherous man.

Around the time of Bradley's death, in the late summer months of 1982, Jackson had demanded conjugal access to Lucy Lonadier, Bradley's mother. Larry Lonadier submitted to Jackson's demand and allowed his wife to sleep with their religious leader, all the while being ordered to bring an allegedly rebellious Bradley into line.

Jasper County Prosecutor Tom Fisher pointed out a major distinction as he wrapped up his case against Jackson. He noted commune members regularly went to the doctor for medical care but suddenly began to rely solely on the power of prayer when Bradley fell ill that August day.

"Christianity got prostituted all over the place in [Jackson's] mind," Fisher told the jury. "There's no reason to think that Larry Lonadier didn't think he'd be closer to salvation for doing it. The only road to salvation, [Jackson] tells Larry Lonadier, is to beat the daylights out of your kid. You'll be closer to God."[13]

Jackson's attorney, William Bontrager of Elkhart, referred to Bradley's death as an unforeseen fluke and said Indiana law protects those who seek healing through prayer rather than traditional medicine.

The jury was unmoved. After just six hours of deliberations, they found Jackson guilty of involuntary manslaughter, battery, two counts of child neglect, and two counts of conspiracy to commit child neglect.

Jasper County Circuit Court Judge E. Duane Daugherty sentenced Jackson to a total of twenty years in prison for his part in Bradley's death remarking, "Except for this defendant, Bradley Lonadier would be alive today."

The judge's sentence of forty years combined was allowed to be served concurrently, meaning the maximum Jackson would be jailed was ten years.

An Indiana Court of Appeals ruling later ordered the court to modify Jackson's sentence, and he won release from the Department of Correction on September 14, 1993.[14]

Larry and Lucy Lonadier were sentenced by Judge Daugherty on January 12, 1983, consistent with the plea agreement they had entered earlier in exchange for their testimony against Jackson. Daugherty gave each of them a ten-year sentence for six felony counts, including involuntary manslaughter, battery, and child neglect charges. The bulk of their ten-year sentence was suspended, with Lucy Lonadier being released from prison in one month, while her husband served about one year. Both were placed on probation, which they were released from in February 1991.[15]

Endnotes

1. *Rensselaer Republican*, Dec. 2, 1982.
2. *Rensselaer Republican*, Nov. 30, 1982.
3. Ibid.
4. *Rensselaer Republican*, Dec. 2, 1982.
5. Ibid.
6. Ibid.
7. Ibid.
8. *Rensselaer Republican*, Dec. 4, 1982.
9. Ibid.
10. Ibid.
11. Ibid.
12. Ibid.
13. *Rensselaer Republican*, Dec. 7, 1982.
14. Jasper County Clerk's Office.
15. Ibid.

JAY COUNTY

VICTIM(S):
Garnet Ginn, 33

PERPETRATOR(S):
None identified.

DATE OF DEATH(S):
February 28, 1950

THE MYSTERY OF MISS GINN'S DEATH

On the night she died, Miss Garnet Ginn attended a meeting of the Portland, Indiana, chapter of Psi Iota Xi Sorority at the Portland Country Club.

The sorority, founded in nearby Muncie, Indiana, in 1897, exists "to be of service with time, money and love in a cooperative effort with the community." In Portland, many young women in 1950 viewed being a part of Psi Iota Xi as important and a valuable way to give back to the community.

As was the custom at the Portland sorority meetings, the night's events ended with a sing-along around the piano. Miss Ginn, later reported to be in good spirits, requested the group sing two songs, "God Be With You 'Till We Meet Again" and "Goodbye Sweetheart." The ladies obliged, and all present reported she seemed to enjoy her evening.

During the meeting, she even offered to host the next meeting of the women at her Portland apartment.

As she left, she offered a ride home to a neighbor who also attended the meeting, Mrs. Gladys Pearson. Mrs. Pearson was the last to see her alive, as Miss Ginn dropped her off around 10:30 p.m.

Garnet, a thirty-three-year-old single woman employed as the home economics teacher at Portland High School, was a reliable, well-mannered, and much-loved woman. Although she reportedly had few gentlemen callers, she was active in her community and well-liked by students at the high school.

"Her family said she was happy in her work, she was not pressured for money, and her health was good," the *Portland Graphic* noted. "They say she loved beauty and harmony and recoiled from crudeness."[1]

The gentleness with which she led her life makes the mystery of how she died even more perplexing.

At 11 a.m. the next morning, Wednesday, March 1, 1950, Portland Schools superintendent Dr. D.S. Weller found Garnet dead beside her automobile in the garage at 318 N. Harrison St., a half block from her apartment at 217 E. Arch St. in Portland. Dr. Weller had gone to her home that morning to investigate why the ever-reliable Miss Ginn had not reported to school to teach her classes.

What Dr. Weller found was a gruesome scene—Miss Ginn's body hung by the throat from the door handle of her 1949 Pontiac, a sewing machine belt tied in a slip-knot around her neck. She sat nearly upright on the floor of the garage in her fur overcoat, lodged in a narrow eighteen- to twenty-inch space between the car door and the outer wall of the garage. A neighbor who shared the garage and removed his car from the two-car garage en route to work earlier that morning had not even noticed her body slumped at the side.

"The tall, brown-haired teacher's pinstripe suit and fur coat were not disarranged, and there was no evidence of a struggle. Her purse, lying open on the front seat of the 1949 green Pontiac, contained a dime and the usual accessories. The car keys were alongside," the *Portland Graphic* reported.[2]

Her wallet and driver's license were missing, police said.

Jay County coroner Donald E. Spahr, MD, ruled Miss Ginn died of strangulation, but police wanted to investigate further before declaring the death either a suicide or a homicide. He said her body was found with her gloves on and her left leg folded under her crumpled body.

Indiana State Police detectives joined the Portland Police Department in its review of the troubling case, but after days, there was little new information to go on.

Witnesses said they noticed nothing wrong with Miss Ginn at the sorority meeting. Mrs. Pearson said she had acted like herself on the short ride home from the country club. Inside her nearby apartment on Arch Street, police found another $30 tucked under a bedroom pillow undisturbed.

A neighbor from across Harrison Street said she noticed Miss Ginn drive her car into the garage between 10:30 and 11 p.m. She later thought she heard "sounds resembling a cat fight and got up [from bed] to investigate." Seeing a cat walk across the street, she returned to bed, but not before noticing that the lights were still on in Miss Ginn's car.[3]

"Friends of the girl said that she was very happy and enjoying her teaching, and as far as they knew, she would have no reason to take her own life," the

Portland Commercial Review reported. "No note was found either in the garage or at her apartment on East Arch Street."[4]

The *Portland Graphic* summed up the mystery this way: "If suicide, why all the contradictory circumstances? If murder, what was the motive?"[5]

The mystery remained, and Miss Ginn's grief-stricken family buried their daughter in a cemetery at Akron, Indiana, in Marshall County, after a short visitation at her parents' home in Mount Summit, Indiana.

Miss Ginn graduated from Brighton High School and later Ball State Teacher's College in 1940 and taught at Albany High School one year before coming to Portland in 1943. She came from a long line of teachers. Her father had served as the principal of Mount Summit High School. Her mother was a teacher in Henry County. Her sister taught at Warsaw High School, and her brother was a teacher and coach in Henry County.

She would not remain in her grave, however. Miss Ginn's family pushed investigators to determine whether she in fact had been murdered, struggling to believe she would have killed herself.

Police investigators exhumed her body on April 12, 1950, and transported it 100 miles away to the Indianapolis General Hospital in order to conduct an autopsy, since one was not conducted at the time of her death. Despite inconclusive evidence of a homicide from the autopsy, two days later, the editors at the *Portland Graphic* had made up their minds and ran a screaming headline declaring, "Ginn Was Murdered."[6]

The autopsy revealed blood clots in Miss Ginn's brain, presumably caused by at least seven blows inflicted on her head, although none of the blows had lacerated the skin of her skull. The body also showed bruises and discolorations of the skin.[7]

Small bloodstains were also later noted on the rear fenders of her car on both sides and above the passenger door—causing some to believe she was attacked as she exited her car and was carried around the back to the passenger's side, where she was hung.

Everyone struggled to accept a suicide ruling, but by early summer, with no new evidence to go on and an inconclusive autopsy finding, Jay County sheriff Clarence Bishop said, "I now lean to the idea that she committed suicide and was not murdered."[8]

Sheriff Bishop added, "There was never enough evidence for us to make any arrests, or even strongly suspect any one person. It is not right to say that the case is closed, though. Something will come up that will change the picture."[9]

No "something" ever did come up to allow police to definitively solve the mystery of Miss Ginn's death. Decades later, some still believe it a suicide, and others believe it a homicide.

Regardless, the happy and peaceful life of one of Portland's finest teachers came to a brutal end.

The lyrics of one of the last songs she asked the ladies of Psi Iota Xi to sing on that night long ago in 1950 were a fitting refrain for her sad passing:

God be with you till we meet again;
When life's perils thick confound you;
Put His arms unfailing round you;
God be with you till we meet again
Till we meet, till we meet,
Till we meet at Jesus' feet;
Till we meet, till we meet,
God be with you till we meet again.[10]

Endnotes

1. *Portland Graphic*, March 9, 1950.
2. *Portland Graphic*, March 2, 1950.
3. *Portland Commercial-Review*, March 1, 1950.
4. Ibid.
5. *Portland Graphic*, March 2, 1950.
6. *Portland Graphic*, April 14, 1950.
7. Ibid.
8. *Portland Graphic*, undated article.
9. Ibid.
10. Rankin, Jeremiah E. "God Be With You 'Till We Meet Again." *Gospel Bells*. Chicago, Illinois: The Western Sunday School Publishing Co., 1880. Music by William G. Tomer, 1882.

JEFFERSON COUNTY

VICTIM(S):
Shanda Renee Sharer, 12

PERPETRATOR(S):
Mary Laurine "Laurie" Tackett, 17;
Melinda D. Loveless, 16;
Hope A. Rippey, 15;
Toni L. Lawrence, 15

DATE OF DEATH(S):
January 11, 1992

THE CRUELEST OF INTENTIONS

What four teenage girls did to twelve-year-old Shanda Renee Sharer on a cold Friday night in Jefferson County is a case that still baffles anyone who has ever heard the details.

The facts are that Shanda's burned and beaten body was found by hunters at about 10:45 a.m. on Saturday, January 11, 1992, along a dirt road in rural Shelby Township of Jefferson County. Her badly burned body was nude except for panties, and was posed in a sexual manner.

Jefferson County Prosecutor Guy M. Townsend said Shanda, a resident of Jeffersonville, Indiana, died of smoke inhalation, but also had been burned, beaten, bound at one time or another, sodomized, and punctured and cut with a knife or other sharp object. The upper part of her body was covered with third- and fourth-degree burns, and her tongue protruded through her clenched teeth, frozen by death.

Smoke in her lungs, pathologists ruled, confirmed she was burned alive on the spot where she was found (although she may have been unconscious by the time a flammable liquid was poured onto her body and lit ablaze).

As the cold reality of Shanda's murder set in, police picked up critical clues to the crime and immediately arrested seventeen-year-old Mary Laurine "Laurie" Tackett of Jefferson County and sixteen-year-old Melinda D. Loveless of New Albany, Indiana, at Loveless's home. They also seized a vehicle used to transport Shanda and other evidence from both Loveless's and Tackett's homes.

Arrests of two other fifteen-year-old girls implicated in the murder quickly followed: Hope A. Rippey and Toni L. Lawrence.

Lawrence proved to be a key figure in uncovering the truth of what happened to Shanda. Eaten up by guilt, on Saturday just hours after Shanda's body was found, Lawrence confessed to her parents what had happened to Shanda the night before. They took their daughter to police to tell her incredible story.

Lawrence told police that she was along with Tackett, Loveless, and Rippey on Friday night in Louisville, Kentucky, and New Albany when Loveless began expressing her repeated concern that Shanda was "trying to steal her girlfriend named Amanda." Lawrence said Loveless wanted to kill Shanda.

Shanda had reason to be scared of Loveless. She had threatened Shanda before while both were students at the Hazelwood Junior High School in New Albany. Loveless, who identified openly as a lesbian, believed Shanda was attempting to steal her on-again, off-again girlfriend, fourteen-year-old Amanda Heavrin. Heavrin was never implicated as having any part in the events unfolding that cold night.

Tackett and Rippey used a ruse of going to meet Heavrin to lure young Shanda from her father's home in Jeffersonville around midnight Friday night. Her father did not know she had snuck out. Hiding under winter coats and a blanket in the back seat of the car was Loveless, a scheming young woman who encouraged the other girls to place Shanda in the middle of the front seat and try to get her to talk openly about her feelings for Heavrin (and her opinion of Loveless). When Shanda did, Loveless jumped up from the back seat and held a knife to Shanda's neck and pulled her hair, the first of many abusive acts in the hours to follow.

Court testimony would later reveal that Shanda pleaded throughout the night to be released, promising not to tell anyone what had already happened and promising to leave Amanda alone.

None of that was good enough for Loveless, whom investigators believed, along with Tackett, led this small band of troubled teens. Loveless had come from an abusive family where sexual boundaries were often violated, and was an angry, vindictive young woman. Tackett had an equally troubling adolescence.

Shanda was in big trouble.

Tackett drove that night, the only one of the girls old enough to have a driver's license. She drove the group back to an abandoned house foundation in rural Clark County known in local lore as the "Witches Castle."

Once there, all of the girls teased and taunted Shanda, with Loveless continuing to threaten her with the knife, pulling her hair and threatening to cut it all off, and even setting fire to a T-shirt and warning Shanda that this was her fate.

Too many cars passed in succession, however, and the girls got spooked and decided to leave the remote "Witches Castle" location. This time with Rippey driving, Tackett and Loveless wedged Shanda in between them in the back seat, still at knifepoint, as the group got lost but eventually made their way to a gravel road near Tackett's home outside of Madison, Indiana.

Once stopped again, Loveless and Tackett ordered Shanda to strip off her clothes and stand naked in the freezing night, wearing nothing but her panties. Loveless scooped up Shanda's blue jeans, blouse, and bra and took them back to the car, gloating over her trophy.

A beating soon commenced with Loveless and Tackett mercilessly punching and kicking Shanda. Rippey and Lawrence remained in the car but witnessed what was happening in front of the car's headlights.

At one point, Loveless's attempt to slit Shanda's throat was unsuccessful because the blade of the knife was too dull. Rippey then jumped out of the car to assist, investigators learned, and sat on Shanda's legs while Tackett sat on her chest and abdomen, as Loveless attempted to strangle the struggling Shanda with her hands. She wasn't strong enough, and Shanda was still fighting for her life, naked in the dirt.

Tackett then retrieved a rope from the trunk of the car, and she and Loveless took turns pulling it tight around Shanda's neck until she was unconscious. Tackett then ordered Shanda's body to be dumped in the trunk of the car, and the group moved on to Tackett's house.

Once inside, the girls began to talk over the night's events, and Tackett offered to "read" Loveless's future using stones or rocks common in ancient Rune magic.

Suddenly, Tackett's dog began barking loudly outside, and the girls quickly discovered why. From inside the trunk of Tackett's car, they could hear the muffled screams of a now-conscious Shanda crying out for help. Tackett quickly took a knife from her mother's kitchen and said she'd take care of it. She returned with blood on her clothing, and Shanda was now silent.

Rippey and Lawrence begged off another car ride to nearby Canaan, Indiana, that Tackett and Loveless had suggested. They both reported they were tired and wanted to go to bed and did so at Tackett's house. Before Tackett and Loveless left, however, they could once again hear Shanda kicking and screaming from inside the trunk. Tackett again "quieted her" and did so again once they had driven north in Jefferson County toward the Ripley County line. At one instance, Tackett went back to the trunk with a tire iron and punched and beat Shanda with it. The investigation would later show she had also sodomized Shanda with the tire tool while the young girl pled for mercy.

No mercy was in sight. This scenario would repeat itself at least three times, with Shanda regaining consciousness and screaming for help, only to be beaten into silence again.

Loveless and Tackett eventually returned to the latter girl's home and picked up Rippey and Lawrence. They wanted to show the girls Shanda's beaten body, gloating that she was "all red" because she was soaked in blood. They also decided they would burn Shanda's body.

As they showed Shanda's beaten and lacerated body to Rippey, Rippey sprayed Windex into her wounds to make them hurt worse. Lawrence refused to get out of the car to look at Shanda's body and cried alone in the front seat.

The four killers stopped one more time, at a Clark Station in Madison to purchase enough gasoline to fill an empty two-litre Pepsi bottle.

Burning Shanda's body was to take place somewhere near the Jefferson Proving Grounds in Jefferson County. The girls got lost again, however, and ended up on County Road 1133 North, also known as Lemon Road, about two and a half miles east of U.S. 421.

As they stopped the car for the final time and opened the trunk, a mumbling and barely conscious Shanda held onto the strings of her life, gurgling blood from her mouth and mumbling the word "Mommy" as she was pulled from the trunk and dumped on a gravel road on top of a red blanket.

Moments later Rippey complied with Tackett's order to pour the gasoline out of the Pepsi bottle onto Shanda, who was now semi-conscious and shivering in the below-zero temperatures. Within moments, she was on fire and not moving.

The girls all fled in Tackett's car, returning only briefly to make sure Shanda was dead. Finding that she was not, Loveless poured the rest of the gasoline on Shanda's body and lit her on fire a second time.

Loveless returned to the car mocking Shanda, whom she said was gasping with her tongue coming in and out of her mouth as she fought for life.

By now, morning light was about to break, and the girls stopped at a McDonald's restaurant in Madison and ordered breakfast. Their night of torture and murder had left them hungry and tired.

Around this time, Shanda's father, Steve, was discovering she had sneaked out of the house the night before. He called Shanda's mother, Jackie Vaught, and told her what he had found. By 1 p.m., they notified police that Shanda was missing. By day's end, the worry surrounding her disappearance would be replaced by a sickening horror that their daughter had suffered unimagineable injuries unto her death.

At about 9 p.m. Saturday night, Clifton and Glenda Lawrence escorted their daughter Toni to the Madison Police Department headquarters and asked to speak to a detective. For the next several hours, Toni Lawrence told a horrific tale of what had happened to Shanda through her tears and growing guilt.

At 1 a.m. early Monday morning, detectives from the Madison Police, Jefferson County Sheriff's Department, and the Indiana State Police awoke a local judge at his home to obtain warrants for a search and arrests. At 2:30 a.m., police raided the Loveless home in New Albany and arrested both Loveless and Tackett, who were asleep together in Loveless's bed.

Prosecutor Townsend's investigation led him to also enter charges against Lawrence and Rippey on March 15, 1992. He charged both girls with murder, arson, battery with a deadly weapon, aggravated battery, criminal confinement, and intimidation—similar charges already leveled against Loveless and Tackett. Loveless and Tackett were also charged with felony murder, child molestation, and criminal deviate conduct.

A month later, on April 22, 1992, Lawrence decided not to take her chances at trial and accepted a plea bargain from the state. In exchange for her testimony against the other three girls, Townsend dropped all the charges except for a guilty plea to a charge of criminal confinement. A judge later accepted the terms of Lawrence's plea deal.

In July, Prosecutor Townsend announced he would seek the death penalty against Loveless and Tackett. Because Rippey was younger than sixteen at the time of the crime, she was not eligible for the death penalty.

In August 1992, Lawrence failed in a suicide attempt in jail and remained at a mental health facility until October. At that same time, Loveless and Tackett's attorneys decided to plea bargain with the state.

Both would plead guilty to the murder and torture of Shanda, as well as the arson and criminal confinement charges. In exchange, the state would drop its request to seek the death penalty against the two and drop the other charges, provided they cooperate with the investigation.

Loveless entered her plea agreement on September 21, 1992.

Rippey's trial was still pending.

Tackett gave an interview from her cell to a Cincinnati TV station in December 1992 in which she said that on the night of the attack, "Shanda had hugged me. She asked me not to let Melinda do it. She was crying ... there wasn't anything I could do."[1]

On December 14, 1992, news reporters from across Indiana, Kentucky, Ohio, and Illinois showed up to cover the sentencing hearings for Loveless. Jefferson County Circuit Court Judge Ted Todd later accepted her plea and sentenced her to the maximum allowable: sixty years.

Shanda's mother, Jackie Vaught, was given a chance to speak at the Loveless hearing. She said, "Melinda [Loveless] has cheated me out of being with my daughter during this life. It is my wish for you [Melinda] that you live your life with memories of her screams and the sign of her burned and mutilated body ... I hope and pray you remember these words for the rest of your life: May you rot in hell."[2]

A similar hearing was conducted on December 28, 1992 for Tackett, and she too was sentenced to sixty years.

After several delays, on June 1, 1993, Rippey's trial finally got underway far from southern Indiana at the St. Joseph County Courthouse in South Bend, where the trial had been moved to on a change of venue. Rippey testified in her own behalf and attempted to show she was dominated by the more aggressive Tackett and Loveless into acts she would not normally have done. Testimony offered by Loveless, Tackett, and Lawrence, however, contradicted Rippey's tale, painting her as a much more active participant than she hoped the court would ever know.

After brief deliberations, Rippey was found guilty, and St. Joseph County Superior Court Judge Jeanne Jourdan sentenced her to sixty years in prison.

Tackett, Loveless, and Rippey are all serving their sentences at the Women's Prison in Indianapolis. With good behavior, Rippey could be released as early as 2017. Tackett and Loveless would have to wait until 2022 for any chance of release, with good behavior.

For her part, Lawrence began to piece back together whatever life she could. She completed her GED and a college degree behind bars, and was released on parole on December 14, 2000. Now a twenty-four-year-old woman, Lawrence was to remain on parole until 2002.

Upon her release, Lawrence told WAVE-TV in Louisville, Kentucky, "I didn't stop it; I couldn't stop it. I don't care what anyone else says. If I would have tried anything different, I would have been dead, lying there with her, and they would never know."[3]

In 2004, the Indiana Supreme Court reduced Rippey's sixty-year sentence to thirty-five to fifty years, moving up her earliest release date from 2017 to 2006. Rippey continued to impress prison officials with her good behavior, completing her GED and a college degree.

On April 28, 2006, Rippey was released from prison on parole. Now twenty-nine-years-old, she served fourteen of the fifty-year sentence.

Shanda's mother remains angry that Rippey was released.

"I do not accept this," Jackie Vaught said. "She murdered my daughter. To me, it's a very small thing to ask [that she remain behind bars]."[4]

Endnotes
1. WKRC-TV, Cincinnati, Ohio, December 1992.
2. CourtTV Web site.
3. Ibid.
4. Associated Press, April 28, 2006.

JENNINGS COUNTY

VICTIM(S):
Willie Todd, 2

PERPETRATOR(S):
George Washington Sage, 35

DATE OF DEATH(S):
March 7, 1866

AN UNTHINKABLE CRIME, TWO BRAVE LITTLE GIRLS

George Washington Sage tried to eliminate all of the witnesses to his heinous, unthinkable crime on March 7, 1866, near Paris, Indiana, in rural Jennings County.

He did not succeed.

Two of his would-be victims, brave sisters only four and six years old, survived the attack to tell authorities who had bludgeoned them unconscious and assaulted their young brother, two-year-old Willie Todd, inside their rural home.

The attack took place around 8 p.m. on March 7 during a rare occasion when both William Todd and his wife, Mary, were away from the home. Mr. Todd needed Mrs. Todd's help in securing a horse for work on their farm, and so the two set out and were away less than an hour.

"The parents, of course, suspected no danger and all their money, etc., was left in the house. In half an hour, however, they returned and were horror-stricken to find all three of the children stretched out upon the floor as if in a dying condition, and weltering in their blood!" the *Madison Courier* exclaimed.[1]

The six-year-old daughter, whose name was never disclosed in news reports about the crime, had been left in charge for the short time her parents were away. Within minutes, however, evil would descend on the defenseless children.

Sage, a former farm hand for Mr. Todd, had returned to the farm to carry out "one of the most fiendish, dark, damning deeds it ever has been our duty to record," the *Courier* reported.[2]

As more details were learned, it became clear the youngest child, Willie, would not survive the assault that left him with a gaping wound on the top of his head.

As the hours passed, however, hope rose for the two daughters.

Thirty-five-year-old Sage was arrested within hours by outraged neighbors who were compelled to stop their plans of lynching him and instead turned him over to the Jennings County sheriff, Samuel Dixon.

The sheriff took Sage back to the Todd farm the next day where the oldest daughter identified him saying, "Washington Sage did it." She said the children had surprised him as he ransacked the Todd home when they came in from playing in the yard.

Sage confessed as well—revealing his take to be two pocketbooks, one with cash and the other just holding Todd family papers.

The investigation would show that Sage knew Mr. Todd had sold a portion of his land about a month before the attack and may have seen the money in Mrs. Todd's purse when he visited the family the day before the assault.[3]

The *Courier* noted that "Sage has always been of suspicious character and generally considered a bad man." They noted he was a suspect in an earlier murder plot against a Jefferson County doctor before 1860.[4]

A two-day trial for Sage was conducted at the Jennings County Courthouse at Vernon on March 21 and 22, 1866. He told the court in a written confession that his motive was his desperation to raise money. He told the court, "I learned our property in Illinois was about to be sold, and knew if we could get there it could be saved, but had no money to pay our way. I was very much troubled about it, and was thinking every day how I could raise the means to go."[5]

He admitted going to the Todd home and finding the parents away and the children out playing in the yard. "Having learned while working for him where he kept his money, I was tempted to take it, and at once commenced searching for it," Sage wrote. "Just as I found it, the children came into the house, and knowing who I was, came to me apparently without fear."[6]

The children's trust of Sage was terribly misplaced. "Something suddenly came over me, and I was so excited that I seemed beside myself. While in this state of mind, I determined to kill them," Sage said.

He detailed taking a brick from the fireplace and "at once commenced to carry out my wicked purpose, striking them as they came to me, the oldest first, and the youngest last. The last one, which was the youngest, I struck a very light blow."[7]

Sage said as he fled the house, he could hear the children crying from their injuries. "I did not expect to escape detection, as the children were not all dead, and as they knew me, I supposed they would tell as soon as someone came in," Sage said.[8]

The deliberations didn't last long—Sage was found guilty and sentenced to death by hanging. Although he had served in the Union Army with the Seventh Illinois Calvary, his life would end in disgrace.

He said, "I still feel truly sorry for all my sins, and have sincerely repented, and believe I have obtained mercy, and enjoy a hope of eternal life."[9]

On his final day, Sage's wife and child visited him at the Jennings County Jail, along with a pastor. As a special gallows was constructed for the first-ever execution in the small county, the sheriff ordered all local taverns closed.

By noon, a large crowd gathered to watch the execution. At 12:30 p.m., an hour-long ceremony began with a local Baptist preacher imploring Sage to "place his whole reliance upon God" and reading the Twenty-Third Psalm. A Methodist minister then read a special homily, followed by a prayer led by the pastor of the Presbyterian church.

"The ministers and friends then bid the condemned a last farewell," the *Courier* reported. "The parting between the father, wife and child of the unhappy man was particularly affecting. As the old, gray-haired man bid his son, whom in childhood he had fondly embraced, a last goodbye, is it strange that tears should flow profusely?"[10]

The *Courier* added, "The prisoner's manner appeared to indicate that he had a faint hope or belief … at the last moment he would be reprieved or pardoned, but as the cap was drawn over his eyes, if he had any such ideas, they all left him, and his whole body tumbled like an aspen leaf."[11]

At 1:45 p.m., Sage was pronounced dead, his dangling corpse cut loose and released to an Illinois mortician for burial.

Endnotes

1. *Madison Courier*, March 9, 1866.
2. Ibid.
3. *Madison Courier*, March 29, 1866.
4. *Madison Courier*, March 10, 1866.
5. *Madison Courier*, May 25, 1866.
6. Ibid.
7. Ibid.
8. Ibid.
9. Ibid.
10. *Madison Courier*, May 26, 1866.
11. Ibid.

JOHNSON COUNTY

VICTIM(S):
Tyler Shanabarger, 7 months

PERPETRATOR(S):
Ronald L. Shanabarger, 30

DATE OF DEATH(S):
June 19, 1999

A LITTLE BOY BORN TO DIE

On Tuesday, June 22, 1999, Ronald and Amy Shanabarger laid their only son, Tyler, to rest in a heartbreaking funeral for a beautiful seven-month-old baby boy who was gone too soon.

Later that evening, Ron confessed to Amy that he had killed Tyler just days before on Saturday, June 19, while she was at work—and he had done so as an act of revenge against her for having missed his own father's funeral three years earlier.

"He said, 'I killed Tyler,'" Amy would tell a court during Ron's murder trial three years later. "I said, 'How?' [And] he said, 'With Saran Wrap.' He put it over [Tyler's] nose and mouth, and got something to eat and brushed his teeth and went to bed."[1]

Amy said she was devastated at what her husband was telling her and said, "He [told me] he couldn't live with the guilt of me hurting him back when his dad passed away, so it was like a revenge."[2]

She said Ron begged her to forgive him, but she refused and immediately took off her wedding ring and declared their marriage over. Ron told her he was willing to turn himself in to authorities, who to this point had followed a coroner's ruling that Tyler's death had been a tragic case of Sudden Infant Death Syndrome (SIDS) and did not suspect foul play.

On Wednesday morning, June 23, Ron and Amy walked into the Johnson County Jail in Franklin and asked to speak to a sheriff's deputy.

"Ron walked up to the window and said, 'Sunday, my son died of SIDS; but that's not what happened. I killed my son,'" Amy testified.[3]

It would be the first of several open admissions Ron would offer that he had wrapped strands of Saran Wrap plastic around his baby son's head and left him alone for twenty minutes to suffocate to death. He confessed that he left him in his crib for his mother to discover when she awoke early on Father's Day, Sunday, June 20.

It was a stunning admission, and Tyler's murder became a national story, covered by national TV networks and newspapers across the country. No one who heard the story of Ron's act could believe it.

"This is like nothing I have ever seen in our country or state or even heard of," said Johnson County Prosecutor Lance Hamner. "It's chilling."[4]

The probable cause affidavit used to secure Ronald's arrest said "... he married her, got her pregnant, allowed time for her to bond with the child, and then took its life."[5]

The trouble started, it seemed, back in October 1996 before Ron and Amy were married. Ron's father took a turn for the worse and died as Amy was about to leave on a cruise with her own ailing mother and her father. Ron asked her to forgo the three-day trip, but she decided to go anyway after consulting with her father.

"[My father] said Ron would have immediate family at the funeral and we would be home right after the funeral, and I would be there for moral support," Amy said.[6]

Amy said Ron was unhappy about her decision. She said he would tell her, "'You weren't there for me when my dad passed away.'"[7]

Ron's former coworkers reported that he had a hard time letting go of the fact that Amy did not attend the funeral. "He said he didn't know if he could forgive her ... I told him to let it go," said Ed McIntosh, a former coworker.[8]

Ron did anything but let it go. The couple married in May 1997, and on Thanksgiving Day 1998, Tyler was born. Ron never came to the hospital to see his wife or his new son.

Amy said Tyler was a happy child who rarely cried, but Ron "wouldn't sit down and play with him. It was almost like Tyler was a brother."[9]

The day after Ron turned himself in to police for killing Tyler, Amy abandoned the couple's Franklin home as local, state, and national news media descended on the community, and she filed for divorce. She was later granted her maiden name back, Amy Parsons.

The Reverend Randy Maynard, chaplain for the Franklin Police Department, agreed to visit with the despondent Ron as he was held in jail without bond.

Maynard said Ron listed all of the things he had lost—his job, his house, his money, his wife, his friends, and on and on.

"I said, 'And you lost Tyler, too,'" Maynard told reporters. "'Oh yeah, I lost the boy, too.' That was it for me. He said the wrong thing. I was out of there."[10]

Johnson County Sheriff's deputies dressed Ron in a bulletproof flak vest to transport him into and out of the Johnson County Courthouse— the officers accompanying him also wore bulletproof vests. Anger in the community remained high.

Within days, news leaked that Ron had insisted that the couple buy a $100,000 life insurance policy on Tyler, although the couple was in financial difficulty already. Amy worked as a cashier at the Kroger Store in Franklin, and Ron worked at the Goodyear Store. While both were employed, they struggled to make ends meet and pay for their new home at 1110 Branifield Court in Franklin, valued at $90,000.

A family friend told the *Louisville Courier-Journal* that Ron was "spending the money in his head" in the two days after Tyler's death. "He told [Amy] he already had $50,000 of it spent in his head," the family friend (who remained anonymous) told the Kentucky newspaper.[11]

As Ron's defense attorneys attempted to defend what seemed indefensible, they announced they would try an insanity plea or at least try to convince the judge and jury that Ron's low IQ meant he was mentally retarded. Under previous examinations, Ron was determined competent to stand trial and had an IQ of 88. An IQ below 70 is generally considered to be equal to mental retardation.

Johnson County Superior Court Judge Kevin Barton ruled out an insanity defense for Ron but said he could cite mental retardation as a reason against a sentence of life in prison without parole. Judge Barton would later remove himself from the case because he was professionally familiar with a proposed member of Ron's defense team. Retired Porter County Judge Raymond Kickbush was appointed as special judge to hear the case. In addition, a jury was selected for the case from Huntington County—at least an attempt to find someone to serve who had not heard the details of the case.

Ron's trial did not open until April 2002, causing Tyler's maternal grandparents to become frustrated. In a January 2002 letter to the *Franklin Daily Journal*, Robert Parsons of Martinsville, Indiana, said, "Three years to bring a case to trial is a disgrace ... the end result is prolonged mental anguish by the victim's family. This case is about a little boy who would be three-years-old now, and about his mother, who will never get the opportunity to see him grow up."[12]

Prosecutor Hamner opened his case with drama fitting the crime.

"While Tyler struggled for air, fought for his life, his father walked out, went to the kitchen, and made himself a sandwich," Hamner said. "And for the final horrific touch, he left the baby for [Amy] to find."[13]

Defense attorney Jay Hoffman said the case was "more complicated, complex, bizarre and strange" than Hamner had indicated and began a relentless effort to point out that Amy stood to gain as much from Tyler's life insurance as Ron did.

Jurors heard two taped confessions Ron gave to police, including one where Ron told the detectives, "I placed Saran Wrap around his head. I came back twenty minutes later ... He was gasping."[14]

On the tape a detective got Ron to admit he did not try to revive the child, although he knew CPR, and asked, "When you put Saran Wrap on Tyler's face and wrapped it around his head, what was your goal?"

"To get revenge," Ron replied.

"And to do what to Tyler?" the detective followed.

"Kill him," Ron said.[15]

During a later interview, Ron also indicated he had a financial motive to kill the baby.

Johnson County Sheriff's major Terry Nichalson testified that under questioning, Ron said, "He wanted to be dead. He asked me to shoot him. He was highly distraught and kept referring to himself as a 'baby killer' or a 'murderer.'"[16]

Defense attorneys argued that Ron was gullible and easily influenced to say what detectives wanted to hear. "He was prepped before the tape was started, and once the tape begins to roll, he is asked predominantly leading questions or questions that suggest an answer," Hoffman said.[17]

That argument wilted as Shanabarger's sister, Bonita Savage, and her husband, Larry, testified for the state that in telephone conversations with Ron following his arrest, he freely admitted he had killed Tyler. Larry Savage said Ron gloated that if he had not told Amy, he would have gotten away with murder.

"He said, 'I had to tell [Amy] to get even with her,'" Larry Savage told the jury.[18]

Ron's defense attempted to show he was a simple man and likely mentally retarded. A former supervisor at a tire shop where Ron had worked said coworkers teased him frequently and even had him convinced that the overhead garage doors were voice activated (although they pushed remote control buttons behind Ron's back as he spoke into what he thought was a microphone to open the doors).

The jury got the case in short order and deliberated for eight hours over two days before returning a guilty verdict on May 8, 2002. Special Judge

Kickbush took up Ron's sentencing a month later and sentenced him to forty-nine years in prison, short of the life sentence prosecutors wanted, and short of the sixty-five-year maximum the judge could have imposed. Defense attorneys requested, and Judge Kickbush agreed, that Ron should be held in protective custody in the Indiana Department of Correction because of the high risk of violence he faced from other offenders.

In August 2003, Amy and her family dedicated a small fountain inside Independence Park in Johnson County in memory of Tyler and other children who had died from child abuse and neglect. Ron's 2003 appeal of his conviction to the Indiana Court of Appeals failed, as did his requests for a new trial in 2004 and 2006.

Endnotes
1. *Franklin Daily Journal*, April 30, 2002.
2. Ibid.
3. Ibid.
4. *Indianapolis Star*, June 25, 1999.
5. Ibid.
6. *Franklin Daily Journal*, April 29, 2002.
7. Ibid.
8. Ibid.
9. Ibid.
10. Associated Press, June 29, 1999.
11. Associated Press, July 4, 1999.
12. *Franklin Daily Journal*, Jan. 29, 2002.
13. *Franklin Daily Journal*, April 29, 2002; Associated Press, April 30, 2002.
14. *Franklin Daily Journal*, April 30, 2002.
15. *Franklin Daily Journal*, May 1, 2002.
16. *Franklin Daily Journal*, April 30, 2002.
17. Ibid.
18. *Franklin Daily Journal*, May 2, 2002.

KNOX COUNTY

VICTIM(S):
Orrel L. Manuel, Jr., 28

PERPETRATOR(S):
Archie Foreman, 27

DATE OF DEATH(S):
January 18, 1961

A POLICEMAN TURNS A GUN ON HIS FELLOW OFFICERS

Vincennes Police Department Sergeant Orrel L. Manuel, Jr. had gained the respect of his fellow officers although he was only twenty-eight years old. As such, it's not surprising that he insisted on following the rules, even when it was a fellow officer in trouble.

Manuel's insistence on doing things by the book, however, would meet up with the desperation of a fellow officer who wanted more than anything to avoid losing his job. It would end with Manuel dead and fellow officer James Mallory, forty-six, critically injured.

The sad tale of a fatal shooting inside the Vincennes city police station began during the early morning hours of Wednesday, January 18, 1961, after Sgt. Manuel investigated a report just after 1:30 a.m. of a hit-and-run driver striking a car parked in front of 116 West Sycamore Street on the city's west side, adjacent to the campus of where Vincennes University now sits.

Sgt. Manuel, whom many officers called "Junior," was joined at the scene by a rookie officer, Charles Robbins, as they followed a trail of water and radiator fluid to a disabled Ford Thunderbird parked in an alley between First and Second streets. A short distance away, Sgt. Manuel found three men familiar to him—fellow officers Archie Foreman, Bobbie Cain, and Ronald Bailey.

Foreman, Cain, and Bailey were all off duty and in street clothes and were on their way to Mundy's Body Shop in the area. The car broke down, however, and was found by Sgt. Manuel.

It was clear that at least Officer Foreman and his twenty-year-old brother Earl Foreman, along for the night, had spent the hours since Officer Foreman went off duty at 10 p.m. the night before drinking and having a good time.[1]

Sgt. Manuel reportedly radioed his shift captain, Loren Willis, and Police Chief Lyman Miller was also notified. Capt. Willis ordered Manuel to return to the police station and write up an accident report and said that the chief would assist in an investigation later.

Sometime later, Officer Foreman telephoned the police station to talk about the accident and to implicate his younger brother Earl as being the one driving at the time of the accident. Sgt. Manuel reportedly told him that if that was the case, he needed to bring Earl to the station to give a statement.[2]

At the station, as Archie Foreman pled with Manuel to not write a report that indicated he had been drinking and driving, "an argument developed [and] Foreman, who was standing, pulled his [police] revolver and fired. The bullet went through Manuel's neck, from left to right, and then entered the abdomen of Mallory, who was standing at the side of the room," the *Vincennes Sun-Commercial* reported in the next day's morning paper otherwise filled with details on the pending inauguration of President-elect John F. Kennedy.[3]

Wounded, Mallory stumbled out the front door of the police station and collapsed on the front sidewalk. Knox County Coroner George Gardner would later rule the bullet had entered the left side of Manuel's neck and came out the right side of his face, slightly lower, and continued on to strike Mallory in the stomach.[4]

Archie Foreman told responding fellow officers that he and Manuel had wrestled for the weapon when it accidentally discharged. Mallory and his son-in-law (and fellow officer Robbins) said that was not the case. Each said that Foreman had just opened fire on Manuel.[5]

Immediately after the shooting, Archie Foreman's younger brother, Earl, grabbed his brother's service revolver, fled the police station, and tossed the weapon into the Wabash River.

As was the case with the hit-and-run accident, Earl was trying to take the blame for shooting the two officers to protect his older brother. Archie had argued with Manuel in part because everyone except the Foreman brothers said Archie had been driving at the time of the car crash and Manuel insisted on writing his report consistent with the facts.

Archie Foreman had reason to fear for his job prior to this incident. Foreman joined the department in 1956, but was suspended from service along with four other officers in 1959 "for conduct unbecoming an officer."

But following the election of a new mayor, he was reinstated to duty in 1960. At the same time, the department remained under heavy community pressure to not only help clean up vice in the community, but clean up its own act as well.[6]

Manuel had also joined the force in 1956, but had enjoyed a better career than Foreman, and won a promotion to sergeant. The injured Mallory, who would recover from his wounds, was a veteran officer, having been sworn in on July 1, 1942.

Police Chief Miller arrested his officer, Archie Foreman, and his brother Earl, and booked them in the Knox County Jail.

The shooting at the police station came at a time when the Vincennes Police Department and the administration of Mayor Holly Kilfoil were already under heavy criticism from some city leaders. Local ministers were particularly upset at what they viewed as lax enforcement of gambling, liquor, and other vice laws.

Following the shooting, the Knox County Ministerial Association issued a statement saying, "We are faced with a tragic breakdown in government and law enforcement in this county and city. Therefore, we ... feel that the righteous indignation of the Christian people of Vincennes and [the] county should arise as a mighty voice and demand the resignation of the City and County officials involved in this gross failure to enforce the law."[7]

The tension in the community was real. The next day, the *Vincennes Sun-Commercial* reported that the city "was at the boiling point Thursday over the fatal shooting of a Vincennes policeman and the wounding of another."[8]

The ministerial association kept the fires stoked by placing a paid advertisement in the *Sun-Commercial* that purported to list the taverns, drive-ins, and other establishments in the city where illegal gambling was flourishing.[9]

On the same day, Archie Foreman was ordered held on a preliminary charge of first-degree murder and a grand jury was called to hear evidence in the case. Police also reported they had found Foreman's service revolver along a bank of the Wabash River.[10]

Foreman's younger brother, Earl, was charged with carrying a pistol without a license, underage drinking, and making a false police report.[11]

Mayor Kilfoil, feeling the pressure created by the ministers and from a meeting of about 800 citizens at Vincennes University to discuss the matter, issued a statement on the incredible shooting among sworn police officers. He noted that the entire city mourned "the tragic death of Officer Manuel and desires to express the deepest sympathy to his wife, family and many friends."[12]

"As mayor of your city, I wish to assure each and every citizen of this fine community that immediate action will be taken to investigate and bring to justice all persons involved in this matter," Mayor Kilfoil said.[13]

With that, the mayor took control of the department away from Chief Miller and placed it in the hands of a civilian Police Merit Commission. He charged the commission with the task of "thoroughly examining the evidence surrounding this tragedy and to take whatever steps it deems necessary not only to correct matters as they now stand, but in the hope that such action as is taken will assist in preventing a reoccurrence of a matter of this nature."[14]

The mayor also took on the criticism of local ministers by saying he did not believe that "a general laxity of law enforcement" existed in Vincennes and pledged to do all he could to ensure "that the laws of the community are enforced during my tenure of office."[15]

On January 30, 1961, a Knox County grand jury indicted Archie Foreman for the murder of Sgt. Manuel and the wounding of Officer Mallory. In March, as he awaited trial, Foreman resigned from the department.[16]

Foreman's trial was transferred to the Daviess County Circuit Court at Washington, Indiana, on a change of venue and opened with jury selection in early June 1961. Ironically, testimony in a murder trial that started from an alleged hit-and-run accident was delayed by another vehicle accident. This one, on the eve of the trial, claimed the life of another one of Foreman's brothers, Woodrow "Cricket" Foreman, seventeen, who died in a one-vehicle crash in Vincennes on Friday night, June 9, 1961.

Officer Robbins was among the first to testify. He reported, "When the gun went off, I looked at Sgt. Manuel and at that time he looked surprised. I heard Officer Mallory say that he was hit and I went to his assistance. When Mallory told me that Manuel had also been hit, I went back to the squad room … Foreman was standing in front of Manuel. Foreman said he was applying pressure to [Manuel's] neck."[17]

Robbins said that when Archie Foreman entered the police station, "he just walked in the front and directly to the squad room … He took out his gun as he walked across the room. He was cocking and uncocking it all the time and talking to Sgt. Manuel."[18]

Archie Foreman kept insisting that Earl Foreman had been driving and began ordering Sgt. Manuel to rewrite his accident report to reflect that. "Sgt. Manuel agreed that we would make out a new report, since we didn't have any idea who was driving," Robbins testified. "Foreman said he was going to show [Manuel] how to enforce the law. He was cocking and uncocking the gun in the area of [Manuel's] head. Manuel was just trying to agree with him."[19]

Officer Darwin Booker, who had assisted in the field investigation of the initial hit-and-run accident, said he returned to the police station when he heard the police radio man call for assistance just after 3 a.m. Booker said that when he arrived at the scene, Foreman was saying out loud that he wanted Manuel to live.[20]

Booker and Captain Willis, who both responded to the assistance call at the police station, said they found Mallory lying on his back on the sidewalk out front. "Sgt. Manuel was laying back in his chair [in the squad room], and Officer Foreman was standing over him, trying to stop the flow of blood," Willis said.[21]

Vincennes Police Chief Miller also testified, saying he rushed to the station house when hearing the report of the shooting. He said he talked briefly with Archie Foreman about what had happened, and that Archie volunteered to get his brother Earl to show the investigators where the gun was thrown after the shooting. Miller said he allowed Archie Foreman to call an attorney from his office after learning Manuel had died, and then arrested him.[22]

The most damning testimony against Foreman came from Officer Mallory, now mostly healed from his abdominal injuries. He told the jury that he witnessed Foreman backhand Sgt. Manuel across the face twice moments before shooting him.[23]

Mallory said he kept his eyes on Foreman's gun for the entire ten-minute episode and that Sgt. Manuel made no moves to defend himself, instead trying to talk calmly to the agitated Foreman.[24]

"[Foreman] was cursing him [Manuel] and telling him he knew about the law and how the wreck report was going to be made out," Mallory testified. "He backhanded Manuel in the head with his left hand, knocking his hat off onto the desk. There was more conversation—a heated argument, then [Foreman] backhanded Manuel again with his left hand, and this time knocked his glasses off on the table."[25]

Mallory said he and Robbins joined Manuel in trying to "talk down" Foreman, saying, "I told him the boys would make out the report anyway he wanted."[26]

Archie Foreman took the stand in his own defense on June 15, 1961, and denied having slapped Sgt. Manuel across the face or threatening him with a gun or with his words. He admitted that he and other officers and his younger brother had spent the evening after getting off work at taverns across the Wabash River in Illinois. He admitted he was driving the car that caused the initial accident but said he wanted to avoid disgracing himself or the police department.[27]

He said he had agreed to bring his brother to the police station, as Sgt. Manuel had suggested, and came in street clothes but had stuffed his .38-caliber service revolver into the waistband of his trousers.

"When I came in, the wreck report was mostly filled out, Junior [Manuel] was writing on it," Foreman said. "I was standing at Junior's left. I took off my jacket and put it on a coat stand. The gun was gouging my stomach, and I reached down with my right hand to take my revolver out and lay it on top of my jacket."[28]

He said it was then that a struggle ensued between Manuel and himself. "I felt a tug on the gun," he said. "I grabbed at it with my left hand and I felt the gun go off. I saw Junior [Manuel] in front of me ... I held [Manuel] in my left arm, took off his glasses and tried to put pressure on the pressure point in his neck," the former officer testified.[29]

"I said, 'My God, Junior! What did you grab that gun for? I didn't intend to hurt you!'"[30]

Under cross-examination, prosecutors pointed out the inconsistencies in Foreman's version of the events with that of the other officers present. Foreman insisted that "I did what I thought was best for the police department, myself and the officers with me."[31]

Earl Foreman testified as well for the defense, backing up every detail of his older brother's version of events. The rest of Foreman's defense consisted of character witnesses.

Knox County Prosecutor Ernest Tilly, Jr. said that Archie Foreman was a man "who went out looking for trouble and found it." Tilly argued strongly that Foreman intended to kill someone when he brought his gun to the police station.

Foreman's attorneys told jurors that their client was a "scapegoat" for a myriad of problems in the police department and that the shooting was nothing more than an accident.[32]

The jury of eight women and four men apparently believed the defense version, voting to acquit Foreman on Friday night, June 16, 1961. Rebuffed but still not convinced of Foreman's innocence, Knox County prosecutors filed new charges against him five days later for leaving the scene of an accident—an offense Archie Foreman had admitted in his trial testimony.[33]

That matter was finally settled on October 31, 1961, when Archie Foreman withdrew his not guilty plea and entered a guilty plea to the charge and was fined $50 and court costs.[34]

Endnotes

1. *Vincennes Sun-Commercial*, Jan. 18, 1961.
2. *Vincennes Sun-Commercial*, Jan. 18, 1961; June 14, 1961.
3. *Vincennes Sun-Commercial*, Jan. 18, 1961.
4. *Vincennes Sun-Commercial*, June 15, 1961.

5.　*Terre Haute Tribune-Star*, Jan. 18, 1961.

6.　*Vincennes Sun-Commercial*, Jan. 18, 1961; *Terre Haute Tribune-Star*, Jan. 19, 1961.

7.　*Vincennes Sun-Commercial*, Jan. 18, 1961.

8.　*Vincennes Sun-Commercial*, Jan. 19, 1961.

9.　Ibid.

10.　Ibid.

11.　Ibid.

12.　*Vincennes Sun-Commercial*, Jan. 23, 1961.

13.　Ibid.

14.　Ibid.

15.　Ibid.

16.　*Vincennes Sun-Commercial*, Jan. 29, 1961; June 8, 1961.

17.　*Vincennes Sun-Commercial*, June 14, 1961.

18.　Ibid.

19.　Ibid.

20.　Ibid.

21.　Ibid.

22.　Ibid.

23.　*Vincennes Sun-Commercial*, June 15, 1961.

24.　Ibid.

25.　Ibid.

26.　Ibid.

27.　Ibid.

28.　Ibid.

29.　Ibid.

30.　Ibid.

31.　Ibid.

32.　*Vincennes Sun-Commercial*, June 16, 1961.

33.　*Vincennes Sun Commercial*, June 18, 1961; June 21, 1961.

34.　Knox County Clerk's Office.

KOSCIUSKO COUNTY

VICTIM(S):
Leroy Lovett, 20

PERPETRATOR(S):
J. Virgil Decker, 19

DATE OF DEATH(S):
March 13, 1921

WHAT A MOTHER'S WORDS CAN DO

The earnest words of a Christian mother from Nappanee, Indiana, were able to do what the Kosciusko County sheriff and seasoned detectives from the Pennsylvania Railroad Company were unable to do: Crack open an incredible murder mystery in March 1921.

Mrs. George E. Walker of Nappanee had read about the incredible crime in the local papers and felt compelled to write to the young suspect, nineteen-year-old J. Virgil Decker (whom she did not know), housed at the Kosciusko County Jail.

The newspapers described the murder of eighteen-year-old Leroy Lovett of Elkhart as a case that would cause "… the most thrilling and perplexing screen productions [to] dwindle into the commonplace" in comparison. But Mrs. Walker was more interested in helping save the soul of the young man accused of the crime.[1]

She wrote, "Dear, dear boy—how my heart goes out to you and how I breathed a prayer to the God of Heaven and Earth who is all power in your behalf and quick as a flash, the thought came back to me—do your duty. God is on the giving hand and so very anxious to help all who are in trouble, no matter what kind of trouble."[2]

Mrs. Walker encouraged Decker, telling him, "God knows you are there and knows you need Him. He will or does know every thought that goes through your mind. And it does not make any difference how faint your prayer, if you are in earnest and mean every word you utter to Him, He will hear you … the way to come is to confess your sins to Jesus and ask Him to take you in His care and forgive you. Then confess everything to men whom you have harmed. You may think it hard, but lean on Jesus and let come what will."

Her letter, coming after about a week of intense questioning and examination by Sheriff Charles B. Moon and the railroad detectives, had its effect. Decker asked to speak to Sheriff Moon's wife, matron of the jail, who had brought him his meals and shared page-worn Boy Scout adventure novels with him. Within moments, he was telling the Sheriff's wife the ugly details of his scheme to stage his own death by murdering Lovett to collect the insurance proceeds on his own life. It was a tale that revealed careful planning and likely involved help from others but was often bungled along the way.

The confession (one of eight different versions Virgil would offer in one week) brought an end to a mystery that fascinated area residents and investigators alike. It also brought special "extra" editions published by both the *Warsaw Daily Times* and its rival, the *Warsaw Union*.

The original claim by Decker's family that the lifeless body of a young man brought to a Marshall County funeral parlor by the Pennsylvania Railroad engineers was Virgil's was exposed as a lie.

Decker, it seems, despite his meager earnings as a farm hand for his brother, Fred Decker of Atwood, had busied himself with purchasing life insurance policies in the amount of $24,000, a tidy sum in 1920s Indiana, the doubled sum paid in the event that his life ended in an accident. The premiums, $500 per year, would have been next to impossible for the young Decker to afford. His older brother, Fred, had told the insurance salesmen he'd help make the premium payments—and he just happened to be named the beneficiary of the policies as well.

Things began to fall apart in Virgil's scheme shortly after Marshall County Coroner Novitas B. Aspinall, MD, began asking questions. Dr. Aspinall, who had jurisdiction over the case because the boy was brought in to the town of Bourbon in Marshall County just before succumbing, was suspicious of the details of the case from the start. The body contained the expected injuries from a twenty-five-mile-per-hour train-buggy mishap (such as a fractured skull and jaw bone) but also included a large amount of dried blood on the head and marks on the neck that indicated someone had attempted to throttle the boy. The clothing on the body was soaking wet from water and covered with sand, despite being found in a dry area along the railroad. Further, Atwood classmates of Virgil Decker, who viewed the body at the coroner's request, said they did not believe it to be their friend.

The Decker family stood firm, the matriarch, Mrs. Lydia Decker, stroking the hair of the young man on the mortician's table, breaking into sobs as she declared, "Yes, it's my boy!" She immediately ordered a casket so the burial could proceed, despite notice from the county coroner that the body had not yet been released to the family, and inquired about how long it would be before she received the insurance proceeds.

Unknown to the Deckers, however, Leroy Lovett's parents, Mr. and Mrs. Sam Lovett of Elkhart, had also viewed the body. "They couldn't fool me even if they did have Virgil's clothes on him," declared Sam Lovett. "The minute I pulled back the sheet, I knew it was Leroy."

Mrs. Hattie Lovett agreed, saying, "I know it is my boy. I couldn't be mistaken. I saw the birthmark on his temple, the tattoo on his arm, and the mark on his wrist. He is my boy ... This is not Virgil, this is my boy."[3]

Dr. Aspinall called an inquest and simultaneously broke down important parts of the scheme. When called under oath to identify the body, Mrs. Decker's demeanor was greatly changed. Gone were her sobs and tears, replaced by suspicion and fear. When pressed, she said, "I won't swear that it is Vigil. I won't swear to a lie for anybody."[4]

In a dramatic scene equal to that of any courtroom, the coroner pressed her, reminding her that she had previously insisted that the body, now displayed before her on a mortician's table, was that of her son. "Surely a mother knows whether it is or is not her son?" Dr. Aspinall asked.

All Mrs. Decker could manage was a non-answer: "Why, I hardly believe it is," she said.

Dr. Aspinall then asked her the color of her son's eyes. When she said blue, the coroner pulled back the eyelids on the young man's corpse revealing them to be brown. "Mrs. Decker swooned, reeled, and was caught by a nearby reporter before she fell. 'I'm sick, take me out of here, take me out of here,' she pleaded and burst into tears," the *Warsaw Daily Times* reported.[5]

As Virgil Decker's deceit, and that of his family, came unwound, the coroner declared the body to be that of Lovett and further declared him to be the victim of "murder by an unknown person."

At nearly the same hour, Sheriff Moon was fifty miles away in Marion apprehending young Virgil Decker after an uncle notified authorities there of his wayward nephew's whereabouts after reading newspaper reports about the sensational events in Warsaw.

Once apprehended, Virgil began offering varying versions of events, including implicating another man from Elkhart named "Guy" and another named "Dago John." He claimed, at varying times, that either of them had beaten Lovett during an argument and attempted to drop his body in the Tippecanoe River and then left him in a horseless buggy on the Pennsylvania rail line running east to west from Warsaw to Plymouth. The train had, in fact, struck a horseless buggy, and an unconscious, but not-yet-dead young man's body was found in the debris by train engineers who stopped. The train workers put the injured man on the train and stopped at the next town, Bourbon, Indiana, to summon help. It was too late, however, and the boy died soon after.

Since he was dressed in Decker's coveralls and carrying insurance papers in his pockets addressed to Decker, Marshall County authorities initially believed the man to be Virgil Decker. They notified his brother, Fred Decker of Atwood, and his mother, Lydia, and another brother, Calvin. All three met up at the Bourbon funeral parlor, and all three declared the body to be that of Virgil.

Decker had perplexed detectives for days, proving an uncooperative inmate, providing petulant responses to their questions about Lovett's death and his possible role in it. The sheriff used "sweatbox" procedures. Decker was housed in a cell directly above that of a Syracuse, Indiana, man, "who keeps a continuous babble that prevents sleep. Decker was beginning to show the effects of the annoyance of listening to the hideous chatter of the crazy man … his condition is pitiful. Short periods of deep silence are interrupted by a bang when he slams some heavy object against the steel walls of the cell and the crash is enough to shake the nerves of a blacksmith."[6]

It was the quiet and apparently convincing letter of Mrs. Walker from Nappanee, however, that broke young Decker.

He offered up a fifth statement to investigators renouncing each of the previous four statements. "I wish to say now in this statement that I myself, James Virgil Decker, killed Leroy Lovett and no one else assisted me."

He detailed striking Lovett unconscious inside a cottage outside Atwood with a piece of iron, then stripping and redressing the young man in some of Decker's clothing, placing him on the driver's seat of a buggy and placing it on the tracks. "The reason I placed my suit of overalls and shoes on Leroy and put him in the buggy and left the buggy stand on the tracks to be struck by the train was that I thought that when the train struck the buggy, it would demolish the buggy and that Leroy would be cut up so bad he could not be identified … and I would have a chance to get away."[7]

However, Virgil's confession would soon be followed by new versions of the events leading to Lovett's death. Frustrated, Kosciusko County officials impaneled a grand jury on March 30, 1921. They returned indictments for murder not only against Virgil, but also against his brothers, Fred and Calvin, and their mother, sixty-three-year-old Lydia Decker.

Following her arrest, Mrs. Decker told reporters she was unable to read and write and that her life had "… been one of hardship, remitting toil and uncongenial surroundings."[8] Mrs. Decker told reporters she was the mother of fourteen children, six of whom were dead. She claimed to have no knowledge of Virgil's life insurance policies and worried often about her twelve-year-old daughter, Leona, who was left in Elkhart when her mother was arrested.

To comfort her, the sheriff's wife, Mrs. Moon, took time to sit and read to her and offer her companionship. She was not to be comforted—at her arraignment, Mrs. Decker cried out to the judge, "Man, why can't I go home? I ain't never done nothing' to be put in jail for. Why, man, they got me locked up with iron doors and bars all around it. Why, man, if you will let me go home, I will come back if you want me. I never done nothing' to nobody." The judge was unmoved and ordered her held until trial without bond.[9]

Virgil's trial was first and drew continued heavy coverage throughout the region and the state. Prosecutors painted a picture of a mentally weak and non-assertive Leroy Lovett who was easily influenced by the more intelligent Virgil. They claimed that Virgil used that edge to lure Lovett to his death. A parade of insurance agents called to the stand testified about the unusually large amount of life insurance Virgil had engaged less than three months before the Lovett murder. Perhaps most devastating, the state produced Lovett's younger brother, sixteen-year-old Fred Lovett, who had been driven to a cottage near Atwood, Indiana, on March 8—just four days before his older brother would meet his death in the same area. Prosecutors contended this was a trial run or a thwarted first attempt by Decker—abandoned because of Fred Lovett's difference in age and size to Decker himself.

While the state called nearly fifty witnesses against Virgil, the defense called only one of little substance. Jurors took little time deciding the matter themselves, announcing during the dinner hour on Friday, June 10, 1921, less than three hours into their deliberations, that they had a verdict: Virgil was guilty. The only disagreement among jurors, the foreman later told reporters, was the degree of murder to be listed. Some jurors wanted Virgil to go to the electric chair, while others felt the circumstantial nature of the evidence did not warrant the death penalty.

As the life sentence was read, "the young defendant blinked in amazement for an instant, then allowed a faint smile to cross his face. He was smiling when he entered the courtroom and was smiling when he left. Decker has maintained a nonchalant manner throughout, and the verdict that sends him to prison for the remainder of his life, failed to break this down."[10]

Upon Virgil's conviction, his mother, Lydia, and two brothers were all released on their own recognizance. She told reporters as she left Warsaw for her home in Elkhart, "You know and God knows that I don't know anything about this."[11] Prosecutors eventually dropped the charges against all other members of the Decker family for what Kosciusko County Prosecutor H.W. Graham cited as insufficient evidence to proceed to trial.

At his sentencing, young Virgil told the Judge L.W. Royse, "I've only got this to say. I'll take the sentence and be glad to fulfill it. And nobody else had anything to do with it."[12]

Endnotes

1. *Warsaw Daily Times*, March 16, 1921.
2. Ibid.
3. *Warsaw Daily Times*, March 15, 1921.
4. *Warsaw Daily Times*, March 16, 1921.
5. Ibid.
6. *Warsaw Daily Times*, March 17, 1921.
7. *Warsaw Union*, March 19, 1921.
8. *Warsaw Union*, April 1, 1921.
9. *Warsaw Union*, April 6, 1921.
10. *Warsaw Union*, June 11, 1921.
11. *Warsaw Daily Times*, June 11, 1921.
12. *Warsaw Daily Times*, June 13, 1921.

LaGRANGE COUNTY

VICTIM(S):
Hattie Dillon, 64

PERPETRATOR(S):
George W. Dillon, 63

DATE OF DEATH(S):
September 26, 1911

A SECOND MARRIAGE IS NOT AS ADVERTISED

The murder trial following the unexpected death of Hattie J. Dillon, second wife of prominent LaGrange County farmer George W. Dillon, prompted "the largest crowd ever jammed into the LaGrange County Courthouse since its construction [in 1879] ... the aisles and entrances and even the stairways leading to the corridors were literally dotted with curious humanity, presenting a spectacle of curiosity unprecedented in the county's history."[1]

Weeks after Mrs. Dillon had expired at the age of sixty-four, a LaGrange County grand jury indicted her husband, George W. Dillon, sixty-three, on a charge of murder.

Feelings among LaGrange County residents about George Dillon were mixed. Some locals knew him mostly as a land-owner who had moved to the county from Fostoria, Ohio in 1909. His first wife, Sarah, had died in June 1910, and her father, John Hallabaugh, died one month later, causing all of Hallabaugh family farmland in Springfield Township of LaGrange County to flow to George. At the time, rumors circulated widely that George had had something to do with the two unexpected deaths, but no investigation was undertaken and no official charges ever leveled.

The death of the second Mrs. Dillon's on September 26, 1911 in a farmhouse near Mongo, came just a little bit over a year after the death of the first Mrs. Dillon, and just months after she and George had wed. When the case came to trial in February 1912 at the stately LaGrange County Courthouse, "Farmers from miles around made their way over bad roads, and long before time for opening court," the *Fort Wayne Journal-Gazette* told its readers in breathless coverage of the trial, "Vehicles were lined on either side of the courthouse. It was the biggest day the local court had ever had."[2]

The trial itself only produced a small handful of witnesses, a doctor who had conducted an autopsy on Mrs. Dillon's body, and had focused particularly on the contents of her stomach to prove a decidedly circumstantial case of murder via strychnine poisoning. It was known that Hattie took quinine tablets to relieve her leg cramps and arthritis.

During the trial. Dr. R.W. Rhamy of Fort Wayne testified as an expert witness and provided an "ocular demonstration" of the tests conducted for strychnine by using a portion of fluid extracted from Mrs. Dillon's stomach at autopsy. "In the presence of the court and jury, he applied the tests and explained the reactions which he declared proved conclusively that the woman died by strychnine poisoning," the *Fort Wayne Journal-Gazette* reported. "A portion of the fluid contents of the stomach was treated with picric acid and the jury was able to see the formation of a white precipitate."[3]

Dr. Rhamy said his tests showed Mrs. Dillon had traces of strychnine in her spleen, liver, stomach, and kidneys. She had no traces of quinine in her system, the tablet that George W. Dillon said he had given her moments before he fell into violent convulsions and died an hour later.[4] Hattie's daughter (identified in accounts only as Mrs. W.O. Sweeny) testified about the quarrels the elderly couple had engaged, starting with a broken promise George had made Hattie that he was not just marrying her to gain a helpmate at his farm, and that Hattie resented the amount of work George asked her to do. She said George Dillon had borrowed money from her family, and often complained that Hattie's disposition was foul, and they spoke to one another in disrespecting tones.

"Mrs. Sweeny said she told [Mr.] Dillon that she wanted to take her mother home with her," reports carrying the trial testimony said, "but that [George] said his wife would not leave him without securing a divorce and alimony, and that he would not do that."[5]

Sarah E. Wisely, Hattie's sister who had first introduced Hattie and George at a party in her home just across the road from Dillon's farm, said she had witnessed arguments between the two. The judge allowed Wisely to retell details of a fight where Hattie had declared she wanted to return to her children and that George had told her, "You'll never go back." [6]

Interestingly, although state witnesses were apparently granted wide latitude in retelling conversations and statements they had heard others say, defense attorneys were blocked in their attempt to call a helpful witness. The state's case centered on the idea that George Dillon wanted to sell his farm and take the money, but that his new wife was unwilling to do so. It was just the latest struggle between the couple.

On Saturday evening, February 24, 1912, jurors returned after a little over two hours of deliberations with a surprise verdict of guilty—not guilty of murder, but guilty of manslaughter.[7]

Dillon received the verdict calmly, but filed an immediate appeal for a new trial. Failing to gain a new trial, in March 1912 Dillon was transferred to the Indiana State Prison at Michigan City. He would not remain a prisoner there for long, however, as on October 7, 1913, Indiana Governor Samuel M. Ralston surprised everyone by granting Dillon a full and complete pardon, and ordered Warden E.J. Fogarty to release him from the prison.[8]

Governor Ralston made no public comments on the case, but his office released the contents of his pardon sentence which noted that George Dillon was "at the time of his conviction, [and] had always been of good character, was of a religious disposition, was industrious and hardworking, his associated were always good, he was not addicted to drink or other vicious habits, had never been charged with crime of any kind, and lived an upright, Christian life."[9] Ralston noted that the prison's warden had reported Dillon was seriously ill and had been housed in the prison hospital for more than four months, and "his recovery is impossible because of his advanced years and general physical disability."[10]

Warden Fogarty's office told reporters that Dillon had been "a model and trustworthy prisoner. He took his imprisonment philosophically and no one has ever heard a word of complaint from him. He appears to be at peace with the world, and has always denied the charge made against him, stating that his wife made a mistake in taking medicine."[11]

The diagnosis of George Dillon's physical state were accurate—he died January 26, 1914, just over three months after he had gained his release.[12] Dillon was later buried alongside his first wife, Sarah, in a prominent grave at Fountain Cemetery in Fostoria, Ohio.

Endnotes

1. *Fort Wayne Journal-Gazette*, Feb. 25, 1912
2. *Fort Wayne Journal-Gazette*, Feb. 25, 1912
3. *Fort Wayne Journal-Gazette*, Feb. 17, 1912
4. Ibid.
5. Ibid.
6. *Fort Wayne Journal-Gazette*, Feb. 18, 1912
7. *Fort Wayne Journal-Gazette*, Feb. 25, 1912
8. *Indianapolis Star*, Oct. 8, 1913
9. Ibid.
10. Ibid.
11. Ibid.
12. *Fort Wayne Journal-Gazette*, Jan. 27, 1914; *Indianapolis Star*, Jan. 27, 1914.

LAKE COUNTY

VICTIMS:
Maxine Walker, 41;
Nakita Moore, 14;
Tonya Dunlap, 23;
Betty Askew, 50;
Michelle Burns, 27;
Debra McHenry, 41;
Sarah Lynn Paulsen, 8;
Cleaster "Precious" McNeil, 29;
Arlinda Smith, 46;
Sarah Harrington, 32

VICTIMS:
James Raganyi, 16;
Michael Dennis, 13;
Nicholas James, 19

PERPETRATOR:
Eugene Britt, 38

PERPETRATOR:
David Edward Maust, 49

TWO SPREE KILLERS HIDE IN PLAIN SIGHT

Throughout history, it seems some criminals have known that often the best place to hide is in plain sight. Two prolific spree killers did just that and succeeded in going undetected for several deadly months in populous Lake County in the northwest corner of Indiana.

Whether it was the shadow of more serious crimes occurring almost daily in Chicago or a dull sense of regularity to violence in the economically challenged areas of Lake County, both Eugene Britt, thirty-eight, of Gary, and David Edward Maust, forty-nine, of Hammond, got away with killing sprees that left at least thirteen women, girls, and young men dead.

Eugene Britt

Eugene Britt surfaced as a threat to public safety as early as April 1978 when he was arrested and charged with the rape of a seventeen-year-old Gary Roosevelt High School girl. A fifteen-year sentence for his conviction sent Britt just down the road to the Indiana State Prison in Michigan City, and he was released in 1993 after serving his full fifteen years.

Back in Lake County, Britt took a part-time job across the county line at the Hardee's Restaurant in nearby Portage, Indiana, about the only job an ex-con with a sex offense on his record could get. Not a model employee, Britt somehow managed to keep the job despite having to get back and forth to Portage from his home in Gary (often riding his blue, ten-speed bike the entire distance).

During his time away from his job at Hardee's, Britt picked up where he left off in 1978, conducting a series of rapes that police believe started in the spring of 1995 and did not end until his arrest in November 1995. Prison time, however, had convinced Britt he had to eliminate witnesses and he began to strangle and kill his rape victims.

His first victim, police believe, was thirty-two-year-old Sarah Harrington of Lake Station, Indiana, who was reported missing in the spring of 1995, and whose strangled body was found in a wooded area near the East Dunes Highway near Lake Michigan on May 16, 1995.

Just a month later, fourteen-year-old Nakita Moore of Gary was reported missing by her mother. On June 24, 1995, her partially decomposed body was found poorly hidden in a vacant lot in the 2000 block of West Fifteenth Avenue, just west of downtown Gary.

Thirty more days passed, and on July 18, 1995, police found the body of Deborah McHenry, forty-one, a Gary resident, lying in the weeds behind a garage at 2940 West Twenty-first Avenue in Gary. Deborah was found just a mile west of where Nakita's body was found.

While police were busy determining who would want to kill any of these women, another call came in just a month later on August 13, 1995, as the body of Michelle Burns, a twenty-seven-year-old Gary resident, was found in a vacant lot near Twenty-first and Broadway. Her body lay exactly two miles directly east of where Deborah was found, and just a block off Gary's main street, Broadway Avenue.

A seemingly unrelated case emerged across the county line in Porter County at Portage, Indiana, a few days later on August 22, 1995, when the partially clothed body of Sarah Lynn Paulsen, just eight years old, was found dumped in a wooded area near her home in the 5000 block of Central Avenue. She had only been missing a short time when searchers in Portage found her.

Unknown to investigators at the time, Britt had been sent home early from work that same day for goofing off and not completing assignments. Before he left Portage, however, he abducted, raped, and killed young Sarah.

But Britt was not on the radar screen yet for any police investigators.

Back in Gary, detectives had little time to reflect as the body count began to grow. On September 2, 1995, police were summoned to an abandoned home in the 500 block of Harrison Street. Just two miles north of where the last body was found, police discovered the body of Betty Askew, fifty, a Gary resident who lived two houses away from where she was found dead.

Ten days later, the alarm sounded again and police began investigating the discovery of twenty-nine-year-old Cleaster "Precious" McNeil of Gary. Her body was found dumped inside an abandoned home at 2144 Massachusetts Avenue in Gary—just two miles from the last body, and just south of the downtown area.

Reporters and citizens were convinced a serial or spree killer was on the loose in Gary. Twenty-four women had been murdered in 1995 in Gary, and city officials felt the pressure. Gary Police Chief Joseph Slay and Mayor Thomas Barnes met reporters on the day McNeil's body was found. Slay told reporters, "We have not found any connections at this time" between the deaths.[1]

Later, Mayor Barnes would acknowledge, "We really did not know we had a serial killer. We collected all our evidence and submitted it to the state so that if there was a serial killer, we could make a statement about it."[2]

Off the record and not allowing their names to be used, Gary police detectives grumbled to reporters that city officials were reluctant to link the cases or call it a spree of murders for fear of creating fear and further damaging the city's image.

The killing likely would have continued, but Britt stepped in front of a South Shore train in Gary and injured his leg on September 14, 1995. A day later, he was released from the hospital and transferred to Refuge House, a homeless shelter in Gary. He later told the Reverend Clyde B. Smith, operator of the shelter, that it was a suicide attempt.

It was at Refuge House that police began to keep a close eye on Britt after Gary police conferred with police in Portage about a possible link between Britt and the killing of Sarah Paulsen. Portage police knew Britt had been sent home early the day Sarah was killed, and eventually linked fibers found under her fingernails to Britt's Hardee's uniform.[3]

Portage police also had a witness statement identifying a man matching Britt's description in the area of Sarah's home just before she went missing. The witness reported the man was riding a blue, ten-speed bike—a bike Britt seemingly always had with him.

On November 3, 1995, Portage and Gary detectives swooped in on Britt at the Refuge House mission and took him in for questioning. Under questioning, Britt began delivering details of his deadly spree, including identifying victims police had yet to find—such as the unidentified skeletal remains of a woman strangled and left dead in a wooded area in the 6800 block of East Melton Road in Gary.

Rev. Smith told reporters, "Upon his confessing to us, my wife and I encouraged him to go to the authorities and wipe the slate clean. So we weren't surprised the next day when the police called us and said, 'Eugene is ready to confess, but he won't talk without you present.'"[4]

Rev. Smith's wife, Delores, who had heard Britt's confessions to her husband just before police arrested him, said, "Just listening to him go in detail, from victim to victim, I really understood the turmoil arising in him that he couldn't control. He was out of control."[5]

On April 26, 1996, Britt pled guilty to murder and two counts of criminal deviate conduct in the murder of Sarah Paulsen. Porter County Prosecutor James Douglas agreed to withdraw his death penalty request and agreed Britt could be sentenced to life in prison without parole, plus an additional fifty years for each count of criminal deviate conduct.[6]

Lake County Prosecutor Bernard Carter had a more complicated set of cases on his hands, although he still had Britt's confession. On October 6, 2006, Britt agreed to a plea agreement that gave him a total of 245 years in prison for the rape and murder of Nakita Moore, Tonya Dunlap, and Maxine Walter. Although he admitted to the other murders under police questioning, the plea agreement allowed those charges to be dropped if Britt gave up his rights to appeal the conviction.

Lake County Superior Court Judge Salvador Vasquez accepted the plea agreement and entered the 245-year sentence for Britt. He wept as he told Judge Vasquez, "I'm truly sorry for my sins and I take full responsibility for my actions, ain't nobody but myself. God knows I'm guilty, God knows I'm guilty."[7]

David Edward Maust

Like Britt, David Edward Maust of Hammond, Indiana, had a long and troubled history as his life had often intersected with not only the criminal justice system, but also mental health services.

Maust moved to a working-class neighborhood of Hammond in 2002 after completing parole for his latest crime, the April 9, 1981, rape and murder of Donald Jones, fifteen, of Elgin, Illinois. Immediately after killing Jones, Maust fled to Texas, where he was eventually arrested and convicted in December 1981 for the rape of another teenage boy there. While incarcerated in Texas, Illinois authorities identified him as Jones's killer and extradited him.

During his often-delayed trial for Jones's murder, Cook County (Illinois) State's Attorney Clifford Johnson noted that Maust was "a bad guy" and "a Gacy type"—comparing him to infamous Chicago serial killer John Wayne Gacy.[8]

Maust was given a thirty-five-year sentence despite pleas by Jones's family that he be given a life sentence. Maust only served about half of that before being released and relocating to Indiana in 2002.[9]

Psychiatric reports prepared for the Illinois court as it tried to determine whether Maust was mentally fit to stand trial for Jones's murder cast a disturbing picture of the man. Dr. Matthew Marcos of Chicago examined Maust and wrote in an August 15, 1986, report that he "has a very long and significant mental history with multiple suicide attempts and homicidal activities … He has a pathological preoccupation with death, mutilation and dying and other bizarre ideations."[10]

Despite such a troubling report, Sister Josephine Migliare, a Catholic nun who counseled Maust while he was held in an Illinois jail cell, said "he is far from being mentally ill. He is intelligent, soft-spoken and not combative. He has helped many young inmates who had backgrounds similar to his. I know that David has spent enough time in the system and is ready to spend the future helping youth with addiction tendencies."[11]

Maust's record clearly established, he still won parole, and trouble soon followed. Living in Hammond, he made quick friends with many of the teenage boys in his neighborhood to whom he was sexually attracted.

In May 2003, the girlfriend of Nicholas James, nineteen, reported her Hammond boyfriend missing. No trace of him was found, and some believed he had just run away from home.

Then in September 2003, two other Hammond youths, James Raganyi, sixteen, and Michael Dennis, thirteen, left a note saying they were running away from home. No one would ever see them alive again.

Hammond police initially focused on Maust after learning from other teenagers in the neighborhood that he sometimes provided beer and marijuana to some of the young men. He was arrested on October 2, 2003, and charged with contributing to the delinquency of a minor for providing beer to two boys, ages twelve and thirteen.

As part of that investigation, police learned he had also been known to spend time with one of the missing boys, Michael Dennis. A probable cause affidavit filed against Maust said Raganyi and Dennis were "hanging around an older man named David over the summer of 2003, and that David had given them money … beer and marijuana."[12] A further check on Maust revealed his violent and criminal past, causing detectives to keep their focus on him.

Eventually, detectives gained a search warrant for Maust's second-floor apartment at 4933 Ash Avenue, just north of downtown Hammond. In addition to searching his apartment, they also checked the basement of the home and noted a fresh patch of concrete in a five by eight-foot section of the floor. Maust told detectives the concrete was placed after he made sewer repairs in the basement.

Unconvinced, detectives brought in a "cadaver sniffing dog," which indicated possible human remains under the cement. Holes drilled into the concrete revealed "coffin flies" from the holes, indicating something was decomposing underneath.

Lake County Coroner David Pastrick announced on December 12, 2003, that his office had supervised the removal of three bodies from under the concrete. They had been positively identified as Raganyi, Dennis, and the previously reported missing Nicholas James.

Pastrick would not give details, but he said it appeared all three had died violent deaths, and that all three were wrapped in plastic and secured with cords and tape.

Questioned by detectives later, Maust confessed he had killed Nicholas James earlier in the summer by striking him in the head after they spent an evening drinking in his apartment. He also confessed to strangling James Raganyi and Michael Dennis in September 2003 after spending an evening drinking with them and attempting to molest them.

The investigation also turned up a startling eighty-seven-page statement Maust wrote to Cook County, Illinois, police in December 1983. Maust disclosed in the statement that he had waged an almost constant struggle to keep from harming people around him.[13]

Having been a patient at an Illinois mental hospital when he was thirteen years old, Maust wrote that he had a terribly strained relationship with his mother, who was violent with him. He admitted that he frequently choked or punched his adolescent friends and got into trouble often, but did not know why.[14]

His statement also contained a confession. Maust said he first killed a boy in 1974 while he was stationed at a U.S. Army post in Germany. He admitted killing a boy named Jimmy he met off base after molesting him. He was arrested and served a three-year federal sentence for manslaughter in the federal penitentiary at Leavenworth, Kansas.[15] He also admitted stabbing a young man in Georgia in 1979, but was acquitted of attempted murder in that case.[16]

"I would say to God, 'please don't let me hurt anyone today.' I would say that over and over to God," he wrote in the statement.[17]

Following the discovery of the three bodies in his basement, Maust's mother, seventy-two-year-old Eva Reyes, told reporters from her Georgia home that she thought her son should have been locked up long ago. "I feel I am to blame somehow," she said. "Yet and still, he has to take some of the responsibility. After all, he was an adult. I'm tired of him now. Yet at the same time, I still love him. It's a hard thing to say, but I think he deserves to lose his life. He's taken so many."[18]

On October 31, 2005, Maust pled guilty to murdering all three of the boys whose bodies were found in his basement. In exchange for his plea, the state agreed to a sentence of life in prison without parole.

On January 19, 2006, Maust took a bed sheet in his Lake County Jail cell and braided it into a rope and attempted to hang himself. Just moments before, Lake County Jail guards had reminded Maust to get his personal items together in order to be transported to the Indiana State Prison.

Maust was rushed to St. Anthony Medical Center in Crown Point, Indiana, where he was listed in critical condition and on life support. He died a day later on January 20, 2006.

Chicago Tribune online blogger Eric Zorg wrote a column titled "David Maust's great escape" in which he detailed a lengthy suicide note Maust had left at the jail before he hung himself.

In his letter, Maust said, "I've lived a wasted life on earth and there is nothing I could say or do to change anything and nobody wants to hear from me anymore. After what I did, there is nothing else to talk about and the taxpayer does not want to hear me talking about God or hear that I've been praying (especially Republicans and parents, and who can blame them) … Life in prison is not what the parents [of the victims] wanted and the Indiana taxpayer does not want to pay the bill. The families wanted me to receive the death sentence and so do many other families and parents across America."[19]

He said he believed "the American taxpayer has had enough when it comes to murdering the innocent and committing crimes against the human race … the time has come for me to move on and end the madness of my life."[20]

Endnotes

1. *Times of Northwest Indiana*, Nov. 12, 1995.
2. Ibid.
3. Ibid.

4. *Times of Northwest Indiana*, Nov. 10, 1995.
5. Ibid.
6. *Times of Northwest Indiana*, April 27, 1996.
7. Associated Press, Nov. 4, 2006.
8. *Times of Northwest Indiana*, Dec. 12, 2003.
9. Associated Press, Dec. 12, 2003.
10. *Times of Northwest Indiana*, Dec. 12, 2003.
11. Ibid.
12. Ibid.
13. Associated Press, Dec. 14, 2003.
14. Ibid.
15. *Times of Northwest Indiana*, Dec. 17, 2003.
16. Associated Press, Dec. 14, 2003.
17. Ibid.
18. *Times of Northwest Indiana*, Dec. 16, 2003.
19. *Chicago* (Ill.) *Tribune*, Jan. 20, 2006.
20. Ibid.

LAKE COUNTY

VICTIM(S):
Ruth Elizabeth Pelke, 78

PERPETRATOR(S):
Paula R. Cooper, 15;
Karen D. Corder, 16;
Denise M. Thomas, 14;
April J. Beverly, 15

DATE OF DEATH(S):
May 14, 1985

WHEN IS A KILLER TOO YOUNG TO DIE?

The horrible crime that put Paula R. Cooper and her friends behind bars was not all that unusual in real terms—thieves and murderers have used lies to gain the trust of their victims for a long time. What stands out about the stabbing death of Ruth Pelke, just a few days short of her seventy-ninth birthday, is the unnecessary violence inflicted upon her and the fact that such violence was perpetrated by young teenage girls.

The murder of Mrs. Pelke would put into motion a criminal investigation, prosecution and sentencing that would eventually draw worldwide attention.

It started during the afternoon of Tuesday, May 14, 1985 when Cooper and her friends decided to skip the rest of the school day at Lew Wallace High School and spend their time on the streets looking for something to do. Coo-. per, just fifteen at the time, landed on the idea of approaching Mrs. Pelke's home at 4449 Adams Street in Gary on the ruse of asking about whether she and her friends could take Bible study lessons from her.[1]

Fifteen-year-old April J. Beverly lived on the same street as Mrs. Pelke and knew that in the past she had invited neighborhood children into her home for Bible lessons using a felt board to depict stories from scripture. Beverly and Cooper were joined on Mrs. Pelke's stoop that day by Karen D. Corder, sixteen, and Denise M. Thomas, just fourteen. The plan was to ask about Bible study lessons to gain entry into the home, and then rob the elderly woman.

The ruse was a clever one and factored in Mrs. Pelke's evangelical Christian beliefs. She often shared her faith with others and was particularly interested in making sure young people knew about Christ. In the past, she had offered her Bible study lessons complete with refreshments for all comers, and saved chocolates for her students who succeeded at memorizing particular verses.

Mrs. Pelke had stopped offering the classes, however, as her age grew and the neighborhood continued to decline. Like many of her neighbors, her home had been subject to petty crimes and thefts. There was no denying that the once-solid working-class neighborhood where she had lived for more than four decades had begun to decay around her. Despite such challenges, and the fact that many other white families had long ago fled Gary's older neighborhoods as part of the "white flight" to the suburbs, Mrs. Pelke remained and enjoyed friendships with several of her neighbors—black and white.

As the girls approached her on this spring day, it apparently didn't occur to her to ask them why they weren't in school. Instead, when they asked about Bible study lessons, she shared with them that she had "retired" from that activity, but had the phone number of another church member who would be glad to instruct the girls. Mrs. Pelke briefly stepped back inside to look for a phone number in a desk drawer.

"When she bent over to go in her desk drawer, [Cooper] grabbed her around the neck and hit her on the head with a vase," Gary Police Sergeant William Burns told a growing horde of reporters from across Indiana and Chicago interested in the sad case. "She then started stabbing her all over her body."[2] It was no simple attack meant just to overcome the frail old woman. It was an attack of extreme viciousness.

Lake County Coroner Daniel D. Thomas would later report that Mrs. Pelke suffered thirty-three separate stab wounds to her chest, abdomen, legs, scalp, and her arms and hands as she tried to defend herself. Police believed that, with so many stab wounds, more than one of the girls had to be involved in the slaying.[3]

Police later recovered a butcher knife used in the attack, stolen from Mrs. Pelke's kitchen and dumped in a trash can at a McDonald's restaurant in Hammond, Indiana.

After stabbing Mrs. Pelke, one of the girls wrapped a towel around her head to hide the gaze of the dying woman's eyes.

"She was still breathing, but the girls said they did not want to see her face," said Gary Police Chief Virgil Motley.[4]

Mrs. Pelke bled to death on the floor of her dining room, and her body was not discovered until the next afternoon, Wednesday, May 15, 1985, when her son Robert Pelke came to her home to check on her since she was not answering her phone. He found his mother, her face wrapped in a towel, dead, and the home's telephone cord ripped from the wall.

A neighbor reported that Mrs. Pelke was a quiet, kind woman. "She wasn't prejudiced," said Nell Hayes, an African-American woman. "She took my kids under her wing since I moved here in 1975. She and I worked our gardens together . . . If you needed something, she always made you feel welcome."[5]

Police picked up two of their suspects, female students from Lew Wallace high School, as they attended classes on Thursday, May 16, 1985. Two other girls were later turned in by their guardians or parents, police said.

Investigators zeroed in on Cooper and her friends after other Lew Wallace students reported seeing the girls driving around Gary in Mrs. Pelke's 1977 Plymouth the day of the murder. The car was later recovered abandoned and out of gas in Harvey, Illinois.[6]

Statements from the girls implicated themselves and each other in the crime, although Cooper was identified by the three other girls as the one who had sustained the attack on Mrs. Pelke—inflicting one of the stab wounds so violently that it pierced the woman's body and shredded the carpeting on the floor beneath her.

Police learned Beverly had first suggested the idea of going to Mrs. Pelke's house, the idea of a robbery quickly hatched from there. Beverly had actually once attended Bible study lessons at the home, and although she was present the day Mrs. Pelke was slain, testimony would later reveal she had remained outside the home and served as a look-out during the attack. She also lost her nerve and asked to be dropped off, not wanting to ride around in the old woman's car after the attack.

There was no question that prosecutors wanted the case moved to adult court—the violence of the crime so severe that a juvenile court proceeding would not suffice. Lake County Prosecutor Jack Crawford, an up-and-coming member of the powerful Democratic Party in Lake County, was determined to get the cases moved, and once he succeeded, he promptly announced that he would seek the death penalty against all four girls.

Crawford later amended his request to include a death sentence only against Cooper, who he was said most responsible for the attack. "By her own admission, she inflicted the majority of the wounds, and the guilty admission does not change our plans to seek the death penalty," Crawford said.[7]

The case was quickly elevated to the front page across the state and the nation, as Cooper, at age fifteen, would be the youngest person ever subject to the death penalty in Indiana. Her case continued to make history as Crawford won a murder conviction against her in 1986, drawing the attention of no less than *The New York Times.*

Sentenced to death, *The Times* reported that Cooper's sentence "rekindled the debate over the appropriateness of capital punishment for juveniles . . . [Cooper's] case has drawn worldwide attention and turned Cooper into what prosecutors and supporters of the death penalty consider an undeserving celebrity."[8]

At the time of the murder, Indiana had the lowest minimum age for a person to be considered for the death penalty, just ten years old. At the time, thirty-six U.S. states had death penalties in place, with nine setting no age minimums.[9]

Some argued that Cooper's sentence gave up all hope of any rehabilitation for young offenders. Others argued that death sentences and other strict penalties for major crimes, such as murder, were meant to punish and had no need to consider rehabilitation.

Corder eventually pled guilty to a charge of murder and received a sixty-year sentence. Her attorneys told the court that Corder was "under the extreme dominance of Cooper" at the time of the crime.[10] Corder would never again walk free—she died in prison on December 30, 2008, at the age of forty, after a long struggle with asthma and heart disease. She had completed twenty-two years of her sentence at the time of her death.

Beverly also took a plea agreement, taking a charge of robbery and causing serious bodily injury and received a twenty-five year sentence. She was released from prison on April 10, 1999, after serving thirteen years.

Thomas took her chances at trial. She told the jury during her November 1985 trial, "I was just standing there screaming and crying" as Cooper and Corder slashed Mrs. Pelke, and recalled that the old woman recited the Lord's prayer as she grew weaker in the attack.[11] There was little question of guilt, and Thomas was found guilty of murder and later sentenced to thirty-five years in prison. With good behavior, she was released from prison on August 25, 2003, after serving eighteen years of her sentence.

It was Cooper's trial, however, that drew the most interest as the death penalty remained an option. Convicted of the crime, as expected, in July 1986, she was sent back to the Lake County Jail to await her sentence. While there, the Lake County sheriff learned that two jail guards and one recreational therapist had allegedly engaged in sexual activity with Cooper at the jail on at least six occasions. Both guards resigned, Sheriff Steven Stiglich said, and the therapist was fired.[12]

On July 11, 1986, Lake County Superior Court Judge James C. Kimbrough took up the issue of Cooper's sentence.

Cooper told the court, "I didn't go there to take anybody's life. It happened. It just happened. Something—it wasn't planned. We didn't sit up and say we was going to kill this innocent old lady. We didn't even know the lady."[13]

She added, "I'm sorry, and I know that's not enough, but taking my life won't bring the lady back."[14]

Although he struggled with his decision, according to what he said in court, Judge Kimbrough was not moved by Cooper's apology or by information that revealed her young life had been one struggle after another. Kimbrough entered the death sentence, but later told reporters that he was uncertain he could do so at the start of Cooper's trial but had become convinced he could not ignore the "wantonness and brutality of the crime" nor Cooper's age, which he believed "was old enough and had the sense enough to be as cold as she was."[15]

As she made history as the youngest person ever on Indiana's Death Row, Cooper's appeals continued to gain national attention including unusual advocates for sparing her life, Mrs. Pelke's grandson, William Pelke of Gary, Indiana, and Pope John Paul II. Citizens in Italy and Germany were particularly appalled, it seemed, by Cooper's sentence and flooded the office of Indiana Governor Robert D. Orr with letters of protest. One Indiana priest delivered to Orr a petition bearing more than two million signatures from across the world. One petition to relieve Cooper of her death sentence came directly in a letter from the Pontiff to Governor Orr.

William Pelke said he did not support executing Cooper for her crime, and said he wanted to help spare her life.[16]

In September 1987, the pope's position was made clearer. "I can affirm that the Holy See and the Holy Father have, through confidential channels, put forward their viewed, aimed at obtaining clemency for Paula Cooper, underlining the human and humanitarian aspects of the case," Vatican spokesman Joaquim Novarro Valls said.[17]

Amnesty International joined the fight to save Cooper's life in November 1988 by filing a "friend of the court" document with the Indiana Supreme Court arguing in favor of Cooper's pending appeal.

On July 13, 1989, the state's highest court voted 5-0 to overturn Cooper's death sentence and said that the young woman must be resentenced, declaring that a fifteen-year-old could not be sentenced to the adult sentence of death.

"The question is whether Paul Cooper may be executed for committing the grisly murder of Mrs. Ruth Pelke," the court's jurists wrote. "We hold that she may not."[18]

They added, "This is a difficult conclusion to reach because of the gruesome nature of Cooper's acts."[19]

The court noted that the Indiana General Assembly had acted to change the minimum age for death sentences in the state and a recent U.S. Supreme Court ruling involving defendants who were sixteen and seventeen years old.

The death sentence reversed, Special Judge Richard J. Conroy handed Cooper a sixty-year sentence in a hearing on August 18, 1989.

In November 1990, the Indiana Court of Appeals upheld Thomas's conviction for the murder of Mrs. Pelke.

Cooper proved, at least initially, to be a difficult inmate for state officials to handle. Often confined to solitary quarters for violations of the rules at the Indiana Women's Prison in Indianapolis, her notoriety also proved challenging for correctional facilities as well. Cooper's behavior began to improve, however, as she grew older behind bars and on May 11, 2001, she was among seventeen women at the prison who received her bachelor's degree during a graduation ceremony behind the prison walls.[20]

Despite her accomplishment, many remained unconvinced that Cooper had changed. Dr. Henry Karlson, a law professor at Indiana University who had studied Cooper's case said, "Although she graduated from college, her problem isn't a lack of ignorance. It's a lack of conscience. She's a completely self-serving person. She'll behave well if it's to her advantage."[21]

Disagreement about Cooper also created tension within the Pelke family. Not all of William Pelke's relatives agreed with him position that Cooper should be spared the death penalty, and his on-again-off-again correspondence with Cooper.

William Pelke said he was acting in a manner that he thought his grandmother would approve of. "After Paula was on death row, I began to think about what my grandmother would have thought about somebody being put to death," he said. "I think she would have been appalled. She was always trying to reach out to girls like Paula."[22]

Once doomed to be executed for her role in the murder of Ruth Pelke, Cooper finally walked out of prison on June 17, 2014, after serving twenty-five years of her new sixty-year sentence.

The last of the girls implicated in the vicious murder to be released, Cooper's new life of freedom came to a surprising end less than two years later in an apparent suicide. On May 26, 2015, Indianapolis Police responded to a report of a body slumped against a tree outside an office building on the city's far northwest side. There, officers found Cooper dead of what was ruled as a self-inflicted gunshot wound to the head. There was a .380-caliber handgun found in her lap and a Toyota Corolla registered to her parked nearby. Cooper, who was forty-five years old at the time of her death, had received forgiveness from Pelke's grandson, William, who visited her in prison fourteen times and often exchanged e-mails with her about plans to engage her in a restorative justice program.[23]

Endnotes

1. *Gary Post-Tribune*, May 17, 1985
2. Ibid.
3. Ibid.
4. Ibid.
5. *Gary Post-Tribune*, May 16, 1985

6. *Gary Post-Tribune*, May 17, 1985
7. *Chicago Tribune*, April 23, 1986
8. *New York Times*, Nov. 3, 1986
9. Ibid.
10. Ibid.
11. *Chicago Tribune*, Nov. 8, 1985
12. *Chicago Tribune*, June 22, 1986
13. *New York Times*, Nov. 3, 1986
14. *Chicago Tribune*, July 12, 1986
15. *New York Times*, Nov. 3, 1986
16. *Chicago Tribune*, May 14, 1987
17. *Chicago Tribune*, Sept. 27, 1987
18. *Paula R. Cooper v. State of Indiana*, Supreme Court Ruling, July 13, 1989
19. Ibid.
20. *Indianapolis Star*, May 12, 2001
21. Ibid.
22. *Times of Northwest Indiana*, June 22, 1993
23. *Indianapolis Star*, May 27, 2015; *Chicago Tribune*, May 27, 2015

LaPORTE COUNTY

VICTIM(S):
A.J. Rumely, Jr., 71;
Frances Rumely, 69

PERPETRATOR(S):
Harold W. Lang, 32

DATE OF DEATH(S):
May 31 and November 25, 1982

A MAN WITH A LIMP AROUSES POLICE SUSPICION

An unusual foot trail in the grass behind the home of LaPorte's popular Mayor A.J. Rumely led to the quick arrest of a disgruntled city worker responsible for shooting the mayor and his wife to death as they slept in their bed on Memorial Day weekend, 1982.

In the last days before his life would change dramatically, Mayor Rumely was actively working with community members to improve a railroad crossing in the city where two LaPorte High School students had been killed in an accident.

Responding to a community need such as this was part of what Mayor Rumely liked about his job. The first-term Republican had run for mayor as he began to think about retiring from his successful career in business. Local Republicans were thrilled—everyone in town, it seemed, knew and loved Rumely and his outgoing wife Frances. The two of them loved LaPorte and the people who called it home.

It would all come to a violent and sad end early on Memorial Day, Monday, May 31, 1982, as the Rumely's slept in their bed in an upstairs bedroom of their home at 95 Keston Elm Drive.

The couple was started awake by a stranger in their bedroom carrying a gun with a homemade silencer on the end of the barrel. The gunman opened fire on both sixty-nine-year-old Frances and seventy-one-year-old Mayor Rumely. The elderly couple never had a chance.

Mrs. Rumely's injuries indicated she had held up her hands to try and shield herself from the shots—two bullets striking her body—one in the chest and one in the hip. The mayor was shot three times, in the abdomen, left forearm, and left thigh. It was a brutal, senseless attack on two defenseless people.

Mrs. Rumely died in her bed before paramedics could arrive to assist her. The mayor, critically wounded, had stumbled to the phone to call 911—the call coming in at 1:36 a.m.

Paramedics rushed Mayor Rumely to the LaPorte Hospital where he underwent four hours of emergency surgery performed by his friend, Dr. Edwin C. Mueller (who was also serving a term as LaPorte County Coroner). Dr. Mueller said the mayor was conscious and alert before the surgery but complained of pain from his wounds.

Dr. Mueller would later oversee the autopsy of Frances Rumely, determining she died of multiple gunshot wounds.

The LaPorte Police Department immediately requested the assistance of the LaPorte County Sheriff's Department and the Indiana State Police. One clue stood out—a homemade silencer found clenched in Mrs. Rumely's hand where she had apparently knocked it loose from the gun, indicating the shooting was more likely an assassination than a botched burglary.

LaPorte Police Chief Larry Miller was tight-lipped about the investigation as media from South Bend, Chicago and all over northwest Indiana descended on his city.

Police searches of Kesling Park directly behind the mayor's home confirmed that the suspect likely approached the home under the cover of dark by slipping through the backyard and entering a window on the first floor of the Spanish-style home.

One investigator, who did not want his name printed, told reporter Tim Brown of the *LaPorte Herald-Argus* that he speculated that Mrs. Rumely "woke when she was hit in the hip [with a bullet], grabbed for the gun, ripping off the silencer, and then was fatally shot. She had a small cut on her chin which she might have gotten in the struggle."

The unidentified police source added, "I'm sure shots were flying all over the place and things happened quickly. [The mayor] was most likely on the bed at her side the whole time."[1]

The mayor's daughter, Martha Scileppi of Chicago, rushed to the hospital to be at her father's side, as did the rest of the nine grown Rumely children. She reported that her father had said the shots sounded like an explosion.

Scileppi said he told her that he looked up and saw a figure wearing dark clothing in the room. "He grappled with the man. My mother was probably dead at that point."[2]

Neighbors had neither heard anything nor seen anyone on the night of the attack—most of them unaware that such violence had erupted inside the Rumely home until police and ambulance sirens broken the silence of the night.

As the news spread across the city of more than 30,000 residents, LaPorte leaders decided to go ahead with the community's annual Memorial Day observances at Fox Park. Mayor and Mrs. Rumely likely would have attended the events, and were mentioned and remembered by those present.

The next day brought some relief, but also shock as police announced the arrest of former city employee Harold W. Lang, a thirty-two-year-old loner with a graduate degree in psychology. News cameras captured Lang, his head bowed, as he was led handcuffed into the LaPorte County Courthouse for an initial hearing.

Lang, who lived with his mother in a modest home less than a mile from the mayor's house, was charged with murder and attempted murder and held without bond at the LaPorte County Jail.

In court for the initial hearing, LaPorte County Circuit Court Judge Paul Baldoni inquired about whether Lang had an attorney or the means to hire one. Lang replied curiously, "I feel there is justice here. I really do feel that."[3]

Investigators revealed that Lang had been fired from his job in the city's sewage treatment plant after five years of service a month earlier, in April 1982, after the latest argument and dust-up between him and his supervisor. He worked at the plant as an operator and lab technician responsible for monitoring the quality of water as it left the plant.

LaPorte County Prosecutor Walter "Skip" Chapala said Lang had given a statement implicating himself in the crime and had led police to a .30-caliber weapon believed to have been used in the attack which he had hidden in a wooded area near his home.

Lang's unusual way of walking—referred to as "reverse pigeon-toed"—had caught the attention of Detective Captain Roger Farley of the LaPorte Police.

"He sort of drags one foot behind him," Farley said. Footprints at the mayor's home indicative of a person who walked while dragging one foot were photographed because plastic casts could not be made.[4]

While responding officers had been able to talk to the mayor briefly before he went into surgery on the night of the attack, he had not identified Lang as the attacker. "The mayor was only able to tell us he was sleeping, felt like he had been stabbed, woke up, saw a dark figure who fled and then made his way to a phone call to call police," Farley said.[5]

"The silencer was the only thing we found at the home we knew the murderer brought with him and left behind," Farley said. "The break-in looked botched so we decided we weren't dealing with an experienced burglar or professional assassin. We did feel murder was the reason [for the home invasion] because nothing valuable was missing from the home."[6]

Ironically, a little over twelve hours after the Rumely shooting. Harold

Lang and his mother, Esther, called police to report an attempted break-in at their East 19th Street home. As detectives talked to Lang about the alleged break-in, they came to "take note of the unusual way Harold walked," Farley said.

At about the same time, other city officials came forward to reveal that Lang had been battling the city in the previous weeks. Co-workers said Lang was quiet and sometimes difficult to get along with.

"He was unpredictable," said coworker Bob Price. "We're coworkers, and one day, he got mad and fired me. Once you get to know a person, you can figure out a pattern, but I could never figure out one for Lang."[7]

Lang's mother, Esther, said her oldest son had asked Mayor Rumely to help him get his job back at the sewage treatment plant. She had even gone to the mayor's home herself during the evening hours of May 7 to plead her son's case and was eventually asked to leave.

She described an altercation between her son and his supervisor, Alex Toth, the city's water works superintendent, which had turned physical. Toth's version differed widely from Lang's take. He said that Lang had telephoned his office after the confrontation and announced he was moving out of town. Toth considered Lang's phone call to be his resignation.

Mrs. Lang said Harold had tried to call Mayor Rumely's office about the matter, but that the mayor had hung up the phone on him and told him to work his appeal through the city's formal personnel procedures. That made Harold angry.

Harold had also sought chiropractic care for injuries he alleged Toth had inflicted on him, and wanted the mayor to authorize payment for those services. Rumely had reportedly told Harold that no such payment could be made.

Mrs. Lang said her son had "a kind heart" and "wouldn't harm a fly" and described him as overqualified for his city job—having completed a master's degree in psychology at Valparaiso University.[8]

Funeral services for Frances Rumely went forward without her husband able to be present as he remained hospitalized in critical condition, trying to recover from his wounds.

In the days that followed, no one could blame LaPorte residents for noting similarities between the Lang case and that of John W. Hinckley Jr., who was pleading not guilty by reason of insanity for an attempted March 1981 assassination attempt of President Ronald Reagan. Lang too would claim insanity during a September 1982 hearing in Marshall County, where his case was moved on a change of venue.

The *LaPorte Herald-Argus* compiled a lengthy profile of Lang's life on the eve of his November 1982 trial. In it, they reported that Lang had always introduced himself to people by stating his full name, "Harold W. Lang," and was known for wearing white socks. "He collected rocks. He talked a little differently, carried his school books like a bushel basket, walking with a slight limp, and turned the jump rope for girls at recess when he was still in school."[9]

The profile added, "Not surprisingly . . . most people cautiously distanced themselves from Harold Lang. Many close enough to speak about him with authority insisted that their names not be used, and many more commented but emphasized they only knew him in passing."[10]

The 1970 LaPorte High School yearbook revealed Lang was a smart student who excelled in math and science and was active in the chess club and debate team. But high school was not a fun time for him.

"He was different all the way," one classmate who wanted to remain anonymous said.[11] As Lang's trial opened at the Marshall County Courthouse in Plymouth, Mayor Rumely's painful struggle, which had stretched over six months, came to an end. He died at 5:22 p.m. on Thanksgiving Day, November 25, 1982, at St. Joseph's Hospital in South Bend. His nine children and many of his grandchildren were with him in his final hours.

Prosecutor Chapala immediately announced he was upgrading existing charges against Lang to two counts of murder and dropping the previously filed attempted murder charge.

The mayor's funeral—attended by more than 600 federal, state and local officials, and community residents—was conducted at St. Peter's Catholic Church in LaPorte. Thirty-five miles away, Lang's trial opened in Plymouth. The mayor's sons and daughters carried his flag-draped casket to his final rest next to his loving wife. Lang's trial would not last long. After hearing the mountain of evidence against him, Lang changed his plea on December 10, 1982, from not guilty by reason of insanity to guilty, but insane. By doing so, he avoided a possible death sentence.

On December 30, 1982, Lang was sentenced to forty years for the murder of each of the Rumely's, and another thirty years for breaking and entering their home.

At his sentencing, Lang told the judge, "Your honor, I can't really explain my actions. I feel that Satan took me over somehow. I want to atone for my actions, although it can never be paid for. I hope in the years ahead, there is some good I can do for someone."[12]

Lang served most of his time in prison under psychiatric treatment. He died at the New Castle Correctional Center on February 27, 2015, after having served thirty-three years behind bars. He was sixty-three years old—about the same age as the Rumely's when they met their death.

Mayor and Mrs. Rumely's son, John, told a reporter that Lang's death "provides no comfort or closure to us as family members" and that since the vicious attack that took his parents as they slept, "his name is rarely, if ever, mentioned among us, simply because we've always focused on our parents' lives together and their legacy to our family, their faith, and to the LaPorte community."[13]

When a LaPorte funeral home listed Lang's obituary, online comments were posted by some of his former schoolmates, who recalled he was consistently teased and bullied as a young man. One recalled even teachers ridiculing Lang and one publicly spanking him in front of an entire gym class of fellow students.

While acknowledging there was "no excuse" for Lang's actions that took the innocent Rumley's lives, one classmate wrote, "I cannot help but think that he was driven mad by what he endured. I do not think he had any friends. Bullies are a threat to all of us, not just the scapegoats who are forced to endure the abuse. Rest in peace Harold. I am sorry I could not help you."[14]

Endnotes

1. *LaPorte Herald-Argus*, June 1, 1982
2. Ibid.
3. *LaPorte Herald-Argus*, June 2, 1982
4. *LaPorte Herald-Argus*, June 3, 1982
5. *LaPorte Herald-Argus*, June 4, 1982
6. *LaPorte Herald-Argus*, June 3, 1982
7. *LaPorte Herald-Argus*, June 2, 1982
8. Ibid.
9. *LaPorte Herald-Argus*, Nov. 27, 1982
10. Ibid.
11. Ibid.
12. *Indianapolis Star*, Dec. 31, 1982
13. *South Bend Tribune*, March 4, 2015
14. Essling Funeral Home web site, LaPorte, Ind., March 6, 2015

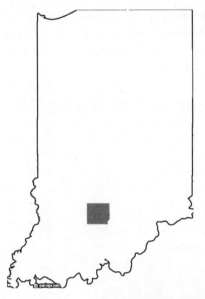

LAWRENCE COUNTY

VICTIM(S):
Erma Prince, 82

PERPETRATOR(S):
Shay White, 33

DATE OF DEATH(S):
September 16, 2002

A GRANDDAUGHTER'S SHAME

Shortly after eighty-two-year-old Erma Prince died in her hospital bed, her granddaughter, Shay White, came into her room and clipped off a small lock of her hair.

"Old Lady, I know you wouldn't like this, but this will be the last thing I get, and I have to have this," a witness said White declared.

White, however, denies she ever did anything but *love* her grandmother. Police and prosecutors believe differently and proved it in a dramatic Lawrence County trial in February 2005.

Jurors believed the version police and prosecutors portrayed that showed White snuck into the Dunn Memorial Hospital in Bedford, Indiana, during the early morning hours of September 16, 2002, and delivered a lethal dose of pain medication.

An autopsy would show the drug propoxyphene in her system—a drug found in prescription drugs such as Darvon, Darvocet, and Novrad. The pathologist, Dr. James Jacobi, attributed her death to "propoxyphene overdose." A laboratory toxicologist testified that Mrs. Prince had between 1,500 and 3,000 milligrams of propoxyphene, administered to her within thirty to ninety minutes of her death.[1]

It was a troubling finding, given that the drug, propoxyphene, had not been used at Dunn Memorial Hospital since March 2002—a full six months before Mrs. Prince's death.

Mrs. Prince had been taken to the hospital after suffering a broken hip during a fall at a Salvation Army Church Camp. White began acting strangely immediately. Witnesses reported she seemed angrier that Mrs. Prince had gone to the camp then concerned about her injury.

When White learned that her pain medication, Darvon, would not be given to her prior to her surgery, White argued with nurses. Hospital nurse Kevin Childers testified, "… As I was admitting her, there was medication [Shay White] said Erma hadn't had yet. She was wanting her to have it … She was very pushy."[2]

When told only hospital personnel could administer controlled substances, she told Childers, "Well, just turn your back, and I'll give it to her."[3]

Childers said Mrs. Prince resisted taking the medicine but eventually relented. "I could tell there was a problem there," Childers told the court.[4]

White and her husband signed consent forms for Mrs. Prince's hip surgery, telling hospital personnel they had power of attorney for the patient. The hospital never requested any documentation nor was it produced to verify that claim.

Doctors and nurses reported Mrs. Prince was alert after surgery and equipped with a patient-controlled analgesia (PCA) device to deliver pain medication as needed. Doctors said they placed it on the lowest setting possible as a matter of caution. "In older people like that, I would always choose the lowest level to not give them too much," Dr. James Rickert, an orthopedic surgeon, testified.

Shay White, however, was not satisfied. Another nurse testified that White became agitated and confronted nurses, telling them that Mrs. Prince could not adequately control the pain medication and needed more medicine.

Following Mrs. Prince's death, two witnesses came forward and said Shay White was reporting her grandmother's death before she had been declared dead. Jason Maddix, a Columbus, Indiana, police officer, said he spoke to White several months after the death, and she said the hospital called and said her grandmother had died at 4:32 a.m. Erma Prince was not pronounced dead, however, until 4:47 a.m.

Another witness, a coworker of White's cousin at a local nursing home, said White called before 4 a.m. to report her grandmother's death.

White's two sisters testified at trial against her. Her older sister, Stacey Barksdale, said White was insistent upon her visiting the hospital immediately after Mrs. Prince's fall. "She told me I should be ashamed of myself for not coming to see my grandmother at the hospital because she might not make it out alive," Barksdale told the court.[5]

Barksdale and other family members supported the idea of an autopsy to learn why Mrs. Prince had died. White opposed that and grew angry when learning from the funeral home that the body had not been released from the hospital, as an autopsy was going to proceed.

Hospital morgue personnel testified that White even called them, demanding to know why the body had not been released.

Another older sister, Jackie Owens, told the court that White could "be hard to get along with ... I think she's controlling ... she just always wanted things done her way or no way."[6]

A nurse, who saw Mrs. Prince alive and sleeping around 3 a.m. on September 16, testified she gave the woman an injection of blood thinner causing her to sit up straight in her bed with large, dilated eyes. Mrs. Prince went back to sleep, and when the nurse checked on her again at 4:45 a.m., she was dead.

Perhaps the most damning testimony came from Donna Flynn Gilmore, Shay White's former best friend. She told the court that White admitted having given her grandmother pain medications while she was hospitalized. "She said that she had given her medication, and she was in the process of being dead if she wasn't dead already," Gilmore said.[7]

Flynn Gilmore had helped police in their investigation, at one point wearing a secret wire and taping device to try to catch White in an open conversation about her grandmother's death.

Two fellow inmates from the Lawrence County Jail were also called to testify and claimed they heard White gloating that she had killed her grandmother and would get away with it.

For her defense, the court allowed White's grand jury testimony to be read to the jury in which she stated, "No, I did not [kill my grandmother]. I loved my grandma and wouldn't kill my grandma ... I couldn't picture anyone killing my grandma. I just can't."[8]

White told investigators that she "just thought she threw a blood clot. It is still hard for me to believe someone did that. It sure wasn't me ... I'd like to know what happened to my grandma more than you guys would. I just know I would never kill my grandmother ... I would never lay a hand on her."[9]

The defense presented another hospital employee, Sara Nikirk, a respiratory therapist, who said she saw a woman in Mrs. Prince's room about midnight on the night she died. She said the woman did not match White's description, and she could not identify her.

Shay White's husband, Ed, also testified saying she was at home with him throughout the night Mrs. Prince died. "I love her, but, myself, I wouldn't lie for her," Ed White said. "Shay was with me in our bedroom."[10]

Jurors took ten hours to review the evidence before finding Shay White guilty of the murder of her grandmother, Erma Prince. The verdict was read at

12:15 a.m. on March 13 in a trial that lasted more than a month and included more than forty witnesses.

For her part, White wept as the verdict was disclosed.

"When the truth comes out, they'll be sorry," White said as deputies led her from the courtroom.

Before her sentencing in early April 2005, White read a statement to the court that said, "This has been a nightmare I can't wake up from. I loved my grandmother dearly. I never once in my life harmed Erma Prince. This verdict was wrong. Maybe your family is normal, but mine never has been."[11]

She said the verdict would make her grandmother sick and read a passage from Luke 21:16 that says, "You will be betrayed even by parents, brothers, relatives and friends, and they will put some of you to death."[12]

She asked Lawrence County Circuit Court Judge Andrea McCord "to do what is right and just. I am innocent ... I have been falsely accused. I committed no crime, certainly not murder."[13]

Judge McCord was unmoved and sentenced White to fifty-five years on the charge, the sentence recommended by the prosecutor. White will be eligible for parole, with good behavior, after serving at least twenty-seven years.

A July 2006 ruling from the Indiana Court of Appeals denied White's request for a new trial. Her attorney said she plans a new appeal before the Indiana Supreme Court.

Endnotes

1. *Bedford Times-Mail*, March 2, 2005.
2. *Bedford Times-Mail*, Feb. 24, 2005.
3. Ibid.
4. Ibid.
5. *Bedford Times-Mail*, Feb. 25, 2005.
6. Ibid.
7. *Bedford Times-Mail*, March 2, 2005.
8. *Bedford Times-Mail*, March 8, 2005.
9. Ibid.
10. *Bedford Times-Mail*, March 10, 2005.
11. *Bedford Times-Mail*, April 9, 2005.
12. Ibid.
13. Ibid.

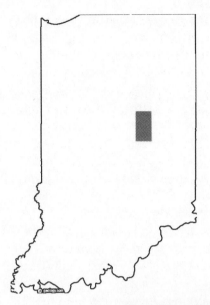

MADISON COUNTY

VICTIM(S):
Erin McKenzie, 7

PERPETRATOR(S):
Kevin L. Carter, 14

DATE OF DEATH(S):
August 24, 1994

THE DEATH OF INNOCENCE

On the sad day that Madison County residents were learning police had arrested a twenty-nine-year-old man for the abduction of a thirteen-year-old girl from her school bus stop, an even more troubling crime was about to rock the community.

The Wednesday morning edition of the *Anderson Herald-Bulletin* on August 24, 1994 carried the news of the man who had allegedly abducted the girl at knifepoint and raped her at his home. Fortunately, the girl escaped her captor and ran for help. Those who assisted her also detained the suspect until police arrived.[1]

It seemed a happy or at least better-than-terrible ending on the city's northeast side. But just three miles away, at the normally quiet Oaks Apartments along Thirty-Eighth Street near Main Street, feelings of panic were setting in as it became clear that seven-year-old Erin McKenzie was missing.

Beth McKenzie had just talked to her daughter Erin on the telephone a few minutes before, agreeing that the second grader from Southview Elementary School could stay at home for the few minutes it would take her mom to drive home from work. Erin had skipped a chance to go with her brothers and a neighbor boy to watch football tryouts at the school.

"Erin would be home [alone] for a matter of minutes," said Troy McCoy, a neighbor who was taking the older boys to the football tryouts. "She was supposed to stay in the house. But when her mother arrived home, Erin wasn't in the house. The door was standing open. The screen door was half open."[2]

Police organized an all-night search for the girl, in and around the Oaks Apartments, using helicopters and, later, bloodhounds to try and catch the scent of the girl last seen around 5:15 p.m. Her mom arrived home just moments later at 5:40 p.m. and notified police quickly of Erin's disappearance.

The search would come to an end not far from Erin's home—a maintenance worker looking in overgrown grass near the apartment complex found the crumpled and bloody body of Erin at about 8:20 a.m. on Thursday, August 25.

The *Herald-Bulletin* declared, "There's a killer on the loose. . . ."[3]

Erin's body was found face-up on the ground, fully clothed in a white T-shirt, shorts, and tennis shoes, police reported. "There was obvious trauma," Sergeant Mitch Carroll of the Anderson Police Department said.[4]

Police said several children in the apartment complex reported Erin was pushing her pink bicycle around the front of the apartment complex at about 5:15 p.m. asking if anyone had an air pump she could borrow to inflate the tire on her bike.

Detectives said it was likely Erin knew her attacker, trying to reassure frightened residents who easily recalled the September 1985 murder of Tamika Nicole Larry who went missing and was later found murdered on Anderson's west side.

"We're not looking for a boogie-man type person," said Captain John Moberly of Anderson Police. "We're looking for somebody who's probably well acquainted with the victim and known to a lot of the people around there who she might have been with."[5]

The autopsy of Erin's body showed she was beaten and stabbed to death. Police said the girl's body, which weighed only fifty-six pounds, showed other signs of trauma, but they refused to elaborate. It was later learned she suffered cuts to her neck and seven broken ribs, some of which punctured her lungs.[6]

A pathologist ruled out any physical evidence of a sexual molestation of the girl, making a motive even more mysterious.

Three weeks to the day that Erin was reported missing, police announced the arrest of fourteen-year-old Kevin L. Carter, a bulky eighth-grade student at South Side Middle School. As Captain Moberly had predicted, he was a resident of the Oaks Apartments, was well known to people in the neighborhood, and was acquainted with Erin. Carter's name was not immediately released—only that a fourteen-year-old boy was under arrest—but everyone in the area knew who the police had nabbed.

"He has given an oral admission that he is responsible for the death of Erin McKenzie," Anderson Police Chief Ron Rheam announced. "The juvenile and his parents have been very cooperative."[7]

Chief Rheam said police focused on Carter after several discrepancies were uncovered in his previous statements to police as a witness. He was known to be one of the last residents of the Oaks Apartments to have reported seeing Erin alive on the day she went missing.

Rheam said the boy admitted that he attacked the girl for fear she would reveal a secret, reporting that Carter had attempted to have sex with the girl and she threatened to tell.[8]

Neighbors at the Oaks were shocked and said it didn't seem possible that the polite young boy, Carter, could be a killer.

"I've got mixed emotions. He appeared to me to be a very normal fourteen-year-old boy," said Jane Banker, Carter's next-door neighbor. "I just can't believe it. They come from football practice and you'd speak to them and it was always, 'Yes, ma'am' and 'no, ma'am.' Very polite."[9]

Another neighbor, however, reported seeing Carter act in a violent way earlier in the summer of 1994 when he attacked another child with a baseball bat during an argument that erupted during a game. Conchita Angelotti said she and another neighbor yelled at Carter to stop hitting the child, and he did.[10]

"He was overwhelmed with anger," Angelotti said, but added he seemed confused about his actions when adults confronted him about it later that day.[11]

Angelotti said the outburst with the bat contrasted sharply with his tender care of his younger sister and the politeness he demonstrated to adults.[12]

Carter lived in a townhouse unit at the Oaks with his mother, stepfather, two younger brothers, and a younger sister. The door of their townhouse was just fifty-five yards from where Erin's body was found, police said. The boy had no prior juvenile record, authorities said.

Madison County Prosecutor William F. Lawler Jr. said that "it appears to be a strong case. The police have done a good job. It's been a rough job for them, but they've done a good job."[13]

Lawler vowed immediately to ask the court to transfer Carter's case from the juvenile court to adult court. He was successful at doing so, and Carter's trial for murder began in May 1995, handled by Lawler's successor, Rodney Cummings, the first Republican elected to county-wide office in Madison County in decades.

The trial would end, however, in frustration as jurors deadlocked 11-1 on whether to convict the young boy, causing Madison County Superior Court Judge Frederick Spencer to declare a mistrial.[14]

Cummings tried again in September 1995 as the Anderson community joined the rest of the nation in the distraction of the ongoing murder trial for O.J. Simpson underway in Los Angeles, California.

Cummings was pitted again against an outspoken court-appointed attorney for Carter, R.C. Dixon. Dixon complained from the start that he lacked adequate time to prepare a defense for Carter. He was appointed on July 17, 1995, and the trial opened on September 6, 1995.

Dixon repeatedly raised the issue of Carter's race, African American, and the victim's race, Caucasian, after no blacks were called for jury selection. He instead suggested the judge order sheriff's deputies to go out into the street and round up African Americans to serve on the jury. Judge Spencer denied Dixon's unusual suggestion.

The first day of testimony also took an unusual turn, as Dixon and Cummings engaged in back-and-forth negotiations outside the jury's presence to reach a plea agreement so that Carter could avoid a trial on the pending charges altogether.

The negotiations broke down, however, because of Cummings's insistence that Carter receive the maximum sentence of sixty years, and that he take the stand "and tell the people of this community exactly what he did."[15]

When testimony finally did get underway, jurors watched a videotape of where Erin's body was found and photographs of her body from her autopsy. A forensic expert then testified that blood found on Carter's shoes contained DNA that matched Erin McKenzie. Further evidence was presented that showed pubic hair found on Erin's body was consistent with that of Carter.

As the evidence against his client grew, Dixon asked the judge to declare a mistrial. He told Judge Spencer that some of the jurors may be aware of plea bargain discussions prior to testimony, and that such information would negatively influence them against Carter.

"Unless somebody tells me that jurors have been influenced by it, I am not going to do this," the judge said in denying Dixon's latest effort to buy more time.[16]

On the third day of the trial, jurors watched another videotape, this one Carter's statement to Anderson police detectives in which he confessed that he threw Erin on his mother's bed, undressed her, and tried to have sex with her, but was unsuccessful. Carter said Erin then laughed at him. He said Erin didn't say anything further or put of any sort of a fight.[17] Afterward, "I took her back in the woods and did what I did," Carter told detectives on the tape.[18]

Dixon told reporters he wanted to ask the court for a linguistic specialist to review the videotape of Carter's statement, which he believed had been edited or manipulated in some fashion by the police.[19]

Erin's grief-stricken mother, Beth McKenzie, testified about the moments after Erin's body was found. She said she saw a friend walking away from the site, and "he had his head down crying saying, 'She's gone, she's gone.'"[20]

Two other Oaks Apartments residents testified they saw Carter and Erin walking together near the front of the complex around 5:15 or 5:20 p.m., but noticed nothing out of the ordinary.

Dixon rested his case without calling any witnesses.

Jurors took not quote an hour to find Carter guilty of Erin's murder on September 12, 1995. As the verdict was announced, Erin's mother sobbed quietly at the back of the courtroom. None of Carter's family members were present for any portion of the trial, including the verdict.

Angered by the verdict, Carter told *Anderson Herald-Bulletin* reporter Ron Wilkins in an interview later that evening that "I'm pissed off because I didn't get a fair trial."[21]

He said the less than sixty minutes jurors used to determine his guilt was poof that it was unfair, the youthful Carter complained. "My age, the race. It's like a black man killing a white girl," he said. "I didn't do this shit. They're trying to get me for something I didn't do."[22]

Carter said he held out hope that an appeal could set him free. That would have to wait. First came sentencing on the conviction at hand, and Judge Spencer gave Carter a fifty-year term. Housing Carter in a state, maximum security correctional facility (which is standard for convicted murderers), however, would prove a challenge since Carter was only fifteen years old at the time of his sentencing.

Carter eventually filed appeals to his conviction that were heard by the Indiana Supreme Court. Carter, through his attorneys, argued that his conviction should be overturned because his confession was not obtained correctly. The justices found, however, that Carter and his mother had been advised of their rights, signed a waiver form, and agreed to answer detectives' questions. The court said, "The evidence indicates that Carter wanted to tell the police something and that the police did not induce him into making an involuntary statement."[23]

Ultimately, Carter served half of his fifty-year sentence, released from prison on October 25, 2012. On the day of his release, he had spent more than half of his life behind bars.

Endnotes

1. *Indianapolis News*, Aug. 25, 1994
2. *Anderson Herald-Bulletin*, Aug. 26, 1994
3. Ibid.
4. *Indianapolis Star*, Aug. 26, 1994
5. *Anderson Herald-Bulletin*, Aug. 27, 1994
6. *Anderson Herald-Bulletin*, Aug. 27, 1994; *Anderson Herald-Bulletin*, Sept. 9, 1995
7. *Anderson Herald-Bulletin*, Sept. 14, 1994
8. *Anderson Herald-Bulletin*, Sept. 15, 1994
9. Ibid.

10. *Indianapolis Star*, Sept. 15, 1994
11. Ibid.
12. Ibid.
13. *Anderson Herald-Bulletin*, Sept. 15, 1994
14. *Anderson Herald-Bulletin*, Sept. 6, 1995
15. *Anderson Herald-Bulletin*, Sept. 7, 1995
16. *Anderson Herald-Bulletin*, Sept. 8, 1995
17. *Anderson Herald-Bulletin*, Sept. 9, 1995
18. Ibid.
19. *Anderson Herald-Bulletin*, Sept. 12, 1995
20. *Anderson Herald-Bulletin*, Sept. 10, 1995
21. *Anderson Herald-Bulletin*, Sept. 13, 1995
22. Ibid.
23. *Kevin Lamar Carter v. State of Indiana*, Indiana Supreme Court, Cause No. 48C01-9411-CF 229

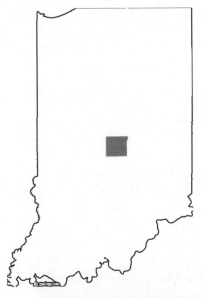

MARION COUNTY

VICTIM(S):
Marjorie V. Jackson, 66

PERPETRATOR(S):
Howard R. Willard, 38

DATE OF DEATH(S):
May 5 or 6, 1977

MOTIVE FOR MURDER: MARJORIE'S MILLIONS

In the years between 1970 and 1977, after Marjorie Jackson's husband died, she faced many of the same dangers and challenges many older widows know.

She struggled to keep up her large ranch-style home at 6490 Spring Mill Road in Indianapolis and over time, became more and more distrustful of those around her. It was a tough time in Marjorie's life—she was on her own and missing her beloved husband, Chester, who had created a good life for her.

As her distrust of others grew, she began to hide her valuables around her house. The big difference was that Marjorie's valuables were in the form of $7.88 million she withdrew from two Indianapolis banks over a period of five months in 1976, along with hundreds of thousands of dollars more in jewelry.

Her bank withdrawals worried bank and law enforcement officials considerably. Bank officials reported having to special order enough currency to fulfill the withdrawals Marjorie would demand. She placed all the money in paper grocery sacks and suitcases, putting them in the trunk of her car and casually driving home.

Marion County Prosecutor James F. Kelley said his office worked closely with the banks, providing a sheriff's deputy to follow her home after the big withdrawals.

"The fact that she was being followed was not to her liking," Kelley said. "We begged her to make other arrangements for the keeping of her money. She told me it was going to a safe place."[1]

Kelley added, "I told her her home was not a safe place. She assured me that it was."[2]

Just a year later, Marjorie would be dead and a big chunk of her millions would be scattered across the United States by thieves who descended on her almost as quickly as word got out that she was hiding money in her home.

The money was left to Marjorie by her successful husband, Chester H. Jackson, the son of Standard Grocery Stores founder Lafayette A. Jackson. Chester took over the stores in 1931 when his father, Lafayette, was shot and killed during a robbery of their flagship store in downtown Indianapolis.

During his tenure as head of the Standard stores, Chester grew the company to 250 stores before selling it to the National Tea Company in 1947. The proceeds allowed him to buy $14 million in coal stocks, $5 million in municipal bonds, $1 million in cash and Treasury bills, and other investments. In all, the Jackson estate was worth more than $25 million.

Marjorie's desire to take her money out of the Indiana National Bank, First Bank and Trust Company, and Peoples Bank, all of Indianapolis, was fueled in part by the embezzlement of almost $700,000 from a trust account by Herbert D. Biddle, a former vice president and trust officer at Indiana National Bank. Biddle was sentenced to ten years in prison for persuading Marjorie to place part of her investment in trust funds he drained.

Marjorie's lonely days at the end of her life came to an end sometime on either Thursday or Friday, May 5 or 6, 1977, after she suffered a single gunshot wound to the abdomen. She was left to bleed to death on her kitchen floor. She was last seen alive on Thursday morning in the yard outside her house, but an exact time for her death could never be determined.

Her body would have most likely lain there for a long time had those responsible for killing her not come back into her home to steal more money and then set it on fire. Washington Township firefighters, who had to cut through multiple locks in the fence surrounding Marjorie's house, put out a blaze at her home just before 7 a.m. on Saturday, May 7, 1977. They found Marjorie dead, although her body had suffered little injury from the fire that was contained to an entry foyer and family room.

What firefighters and deputies from the Marion County Sheriff's Department found next startled them even more than Marjorie's dead body. Scattered throughout the house were all the signs of a burglary, dumped-out drawers and jewelry boxes (some jewelry even dropped outside near a rear fence where the perpetrators had fled). But there were also trash cans, tool boxes, sewing kits, vacuum cleaner bags, and even the master bedroom headboard stuffed with more money than any of them had ever seen. Thousands of brand-new $100 bills were hidden, it seemed, everywhere. They also found a checkbook listing a remaining balance of $1.7 million.

In all, police counted at least $5,015,489 as being present in the house, Marion County Sheriff's Department Lieutenant Robert W. Kirkman told reporters. There was so much money; in fact, police displayed it in several grocery carts packed full. With that, Marjorie's murder went from a "standard" robbery-murder to one that would attract worldwide attention. All by itself, the $5 million left behind by the suspects made Marjorie's robbery the largest such robbery ever in U.S. history—and that didn't even count the still unknown amount the suspects had taken for themselves.

It was a predictable ending for those who were familiar with Marjorie. Five months earlier in January 1977, the Marion County Sheriff's Department and Marion County Prosecutor's Office had attempted to pursue burglary and robbery charges against two men who allegedly stole more than $800,000 from Marjorie's home during a bold heist while Marjorie reportedly hid out of sight inside the house. Marjorie, however, refused to cooperate with investigators and never acknowledged such a theft had occurred, and no charges were brought.

Marjorie's life had begun to come undone in other ways as well. Neighbors often complained that she did not keep her yard in good order or trim weeds or overgrown trees on her property. She refused to hire anyone to help keep up her land, despite having millions to her name. When one neighbor attempted to help her clear brush, she threatened him and ordered him off her property. The house fell into such disrepair (despite the fact that it sheltered millions of dollars within its walls) that most passersby thought it was abandoned or vacant.

Investigators had their hands full trying to figure out what was actually missing from the home after the fire was extinguished and Marjorie's body was discovered. Kirkman said all over the house, a variety of unusual finds popped up: Fifty loaves of bread, 150 pounds of coffee, about 200 dozen boxed cookies, and many large, fancy cakes bearing religious messages, such as "To God, from Marjorie."[3]

The cakes were not the only "gifts" left for God and Jesus. Kirkman said many more packages wrapped in aluminum foil were found, each bearing cards that said, "To God, from Marjorie," or "To Jesus Christ, from Marjorie Jackson." Police opened the packages, believing they contained more currency but found only items such as washcloths and other household items wrapped up.

Lieutenant Kirkman said, "I can't understand why a burglar would want to shoot her. He could have come by and hit [robbed] her again and again and again."[4]

Police at first worried that anyone smart enough to know that Marjorie's house was the ultimate burglar's "jackpot" may be difficult to apprehend. They needn't have worried. Those responsible for the heist and murder seemed incapable, from the start, of knowing what to do with the millions they took.

On Monday, May 9, 1977, just two days after Marjorie's body was found in her burning house, police arrested two men and confiscated more than $1.7 million in cash they believed was stolen from the Jackson home.

Twenty-nine-year-old Manuel E. Robinson and thirty-eight-year-old John Williams, both of Indianapolis, were detained after they attempted to trade in a brand-new Lincoln Continental just two days after purchasing it with $13,500 in cash. Serial numbers on the cash used to buy the car matched those on record with the Federal Reserve (which kept records of Marjorie's massive 1976 bank withdrawals). Robinson's girlfriend, twenty-two-year-old Annie K. Young, was also held after investigators found a half million dollars in her modest near north side apartment, the currency stuffed in her nightstand, her dresser, behind a wall hanging, and in a suitcase.

The FBI was called in to assist when investigators learned that other co-conspirators in the heist and murder had fled the state. On Thursday, May 12, 1977, authorities publicly announced they were also seeking thirty-eight-year-old Howard R. Willard of Mooresville, Indiana, and his forty-eight-year-old ex-wife, Marjorie L. Pollit, whom he divorced twice and with whom he was now living.

Investigators identified Willard as "the mastermind" of the heist as charges of first-degree murder, burglary, and arson were leveled against Robinson. Williams and Young were charged as accessories to murder. Williams later had his charges reduced when he led police to a bank safety deposit box where he had hid $40,000 in cash Robinson had given him.

Police said Willard, a maintenance man earning just $115 a week after being laid off from Kendrick Hospital in Mooresville, had led a series of burglaries at Marjorie's home in the two or three days before her body was discovered. They said he had met Robinson at the Shalimar Club, an inner-city bar located at 418 E. 22nd Street, and had plotted the heist with him there.

Police also learned that the day before Marjorie's body was found, Willard was buying drinks for all takers at Pat's Bar in Mooresville and at one point, lit a cigar with a $100 bill to prove his new-found wealth. That remarkable scene, where Willard was quoted by bar patrons as saying he was going to buy up the town of Mooresville and rename it "Willardsville," was preceded by an unusual car accident two days before when Willard totaled *his* brand-new 1977 Lincoln Continental purchased days earlier for $13,000.

Just before Willard and Pollit fled the area in a newer model Oldsmobile pulling a camper trailer, they stopped off at their daughter's Indianapolis apartment and gave her $400, which the daughter promptly spent.

Marion County Sheriff Donald E. Gilman, who along with investigators was fielding questions about the case from reporters around the world, made a personal appeal to Willard and Pollit to "turn yourselves in to the FBI in the interest of your own personal safety. Exaggerated stories and rumors that you have millions of dollars in your possession put your lives in great danger from unscrupulous persons."[5]

He reminded the two fugitives that the police knew the serial numbers of the money taken from Marjorie's home and "there is very little chance you will escape apprehension, and a great chance that harm will come to you at the hands of persons looking to gain whatever money you have in your possession."[6]

On Friday, May 20, 1977, police got their wish as an alert trailer park owner in Tempe, Arizona, notified authorities that a new couple had just arrived and were trying to buy a trailer from him for cash. Agents surrounded the small trailer Willard and Pollit had rented—inside, they found just $170,745 in cash stuffed in clothing and suitcases. Police also found the business card of noted defense attorney F. Lee Bailey in Pollit's purse as the couple had sought his advice during their two-week cross-country lam.

Eventually, investigators would find more of Marjorie's money. In July 1977, Pollit led FBI agents into the 114-degree heat of the Arizona desert outside Phoenix, where they dug a five-foot hole and found $1.67 million buried in boxes wrapped in duct tape. Pollit also led police to a bridge over the White River in Indianapolis where the .22-caliber weapon used to shoot Marjorie had been thrown. It was later recovered by police divers.

The total amount of funds recovered so far equaled $3,571,082, in addition to the $5,015,489 police reported finding stuffed in Marjorie's home.

"With the recovery of the money in Phoenix, we believe we have recovered substantially all of the money from the Jackson case," Prosecutor Kelley said.[7]

Police arrested Pollit's sister, fifty-three-year-old Robertina Harroll of Ringgold, Georgia, who they said traveled with Willard and Pollit to Arizona and received some of the money. She was arrested outside Atlanta, Georgia, but had only $4,000 in her purse at the time. Both sisters entered guilty pleas to federal charges of transporting stolen money across state lines and began cooperating with investigators.

"I am [pleading guilty] because I've prayed," Pollit told U.S. District Court Judge James E. Noland. "I am going to spend my life in heaven even if it means going to prison and living behind bars."[8]

Willard stood trial on an eight-count indictment for murder, burglary, robbery, conspiracy, and arson in November and December 1977 in Marion County—a trial initially broadcast nearly live on local television until an order from the chief justice of the Indiana Supreme Court warned the judge that the state's high court would not tolerate violations of Indiana's prohibition against cameras in the courtroom.

At Willard's trial, a pathologist testified that Marjorie's gunshot wound would not have been lethal had she received medical treatment in time. However, testimony revealed Willard had cut the phone lines to her home during one of the burglaries, making it impossible for the elderly woman to summon help.

A surprising witness came in the form of Ralph A. Wadsworth II, a former aide to the Indianapolis city controller. Wadsworth, an elected Republican precinct captain in Indianapolis, said he knew details of the January 1977 burglary of Marjorie's home that netted more than $800,000. Wadsworth told a tale of having met Willard earlier that year when someone told him Willard was an expert safe cracker, and he sought his help for a heist he was planning from the safe of a downtown store.

Wadsworth quoted Willard as saying, "I don't mind blowing the bitch away if she gives us any trouble."[9]

One of Willard's other ex-wives, Osa Willard, testified that she gave her former husband a gun in the weeks before Marjorie's death because he said he "had to have a gun." She added, "[Willard] said he didn't have enough guts to use it, that the other guy would have to use it."[10]

Pollit's testimony against the man she had married and divorced twice drew heavy interest as well. She testified that on Saturday night, May 7, 1977, Willard and Robinson came back to the Indianapolis apartment of Robinson's girlfriend, Young, with large amounts of cash. They spent hours dividing the money between them—about $1 million each for Willard, Robinson, Pollit, and Young. She also testified about helping dispose of the murder weapon.

She said Willard began drinking heavily in the next few days, complaining that he could still hear in his head the moans of the dying woman.

Pollit told jurors that it was attorney F. Lee Bailey's idea that she bury the money in the desert, but that Bailey had said Pollit and Willard would have to turn themselves in to authorities before he would represent them. A spokesman for Bailey told the *Indianapolis Star* that he had advised burying the money for safekeeping until he could negotiate the couple's surrender.[11]

On December 6, 1977, jurors found Willard guilty on all eight counts. On December 24, 1977, he was sentenced to life in prison. A federal judge added another fifteen years in January 1978 on federal charges leveled against Willard—to which he pled no contest.

Pollit and her sister, Robertina Harroll, were sentenced in the first week of January 1978 on lesser charges, having completed their deal to testify against Willard. Pollit received a five-year sentence from a federal judge, while Harroll was given a two-and-a-half year sentence. State charges against the two women were later dropped.

In April 1978, the trial of Manuel Robinson opened and included testimony by Pollit and his former girlfriend, Young. Marion County deputy prosecutor John Schwartz said they did not plan to call Willard because he was "so unpredictable and we can't depend on his testimony."[12]

Pollit testified that Robinson said he had to "shoot the woman" during the invasion and that Willard "was mad at Manuel because he almost got shot, too...."[13]

She testified that Robinson came up with the idea of starting the fire at Marjorie's home because he worried that his fingerprints were all over the house.

Young testified that Robinson and Willard "put the money on the floor and they divided it up. There were stacks of it ... and [Willard and Pollit] left and Manuel said, 'they stole it' and Manuel put his money on the bed and laid in it. The money stayed on the bed all night as we slept." [14]

On April 25, 1978, jurors delivered a surprise verdict. They found Robinson guilty on six counts of burglary, arson, and conspiracy but found him not guilty of murder and armed robbery. For his convictions, Robinson was given a ten- to twenty-year sentence and fined $17,000, although Robinson now claimed to be broke.

In July 1978, the final chapter was written when the last of seven men were sentenced for their roles in the January 1977 burglary at Marjorie's home. Police could not charge them before because she refused to cooperate with the investigation.

Endnotes

1. *Indianapolis Star*, May 9, 1977.
2. Ibid.
3. *Indianapolis Star*, May 8, 1977.
4. *Indianapolis Star*, May 9, 1977.
5. *Indianapolis Star*, May 14, 1977.
6. Ibid.
7. *Indianapolis Star*, July 2, 1977.
8. *Indianapolis Star*, July 15, 1977.
9. *Indianapolis Star*, Dec. 2, 1977.
10. Ibid.

11. *Indianapolis Star*, Dec. 3, 1977.
12. *Indianapolis Star*, April 19, 1978.
13. *Indianapolis Star*, April 20, 1978.
14. *Indianapolis Star*, April 21, 1978.

MARSHALL COUNTY

VICTIM(S):
Jacob Russell Saine, 43

PERPETRATOR(S):
John R. Burns, mid-20s;
Arthur Silbert, mid-20s;
Peter J. Fox, mid-20s;
Joseph Beyers, 21

DATE OF DEATH(S):
December 29, 1920

THE CITIZENS OF CULVER CONFRONT A ROBBERY-MURDER

Fifteen minutes after the Exchange Bank of Culver, Indiana, opened for business on Wednesday morning, December 29, 1920, three masked men entered the bank and began a bold robbery of the venerable institution. Before they were done, forty-three-year-old local hardware merchant and Culver Fire Chief J. Russell Saine would be dead, trying to defend the bank and the community.

Bank cashiers and tellers complied with orders barked to them by the heavily armed men to produce all of the bank's cash. Bank manager William O. Osborn was meeting in his private office at the time with William O'Connor, a Culver resident, when they overheard the robbery starting in the bank's main lobby.

O'Connor said two men in masks came into Osborn's office and ordered both of them to put their hands up and face the wall. The three men inside the bank worked quickly to gather up almost $20,000 in cash, O'Connor said, and noted one of the men struggled to put more than $5,000 in the pockets of his coat.

Osborn suffered a single blow to the back of his head from the butt of a revolver when he did not respond quickly enough to the bandits' demands.[1]

Henry Speyer, proprietor of a store near the bank, was alerted to the robbery when his young son discovered the holdup was underway and rushed in to tell his father. A postal clerk also saw the robbery starting and notified the town's telephone operator to sound the fire alarm.

At that news, "... the fire whistle aroused the citizens who hurriedly rushed to the scene, some of them arming themselves," the *Plymouth Daily Democrat* reported.[2]

Witnesses said a total of five bandits had approached the bank on Main Street in Culver in a black Marmon automobile sporting yellow wheels. They said three men entered the bank and two men remained outside, one behind the wheel of the car and the other on the sidewalk outside the bank.

As the fire whistle blew alerting residents to the robbery in progress, Fire Chief Saine exited his hardware store just across the street from the bank, armed with a shotgun. He got within thirty feet of the getaway car and ordered the driver to put his hands up when shots rang out. Saine was hit almost immediately, as was local salesman Jerome Zechiel, a bystander. The bullet pierced Saine's jaw, and he lay mortally wounded in the street. Zechiel was also seriously wounded with a bullet lodged in his hip. Ray Swigart, an employee of a diner on Main Street, had a bullet pierce his hat during the melee but escaped uninjured.

Both Saine and Zechiel were dragged inside nearby stores to get them away from the continued gunfire and later were transported to the hospital at the Culver Military Academy.

The Plymouth newspaper reported, "The timely arousal of the citizens was a surprise to the robbers as they had evidently contemplated that their deal could be pulled off without general knowledge and that they would be on their way with the loot before the Culver citizens in general were advised."[3]

"As the citizens collected, the two men in the car became alarmed and started their car, leaving the men inside the bank to find their own get-away," the *Democrat* noted.[4]

The *South Bend Tribune* reported it was Osborn who identified an exit for the men still inside the bank when the shooting started outside. "Show us another way out of this place, and be damned quick about it," Osborn said one of the men demanded.[5]

Osborn then led the three men to a trap door at the back of the bank that led to a basement room and exit to the alleyway behind. As the robbers made their way in the alley, the now growing Culver citizens' posse surrounded them and held them for the town marshal, William Murphy, and later the sheriff. Money from the bank was found in each of the men's pockets.

For a time, there was "grave danger of Culver citizens forgetting their good citizenship. However, some of the older more conservative heads got the ear of the crowd and advised moderation, appealing to the excited men to let the law take its course."[6]

A large crowd gathered later that same day in Plymouth, the county seat of Marshall County, when news spread that the captured suspects would be arriving on the afternoon train in order to be jailed at the Marshall County Jail.

Concerned about the growing crowd of the curious and the angry (for this was the first bank robbery ever in Marshall County), Sheriff W.H. Franklin snuck the men into town in a private automobile and lodged them in their jail cells before the crowd was ever aware the men were incarcerated.

One of the bandits who had fled in the getaway car, twenty-one-year-old Joseph Beyers of Knox, Indiana, was captured the next day in Starke County; he was injured. The driver of the car, later identified as Earl Wilt of Chicago, escaped and was never apprehended.

Police said Beyers was struck by buckshot from Saine's gun that penetrated the getaway car and was reported to be "suffering severely from his wounds" but remained lodged at the county jail in Plymouth—not the hospital.[7]

When Saine eventually succumbed to his injuries in late January 1921, the Marshall County grand jury promptly indicted Beyers and three of his accomplices, John R. Burns, Arthur Silbert, and Peter J. Fox, all of Chicago, for murder. The state would seek the death penalty against the men.

A judge later granted their request that their trial be moved one county east, to Kosciusko County, because of the intense publicity the case had generated in Culver and Plymouth. The four defendants guaranteed, however, that their May 1921 trial would continue to be big news in Indiana—even if it was moved to Warsaw—when they hired "famed and celebrated" defense attorney Clarence S. Darrow.[8]

"It is expected that Darrow will stage one of the most bitter fights ever waged in the county to save his clients from the electric chair," the *Warsaw Union* reported.[9]

It was unclear, however, how vigorous a defense the now sixty-four-year-old Darrow could handle as he suffered the continued effects of age.

The state relied heavily on eyewitness testimony, including that of Bert Rector, owner of the Rector Pharmacy in Culver, who grabbed his shotgun when he heard the alarm and witnessed Saine exchanging fire with the driver of the car (Wilt) and falling. Charles Pettis, the Main Street barber in Culver, also got off a few rounds into the fleeing car and provided witness testimony.

Charles McLean, a post office clerk at Culver, testified that he saw the men as they placed the masks over the faces and prepared to enter the bank. He positively identified them in court as Burns, Fox, and Silbert.

Jerome Zechiel, who was wounded in the shootout but survived, testified that as he drove into downtown Culver that morning he thought it odd that the town barber and Mr. Saine were both out on Main Street without their winter coats on.

He quickly noticed Saine was carrying a rifle. He said, "Saine raised his rifle and ordered the men to halt. The car was gaining speed when he shouted to the driver to halt. At this command, the car slowed down, and it appeared as if the two men were about to surrender ... as the car slowed down, both guns flashed. Almost instantly, the rifle of Mr. Saine fired, then his body tumbled to the ground."[10]

Despite huge expectations about the type of defense Darrow would raise, only one witness was presented by Darrow—defendant Beyers, the only local boy charged in the case.

Beyers told the court that he and Fox had planned the robbery the night before at his home in Knox and drove to Culver early the next morning. He said he had met Fox months before at a bar at the corner of State and Van Buren Streets in Chicago where they liked to drink. He said he did not know the other defendants from Chicago prior to the day before the robbery and was introduced to them by Fox.

Beyers said Fox had come up with the idea of the robbery because "he thought Culver would be a good place as it was a small town and dead in the winter time."[11]

In closing arguments, "Attorney Darrow delivered one of the finest pleas ever heard in this court room, it was a masterful piece of work and one that all who were fortunate enough to hear it will remember for the rest of their lives," the *Warsaw Union* gushed.[12]

In his statement, Darrow said, "I came to this town without any loot and no doubt will go back without any. I knew the robbery had taken place in such a manner as to attract a great deal of public notice. I knew every citizen had formed an opinion against the men implicated and that opinion was almost impossible to change. I also knew my clients had committed a robbery. I came down [here] because all my life I have been drawn by people who had no friends."[13]

Darrow focused his effort on trying to save the men from execution.

"The people [of Culver] went out with the intention of killing the defendants. I don't blame them for that, that's human nature ... but I don't believe there is a man in this county who would not save a life, if he could. I don't know why they should expect you to take their lives."[14]

He said, "The lives of these boys are in your keeping; if you sentence them to death, that power is yours and the Supreme Court of Indiana will never interfere ... This is your case. [The prosecutor] won't have to kill these men, it's your job. He won't have to turn on the electricity; he won't have to pronounce the doom upon a human being. That's your job, and it will rest upon you for the rest of your lives."[15]

Darrow told the jurors that the state "will ask you to kill these four boys so there won't be any bank robberies. If you think that will do it, go on and do it. It will be tough on the boys, but well worth the price. But people can't be scared into good by killing a few boys."[16]

Prosecutor Henry Graham countered, "It is not necessary for the state to introduce a single bit of evidence to show that these men, through premeditation or malice killed Jacob Saine. It is our law that anyone who kills any human being during a robbery is guilty of murder."[17]

Despite Darrow's apparently brilliant oratory, facts are facts, and the evidence presented by the state of the guilt of the four men was overwhelming. Jurors returned a guilty verdict just after 9 p.m. on May 19, 1921, but recommended a sentence of life imprisonment.

Kosciusko County Circuit Court judge L.W. Royse took up the issue of sentencing on May 27, 1921, and asked each of the young men if they had a statement to make. Burns told the judge, "We didn't get a square deal," and Fox repeated the theme by saying, "We sure got a dirty, rotten deal." Judge Royse then sentenced all four men to life in prison.[18]

Endnotes

1. *Warsaw Union*, May 13, 1921.
2. *Plymouth Daily Democrat*, Dec. 29, 1920.
3. Ibid.
4. Ibid.
5. *South Bend Tribune*, Dec. 30, 1920.
6. *Plymouth Daily Democrat*, Dec. 29, 1920.
7. *South Bend Tribune*, Dec. 30, 1920.
8. *Warsaw Union*, May 9, 1921.
9. *Warsaw Union*, May 10, 1921.
10. *Warsaw Union*, May 16, 1921.
11. *Warsaw Union*, May 18, 1921.
12. *Warsaw Union*, May 19, 1921.
13. Ibid.
14. Ibid.
15. Ibid.
16. Ibid.
17. Ibid.
18. *Warsaw Union*, May 27, 1921.

MARTIN COUNTY

VICTIM(S):
Tom Archer, 60;
Martin "Matt" Archer, 45;
John Archer, 30

PERPETRATOR(S):
Unknown members of a Shoals,
Indiana, lynch mob

DATE OF DEATH(S):
March 10, 1886

'JUSTICE BY JUDGE LYNCH'

The "hands of Judge Lynch" dealt with notorious brothers Tom and Martin Archer on the Martin County Courthouse lawn in Shoals, Indiana, a few moments after midnight on Wednesday, March 10, 1886.

"Precisely at 11:30, a vigilante committee of about one hundred, comprised of men from Martin and Orange counties, surrounded the jail," the *Indianapolis Times* reported. "The lynchers were very quiet and orderly."[1]

The members of the mob did not accept Martin County Sheriff John A. Padgett's refusal to open the doors of the jail, and "heavy blows demolished the door," but they were unable to open the cells holding Tom, age sixty, and his brother, Martin, age forty-five, with the rocks they had brought. A third cell held Tom's son, thirty-year-old John Archer. However, a key was produced, and all three men were led quietly from the jail where the men were lodged on a charge of murder in the death of John Bunch of Martin County.

"When the Archer gang saw the lynchers, they offered no resistance, and when asked if they had anything to say they refused to speak," the *Times* account continued. "Their hands were tied behind their backs and they were taken over to the Courthouse yard. They were again asked if they had any confession to make, and still no reply being given by any of them, they were unceremoniously strung up to young maple trees."[2]

"A farmer from Lost River Township, the home of the Archer's, extended the loop and attempted to slip it over the victim's head," Harry Q. Holt's *History of Martin County, Indiana* explains in his review of events. "However, his hands shook so badly that he made three or more futile attempts. A Shoals saloon keeper is said to have been standing nearby and stepped forward saying, 'Give it to me, I will put it around the son of a bitch's neck!'"[3]

A reporter on the scene dispatched that Tom Archer was hung first, although he was so tall his feet touched the ground as he died. His brother Martin was next, hanging right next to his brother on a big branch of the tree. John was hung last on another tree about thirty feet away.

"The eyes of both [Tom and Martin] are staring wide open, making a most horrible and ghastly site," reported a correspondent from Shoals.[4]

Holt wrote, "The sin-stained criminals asked for no prayers for their souls as they were transferred to God from the ends of hemp ropes fastened to the limbs of beautiful maple trees."[5]

The Archers, collectively, were blamed for a long line of crimes, whether they were responsible or not. The crimes charged against them included murder, robbery, and theft. "For 25 years, they have been a reigning terror in both Martin and Orange counties, and have terrorized the community in which they lived until the people didn't know when they went to bed at night whether they would be murdered before morning or their houses burned down," the *Times* report included.[6]

"After [the mob] had hung the Archers to the trees in the Courthouse yard, they stood quietly around until satisfied that the last breath had left their victims," the *Times* reported.[7]

Holt, in his account, added, "The mob completed its ghastly assignment with military precision and as a final gesture of triumph, stopped on the river bridge and fired revolvers."[8]

The Martin County coroner refused to cut the men's bodies down from the trees, although daylight had begun to break in the small town. "Word was sent in from the country not to cut them down, but to let them hang, as the country people wanted to see them hanging," it was reported.[9]

It was to be the first and only such hanging in Martin County history.[10]

Another member of the Archer gang, John Lynch, had been arrested as well and while held at the Daviess County Jail at Washington, Indiana, gave a confession implicating the Archers in the murder of Mr. Bunch.

Martin "Matt" Archer then told reporters on Tuesday, March 9, 1886, that Lynch was "playing a big game of bluff on the officials, for I am positively certain that he can make no confession that will criminate any of us."[11]

Martin Archer added a prophetic statement just hours before he would die at the hands of a lynch mob: "The people in this part of the country are down on us, and will not be satisfied until every last one of us are dead. For myself, I do not care, for I am not afraid of death, but the thought of leaving my wife and my little ones to the charity of the people completely unmans me."[12]

He added that he knew of rumors in the community of a possible lynching. "Life is sweet," he said, and if a mob came, "I will fight dearly for it."[13]

The *Indianapolis News* reported that the lynch mob was finally formed after a local man followed the Martin and Daviess county officials to a site where John Lynch pointed to the decomposed remains of Mr. Bunch that he said Martin Archer had forced him to help dump.[14]

Back in Shoals, the coroner finally relented at 10 a.m. and agreed to cut down the men's bodies, but not before a large throng of men, women, and children gathered to see the sight, "just in front of the entrance to the temple of justice, presenting a sight that appalled the stoutest hearts."[15]

The coroner ordered the bodies displayed on benches inside the Martin County Courthouse "and all during the day, hundreds of people from far and near swarmed in to gaze on the remains."[16]

No suspects were identified by Sheriff Padgett in the lynching, and no arrests were made. The confessing suspect, John Lynch, was reported to be "greatly affected" by the news of the lynching and had been "fear-stricken all day, crying and bemoaning his condition."[17]

The Archer family eventually retrieved the bodies for burial, although they remained "frantic over the affair."[18]

"The [Archer] women will be left destitute," the *Times* reported. "It was developed today that a letter was found from one of the Archers to his wife ordering her to warn all witnesses against the outlaws to refuse to testify against them, and that if any ... refused to keep silent, to kill them."[19]

John Lynch was eventually released from jail, not charged with the murder that was attributed to the Archers but that he admitted he assisted with under duress.

After learning the Archers were in fact dead, Lynch gave an interview to newspaper reporters and said, "John Archer was the cause of it all. These Archers forced me to assist in killing Bunch and I did it to save my life."[20]

"The three empty cells today presented a spectacle," the *Times* dispatch detailed. "The hats, coats and boots of the gang lay strewn around. The three cots where the outlaws slept remain just as they were when they arose from the cell of 'Judge Lynch' and went speedily to their doom."[21]

Endnotes

1. *Indianapolis Times*, March 10, 1886.
2. Ibid.

3. Holt, Harry Q. (1953) *History of Martin County, Indiana* Stout's Print Shop, Paoli, Indiana, page 183.
4. *Indianapolis Times*, March 10, 1886.
5. Holt, page 184.
6. *Indianapolis Times*, March 10, 1886.
7. Ibid.
8. Holt, page 184.
9. *Indianapolis Times*, March 10, 1886.
10. Ibid.
11. Ibid.
12. Ibid.
13. Ibid.
14. Ibid
15. *Indianapolis Times*, March 11, 1886.
16. Ibid.
17. Ibid.
18. Ibid.
19. Ibid.
20. *Indianapolis Times*, March 13, 1886.
21. *Indianapolis Times*, March 11, 1886.

MIAMI COUNTY

VICTIM(S):
James H. "Jimmy" Grund, 47

PERPETRATOR(S):
Susan A. Grund, 34

DATE OF DEATH(S):
August 3, 1992

A DIFFICULT WOMAN TO KEEP HAPPY

Susan Sanders was born into an impoverished Indiana family in October 1958, headed by a raging alcoholic father and a mother unable to control him. She would grow into a beautiful woman who found a way to make her looks work for her.

Her journey ends, however, in the same desperation in which she seemingly started life. At age thirty-four, Susan was arrested and eventually convicted of the murder of her once-loving and always-prominent husband, forty-seven-year-old former Miami County Prosecutor James H. "Jimmy" Grund.

Married three times, Susan's latest marriage to Jimmy, who was divorced from his first wife, represented a big achievement in her life. It seemed her life of poverty and all the struggles it brought were finally behind her. Susan was active in the Miami County 4-H Fair and briefly ran a woman's apparel shop in downtown Peru that later failed. As the wife of a former county official, she had "arrived"—albeit on a very small scale in the county-seat community of Peru, Indiana.

Susan's dream began to unravel for good on the evening of Monday, August 3, 1992. At 11:55 p.m., Susan frantically dialed the emergency room at Dukes Memorial Hospital in Peru (rather than 911) and reported she had found her husband shot in the couple's bedroom.

The community of Peru and Miami County was shocked. The son of a prominent Republican family and a former county prosecutor, James A. Grund—Jimmy Grund—had succeeded his father as prosecutor for one term from 1978 to 1982. Active as the attorney for the Peru Community Schools and owner of several businesses, Jimmy's life was one of accomplishment and respect.

"I knew him well on a professional basis, and that's probably why I am sitting here in my own shock," said Peru Schools superintendent Tom McKaig.[1]

Christian Sands, who worked in Jimmy's law practice in Peru, expressed what many were feeling: "This type of thing is not supposed to happen—not here. What a shame for the community."[2]

An autopsy helped authorities rule out the possibility of a suicide, consistent with the fact that no weapon was found in the expansive Grund home at 7 Summit Drive. There was no evidence of forced entry either.

Miami County Coroner Daniel Roberts, MD, was circumspect in listing a cause of death (in order not to jeopardize the criminal investigation), although the pathologist who performed the autopsy said Jimmy died of a gunshot wound to the head. Investigators quickly ruled out the idea that a defendant that Jimmy had sent to jail had anything to do with the crime. Detectives called that idea "unlikely."

On Friday, August 8, a memorial service for Jimmy was conducted in the chambers of the Miami County Courthouse in Peru. Among the speakers was Jimmy's father, James A. Grund, who told those assembled, "I will miss counseling with him. He did his very best to see that justice was done."[3]

Quietly, behind the scenes, investigators began to turn their focus on Jimmy's second wife, Susan. Her behavior was sometimes odd, and her relationship with investigators varied—from cooperative to dismissive.

Just a week after Jimmy's death, a struggle between Susan and the rest of Jimmy's family had begun over his will. By October, the first public fracture was reported.

Jimmy's children from his first marriage, James David Grund and Jama A. Lindral, contested the will filed by Susan saying it was a fake. In their complaint filed in the same court where their father had been memorialized just two months earlier, they declared, "The pretended will was a fraud. It was contained under coercion of Susan A. Grund, who is under investigation for the homicide of James H. Grund."[4]

It was the first time Miami County residents saw in print what many people thought and had said: Susan killed her husband.

Jimmy's kids became enraged when Susan attempted to open the will just five days after Jimmy died. The will itself was signed just three weeks before Jimmy was shot and just before he left for an Alaskan vacation—without Susan. The latest version left almost his entire estate, estimated to be worth more than $250,000, to Susan.

The suit by Jimmy's kids also revealed a fact that few knew about the social-climbing Susan: She was a convicted felon and therefore not allowed to be an executor of an estate under Indiana law.

Oklahoma City, Oklahoma, officials confirmed that Susan (who was then using the name Sue Ann Whited) had pled guilty to a felony child beating case on November 14, 1983. She had received a five-year sentence, all of it on probation.

The case centered on Susan's attacks on her three-year-old stepson, Thomas R. "Tommy" Whited III in May of 1983. The child was left with severe hearing and sight impairments and brain damage and was bedfast as a result of the beating.

By Monday, October 12, Miami County Prosecutor Wil Siders had no choice. He had to acknowledge publicly what the civil case brought by Jimmy's children had revealed: Susan Grund was a suspect in her husband's murder.

"She certainly is a suspect," Siders said. "She is not the only suspect."[5]

Siders and detectives continued their nearly round-the-clock work on the case until Tuesday, November 3, when headlines in the *Peru Daily Tribune* carried the news: "Susan Grund faces murder charge."

Indiana State Police arrested Susan at 4 a.m. that day at her mother's home in Vincennes, Indiana. Susan's sister, Darlene Worden, had given detectives a statement saying Susan had admitted she killed Jimmy.

Miami County Circuit Court Judge Bruce Embrey conducted the initial hearing for Susan where a not guilty plea was entered and she was ordered held without bond. Judge Embrey then immediately excused himself from the case because of his friendship with the victim, Jimmy Grund.

Prosecutor Siders' charges filled in some missing pieces of information. In addition to listing the will and its proceeds as a possible motive, Siders said Jimmy had been shot with a 9-mm pistol, the same type of gun stolen from Jimmy's oldest son, J. David Grund, on July 4. The prosecutor said Susan knew David had the gun and had been at his home unexpectedly on July 4. He said she asked to see the gun and asked how it worked—all of which was shown to her.

Susan's sister, Darlene, said had she insisted they take two stuffed teddy bears from the home after Jimmy's shooting. Both of those bears were recovered at Susan's mother's home in Vincennes, and police said one of them had been re-sewn shut in the back.

Susan's trial finally got underway a year later in September 1993. Jurors were selected from Kosciusko County in Warsaw and brought to Miami County to hear the case.

Right off the top, firearms experts testified that J. David Grund's 9-mm gun had been used to kill his father. A pathologist provided startling testimony when he reported that powder burns on Jimmy's face indicated the gun was held virtually up against his eyelid when it was fired, killing him instantly.

Jimmy's namesake son, J. David, then testified about Susan's July Fourth visit to his rural Miami County home and her intense curiosity about the gun. Siders surprised observers by asking J. David if he had ever engaged in a sexual affair with his step-mother, the defendant Susan Grund.

"I never had an affair with that woman," J. David said, looking at Susan.[6]

Zoyla Henderson, one of Susan's friends, testified that Susan often said she would kill her husband if he ever had an affair or tried to leave her. She said Susan was serious when she said, "I've been very explicit about it. He knows it."[7]

Henderson also told of an odd answer Susan gave to State Senator Thomas Weatherwax of Logansport at a Republican fundraiser. Senator Weatherwax inquired about what Susan did for a living, and Susan replied, "My full-time job is to set Jim up so well that if he ever leaves me, he'll leave with nothing."[8]

Susan's mother, Nellie Sanders, testified about a flowerpot found in her home (and one Susan had asked her to keep) filled with cement where police later found the murder weapon encased.

Her sister, Darlene Worden, testified as well and said Susan had told her the shooting at their home was supposed to be a murder-suicide. Worden told the jury that Susan said, "I shot Jimmy."[9]

Worden also said, "[Susan] said, 'Jimmy didn't want to go on living because I'm beautiful and he's getting fat and old. He thought he was losing me.'"[10]

Under cross-examination, Worden didn't mince words. When asked about her sister Susan, Worden said, "She's a liar. She's always been a liar."[11]

As the defense opened its case, Susan Grund took the stand and immediately admitted hiding the gun when she found her husband shot on the sofa in their bedroom. She said it was to protect his son, J. David, whom she thought might have shot his father.

During her testimony, Susan broke down frequently (as she had between hearings, complaining of headaches and dizziness). Asked why she had never told police about finding the gun, she said, "Because I didn't want them to know, because I'd touched it, and it was David's gun."[12]

She then contradicted J. David's earlier testimony and said she and her young stepson had carried on a sexual affair from May 1990 to June 1992, without her husband Jimmy knowing. Her continued testimony attempted to implicate J. David as the one who wanted Jimmy dead—detailing fights and arguments the two had engaged in over the years.

Jurors soon got the case—but *without* knowing about Susan's previous conviction for the brutal beating and maiming of her stepson in Oklahoma.

With just over fifteen hours of tedious deliberations completed, the trial came to a surprising end. Just before 1:30 a.m. on Friday, October 1, 1993, Special Judge John F. Surbeck, Jr., declared a mistrial after jurors announced they were hopelessly deadlocked.

"We feel we will not come to a unanimous decision," jury foreman Joe Shoemaker told Judge Surbeck. Shoemaker said twelve separate votes had been taken, and they remained deadlocked.[13]

Prosecutor Siders was not giving up. He re-filed murder charges, and a second trial started in March 1994, again with a jury selected from Kosciusko County. Prosecutors called thirty-seven witnesses, but everyone just wanted to hear from one witness: Susan Grund.

In her testimony this time, she met with the anger of Judge Surbeck when she continually made statements such as, "It's difficult [to respond] when you're confined as to what you can say," and "There's so much I can't say."

Siders argued that Susan was intentionally trying to mislead the jury into thinking there was other evidence they were not hearing. Judge Surbeck directed Susan, "You are not to editorialize on my evidentiary rulings." He warned her if she continued to respond as she had so far, "I'll have no choice but to mistrial this case and we'll do it again in six months."[14]

This time, jurors again deliberated at length—more than thirteen hours— but the outcome was different. Just after midnight on Wednesday, March 16, 1994, jurors declared Susan guilty as charged.

Susan was back in court a month later to face sentencing. Judge Surbeck sentenced her to sixty years in prison, the maximum sentence allowed.

J.M. Eichorn, an Oklahoma City Police detective who had investigated the beating of Susan's stepson in 1983, testified about the previous case. He told the judge that Tommy, now thirteen years old, was deaf, mentally disabled, nearly blind, and required the constant care of a nursing home. He said Tommy had to be strapped into a chair or his bed to remain in place, had one hand permanently curled, and had frequent seizures. He knew one word—"food."

"Today is his day," Eichorn said. "Tommy got justice for the suspended sentence she received. I'm sure Tommy would thank that judge if he could."[15]

Eichorn said Susan was "a pretty woman, but she's deadly." He recalled in anger the photos showing the extent of Tommy's beating and his severe sunburn after Susan decided he had been bad and was forced to stay in the bed of a pickup truck for hours in the blazing Oklahoma sun.

Susan is not eligible for parole before 2034—when she'll be seventy-six years old.

Endnotes

1. *Peru Daily Tribune*, Aug. 4, 1992.
2. *Peru Daily Tribune*, Aug. 5, 1992.
3. *Peru Daily Tribune*, Aug. 8, 1992.
4. *Peru Daily Tribune*, Oct. 10, 1992.
5. *Peru Daily Tribune*, Oct. 13, 1992.
6. *Peru Daily Tribune*, Sept. 28, 1993.
7. *Peru Daily Tribune*, Sept. 29, 1993.
8. Ibid.
9. *Peru Daily Tribune*, Sept. 30, 1993.
10. Ibid.
11. Ibid.
12. Ibid.
13. *Peru Daily Tribune*, Oct. 1, 1993.
14. *Peru Daily Tribune*, March 15, 1994.
15. *Peru Daily Tribune*, April 16, 1994.

MONROE COUNTY

VICTIM(S):
Won-Joon Yoon, 26;
Ricky Byrdsong, 43

PERPETRATOR(S):
Benjamin N. Smith, 21

DATE OF DEATH(S):
July 4, 1999

HATE COMES HOME

On the Fourth of July in 1998, Benjamin Smith made his presence known in Bloomington and around the Indiana University campus with a series of racist, white supremacy leaflets that he diligently distributed.

One year later, police and the community would again notice Smith, but this time, with fear and loathing as he concluded his three-day killing spree by finding his last victim—twenty-six-year-old Korean doctoral student Won-Joon Yoon—in Bloomington.

Smith would never answer for his crimes. He engaged police in a low-speed chase as he fled in a stolen minivan. Near Salem in southern Illinois, around 9:30 p.m. Sunday evening, the suspect shot himself twice at close range. As the van crashed and with his shirt already soaked in blood, he fired a third, fatal shot into his own neck.

In his wake, two people, including Won-Joon, were dead and fifteen others were injured.

The investigation would reveal that the life led by Smith was spiraling out of control, although experts said his July Fourth killing spree would have been difficult to predict.

In Indiana, he waited until just before 11 a.m. Sunday morning, July 4, 1999, to attack as Won-Joon and others walked to the Korean United Methodist Church for Sunday morning worship services. Witnesses reported hearing loud shots ring out in front of the church at 1924 E. Third Street in

Bloomington and seeing Won-Joon fall to the ground. A blue Ford Taurus was seen fleeing the scene.

As worshipers inside the church rushed outside to aid him, it was clear Won-Joon was mortally wounded. Two of the bullets had struck him in the back. He was dead on arrival at Bloomington Hospital.

One witness who heard the shots and saw the Ford fleeing and running red lights followed it east all the way to Nashville, Indiana, and provided police a license plate number and a good description. Both matched Smith—a figure familiar to Monroe County officials.

The Bloomington shooting was just the latest to capture national attention during the long Independence Day weekend. Two previous days of hate-motivated shootings had already occurred in Illinois. Now, the hate crimes had come home to Indiana.

On Friday night, July 2, police were busy in the Chicago area investigating the shooting of six Orthodox Jews who were shot and wounded as they left a synagogue there. Within an hour, a second shooting, this one fatal, was reported in nearby Skokie, Illinois, that left former Northwestern University basketball coach Ricky Byrdsong dead as he walked along a neighborhood street. Finally, just before 9:30 p.m., police responded to a call in Northbrook, Illinois, where an Asian-American couple reported being shot at several times following a traffic accident—both were uninjured.

The FBI and Illinois and Indiana law enforcement agencies were on high alert. Police had already begun to suspect Smith—and knew for certain the crimes so far were hate-motivated.

Then, just after 1:15 p.m. Saturday, July 3, a thirty-one-year-old black man crossing the street further downstate in Springfield, Illinois, was shot in the buttocks. Fifteen minutes later, two other men were fired upon but not hit by a passing motorist driving a blue Ford Taurus.

Just before 3 p.m., shots rang out again as a black minister crossing the street in Decatur, Illinois, was shot twice—a third shot knocking a cell phone from his hands.The shooting was not over, however. Around midnight near the University of Illinois campus at Champaign-Urbana, Illinois, six Asian students reported being shot at as they stood on a street corner. One man was seriously injured when bullets struck him in the leg and the arm. Again, the vehicle description matched the earlier assaults.

All was quiet until the attacks resumed the next morning, a sunny July Fourth Sunday morning in quiet Bloomington. Again, the shots were deadly.

"This is a nightmare come true," said Jeffrey Willsey of Bloomington United, a group that had formed a year earlier after the prolific Smith plastered the town with hate-filled leaflets and brochures. Smith was eventually traced to a dozen incidents of placing offensive leaflets, most of them linked back to the dubious World Church of the Creator, throughout Bloomington and nearby Ellettsville.[1]

Smith had appeared in a 1998 documentary on WTIU-TV, the PBS affiliate in Monroe County, in which he defended the leaflets. As he put it, "All it really is is the truth."[2]

In a videotaped interview completed just two weeks before the shootings, Smith told an interviewer that the nation's whites were involved in "a life or death struggle for the future of our race."[3]

After the shootings, Bloomington Mayor John Fernandez said the city had "a great deal of work to do ... to try and begin the healing process. It's the same throughout our country, where we have to bring this kind of hate-driven violence to an end."[4]

President Bill Clinton offered remarks on the two-state killing spree that had become headline news across the U.S. Clinton called the shootings "a rebuke of the very ideals that got us started." He added that the acts were a stern reminder that "... we should rid our hearts of hatred immediately."[5]

The Indiana victim, Won-Joon, had just moved to Bloomington and had yet to begin his doctoral studies in economics at Indiana University. His family said he had wanted to travel to his home in Seoul, South Korea, that summer, but they had decided he should stay in Bloomington and make friends and get acquainted with his new community.

His father and mother, Shin Ho and Kang Soon Lee Yoon, traveled through the night to reach Bloomington to see their son's body before it was turned over to a funeral home. At the hospital where Won-Joon's body rested, ten of his fellow students had maintained a vigil in an adjacent room until his parents could arrive.

Shin Ho, in an emotional news conference on the sidewalk outside the very church where his son had been shot, said he had just talked to his son a day before. He had told him, "You have to be sincere, you have to be amicable, and you have to be hospitable to all."

Nearby was a makeshift memorial that Indiana University students and community members had begun to create in Won-Joon's honor.

"With his death, gone are the dreams, hopes, and happiness my family has had with my son, Won-Joon," Shin Ho said. "He was kind, generous, and caring to everyone he met in his community."[6]

Shin Ho tried to remain focused on his "quiet, young bright [son] from Korea who wanted to pursue his career in this country."

His voice rose with emotion, however, as he stated, "He was gunned down by one insane, full of racial hatred, young American man. What is America, which is known as the world model country, doing while the American flag, a symbol of freedom, equality, and justice, is being torn apart by a gun spree? We believe Won-Joon, my beloved son, sacrificed himself to prevent Benjamin Smith from killing innocent people anymore."[7]

At the time of his death, Won-Joon had already completed a degree at Southern Illinois University and had studied during breaks at Harvard University.

On Monday, July 12, an overflow crowd of mourners and supporters packed the Indiana University Musical Arts Center for a two-hour memorial service for Won-Joon and the other victims. U.S. Attorney General Janet Reno attended on behalf of President Clinton and read remarks the president wrote for the event.

Clinton said, "This ceremony of healing and unity is a powerful and moving response by the Bloomington community to the violence that ended the lives of Won-Joon Yoon and Ricky Byrdsong, and that injured and terrorized so many others."[8]

Reno praised the efforts of the Bloomington United group by saying, "The people of this community came together not quite a year ago to speak out against intolerance. You confronted the message of hatred. It was the right thing to do. This nation must follow your example."[9]

Meanwhile, the investigation into Smith and his path of destruction focused quickly on how a man with such a record and hateful political perspective so easily obtained weapons and so easily moved about undetected across two states in three days.

A native of Illinois, Smith had moved to Bloomington after dropping out of the University of Illinois in February 1998 after facing disciplinary action for fighting and possession of marijuana and knives in a university dorm. He also had prior arrests for battery against a girlfriend in Skokie and Wilmette, Illinois, (the latter community being his hometown).

Initially, his leaflets distributed at Indiana University—met with anger by most that received them under their windshield wipers or in their mailboxes— were from the White Nationalist Party. Later, the materials supported the World Church of the Creator, also known as the Creativity Movement.

Most considered Smith non-violent but weird. Most also knew that the World Church movement in liberal Bloomington consisted of only one man: Smith himself.

As Smith's 1999 crimes came into focus, Matthew Hale, the twenty-seven-year-old leader of the World Church, told reporters that he thought Smith was upset because of Hale's struggles to win a law license in Illinois. The Illinois State Bar Association had determined Hale's activities as leader of the white supremacy group rendered him unfit to practice law in that state, despite having completed law school.

"I strongly suspect that the denial of my law license set him off," Hale told CNN. "Why? Because of the timing involved and because I know he was very passionate about me getting my law license. He had testified for me at the hearing I had on the matter."[10]

Hale also made certain reporters knew Smith was no longer considered a member of the World Church since his $35 annual membership fee had not been received for 1999.

Hale called Smith's actions "sad" and said, "If I had any inkling of this [violence], I would have, of course, taken him aside and said, 'Ben, brother, this isn't the way.'"[11]

It was not the first time, however, the "church" had been linked to murder. In fact, Hale had become leader of the church when its founder lost a civil suit in Florida pertaining to the murder of a black sailor there by members acting on behalf of the group.

Hale and his organization faced multiple civil suits following Smith's rampage that many believed was inspired by Hale himself. It was a futile effort. In April 2005, Hale was sentenced to forty years in prison for his role in trying to hire an FBI informant to kill U.S. District Court Judge Joan Humphrey Lefkow of Chicago.[12]

Harlan Loeb of the Anti-Defamation League noted the "church" had no building, no physical presence beyond Hale's Web site and home-based office, and was nothing more than a group set up to promote "gutter-level racism and bigotry."[13]

In the wake of Smith's shootings, federal authorities arrested sixty-four-year-old Donald R. Fiessinger of Peoria, Illinois, who they said illegally sold Smith two firearms used in the rampage. Fiessinger told ATF agents that Smith said he planned to use the guns for hunting and that he did not know of Smith's bigoted views.

Smith's parents, Kenneth and Beverly Smith of Wilmette, Illinois, issued a public apology for their son's deadly actions. "We have tried to think what we could have done differently, but like the parents of other good children who become criminal ... we found no answer," their statement said.[14]

In the years following Won-Joon's death, Indiana University students erected a stone monument in his honor, and the university has annually awarded an academic scholarship to a worthy student in his name.

Shin Ho, Won-Joon's father, has returned to Bloomington frequently, a city he had never seen prior to the day he came to collect his son's remains. A year after the murder, he said he came back not to portray his son as a "martyr," but to help the world remember "a simple Korean student" whose death calls people to love and peace.

He told reporters, "We found the presence of God … and we are meeting every day with the amazing grace and love of God."[15]

In a moving account in the *Bloomington Herald-Times*, reporter John Meunier noted, "[Shin Ho] paused for a moment, his hands together as if ready to pray. In the silence—in the passing of an unspoken memory—the tears welled up in his eyes, the red blush of grief erased the bliss from his expression and the sorrow poured forth."[16]

Won-Joon's fiancée, Catherine Matthews, a doctoral student in education, said she hated living in Bloomington where the man she was to marry was murdered "because someone thought he wasn't good enough." But the Tennessee native said she stayed for her studies and to be somewhere where people remember Won-Joon's death and its meaning.

"I realized that I couldn't be in a place that didn't know what had happened to the most important person in my life—the most important event in my life," she said. "… So as difficult as it is to be here, I think it would be more difficult to be someplace else … His death has to matter."[17]

Endnotes
1. *Bloomington Herald-Times*, July 4, 1999.
2. CNN, July 6, 1999.
3. Associated Press, Aug. 28, 1999.
4. CNN, July 4, 1999.
5. CNN, July 6, 1999.
6. *Bloomington Herald-Times*, July 7, 1999.
7. Ibid.
8. *Bloomington Herald-Times*, July 13, 1999.
9. Ibid.
10. CNN, July 5, 1999.
11. CNN, July 5, 1999.
12. Associated Press, April 7, 2005.
13. CNN, July 5, 1999.
14. Associated Press, Aug. 28, 1999.
15. *Bloomington Herald-Times*, July 5, 2000.
16. Ibid.
17. Ibid.

MONTGOMERY COUNTY

VICTIM(S):
Nadine Baird, 32;
Kathryn Baird, 78;
Arthur Paul Baird I, 68

PERPETRATOR(S):
Arthur Paul Baird II, 39

DATE OF DEATH(S):
September 6 and 7, 1985

THREE MURDERS PROMPT A DEATH PENALTY DEBATE

On Friday night, September 6, 1985, Arthur Baird II began a series of murders that would baffle investigators and his community for decades. On that night, Baird strangled to death his thirty-two-year-old wife, Nadine, who was six months pregnant, inside the trailer home they shared on property owned by Baird's parents in rural northeast Montgomery County.

For the next several hours, he sat watching TV, holding the limp body of his dead wife until it was time to go to bed. The next morning, Saturday, September 7, 1985, he awoke and fed the chickens on the property as he was expected to do and visited his parents' farmhouse several hundred yards from his own trailer. He asked his mom, seventy-eight-year-old Kathryn Baird, to give him a haircut. She obliged and also began preparing a meal for Baird and his namesake father, sixty-eight-year-old Arthur Paul Baird I.

Before the morning was out, his parents would also be dead, victims of multiple stab wounds, just one year before their fiftieth wedding anniversary. His mother was found slain on the kitchen floor where she had begun meal preparations. His father lay on the floor just inside the back door of the farmhouse. Initial fears that Baird's grandmother, Nora Fleming, who lived in a second trailer on the Baird farm may also have been harmed were relieved when it was learned she had been away visiting other relatives when the attacks occurred.

Police learned of the murders when Nadine's father came to visit his daughter and found her dead.

The case would prove not only a baffling for investigators—but was a historic one: It was the first triple murder case in Montgomery County history. It was the first murder in the county in seven years.

Baird himself left a letter asking for forgiveness and inexplicably fled south about 180 miles to Huntingburg, Indiana, where he was arrested as he sat watching a softball game in a city park there on Sunday, September 8, 1985.

Baird's actions were hard to understand. Described as kind but shy and quiet, he had always projected an image of being a highly religious man. He was selected to be a deacon at the church of which Baird and his wife, Nadine, were active members. Baird was unemployed at the time, laid off months earlier from his job at United Farm Tool Company. Investigators wondered if a large stack of past-due bills they found inside the couple's trailer combined with Nadine's pregnancy may have led Baird to act in a rash fashion.

Montgomery County Prosecutor Wayne Steele announced immediately that he would seek the death penalty against Baird and added charges for feticide because of the death of Nadine's unborn child—the couple's first. While an exact motive remained unknown, Steele reminded reporters that a motive was not required under Indiana law to prove murder.

One of Nadine's friends, Kemla Gerde of Romney, Indiana, told the *Crawfordsville Journal Review* that Nadine was very excited about the prospect of being a new mother. "She was a very sweet, caring person," Gerde said. "I never heard a hard word out of her."[1]

She said Nadine had approached her pregnancy seriously, following her doctor's orders precisely and altering her diet just has he had instructed. "Nadine was the type of person who made sure she did everything just right," Gerde said. Her baby was due in mid-December.[2]

Gerde may have been one of the last people to see Nadine alive. She visited with the couple at their trailer on Wednesday evening, September 4, and played cards with them. She told police Baird was extremely quiet that evening, saying little.

She added a fact Nadine had confided to her, and one apparently few knew. Nadine feared Baird, but she could never get her to say why.

The contents of the letter Baird left at his parents' farmhouse were revealed in the subsequent days. In it, he wrote, "I failed God, wife, parents and everybody else. I am sorry I had to do what I have done."[3]

Baird's letter also said, "My mind broke and I had complete breakdown. I did not plan on this happening. I planned on taking care of Nadine and everybody else. I was looking forward to farming and having a family. I do love Nadine and parents."[4]

The note suggested Baird planned to turn himself in but asked police to not come looking for him. "I know I've done wrong. I need time alone to make my peace with God. I have to live with what I have done, so please leave me alone. I will turn myself in, in time … I will come for punishment in due time."[5]

Baird rejected plea agreements offered by the state and so a six-day trial to consider his fate began in February 1987. At trial, he claimed he was insane at the time he killed his family. His lawyers presented evidence that Baird had become extremely delusional. He had become convinced the federal government was going to pay him $1 million for his advice on how to solve the national debt. Baird was so convinced of the $1 million coming his way, he had made plans to purchase a $575,000 farm in Montgomery County.

Dueling psychiatrists testified at trial. Some said that Baird was not insane, while others said he lacked the requisite capacity to understand the wrongfulness of his acts.

Regardless, jurors found him guilty of three counts of murder and one count of feticide on February 17, 1987. The jury recommended the death penalty for the murder of Baird's parents but not for the murder of his wife. The judge subsequently sentenced him to death for his parents' deaths and to another sixty-eight years in prison for the death of Nadine and her unborn baby.

Baird lost various appeals of his sentence along the way through state and federal courts. His later appeals continued to argue that because of his mental illness, he was not competent to be put to death for the crimes.

In one appeal, he noted that he "did not choose to murder his wife and parents" since "his *hands* murdered his wife and parents while under the control of unseen forces and persons."[6]

In July 2005, Baird's court-appointed appellate attorney, Sarah L. Nagy, asked the state to delay his execution scheduled for August 31, 2005, so that an independent psychiatric review of his condition could be conducted. She said, "His thoughts are as real to him as a sane man's, though they be insane thoughts. Baird cannot prepare for his death because he does not believe it will occur. He operates under the delusion that he will wake up and God will make [time turn] back to the day before the murders occurred."[7]

Nagy backed up her claims with a report from Dr. Phillip M. Coons, a retired professor of psychiatry from the Indiana University School of Medicine. Dr. Coons concluded that Baird was "grossly psychotic and delusional" and "thinks his sentence is unjust" because "his *hands* murdered his wife and parents."[8]

As his scheduled execution date closed in, members of the Indiana Parole Board conducted a lengthy hearing to determine whether to recommend a stay for Baird. The board voted three to one against clemency on August 24, 2005, despite a report from a state-hired psychiatrist, James H. Lowery, who said Baird appeared to be highly psychotic and unable to distinguish reality from imagination.

Despite that information, Parole Board member Thor R. Miller declared that Baird "has played an elaborate game of deceit and misrepresentation that has served to delay the imposition of the death penalty for nearly two decades. This is nothing more than a brutally cruel man."[9]

Parole Board Chairman Raymond Rizzo said he did not know why Baird had killed his family, but "each time he tells the story of what happened on that day, it's embellished."[10]

Days later, the Indiana Supreme Court once again ruled that Baird's execution should go forward (although on a divided three to two vote). On the same day, the editors of the normally conservative *Indianapolis Star* editorialized that Baird should not be executed until serious questions about his mental status were resolved.[11]

The issue of Baird's sanity and the appropriateness of the death penalty came to a head on Monday, August 29, 2005, just forty-eight hours before he was to be executed. Governor Mitch Daniels commuted Baird's sentence to life in prison without parole, sparing him death. Daniels' move, however, did not end the ongoing debate of whether the mentally ill should be executed.

Governor Daniels said, "I reached today's decision without substituting my judgment for others on the ambiguous issue of Mr. Baird's degree of insanity. To me, it suffices to note, had the sentence of life without parole been available in 1987, the jury and the State would have imposed it with the support of the victims' families."[12]

Endnotes

1. *Crawfordsville Journal Review*, Sept. 10, 1985.
2. Ibid.
3. *Crawfordsville Journal Review*, Sept. 11, 1985.
4. Ibid.
5. Ibid.
6. Psychiatric report contained in appeal documents, Indiana Supreme Court Order, Case No. 54S00-0505-SD-240, Aug. 22, 2005.
7. *Indianapolis Star*, July 26, 2005.

8.   *Indianapolis Star*, Aug. 23, 2005.
9.   *Indianapolis Star*, Aug. 25, 2005.
10. *Indianapolis Star*, Aug. 28, 2005.
11. *Indianapolis Star*, Aug. 26, 2005.
12. *Indianapolis Star*, Aug. 30, 2005.

MORGAN COUNTY

VICTIM(S):
Carol M. Jenkins, 21

PERPETRATOR(S):
Kenneth C. Richmond, 70

DATE OF DEATH(S):
September 16, 1968

THIRTY YEARS OF SILENCE BROKEN, AN UGLY TRUTH REVEALED

On September 16, 1968, Carol Jenkins of Rushville, Indiana, began a new temporary job—one that would take her to her death.

Three decades of questions and suspicion cast a shadow over the community of Martinsville, Indiana, until the truth was finally known about what happened to Carol that Monday night so long ago.

What was always known was that twenty-one-year-old Carol was an attractive but shy black woman working in a predominantly white community as part of a group of young people dropped off in quiet Martinsville that afternoon to go door to door and sell Colliers encyclopedias. A petite 5'3", 110-pound woman, Carol had already called on several homes in the east end of Martinsville when her troubles first started.

Around 7:40 p.m., as she called on the Don Neal home at 1242 E. Columbus Street, she told Mrs. Neal that two men in a black, four-door 1965 Mercury Comet had been harassing her as she walked down the street. They called Martinsville Police and Officer Clarence Richards questioned Carol about her encounters with the men and patrolled the area in his squad car trying to locate the car.

Mrs. Neal, still concerned for Carol, offered to drive her to meet her friends who were on other streets in the area trying to sell encyclopedias. Carol declined her offer and said she would be okay. She was last seen walking

271

about 8:30 p.m. near Home Avenue and Washington Street. She got as far as Morgan Street and walked west to Lincoln Street where she dropped her sales notebook. Her body was later spotted 105 feet further west.

Morgan County Coroner James Summers said Carol had suffered a fatal stab wound to the heart. He found another gash on her chin (caused either by the knife or her fall). She had not been molested or robbed (her purse was intact and with her when she fell). She was pronounced dead at 9:25 p.m.

Carol had taken the encyclopedia sales job to help make some money while she was off work from the Philco Plant in Connersville, which was enduring a lengthy strike at the time.

Police questioned numerous witnesses and potential suspects but made no arrests. They also defended themselves against accusations they had not responded appropriately enough when Carol first called them to report the two men bothering her.

"When the officer spoke to her that night, he offered to take her to her friends, but she thought it was unnecessary," said Morgan County Prosecutor Richard Bray.[1]

Carol's Rushville funeral on September 18, 1968, drew "mourners and the curious and the disbelieving" as "each sorrowful exclamation was followed by a heartfelt epithet which recalled Miss Jenkins as a fine and wonderful girl."[2]

Martinsville Mayor James D. Garner wired Rushville Mayor Raymond Gibson with this message: "Martinsville citizens deplore the terrible murder of Carol Jenkins. Investigation is being pressed by authorities. Please convey my condolences to the family."[3]

And that was where the mystery of the murder of Carol Jenkins would stay—in a sad part of everyone's memory and with the realization that no one had been held accountable. The case was never closed by Morgan County officials, but it was considered terribly cold.

It would remain that way until a startling development in May 2002, when Indiana State Police and Morgan County officials announced the arrest of seventy-year-old Kenneth C. Richmond of rural Hendricks County for the murder of Carol Jenkins. His arrest would be national news, as the *New York Times* and other national media dispatched reporters to Martinsville to cover the stunning development.

The frail and sickly Richmond had been a focus of the investigation since an anonymous letter was delivered to investigators months earlier implicating him in the death. The letter came from someone who knew a lot of the details of Carol's brutal death. The letter, it turns out, came from Richmond's daughter, Shirley McQueen, who witnessed the murder as a seven-year-old girl on that night long ago.

McQueen's story was made all the more believable because of a key detail she remembered: Carol was wearing a bright yellow scarf the night she died, a fact never revealed publicly.

McQueen, now forty years old, told an incredible story that her alcoholic father, a vitriolic racist and former member of the Ku Klux Klan, was incensed to see a black woman walking a neighborhood street in Martinsville. After harassing Carol verbally, he eventually jumped from his car and plunged a screwdriver he found in the car into Carol's heart.

Devastated by what she saw, McQueen said she sat silently in the car as her father attacked Carol. She quoted him as saying, "She got what she deserved." When they got home, Richmond gave his little daughter $7—one dollar for each year of her life—to buy her silence about what she had seen. "He said, 'It was our secret,'" McQueen said.[4]

Morgan County Prosecutor Steven Sonnega admitted it would be difficult to proceed to trial on the now thirty-four-year-old memory of a witness, but he was proceeding regardless.

Carol's father, Paul Davis, was also overjoyed. "At least I know that my daughter can rest in peace. I just felt like she was always saying, 'Daddy, why couldn't you find out who did it?'"[5]

His daughter, a 1965 graduate of Rushville High School, had dreamed of moving to Chicago to try her hand at being a fashion model. "I always felt like she was a very sweet, sort of naïve girl. She had a smile for everybody. Carol didn't like imposing on anybody," her father said.[6]

Richmond, it turns out, had faced murder charges before. In 1985, he had been acquitted of murder and attempted murder charges in Owen County, Indiana. In 1987, he was accused of attempted murder in Florida but found not guilty by reason of insanity. Richmond was a troubled man, fixated on the idea of castrating himself. He succeeded in partially castrating himself in 1982, police said.

A trial was set for Richmond for August 2002 but was delayed after doctors reported his physical and mental condition would not permit him to be a part of the trial. A cancer specialist said Richmond was suffering from the end stages of bladder cancer and had suffered numerous small strokes. He estimated Richmond had less than three months to live.

It would prove an accurate prognosis, as Richmond died on August 31, 2002, while being treated at LaRue Carter Memorial Hospital, a state mental hospital in Indianapolis.

Carol's family was disappointed that no trial could be held and angry that Richmond had never publicly admitted his guilt or apologized. There was no funeral conducted for him. "I feel [his death] is God's will. It's his punishment. It's his judgment and I can accept that," Paul Davis said.[7]

In February 2007, a spokesman for the Indiana State Police confirmed that Richmond had "acknowledged his involvement in the death of Carol Jenkins" to a jail guard at the Morgan County Jail but had not implicated any other people.[8]

Endnotes

1. *Bloomington Herald-Telephone*, Sept. 18, 1968.
2. *Bloomington Herald-Telephone*, Sept. 19, 1968.
3. *Rushville Republican*, Sept. 20, 1968.
4. *Indianapolis Star*, May 9, 2002.
5. Ibid.
6. Ibid.
7. WISH-TV, Channel 8, Indianapolis, Sept. 3, 2002.
8. WTHR-TV, Channel 13, Indianapolis, Feb. 14, 2007.

MORGAN COUNTY

VICTIM(S):
Terry Lee Chasteen, 21;
Misty Ann Chasteen, 5;
Steven Michael Chasteen, 4;
Mark Lewis Chasteen, 2

PERPETRATOR(S):
Steven T. Judy, 22

DATE OF DEATH(S):
April 28, 1979

INDIANA EXECUTES A KILLER WITHOUT REMORSE

Terry Chasteen had a busy day ahead of her on Saturday, April 28, 1979, so she got an early start.

Scheduled to be at work at 7 a.m. for her shift at the Marsh Supermarket on Lafayette Road in Indianapolis, the twenty-one-year-old single mom woke, bathed, and fed her three children: five-year-old Misty, four-year-old Steven, and two-year-old Mark. She then loaded them into the car to be dropped off at a babysitter's house.

Terry would never make it to the babysitter's house or to work that day. Her brutalized body was found about 9:30 a.m., just over two hours after she was killed and each of her three children were tossed into the White Lick Creek in rural Morgan County—like someone throwing away trash.

Mushroom hunters found Terry's body about 250 yards from the Indiana 67 bridge over the creek. A scarf was pulled tight around her neck indicating she had been strangled. She was found naked with her hands bound behind her back with ripped shreds from her Marsh Supermarket uniform. Her feet had also been bound. Her killer had stuffed a rag into her mouth to muffle her screams.

Just a short distance away were the bodies of her three children, all drowned in the icy spring waters of the creek, a White River tributary.

Police retraced Terry's steps and found her Ford Granada abandoned along I-465 on the west side of Indianapolis near the junction with Interstate 70—about ten miles north of where the bodies were found. She had had a flat tire replaced on that spot by someone, but police would later find the car's motor had been disabled.

Terry's ex-husband, Mark Chasteen, was immediately ruled out as a suspect. Stationed with the U.S. Navy in California, he was not in Indiana that day. He was devastated by the loss of his children and his ex-wife with whom he had reportedly had an amicable divorce.

Jack Lane, Terry's live-in boyfriend, was also ruled out as a suspect. He was at work at a downtown Indianapolis hotel at the time Terry and her children were attacked.

The men closest to her ruled out, police began to look more closely into Terry's disabled car and began to wonder whether she had been picked up by a "good Samaritan" who saw the young mother and three children stranded along the busy interstate highway.

Morgan County Sheriff Richard Allen said, "The person who did this is an animal as far as I am concerned." He said the murders were "very brutal" and noted that the three children were held forcibly under the water until they drowned.[1]

Sheriff Allen would get his man just thirty-six hours after the bodies were found with the arrest of a baby-faced twenty-two-year-old Steven T. Judy, an Indianapolis construction worker. Judy was arrested, Allen said, after several hours of questioning by police at Mooresville.

Witnesses who reported seeing a particular type of pickup truck near the site of both Terry's broken-down car and the bridge over White Lick Creek helped detectives zero in on Judy who had worked on many home construction sites in the Morgan County area. The gray pickup truck stood out because of a large tool box at the back of the cab.

Although just twenty-two years old, Judy was already familiar to police in two states.

He had served twenty months in Illinois for severely beating a Naperville, Illinois, woman whom he assaulted while offering to help her when her car broke down.

Paroled by Illinois in March 1977, he was arrested twenty-three days later in Indianapolis for the abduction of a twenty-four-year-old woman and taking her car. The woman had succeeded in grabbing the steering wheel and escaped the knife-wielding Judy. For his second violent crime against a woman, he was given a one-year sentence which he completed just thirty-five days before abducting, raping, and killing Terry Chasteen.

Judy also had a frightening juvenile record, including charges of burglary and molestation against three young girls at the age of twelve in 1968, followed by assault, battery, and criminally deviant conduct charges at age thirteen. The latter incident involved Judy using the ruse of selling tickets to a youth-sponsored event to gain entry into a twenty-three-year-old woman's apartment where he used a hatchet and a butcher knife to terrorize her. The woman suffered forty separate knife and ax cuts to her head, chest, and abdomen but was able to escape. For that attack, he was sent to Central State Hospital, an Indianapolis mental hospital, for treatment.

During one of his criminal proceedings, a court-appointed psychiatrist called Judy "an extremely unstable and dangerous individual" and said his problems were "linked to unresolved hostilities toward females."[2]

On the same day Terry and her three young children were mourned and buried at a funeral in Brownsburg, Indiana, Judy wept during his initial appearance in Morgan County Superior Court where he was to face multiple charges that would lead to the death penalty.

The investigation began to give more details about what had happened to Terry and her children. Judy may have actually known her in passing. At one time, he had dated one of Terry's coworkers at Marsh. Police also learned that after fixing the flat tire for Terry, Judy meddled with the car's motor, giving him a chance to offer Terry and her three children a ride in his truck.

As awful as his criminal history was, Judy was not without at least one defender. Mary Carr of Indianapolis had served as his foster mother since he was thirteen years old. She said, "Steve's whole childhood was pure hell. He came from a broken home. He practically has no family."[3]

Mrs. Carr said, "I'm not saying he did it or didn't do it, I just don't understand it. [My] kids really loved him. One of our daughters is the same age as one of the children who died. If he did do it, I believe something snapped."[4]

She said Judy was popular with the girls and had carried on formal courtships with several. "He never treated any of them bad," she said. "This thing does not go with his whole personality."[5]

Robert Carr, his foster father, described Judy as "a real good worker. He worked for me as a laborer … Oh, he's been in and out of a few scrapes, but I never had any trouble with him."[6]

It was Mr. Carr who had loaned his pickup truck to Judy on the Friday night before Terry and her children were attacked—the same truck that witnesses later told police was near the crime scene.

A February 1980 trial attracted heavy media attention across Indiana. Judy attempted to use an insanity defense and testified that he had motioned for Terry to pull her car off the road because of the flat tire. Once there, he told jurors he had removed a coil wire so the car would not start.

The personable, almost friendly Judy testified that once at the White Lick Creek site (far from where he had promised to take Terry and her kids), he sent the bewildered children ahead of Terry and himself along a small path near the creek. As they walked ahead, he raped Terry causing her to scream. He said her screams caused the children to come back and gather around him and yell at him. Scared and losing control of the situation, Judy strangled Terry to death and then picked up each of the children and threw them as far as he could into the creek.

A shocked courtroom listened as he said he remembered seeing one of the children trying to stand up in the water of the creek, only to fall down again and drown in the rushing waters.

Jurors returned a guilty verdict against Judy for four counts of murder on February 2, 1980. All that was left was a sentencing hearing to determine whether he should be executed by the State of Indiana. At the hearing, Judy asked his defense attorneys to present no mitigating evidence in his favor. He "testified" at the sentencing hearing by threatening the judge and members of the jury—saying if they did not recommend the death penalty against him, he would someday get out of jail and try to kill each of them. The jury and judge obliged, and on February 25, 1980, he was sentenced to die for his crimes.

Over the coming weeks and months, Judy's case would gain national attention as he stubbornly refused any effort to appeal his sentence and perhaps save his life. If his execution were to go forward, it would be the first in Indiana since 1961. It would only be the fourth execution in the United States since the landmark 1976 U.S. Supreme Court ruling that overturned death penalties in most states.

"We're kind of disappointed that he just won't fight for his life," foster mother Mary Carr said. "He won't let anybody help him, and we can't figure it out."[7]

Mrs. Carr said she was angry that the state was so eager to execute her foster son but had not offered him the help he needed when he was young. "Our system helped nurture this, helped turn him into a murderer," she said. "You know a 12-year-old boy who attacks a woman needs help, but Steve back on the streets nine months after that attack."[8]

Since Judy was unwilling to help himself, the American Civil Liberties Union and ten clergy members stepped up in March 1981 to file an appeal of Judy's death sentence. The ACLU and the ministers also asked Governor Robert D. Orr to intervene and grant a delay or clemency for the convicted killer. Governor Orr said he could see "no reason" to delay the execution. Judy issued a statement rebuking the efforts by others to appeal on his behalf.

On March 6, 1981, the U.S. Supreme Court refused to block Judy's scheduled execution, now just forty-eight hours away. On the same day, the Indiana Clemency Commission also rejected the appeal request the ACLU had filed.

The next day, Judy conducted a news conference of his own from inside the Indiana State Prison at Michigan City. He said he had no regrets about the murders and preferred being executed.

"I don't lose sleep over [the murders]," he said. "It's just something that happened. I'm not sorry for the things that I've done. I've lived my life the only way I know how."[9]

Judy said he felt he had been given a fair trial. He said, "The death penalty for me is a release ... I just can't see spending the rest of my life in prison."[10]

He placed at least partial blame for his crimes on society, saying that the events in his life were "crying out saying, 'Hey, stop me. Something is wrong.' Society hasn't been able to help me. They've had their chance. They haven't really tried. They have known since the time I was 10 years old I was a very dangerous person, that something like this would happen, but nothing was ever done about it."[11]

He added the obvious—"I'm not the type who puts blame on myself."[12]

The *New York Times* editorialized against Judy's pending execution, noting, "If Judy is executed tomorrow, as scheduled, the State of Indiana runs no risk of executing the wrong man ... [Judy's] contempt for life, it seems, is absolute. But though his death may be, so far as one can gauge such imponderables, no loss to society, the manner of his dying is a blow to civilization."[13]

The *Times* acknowledged that Judy was "for whatever reason, a barbarian" but believed that "a civilized country can afford to deal with people like him in other, wiser ways ... To endorse execution, however understandable the impulse, is quite simply to come down to his level."[14]

Regardless of views elsewhere, most Indiana citizens were highly supportive of the death penalty and had grown particularly tired of any delays in ending the life of a murderous sociopath such as Judy.

Hoosiers had reason for disgust. In his last news conference, the unrepentant Judy had told reporters that "all women are gullible, all that I've met" and that "I don't know why I committed the crimes. I am what I am."[15]

At 12:12 a.m. on Monday, March 9, 1981, the now twenty-four-year-old Judy was placed in the state's electric chair and had 2,300 volts of electricity run through his body for ten seconds and then another 500 volts for twenty more seconds.

Judy's lawyer, Steven L. Harris, convinced him to write a confession letter that could be opened after his death that may clear up any additional crimes in which he had been involved. Police were particularly interested in the November 1978 murder of Linda Unversagt who was found strangled in an abandoned house Judy was known to visit.

In his letter, Judy wrote to his attorney, "I'm sorry, Steve, but I've decided to handle it this way because I care too much for my foster mom and family. I hope you can understand. Thank you for all your love for me."

What followed were seven blank pages of paper.[16]

Endnotes

1. *Indianapolis Star*, April 30, 1979.
2. *Indianapolis Star*, May 1, 1979.
3. *Indianapolis News*, May 1, 1979.
4. Ibid.
5. Ibid.
6. Ibid.
7. Associated Press, Feb. 18, 1981.
8. Ibid.
9. *New York Times*, March 8, 1981.
10. *Indianapolis Star*, March 8, 1981.
11. *Indianapolis News*, March 7, 1981.
12. Ibid.
13. *New York Times*, March 8, 1981.
14. Ibid.
15. *Indianapolis News*, March 7, 1981.
16. *Indianapolis Star*, March 9, 1981.

NEWTON COUNTY

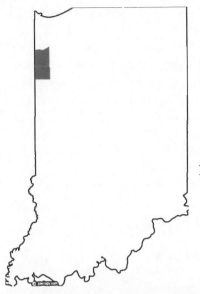

VICTIM(S):
Anthony "The Ant" Spilotro, 48;
Michael Spilotro, 41

PERPETRATOR(S):
14 men indicted; 2 died prior to trial,
7 pled guilty, 5 faced trial in 2007

DATE OF DEATH(S):
June 14, 1986

A MOB-INSPIRING MURDER FROM THE HEARTLAND

In the closing scenes of Martin Scorsese's award-winning 1995 film, Casino, actor Joe Pesci's character "Mickey" and his brother are brutally bludgeoned and buried alive in a grave in a remote cornfield. It was not just a dramatic scene that made its point about alleged "mob justice," it was at least partially inspired by actual events in rural Newton County, Indiana.

Two Chicago brothers, alleged members of the "Chicago Outfit" met such a horrifying end just outside Enos, Indiana, on June 14, 1986. Forty-eight-year-old Anthony "The Ant" Spilotro and his forty-one-year-old brother, Michael, left their suburban Chicago homes on that Saturday for a planned meeting with some of their colleagues.

They were never seen again.

Anthony's 1986 Lincoln Continental was later recovered from the parking lot of a Howard Johnson's motel in Schiller Park, Illinois. Investigators said the car showed no signs of a struggle, and no one at the motel reported seeing the men. Speculation quickly centered on the idea that the Spilotro brothers had met trouble.

Their disappearance would mean the delay of Anthony's scheduled trial, which was to open in Las Vegas, Nevada, the following Monday morning. Anthony was facing charges that he had directed a burglary ring that netted thousands. Nevada authorities had released Anthony on a $200,000 bond, but he was due back in Nevada the day he disappeared.

Anthony had been in trouble before – charged many times with various offenses, including murder, but convicted only once, for lying on a home loan application. He was fined $1 for that offense.[1]

His brother, Michael, a restauranteur and part-time actor whose acting credits included ironic roles such as an FBI agent on the CBS series *Magnum, P.I.*, was facing his own troubles. A federal indictment brought against him in April 1986 charged him with extortion for allegedly shaking down bribes and kickbacks from organized prostitution operations in Chicago. He was free on a $25,000 bond when he disappeared.

Reporters who covered the "Chicago Outfit" quickly settled on the idea that the Spilotro brothers were likely dead – "an emergences of a new power in the Chicago crime syndicate" – to silence them, an anonymous federal investigator told the *Chicago Tribune*.[2]

The *Tribune* further reported on June 21, 1986, that the "Chicago crime syndicate bosses reportedly decided that [Anthony], the Nevada underworld boss, and his brother were to be killed," according to federal agents speaking anonymously.[3]

Former mobster Frank Cullotta, a Spilotro lieutenant who became a federal informant in 1982, said Anthony "told me in 1978 when I first arrived in Las Vegas that no one was to know that he was getting a cut [of the burglary proceeds] because he didn't want any problems with the people back in Chicago." Cullotta's remarks came during an April 1986 trial against Anthony that ended in a mistrial.

Anthony may not have known his life was in danger, however. He was banking on the fact he had accumulated a large amount of respect in the organization since earning a leadership role in Las Vegas from the "outfit" as early as 1971.

On Monday, June 23, 1986, a farmer getting ready to work in his cornfield along Newton County Road 100 North, about a half mile west of County Road 400 West, stumbled upon a freshly dug grave where the four-inch high corn he had planted had been disturbed. He knew enough to call the police, and they quickly unearthed the end of the line for the Spilotro brothers.

Newton County Coroner David Dennis ordered the bodies removed and transported to Indianapolis for an autopsy. Both men had suffered massive blunt force injuries, including broken hands and arms as they had attempted to defend themselves from a fury of blows from a blunt object. There were no indications that either man had ever been bound.

Dennis said the grave measured five feet deep and three feet wide, indicating that it likely had been dug in advance. Scorsese used the same measurements in his film, *Casino*, showing both men being dumped into the hole, piled one on top of the other, clad only in their underwear.

Identification of the two men was made extremely difficult, Dennis told reporters, because of the intensity of the beatings they had endured. Fingerprints and dental records later confirmed the identity of the two men. Another Spilotro brother, dentist Patrick Spilotro of Chicago, provided the dental records used.

Indiana State Police investigators said two sets of footprints leading 190 feet to and from the gravesite from County Road 100 were found. Police also believed a burned stolen car found dumped about two miles west of the gravesite on June 16 may have been used by the perpetrators. Edward Hegerty, special agent in charge of the FBI's Chicago office, called the disposal of the bodies "botched in that the grave was dug inside a newly planted cornfield," and thus discovered.[4]

"It is very likely that the persons responsible for this left the scene of the crime with the anticipation that the bodies would never be found," Hegerty said.[5]

Attorney Doug Roller, former head of the Justice Department's Organized Crime Strike Force in Chicago, told the Associated Press that the crime "looked like punishment, pure and simple. I don't think [the killings] were intended to be a message, because the bodies weren't supposed to be found."[6]

Roller said Anthony Spilotro "screwed up and the mob doesn't tolerate this kind of thing," and that his brother Michael's murder was probably was a result of him being in "the wrong place at the wrong time."[7]

As Anthony and Michael's bodies were released to their grieving families, the Archdiocese of Chicago announced that the brothers would be denied a funeral mass in the church because of their alleged ties to organized crime. Coroner Dennis said a month later fixed the cause of death for Anthony and Michael as "asphyxiation due to blunt force trauma." He said the men appeared to have died from suffocating on their own blood as a result of the beatings.

He said their injuries were sufficient enough "to render them lifeless, but multiple head wounds is not a cause of death and the presence of aspirated blood leads me to conclude they were asphyxiated."[8]

Publicly, the FBI and Newton County officials said they were optimistic arrests could be made in the case, but seemed to understand that cooperation with law enforcement officials by associates and members of the Chicago Outfit would be virtually non-existent.[9]

A three-month federal grand jury probe proved that conclusion right. In September 1986, the Justice Department reported they had no solid leads in the case, no motives, and no identified suspects.

A new twist in the case emerged in October 1989 when Betty Tocco, wife of alleged Mafioso Albert "Caesar" Tocco, said she would implicate her husband in the burial of the Spilotro brothers. Sixty-one-year-old Albert was facing multiple charges of extortion, racketeering, and car theft.

"In the early morning hours of June 15, 1986, Albert Tocco, his clothing covered with dirt, told his wife he had just dug the grave of reputed mobsters

Anthony and Michael Spilotro and feared he had left his fingerprints on the shovel," the *Chicago Tribune* reported from federal court documents.[10]

The *Tribune* said Betty Tocco had begun to expose her estranged husband in exchange for a possible deal with the feds for a new identity for herself and her eight-year-old son. Albert Tocco's attorneys dismissed Betty's claims as those of a "vindictive, bitter woman."[11]

Betty told a reporter from the *Chicago Sun Times* that she did not believe Albert's frequent claims of being involved with the mafia until he asked her to pick him up near Enos, Indiana, in June 1986. As they drove back home to Chicago, she said he confessed that he had buried the Spilotro brothers. "I couldn't believe what I was hearing," Betty said. "I was shocked, nauseated, disgusted. It was Father's Day. His sister and mother were coming over for a barbeque. What was I supposed to say, 'Albert just buried the Spilotro's last night, so we can't barbeque today?'"[12]

In December 1990, a twenty-nine count indictment of reputed mobsters was released by the U.S. District Court in Hammond, Indiana, that charged fifteen separate men with crimes. Along with Tocco, both Dominic "Tootsie" Palermo, seventy-two, and Nicholas "Nicky" Guzzino, forty-nine, were identified in testimony at Tocco's trial as two of three men who helped bury the Spilotro brothers.

The indictment hearing for Palermo and Guzzino revealed that Tocco referred to the burial as a mess and that passing cars near Enos that night had caused the men to initially dump the bodies in a nearby ditch and then had to drag them a long distance to the prepared grave.

Tocco was later sentenced to two-hundred years in prison on a variety of charges and died behind bars, fifteen years into his sentence at the federal prison in Terre Haute, Indiana on September 21, 2005. He was seventy-one. Tocco was never charged in the Spilotro murders.[13]

Federal authorities had enough to hold Palermo and Guzzino on other charges, but they were never charged with the Spilotro murders either.

Another big break came in 1998 and 1999, when mafia son Frank Calabrese, Jr., decided to don headphones holding a tiny microphone and pulled incriminating statements about the Spilotro murders from a reliable source: his father, "made" mobster Frank Calabrese, Sr.

Senior citizen Frank, Sr., was sixty-nine-years-old and reportedly interested in grooming his son to help take over what remained of the "Chicago Outfit." Jailed along with his son and brother in a federal penitentiary in Michigan, the secret tapes were made by Frank, Jr. over a two-year period. The tapes were played during the sensational "Family Secrets" trial in Chicago in June 2007. During several hearings, tapes showed Frank, Sr. describing details of the Spilotro murders as well as seventeen other homicides.

Frank, Sr. told his son that Anthony and Michael Spilotro were lured to the basement of a Bensenville, Illinois home on that Saturday in June 1986 on the pretense of being "initiated" or "made" in the Outfit. Instead, the men were brutally beaten to death by as many as six men, and their bodies later dumped in the makeshift grave in Newton County.

Anthony Spilotro was killed on the orders of Chicago Outfit kingpin Joseph "Joey" Aiuppa, Frank, Sr. said on one tape. The powerful Aiuppa, who died of natural causes in 1997, was angered that Anthony had engaged in a sexual affair with the wife of another mobster and that Michael was throwing his weight around Chicago to further his personal interests.

Indicted along with Frank, Sr., for the crime originally in 2005 were fourteen other men, although two died before they could face trial, and seven others entered guilty pleas in deals to a variety of charges with federal authorities. Among those who plead guilty was Frank, Sr.'s brother Nicholas "Joy" Calabrese who cooperated fully with federal authorities and was released from federal prison on May 25, 2005.

At the end of the "Family Secrets" trial, Paul "Paulie the Indian" Schiro, was convicted of racketeering and conspiracy and won a 20-year sentence in January 2009. Frank Calabrese, Sr., and James Marcello were both sentenced to life in prison for murder and conspiracy. Frank, Sr. died on Christmas Day 2012 at the age of seventy-five. Joey "The Clown" Lombardo was also given a life sentence that he continues to serve time as he approaches the age of ninety.

A former Chicago cop, Anthony Doyle, was not charged with murder, but conspiracy for allegedly assisting his mob friends and received a 12-year sentence. Another defendant, Frank "The German" Schweihs, escaped conviction and sentencing when he died of cancer on July 24, 2008.

Frank Jr., who turned on his father in prison and made the incriminating audio recordings for the FBI, was released from prison on February 3, 2000.

Endnotes

1. *Gary Post-Tribune*, June 24, 1986
2. *Chicago Tribune*, June 19, 1986
3. *Chicago Tribune*, Feb. 13, 1986
4. *Chicago Tribune*, June 24, 1986
5. *Hammond Times*, June 24, 1986
6. Associated Press, June 25, 1986
7. Associated Press, June 25, 1986
8. *Hammond Times*, July 25, 1986
9. FBI Informational Memo, May 19, 1993
10. *Chicago Tribune*, April 4, 1990
11. Ibid.
12. *Chicago Sun-Times*, May 17, 1990
13. *Chicago Tribune*, Sept. 25, 2005

NOBLE COUNTY

VICTIM(S):
Angela Teresa Adams, 24

PERPETRATOR(S):
Eric Lee Adams, 27

DATE OF DEATH(S):
September 13, 2002

AN IMPROPER BURIAL FOR ANGELA

Eric Lee Adams of Rome City, Indiana, said he always intended to give his ex-wife, twenty-four-year-old Angela Adams, a proper burial, but he never got the chance.

Twenty-seven-year-old Eric, the father of Angela's three children, first told police on September 22, 2002, that Angela had left her apartment to go help a friend in Southern Indiana move into a new home and had never returned. He hoped people would believe the young mother had just "run away" from her life.

It was a lie.

Angela was last seen alive on September 13, 2002, about a week before she was reported missing. Six months of intensive searching followed, including help from the *America's Most Wanted* television series. Then, on March 21, 2003, workers clearing brush behind a factory in Kendallville, Indiana, made a gruesome discovery.

Angela's tiny, four-foot-nine-inch, ninety-pound body was discovered wrapped in plastic garbage bags and stuffed into an abandoned fifty-five gallon barrel. The barrel, resting just twenty-five to thirty feet from a gravel parking lot for the Group Dekko Industrial Complex in Kendallville, was partially hidden with brush and other debris. It was found lying on its side in a ditch along the Norfolk and Southern railroad tracks.

By coincidence, the barrel was found behind the PVC Compounders facility where Eric worked and his father, Dave Adams, served as the plant manager.

Police were dubious of Eric's claims from the start, particularly given the volatile nature of his past relationship with Angela and his growing anger over court-ordered child support payments he continually missed.

Identification of Angela's body took some time due to the advanced decomposition. Dental records confirmed her identity, and police zeroed in on Eric as a prime suspect.

Described as a "free spirit," friends and family said Angela was working on getting her life in order, and they never believed claims by Eric six months earlier that she had just walked away from her life in Noble County. She had suffered physical and verbal abuse in her marriage and in her dating life, family members said.

Angela and her two daughters, ages three and four, lived in subsidized, low-rent housing in Rome City for about a year prior to her disappearance. Her son, her oldest child, lived with his father, Eric Adams.

At the time she disappeared, Angela was unemployed and counted heavily on welfare, food stamps, and child support payments to clothe, feed, and house her children. In fact, on March 12, 2002, a Noble County judge ordered Eric Adams to pay her $40 a week in child support and make up for the $1,280 he was behind. It was an order he defied.

Eric continually challenged the child support orders, and his unwillingness to show up in court for hearings to explain his actions dragged out the argument between Eric and Angela over months. Some believed that Eric was angry at not only having to pay child support, but that Angela had begun dating other men.

Following her disappearance, police used trained search dogs, helicopters, and aerial photography in and around Rome City to find any clues as to Angela's whereabouts. The searches turned up nothing.

The child support battle gave police continued access to Eric, however.

On August 26, 2002, less than two weeks before Angela was last seen alive, Angela and Eric were in Noble Circuit Court to further determine child support requirements. The court found Eric in contempt of its order to pay child support and ordered him to appear on October 7, 2002, for sentencing.

It was between the August and October court hearings that Angela would go missing.

Police picked up Eric on the outstanding child support warrant on November 11, 2002. At the time, Eric submitted to a "voice stress test" where he denied having anything to do with Angela being missing.

Analysis of the test indicated Eric was being deceptive.

Whether or not he was deceptive, the investigation would have to grind on many more weeks before Eric could be arrested. The discovery of her body in March 2003, however, jump-started the investigation, and Eric was arrested ten days later.

Under questioning from police, Eric reportedly spun a tale of the couple arguing in their apartment. He said that he shoved Angela in anger, and she accidentally struck her head on a towel bar in the bathroom.

In another interview, Eric told a version police believe was closest to the truth; however, he told police he did not kill her. He said he went to the apartment and found her dead body in a half-full bathtub on September 13, 2002. Fearing that he would be implicated, he told police he put a T-shirt on Angela, placed her in two trash bags, and placed her body on the floor beside her bed. He said he covered her corpse with clothing so her two young daughters would not see her there.

Eric said he left Angela's body there for a day and a half and admitted placing the body of his wife in the trunk of his car while her two daughters slept in the backseat of the same car.

Eric's idea of "proper burial" for Angela included a half-baked attempt to dig a shallow grave for her behind the PVC Compounders facility where he worked. Police did find a small, four-foot-long, two-foot-wide, and one-foot-deep hole. But Eric said he grew too tired shoveling while his two daughters slept in a car nearby and gave up.

It was then, Eric told police, he decided to dump her body in the barrel and hide it in the ditch.

Eric and Angela Adams' son told police that he saw his parents fighting in the bathroom on the last day he saw his mother and that he saw his father, Eric, holding his mother's head under the water in a bathtub. He told investigators, "Mommy" was "resting" in the bathtub with her eyes open.

Noble County Sheriff Gary Leatherman arrested Eric on March 31, 2003, on multiple charges, including murder and removal of a body. At Eric's initial hearing at the Noble County Courthouse in Albion, he told the court, "I didn't do it," but was held without bond. The judge appointed a public defender as his defense attorney.[1]

Just as Eric's trial was to begin more than a year later in May 2004, he shocked all by entering into a surprise plea agreement to plead guilty to lesser charges and admit that he had killed his wife.

Eric admitted that he held his wife's head under the water in the tub until she drowned and then placed her body in the barrel at the factory where he worked.

Noble County Prosecutor Steven Clouse accepted a deal in which Eric pled guilty to an amended charge of voluntary manslaughter, a charge of moving a body from the scene of death, and two charges of manufacturing methamphetamine.

Clouse told reporters he could accept the deal with Eric's full confession and with the intent of sparing the couple's young children from having to testify in court about their mother's murder, which at least one of them witnessed.

Eric Adams told the court he had acted under "sudden heat" when he attacked his wife in the bathtub during their argument. The designation of acting in "sudden heat" allowed for the voluntary manslaughter charge, rather than murder.

The methamphetamine charges resulted from admissions by Eric that he had manufactured the drug for sale and use both in Angela's apartment after he had killed her and again in 2003 at his parents' home in Rome City.

Eric Adams was sentenced on July 13, 2004 to fifteen years on the voluntary manslaughter charge, two years for moving the body from the scene of death, and fifteen years for two additional charges of manufacturing or dealing in narcotic drugs.

Endnotes

1. *Fort Wayne News-Sentinel*, April 1, 2003.

OHIO COUNTY

VICTIM(S):
Elizabeth Gillespie, 35

PERPETRATOR(S):
James S. Gillespie, 35

DATE OF DEATH(S):
December 10, 1903

A GRUDGE BETWEEN TWINS TURNS DEADLY

As James S. Gillespie was removed from the Ohio County Jail in Rising Sun, Indiana, on Saturday morning, January 7, 1905, to be transported to the Indiana State Prison at Michigan City, only a handful of townsfolk stood by to witness the spectacle.

Gillespie, the son of a Civil War veteran and a prominent family in Rising Sun, was headed to prison for the incredible act of shooting his twin sister, Elizabeth Gillespie, who died two days later on December 10, 1903.

As he left the jail, one man said, "Goodbye, Jim," to which Gillespie replied in a firm voice, "Goodbye, boys, all of you. I'll be back with you again ..."[1]

His statement would prove true—just over two years later in April 1907, Gillespie was free and returned to his home in Rising Sun, across the street from where Elizabeth had been shot to death with a 16-gauge shotgun.[2]

The case against Gillespie would gather nationwide attention to Indiana's smallest county. For its time, a brother accused of murdering his twin sister was a crime simply unheard of before.

The story began on a quiet Tuesday evening in December 1903 as Elizabeth, thirty-five, prepared the parlor of the home she shared with her mother for the regular meeting of the Women's Literary Club. Before her guests arrived, however, a shot rang out and struck Elizabeth in the head behind her left ear.

The shot also extinguished the oil lamp in the room, and Elizabeth's elderly mother, Margaret Gillespie, fumbled in the darkened room crying out for her daughter, eventually finding her near death on the floor.

"Miss Gillespie is still alive, but is sinking fast, and the attending physicians give her but a few hours to live," the *Indianapolis Star* reported. "She has never regained consciousness since the tragedy."[3]

Police declared immediately that "a strong chain of circumstantial evidence" existed to charge a suspect they had identified. Investigators didn't have to look far. Suspicion seemed to fall immediately on Elizabeth's twin brother, James, to whom she had been estranged for years.

If he had hoped to avoid suspicion, his actions after his sister was shot did not help. Despite living just across Poplar Street from his sister's home, Gillespie did not come outside his home to investigate the shot or the cries of his elderly mother for help, although most others in the neighborhood nestled along the Ohio River did.

Elizabeth was well known in Rising Sun and throughout the county as a leader among the women's social scene, active in the Presbyterian church and other organizations. She was a well-respected woman, if not considered a spinster. The *Star* reported that she had "shown a distinct religious bent ever since an unfortunate love affair 10 years ago" that ended in a broken engagement for marriage.[4]

Elizabeth succumbed to her mortal wounds on the afternoon of December 10, 1903. Two gun "wads" were removed from her head by the coroner, who declared her death a homicide.

"If these bloody wads prove to be sixteen gauge, the size of the shotgun in the possession of James Gillespie, brother of the murdered girl, doubt will exist no longer in the minds of the people as to the identity of the guilty man," the *Indianapolis Star* declared.[5]

Reports emerged that James and Elizabeth had stopped speaking to each other sometime in 1901, after the death of their father, Dr. William Gillespie, Sr., a Civil War veteran and prominent physician in the community. James, reportedly, was angry that his father's will favored his twin sister. Other siblings discounted that as the cause of the row between the two, noting that Dr. Gillespie's widow (who was still alive) was actually the primary beneficiary of the estate.

After their fight, James moved across the street into the home of an older sister, Mrs. Belle Seward, a widowed woman.

"The enmity grew, and the old time love which had existed between Elizabeth and her brother turned almost to hatred," the *Star* reported.[6]

When Elizabeth died, Gillespie was summoned to appear before the Ohio County grand jury but remained uncooperative with the investigation.

He refused, initially, to deliver his shotgun as the subpoena from the court ordered but eventually relinquished it.

As the prosecutor questioned Gillespie in front of members of the grand jury at the Ohio County Courthouse, he remained cool and unmoved. "Too many people of this town are accusing me of murder," he said and declined to answer any questions.[7]

James and Elizabeth's older brother, Dr. William Gillespie, Jr. of Cincinnati, Ohio, was also called to testify, but he spoke only to his treatment of his sister's wounds.

When reporters gathered at the courthouse told Dr. Gillespie that his brother James was a prime suspect in the murder, he said, "On that suspicion, you are altogether wrong. We will fight this thing to the bitter end."[8]

A day later, disturbed by news reports that his brother had killed his sister over their father's estate, Dr. Gillespie issued a written statement saying, "There was no difficulty in the family over my father's estate. In fact, his will was not drawn until he had consulted each of his legal heirs and found that they were not only willing, but serious, that the whole estate should go to my mother."[9]

He added, "There were no estrangements over business troubles in the family at all. My sister was not only on good terms with my brother and sister, but was on equally bad terms with my other brother and myself. The estrangement was not due to any one cause but to separate and distinct conditions in each individual case."[10]

Despite Dr. Gillespie's statement, news reports continued to refer to "longstanding" and "deeply held resentments" between the Gillespie children, all of whom were described as being "quick tempered and having a reputation of being firm in their convictions."[11]

Reporters also seemed fascinated that a set of twins could be enemies of any sort.

"The ill feeling between the twins ... is considered remarkable by the medical fraternity," the *Indianapolis Star* reported. "Twins are usually close to each other throughout life, and a case cannot be recalled when a twin has been known to have intentionally harmed the other ... Doctors say that it is not uncommon that twins possess minds more or less susceptible to influence by others, but it is quite unusual for ill feelings to spring up between them."[12]

Other witnesses called before the grand jury included Myron and Carrie Barbour, a married couple who shared the home across the street from Elizabeth with James and his older sister, Mrs. Seward.

Initially, Myron Barbour refused to answer any of the questions put before him until threatened with a stay in the county jail by Ohio County Circuit Court Judge Downey.

Investigators were interested in how the Barbours reacted as well as Gillespie. They believed a "deep-laid plot" involving as many as four people was behind Elizabeth's murder. Reporters also learned that Elizabeth may have known her life was in danger. Shortly before her murder, she told a friend, "Oh, I have troubles that you know nothing about."[13]

As Elizabeth's funeral went forward on Sunday, December 13, 1903, at the Presbyterian Church in Rising Sun, two family members were conspicuous in their absence: James Gillespie and the sister with whom he shared a home, Belle Seward. Among the pallbearers for Elizabeth's casket were the mayor of Rising Sun and the Ohio County treasurer, two of the deceased woman's many friends.

Two days later, reporters in Indianapolis and Cincinnati began suggesting another new possible motive for Elizabeth's murder. Both reported heavily on a $3,000 life insurance policy James stood to gain by Elizabeth's death.

The New York Life Insurance Company reported that Elizabeth purchased the policy in July 1901 and paid for five years in advance, receiving a discount on her total premium of $347. The agent who sold the policy believed she bought it as an investment only. James was named recipient of the policy, it turns out, before he and Elizabeth fought and was never removed from it.

Reporters also zeroed in on the fact that while Elizabeth was active and popular in many circles in Rising Sun, she was also viewed as pious and judgmental at times.

"Her life was devoted to social purity and misconduct on the part of others evoked from her severest condemnation," the *Indianapolis Star* offered. "It may be said that she gave up her life because of her denunciation of what she considered an unpardonable transgression of social laws."[14]

As the media frenzy continued, grand jury testimony revealed that Carrie Barbour held an intense hatred of Elizabeth Gillespie, and held a "hypnotic influence" over James Gillespie. One witness reported that Carrie had struck Elizabeth twice with a broom handle after becoming angry at what Elizabeth told others about her alleged immoral behavior. Carrie also had threatened to splash vitriol (sulfuric acid) on Elizabeth's face to try to blind her permanently.[15]

Carrie Barbour and Belle Seward were also called before the grand jury, but not before some excitement on the courthouse lawn. Photographers from Indianapolis and Cincinnati had arrived in town and attempted to take pictures of the two women as they appeared to answer questions. James Gillespie reportedly attacked one of the photographers, and successfully blocked their view. The judge later refused his request that the photographers be ordered to stop taking photos of the women.[16]

On December 21, 1903, the grand jury ordered Elizabeth's body exhumed from the grave she had held for just over a week. They ordered that all of the "wads" or bullet fragments in her head be removed and compared to James's shotgun, "the only 16-gauge gun in Rising Sun."[17]

The next day, December 22, 1903, the indictment of four people for the murder of Elizabeth Gillespie was front page news across Indiana, Ohio, and Kentucky. Indicted for murder were James Gillespie, thirty-five, his sister Belle Seward, forty-eight, and Myron and Carrie Barbour, both thirty-five.

While Seward and Gillespie remained calm during a two-hour preliminary hearing, Myron Barbour appeared almost panicked at the charges. The two women were released on bond, but Gillespie and Myron Barbour were ordered held at the Ohio County Jail. Mr. Barbour would eventually be granted bail, but Gillespie would not.

"Only twice did Barbour attempt to speak to his wife [in court]. Mrs. Seward sat between them. Once when Barbour apparently attempted to suggest something to Mrs. Barbour, she made a quick retort as if angry. The coolness between them was quite noticeable," the *Star* reported.[18]

Carrie Barbour was an attractive woman described as "possessing fiery eyes and a winning smile" and as "a determined little woman" who "held a strange influence over James Gillespie."[19]

Suggested in news reports, but not stated outright, was that Carrie Barbour had engaged in a sexually intimate relationship with James Gillespie, despite being married to Myron Barbour.

"Behind the whole affair is a story of hate and malice," the *Star's* unnamed correspondent reported. "The jury is believed to have been told a story to the effect that Mrs. Barbour bore intense hatred toward Elizabeth Gillespie because the latter had accused her of improper conduct."[20]

The *Indianapolis Star* report added, "It is a fact that for several years, Mrs. Barbour has not mingled in society in this town. She has had only a small circle of woman friends in Rising Sun. This social ostracism was attributed ... to Miss Gillespie who was the acknowledged social leader of the town."[21]

James Gillespie engaged Captain John B. Coles to lead his defense and in doing so created a precedent in Indiana. Captain Coles' twenty-three-year-old daughter, Cynthia Coles, was also an attorney and joined her father on the defense team and thus became the first woman to represent a murder defendant in an Indiana courtroom.[22]

Gillespie spent the holiday in jail, "while Christmas cheer abounded in most places in Rising Sun, [and] he was peering from behind the bars."[23]

In May 1904, Gillespie's case was finally called in Ohio County Circuit Court and ended on June 4, 1904, with no verdict returned against him. An impaneled juror had failed to disclose that he or she was actually related to Gillespie during jury selection, and the equivalent of a mistrial was declared.[24]

A new trial was called for January 1905, and the state continued to use the 16-gauge gun as its strongest evidence against Gillespie. This time, Gillespie used the power of his family's name to secure U.S. Congressman Francis M. Griffith of Vevay, Indiana, to lead his defense. Congressman Griffith and Captain Coles argued that the circumstantial evidence against Gillespie was not enough to convict. They also argued a conviction subjected him to "jeopardy" (presumably what is known as "double jeopardy" now) because of the aborted 1904 trial.

The prosecutor attempted to match the prominence of Congressman Griffith in the courtroom by engaging State Senator William A. Kittinger of Anderson, Indiana, to lead the state's case. Kittinger told jurors, "Take all the evidence together, the motive of property, life insurance and bitter hatred, the conduct of James, the statements of Bell Seward, Carrie Barbour and Myron Barbour; the running footsteps [heard after the shooting], the click of an iron gate, and his guilt is shown beyond question."[25]

Jurors apparently agreed, taking just three hours to convict Gillespie of murder and recommending a sentence of life in prison. The Barbours and Seward faced separate trials on charges that were eventually reduced to being accessories before and after the crime.

Gillespie's continued prominence apparently helped in the duration of his sentence. He was paroled from the prison after only a little over two years, in April 1907.[26]

He returned to the Poplar Street home across from where his sister Elizabeth had been murdered and lived a quiet life there for nearly four decades.

On September 16, 1938, his name was once again on the front page, but this time for his own death. The Ohio County coroner ruled Gillespie killed himself by placing a shotgun in his mouth and shooting himself on the back porch of his home. He was seventy-two years old.

He left a note for the coroner that read, "Coroner, I cannot bear the pain any longer."[27]

The notice of his death made no mention of his illustrious past, and instead said he was a member of "a well known family in this community and [he] had been a life-long resident of this town."[28]

Endnotes

1. *Indianapolis News*, Jan. 7, 1905.
2. *Rising Sun Recorder*, April 5, 1907.

3. *Indianapolis Star*, Dec. 10, 1903.
4. Ibid.
5. *Indianapolis Star*, Dec. 11, 1903.
6. Ibid.
7. Ibid.
8. Ibid.
9. *Indianapolis Star*, Dec. 12, 1903.
10. Ibid.
11. Ibid.
12. Ibid.
13. *Indianapolis Star*, Dec. 13, 1903.
14. Ibid.
15. *Indianapolis Star*, Dec. 12, 1903; Dec. 16, 1903.
16. *Indianapolis Star*, Dec. 19, 1903.
17. *Indianapolis Star*, Dec. 16, 1903; Dec. 22, 1903.
18. *Indianapolis Star*, Dec. 23, 1903.
19. Ibid.
20. *Indianapolis Star*, Dec. 23, 1903.
21. Ibid.
22. *Indianapolis Star*, Dec. 25, 1903.
23. *Indianapolis Star*, Dec. 26, 1903.
24. *Rising Sun Local*, May 14, 1904; June 4, 1904.
25. *Indianapolis Star*, Jan. 6, 1905.
26. *Rising Sun Recorder*, April 5, 1907.
27. *Rising Sun Recorder*, Sept. 16, 1938.
28. Ibid.

ORANGE COUNTY

VICTIM(S):
John E. Thacker, 31

PERPETRATOR(S):
Lois A. Thacker, 26;
Donald R. Buchanan, Jr., 27;
James L. Hart, 24;
Charles Matthew Music, 17

DATE OF DEATH(S):
November 2, 1984

A POORLY EXECUTED PLAN

As John Thacker made his way home just after midnight on Saturday, November 2, 1984, he came across a pine log blocking Qualkenbush Road, about a half mile south of State Road 56, east of Paoli, Indiana. He was just 200 yards from the driveway to his trailer home as he got out of his truck to move the log so he could pass.

In an instant, shots rang out, and John fell to the roadway, dead.

Within thirty minutes, Orange County Sheriff's deputies would be on the scene and would find John dead where he was struck by twelve-gauge shotgun and deer slugs. Before twenty-four hours had passed, police had pieced together a hasty and poorly executed plan cooked up by John's twenty-six-year-old wife, Lois A. Thacker. It was a plan for murder that Lois thought would set her free from a marriage she hated and put $100,000 in insurance money in her pocket.

Orange County Sheriff's Lieutenant Tony Underwood said investigators determined that as John stepped from his pickup truck (which was still running in the roadway when deputies arrive), "three men were on the west of the road lying in wait, as he moved the log and started to stand up, he was shot in the back and then shot at point blank [range] in the head."[1]

Tammy Lake and Gregory M. Bird, both twenty-one, of Paoli, told police they came upon John's body lying in the roadway in front of his truck, near the log. The couple had been "parking" in the area and did not hear the shot because of their car stereo. Both Lake and Bird went to the home nearest the scene—the Thacker trailer.

When they entered the trailer, they saw a relaxed Lois Thacker lying on the sofa under a blanket. She told them she did not have a phone, and they would have to go somewhere else to call for help. Thacker's sister, eighteen-year-old Connie L. Busick, was also present and seemed disinterested as well in what the couple was reporting about a dead man in the roadway.

Lieutenant Underwood said that as police questioned Lois and Connie, "We got conflicting stories that weren't matching up. We finally came up [to the] two guys from Salem [Indiana] that say they were with them."[2]

The two men from Salem, twenty-seven-year-old Donald R. Buchanan Jr. and twenty-four-year-old James L. Hart, were both picked up later on Saturday and gave statements implicating themselves in the attack. Police also detained Thacker and Busick's cousin, seventeen-year-old Charles Matthew Music of Paoli.

The suspects were not holding up well under initial police questioning. Underwood reported, "We have some confessions. We taped some of them, and we have a confession from one . . . of what happened."[3]

Police learned that Thacker had taken out a $100,000 life insurance policy on John just two months earlier and that the couple had significant marital problems.

John, an employee of the Essex Corporation in Orleans, Indiana, where he built and repaired water pumps, was the father of three children from a previous marriage and had only been married to Lois Thacker seven months when he was killed.

As investigators pieced together what had happened, it became clear that Lois Thacker was at the head of this ragged band of scoundrels and had promised the men money if they would help kill John. Her teenage cousin, Matthew, and her sister Connie, seemed to need little prodding to go along with her plan.

Orange County Prosecutor Darrell F. Ellis felt he had enough information to try to avoid a costly trial. A plea agreement was offered to Thacker, but she refused (despite knowing some of her alleged co-conspirators were cooperating with prosecutors). Thacker's trial was moved to Dubois County and open at the courthouse in Jasper in May 1985. Unsuccessful in avoiding a trial through the plea deal, Ellis was all in, seeking the death penalty against Thacker.

Among the key witnesses the state had lined up against her was Buchanan who had already pled guilty to a charge of conspiracy to commit murder and received a thirty-year sentence.

Prosecutor Ellis did face one obstacle. Jurors in the current case would not hear about the fact that Thacker had admitted she was involved in the shooting death of her first husband, Phillip E. Huff, who died February 5, 1983. An Orange County grand jury had reviewed that case at the time, including

Thacker's claims that she was in fear of her life at the hands of her husband. She claimed self-defense in shooting her husband. Cleared in his death, she collected a $5,000 life insurance payout for Phillip's death.

The first witnesses in the Thacker trial were the young couple who encountered a disinterested Lois Thacker as they tried to report finding John's body. A pathologist also testified, offering graphic testimony using scale models to show the extent of the injuries John had suffered in the ambush.

Dr. James Jacobi told the jury that John suffered a massive open wound to the left side of his back when first shot – a wound so severe he would have bled to death in less than five minutes. He also suffered a close-range shot to the skull that blew off a large portion of the side of his head and forehead. Police located the .12-gauge shotgun used to kill John, broken into three parts, after suspect John Hart led them to it.

Prosecutors also called John's first wife and the mother of his three children, Linda Doan, who testified that Lois had threatened to kill John if he was ever unfaithful to her, just as she had killed her first husband. Judge Hugo C. Songer ordered jurors to disregard Doan's remark—clear hearsay—about the killing of Thacker's first husband but refused a defense motion for a mistrial.

Thacker's sister, Connie Busick (who had earlier pled guilty to a lesser charge and received a five-year sentence), testified that she had engaged in sexual affairs with both of her sister's husbands and was present during a meeting at the Thacker trailer on November 1, 1984, when Lois had assembled Buchanan, Hart, and their cousin Matthew Music to begin planning her husband's murder.

Busick said her sister did not approve of a suggestion by Buchanan to strike the victim over the head with a blunt object. "Lois said she wanted it done with a deer slug because Phillip [Huff, her first husband] was killed that way," Busick said.[4]

Again, defense counsel objected to the introduction of Huff's name into the proceedings, but Judge Songer overruled the objection.

Busick said Thacker had agreed to her having sex with her husbands because she wanted her sister to carry a baby for her. Busick did get pregnant by one of the men, but told jurors she decided to obtain an abortion rather than turn the child over to her sister.

Detailing the night of John's murder, Busick said she and her sister, Lois, calmly watched TV as they heard the two shots outside the trailer.

Moments later, Buchanan and Music came to the trailer and "[Buchanan] was crying and got down on his knees and said, 'Get me out of here.' When I asked who did it, he pointed to Matt [Music]. He asked me why did I let him do it, and I told him that I had told him not to, but he said I didn't try hard enough [to convince him]."[5]

Co-conspirators Buchanan and Hart testified next and admitted that the shooting death of John Thacker on November 4, 1984, had actually been preceded by an aborted attempt to kill him in some manner the night before.

Buchanan said Lois asked him repeatedly if he knew anyone who could kill her husband John. "I thought she was joking," he said. "But on other occasions, she asked me [again] if I knew anyone who would kill her husband."[6]

Hart, who had no deal yet with prosecutors but hoped his testimony would help reduce pending charges against him, said he helped drag the log across the road and backed up Buchanan's claim that it was the seventeen-year-old Music who did the shooting. Hart claimed a gun he was carrying at the time was unloaded.

Music's testimony would startle most observers. He calmly discussed his involvement.

"I shot and killed John Thacker," he said. "But I'm a reasonable person, not a killer. I don't go out and kill people just to have something to do for a hobby."[7]

Music said Lois Thacker had convinced him that it was John, and not Lois, who had shot and killed Phillip Huff (one of Music's friends) and that John wanted to have sex with Music's young girlfriend.

"When I told [Lois] it was crazy and I didn't want any part of it, she said I was already a part of it and kept asking if I was going to help do it," Music testified.[8]

Thacker's defense team attempted to implicate particularly Music in the murder of John Thacker, calling several of Lois's relatives who testified that the young man had previously spoken of killing John. Lois testified that she had nothing to do with the plot to kill her husband and that she had loved him from the time she was thirteen years old.

Jurors got the case on May 17, 1985, and deliberated just ninety minutes before returning a guilty verdict of murder against Lois Thacker. She had not only turned down a pre-trial offer to avoid a long prison sentence (and perhaps even a death sentence), she also refused to allow jurors to consider lesser included offenses (such as assisting a criminal) which would have resulted in a better sentence.

On June 27, 1985, Judge Songer sentenced Thacker to death. However, in July 1990, the Indiana Supreme Court voted three-to-two to overturn that sentence saying insufficient evidence existed to warrant the death penalty. They ordered Songer to re-sentence Thacker, which he did: forty years in prison for murder, plus another twenty years for aggravating circumstances revealed in the case.

Music was sentenced in August 1985 to forty-five years for his role in the murder. Buchanan was sentenced to thirty years for conspiracy to commit murder. James L. Hart was convicted on a lesser charge of burglary in a plea agreement and served five years of a ten-year sentence, leaving prison on November 19, 1991. Buchanan was released on January 2, 2001, after serving sixteen years, and Music served twenty-two years in prison before being released on April 29, 2008.

In the weeks after her trial and before she knew her death sentence would be overturned, Thacker talked to reporter Wanda Williams from the *Bloomington Herald-Times*. She told her, "I've always had a fear of being by myself. I want somebody for companionship. I don't know if I could stand being in a cell by myself."[9]

As she spoke, Thacker held the distinction of being the only woman on Indiana's death row and only the second woman in the state's history to be so sentenced to that point. "I believe in God," she said. "I don't think God will let the state kill me. I think he knows I've been through enough. If they do kill me, it won't be God doing it, it will be the state doing it."[10]

In jail, Thacker said she worried about her three children. She said, "I was all they had, and now they ain't got nothing," her remark missing the irony that the same was true for John Thacker's three children who were left without their father.[11]

Once condemned to die, Thacker finally won parole on April 5, 2013 after serving twenty-three years of her sentence.

Endnotes

1. *Bloomington Herald-Times*, Nov. 4, 1984.
2. Ibid.
3. Ibid.
4. *Bloomington Herald-Times*, May 14, 1985.
5. Ibid.
6. *Bloomington Herald-Times*, May 15, 1985.
7. *Bloomington Herald-Times*, May 16, 1985.
8. Ibid.
9. *Bloomington Herald-Times*, July 7, 1985.
10. Ibid.
11. Ibid.

OWEN COUNTY

VICTIM(S):
Francis Edward Drescher, 48

PERPETRATOR(S):
None ever arrested or charged.

DATE OF DEATH(S):
June 9, 1915

THE UNSOLVED MYSTERY OF 'THE POISON PLOT'

The death of Owen County Coroner Francis Edward Drescher on Wednesday evening, June 9, 1915, did nothing to help solve the mystery of the "poison plot by mail" scandal that rocked this southern Indiana county for several months in 1914-15.

Drescher, who was a Spencer undertaker and owned a furniture store there, died unexpectedly and amidst an already simmering controversy.

Although his death was eventually ruled a suicide by poisoning by the acting coroner named to succeed him in office, his family and many community members never accepted that conclusion. They believed then, and many still do, that Drescher died of heart disease or some other natural cause, the result of a short illness that set upon him in the hot days of early June 1915.

Disagreement has lingered not only about how and why Drescher died, but also about any possible involvement by him in sending "free samples" of cold and flu remedies to local residents, laced with poison. Drescher, nor anyone, was ever charged with the scandal, but the questions linger a century later.

The controversy began just after Memorial Day in 1915 when Owen County Recorder Charles P. Surber disclosed to reporters from the *Owen County Democrat* that a sample bottle of quinine (a common cold and flu remedy in the early part of the twentieth century) sent to him was confirmed by state investigators to be laced with strychnine poison.

In quick succession, seven other leading citizens of Owen County came forward to disclose they too had received a free sample of quinine by mail— including the county health officer, an undertaker, and two local physicians. Before it was over, twenty-six area residents would report having received samples of the medicine.[1]

Surber disclosed the free sample had come to his home in early November 1914, just before that fall's election where he won a term as Owen County recorder. "He looked upon the package [sent to him] with suspicion at the time, but waited until a few days ago to have the 'medicine' analyzed," the *Owen County Democrat* reported.[2]

Surber told reporters that the typewritten label on the bottle that said "free sample" matched that of anonymous typewritten letters mailed to many county voters just before the November election declaring him incompetent to serve as county recorder.

"It is the supposition of Surber that the same person who sent him the poison was responsible for the circulation of the anonymous letters," the *Democrat* report indicated.[3]

"I had a bad cold and was in need of quinine at the time the package was delivered just a few days before I was to be voted upon for county recorder," Surber said. "But I never had heard of free samples of quinine being distributed and this aroused my suspicion. The quinine was in a bottle and the bottle was wrapped in cotton."[4]

Surber, a Gosport, Indiana farmer, stopped short of naming who he thought was responsible for sending the poison, but said he had a good idea of who it was.

Surber, the Republican nominee for county recorder, said "just after my nomination, a certain person told another man in Spencer that, although I had won the nomination for recorder, I would never serve. That was repeated to me and it is the one thing that made me suspicious."[5]

Surber won the election by defeating County Commissioner John W. Black in the November balloting. Black had won the Democratic nomination by defeating Drescher in the May primary. Coincidentally, Black also reported receiving an anonymous quinine sample in the mail.[6]

Despite holding the position of secretary of the Owen County Democratic Central Committee, Drescher had struggled to win countywide office. Elected previously to the county coroner's position, he had sought the higher-paying post of recorder in the 1914 election but lost. He was subsequently named coroner again in early 1915 when the winning candidate "failed to qualify" for the office.[7]

Dr. H.E. Barnard, state chemist in Indianapolis, confirmed that the strychnine present in the quinine remedy was of sufficient quantity to cause death. Most of the samples analyzed showed that the quinine was adulterated with 15 to 26 percent of strychnine, Dr. Barnard reported.[8]

Owen County Prosecutor Joseph K. Barclay was joined in his investigation of the matter by postal inspectors from Indianapolis since the "poison plot" letters had been mailed from an Indianapolis post office to Owen County addresses.

William Blair, an undertaker at Patricksburg, Indiana, and one of Drescher's business competitors, said he too had received a free sample of the quinine. "I am thankful that I heard of the attempt to poison Mr. Surber," Blair said. "I might have taken some of the poison, believing that it was pure quinine, as it was I was suspicious at once."[9]

Blair told reporters that he and Drescher had a small feud between them because of an incident when Drescher was in one of his earlier terms as county coroner. Blair said Drescher had advised at least one family not to send the body of their loved one to Blair's funeral parlor for preparation, alleging that Blair did not possess an embalmer's license. The body was instead sent to Drescher's funeral parlor in Spencer.

"This caused bitterness on Blair's part and was only one of a number of similar incidents in connection with the relations between the two men," the *Indianapolis Star* reported.[10]

Two physicians, Dr. William McQueen of Quincy, Indiana, and Dr. G.E. Willoughby of Gosport, Indiana, also received free quinine samples in the mail, later determined to be laced with poison. Dr. R.H. Richards, the deputy Owen County health officer, also received a sample in powder form. All three physicians believed the samples were sent to them in order to cause them to offer the medicine to their patients, rather than to kill them individually.[11]

Barclay and other county officials warned Owen County residents to be suspicious of any "free samples" of medicine or any other consumable goods sent to them. As the investigation wore on, so did the rumors, with the *Owen County Democrat* noting excitedly in a front page article, "It is only a question of time that the guilty one will be apprehended. Something is liable to happen any day that will create a big sensation in this part of the state."[12]

Residents also began recalling an incident dating back to 1908 when a quart-size bottle of whiskey was delivered to the home of local furniture store owner George W. Edwards. Edwards, whose Spencer store directly competed with Drescher's downtown store, had just been elected Owen County auditor at the time.[13]

Edwards said eight men had tasted the whiskey at his home, all of them becoming violently ill, including convulsions and other symptoms of poisoning. "An investigation was made, but no evidence of any value was obtained, and the matter was dropped," the *Owen County Democrat* reported.[14]

On Wednesday, June 9, 1915, the poison by mail story emanating from Owen County to newspapers across Indiana, took one more step into the bizarre with the report of the unexpected death of Drescher at his Spencer home.

As the evening shadows drew longer, Drescher's lifeless body was found on the floor of his home by his wife at about 7:30 p.m., the drapes of his home all drawn (which stood out to neighbors who said the drapes were always open). Drescher's children were all downtown in Spencer at the Majestic Theatre watching "a moving picture show" at the time, but were immediately summoned home by their grieving mother.[15]

News reports indicated a note was found under Drescher's body that read, "I ate a radish and my heart has broken. It hurts me today. Pocketbook. Goodbye, mom and children."[16]

Drescher's friend and physician, Dr. O.E. Gray, was immediately summoned and he declared the man dead. Dr. Gray and Dr. Allen Pierson, another Spencer physician, performed an autopsy on Drescher's body, including removing his stomach and delivering it to an Indianapolis chemist for analysis.[17]

Drescher's family reported that he had returned ill two weeks ago from a meeting of the Indiana Funeral Directors' Association at Indianapolis. At the time, he complained of "ptomaine poisoning" (or food poisoning) believed caused by something he ate at the meeting.[18]

The unexpected death of the county coroner and local business leader fanned the already intense flames of rumor surrounding the poisonous mailings.

Dr. Pierson told an *Indianapolis Star* reporter that Drescher was "a peculiar man" who was a "paranoiac of pronounced type" and that "the man had a tendency toward kleptomania." The *Star* noted that "it is generally known that while not an outright criminal, Drescher had been known on many occasions to show kleptomaniac tendencies. He was openly distrusted by many persons because of this."[19]

"Opinion is not wholly against Drescher in Spencer," the *Indianapolis Star* report added. "There are many prominent persons who are not ready to believe that he had a part in the poison mystery. They accept the theory of natural death" and pointed out that Drescher "had hoed a hard row in Spencer. Unable to make ends meet as an undertaker, he had accepted the onerous duties of secretary of the county Democratic committee and became the 'political goat' of the county. His work had been drudgery with small thanks, little pay and no other reward."[20]

The rumoring and sensational reporting occurring on the story by reporters from Indianapolis and other cities caused the *Owen County Democrat* to repeat its assurance that the responsible party would be apprehended or named. "But until the guilty ones are apprehended, the *Democrat* prefers to not cast reflections upon anyone. It is a good time for the people of Owen County to 'keep their heads on their shoulders,'" the local paper advised.[21]

A week later, the *Democrat* took the unusual step of printing in its entirety the report of James McClure, the county's new acting coroner, on Drescher's death, including word-for-word transcripts of testimony given before a coroner's inquest into the matter.

Next to that, the paper ran a story titled "Excitement dying down" to further quell rumors and accusations now swirling openly in Indianapolis and Bloomington newspapers that more than suggested Drescher was responsible for the poisonous medicine.[22]

"It is stated here [in Spencer] that Drescher was to have been arrested today and charged with sending poisoned quinine through the mails to a number of county officials and other persons," the *Indiana Daily Times* reported in its front page story following Drescher's death.[23]

The *Indianapolis Star* was equally candid, noting, "Drescher's name has been mentioned frequently in connection with the search for the person who mailed 'free samples' of quinine adulterated with strychnine, to many persons in the county."[24]

The *Star* report added, "It is known that a postal officer inspector was in [Spencer] today and it was reported tonight that Drescher was to be arrested tomorrow morning."[25]

Indianapolis newspapers also reported that maybe more than one person was responsible for the poison mailings since one of the mailings from Indianapolis was completed at a time when Drescher was known to be in Spencer.

"So convinced, however, are local officials that Drescher had a part in the attempted poisoning that they regard this evidence in the light of proof that a second person was concerned, rather than as an alibi for Drescher," the *Indianapolis Star* reported in a front page story that included a photograph of federal postal inspectors and Owen County officials at the center of the probe.[26]

Indianapolis Star correspondent W. C. Mattox, reporting from Spencer, did take a momentary breath in the excited coverage of the story to note, "If Drescher did not commit suicide, then his death was a weird stroke of fate and a most remarkable coincidence...."[27]

Suspicion and speculation was also cast on the sudden death years earlier of the domestic worker in the Drescher home, Miss Maude Clark, who died of what was then believed to be a cerebral hemorrhage when she was alone in the Dresher home. Questions also swirled around the sudden death of the Reverend A. B. Banta, pastor of the Presbyterian Church in Spencer attended by the Drescher family. In each case, Drescher prepared the bodies for burial.[28]

Even more questions were raised about the November 1914 death of Alice McHenry, a twenty-two-year-old young bride in Owen County, who died without warning. A neighbor, Emma Grounds, who had originally accepted Drescher's ruling that Mrs. McHenry died of a cerebral hemorrhage, later noted that the woman had taken quinine for an illness shortly before suffering violent convulsions and dying. After her death, Drescher had embalmed her body and handled her funeral.[29]

One report surfaced that Mrs. McHenry's body would be exhumed for examination, but no follow-up reports indicated that this was ever actually undertaken.[30]

As the rumors swirled and more and more previous deaths were recalled, an unusual ruling on Drescher's death was offered.

While Dr. H.P. Noble, a private Indianapolis chemist, noted that there was no trace of strychnine poison found in Drescher's stomach, acting Owen County Coroner McClure nonetheless declared Drescher's death a suicide by poisoning.

McClure relied heavily on autopsy results that showed heavy discoloration of Drescher's stomach and other organs, and the immediate and significant onset of rigor mortis in the man, moments after his death.[31]

"I have completed a very careful examination for strychnine in the stomach which you submitted to me," Dr. Noble wrote to McClure. "I have made separate examinations of the stomach contents and of the stomach itself. Neither contains detectable quantities of strychnine."[32]

Dr. Noble added, "This fact does not exclude the possibility of poisoning by strychnine since the substance might have passed out of the stomach and since, generally speaking, the poison which kills is not that which remains there."[33]

He said "a more conclusive finding might have resulted from an examination of the liver and of the kidneys" although those organs were not preserved before burial.[34]

Regardless of Dr. Noble's analysis, McClure declared that "from a careful examination of all evidence heard and seen and from all circumstances surrounding the death of the descendent, I find that the probable cause of death was from poison administered from his own hand."[35]

The *Indiana Daily Times* reported that "friends of Drescher assail the verdict of the acting coroner. They declare he is trying to place the blame for the poison plot on a dead man rather than go to the trouble of finding the persons really guilty."[36]

Despite the concerns of Drescher's family and friends that he had been wrongly accused and convicted in the minds of local citizens and in media accounts of the "poison plot," the investigation by federal and local officials quickly fizzled after his death.

Deputy Owen County Prosecutor J.L. Duncan said, "For my part, I don't believe there would be anything gained by exhuming and examining bodies unless we have strong evidence not only that Drescher might have had a hand in the deaths, but that some other person aided him. We can't take criminal action against a dead person, of course, but it may be that some other person was involved. In that case, it might be necessary to exhume some bodies."[37]

No exhumations were known to have taken place, and no other suspects were ever publicly identified, leaving the questions swirling around Francis Edward Drescher to follow him long after his death.

Endnotes

1. *Owen County Democrat*, May 27, 1915; June 17, 1915.
2. *Owen County Democrat*, May 27, 1915.
3. Ibid.
4. Ibid.
5. *Bloomington Evening World*, June 8, 1915.
6. *Bloomington Evening World*, June 7, 1915.
7. *Indianapolis Star*, June 3, 1915.
8. *Owen County Democrat*, May 27, 1915.
9. Ibid.
10. *Indianapolis Star*, June 4, 1915.
11. *Owen County Democrat*, June 3, 1915.
12. Ibid.
13. Ibid.
14. Ibid.
15. *Owen County Democrat*, June 10, 1915.
16. Ibid.
17. Ibid.
18. Ibid.
19. *Indianapolis Star*, June 4, 1915.
20. Ibid.
21. *Owen County Democrat*, June 10, 1915.
22. Ibid.
23. *Indiana Daily Times*, June 3, 1915.

24. *Indianapolis Star,* June 3, 1915.
25. Ibid.
26. *Indianapolis Star,* June 4, 1915.
27. Ibid.
28. *Indianapolis Star,* June 5, 1915 and June 8, 1915; *Bloomington Evening World,* June 8, 1915.
29. *Indianapolis Star,* June 10, 1915.
30. *Indiana Daily Times,* June 12, 1915.
31. *Indiana Daily Times,* June 11, 1915; *Bloomington Evening World,* June 5, 1915.
32. *Indiana Daily Times,* June 11, 1915.
33. Ibid.
34. Ibid.
35. *Bloomington Evening World,* June 12, 1915.
36. *Indiana Daily Times,* June 12, 1915.
37. *Bloomington Evening World,* June 9, 1915.

PARKE COUNTY

VICTIM(S):
Gregory D. Brooks, 22;
Raymond Spencer, 17;
Reeve B. Spencer, 16;
Ralph B. Spencer, 13

PERPETRATOR(S):
Roger C. Drollinger, 23;
Michael W. Wright, 23;
Daniel R. Stonebraker, 22;
David W. Smith, 19

DATE OF DEATH(S):
February 14, 1977

THE HOLLANDSBURG MASSACRE

It's a case that has lived on in Indiana lore for decades and is known by most simply as "The Hollandsburg Massacre."

The story is one that has frightened and saddened generations of Hoosiers who learned how forty-one-year-old Betty Jane Spencer and her four sons were forced to lie face down on the floor of their northern Parke County mobile home near Hollandsburg, Indiana, while four unknown gunmen summarily executed the boys with shotgun blasts to the back of their heads. Police counted a total of twelve shotgun shells at the scene.

Mrs. Spencer, who survived a gunshot wound to the head by pretending to be dead, fooled her would-be murderers when the shot blew off the wig on her head, causing the gunmen to think they had blown off a portion of her skull. After the men ransacked the home for any valuables they could find, they fled. Mrs. Spencer pulled her wounded body up to discover the phone lines to the trailer had been cut. She then stumbled down a snowy lane to a neighbor's house to call police just before 1 a.m. on Valentine's Day 1977.

Mrs. Spencer's neighbor, Harold Escue, told sheriff's deputies that he heard her "knocking at the door. She was hollering, 'Get up and help me, please!' I got up and went to the door and then she said, 'Please help me! I've been shot and my boys are all dead!'"[1]

Escue said Mrs. Spencer pleaded as they waited for the police to arrive, "If you don't keep talking to me, I'm going to pass out."[2]

Mrs. Spencer was rushed to Union Hospital in Terre Haute suffering from shotgun pellet wounds to the head, neck, back, and shoulder.

Based on Mrs. Spencer's account, two men entered the trailer by bursting in the unlocked front door, and two more kicked in a back door, which was locked. As they left, they stole the family's car. It was found a short time later elsewhere in Parke County. Although the men stole some stereo equipment, they found only about $30. The manner of the "take over" robbery of the Spencer home matched similar cases reported in the prior week in the Parke County area, Indiana State Police detectives said.

"Police said they found the bodies lying in a pool of blood near a chair in the living room," the *Crawfordsville Journal-Review* reported. "Three of the bodies were next to one another and the other body was found about two feet away from the others. Police believe the space between the bodies was where Mrs. Spencer was lying."[3]

Police cleared Keith Spencer, the boys' father, as he was at work at the time of the assault as an overnight engineer at an Indianapolis TV station. The Spencer's daughter, Diane, was away at Purdue University at the time of the attack.

As news of the execution-style murders spread, community members expressed shock.

At Turkey Run High School where Raymond was a junior, Reeve was a sophomore, and Ralph was an eighth grader, the news hit especially hard. The boys were described as "good students and super-fine, clean-cut boys" and were active in the high school's Future Farmers of America chapter.

A funeral for all four boys was conducted at Rockville Christian Church, and they were buried side-by-side in identical caskets at the Mount Moriah Cemetery at Hollandsburg. Betty Jane was well enough to attend the funeral for her son, Gregory Brooks, and her three stepsons. She and her third husband, Keith, sat united in their grief with Keith's ex-wife, Carol Spencer, the mother of the other three boys.[4]

Based on Betty Jane's descriptions of the assailants (and those of a Veedersburg, Indiana couple also robbed in their home by intruders during the same week), state police issued composite drawings of three suspects on February 17, 1977, and asked for the public's help in finding those responsible. More than 1,000 separate leads were called in, all of them run down by investigators

Captain Stan Kenney, head of the state police's Criminal Investigations Division, said, "In most serious crimes, there is a motive that you can sink your teeth into. What I think we have here is a petty theft coupled with a senseless killing."[5]

Several weeks went by before headlines across Indiana carried the news of the March 9, 1977 arrest of one of four Montgomery County suspects in the case, twenty-two-year-old Daniel R. Stonebraker of Darlington, Indiana. Stonebraker was charged with murder. Three other suspects were also named, including twenty-three-year-old Roger C. Drollinger of Waynetown, Indiana; twenty-three-year-old Michael W. Wright of Crawfordsville, Indiana; and nineteen-year-old David W. Smith of Wingate, Indiana.

Detectives said Stonebraker had been under surveillance for about two weeks based on tips received from the public and was picked up by police in Crawfordsville and taken to an Indiana State Police post for questioning. During that questioning, Stonebraker said enough to be charged with murder.

Drollinger, a known local drug dealer, failed to appear for a March 4, 1977, sentencing hearing in Montgomery County, and authorities feared he had fled the state. Smith, the youngest suspect, was believed to be in Drollinger's company. Police detained a thirty-two-year-old Crawfordsville woman who they believed drove Drollinger and Smith to the Daytona Beach, Florida area in the days following the Hollandsburg murders.

Wright, a graduate of the U.S. Naval Academy Training Center, was picked up without incident by FBI agents on March 11, 1977, in Santa Clara, California, where he was working as a gas station attendant.

As Drollinger and Smith continued to elude capture, the FBI issued wanted posters for both men saying that they were "being sought for the brutal execution-style shotgun slayings of four young male members of an Indiana family, and the serious wounding of their mother." The poster said the men were "believed to be heavily armed with a sawed-off shotgun and revolver" and that "both individuals should be considered armed and extremely dangerous."[6]

Smith would be the next domino to fall. Police in Lexington, Kentucky picked him up on March 31, 1977 at a Holiday Inn where he had convinced two railroad employees that he was an AWOL soldier trying to make his way home to Indiana. The railroaders had sympathy on the boy because he looked like he needed to clean up and complained of heavy blisters on both of his feet from having walked long distances to reach Kentucky. When arrested, Smith was carrying a handgun and initially fought attempts to extradite him to Indiana to face charges.

Smith's mother, Lois Lyons, told reporters her son was relieved to be captured and not having "to worry about looking over his shoulder. He's scared. He lost his security when Roger (Drollinger) walked out on him. He was scared . . . he wanted to come home."[7]

On April 11, 1977, Drollinger ended his long run by voluntarily turning himself in to FBI agents from the Indianapolis office of his attorney. Drollinger said he had spent Easter weekend at an Indianapolis motel with his family. He claimed he was innocent in the case and blamed Stonebraker for implicating him. He said he worried for his family's safety as the manhunt for him dragged on.

Parke County Prosecutor Clelland Hanner said they had begun to build a good case against the four men and had recovered three sawed-off shotguns believed to have been used in the slayings (the guns found in a rural area near Shades State Park). One of the shotguns was confirmed as having been stolen in a home robbery in Fountain County the weekend before the four murders.

Drollinger's trial was the first to go forward, opening in September 1977 at the Blackford County Courthouse in Hartford City, Indiana, where it was moved on a change-of-venue motion. Hanner told jurors that Mrs. Spencer would take the stand and identify Drollinger as "the bossman" of the murderous gang of four young men. Drollinger's defense focused on how the others had blamed him and planned to highlight that he had an alibi for the time of the murders.

Daniel Stonebraker was a key witness against Drollinger and provided grisly testimony about how the four men had terrorized their victims. He testified that the four men went out looking for someone to rob and kill before they settled on the Spencer's home that night. He said Drollinger had told the other three that it was important that "they shoot or be shot" and that Drollinger said wearing masks was not necessary during the robbery "because no one would be left alive."[8]

As they entered the Spencer home, Stonebraker said Mrs. Spencer pleaded with the men, "Take anything you want, but don't hurt us."[9]

He said Gregory Brooks, the oldest of Mrs. Spencer's sons, was the first one shot and after being shot once, "he raised up and said, 'Don't shoot me again.'" At that, Stonebraker said Drollinger took a shotgun, pulled Brooks up from the floor by the back of his hair, and fired the muzzle of the gun less than one foot away from his face.

Stonebraker said the men had planned to write the words "helter skelter" on the refrigerator of the home using the victim's blood (and mimicking the infamous Manson family killings in California), but they forgot to do so before they fled.

He said he could not recall why the shooting started but said, "Mike [Wright] shot three times, David [Smith] fired three times, I fired once or twice, Mike shot again, David fired another time, and Roger [Drollinger] took Smith's gun and fired a shot." He added that Drollinger then kicked each of the victims in an attempt to make sure they were all dead.[10]

Stonebraker said it was because of him that Mrs. Spencer survived. He said Drollinger was concerned that she was still breathing, but the shotgun had jammed and would not fire again. A second attempt was made and Stonebraker said he missed Mrs. Spencer's head and struck the already-dead Brooks lying next to her.

Prosecutor Hanner had Stonebraker confirm that he knew the testimony he was providing could be used against him in his own upcoming murder trial, but Stonebraker said, "I couldn't live with the death of those people on my conscience. I wanted to be caught but I couldn't turn myself in. I wanted them to catch the ones who done it—which was us. They have got the right people. I want to make sure justice is brought forth for the death of those people."[11]

Stonebraker said the other three men feared Drollinger and did what he told them to do. "I went along because I didn't want to get shot," he said.[12]

As stunning as Stonebraker's testimony had been, Betty Jane Spencer's testimony on Thursday, September 15, 1977, would be heartbreaking.

She described in horrifying details the shootings in her home. As the men fled, she "wiggled her feet" and realized she was still alive. "I went to the window and saw two cars take off at a high rate of speed. I turned from the window and asked, 'Is anyone alive?' Nobody answered. As I stood there—a terrible sound. It took me a moment to realize it was blood rushing from our boys. It sounded like a waterfall or something like that."[13]

Betty Jane described Drollinger as the one who gave the orders to the other men. She said that after the men had searched the trailer for valuables, "I heard some kind of clicking sound behind us. At that time, I didn't know one gun from another . . . Suddenly, there was a shot fired . . . and a piece of Greg's [Brooks] head fell off beside my face. I turned my head toward him, and he was wiggling. It was so quiet, then Greg said, 'My God, I'm flying.' Then they shot him again. Then I felt him die next to my side."[14]

She said the shooting then intensified, and she soon felt her step son Raymond die on the other side of her. Michael W. Wright also testified for the prosecution, with the agreement that his testimony would not be used against him at his upcoming trial. He admitted in open court that he was the first to fire a shot, but claimed he had aimed at a sofa and had tried not to hit anyone, but his shot partially hit Mrs. Spencer.

Drollinger took the stand in his own defense as the centerpiece of his effort to avoid conviction. He quickly implicated each of the other three defendants in the killings, but not himself. Drollinger's wife and father took the stand in an attempt to provide an alibi for their loved one.

In his testimony, Drollinger challenged Mrs. Spencer's identification of him in her testimony as the man who led the killings. "If she says I was there that night, she's incorrect," he said. "I don't understand why she wanted to pick me out, but she's just confused."[15]

Confused or not, jurors believed Mrs. Spencer and the prosecution, and took less than an hour to convict Drollinger on September 21, 1977 on four counts of murder. A month later, Drollinger was sentenced to four life terms without the possibility of parole.

David W. Smith's trial opened less than a month later at the Jasper County Courthouse in Rensselaer, Indiana, also on a change of venue. Prosecutors repeatedly referred to Smith as "Drollinger's lieutenant" or "second in command" in the killings.

As they had in Drollinger's case, Stonebraker and Wright testified for the state offering damning testimony against Smith for his part in the murders. Smith's defense attorneys attempted to paint the youngest of the accused conspirators as being led by the older men, but Stonebraker testified that it was Smith who liked to gloat about killing people and said Smith had called him "a chicken" for not wanting to take part in a killing.

Mrs. Spencer testified again, telling the jury that of the four men who entered her home that night, she got the best look at Smith and remembered him because of his younger age.

In his defense, attorneys called on psychiatrists who had examined Smith to offer their insights. Dr. Edward Stuntz said, "David has the capacity to appreciate the wrongfulness of his conduct, but lacks the capacity to conform his conduct to the requirements of the law."[16]

Dr. Stuntz also said that Smith's "hunger for a father figure" in his life drew him to the older Drollinger whom he described as "a great influence" on Smith's young life.[17]

Jurors returned a verdict of guilty on all four counts against Smith on October 13, 1977. Although he had openly wept during some of the testimony during the trial, Smith was dry-eyed and showed no emotion as the verdict was read. Like Drollinger, Smith was sentenced to four life terms without the possibility of parole.

Stonebraker and Wright would both enter into plea agreements with the state rather than go to trial. Each pled guilty to one count of first-degree murder and three counts of second-degree murder. Both were sentenced to two life terms and two additional terms of fifteen to twenty-five years for the second-degree charges.

Betty Jane Spencer told reporter Anne Ryder of WTHR-TV, Channel 13 in Indianapolis, during a 2002 interview that she suffered from "survivor's guilt" for not having died alongside her boys. "I didn't feel I deserved to be alive, and I finally decided I did," she said.[18]

In the years after the "Hollandsburg Massacre," Mrs. Spencer used the notoriety of the case to help fifty-six separate state and federal laws pass addressing victims' advocacy rights. In 1983, she was the guest of President Ronald Reagan at the White House who honored her efforts. In 1988, Betty Jane and her husband Keith separated, and she moved from Indiana to Florida.

"Family members who have been traumatized by violent crime come out of their ordeal very different people," she said. "We see a high level of estrangement and divorce in victimized families. Unfortunately, Keith and I had to pay that hidden cost of crime."[19]

Betty Jane, diagnosed with lung cancer after years of smoking, succumbed to her illness on October 26, 2004.

Roger C. Drollinger, long believed to be the "ring leader" of the Parke County killers, was found dead in his cell at the Wabash Valley Correctional Center in Carlisle on January 29, 2014. He was sixty-one years old. Indiana Department of Correction officials indicated no foul play was suspected in Drollinger's death.[20]

Endnotes

1. *Terre Haute Tribune-Star*, Feb. 15, 1977
2. *Crawfordsville Journal-Review*, Feb. 14, 1977
3. Ibid.
4. *Crawfordsville Journal-Review*, Feb. 17, 1977
5. *Rockville Republican*, Feb. 21, 1977
6. FBI posters, March 15, 1977
7. *Rockville Republican*, April 4, 1977
8. *Terre Haute Tribune-Star*, Sept. 13, 1977
9. Ibid.
10. Ibid.
11. *Terre Haute Tribune-Star*, Sept. 14, 1977
12. Ibid.
13. *Terre Haute Tribune-Star*, Sept. 16, 1977
14. Ibid.
15. *Terre Haute Tribune-Star*, Sept. 20, 1977
16. *Terre Haute Tribune-Star*, Oct. 12, 1977
17. Ibid.
18. WTHR-TV, Indianapolis, Ind., Nov. 13, 2002
19. Protect the Innocent web site, undated entry
20. *Indianapolis Star*, Feb. 8, 2015

PERRY COUNTY

VICTIM(S):
Mary (Kennedy) Artman, 36;
Charles Artman, 12

PERPETRATOR(S):
William H. Artman, 34

DATE OF DEATH(S):
February 11 and 12, 1894

NO HELP AVAILABLE WHEN IT WAS NEEDED

The mental health treatment William H. Artman of Perry County needed wasn't available in his time, and was developed in Indiana and other states far too late to save his family. On February 11 and 12, 1894, he bludgeoned his thirty-six-year-old wife Mary to death, along with their oldest child, twelve-year-old Charles.

Unable to coherently explain why he had killed his family, Artman freely admitted he had beaten them to death and then mutilated their bodies. Suffering from untreated mental illness, there seemed little that could be done to prevent such acts. In rural areas such as Perry County, Indiana, just before the dawn of the twentieth century, mental illness often went undiagnosed, and as a result, untreated.

It wasn't until 1894 that U.S. states such as Indiana began enacting "State Care Acts" that centralized responsibility for the care of people with mental illness with state governments.[1]

Indiana was slightly ahead of the national trend, however, in opening the state's first "Asylum for Feebleminded Children" in 1879 but mostly because such "feeble minded" people were viewed as a drain on the social and economic fabric of Indiana. In those days, the term "feeble minded" took in both the now-defined distinct and separate disabilities of mental illness and mental retardation.[2]

Treatment options in William Artman's era were dubbed "mental hygiene" and were scientifically based, but relied upon institutional care that heavily restricted patients and provided little active treatment.[3]

It seems any help, however, *could* have saved the Artman mother and son—even locking up William Artman.

Described as "an upright, honest citizen" who was "well respected," the arrest of Mr. Artman and the disclosure of Mary and Charles's murders were received in a rather straightforward manner by the "town folks" in nearby Tell City, Indiana, when the *Tell City Journal* reported on the case in its February 14, 1894, edition.

Under a headline reading "A Dark Deed," the *Journal* noted, "Another wife and child has been sacrificed on the altar of butchery" and that responding neighbors to the Artman place, about five miles northeast of Tell City (near the settlement of Lily Dale, Indiana), reported "a crime scene they will not likely forget for many long days."[4]

The report said Mrs. Artman and her son were found on the floor of their home with "their features mutilated almost beyond recognition by the boot heel of the murderer."[5]

Mr. Artman was on the scene when investigators arrived "and jumped up and rushed at them like an infuriated wild beast and it was with great difficulty they overpowered him," the *Journal* reported.[6]

The farmer quickly confessed to one of his neighbors, saying, "Yes, Henry, I killed them both," but said he did not know why he committed the crime and "relapsed into religious mutterings. Before being taken to the county jail, he begged to be allowed to see the remains of his victims, which request was granted."[7]

Sheriff's investigators learned that as Artman stomped his wife (and later his son) to death, two of their five children, Laura, nine, and Albert, eight, slipped away from the home. It was unclear how the youngest children, Eddie, four, and Mary Orilla, one, survived the attacked unscathed.[8]

Perry County Coroner Charles Labhart determined at an inquest that Mrs. Artman was killed between 8 p.m. and midnight on Sunday, February 11, 1894, and that the boy was not killed until around 8 a.m. Monday morning, February 12, 1894. Few details about the intervening hours were learned, but Laura Artman said her father had been agitated for some time on Sunday, accusing his wife of "consorting" with a neighbor man who lived about two miles south.[9]

Coroner Labhart's report detailed the grisly nature of the attack. He said Mrs. Artman "had her right eye gouged entirely out of her head, and otherwise, badly bruised and mutilated—had no clothing on except the sleeves and shoulder yoke of an old torn waist part of a dress."[10]

Young Charles Artman "had his face and head badly bruised with the brain protruding from his forehead, was fully dressed in plain common youths' clothes, and his coat on, and barefooted," the coroner said.[11]

In the months leading up to the attack, neighbors and relatives reported that Artman had become interested in spiritualism, an interest that his wife Mary did not share. During his trial for the murder of the two loved ones, he indicated that he believed his mind had been affected by some of the tenets of spiritualism. "His behavior during the three days before the murders, during his four months in jail, and during the trial earned opposing opinions from neighbors and acquaintances as to his state of mind," Perry County historian Michael F. Rutherford wrote.[12]

Four doctors who examined Artman said they either did not have sufficient evidence to make a ruling as to his mental state or believed that he was sane enough to know right from wrong.

Artman, while held at the Perry County Jail at Cannelton, Indiana, attempted to escape on May 8, 1894, "but was overpowered after an interesting fight," the *Tell City News* reported.[13]

His trial for murder was conducted for three days beginning on May 24, 1894, and provided even more details about the gruesome assault that the coroner had not originally disclosed. A pathologist testified that Mary Artman, in addition to losing one of her eyes at the hands of her husband, had a dozen cuts on her body, a probe rammed through her brain, and her womb cut out. The dead boy's body was found thrown over the top of his mother, the pathologist testified.[14]

Artman testified himself but gave testimony that was reported to be "rambling, vague and inconsistent with itself" and the statements of others. He was found guilty of murder on May 26, 1894, and sentenced to life in prison.[15]

Mary and Charles Artman were buried at Deer Creek Cemetery in Perry County, but it is unclear what happened to the four surviving Artman children.[16]

The *Tell City Journal*, poetic in its coverage, said that Artman had "struck down the citadel of [Mary's] earthly life and her soul had crossed the borderlands of eternity. For him, no more would she give a smile of recognition."[17]

Endnotes

1. Overview of Mental Health Services, *Mental Health: A Report to the U.S. Surgeon General*, Centers for Disease Control & Prevention, Atlanta, GA, Chapter 2, Section 7.

2. Osgood, Robert L. (2001) The Menace of the Feebleminded: George Bliss, Amos Butler, and the Indiana Committee on Mental Defectives, *Indiana Magazine of History,* December 2001, Indiana University Trustees, Bloomington, IN, pages 253-254.
3. Morrissey, J. P., & Goldman, H. H. (1984). Cycles of reform in the care of the chronically mentally ill. *Hospital and Community Psychiatry, 35,* 785–793.
4. *Tell City Journal,* Feb. 14, 1894.
5. Ibid.
6. *Tell City Journal,* Feb. 21, 1894.
7. *Tell City Journal,* Feb. 14, 1894; Feb. 21, 1894.
8. *Tell City Journal,* Feb. 14, 1894.
9. Rutherford, Michael F. (2000) *Perry County: Then and Now,* Turner Publishing Company, Paducah, KY, pages 144-145.
10. Rutherford, page 144.
11. Ibid.
12. Ibid.
13. *Tell City News,* May 12, 1894.
14. *Cannelton Telephone,* May 31, 1894.
15. Ibid.
16. Rutherford, page 145.
17. *Tell City Journal,* Feb. 14, 1894.

PIKE COUNTY

VICTIM(S):
Shannon L. Wentzel, 15

PERPETRATOR(S):
J. Brian Powell, 24;
Kelly S. Craig, 17;
Leon R. Jones, 21

DATE OF DEATH(S):
December 9, 1995

A VERY MEAN MURDER

Fifteen-year-old Shannon Wentzel spent Friday night, December 8, 1995, doing what many of her peers liked to do—hanging out between the La Cappucino's coffee house on Division Street in downtown Evansville and the McDonald's just two blocks down at the corner of Main and Division Streets.

It would be the last place she would be seen alive. Around 10:30 p.m., she got into the pickup truck of a man described as a white male in his twenties. She would soon be murdered in a mean, vicious way that shocked even veteran police investigators.

Indiana State Police detective Mike Hildebrand said the group of kids Shannon was with was getting ready to head home for the night, when Shannon announced she was going to leave with the young man in the McDonald's parking lot. She told her friends his name was Kelly.[1]

Saturday morning, Shannon's worried family called the police asking for their help in locating her. What they didn't know was that Shannon was already dead, callously dumped along a Pike County road, miles from home.

On Sunday, news broke that Pike County officials had found a body. Shannon's family helped identify the victim as the young Bosse High School freshman.[2]

322   *Andrew E. Stoner*

Her body had been found by a water well worker on Saturday morning in a rural area of southern Pike County known as Five Points, Indiana (west of Stendal, Indiana). An immediate cause of death could not be determined, but Hildebrand said he could not rule out exposure because overnight temperatures had plunged into the single digits as the season's first major snowfall, measuring five inches in some areas, blanketed the community on Friday and Saturday.[3]

The murderers had disposed of her remains on a snow- and ice-covered gravel road. Because of these difficult road conditions, Detective Hildebrand speculated that the body had most likely been dumped by someone driving a truck. "It was pretty slick. The road that led to where she was at, I just don't think a car could get there," he said.[4]

Police soon picked up seventeen-year-old Kelly Craig of Newburgh, Indiana. After questioning him about meeting Shannon at the McDonald's that night, they arrested him and charged him with murder. Craig's friend, twenty-four-year-old J. Brian Powell, of Chandler, Indiana, was also arrested and charged with murder.

As details emerged about Shannon's final moments, residents were shocked and horrified.

"What Shannon Wentzel thought would be a ride home from a former boyfriend turned into a violent and ugly end to her young life," wrote a reporter for the *Evansville Courier*.[5]

Documents filed in the charges against Craig and Powell indicated Shannon had been beaten, raped, and then run over by a pickup truck as many as nine times to ensure she was dead. Prosecutors said Craig had given a statement implicating himself as well as a third man, twenty-one-year-old Leon R. Jones of Ann Arbor, Michigan, in the crime. Jones was under arrest in Traverse City, Michigan.

"This all came together very fast," said Pike County Prosecutor Jeff Biesterveld. "We wanted to get the warrants and arrest them as soon as possible."[6]

Investigators said the three suspects fled to Michigan from Southwestern Indiana shortly after killing Shannon. Craig and Powell later returned to Indiana.

Investigators soon learned some of the specific details of what happened to young Shannon in Jones's black four-wheel-drive Ford Ranger pickup truck: truly a night of terror.

After stopping off for beer, the trio said they planned to go "mudding" on a rural road in Pike County. Craig and Powell's statements said that "fun" ended about midnight when Jones stopped his truck, and the three men and one woman got out.

Statements given by Craig and Powell said Jones was the first to strike Shannon in the head with a beer bottle, knocking her to the ground. At that point, all three began beating and kicking the girl.

After she was subdued, Powell said Craig and Jones both took turns raping the girl and that all three of the men took turns sodomizing the young woman who by then was lying motionless on the frozen roadway.

To ensure that she was dead, Jones came up with the idea of running over her body with the truck. After doing so, they loaded her body into a blanket and drove to a spot about a mile away near Pike County roads 1200 South and 400 East where they planned to dump her body.[7]

Shannon's mother, Lori, was beside herself with grief over what her daughter had endured. "Shannon's life was wasted for what? I don't know," she said.[8]

Lori said her daughter, Shannon, trusted Kelly Craig. "That's the only reason she went with him. She wanted a ride home, and that's the only reason she got in."[9]

"When they were doing this to her, she needed my help," Lori said through tears to *Evansville Courier* reporter Lou Bubala. "I wasn't there. That's hard to deal with. That's hard."[10]

On Friday, December 15, 1995, Powell and Craig hung their heads and looked at the ground as both were led into the Pike County Courthouse at Petersburg to answer the charges against them. Pike County Circuit Court Judge Marvin Stratton read the charges against the men, both high school dropouts, and noted they faced a maximum sentence of sixty-five years in prison if convicted. Powell began to weep. Craig showed no emotion.[11]

Prosecutor Biesterveld said he was still considering seeking the death penalty against the men. "It is a very difficult case to try," he said. "I have children of my own, and I empathize with the victim's family. That's one reason I want to talk to the family [before deciding on a death penalty charge]."[12]

Back in Michigan, prosecutors worked to complete Jones's extradition to Pike County, Indiana. Jones eventually appeared in Pike County Circuit Court in early January 1996 facing charges similar to those leveled against Craig and Powell.

Jones quickly decided to enter a plea in the case and avoid a trial. He was the only African-American defendant in the case. It would have been a struggle to find anything other than an all-white jury in Pike County where the overall population is 99 percent white, according to U.S. Census records.

Jones pled guilty on December 13, 1996, to the murder and rape of Shannon Wentzel. During his sentencing hearing in January 1997, Dr. John

Heidingsfelder, a forensic pathologist, testified that Shannon had died as a result of "the cumulative effect of the injuries" including blunt force trauma to the head, face, chest, abdomen, legs, arms, and hands. Heidingsfelder indicated she may have also suffered stab wounds and confirmed that her ribs were broken in multiple places. The girl's lungs and liver had also been punctured.

A tennis shoe tread found on her face, Dr. Heidingsfelder said, indicated she was brutally beaten before being run over by the truck. He confirmed that injuries consistent with her being sodomized before death were also present.[13]

Powell also testified in the sentencing hearing against Jones, offering another gruesome detail. He said after the initial assault on Shannon, as the men drove her body to where they planned to dump her, Shannon sat straight up in the back of the pickup truck startling the men. Powell quoted Jones as saying, "The bitch still ain't dead; we're going to have run over her again."[14]

Judge Stratton had heard enough.

"The victim's death was apparently slow, painful, and torturous," he said. "Less than the enhanced term [in prison] would depreciate the seriousness of the crime."[15]

Stratton sentenced Jones to a total of ninety-five years in prison, sixty-four years and eleven months for murder and thirty years for criminally deviant conduct. Housed at the Indiana State Prison in Michigan City, Jones would be sixty-nine years old before being eligible for release in 2043.

Powell, who never went beyond eighth grade in school, but who gave police the most detailed description of the crimes against Shannon during the early stages of the investigation, entered guilty pleas to charges of aiding in murder and criminally deviant conduct. He was sentenced on February 27, 1997, to forty-five years for aiding in murder and twenty-nine years and eleven months for criminally deviant conduct. He is being held at the New Castle Psychiatric Correctional Facility in Henry County and is not eligible for release prior to 2033 when he will be sixty-two years old.

Craig took the next plea deal and was sentenced on October 23, 1997, to forty-five years in prison for aiding in murder and another nine years and eleven months for attempted rape. He is being held at the Wabash Valley Correctional Facility at Carlisle, Indiana, and is not eligible for release prior to 2020 when he will be forty-one years old.

In 1999, Jones filed an unsuccessful appeal of his sentence to the Indiana Supreme Court arguing that Judge Stratton's requirement that he serve his two sentences, totaling ninety-five years consecutively, was unfair and failed to consider his possible mental illness and his dysfunctional childhood. The high court disagreed, saying, "We conclude that [Jones'] sentence is not manifestly unreasonable and affirm the judgment of the trial court."[16]

Endnotes

1. *Evansville Courier*, Dec. 11, 1995.
2. Ibid.
3. *Evansville Courier*, Dec. 13, 1995.
4. *Evansville Courier*, Dec. 12, 1995.
5. *Evansville Courier*, Dec. 14, 1995.
6. *Petersburg Press-Dispatch*, Dec. 14, 1995.
7. *Evansville Courier*, Dec. 14, 1995.
8. Ibid.
9. Ibid.
10. Ibid.
11. *Evansville Courier*, Dec. 15, 1995.
12. Ibid.
13. *Petersburg Press-Dispatch*, Jan. 15, 1997.
14. *Evansville Courier*, Jan. 15, 1997; Petersburg Press-Dispatch, Jan. 15, 1997.
15. *Evansville Courier*, Jan. 15, 1997.
16. *Leon R. Jones v. State of Indiana*, Indiana Supreme Court ruling, (1999).

PORTER COUNTY

VICTIM(S):
Lorraine "Lorie" A. Kirkley, 34

PERPETRATOR(S):
David F. Malinski, 33

DATE OF DEATH(S):
July 21, 1999

A 'SELFISH, UNGODLY AND WICKED' ACT

Six years after he stalked, abducted, tortured, and finally killed Lorraine "Lorie" Kirkley, David Malinski directed authorities to where they could find her body.

It was a secret he had intended to take to his grave—but meetings with a prison chaplain and a desire to join the Christian fellowship at the Indiana State Prison drove him to come clean.

Malinski told police they could find Lorie's body in a five-foot grave he dug for her from midnight to 5 a.m. on a hot summer night in late July 1999 on his father's property near Rensselaer, Indiana, in Jasper County.

Just a few feet removed from his father's cabin, Malinski had wrapped Lorie's body in a tarp and tied it with bungee cord and convinced himself he had buried any proof of his evil acts once and for all. A rusted can of Deep Woods Off that Malinski had used to keep from being bitten by mosquitoes as he worked through the night to bury Lorie's body was the clue to help authorities find the grave.

It was the end of a long and earnest search for Lorie that police, firefighters, the FBI, family members, and volunteers from the community had carried on for months in Porter, LaPorte, and Lake counties.

Thirty-four-year-old Lorie Kirkley was last seen alive on Wednesday, July 21, 1999, as she left her job as a cardiac rehabilitation nurse at Porter Memorial Hospital. Her husband of eleven years, Robert Kirkley, returned home after her that evening and found the garage door open, and Lorie's vehicle gone. He also found blood and evidence of a struggle.

Taped to a wall nearby was the latest taunting note left in the Kirkley home that convinced him Lorie was in terrible danger.

Local, state, and federal police began a massive investigation into Lorie's disappearance. No one was convinced she ran away—a lens from her eyeglasses and important thyroid and asthma medicine that she needed were left behind. Her 1994 Ford Explorer was also missing.

Further, Lorie and Robert had listed their house for sale and begun building a new one further east in South Bend where Robert's job was taking him. Lorie had even applied for jobs at hospitals in South Bend and Mishawaka preparing for their move. It seemed unlikely she would just walk away.

A neighbor reported seeing a man ride up to the Kirkley home in the Hunter's Pointe subdivision of Valparaiso on both Tuesday and Wednesday and both times enter the home by opening the garage door. He also noticed Lorie's vehicle as she arrived home from work on Wednesday evening and played with her dog Patches in the yard. The Explorer was driven away soon afterward, with two people inside.

The break-in at the Kirkley home was the second in seven months, although no forced entry was used either time. Police would eventually learn why: Malinski had stolen the overhead garage door opener from Lorie's Explorer in the employee parking lot at the hospital.

Malinski knew Lorie well—he was a colleague of hers in the cardiac rehab unit where he worked as a physical therapist. Their careers, however, were on very different paths. Lorie was considered a valued, model employee. Malinski, on the other hand, seemed to slip in and out of trouble (as he did in a previous job at a Michigan City hospital) and was socially awkward with others.

Unknown to investigators until later, however, Malinski had systematically stalked Lorie for months, perhaps more than a year. In a February 2, 1999, break-in at their home, he left behind a computer-written note alleging Lorie was having an affair with another man and included a collage of nude, grainy photos of Lorie taken at an unknown time. Among the items stolen were some of Lorie's underwear.

The incident scared the Kirkleys—causing Lorie to cut back on her cycling club activities. They installed a home alarm system. Robert was concerned, too, but along with Porter County Sheriff's detectives, who investigated the break-in, was unsure what it all meant.

Sheriff's detective Jerry Kratowicz would later describe the break-in as "absolutely bizarre" and said that Lorie was "upset, very upset ... and afraid."[1]

Although he had little to go on, Kratowicz kept the case file on top of his desk. "I couldn't, in all conscience, close it out," he said.[2]

The new break-in and Lorie's disappearance included two handwritten notes threatening the Kirkley family.

As news broke of Lorie's disappearance across Porter County, so did Kelley Malinski's willingness to continue to keep her husband David's secrets.

Kelley frantically called her mother, and they both met with an attorney to hear Kelley declare, "I think he did it to her."[3]

Kelley told her mother and the attorney that she knew David had broken into the Malinski home in February after she found some of Lorie's belongings in her home. Kelley would soon tell her story to detectives and turn over a .357-Magnum handgun that she said David kept hidden in their large, $250,000 Chesterton home.

David, meanwhile, was at the home of his brother Charles in Griffith confessing that he had done "something stupid."[4]

Police picked up David in Griffith about an hour after Kelley told her story and began questioning him about the break-in at the Kirkley home. He freely admitted to the February invasion, to leaving the notes and pictures, and taking Lorie's Ford Explorer, and burning it on a rural LaPorte County road, but denied having anything to do with her disappearance.

No one believed his story, and prosecutors charged Malinski with two counts of burglary, one count of auto theft, and one count of arson on July 29, 1999. Although not initially charged with harming Lorie, "the main suspect in the disappearance is obviously Mr. Malinski," police spokesman Tim Emmons said.[5]

On Wednesday, August 4, 1999, prosecutors took the next step and charged Malinski with the abduction and murder of Lorie Kirkley. Their case had been helped considerably when a citizen in Valparaiso turned in a plastic bag they found near an apartment complex dumpster. The note said, "Give this to Bob Kirkley [Lorie's husband]" and also said, "I'm sorry about your wife." The bag contained the keys to Lorie's Explorer and an anonymous note addressed to her husband. The note said that "he killed Lorraine Kirkley because she recognized him during the July 21 burglary. The author further described Lorraine biting his right middle finger during the confrontation," according to court documents.[6]

Porter County Chief Deputy Prosecutor Brian Gensel (who would later be elected county prosecutor) said Malinski admitted to being the author of the note and that he was responsible for blood found in Lorie's kitchen, although his story continued to evolve.

Malinski had a severe bite wound to one finger on his hand and other scratches and bruises, consistent with the note found indicating Lorie had bitten her attacker.

John Martin, Malinski's attorney, described the evidence to charge his client as "flimsy" and unsuccessfully asked the court to release him on bond.

Just a month later, another major break came in the growing case against Malinski. Police found a set of sixteen Polaroid photographs taken of Lorie that showed her bound, gagged, nude, and posed, and being sexually molested. Police were tipped off to the location of the photos along a county road near Malinski's Chesterton home after Malinski asked his fellow inmate to go and get them once he was released from jail.

Further buttressing their case, multiple searches of Malinski's home turned up a secret "porn room" Malinski had set up to display his pornography. An observant detective noted the home's roof line and discovered officers had not been inside the entire attic of the home. A subsequent search turned up Malinski's secret "porn room" that he had partitioned off with drywall in a portion of the home's attic.

Also found was a letter from David to his wife, Kelley, that indicated the level of loyalty he required of her—even though she had been the one to finally tell police of David's secrets. The letter was titled, "See Proverbs 31, 10-31," offering the Biblical passage, "Her husband has full confidence in her … She brings him good, not harm, all the days of her life …"

Computer files at Malinski's house revealed plans for an alibi and detailed descriptions of how Lorie normally traveled to and from her job to home.

For those who had known David Malinski since he was young, the mounting evidence against him was startling. Best known for his football ability, Malinski had been an all-state lineman for Munster High School and a starting offensive lineman for the Ball State University Cardinals (winning all-conference honors his senior year).

"A lot of guys I played [football] with were violent off the field. David was not violent," said one of his former Ball State teammates, Jason Whitlock. "David was a quiet, intelligent individual."[7]

Those who didn't know David Malinski personally but only through the growing evidence against him were disturbed. "The photos [police recovered] are rather shocking in and of themselves because of the subject matter," said Joseph Prahlow, a board certified forensic pathologist, who examined the photos.

Malinski offered a defense that sought to kill Lorie a second time—he said Lorie willingly posed for the pictures as part of a plot the two of them had hatched to run away together to North Carolina. He claimed this was the result of their long-standing sexual relationship.

Beyond Malinski's delusional idea that Lorie was his lover and willing torture participant, no evidence was ever presented to support his libelous claim.

After several delays, Malinski's trial was scheduled to go forward at the start of 2000, despite the fact that multiple searches, in which the FBI assisted, had yet to turn up Lorie's body. A jury was selected from Tippecanoe County and brought 100 miles north to Valparaiso to hear the case.

Porter County Superior Court Judge Roger Bradford opened the trial on Malinski's thirty-fourth birthday with prosecutors showing slides of Lorie as she once was and then as she sat bound, gagged, and tortured in the photos recovered by investigators.

A videotape of Malinski's multiple statements to police was played for jurors in which he admitted he "was always" thinking about a possible romantic relationship with Lorie but said he did not ask her out because they both were married.

In a second statement, he changed his story to say he and Lorie had carried on a sexual relationship and planned to run away together.

He also admitted stealing the garage door opener from Lorie's car, driving to her home during his lunch break, unlocking a door from inside, and then leaving and returning later to burglarize the home. He admitted taking photos of women, including Lorie, using the locker room showers at Porter Memorial Hospital, which he used to make the photo collage he left behind at her house.

He denied abducting or killing Lorie, sticking to his story that she ran away from an allegedly unhappy marriage. He said he refused to go with her because he "didn't want to change anything. I just wanted to keep having fun. I love my wife. This woman [Lorie] was just sexual convenience. It was lust."[8]

Lorie's husband, Robert, gave tearful testimony in which he told the court how much they loved one another, loved cycling together, shared church activities together, and were making plans to move to a newly built home in South Bend. In fact, a real estate agent working with them to sell their Valparaiso home described them as "newlyweds" because of how much they seemed to love one another.

An FBI agent testified he talked to more than 500 people who knew Lorie, including about 350 of her former patients in the cardiac rehab unit. None of them reported any knowledge or suspicion of any type of relationship between Lorie and Malinski.

Malinski's defense team called only one witness—noted Indiana pathologist John Pless. They were able to get Pless to contradict a prosecution witness who said they believed the photos taken of Lorie showed she was an "unwilling participant."

As the two-week trial came to an end, jurors took only two hours to find Malinski guilty on seven separate charges. One juror, who asked to remain anonymous, later told reporter Mark Kiesling of the *Times of Northwest Indiana* that she would have voted for the death penalty had prosecutors sought it.

She said the prospect of a death penalty "… troubled me a little bit going in … but I think all the evidence added up. [Malinski] had a whole lot of holes in his story."[9]

The juror denied that the photographs that Malinski had taken of his victim were the deciding factor in spite of their shocking scenes. Key elements were his statements he made to his brother, his wife, and the note found by a citizen in a bag of Lorie's possessions.

Judge Bradford later sentenced Malinski to 155 years in prison. He would be 111 years old before he was eligible for parole.

As he was sentenced, Malinski gave an angry, defiant interview to reporter Ken Kosky of the *Times*. He said he had turned to God since he was arrested and blasted police and prosecutors for treating him unfairly.

He added, "I think I had an evil spirit" in me, "… but I'm going to heaven now."[10]

He explained that investigators had twisted his story around to suit their purposes—"they made me out to be a monster. It's ridiculous," he said.[11]

Particularly troubling to him was the revelation of his secret "porn room" in the attic of his home which he defended as a room he built just to practice hanging drywall, running electrical wires, and installing air conditioning.

"I made the room out to be a dungeon," Malinski said. "If it was successful, I'd finish our bonus room. It was harmless."[12]

As time passed, most people forgot about the angry, lonely David Malinski locked away just twenty-six miles down the road at the Indiana State Prison in Michigan City. Most ignored the fact that he lost in September 2003, as expected, the appeal of his conviction. That is, of course, until Malinski surprised everyone again.

A September 16, 2005, meeting between Malinski and the man who had put him behind bars, Deputy Prosecutor Gensel, revealed Malinski was ready to disclose the location of Lorie's body—a woman he had vehemently denied ever harming.

In an odd public statement where he referred to himself in the third person, Malinski said he had "concealed the truth to avoid the death penalty and out of fear of losing his family. But he has been tormented by the fact that he took Lorraine Kirkley's life and has not revealed her location to her family or authorities. Now, he is no longer concerned about protecting himself but wants to resolve this matter for the families involved."[13]

Malinski said he had been born again and "accepted Jesus' leadership" over his life. Still writing in the third person about himself, he said, "Originally, he had planned to take this secret to the grave; but Jesus has changed his heart and revealing this secret has become urgent."[14] He described his acts against Lorie as "selfish, ungodly and wicked."[15]

For his part, Robert Kirkley said, "I would like to express deepest appreciation to all those who have worked on this case and who have kept us in their prayers and good thoughts … our hope lies in knowing that we … will see her again some day."[16]

Anthropologists, forensic experts, and police unearthed Lorie's body on Friday, September 30, 2005, in the area Malinski pointed to at the scene. An autopsy on her remains revealed Lorrie had been manually strangled to death by Malinski. Evidence of a sexual assault could not be determined because of the state of decomposition of the body.

On Saturday, October 16, 2005, Robert Kirkley and Lorie's parents, William and Patricia Jones of Kewanna, Indiana, gathered with family and friends at the Fulton Baptist Church to properly memorialize her. She was buried in a quiet cemetery at Grass Creek, Indiana, about five miles from the Fulton County farm where she grew up.

Endnotes

1. *Times of Northwest Indiana*, Jan. 27, 2000.
2. Ibid.
3. *Times of Northwest Indiana*, Feb. 3, 2000.
4. Ibid.
5. *Times of Northwest Indiana*, July 30, 1999.
6. *Times of Northwest Indiana*, Aug. 5, 1999 and Jan. 27, 2000.
7. *Muncie Star Press*, Feb. 5, 2000.
8. *Times of Northwest Indiana*, Jan. 28, 2000.
9. *Times of Northwest Indiana*, Feb. 9, 2000.
10. *Times of Northwest Indiana*, March 17, 2000.
11. Ibid.
12. Ibid.
13. *Times of Northwest Indiana*, Oct. 1, 2005.
14. Ibid.
15. Ibid.
16. Ibid.

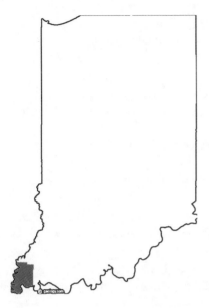

POSEY COUNTY

VICTIM(S):
Stacey Lynn Forsee, 20;
Tia Maranda Forsee, 3;
Jordan Michael Forsee, 18 months

PERPETRATOR(S):
James P. Harrison, 41

DATE OF DEATH(S):
January 17, 1989

AN EVIL OBSESSION

Stacey Lynn Forsee was at the Mount Vernon Church of God one Sunday morning in 1988 when she met the man who would develop a strong, obsessive interest in and attraction for her that would eventually lead to three ugly murders.

A mother at the young age of seventeen, Stacey suffered from asthma so badly she required an oxygen tank in her home to keep her breathing normal. Nevertheless, she was a doting and loving mother to the two children she was raising on her own by the time she was twenty.

Stacey's mom, Gloria Forsee, said her daughter knew asthma was shortening her life, but she remained upbeat. Another family friend noted how well she kept her two children dressed, and her home neat and tidy, and how she always wore a smile.

All of that would change in the freezing early morning hours of Tuesday, January 17, 1989, inside Stacey's simple, one-story home at 235 Elm Street in Mount Vernon, Indiana.

After neighbors and a newspaper delivery person noticed heavy smoke pouring from Stacey's home, they called the fire department. Firefighters could not save Stacey and her two children. Stacey and her eighteen-month-old son Jordan were found dead on the sofa in the living room, apparently where they had slept for the night. Tia Forsee's lifeless three-year-old body was found in her bed in a back bedroom.

It took just forty-eight hours before police and the coroner declared the deaths were "fire related," but that Stacey had not died from fire- or smoke-related injuries. Although the fire had been intentionally set, investigators believed, trauma on Stacey's body indicated she had died of multiple stab wounds and likely had bene raped as semen was found inside her mouth.

Her daughter, Tia Foresee, died of burns suffered in the fire, and her son Jordan Forsee, had died of smoke inhalation.

The investigation into who killed Stacey and her two young children would drag on for months and eventually years. Police did not give up, eventually arresting and charging James P. Harrison, forty-one, with the murders more than two years after the offense.

Police and prosecutors based their case on the fact that Harrison was observed near Stacey's home on the night of the fire before the fire trucks arrive. He had also purchased kerosene in the days before the murder, and he regularly carried a hunting knife of the type that was used to kill Stacey. He also implicated himself in the crime to fellow inmates while he was being held in a Maryland jail.

Harrison's trial finally got underway in Posey County in November 1991 and opened with one of Harrison's poems presented by prosecutors to reveal his obsessive interest in the younger Stacey.

Church members testified that Harrison had become enamored with Stacey (even though she was twenty years younger than him) shortly after one church member pointed her out to him and said, "There's a woman who would probably use a good Christian husband."[1]

One church member, Allan Baker, said Harrison "… made the comment shortly after he met her that she was *his* woman."[2]

A problem arouse, however, as Stacey was not available to date Harrison or anyone else, even if she had wanted to. Witnesses said she was devoted to Scott Rickard, a Terre Haute man incarcerated in a correctional facility on a DUI charge. Stacey believed she and Rickard would someday get married.

Stacey was not oblivious to Harrison's affections for her. In November and December of 1988, she became upset with him when he continued to bring gifts for her and her children to her home.

Karen Sue Baker, another church member, testified that Stacey had discussed the situation with her and said she only wanted to see Harrison at church, and only as a friend, not as a love interest. Allan and Karen Sue Baker attempted to tell Harrison that his advances were unwelcomed, but he seemed insulted.

He continued to attend the church, however, except for the Sunday before the deadly assault and fire at Stacey's home. "I noticed he looked at her a lot [during church], had his eyes fixed on her quite a bit, but he never spoke to her," Karen Sue Baker said.

One of Stacey's neighbors identified Harrison from a photo lineup as the man she had seen in the neighborhood during the early morning hours of January 17, 1989.

Prosecutors also successfully introduced a statement Harrison gave to Mount Vernon Police Chief Kenneth R. Rose when he was questioned by Rose at a jail in Baltimore, Maryland.

Harrison's half-brother, William Cross, Jr., testified against his kin. However, he proved to be a confused witness. He originally gave police a statement that at least partially implicated his half-brother in the crime. He later recanted and said he felt pressure from the police to make the statement, and did so only because he feared they would put him back in jail.

Portions of Cross's statement were true, he said, including parts about seeing Harrison with a knife two days before the fire and that Harrison had written him letters saying he was disappointed Stacey had ended their alleged relationship.

The most damaging blow to Harrison, however, was testimony that DNA samples taken from the semen in Stacey's mouth matched only 7.4 percent of the white male population of the United States, inclusive of Harrison.

Defense attorneys attempted to raise an alternate theory for why Stacey had been killed, saying she had approached a detective with the Indiana State Police during the last week of her life complaining about being followed by a man in a white van. Defense attorneys contended Stacey may have had incriminating evidence against some local drug dealers.

Harrison's trial lasted six days, and deliberations would cover another twenty hours over four more days, before guilty verdicts were returned.

In a surprise move, however, guilty verdicts were only rendered for the deaths of Tia and Jordan Forsee. The jury acquitted Harrison in the death of Stacey. Jurors did convict him on the charges of arson and found him also to be a habitual offender. (The latter designation was made possible by Harrison's two previous convictions for a 1971 voluntary manslaughter case in Arlington, Virginia, and a later conviction for second-degree murder, also in Virginia.)

In separate deliberations, the jury recommended Harrison be put to death for his crimes. He was so sentenced on December 14, 1991, for his convictions on two counts of murder and one count of arson.

Harrison lost a 1995 appeal of his conviction and sentence before the Indiana Court of Appeals but was more successful on the federal level. In January 2004, U.S. District Court Judge Sarah Evans Barker of the Southern District of Indiana, threw out Harrison's convictions saying Posey County Circuit Court Judge James Redwine had demonstrated "actual bias" before and during the trial. Barker's ruling gave prosecutors the option of retrying Harrison.

Judge Redwine defended his actions in the case saying, "I had no prejudice against him. I know he got a fair trial."[3]

The Seventh U.S. Circuit Court of Appeals affirmed Barker's ruling on October 27, 2005, agreeing that Harrison had been denied due process because of questions raised about the impartiality of the original trial. A new special judge was appointed to rehear Harrison's case. The second time through, Harrison was once again convicted and finally sentenced on May 5, 2008 to one-hundred fifty years for the deaths of the two children—nearly two decades after the original incident.

Endnotes

1. *Evansville Courier*, Nov. 8, 1991.
2. Ibid.
3. Indiana Law Online Blog, Nov. 5, 2005.

PULASKI COUNTY

VICTIM(S):
Milo Lewis, 47

PERPETRATOR(S):
Arthur James Lewis, 29

DATE OF DEATH(S):
October 11, 1967

A GUN HIDDEN IN A BOOK IS USED TO KILL THE SHERIFF

In a scene straight out of a black-and-white film noir, Pulaski County Jail inmate Arthur James Lewis successfully shot his way to freedom on October 12, 1967, using a gun smuggled to him inside a carved-out book.

Twenty-nine-year-old Lewis of Gary, Indiana, fled the jail at Winamac after shooting Pulaski County Sheriff Milo Lewis (no relation to the suspect) in the neck and shoulder and locking him and the sheriff's radio man in another cell. The suspect then fled in a county sheriff's vehicle.

Winamac Town Marshal Claude Lloyd, stopping by the jail to visit the sheriff just before 9 a.m., discovered the two officers locked in the cell and freed them. The sheriff was critically wounded and was rushed to Pulaski Memorial Hospital where he died three hours later at 11:50 a.m.

Milo Lewis was the first Republican to be elected sheriff in Pulaski County in a dozen years and was just ten months into his first term in office when he died.

Pulaski County Coroner Henry Eshelman, MD, said a bullet had ruptured the main artery in his neck, and "the wound was probably fatal from the beginning." The bullet had been coughed out of the sheriff's throat as he gasped for breath at the hospital. The second bullet lodged near his esophagus.[1]

The sheriff's radio man, Fred Anderson, told other officers that the incident started at about 8:30 a.m. on that Wednesday morning while a second deputy was out of the building.

Anderson explained the ruse Lewis used to get out of his cell. "He wanted to call his lawyer, he said he wanted to plead guilty," so Sheriff Lewis granted him permission to use the phone. "First thing I knew, I looked up and this guy pulled a small gun from his pants pocket," Anderson said.[2]

As the sheriff attempted to talk him out of using the gun and tossed the cell keys he was demanding out of his reach, Lewis shot the sheriff twice. Anderson said Lewis forced him to help drag the dying sheriff to the cell where both men were locked up.

Police later found a carved out paperback book where Lewis had hidden a .25-caliber, nickel-plated handgun. As he left the jail, he also grabbed two other .38-caliber handguns to take with him. Investigators learned he had received a visitor at the jail the night before the shooting—possibly the person who slipped him the gun.

Arthur Lewis was being held in Pulaski County as he awaited trial on an armed robbery warrant from South Bend. His trial had moved from St. Joseph County to Starke County. Starke County officials asked the Pulaski County sheriff to hold the man since the jail at Winamac was considered more secure than the one at Knox.

The incident sparked a massive manhunt across Northern Indiana which quickly centered on the towns of Wanatah, Indiana (in adjacent LaPorte County where the sheriff's vehicle was abandoned), and Kouts, Indiana, the latter a Porter County town where the fugitive stole a car. At Wanatah, officers conducted a door-to-door search of residences to find Lewis, just as they had done in July 1966 at Rolling Prairie, Indiana, when they arrested him for the armed robbery of Sule's Tavern in South Bend, which netted him $2,500.

The FBI joined with 150 Indiana officers in the search for Arthur Lewis and continued to focus on areas north and west of Pulaski County. Eventually K-9 and helicopter units were also employed in a fruitless attempt to find the man. Leads that would turn out to be false had even led authorities to burn off a wheat field ready for harvest near Fowler, Indiana, after a resident reported seeing a "negro" walking in that area.

Friday the thirteenth of October would prove unlucky for Arthur Lewis— the stolen car from Kouts was located by police parked in the 3400 block of South Michigan Street in South Bend.

As South Bend and FBI officers zeroed in on a house at 121 S. Lake Street, Lewis, referred to by one reporter as a "will-o'-the-wisp escape artist" attempted one more try at freedom, dashing about two blocks away from the house before Indiana State Police sergeant Charles Neary caught him in a vacant lot.

In the Lake Street house, police found the stolen weapons Lewis had used to gain his freedom. A resident of the home, twenty-seven-year-old Arthur L. Wells, was arrested and charged with aiding an escaping prisoner. A second man, thirty-two-year-old Aubrey McCaskell of Gary, was also held on an aiding and abetting charge for allegedly smuggling the gun into Lewis's cell.

Two others, Faye Walker of Gary and Carl W. Myslinski of LaPorte, were also later indicted for "counseling, encouraging, hiring and commanding [Arthur Lewis] to commit murder."[3]

In a rare Saturday morning court hearing, Pulaski County Circuit Court Judge Robert Thompson ordered Lewis held on a preliminary charge of murder. For safekeeping, he was immediately whisked away to the Indiana State Prison at Michigan City.

The next day, funeral services for Sheriff Lewis were conducted at the Monterey Methodist Church which included an honor guard of hundreds of police officers from across the state. A World War II veteran, he was afforded full military rites at the Monterey Cemetery.

Ironically, Sheriff Lewis was killed in the line of duty almost 60 years to the day after Pulaski County Sheriff Charles H. Oglesby was gunned down by a train robber in October 1907.

For his part, Lewis was convicted of second-degree murder in the death of Sheriff Lewis following a trial conducted in Cass County on a change of venue. He was sentenced to life in prison on September 26, 1968. He would not remain behind bars for long. In a rare escape from the Indiana State Prison at Michigan City, Lewis and another inmate stowed away on a garbage truck and escaped to freedom on November 18, 1968. He was recaptured a short time later and remained in prison for the next quarter century until winning parole in 1992. He completed his parole in 1999, and was finally a free man at the age of sixty-one.[4]

Endnotes

1. *Pulaski County Journal*, Oct. 12, 1967.
2. *South Bend Tribune*, Oct. 14, 1967.
3. *Pulaski County Journal*, Oct. 26, 1967.
4. *Michigan City News-Dispatch*, Nov. 19-20, 1968; Indiana State Prison Records.

PUTNAM COUNTY

VICTIM(S):
Zachary Snider, 10

PERPETRATOR(S):
Christopher M. Stevens, 20

DATE OF DEATH(S):
July 15, 1993

TRYING TO MAKE A DIFFERENCE FROM ZACHARY'S DEATH

The gruesome discovery of the decomposing body of ten-year-old Zachary Snider on Wednesday, July 21, 1993, would change Indiana in very important ways in the years that would follow.

Sadly, child abduction and murder in Indiana (or any state) did not stand out as particularly unusual. Crime-jaded Hoosiers feared such things but had begun to understand that such evil did exist in our midst.

However, there would be many things different about the murder of the boy with a wide, toothy smile known as Zachary. When the circumstances of his abduction and murder became known, Hoosiers from all walks of life took notice and decided his death had to mean something and worked to bring change in the growing state.

The case began as a missing child report on Thursday, July 15, 1993, as Zachary's frantic Cloverdale, Indiana, parents reported him missing to Putnam County authorities. A massive search commenced. Police enlisted the help of community and neighborhood volunteers. The search proved fruitless until days later when an anonymous tip came in to police and officers found Zachary's body dumped along a rural road about six miles northwest of Cloverdale.

For Zachary's parents and all the residents of the lush, close-knit Stardust Hills subdivision, the news was devastating. "Our neighborhood has become a wasteland," neighbor Becky Galvan told reporters. "We felt we could let our kids run [around] the neighborhood, but not anymore . . . They don't feel safe anymore."[1]

Even more troubling for parents, the man arrested for Zachary's murder was someone who had helped search for him. Police held twenty-year-old Christopher M. Stevens, a curly-headed man who had just moved to Cloverdale from Indianapolis, on suspicion of Zachary's murder. Although new to the area, he was well-known and often seen in the company of neighborhood children—despite being almost a decade older than most of them.

Police began to focus on Stevens, despite his proactive move to load children into his car and search the area for Zachary. A witness reported that they saw Zachary's bicycle parked outside Stevens' house the day he went missing.

Galvan said the children in the subdivision seemed to look up to Stevens because "he was a cool, older guy who did things with them."[2]

Stevens had been in Galvan's own home and had been the one to tell her that Zachary was missing. He warned her to keep her children inside the house until case was solved.

It seems Stevens's intentions had never been innocent or "cool."

It also seems no one in the area knew who Stevens was or that he had a troubling past that would cause any parent to keep their child away from him, if they had only known. Stevens had been free from jail for only sixty days after his latest run-in with the law for inappropriate behavior with children when he moved to Cloverdale.

Marion County authorities placed Stevens on parole in May 1993 after he had served four months of his one-year sentence for a conviction for fondling a ten-year-old boy and his eleven-year-old sister beginning in November 1991. After his release, his probation was transferred from Marion to Putnam County so Stevens could go live with his father and stepmother at Cloverdale. Stevens and his family were under no legal obligation at the time to inform anyone of his past record, and they didn't.

"We're just still in shock about the whole situation," his father, Joe Stevens told the *Terre Haute Tribune-Star*. "We had tried to get [Chris] to stay away from Zachary because of his past situation."[3]

As police questioned Stevens about Zachary's death, he eventually admitted he had killed the boy because Zachary had threatened to tell his parents that the two of them had engaged in oral sex. Stevens detailed how he made multiple attempts to kill the boy inside his home, finally succeeding by placing a plastic trash bag over the boy's head as he strangled him with an electrical cord.

Stevens's death penalty trial in February 1995 was moved to Tippecanoe County because of the intense statewide and national publicity. Jurors watched a videotape of Stevens' initial statement to police saying Zachary had come to his house that day to confront him about rumors that Stevens was claiming to be having an affair with Zachary's mother.

"He was mad. Real mad. He threatened to tell, not about me and his mom, but about me and him," Stevens told detectives on the tape.[4]

He also told detectives, "As soon as [Zachary] said he was going to tell, I remember thinking, 'I'm not going to go through this again.'"[5]

Putnam County Prosecutor Robert Lowe said the rumor about an affair between Stevens and Zachary's mother was made up by Stevens to divert other, growing rumors that some thought he was gay.

Stevens described how he led Zachary into his bedroom and tried to smother him with a pillow, "but that wasn't doing anything," so he retrieved a trash bag and the cord from a nearby video game.

Stevens admitted that as he worked to kill Zachary, the boy said, "Why are you doing this to me?" and "I love you Chris, I love you."[6]

After killing the boy, Stevens said he placed his body and his bicycle into the trunk of his car and drove to a secluded area and tossed both of them off a bridge. He even detailed having to climb down below the bridge to dislodge the bicycle from the tree branch where it had become stuck.

Further damaging evidence came from Stevens's older brother, twenty-four-year-old Mark Stevens, who told the court that his brother admitted killing the boy and disposing of his body. It was Mark Stevens who tipped off police about the location of Zachary's body based on what his brother had told him.

Stevens' stepmother, Marsha Stevens, testified about a 1993 letter she received from her stepson while he awaited trial for Zachary's murder. In it, he said, "I'm sorry for killing someone in your house and causing you guys so much grief. I guess it is like everybody had always said. I'm nothing but a worthless, perverted piece of trash."[7]

Prosecutors then called Zachary's father, Todd Snider, who burst into tears as he identified photographs of the boy's bike found where the body had been dumped. It was a bike Zachary had loved ever since his father bought and assembled it for him.

Todd Snider composed himself to say that he had become highly suspicious of Stevens as early as June 1993 when Stevens took Zachary fishing. When he went to join the two fishing, he had trouble finding them and eventually located them far from the Stardust Hills subdivision.

The father said he confronted Stevens immediately. "I said something to the point that I didn't know what was going on here, but I didn't like it and that Zachary was not to be in Mr. Stevens' car and that Mr. Stevens was to stay away from my son."[8]

The trio returned home, and Todd Snider resumed working on a motorcycle he was building in the family's garage. When he went inside the house to get Zachary to ask him for some help, he was gone. By 7 p.m., when he still had not returned, Snider and his wife, Sandy, were frantic. Snider reported that Stevens had come to their home multiple times that evening pretending to assist in the ad hoc search for the boy that neighbors had assembled.

Stevens' defense attorneys referred to their client as a "twenty-year-old boy" and said the letter from his jail cell to his stepmother reflected Stevens was worthy of pity. "How low do you have to sink to write something like this? How can a twenty-year-old feel that way about himself?" defense attorney Robert Clutter asked jurors.[9]

Stevens' three-day trial came to an end on February 9, 1995, without any testimony from Stevens himself and after only two hours of deliberation by jurors. They found Stevens guilty on all counts and recommended the death penalty.

After the verdict was read and jurors were removed from the courtroom, Stevens spoke up unexpectedly and complained to Tippecanoe County Judge George Heid: "I agreed not to testify on my own behalf on the basis that voluntary [manslaughter] was already in the [jury] instructions. They deliberately lied to me to keep me from testifying." He added, "I just want it on the record that I was denied my right to testify."[10]

During the sentencing phase of Stevens' trial, a court-appointed counselor said his review revealed Stevens had often been suicidal in his life and had engaged in self-mutilation in the past. The counselor said Stevens appeared to suffer from severe depression, had eating and sleeping disorders, and had begun drinking alcohol as early as age five.

Prosecutor Lowe stomped out any growing feeling of pity for Stevens when he presented a former fellow inmate of Stevens from the Marion County Jail. A twice-convicted child molester, Tracy Eaton testified that the night before Stevens was released from jail in May 1993, the other jail-isolated child molester suspected that he'd be back in jail soon.

"He said, 'No I won't—next time I'll kill him,'" Eaton quoted Stevens as declaring.[11]

Judge Heid was unconvinced by any arguments raised for sparing Stevens. He ruled that Stevens should be executed for Zachary's murder. As Heid announced the sentence, Stevens's mother, Shirley Plowman, began sobbing in the courtroom.

A now-defiant Stevens then turned to a juror present in the courtroom audience for the sentencing hearing and said, "I hope you're happy now, bitch."[12]

Zachary's parents and their friends decided that the young boy's death had to create change in Indiana. They didn't want other neighborhoods having to live next to convicted child predators without knowing it. In response, they approached State Representatives Susan Crosby of Roachdale and Jerome Kearns of Terre Haute to create a child abuse registry in Indiana.

The registry, which would become known as "Zachary's Law," required public disclosure of the whereabouts of all persons convicted of child abuse or neglect anywhere in the state as soon as they are placed on probation or parole.

Governor Evan Bayh signed the bill into law on May 14, 1994, at the Indiana Statehouse with Zachary's parents at his side. Within the first decade of its existence, the list of names available had grown to more than 1,000 and was expanded to include the photographs and addresses of sex offenders posted online.

In July 2007, the U.S. Court of Appeals in Chicago overturned Stevens' death penalty sentence, agreeing with his lawyers that jurors were not presented adequate information about Stevens' mental illness. The court determined that jurors may have made a different sentencing recommendation had they known of Stevens mental health problems.

"In this case, we find reasonable probability . . . that the result would have been different if the jury had heard mainstream expert psychological testimony," Judge Diane P. Wood wrote in a 2-1 ruling in Stevens' favor.[13]

The high court stopped short of releasing Stevens, or ordering a new trial, and instead ordered a new sentence be given to Stevens for his conviction. The Putnam County court obliged, with Stevens sentenced to life in prison, without the possibility of parole, on November 23, 2009.

Endnotes

1. *Terre Haute Tribune-Star,* July 23, 1993.
2. Ibid.
3. Ibid.
4. Associated Press, Feb. 8, 1995.
5. *Lafayette Journal & Courier,* Feb. 8, 1995.
6. Associated Press, Feb. 8, 1995.
7. Associated Press, Feb. 9, 1995.
8. *Lafayette Journal & Courier,* Feb. 9, 1995.
9. *Lafayette Journal & Courier,* Feb. 10, 1995.
10. Ibid.
11. *Lafayette Journal & Courier,* Feb. 11, 1995.
12. *Lafayette Journal & Courier,* March 15, 1995.
13. Associated Press, June 28, 2007.

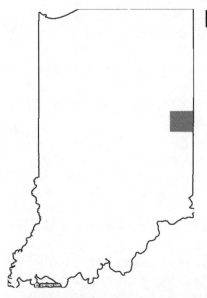

RANDOLPH COUNTY

VICTIM(S):
Donald Saunders, 32

PERPETRATOR(S):
Janet L. Blakeslee, 35

DATE OF DEATH(S):
February 9, 2004

A WOMAN INSISTENT ON GETTING HER OWN WAY

Janet Blakeslee was a woman who was used to getting her own way—any way she could. So when a Randolph County judge told her in early 2004 that she would have to grant her ex-husband, Donald Saunders, visitation with their two children, ages seven and two, she was incensed.

It was the latest defeat for Blakeslee in her attempts to take total control over the lives of her children and to cut Saunders out forever. No one could predict she would take her need for control to such extremes.

On Monday, February 9, 2004, a judge ruled that Saunders should be granted visitation and ordered Saunders and Blakeslee to meet with officials in the Randolph County Office of Family and Children to work out how that would occur. It was a major victory for Saunders who had been denied visitation for months. Blakeslee had not attended the court hearing but instead, was elsewhere making other plans.

"He was a caring man who only wanted to see his children," Saunders attorney Jay Toney said. "He was patient with the system, understanding it was slow. When he left [the courthouse], he was happy. He was going to see his kids."[1]

Saunders' happiness would be short-lived.

Just before 3 p.m. that day, Steve Cox, director of the local OFC office, placed a call to 911 reporting that a woman had shot a man inside a conference room in their downtown Winchester offices.

When police arrived, they found Blakeslee had already been subdued and disarmed by office staff and other visitors. She was seated on the floor yelling her case to anyone who would listen. Nearby, Saunders lay dead from multiple gunshot wounds—one to his back and four to the back and side of his head.

Blakeslee told the first Winchester Police Department officer arriving on the scene, "I killed him. He's dead. And he's in Hell."[2]

Fortunately, Blakeslee's five children, including the two she had during her two-year marriage to Saunders, were outside the offices waiting in Blakeslee's van with their grandfather. They had not witnessed the shooting, only the arrival of police cars and ambulances.

Saunders' family back in Bargersville, Indiana, in Johnson County were devastated at the news. They knew how hard he had fought to stay in his children's lives. He had even tried to get custody of them himself.

"[Janet] wanted to take them away from him entirely, and he was determined to try and keep a connection with them," Saunders' grandmother Wilma Nelson said. "We had been worrying for a long time that something like this was going to happen because we knew the kind of person she was. She was very controlling and didn't like it when she wouldn't get her way."[3]

The Saunders family knew Janet well. She had previously been married to Donald Saunders' brother, Steven, who died in a traffic accident years earlier. Following his death, Janet and Donald became friends, started dating, and married in 2001—although it apparently was a "common law" relationship, because no marriage license was ever located.

As their relationship soured, Saunders moved out of their shared Losantville, Indiana, home and Blakeslee began making allegations that he had molested some of the children. Those allegations never resulted in any criminal charges against Saunders, but the court did award Blakeslee custodial care of the children and ordered Saunders to pay child support.

In the wake of the startling shooting in a public building, Randolph County officials began a review of security measures. Randolph County Prosecutor David Daly was vocal in his desire that security be increased and said in the meantime, he had decided to keep a handgun near him at all times.

"If someone comes in here and starts firing in my office, I at least want to be able to fire back," Daly said.[4]

Justice in the case was quick. Blakeslee's trial began in August 2004, just six months after the shooting. Blakeslee told the jury that she had "freaked" and killed Saunders because she believed he was going to rape her children during a court-ordered visitation at the Office of Family and Children.

Blakeslee's attorneys argued she was mentally ill at the time of the shooting, although two court-appointed experts said she was not mentally ill.

"I was scared for my children," Blakeslee said. "I was a mess. All I was trying to do was keep my kids safe."[5]

Testimony revealed that Blakeslee, worried that she would have to cooperate with visitation for Saunders, had skipped the court hearing the morning of the shooting so she could pack her van and prepare to flee with her children. Police later recovered clothing, 300 rounds of ammunition, and $17,000 in cash from the van.

Blakeslee apparently agreed to bring the children to the Office of Family and Children after being wrongly told that the visit with Saunders would be supervised by an armed guard. As the meeting started, "Donnie [Saunders] said something. I don't remember what it was. I remember feeling sick," Blakeslee said in court. "The next thing I knew, Donnie was on the floor."[6]

Under cross-examination, she denied she hated Donald and said, "I didn't want my kids raped anymore."[7]

Jurors took just two hours on August 16, 2004, to deliberate Blakeslee's fate and returned a verdict of guilty but mentally ill for the murder. A month later, Special Judge Brian Hutchinson of Jay County sentenced Blakeslee to fifty-five of the sixty-five-year maximum sentence.

On August 4, 2005, however, the Indiana Court of Appeals overturned Blakeslee's conviction and ordered a new trial, saying Judge Hutchinson had erred in not allowing certain jury instructions defense attorneys had sought.

A second trial conducted in September 2006 resulted in Blakeslee being convicted of voluntary manslaughter. She was sentenced to twenty-four years and eleven months in prison on October 2, 2006. She is serving her sentence at the Indiana Women's Prison in Indianapolis and is not eligible for parole before 2016.

Endnotes

1. *Muncie Star-Press*, Feb. 11, 2004.
2. Ibid.
3. Ibid.
4. *Muncie Star-Press*, Feb. 12, 2004.
5. *Muncie Star-Press*, Aug. 13, 2004.
6. Ibid.
7. *Muncie Star-Press*, Aug. 14, 2004.

RIPLEY COUNTY

VICTIM(S):
Lyle S. Levi;
Clifford Gordon;
Henry Schutter, Jr.;
Bert Andrews;
William Jenkins

PERPETRATOR(S):
Unknown members of Versailles,
Indiana, lynch mob

DATE OF DEATH(S):
September 15, 1897

THE PEOPLE OF VERSAILLES TAKE JUSTICE INTO THEIR OWN HANDS

The people of Versailles, Indiana, had grown impatient with a marauding group of robbers who stole hard-earned wages from Ripley County farmers and others, and so, during the early morning hours of Wednesday, September 15, 1897, the people took justice into their own hands.

As the *Versailles Republican* reported, "The peaceful citizens of the quiet town of Versailles were aroused from their slumbers at an early hour Wednesday morning with the startling news that one of the most terrible tragedies of modern times had taken place within her borders."[1]

The report continued, "The awful news spread like fire, and the horrid spectre of five human beings, hanging cold in death to the same tree, met the gaze of all who cared to look. Mob law had done its work ... [and five men] had paid the penalties of their supposed crimes, according to the law of 'Judge Lynch.'"[2]

It wasn't as if lynching were new to Indiana—in fact, throughout its history, the state has produced more than one ugly tale of lynching. However, by 1897, the reports of lynching had grown scarcer and were separated by more and more years. The last known public lynching in Indiana occurred in Marion, Indiana, on August 7, 1930, when two black men were lynched by an angry mob of white citizens; a third escaped death.

In the Versailles incident, all five of the victims—Lyle S. Levi; Clifford Gordon; Henry Schutter, Jr.; Bert Andrews; and William Jenkins—were white, but their fate was the same.

The five men hung at Versailles were all residents of Osgood, Indiana, and had been jailed just a day or two before on various charges related to a robbery and shootout with police at Correct, Indiana, a village about four miles south of Versailles. Sheriff Henry Busching suffered a minor hand wound from a bullet in the shootout.[3]

The men were also suspects in a series of armed robberies perpetrated against unsuspecting farmers who had brought grain or livestock to town for sale. The men allegedly robbed the farmers while they were en route home with their earnings.

It seemed stealing a man's hard-earned wages was more than folks in Ripley County were willing to accept. And they grew tired of local officials' inability to capture those responsible.

The *Versailles Republican* reported that the Ripley County jailer was awakened just after midnight by the sounding of a bell at the jail. "He was met at the door, face to face, by three stalwart men, masked, armed and resolute. The keys of the jail were demanded of him," the newspaper reported.[4]

The night jailer, Will E. Kenan, refused to release the keys to the men, but at gunpoint, Kenan eventually relented and gave up the keys. Immediately, another ten to twelve "lynchers" climbed the stairs of the jail and placed ropes around the necks of the men "and they were pulled or hauled down stairs."[5]

"The order was given to 'pull on those ropes and pull fast,'" and the men were strung up to a tree near the jail known as "Gordon's Leap," and each was summarily hung to death.[6]

Another inmate in the jail, Charlie Kelley, who was not harmed by the lunch mob, told the coroner's inquest that, "The jail was unlocked; 10 or 12 persons came in and told us to throw up our hands. They had black masks on their faces."[7]

He said Schutter and Jenkins were the first two grabbed, and both were struck on the head with blunt objects by the mobbing men as they attempted to resist being dragged from the jail.

Although aiding in the investigation, Kelley remained a man who garnered little respect, it seems. A few days after the lynching, the *Versailles Republican* reported that "the depravity of Charles Kelley was displayed when he stated, that while the bleeding corpse of Schutter was lying on the cell floor and before the mob dragged it from the jail, he robbed it of three silver dollars, and hid them in his bed."[8]

Another overnight jail guard, William H. Black, told the coroner that the men dragged from their cells begged for mercy, but none was shown to them. He noted that as the mob left the jail, "A fellow came to us [Black and William Kenan] and bid us good night and said, 'Don't give any alarm for one hour' ... I did not recognize any of them."[9]

Deputy Sheriff Robert Bassett also testified that he saw 250 to 300 men outside of the jail that night but said he could not recognize any of them.[10]

Versailles physician, Dr. R.T. Olmsted, told the coroner's inquest that one of the men, Lyle Levi, had suffered a gunshot wound, likely inflicted as he resisted efforts to pull him from the jail. He said the gunshot wound was most likely fatal, although his body was still strung up from the tree branches.[11]

Dr. Olmsted said Schutter suffered wounds on his head and had a fractured skull but died as a result of being strangled while hanging from the tree. William Jenkins "... had contused and lacerated wounds on the right side of his head, and his skull was fractured, [and] his body also indicated strangulation [by hanging]," Dr. Olmsted reported.[12]

The doctor also said, "The rope was tied tightly around [Clifford Gordon's] neck with noose, and hanging from the limb of a tree. In my opinion, his neck was fractured, which produced death."[13]

Regarding Bert Andrews, he reported, "... his body was hanging to a tree, his feet touching the ground; suspended by rope around the neck by slip-noose. From appearance of the body, death was caused by strangulation."[14]

News of the lynching reached the state house in Indianapolis, and Governor James A. Mount said, "News of the lynching at Versailles fills me with inexpressible regret ... and mob violence must be stopped."[15]

Ripley County authorities continued to investigate via the coroner's inquest and a subsequent grand jury. As the *Versailles Republican* reported, "The investigation has proceeded quietly, and has caused no excitement."[16]

If state officials were outraged at Indianapolis, that sentiment did not seem to prevail in Ripley County. "Relic hunters had nearly carried away the elm tree where the lynching took place, only the body of the tree remains," the *Versailles Republican* reported. "It is to be hoped that further damage to the tree will cease."[17]

"Large crowds of people daily visit the place where the lynching took place, and considerable interest is still maintained in listening to a reciting of the remarkable story," the report in the Versailles newspaper added.[18]

Governor Mount continued to express his concern from Indianapolis, sending another telegraph directly to the sheriff saying, "Wire me at once the particulars of the lynching that has occurred in your county. I further direct that you proceed immediately with all the power you can command to bring to justice all the parties guilty of participation in the murder of the five men alleged to have been lynched."[19]

The governor added, "Such lawlessness is intolerable and all the power of the State, if necessary, will be vigorously employed for the arrest and punishment of all the parties implicated."[20]

Sheriff Busching sent his own message to the governor, assuring him, "Have my men actively at work. Will use every means in my power to bring 'lynchers' to justice. Nothing tangible yet. Will keep you informed of developments."[21]

The governor also telegraphed Ripley County Prosecutor Marcus R. Connelly and urged him to act swiftly to bring the lynch mob to justice. He informed Connelly that he was dispatching a deputy attorney general from Indianapolis to Versailles to investigate on behalf of the state.

Governor Mount acknowledged that "thieving and systematic robbing have been carried on there [in Ripley County], and that criminals have not been promptly brought to justice; while this failure to enforce the law may have occurred, yet it is no justification for mob law. No violation of law and no such crime is justifiable."[22]

All of the lynching victims were buried on September 16, 1897. Bert Andrews' private funeral was conducted inside the home of his Osgood, Indiana, parents as family and friends stood outside. "The body was taken to another village, followed by four carriages and two buggies, where it was consigned to the earth in the quiet country churchyard."[23]

A funeral for Clifford Gordon occurred less than an hour later and just four blocks from Andrews' parents' home. His body was then transported to a cemetery at Nebraska, Indiana, in Jennings County.

The other three men, Schutter, Jenkins, and Levi, the latter being "the supposed leader of the gang," were also eulogized that day, and all were buried at Greenview Cemetery in Osgood.[24]

Two Ripley County farmers, Jacob Schumacher and Nicholas Volz of Morris, Indiana, said news of the lynching was welcomed in the county. "They said the feeling among the people was one of relief and not of horror. There is no possibility, they say, that any of the men lynched were innocent," the *Madison Courier* reported.[25]

"The men have been known for years in the community as men who would not do an honest day's work and would turn their hands to crime," the *Madison Courier* added.[26]

"I had known Schutter, one of the men lynched, for years and I have never known any good of him," Schumacher said. "He and his gang have terrified our part of the country. When a man went to Osgood to get any money he had to be careful that no one saw him put the money in his pocket or some of the gang would be after him as soon as he got out of town."[27]

Volz said the gang was probably as large as ten men, and "when any of the gang were caught, it seemed that their pals would 'swear them out' [of jail]. The people bore it as long as they could, and then took their own course to relieve themselves."[28]

No one would ever be arrested or tried for the lynching. The only arrests would be of the widow of William Jenkins and another woman from Madison, Indiana, for allegedly receiving stolen property from the now deceased men.

Deputy Attorney General Merrill Moores sent a telegraph to Governor Mount and assured him that peace had been restored in Versailles and that Ripley County Circuit Court Judge Willard New was taking the matter seriously, although Prosecutor Connelly was conspicuous in his absence from the county and the grand jury proceedings.[29]

On March 2, 1898, Deputy Attorney General Moores' investigation concluded in a fantastic theory forwarded by Ripley County officials and reported to the governor by Indiana Attorney General William A. Ketcham.

Ketcham reported that the investigation showed that Sheriff Busching was not present at the jail the night of the attack but had left the jail in command of five of his deputies. The deputies, however, were armed with unloaded shotguns. The deputies had withdrawn the shells "in order to make their weapons more efficient" and said that "undoubtedly in the case of an emergency requiring action, a sufficient charge could be placed in the gun"—but no guns were ever fired by the deputies.[30]

Ketcham said the investigation showed "… no person whatever, either of the county, or from any other place, participated either directly or indirectly in the killing of those five men …"[31]

Ketcham said local residents implicated Levi in the killing of the other four men. Their theory was that Levi had broken out of jail undetected, secured a gun, returned to the jail undetected, and then single-handedly led his four co-conspirators out of the jail, lynched them from the tree by himself, and then killed himself by hanging himself and then shooting himself as well.

The attorney general added a postscript to his report to the governor: "When you are at leisure, I will be glad to report further orally in the matter, and if there be any lingering doubts in your mind as to the correctness of this 'theory' which, I admit, at first blush would seem to be somewhat unreasonable, to remove those doubts and convince you that no other explanation is either tenable or possible."[32]

Governor Mount told reporters at Indianapolis that he never held out hope for a conviction. Instead, the governor said, he hoped the general discussion of the subject would help put an end to lynching in Indiana and help move along legislation to "put a quietus upon whitecapping as well as lynching," he said.[33]

"Governor Mount said yesterday nothing additional would be done by the state in the immediate future," the *Madison Courier* reported. "It is now believed that the state authorities are disgusted in their efforts to prosecute the Ripley County lynchers, and that nothing further would be done."[34]

The *Courier* added, "The Attorney General in his sarcastic report filed with the governor uses several expressions which seem to indicate that the last effort has been made by the state and nothing else can be done."[35]

Endnotes

1. *Versailles Republican*, Sept. 15, 1897.
2. Ibid.
3. *Madison Courier*, Sept. 13, 1897.
4. *Versailles Republican*, Sept. 15, 1897.
5. Ibid.
6. Ibid.
7. Ibid.
8. *Versailles Republican*, Sept. 22, 1897.
9. Ibid.
10. Ibid.
11. *Versailles Republican*, Sept. 15, 1897.
12. Ibid.
13. Ibid.
14. Ibid.
15. Ibid.
16. *Versailles Republican*, Sept. 22, 1897.
17. *Versailles Republican*, Sept. 15, 1897.
18. Ibid.
19. *Madison Courier*, Sept. 15, 1897.
20. Ibid.
21. *Madison Courier*, Sept. 18, 1897.
22. *Madison Courier*, Sept. 17, 1897.
23. Ibid.
24. Ibid.
25. Ibid.
26. Ibid.

27. Ibid.

28. Ibid.

29. *Madison Courier*, Sept. 18, 1897.

30. Indiana Attorney General's Biennial Report, 1897-98, page 47.

31. Ibid.

32. *Madison Courier*, March 3, 1898.

33. *Madison Courier*, March 2, 1898.

34. *Madison Courier*, March 3, 1898

35. Ibid.

RUSH COUNTY

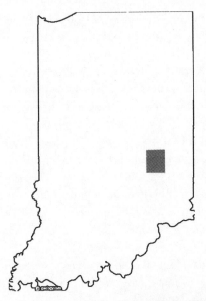

VICTIM(S):
Ray Compton, 41

PERPETRATOR(S):
James W. Webster, 35

DATE OF DEATH(S):
October 3, 1932

A MOONSHINE MURDER

Rush County Sheriff Ray Compton set out about noon on Monday, October 3, 1932, to serve a "John Doe" warrant at a farmhouse at the end of a long lane in the Circleville settlement, just south of Rushville, Indiana. It was the last run the two-term sheriff would ever make.

The sheriff's brother, Deputy Sheriff Clarence "Ed" Compton, and Special Deputy S.L. Hunt accompanied the sheriff that day as he sought to investigate reports of an illegal still and illegal liquor sales occurring on the property.

As Sheriff Compton approached the front door of the rundown farmhouse, "a woman suddenly threw herself against the Sheriff while a man quickly darted upstairs. As the Sheriff threw aside the woman, the man on the stairs fired twice at the official, one bullet striking him in the face. He was killed practically instantly," the *Rushville Republican* reported.[1]

The suspect was able to escape by climbing out an upstairs window and then jumping to a porch roof below. Deputy Sheriff Compton stayed with his dying brother, while Special Deputy Hunt raced back to Rushville to summon Rushville Police Department officers to assist in a search for the suspect.

The suspect's wife who had thrown herself into the sheriff's path, eighteen-year-old Anna May Webster, was "sullen and silent" and "although she admitted she was the wife of the man who shot the Sheriff, the woman would make no further comments."[2]

A search of the property revealed a twenty-five-gallon still operating in an outbuilding on the property and twenty gallons of whiskey, which was also confiscated.

A posse quickly formed and scoured the woods and countryside south of Rushville and the Circleville settlement. The suspect's wife eventually identified him as thirty-five-year-old James W. Webster. Webster and his wife had just recently moved to the rented farmhouse from their previous home at Milroy, Indiana. They were originally from Ohio.

An autopsy showed Sheriff Compton suffered a single but mortal gunshot wound to the lower right jaw. He was shot and killed just a short distance from the site where Rushville Police Department patrolman Walter Garrison was killed as he checked on a car parked in a lane there in February 1931. Dr. Lowell M. Green, county coroner, took over temporarily as the new Rush County sheriff.

Sheriff's deputies later raided another Circleville home, that of George Lee Rowland, whose wife was Anna May Webster's sister. "A large still and a quantity of mash and liquor" were confiscated, and everyone in the house was jailed, the *Rushville Republican* noted.[3]

Webster was a desperate man—at the time of the Rush County shooting, he was sought as a fugitive from Iowa. He had escaped prison there where he was serving a life sentence for murder. He had served ten years earlier in Missouri for the death of another man.[4]

Days of searching turned frustrating as it became "the general supposition that Webster slipped through the volunteer picket lines composed of authorities and hundreds of armed posse men, and vanished to other haunts far away from Rush County."[5]

Hopes were raised when police in Lima, Ohio, arrested a man who matched Webster's description. Men who knew Webster went with Rush County authorities to Lima but confirmed the man was not Webster. A man spotted in a field in eastern Shelby County also raised hopes briefly, but no apprehension was made.

On Thursday, October 6, 1932, the Rush County grand jury returned an indictment of murder against Webster and ordered his young wife held as a material witness, along with sixty-seven-year-old Fred "Froggy" Clevenger, Sr., who owned the farm where Webster was running the still. His brother-in-law, George Rowland, was also indicted for operating an illegal still and pled guilty three days later. He was sentenced to one to five years in the state reformatory.

A day later, on Friday, October 7, 1932, the Rush County commissioners voted to offer a $500 reward "for the capture of the Sheriff's murderer, dead or alive."[6]

The commissioners also selected the deceased sheriff's brother, "Ed" Compton, to be the new Rush County sheriff with the understanding that the widow of the sheriff would remain as the county jail matron and receive the same salary her husband would have earned, had he lived.

The last hope for finding Webster in Indiana came in the form of an unusual report from Milan, Indiana, fifty-three miles away from Rushville in Ripley County. A barber there reported he gave a haircut and a shave to a man who was likely Webster. The barber said he noticed a revolver in the man's coat pocket and that he matched a description he had heard of Webster.

The trail to find Webster continued to grow cold until a report was received that Webster committed suicide later during a violent shootout with police at Cincinnati, Ohio, rather than return to jail.[7]

Endnotes
1. *Rushville Republican*, Oct. 3, 1932.
2. Ibid.
3. *Rushville Republican*, Oct. 4, 1932.
4. Indiana Police Officer Memorial Web Site; Officer Down Memorial Page, Inc.
5. *Rushville Republican*, Oct. 5, 1932.
6. *Rushville Republican*, Oct. 7, 1932.
7. Indiana Police Officer Memorial Web Site; Officer Down Memorial Page, Inc.

ST. JOSEPH COUNTY

VICTIM(S):
Lisa Marie Bianco, 29

PERPETRATOR:
Alan L. Matheney, 38

DATE OF DEATH(S):
March 4, 1989

A BRUTAL END FOR A WOMAN WHO TRIED TO CHANGE THINGS

Sadly, among the some 400 murders each year in Indiana, domestic violence-related killings are entirely too common.

Nothing was common, though, about the startling and brutal slaying of twenty-nine-year-old Lisa Marie Bianco of Mishawaka, Indiana, on Saturday, March 4, 1989.

Bianco was bludgeoned to death on the snow-covered sidewalks outside her home as she desperately attempted to flee the latest assault on her by her abusive ex-husband, thirty-eight-year-old Alan L. Matheney.

Lisa Marie's last moments on earth were filled with terror. As she finished her shower inside her simple home at 503 Laurel Street in Mishawaka, she had reason to feel more secure than she had in a long time. Her abusive ex-husband, Matheney, was locked away at the Pendleton Reformatory 141 miles away.

It was a false sense of security that would be shattered as quickly as the back door of her wood-frame home as Matheney kicked it in and Lisa Marie began to run. Armed with a .410-gauge shotgun, Matheney chased Lisa through the house and out the front door onto the sidewalk as their two young daughters, seven-year-old Amber and ten-year-old Brooke, screamed and cried for their father to stop. Brooke ran next door to call police as her father continued chasing her mother.

358

Lisa Marie, clad only in her underwear, got as far as the sidewalk in front of 703 E. Sixth Street, just across the street, when Matheney grabbed her from behind and began viciously beating her with the butt of the shotgun.

A neighbor, Helen Szabo, would later report she saw Bianco trying to reach the front door of a house to get help. She said. "I saw a man grab her as she was about to put her hand on the storm door. He had what looked like a big stick with a thick end. He came up and hit her. He hit her a second time and she fell."[1]

After Lisa Marie fell, Szabo said she saw the man raise it up over his head and "hit the woman as hard as he could" multiple times. Another neighbor came out and shouted at Matheney, and he fled the scene.[2]

Dr. Louis Grwinski, a deputy coroner for St. Joseph County, said Lisa Marie had suffered at least twenty blows from the shotgun, reducing part of her skull to pulp. The force of the blows had broken the shotgun into three pieces, Mishawaka police said.[3]

Within hours, off-duty South Bend police sergeant Norvall Williams received a telephone call from Matheney saying he wanted to turn himself in for the murder. Williams arranged to pick up Matheney and delivered him to the Mishawaka Police Department for questioning.

Under questioning, police learned that Matheney was in the area on an eight-hour pass from the Pendleton Reformatory and had disobeyed orders from the Department of Correction and went to Mishawaka from Pendleton, instead of Indianapolis. Matheney was housed at the reformatory serving a sentence for battery for a January 1987 attack on Lisa Marie.

As news spread that Matheney had committed a murder while on an approved leave from a correctional facility, the waves were felt as far south as the statehouse in Indianapolis. Governor Evan Bayh announced he was suspending the release or furlough program immediately until a determination could be made about how Matheney was ever approved to leave the prison.

Bayh told a large gathering of reporters at Indianapolis that it was his understanding that Lisa Marie should have been notified that Matheney was being given a pass before he was allowed to leave. The governor, at the time the nation's youngest governor, said he was concerned about the program from his very first day on the job—having been sworn into office just a little over sixty days before.

"I was worried about this from the very beginning," Governor Bayh said. "As a matter of fact, I was worried about this during the campaign ... we're going to completely review this program to make sure it doesn't happen again."[4]

Bayh said Matheney's actions proved the program should be abolished. The release or furlough program began in 1982. Correctional officials said this was the first major incident reported since that time.

The DOC said they released Matheney to his mother's custody on Saturday morning, March 4, 1989, under the agreement that he could go to Indianapolis but had to be back within eight hours. He was actually eligible for a full forty-eight-hour pass, but DOC officials had decided to limit him to just eight hours since this was his first trip outside the prison.

Instead of following the agreement, however, police learned Martha Matheney, the suspect's mother, followed his orders and let him drive himself directly to St. Joseph County where he subsequently killed Lisa Marie.

Charles Miller, a DOC superintendent at Pendleton, said, "There was no hint or indication from the attitude [Matheney] displayed in the institutions or on the job that he was anything but a good inmate."[5]

A closer look at Matheney's record, however, would reveal he was struggling terribly in letting Lisa Marie go. Divorced in 1985, Matheney had continued to stalk and harass her and had been arrested for breaking into her home on at least one occasion.

A closer look would also have revealed that Lisa Marie's family and St. Joseph County Prosecutor Michael P. Barnes had attempted to keep Matheney from being released on furlough passes. Barnes had personally intervened in the past, causing DOC officials to cancel Matheney's passes— and greatly angering him. Matheney's family members reported he soon became convinced in the heat of his anger that Lisa Marie and Barnes were having an affair. In reality, it was a case of a diligent prosecutor trying to do what he could to keep someone he considered dangerous behind bars.

Lisa Marie's father, Eugene Bianco, said it was Matheney's mother, not state officials, who had notified her once before that he was getting ready to receive a weekend pass. It was then that Barnes intervened.

"Alan's mother called Lisa about a month before and said he was getting out for the weekend and was out for revenge, so Lisa should get out of town," Eugene Bianco said.[6]

By the summer of 1997, Lisa Marie had taken back her maiden name of Bianco and had begun to put distance between her and the violent past she had endured at Matheney's hands. Active as a volunteer at a domestic violence shelter in adjacent Elkhart County, she told *South Bend Tribune* reporter Judy Bradford about some of her experiences.

In a *Tribune* essay published after her death, Bradford wrote that hearing of Lisa Marie's murder had "brought chills and a wave of nausea to me … I remembered a short, dark woman who felt powerless in the late summer of

1987. I remembered a woman who was asking for help, but who wasn't sure what to ask for or how to ask it."[7]

Bradford noted that her meeting with Lisa Marie had been part of background research for other stories she planned on domestic violence. She was drawn to talking to Lisa Marie because "she was not the stereotypical 'battered wife.' She had not accepted the beatings and rapes. Every time he had abused her, she had let the authorities know."[8]

The notes Bradford took that day included Lisa Marie's comment: "If only I could get him put away for a year, I could put my life back together again." She had expressed frustration with the legal system that did not lock people up for as long as they should be.[9]

On March 7, 1989, police officially charged Matheney with murder and burglary.

The investigation had shown so far that Matheney arrived in St. Joseph County about midday that Saturday and made a bee-line for the Granger, Indiana, home of a friend on the ruse of changing his clothes. Once there, Matheney stole the shotgun he would later use to kill Lisa Marie.

As the firestorm of questions continued to grow over how Matheney was ever released in the first place, Governor Bayh suspended seven Department of Correction employees for approving the release.

Bayh added he personally thought Matheney should be subjected to the death penalty. Prosecutor Barnes, a fellow Democrat, responded, "The governor is entitled to his opinion, but we are not going to let that pressure us or cause us to make a decision before we have all the information."[10]

On March 13, 1989, former U.S. Attorney Virginia Dill McCarty released a special report she had written at Governor Bayh's request that indicated Matheney had been denied six previous attempts at furlough passes. She said a "blurring of the lines" had occurred within the DOC regarding who was responsible for granting releases and that the program appeared to become more lenient over time in granting furloughs.

"Somehow, the whole thing fell through the cracks," McCarty said.[11]

"The [release] program was ill-conceived from the very beginning," the governor said. "Someone of reasonable intelligence looking at this fact situation should never have released him ... It was a bad decision and a bad program. There's no other way to explain it."[12]

The trial for Matheney began in April 1990 using jurors selected from Lake County who were then transferred to St. Joseph County to hear the case.

Matheney's mother, Martha, testified that her other son, Ray, had driven her to Pendleton that Saturday morning in March to pick up Alan but that Alan had insisted on driving as they left. Mrs. Matheney said that as they drove, she told him he was missing the signs for Indianapolis, but that he insisted on driving north to Mishawaka instead of where he was supposed to go.[13]

Mrs. Matheney, however, admitted under cross-examination that she had called Lisa Marie after one of Matheney's earlier attempts to get a furlough pass was canceled because of her complaints.

She admitted she said to Lisa Marie over the phone, "You bitch, you, I hope you get what you deserve," but denied that she thought her former daughter-in-law would be killed by her son and said she was only speaking in anger for losing a chance for a visit with her son.[14]

Matheney's brother, Ray, testified that his brother was "macho" and that after he attacked Lisa Marie, his brother hugged him and told him, "It's over. Take care of mama."[15]

Both of Matheney's two daughters testified as well. The older daughter, Brooke, said she and her sister were watching television when they heard the back door being kicked in. Their mother, she said, had just finished taking a shower and was not fully dressed when their father burst in. Both girls described hearing their mother's screams as she fled nearly naked into the snowy front yard.

Under cross-examination, Matheney's attorneys elicited statements from the two girls that they loved their father and that he had never been mean to them or hurt them.

Kenneth Carrick, Matheney's former friend and coworker from Elkhart, testified that Matheney had often complained about his ex-wife and said, "I should have killed the bitch. I'd get ten years and be out in five."[16]

Prosecutors also called Department of Correction employees who testified about the breakdowns in the furlough program, including a counselor at Pendleton who said he spoke often to his superiors about making sure Matheney remained behind bars. Matheney's former divorce lawyer, Michael Scopelitis, testified that Alan and Lisa Marie were "obsessed with each other" and that Alan's behavior had grown increasingly more bizarre over the time he had worked with him.[17]

A Chicago psychiatrist who examined Matheney, Dr. Helen Morrison, told the jury that the defendant suffered from a paranoid personality disorder and often believed people were plotting against him. Morrison said it was her opinion he had suffered from these feelings since adolescence and that incarceration had made them worse.[18]

On April 11, 1990, jurors found Matheney guilty on all counts in the beating death of Lisa Marie. Matheney smiled widely at each of the jurors as the verdict was read and did so again before reporters as he was led from the courtroom. On April 13, 1990, jurors recommended that Matheney be executed for his crimes. Lake County Superior Court Judge James E. Letsinger, who presided over the case, followed their recommendation and ordered Matheney to be executed.[19]

Confined to death row at the Indiana State Prison in Michigan City, Matheney began a long series of unsuccessful appeals of his conviction, and his sentence. After many delays, he was finally executed on September 28, 2005.

Endnotes

1. *South Bend Tribune*, April 4, 1990.
2. Ibid.
3. *South Bend Tribune*, March 5, 1989.
4. *South Bend Tribune*, March 6, 1989.
5. Ibid.
6. *South Bend Tribune*, March 10, 1989.
7. *South Bend Tribune*, March 7, 1989.
8. Ibid.
9. Ibid.
10. *South Bend Tribune*, March 8, 1989.
11. *South Bend Tribune*, March 14, 1989.
12. Ibid.
13. *South Bend Tribune*, April 5, 1990.
14. *South Bend Tribune*, April 5, 1990.
15. Ibid.
16. Ibid.
17. *South Bend Tribune*, April 9, 1990.
18. *South Bend Tribune*, April 10, 1990.
19. *South Bend Tribune*, May 11, 1990.

ST. JOSEPH COUNTY

VICTIM(S):
Rev. Robert Pelley, 38;
Dawn Pelley, 32;
Jonell Pelley, 8;
Joleen Pelley, 6

PERPETRATOR(S):
Robert J. "Jeff" Pelley, 17

DATE OF DEATH(S):
April 29, 1989

A PASTOR'S SON RESPONDS WITH UNSPEAKABLE SIN

On Saturday evening, April 29, 1989, Reverend Robert Pelley had offered a compromise to his otherwise "grounded" son Jeff, seventeen. He would allow Jeff to attend the previously planned LaVille High School prom in nearby South Bend, Indiana, but he would not be allowed to attend all-night "after-prom" activities that most of his friends would attend. Further, Rev. Pelley said he would drive his son and his date to and from the prom since Jeff officially remained grounded for a previous row the two had engaged in.

What seemed a reasonable compromise was apparently anything but in Jeff's troubled mind. Police believe that shortly after company departed the Pelleys' church parsonage just outside Lakeville, Indiana, that Saturday evening, Jeff took his father's shotgun, murdered his father, step-mother, and his two step-sisters, and casually attended the prom and after-prom activities as if nothing was wrong.

It was a story that startled everyone in St. Joseph County. Lakeville is a quiet, mostly rural community on the southern edge of the more populous South Bend and Mishawaka. Violent crimes such as this were more common in the city, not out in the rural farmlands of the county.

But violent it was. On Sunday morning, April 30, 1989, when Rev. Pelley and his family did not show for regular morning services at the Olive

Branch United Brethren Church next door to their home on Osborne Road, parishioners went to investigate.

Some thought it was another practical joke by their beloved pastor, who the week before had sat in the front row of the sanctuary wearing a T-shirt and reading the Sunday paper to try to make a point about the importance of weekly worship.

It was not a prank, however. When 10 a.m. came and went that morning and still no sign of the Pelley family, church trustees obtained a key to the parsonage and cringed at what they found.

In an upstairs hallway lay Rev. Pelley, thirty-eight, dead from two massive shotgun blasts to the chest and head. In a downstairs family room, the pastor's wife, Dawn Pelley, thirty-two, and two of her daughters, eight-year-old Jonell and six-year-old Jolene, were also dead from shotgun blasts. Both of the girls were found "huddled" next to their mother as if trying to avoid being shot. Police later said Jolene's hand was blown off by the shotgun blast as she attempted to block herself from the shot.

Later, a lay leader of the congregation took up the grim task of announcing to the eighty congregants who had arrived for morning worship services that Rev. Pelley and his family were dead in the parsonage next door. Amidst heavy weeping and praying, the congregation drew close to one another, dumbfounded at the idea that someone would want to harm their pastor and his family.

Three of the Pelley children were not at home that weekend. Jackie Pelley, fourteen, was away overnight at a church-related event at Huntington College. Ten-year-old Jessica Pelley was visiting relatives in Kentucky. Police wanted to know the whereabouts of the Pelley's oldest child, seventeen-year-old Jeff, who had graduated from LaVille High School in January 1989. They learned he had attended the high school prom the night before in South Bend, and was likely at the Great America Amusement Park north of Chicago with his date and other friends.

Police said no forced entry was found at the Pelley home and that no immediate motive could be determined. Robbery was quickly ruled out as nothing appeared taken from the home. The fact that the parsonage was locked up tight and had to be opened with a key that Sunday morning would someday prove an important fact.

A look into the Pelleys' lives revealed no obvious motive. The couple had married just over two years ago, just before accepting the call to serve the small Lakeville congregation. Both Robert and Dawn had been married previously, but both of their spouses had died, leaving them single parents. Jeff and Jackie were Robert's children from his first marriage, while Jessica,

Jonell, and Joleen were Dawn's daughters from her first marriage. The blended family they formed settled in Lakeville.

As the investigation proceeded, St. Joseph County Sheriff's Department divers searched nearby bodies of water for a possible murder weapon, but never located one. Sheriff Joseph F. Nagy also led a horse posse of eight officers to search farm fields and rural areas near the home, but also failed to locate a discarded weapon.

Police questioned Jeff Pelley, but he was not held as a suspect. Sheriff's Sergeant Charles Feirrell said, "We're not eliminating anyone [as a suspect] at this time."[1]

Dr. Louis Grwinski, deputy coroner of St. Joseph County, said autopsies revealed that all four victims were each shot at least once with a shotgun fired at close range to their faces. Grwinski said it appeared the four were killed sometime late Saturday afternoon or early Saturday evening.[2]

Funerals for the four victims were conducted at the Olive Branch United Brethren Church on Wednesday, May 3, 1989, with an overflow crowd of mourners present.

"We are not here to discuss the events of their deaths," said United Brethren Church Bishop C. Ray Miller. "Nor are we here to give reports or interviews. What we are here for is what the family would have wanted. We are here to worship God."[3]

Rev. Alfred G. Price, superintendent of the United Brethren Church's Northern Ohio Conference, said the small congregation's pastor was excited about the opportunity to grow the church and "followed Jesus" and sought to "serve Jesus" in that place. "God is counting on you to carry it out," Price said.[4]

Following the funeral, the four Pelley family members were laid to rest at Southlawn Cemetery in South Bend.

And that is where things stood for a long time. Almost an entire family gunned down, no known reason for their deaths, and no arrest made for those responsible.

As sad as those realities were, the case began to fade into the background memory of most St. Joseph County residents.

There was brief renewed interest in the case when a new St. Joseph County prosecutor, Christopher Toth, came to office—the first Republican in decades to win election to county-wide office in traditionally Democratic St. Joseph County. Toth told reporters in April 2000 that he was forming a "cold case unit" that would focus on, among other cases, the Pelley murders.

Toth was a man of his word. On Monday morning, August 12, 2002, the front page of the *South Bend Tribune* displayed a shocking headline: "Pelley arrested; Son held in 1989 slaying of family." Once suspected, often rumored about—now here was confirmation for many that Jeff Pelley *did* have something to do with the awful slaying of his family.[5]

Pelley family members confirmed for the *Tribune* that the now thirty-one-year-old Pelley had been arrested on Saturday, August 10, 2002, as he left an airplane at the Los Angeles International Airport, while en route home from a business trip. Two days later, Toth and his staff made it official; they were charging Jeff with murder for the unsolved cases from thirteen years ago.

A probable cause affidavit filed in support of those charges revealed more about what police had known back in 1989 than was ever released before. Among those facts was the odd question Jeff had asked investigators back then about whether he could go to the electric chair if he talked to the police about certain things.

"When the investigator replied that it might make a difference, but that Jeff would have to let the investigator know what those things were, [Jeff] slumped in his chair, his head down, with his hands covering his face," the affidavit stated.[6]

Police said in the week before the April 1989 LaVille prom, Jeff continued to tell his date and friends that he would be attending all of the prom events, even though his father had grounded him. "The evidence shows that the murder was premeditated," the state said in its filing. "Plainly, even as late as early afternoon on Saturday, Robert Pelley conveyed that he did not intend to permit his son to go to any prom event other than the dance."[7]

More than a decade later, some of Jeff's friends still remembered that prom night from 1989 vividly. Classmate Beth Platz said she recalls exiting the Great America Amusement Park to find police gathered around Jeff Pelley's car to inform him that his family had been killed.

Platz said that when Pelley began telling everyone that he was attending the prom and related events, "everyone was shocked and confused because he'd been in trouble, and his father said he couldn't go. It turned out he was going to go, and then he showed up late for dinner [prior to the prom]."[8]

Dana Munger, another classmate who lived near the Pelleys, said Jeff had been grounded by his father because of some sort of theft-related incident in the weeks prior to the prom.

"I lived fairly close to [Jeff] when it happened, and that was kind of scary," Munger recalled. "Not knowing for sure what happened … you kind of looked at him. Did he or didn't he? I would have to say, yeah, I did suspect him."[9]

Carol Jensen, leader of the Olive Branch church choir when the murders happened in 1989, said many church members knew Jeff struggled to get along with his father and resented the attention his father gave to his new step-daughters who were many years younger than Jeff.

If people thought Jeff acted oddly during those days thirteen years ago (including a lack of tears at his family's funeral), they were not alone. Odd behavior had punctuated the years following as Jeff grew into adulthood. A college dropout, in December 1993, Jeff married Kimberly A. Singletary in Lee County, Florida.

Six months later, he was convicted on two counts of wire fraud for attempting to defraud a trust fund left to him after his father's death. He was sentenced to six months' home detention for cooking up a scheme to convince the administrators of the trust fund that he had cancer and that he required more than $20,000 in cash to pay for medical bills.[10]

Jeff and Kimberly would divorce in August 1997, court records show, only to remarry each other again in December 1999. At the time of his arrest, Jeff and Kimberly were the parents of one child and living in Tarpon Springs, Florida. Jeff was employed by IBM.[11]

Jeff and his new family immediately declared his innocence, and unsuccessfully conducted a protracted battle to prevent him from being extradited to Indiana to face murder charges. Regardless, a trial for Jeff opened in July 2006 at the St. Joseph County-City Building in South Bend. It would be handled not by Toth, but by new Democratic Prosecutor Michael Dvorak, who defeated Toth in his 2002 re-election bid.

An early witness in the high-profile case, St. Joseph County Sheriff's Detective John Pavlekovich told the jury that investigators focused almost immediately on Jeff as a likely suspect based on what they were being told about the teen by others. Pavlekovich said Jeff was an early suspect "because the opportunity was there" and because the home showed no signs of forced entry.[12]

Prosecutors zeroed in on a twenty-minute window they said existed on that Saturday evening between the time church members who had stopped in at the Pelley home left, and the time Jeff was witnessed en route to dinner with his prom date.

Jeff was demonstrative during the proceedings, emitting a loud sob on the first day of testimony when a crime scene photograph was introduced that showed his father's body in a blood-soaked hallway of the home.

One church member, Joyce Schafer, said she witnessed a tense discussion between Jeff and his father on the Saturday afternoon before the prom. She said Jeff was busy washing and waxing his Ford Mustang in the driveway of the parsonage when his father asked him why he was bothering to do that because he was not going to allow him to drive the car to the prom.

Jurors also heard from a Lakeville gun store owner who said Rev. Pelley had purchased a 20-gauge shotgun in December 1987 that he said he wanted for rabbit hunting. Ironically, Steve Diller, the gun store operator, said that

Rev. Pelley had stopped by his store on the morning of Saturday, April 29, 1989, but did not purchase anything. The Pelleys were found dead the next day.

Prosecutors also called Jeff's prom date, Darla Emmons Adams, who said Jeff told her he had "a bad feeling" about his family in the hours before police showed up at the amusement park with the grim news that the Pelley family was dead. While Jeff's behavior was odd on Sunday at the amusement park, she said, on Saturday night at dinner, at the prom, and at after-prom activities, she said Jeff acted "normal."[13]

As a final piece, prosecutors played the videotape of a statement Jeff gave to detectives on May 1, 1989, the after day the bodies were found. On the tape he said he did not know who would have wanted to hurt his family, and denied any personal involvement.

Jeff said on the tape, "We had a real good day Saturday. We got along real well," despite testimony by others that he and his father were still feuding.[14]

He claimed on the tape that he loved his step-sisters, but that he and his step-mother Dawn "tolerated each other," but that he did not hate her.[15]

Pelley's defense attorney, Alan Baum of California, opened his case by reminding jurors that the state had collected a lot of evidence in the murders but had not connected any of it to Jeff Pelley. In fact, the state had presented no fingerprints, no bloody clothes, and no eyewitnesses to link Jeff to the murders.

"I think the truth is coming out," Baum said.[16]

He added, "This was a rush to judgment ... There were areas that should have been investigated as a matter of course and there was information they received that they didn't follow up on."[17]

Called as a defense witness, step-sister Jackie (Pelley) Delp said that Jeff and his father had disagreements, although they were not violent. She confirmed under cross-examination, however, that she had witnessed an argument between the two on the front lawn of their home that resulted in Rev. Pelley pushing Jeff in the chest and Jeff landing on his butt.[18]

The six-day trial drew to a close on July 19, 2006, after about forty witnesses had testified. Jurors would take three days to consider the evidence presented, and on July 21, 2006, found Jeff Pelley guilty of four counts of murder. Jeff "cringed and began to cry" as St. Joseph County Superior Court Judge Roland W. Chamblee read the verdict. Judge Chamblee sentenced Jeff to 160 years in prison on October 17, 2006.[19]

Just a month later, Jeff, now thirty-four years old, began filing a series of appeals on his conviction. He blamed shoddy police work and St. Joseph County politics as the reason for his conviction. He also raised the issue of previously unheard-of statements by some Lakeville area youth who were allegedly bragging they were going to kill a local pastor. Among evidence prosecutors could not present were "progress notes" kept by a family counselor at the Family and Children's Center in South Bend from ongoing counseling sessions Jeff and his parents had attended from May 1986 until two days before the murders in 1989. Defense and prosecutor battles over these records delayed proceeding with the Pelley trial for more than two years.

The Indiana Supreme Court ruled in June 2005, however, that a St. Joseph County judge (and later the Indiana Court of Appeals) was in error in blocking prosecutors' access to the notes written by a social worker. The "statutorily created privilege" between a client and a counselor that is protected from disclosure was not in place, the court ruled, at the time the Pelleys were attending counseling. They ruled prosecutors could have access to some but not all of the records of the Pelley family counseling sessions.

Jeff and his wife continue to fight for his release and started a Web site called "Justice for Jeff" encouraging people with information about others who may have killed the Pelleys to come forward and tell police.

On February 19, 2009, the Indiana Supreme Court voted unanimously to deny Pelley's appeal of his convictions for the murders. The high court rejected all of Pelley's claims, including that he had been denied a speedy trial under Indiana law.

Endnotes

1. *South Bend Tribune*, May 2, 1989.
2. *South Bend Tribune*, May 3, 1989.
3. *South Bend Tribune*, May 4, 1989.
4. Ibid.
5. *South Bend Tribune*, Aug. 12, 2002.
6. *South Bend Tribune*, Aug. 13, 2002.
7. Ibid.
8. Ibid.
9. Ibid.
10. *South Bend Tribune*, Aug. 12, 2002.
11. Ibid.
12. *South Bend Tribune*, July 12, 2006.
13. *South Bend Tribune*, July 14, 2006.
14. *South Bend Tribune*, July 18, 2006.
15. Ibid.
16. *South Bend Tribune*, July 15, 2006.
17. *South Bend Tribune*, July 17, 2006.
18. *South Bend Tribune*, July 19, 2006.
19. *South Bend Tribune*, July 22, 2006.

SCOTT COUNTY

VICTIM(S):
Harold Amick, 25;
John Pfaffenberger, 38

PERPETRATOR(S):
Lacell "Toots" Long, 25;
Robert Neal, 20;
Ed Coffin, 22

DATE OF DEATH(S):
June 4 & 6, 1934

A TRIO OF THIEVES TURNS DEADLY

Three young Hoosier men took one day to go from small-time thieves to big-time murderers and desperados.

Perhaps enamored with the images of 1930s gangsters splashed across movie newsreels and daily newspapers and facing the realities of Depression-era Indiana, the three took their crimes up several notches on Monday, June 4, 1934 as they engaged in gun battles with a Seymour Police officer and later deputies from the Scott County Sheriff's Department.

Before they were done, twenty-five-year-old Scott County deputy sheriff Harold Amick was dead. Thirty-eight-year-old Seymour police officer John Pfaffenberger would succumb to his wounds two days after being shot by the men.

The day of terror undertaken by the young men, all Hoosier natives, was inexplicable and set in motion a manhunt throughout south central Indiana. In the end, all three were nabbed, the first caught was twenty-year-old Robert Neal of Bloomington, who left his new bride of three weeks at home as he went out for a day of crime.

Neal's confession implicated his friend, twenty-two-year-old Ed Coffin of Helmsburg, Indiana. Neal said Coffin had supplied the getaway car, a 1932 Chevrolet coupe, but Neal had done the driving. A third man, the alleged "mastermind" of the crimes, twenty-five-year-old Lacell "Toots" Long of Shelbyville, Indiana, was also captured.

The industrious thieves started their day early, Neal told detectives. He said they left his Bloomington home at 6 a.m. that Monday morning intending to rob a filling station at Helmsburg, a tiny community just west of Bean Blossom, Indiana, and northwest of Nashville in Brown County.

"Coffin told me he was supposed to meet Long at Helmsburg to rob a filling station," Neal told detectives. "The car had Ohio plates. We drove to Nashville to get a road map [and] Coffin stole a rope out of a church near Stonehead [between Nashville and Brownstown] ... to tow a car he expected to steal."[1]

After the robbery at Helmsburg, the trio traveled south into Jackson County and stopped for gas at a station in Brownstown, Indiana. After filling up, Coffin asked for a pack of cigarettes, and the trio drove off without paying for seven gallons of gasoline as the attendant was inside the station retrieving them.

"We went to Seymour and made our first stop at a red light," Neal said. "A policeman drove in front of our car and blocked us off. The policeman got out of the car and Coffin yelled at me to get the hell out of here. I started off and heard some shooting."[2]

In the shootout, at Chestnut and Tipton Streets in Seymour proper, Patrolman Pfaffenberger was mortally wounded. Doctors said he suffered a serious gunshot wound to his right side, and another one to his arm, but remained conscious until he died shortly after 10 p.m. on Wednesday, June 6, 1934, while receiving treatment at Schneck Memorial Hospital in Seymour. An autopsy showed the bullet had pierced his right intestine and created serious hemorrhaging in his body. He was the married father of five young children.[3]

Seymour Police and Indiana State Police radioed to all officers in the area a description of the suspect vehicle involved in the shootout.

Scott County authorities, however, were hot on the trail of reported chicken thieves in the southern part of the county. Deputy Sheriff Harold Amick, brother of Scott County Sheriff Wilber Amick was among them. Also along on the routine chicken theft report were the sheriff's son, nineteen-year-old Kenneth Amick, and Fred Groves, the Scottsburg town marshal.

Unknown to them, the trio of thieves-turned-killers was headed straight for them at Underwood, Indiana, a settlement just inside Clark County on the Scott-Clark county line.

"I heard the noise of tires on the road and knew [the car] was coming fast," Marshal Groves said. "The bandits tried to turn into a side road and the car hit the front of the filling station. [Sheriff Amick] remarked, 'There's some drunk,' and we went around to investigate."[4]

Groves continued, "As we went around, one of the men climbed out of the left side of the car. Two others got out of the right. Without a word, the first man fired two shots at into Deputy Amick's face. He fell. [The sheriff] and the same man exchanged shots as he ran around the side of the station."[5]

Groves said the men then scattered in three directions across adjacent farm fields.

Deputy Harold Amick and his brother, Sheriff Amick, were both rushed from the scene. Harold was dead on arrival at St. Edward's Hospital in New Albany. The coroner later ruled he died of a bullet wound to the face and brain. The victim's brother, Sheriff Amick, struggled to breathe after witnessing the shooting death of his brother.[6]

From there, the bandits fled on foot and separated. One of them resurfaced the following morning around 7 a.m. at the town of Leota, Indiana, farther northwest of the Underwood shooting, but still in Scott County. As eighteen-year-old Ralph Shields went to the barn to retrieve his car, he was held up at gunpoint by "Toots" Long and ordered to drive from the scene. Ralph's uncle, Gilbert Shields, saw what was happening and attempted to intervene but was pistol-whipped by the man.

Ralph Shields later told police Long ordered him to drive somewhere where he could get some breakfast. Ralph drove to the home of his grandmother, Ada Shields, who prepared breakfast for the men but became suspicious and fled the house seeking help. After the grandmother fled the house, Long ordered Ralph to again drive him, this time west out of Scott County toward the Jackson County town of South Boston.

Long eventually dumped Ralph off as far west as Bedford, Indiana, and headed east again. He was captured the next day near Nashville, Indiana, where he had attempted to hide out by taking a day laborer's job in a local orchard.

Upon his capture at Neal's Bloomington apartment, police noted that the handle of Coffin's .38-caliber handgun contained four notches. "One of the notches, newly cut, is believed to have been placed there by Coffin after he learned that he had killed Harold Amick," the *Jeffersonville Evening News* reported.[7]

All three men were quickly transferred to the custody of the Clark County sheriff since the first fatal shooting had occurred just inside Clark County at Underwood. Clark County Prosecutor Clyde F. Crooks said he would seek the death penalty against all three men.

Authorities didn't wait long to get going on a trial—"the three prisoners, manacled to each other, were rushed to Jeffersonville at 8:25 o'clock Friday morning by heavily armed officers in seven automobiles. Sounding sirens to clear the traffic, the party sped to the Jeffersonville courthouse, where a detachment of eight state patrolmen and two Clark County officers guard the alleged bandit(s)."[8]

The trial for Long and Coffin opened promptly in Clark County Circuit Court on Friday, June 8, 1934—just days after the shootings. Neal was returned to the jail at New Albany, presumably to be called later as a witness against his two co-defendants.

Prosecutor Crooks said that "evidence will show these boys committed the most heinous crime ever committed in the state of Indiana ... We will show that these defendants had the audacity to brag about this crime. They boasted of knocking the rear glass out of an automobile so they could shoot back at pursuing officers. Marks on the butt of the gun will show scars."[9]

Neal's new bride, sixteen-year-old Martha (Marshall) Neal of Bloomington, and Long's "sweetheart," eighteen-year-old Pauline Meadows, were called as early witnesses. They both gave statements that Coffin admitted shooting the two officers.

Scott County Sheriff Wilber Amick, who had suffered physically from the grief of losing his brother and the determination to find the men, also testified. He identified Coffin as the man who fired upon his group.

"Tensed with the drama of the moment, the crowded courtroom was silent as the Sheriff sat on the witness stand and told of the ruthless slaying of his brother at Underwood when the party of officers were approaching a wrecked car intent on giving whatever assistance they could to the unknown occupants," the *Seymour Daily Tribune* reported dramatically.[10]

The jury quickly reached a verdict, and Coffin and Long were both found guilty on Saturday, June 9, 1934. Clark County Judge George C. Koop sentenced Coffin to be electrocuted by the state and sentenced Long to life in prison without parole. Both were immediately transferred under heavy guard to the Indiana State Prison at Michigan City "laughing and chatting with apparent indifference to their fate," the *Jeffersonville Evening News* reported.[11]

The third member of the gang, Robert Neal, was tried separately in June 1934 in Jeffersonville and received a life sentence from Judge Koop as well. The jury deliberated only eight minutes in his case.[12]

Coffin was electrocuted on October 9, 1934.

Endnotes

1. *Jeffersonville Evening News,* June 6, 1934.
2. Ibid.

3. *Seymour Daily Tribune,* June 7, 1934.
4. *Jeffersonville Evening News,* June 5, 1934.
5. Ibid.
6. *Seymour Daily Tribune,* June 5, 1934.
7. *Jeffersonville Evening News,* June 7, 1934.
8. *Jeffersonville Evening News,* June 8, 1934.
9. Ibid.
10. *Seymour Daily Tribune,* June 8, 1934.
11. *Jeffersonville Evening News,* June 11, 1934; *Scottsburg Chronicle,* June 13, 1934.
12. *Scottsburg Chronicle,* June 20, 1934.

SHELBY COUNTY

VICTIM(S):
Shirley F. Sturgill, 42;
Barbara Foote, 32

PERPETRATOR(S):
John Dell Carr, 30

DATE OF DEATH(S):
October 6, 1990 and July 4, 1991

A WIFE FINALLY TELLS OF A DEADLY SECRET

Angie Carr of Shelbyville lived in fear of her husband, John Dell Carr—in so much fear that she kept hidden for more than five years that her husband had brutally sodomized and murdered her mother in October 1990.

Angie finally came forward after John had already been arrested and convicted for a second murder, the July 4, 1991, murder of thirty-two-year-old Barbara Foote of Fishers, Indiana, and the rape of her seven-year-old daughter.

Angie did not come forward, however, until another man, forty-three-year-old Orville Jack Dobkins, was arrested and held from just shortly after the murder of Angie's mother, Shirley Sturgill, in October 1990, until May 1991 when evidence began to clear him.

The trail of death and destruction created by John Dell Carr began on Saturday, October 6, 1990, when police and firefighters found the burned, beaten, mutilated, and strangled body of forty-two-year-old Shirley F. Sturgill inside her gutted Apartment Number 4 at 523 Miller Avenue in Shelbyville. The divorced woman lived alone but was friendly and well acquainted with her neighbors.

Neighbors said they last saw Sturgill alive as she sat on the sofa in front of the window in her apartment, watching television around 9:30 p.m. that Saturday night. Sturgill had lived in the ground-unit apartment for about two years ago.

Shelby County Coroner Norman F. Richard, MD, reported that Sturgill had been strangled by an assailant who used his hands but refused to confirm initial reports that she had also been sexually assaulted. The autopsy indicated she was dead before the fire was set and that her corpse had suffered severe burns in the fire.

Dr. Richard said he was purposefully withholding some information from the media. "I'm keeping my mouth shut until I know what's going on. I'm not going to interfere with [the police] investigation," he said.[1]

"There are a lot of things we saw that we don't want to tell because only us and the bad guy know," said Shelbyville Police captain Kehrt Etherton.[2]

Etherton did confirm there was no sign of forced entry and that firefighters had to kick in the locked front door of Sturgill's apartment when they first responded to the 911 report of a fire.

On October 24, 1990, police announced the arrest of Orville Dobkins, a local car salesman and neighbor of Sturgill's in the apartment building where she lived. He was charged with murder and arson and held without bond.

Police said upon Dobkins' arrest that they had physical, medical, and forensic evidence linking him to the crime. His arrest came at the Indiana University Medical Center in Indianapolis moments after he underwent a court-ordered dental examination, police said.

Etherton called Sturgill's murder "bizarre" and said no motive had been determined yet.[3]

As Dobkins was brought to the Shelby County Courthouse for his initial hearing, members of Sturgill's family gathered outside, including Angie Carr. She told a *Shelbyville News* reporter that her mother "always made time for us. She had three grandkids and she thought a lot of them."[4]

Friends of Dobkins' said they could not believe he would ever harm anyone and described him as spiritual and a man who enjoyed reading the Bible.

Detectives admitted that Dobkins was adamant that he did not kill Sturgill but said that he was the only resident of the apartment complex without an alibi for the time police believed Sturgill was killed.

"He really feels he has been persecuted," said Dan Comstock, an employee of the *Shelbyville News* who said he had known Dobkins for three years. "He felt like he was locked into a corner."[5]

At his initial hearing, prosecutors announced they might seek the death penalty against Dobkins because of aggravating circumstances in Sturgill's death. Without offering details, they noted that in addition to being strangled, Sturgill had been beaten, bitten, and partially dismembered or disfigured while she was still alive. They refused to elaborate.[6]

On May 17, 1991, seven months after jailing Dobkins on charges of murder and arson, a shocking development occurred as Shelby County Prosecutor James R. Lisher announced that his office was dropping the charges against Dobkins "with prejudice," meaning he could file them again later. Shelby County Superior Court Judge Jack A. Tandy ordered Dobkins released from the Johnson County Jail at Franklin, where he was held.

Lisher said about the latest development, "The dismissal of the charges came after three additional forensic experts reviewed particular evidence and different conclusions were made."[7]

The "particular evidence" had to do with bite marks on Sturgill's body that a forensic expert, Dr. Donnell Marlin of the Indiana University School of Dentistry, had said matched teeth patterns belonging to Dobkins. However, an additional review by two other forensic odontologists found that the bite marks were not a match for Dobkins.

Lisher said, "The appropriate course of action at this time is dismissal of the charges against Dobkins. The investigation continues, and Dobkins remains a suspect with others in this case."[8]

The prosecutor said evidence that remained, beyond the dental bite analysis, was all circumstantial and not enough to go forward with charges against Dobkins. "My citizens expect our collective wisdom to present a case that will prove guilt beyond a reasonable doubt," he said. "… we do not have that proof at this point."[9]

Sturgill's family was informed privately of Lisher's move just before it was announced publicly. Among those attending the briefing with Lisher and his staff was Angie Carr, who told reporters, "I guess we figured right," indicating that she had guessed Lisher might be dismissing charges and that was the reason for asking to meet with the family privately.[10]

That was where things remained until just over a month later when headlines on July 6, 1991, carried the startling news that a seven-year-old girl had worked herself free from ropes around her hands and walked for help to a neighbor's house early on that Sunday morning.

The girl, left for dead in a farm field about three miles south of St. Paul, Indiana, in Shelby County, told police she had witnessed her mother being murdered late on Friday night, July 4, 1991.

Investigators soon found the body of Barbara Foote inside her home in the 11200 block of Cumberland Road in Fishers. Barbara had been strangled to death by someone's hands, and the little girl also had been strangled, although the assailant apparently stopped before actually killing the youngster.

Hamilton County authorities quickly picked up thirty-year-old John Dell Carr of Shelbyville and charged him with murder, rape, attempted murder, criminal confinement, sexually deviant conduct, and burglary. Hamilton

County zeroed in on Carr after Shelby County authorities notified them that he had contacted a detective there and said he wanted to turn himself in for the crime. At the time of his arrest, Carr was on parole for a 1989 sexual assault in New York.

Hamilton County Prosecutor Steve Nation said he had no idea of what motive might exist for the crime and that Carr had not confessed. They had learned that Carr was familiar with Foote since he was employed as a roofer by Foote's ex-husband.[11]

A further review of his background revealed he had enjoyed a commendable, decade-long career in the U.S. Army, winning a promotion to staff sergeant before being arrested and convicted of the 1989 sexual assault in the small town of Watertown, New York. The sexual assault at knifepoint occurred during the period Carr was assigned to nearby Fort Drum and involved a thirty-two-year-old woman he met while she worked her shift at an all-night gas station.[12]

His parole was later transferred to Indiana so he could move home closer to his native Shelbyville. Officials reported he was dutiful about reporting for regular meetings with his parole officer and had caused no known trouble while on parole.

As the investigation into Foote's murder wore on, Carr eventually agreed to a plea agreement with Hamilton County prosecutors that allowed him to plead guilty to charges of murder and kidnapping, while the other charges were dropped. He blamed his actions on days of drinking and smoking marijuana before the attack and said he could not remember assaulting Foote or her young daughter.

On May 29, 1992, Carr was sentenced to eighty years in prison for Foote's murder and told the judge, "I have great remorse [but] I can't turn back time."[13]

Shelby County officials now had added interest in Carr and whether he had been involved with the Sturgill slaying back in 1990. Evidence, which at first was not linked to Carr, now seemed to fit into place, including a pair of U.S. Army-issued men's boxer shorts found at the murder scene and a cigarette butt later traced via DNA to match Carr.

A Shelby County grand jury indicted Carr for Sturgill's murder on February 15, 1996.

"Carr was always on our list of suspects," detective Etherton told reporters. "In the pecking order we were going by, he would have been the next one after Dobkins."[14]

With Angie Carr safely assured that her violent and now ex-husband was staying behind bars, she had begun talking to investigators, helping to fill in the holes in the case that led to Carr being charged.

The tale Angie would tell then and again later in her ex-husband's April 1997 trial for the Sturgill murder was shocking and sad.

Angie said that on the day her mother was killed, October 6, 1990, she and her husband had argued because she wanted to take her two daughters over to her mother's apartment for a visit. John Dell Carr resented the time Angie wanted to spend with her mother and would not allow her to take the car for the visit.

Angie accepted what she was told that day, and John left their Shelbyville home on the excuse of going to visit his worksite. Instead, he spent the day and evening drinking and eventually went to his mother-in-law's apartment and brutally killed her.

She said John did not return until almost 11 p.m. that Saturday night and talked little when he returned. As he took a shower, Angie searched his clothes and discovered that the Army-issued boxers he always wore were missing.

"I thought he was seeing another woman," she said.[15]

Angie said after John ate his dinner late that night and the couple settled into bed, he got up and retrieved a shotgun from his gun case. Carr pointed the gun at her. She said, "He said he had hurt my mother, he had choked her. I looked at him and asked him what he meant by that. He repeated it again. He said he hurt and choked my mother."[16]

She said her husband then grabbed her by the hair and dragged her to the doorway of the bedroom of their one- and three-year-old daughters, who were sleeping. "He pointed the gun at them, my babies," she said. "He said if I said anything to anybody that he would kill my kids and me."[17]

Scared into silence, Angie said nothing as one of her mother's neighbors was arrested, charged, and held for months for the murder which she knew he had not committed. She said she only felt safe to come forward after the arrest was made in Foote's murder.

Carr's defense attorneys hit her hard about the fact that she had remained silent as Dobkins was arrested and charged. "I hope he can forgive me," Angie said. "It haunts me to this day, but I had to protect my babies."[18]

At the April 1997 trial for Carr, Dr. Michael A. Clark, a forensic pathologist from the Indiana University School of Medicine, said his review of Sturgill's death revealed four distinct bite marks on her body meant to mutilate or remove her nipples and the forced insertion of a toilet cleaning brush into her vagina.

Dr. Clark said both of those facts indicated "ritualistic behavior." He added, "It can mean the person has done something like this before."[19]

The pathologist said Sturgill was not alive when her body was set on fire in two places, but that she was alive when bitten and sodomized. In addition, she suffered a blunt force injury to the head, a large gash above her eye, and was eventually manually strangled.

A review of the bite marks on Sturgill's breasts were "consistent" with Carr's dental impression, Dr. John P. Kenney, chief forensic odontologist for Cook County, Illinois, testified. Other forensic experts said Carr's blood type and DNA matched saliva found on a cigarette butt found in Sturgill's bedroom.[20]

Expected to be called as a defense witness, the originally-charged Dobkins was instead called as a rebuttal witness by prosecutors. He flatly denied he had killed Sturgill and said he was "devastated" to have been charged in her murder.[21]

Jurors took eight hours before returning a verdict on April 22, 1997, that Carr was guilty of murdering his mother-in-law. On May 21, 1997, Carr was sentenced to sixty years in prison in addition to the eighty years he was already serving for the murder of Barbara Foote.

Carr filed an unsuccessful April 2000 appeal of his conviction in the Sturgill murder before the Indiana Supreme Court. In it, he claimed his Fourth Amendment rights were violated after prosecutors and police had to have him anesthetized in order to collect a dental impression from him. Carr had refused to voluntarily submit to the dental procedure.

As for Jack Dobkins, he said, "You don't know the load that was lifted off me," when Carr was arrested and convicted of Sturgill's murder. "I had always hoped the investigation would be continued," after he was released, he said.[22]

Now forty-eight-years-old, Dobkins moved to Somerset, Kentucky, to get away from doubters in Shelby County. He said he did not plan to pursue a lawsuit against Shelby County for his arrest, but that "The perception of being falsely accused never leaves."[23]

Endnotes

1. *Shelbyville News*, Oct. 9, 1990.
2. Ibid.
3. *Shelbyville News*, Oct. 25, 1990.
4. Ibid.
5. Ibid
6. Ibid.
7. *Shelbyville News*, May 17, 1991.
8. Ibid.
9. Ibid.
10. Ibid.

11. *Indianapolis Star,* July 9, 1991.
12. *Indianapolis Star,* July 10, 1991.
13. *Shelbyville News,* April 7, 1997.
14. *Shelbyville News,* Feb. 16, 1996.
15. *Shelbyville News,* April 17, 1997.
16. Ibid.
17. Ibid.
18. *Shelbyville News,* April 18, 1997.
19. *Shelbyville News,* April 14, 1997.
20. *Shelbyville News,* April 15, 1997.
21. *Shelbyville News,* April 22, 1997.
22. *Shelbyville News,* Feb. 20, 1996.
23. Ibid.

SPENCER COUNTY

VICTIM(S):
Kathleen M. Kohm, 11

PERPETRATOR(S):
None ever criminally charged.

DATE OF DEATH(S):
April 5, 1981

MURDER IN A TOWN CALLED SANTA CLAUS

On the cold night of January 31, 1984, firefighters were called to a fire at the two-story log cabin home of Indiana State Police Trooper Jerry Wayne Cliver of Sullivan County.

Fire officials said the fire was reported at 1:55 a.m. as Cliver home and discovered a fire on the bottom floor of the cabin home. Firefighters extinguished a fire in the living room, although damage to the rest of the home was extensive. Firefighters left a short time later, but were called back at 3:45 a.m. when Cliver reported the house was on fire again—this time a blaze erupting on the second floor.

On the second run, twelve firefighters fought the blaze for almost three hours but could not save any of the home this time. Efforts to save the home were hampered by a lack of fire hydrants in the unincorporated area just southeast of the Sullivan city limits.[1]

A state fire marshal's investigator joined with investigators from the Sullivan County Sheriff's Department to determine if the fire was arson. A Sullivan County grand jury to hear evidence about the fire beginning March 28, 1984. Among the twenty-five witnesses receiving subpoenas was Trooper Cliver.[2]

The grand jury were never hear testimony from Cliver. Events in Trooper Cliver's life would interrupt those proceedings and supersede any arson investigation. At about 10:30 p.m. on Friday, March 23, 1984, for reasons that are still mostly inexplicable, Trooper Cliver went to the Dugger, Indiana, home of his ex-wife, thirty-year-old Jerri Lynn Cliver, and summarily shot her and her new boyfriend, thirty-eight-year-old Donald L. Clayton. Jerri Lynn was critically injured, and Donald was killed instantly.

Trooper Cliver, who had been remarried less than a month before to another woman, came home to his new wife, Amy Noble Cliver, and she instantly knew something was terribly wrong.

"He stood at the door for a minute," Amy Cliver said. "He was kind of shaking. I noticed as soon as he walked in, something was wrong. I could tell by the look on his face."[3]

Amy said her new husband Jerry told her, "You won't believe what I've done," and then admitted he had shot his ex-wife, Jerri Lynn, and her new boyfriend.

Amy's comments came during a hearing in Sullivan County Circuit County on March 24, 1984, as prosecutors sought an arrest warrant for the now-unaccounted-for state trooper. Judge George E. Taylor issued warrants for Cliver's arrest on charges of murder and attempted murder. Amy told the court her husband was at their Sullivan home from about 4 to 9 p.m. Friday night, and "he was perfectly all right—in a good mood," she said. He abruptly got up from a chair at 9 p.m. and announced he was going to "get a couple of drinks," although he left their home in his marked Indiana State Police patrol unit.[4]

From there, police were unsure where Cliver went, but they do know he phoned Jerri Lynn's home at about 9:30 p.m. on the night on the shooting on the pretense of making arrangements to pick up the couple's two children, five-year-old Carly and two-year-old Caleb, the following day.

Jerri Lynn's mother, Mary Jo Delph, told the court that she listened in to the first few moments of the conversation between Cliver and her daughter on an extension phone and noted no real hostilities. Amy told the court, however, that Cliver had become upset when he heard Clayton's voice in the background when he would call her on the phone. Although divorced and remarried, it appeared Cliver was still unhappy his wife had moved on and had a new boyfriend.

At about 10:30 pm., after she had retired for the evening, Delph (who lived in another home on the same rural Sullivan County lot as her daughter's trailer), said she heard "a horrible sound." She said he looked out the window in time to see Cliver entering the front door of her daughter's home after having kicked in the door. As Delph woke her husband to alert him to the happenings, she said he heard gunshots ring out. Seconds later, she said, Cliver came running out of her daughter's house and fled to a nearby woods.

Although she screamed out, "He acted like he had no knowledge of my screams," Mrs. Delph said.[5]

Mrs. Delph ran to her daughter's trailer and found her two grandchildren seated on the floor in the living room frightened and confused, but still watching TV. One was crying, she said, but both were unharmed.

In the kitchen, Mrs. Delph found her daughter on the floor, bloody and moaning. She had gunshot wounds to her head, chest, and abdomen. Police determined she had suffered two separate gunshot wounds.

The nude body of Donald Clayton, a Linton, Indiana, resident was found slumped over a hobby horse toy in the children's bedroom. Coroner William Tennis said he had been shot three times and died instantly.[6] Tennis told reporters the bullets used on both Jerri Lynn and Clayton were "high caliber, copper clad, hollow-point shells."[7]

Detectives were able to get a brief statement from Jerri Lynn before she was taken to the intensive care unit at Terre Haute Regional Hospital for treatment of her wounds. Her statement confirmed it was her ex-husband who had attacked her and her boyfriend.

Sullivan County Prosecutor John S. Elmore said Jerri Lynn's statement was key. A search was underway to find Cliver. Elmore warned residents that Cliver should be considered "extremely dangerous." Armed guards were placed on Jerri Lynn's hospital room to ensure that Cliver had no chance to finish his deed.[8]

Cliver's new wife, Amy, told detectives that her husband had returned to their home in his state police car following the shootings, but left almost immediately driving her 1974 Chevy Malibu.

Jerry Lynn's mother, Mrs. Delph, said the entire incident baffled her. She said Cliver had made it clear he did not want to be married to Jerri Lynn anymore, "but he didn't want anyone else to have her," she said.[9]

Added to the mix was the suspicious fire that destroyed his log-cabin home – what some suspected was an attempt to collect insurance proceeds to meet the new financial demands of child support and other expenses.

If his personal life was in flux, so was his professional life. His superiors in the Indiana State Police had grown weary of Cliver. He was assigned to the Terre Haute post and patrolled quiet Sullivan County, something Cliver was not happy about. He had requested transfers back to the Jasper post, requests that had been denied.

"I denied his transfer," said state police supervisor Robert McClure. "I will not transfer a poor quality performer. His performance was not meeting my expectations."[10]

Despite such an assessment, Coroner Tennis, who had worked with Cliver on many cases, said he was an intelligent man and was very skilled in police training.[11]

A native of Dugger, Indiana, Cliver had been a state trooper for a decade when his life began to crumble in 1984. Just before the shootings at his ex-wife's trailer, he reported his service revolver had been stolen (a suspicious and significant foul-up for a police officer), and he was issued a new one.[12]

Three days after the shootings and with few clues to go on regarding Cliver's whereabouts, state and local officials called upon the FBI to help locate the wanted police officer on the run. In Indianapolis, embarrassed state police brass moved quickly to fire Cliver based on the pending charges against him.

On April 1, 1984, a railroad employee turned in a gun found along a rail line running parallel to U.S. 41 near Evansville. Indiana State Police investigators confirmed it was the replacement weapon issued to Cliver a few weeks before the shootings and was likely the one used in the attacks.[13]

From that point on, state, federal, and local investigators were stumped and simply could not locate Cliver. That was until more than a year later on April 23, 1985, when the front page of the *Sullivan Daily Times* declared the news, "Cliver captured in Florida."[14]

Cliver's thirteen months on the run had come to an end earlier that morning, just before 8 a.m., as he reported for work at a construction site in Fort Lauderdale, Florida. FBI agents had tracked him to the site and swooped in to arrest him without incident. The FBI said Cliver had been using the alias "James George Zoeller," and had tracked him to Fort Lauderdale after a man using that name was arrested by police in nearby Sunrise, Florida, earlier for using a stolen license plate on his car.

Amazingly, Cliver had successfully avoided detection while under arrest in Sunrise as "Zoeller," posted a $2,500 bond, was set free until nabbed by the FBI weeks later. Routine fingerprint checks on the suspect "Zoeller" weren't conducted, however, until after he had been released.

The arrest of Cliver was not only good news back in Indiana, but good news for FBI officials who had placed the wayward cop on their "Top 20 Most-Wanted Fugitives List" for 1984.[15] As more of Cliver's run from the law became known, Prosecutor Elmore and Sullivan attorney Douglas S. Followell acknowledged to reporters that each had received phone calls from Cliver during the thirteen months he was at large. The calls to Elmore and Followell followed known calls Cliver had also made to his new wife, Amy Cliver.

Elmore said the call from Cliver covered general topics. "It was the first of what I hoped would be a series of communications that would lead him to turning himself in. He did tell me that he'd thought about turning himself in a thousand times."[16] Although Cliver would not disclose where he was during the phone calls, he told Elmore he had recently slipped undetected in and out of police custody.

Followell was circumspect about his conversations with a man he considered his client, but said, "I don't think he was trying to avoid capture to any great extent. He was probably very apathetic to the situation."[17]

Cliver's return to Sullivan County on May 6, 1985, was big news in Indiana. Cliver was now sporting a full beard and large eyeglasses. State police ensured heavy security was in place for his arrival at the Sullivan County Airport after death threats were received against him.[18]

At the courthouse in Sullivan, Judge Taylor entered the standard not guilty pleas for Cliver and ordered him held without bond at the Sullivan County Jail. Because of his past as a state trooper, jail authorities would have to make special arrangements to keep their murder suspect away from other inmates.[19]

"It was my idea [to isolate him] and he agreed to it," said Sullivan County Sheriff Joe Fitch. "I don't anticipate any problem with Jerry. He's promised me he'll be no problem. But we still must treat him as a prisoner."[20]

It was a promise, Sheriff Fitch would learn, that Cliver had no intention of keeping. At 1:55 a.m. on October 12, 1985, just sixteen days before the start of his scheduled trial, Cliver escaped from the Sullivan County Jail prompting another massive manhunt.

Prosecutor Elmore said it appeared that human error appeared to be at fault in allowing Cliver to slip away. "I know the natural reaction will be that faulty [jail] design aided his escape," Elmore said. "But what I've found so far in my investigation is that human error and mistakes were responsible for Cliver's escape."[21]

Sheriff's Department officials did cite jail design problems as the reason for the escape. Deputy Sheriff Ray King told the *Sullivan Daily Times* that the section of the jail where Cliver was held, normally a women's dorm, did not lock down correctly at night.

"It's a design flaw in the jail, but that area cannot be locked down electronically like the other areas in the jail," King said.[22]

King explained that Cliver had slipped out of a crank-style window in the jail the opens out about ten inches. Although covered by a metal mesh netting on the outside, "some of them are so loose you can open them with your fingers," King said.[23]

Elmore was incensed. "You don't keep your most serious offenders in the least secure place in the jail," he said."[24]

State police immediately joined local officials in the search for Cliver, bringing in helicopters and hound dogs to try and track his path. Guards were again placed on Jerri Lynn Cliver, who was at home but still recovering from her gunshot wounds.

Cliver's attorney Followell said he was stunned by Cliver's escape and said he thought they were developing a good case in his defense for the upcoming trial.[25]

Once again, the FBI stepped in to try and track the elusive Cliver as state police investigators acknowledged that he was likely "long gone" from Indiana.[26] Also like last time, Cliver would remain free for about a year, finally being captured in dramatic fashion following a shootout and a four-hour chase with Florida Highway Patrol (FHP) officers on October 9, 1986, between Gainesville and Orlando, Florida.

The drama started at 4 a.m. that day as an FHP officer attempted to pull Cliver over for a burned-out taillight. After he stopped, Cliver jumped from his car and fired one shot from a .22 caliber pistol at the trooper who was still seated in his vehicle.

It was a sickening scene. Cliver, once a state police officer himself, had struck Trooper Harry Dennard, Jr., in the chest with a bullet. A bullet-proof vest, however, saved the officer from death. Seriously wounded, the Florida trooper returned fire, striking Cliver in the legs. Despite his injuries, the desperate Cliver commandeered an *Orlando Sentinel* newspaper delivery truck that had stopped in traffic near the scene. In doing so, Cliver kidnapped the driver and fled toward Gainesville.

As the bullet wounds in his leg weakened him, Cliver ordered the newspaper truck driver to take over the wheel. Eventually, "the driver slammed on the brake, stopped the vehicle, jumped out and fled," said Lieutenant Robert McClure of the Florida Highway Patrol.[27] From there, Cliver was able to drive another twenty-three miles before finally surrendering without further incident, McClure said.

The violent incidents in Florida would greatly impact the pending cases against Cliver back in Indiana. Orange County, Florida prosecutors were insistent that they try Cliver on their various charges before turning him over to Indiana authorities for prosecution.

On March 30, 1987, Cliver was sentenced on four separate charges in Orange County, Florida, including attempted murder, attempted negligent homicide, kidnapping and carrying a concealed firearm. He received a sentence of forty-six years for his Florida crimes.

In June 1988, Cliver was returned to Indiana to face charges for the murder of Donald Clayton and the attempted murder of his ex-wife, Jerri Lynn. In court testimony, Cliver said he did not remember the shooting but did recall that he and his wife had talked calmly on the phone earlier in the evening.[28]

Cliver pled guilty to the Indiana charges in an agreement with prosecutors that his Indiana sentence of forty-years run concurrently with the Florida sentence. Indiana officials reserved the right to force Cliver to serve the remainder of his Indiana sentence should he ever gain an early release in Florida.

Cliver was released from prison in Florida in 2009 and returned to Indiana a free man. Because his sentences in Florida ran concurrently with his Indiana charges, the twenty-two years served in a Florida penitentiary fulfilled the sentencing terms in both states. Cliver, now in his sixties, has maintained a low profile since returning to Sullivan County and reportedly lives a quiet life in a rural area of the county.[29]

Endnotes

1. *Sullivan Daily Times*, Jan. 31, 1984
2. *Sullivan Daily Times*, March 26, 1984
3. Ibid.
4. Ibid.
5. Ibid.
6. Ibid.
7. Ibid.
8. Ibid.
9. *Terre Haute Tribune-Star*, March 25, 1984
10. *Sullivan Daily Times*, March 26, 1984
11. Ibid.
12. *Sullivan Daily Times*, March 27, 1984
13. *Sullivan Daily Times*, April 2, 1984
14. *Sullivan Daily Times*, April 23, 1985
15. Ibid.
16. *Sullivan Daily Times*, April 29, 1985
17. Ibid.
18. *Sullivan Daily Times*, May 6, 1985
19. Ibid.
20. Ibid.
21. *Sullivan Daily Times*, Oct. 14, 1985
22. Ibid.
23. Ibid.
24. Ibid.
25. *Terre Haute Tribune-Star*, Oct. 13, 1985
26. *Terre Haute Tribune-Star*, Oct. 14, 1985
27. *Sullivan Daily Times*, Oct. 10, 1986
28. *Terre Haute Tribune-Star*, March 20, 1994
29. *Greene County Daily World*, Sept. 1, 2009

STARKE COUNTY

VICTIM(S):
David Garland, 48

PERPETRATOR(S):
Sharon S. Garland, 44;
Allen Garland, 22

DATE OF DEATH(S):
January 24, 1996

A CONSPIRACY TO KILL

Police made it clear when they began investigating the January 24, 1996, murder of David Garland of rural Knox, Indiana, that they were not looking for a "murderer running loose." There was no forced entry to the Garland home, and nothing had been stolen. Only a married man and father shot dead.[1]

Forty-eight-year-old Garland was found shot to death on the kitchen floor of his mobile home at 9275 E. Division Road, about five miles east of Knox in Starke County. He shared the trailer home with his forty-four-year-old wife, Sharon, and their son, twenty-two-year-old Allen, both of whom found the body, the two told police, after returning home from a shopping trip at 9:30 p.m. that Wednesday evening.

Starke County Coroner Howard Bailey said Mr. Garland suffered five separate gunshot wounds to the head and was killed instantly. The coroner said a .25-caliber weapon was used in the assault. It appeared the man was making a sandwich at the time he was killed—a bottle of mustard lay on the floor next to his body.[2]

The police investigation never left its focus on Sharon and her son, and on February 15, 1996, both were hauled into Starke County Circuit Court and charged with murder and conspiracy to commit murder. Both were held at the Starke County Jail without bond.

Investigators based the arrests in part on statements provided to them by marriage and family counselor, forty-two-year-old James Lloyd, previously employed by the Starke Memorial Hospital Community Recovery Center and Culver Community Schools. Lloyd told police that Allen had told him two days after the shooting that he "felt a great release" that his father was now dead.[3]

Lloyd also told detectives that Sharon said she was "glad it is over" and gloated that "the police have nothing on us."[4]

A probable cause affidavit filed in support of the charges against Sharon and Allen said the Garland family was in turmoil over Allen's homosexuality and his desire to lead an openly gay lifestyle. David Garland was also angry that his wife openly engaged in extra-marital affairs with other men.[5]

Starke County Prosecutor Kim Hall said the family had been attending counseling sessions with Lloyd for some time and Lloyd told detectives that Sharon and Allen "talked and acted with hostility, anxiety and extreme anger—they appeared homicidal."[6]

"I am going to kill David," Mrs. Garland allegedly told Lloyd. "I hate him. I am not going to take it anymore. I want to do him in."[7]

Lloyd's story to police also led to a possible murder weapon. He told detectives he kept a loaded .25-caliber handgun in his office for protection, hidden under the cushions of a sofa. He accused Allen Garland of stealing the gun during a counseling session shortly before David Garland's murder.

Further implicating the two, Lloyd said they had called him and asked to talk to him two days after the murder. While they walked and talked, Lloyd reported that Allen said, "I shot him in the head and he fell. But it wasn't enough," indicating that he had to shoot him additional times.[8]

Police were not done talking to Lloyd, and before it was over, he went from "star witness" to "additional suspect." Police used the excuse of wanting to interview him again and asked Lloyd to report to the Starke County Sheriff's Department. When he did on August 16, 1996, he was arrested and charged with murder. On an unrelated matter, Lloyd faced additional charges related to an alleged theft from Starke Memorial Hospital for allegedly taking fees for counseling sessions from clients but not turning it over to the hospital's addiction center.

Lloyd's arrest came just days before the trial for Allen Garland was to begin, causing a delay. It also caused a major change in strategy since prosecutors had originally planned to use Lloyd's testimony against both Allen and his mother, Sharon.

After Lloyd's arrest, Allen Garland sought to be granted bond from the jail, and a bond hearing was conducted in which one of Allen's friends testified that he told her about the plot, hatched by Lloyd, to kill his father before it happened. Starke County Sheriff's detectives Robert Sims, Oscar Cowen, and Ron Lawson also testified that it was now their belief that Lloyd had actually shot and killed David Garland.[9]

All three detectives said there was no physical evidence linking Allen to his father's murder and they believed Lloyd to be a liar.[10]

Despite the testimony, Starke County Circuit Court Judge David P. Matsey denied Allen's request to receive bond and ordered that he continue to be held without bond (along with Sharon Garland and James Lloyd) at the Starke County Jail.

In October 1996, the trial against Allen and Sharon Garland finally got underway with prosecutors presenting their theory that the two had conspired with Lloyd to murder David Garland.

Glenn Garland, one of David's and Sharon's older sons, testified that he was distraught when he learned his mother and brother had lied to him about the details of his father's death. He had visited his brother at the jail shortly after his arrest but later became convinced the two had something to do with the murder.[11]

On Friday, October 31, 1996, prosecutors said they intended to call Lloyd as a witness in the trial against the two Garlands. Outside of the jury's presence, however, Lloyd said he would invoke his Fifth Amendment rights and not answer any questions. Prosecutors gave up on their attempt, and Lloyd was returned to the jail.

Jurors also watched a videotaped statement Allen Garland gave to police shortly after his arrest. In it, he said he went to Lloyd's office, and Lloyd told him "all the plans are in the works." Allen said he was confused by what that statement meant.[12]

On the tape, Allen implicated his mother in having a sexual relationship with Lloyd, their counselor, and said from how Lloyd was talking, "It sounded like he wanted to kill my Dad. I don't know if it was his plan, Mom's plan, or I don't know whose."[13]

Allen then detailed a trip in Lloyd's car the two took around Lake Maxinkuckee in adjacent Marshall County. Allen said Lloyd kept saying "he owed your mother" and kept encouraging the young man to kill his father. An earlier attempt to kill David Garland on January 19, 1996, was aborted, Allen said, when Lloyd spotted a police car driving near the Garland family trailer.[14]

Defense attorneys placed Allen's friend, Melissa Collins Boller, on the stand who confirmed many of the details of Allen's version of events.

Sharon Garland then took the stand in her own defense providing a lengthy description of her life with David and Allen and her interactions with Lloyd. Mrs. Garland said David could be abusive to her and her children. She said she filed for divorce earlier in their marriage after he exposed himself to a family friend—but later reconciled with him.[15]

Sharon also told of a history of sexual abuse in their family, helping defense attorneys in their theory that Lloyd wanted David Garland dead because he personally abhorred molesters.

She repeated Allen's claims that Lloyd had planned and executed the murder of David Garland and that they were threatened into silence because of their fear of Lloyd.

Sharon recalled that Lloyd came to their home the night of the murder unexpectedly and that she asked him what he was doing there. "'I came to talk to David,'" she quoted him as saying as she permitted him to enter their home. "James Lloyd was already in the house ... I looked up and I heard David say, 'Hi, James.' My back was to them. I heard a gunshot and a thud. I raised up and I turned my head, and I looked at James ... James was at the counter [in the kitchen near where David lay dying]," she testified.[16]

She added that Lloyd "pointed his gun at me and said, 'You're going to keep your fucking mouth shut or I'll kill you and your fucking family!' ... It was like a nightmare."[17]

Although Lloyd did not testify, he was "brought to the courtroom in order for the jury to see him in person" the *South Bend Tribune* reported—an interesting approach given that Lloyd was an African American living in a predominantly white community and the Garlands were white, as were all the members of the jury.[18]

The trial of Sharon and Allen Garland came to a close on Saturday, November 30, 1996, and set a record as the longest trial in Starke County. Jurors found both of them guilty of all charges, including murder and conspiracy to commit murder.[19]

One juror, who asked to remain anonymous, told the *South Bend Tribune* that jurors found the decision a "very, very difficult one" but said defense attorneys' attempts to take the jury's focus off the actual crime "insulted our intelligence."[20]

On December 20, 1996, Judge Matsey took up the issue of sentencing for both Sharon and Allen. Prosecutor Hall told the judge that "evidence in the record clearly indicated this was a murder for hire" and that the Garlands had participated in a plan or conspiracy to kill David.[21]

Matsey sentenced both defendants to identical fifty-five-year terms in prison.

Preparations for Lloyd's long-delayed trial finally began to move in 1997 when Matsey denied a request to move the case out of Starke County but approved a motion to import a jury from another county.

In August 1997, during a pre-trial hearing to consider motions to quash some of Lloyd's statements to police, his defense attorney, Cleo Washington, a former state senator from South Bend, questioned detective Ron Lawson about whether offers of immunity had ever been made to Lloyd.

Lawson volunteered a surprise answer during the hearing by replying, "If you're asking me if I ever said the 'N' word, I'm not going to sit here and say no," Lawson said.[22]

Washington and Prosecutor Hall seemed baffled by the response. "I don't know why he said what he did," Hall later told reporters.[23]

Washington told reporters that Lloyd's race "may or may not be a part of the testimony in the trial ... I find it interesting that four days before the trial, they bring in a black man as co-counsel for the prosecution."[24]

A day later, Hall surprised everyone by announcing that murder charges against Lloyd were being dropped, although battery and unrelated theft charges were still pending. Hall made his decision after Sharon and Allen Garland notified the state that they would refuse to testify against Lloyd at trial—for fear of harming planned appeals of their fifty-five-year sentences.

Hall said he was dismissing the charges "with prejudice" and reserved the right to file them again.

"James Lloyd can only be tried once on these charges," Hall said. "The best evidence [testimony from the Garlands] is not available at this time. We wanted to preserve the state's right to prosecute this case when the jury can hear all of the evidence against James Lloyd."[25]

As a result, Lloyd was able to bond out of jail after a year.

Lloyd told a *South Bend Tribune* reporter that the year he had spent in the Starke County Jail had nearly "demonized" him and blamed racism for the case against him.

"I did not kill David Garland," Lloyd maintained in the interview. "Why would Allen [Garland] sit in jail all those months and not talk about someone else killing his own father? It doesn't add up. [The Garlands] have changed their stories so many times. If they do testify, I'll walk all over that."[26]

Lloyd revealed that he had originally assisted investigators in reviewing the murder of David Garland, even at one point wearing a wire to secretly tape record comments by Sharon and Allen in a meeting at his office.

"I could have been implicated right there by something the Garlands might have said with the wire," Lloyd said, indicating he believed the secret recording verified he was not involved in the murder or the plot.[27]

Lloyd said he feared going to trial in Starke County, one he described as being "the most racist and segregated county in the state of Indiana."[28]

After months of continued negotiation, Lloyd returned to Starke Circuit Court on Friday, October 31, 1997, and entered a plea agreement on the theft charges filed earlier. He was sentenced to serve an additional six months in prison (in addition to the year and a half he had been held already on the dismissed murder charge) and pay fines.

As of 2007, the murder charge or conspiracy charges against Lloyd have never been refiled.

Allen and Sharon Garland began pursuing separate appeals of their cases. Allen's 1999 appeal would produce a bombshell. The Indiana Supreme Court reversed his murder conviction and ordered the court to enter a new judgment on the charge of assisting a criminal only. Justices agreed with Allen's assertion that there was insufficient evidence to prove he had in any way participated in killing his father.[29]

As a result of the ruling, Allen Garland was sentenced to an eight-year term on the assisting a criminal charge on April 7, 2000. He was released from prison in February 2002.

On the same day Allen won a new sentence, the Indiana Supreme Court also ruled Sharon had received inadequate counsel at trial.[30]

A new trial was held, and Sharon was again convicted of murder and sentenced on October 5, 2000 to fifty-four years and eleven months in prison.

Sharon would not succeed on a second appeal filed in 2003 when the court ruled that the state, in her new trial, *had* produced "sufficient evidence to convict Sharon of aiding in the murder of her husband David Garland" and ruled against her claim that a new judge should have been appointed to hear her case.[31]

Endnotes

1. *South Bend Tribune*, Jan. 26, 1996.
2. *South Bend Tribune*, Feb. 16, 1996.
3. Ibid.
4. Ibid.
5. Ibid.
6. *South Bend Tribune*, Feb. 16, 1996; *Knox Leader*, Feb. 21, 1996.
7. *South Bend Tribune*, Feb. 16, 1996.
8. Ibid.
9. *South Bend Tribune*, Aug. 28, 1996.
10. Ibid.
11. *South Bend Tribune*, Oct. 30, 1996.
12. *South Bend Tribune*, Oct, 31, 1996.
13. Ibid.
14. Ibid.

15. *South Bend Tribune*, Nov. 12, 1996.
16. *South Bend Tribune*, Nov. 13, 1996.
17. Ibid.
18. *South Bend Tribune*, Nov. 12, 1996.
19. *South Bend Tribune*, Dec. 1, 1996.
20. Ibid.
21. *South Bend Tribune*, Dec. 21, 1996.
22. *South Bend Tribune*, Aug. 15, 1997.
23. Ibid.
24. Ibid.
25. *South Bend Tribune*, Aug. 17, 1997.
26. Ibid.
27. Ibid.
28. Ibid.
29. Indiana Supreme Court Ruling, *Allen Garland vs. State of Indiana*, Nov. 19, 1999.
30. Indiana Supreme Court Ruling, *Sharon Garland vs. State of Indiana*, Nov. 19, 1999.
31. Indiana Supreme Court Ruling, *Sharon Garland vs. State of Indiana*, May 14, 2003.

STEUBEN COUNTY

VICTIM(S):
Thomas L. "Tommy Boy" Burke
(alias E.S. Bliss), 30

PERPETRATOR(S):
(None ever convicted)

DATE OF DEATH(S):
August 22, 1928

THE AMAZING TRIALS OF SHERIFF ZIMMERMAN

On a warm August evening in 1928, farmers from several miles away could see the flames of a barn burning near the settlement of Ray, a tiny Steuben County village that straddles the Indiana-Michigan state line. By morning light, the fire revealed an incredible mystery.

In the ashes of the barn and charred farm implements, police found the torso of a white male, estimated to be 5 feet, 1 inch tall and weighing only 140 pounds. Although the body was described as "burned beyond recognition," after several days of back and forth, the county coroner settled on the identity of the man as being an ex-con on the run from Florida and Ohio authorities named Thomas L. "Tommy Boy" Burke (who also used the alias E. S. Bliss).

Burke was a suspect in the May 1928 robbery of the First National Bank of Angola, a heist that reportedly yielded more than $100,000 for Burke and his cohorts. Burke's body was, in fact, "identified" by one of his former bank robbing colleagues who was awaiting trial in Toledo, Ohio, on another charge. The coroner also said the initial "B" was found on what remained of his underwear not lost to the fire, although fingerprinting was impossible since the intensity of the fire had burned off Burke's hands. Six gunshot cartridges found in the ruins of the fire with Burke, but the local coroner determined he died of blunt force injuries to the skull.

The timing of the murder and subsequent fire used to cover the crime represented some very bad timing for Steuben County Sheriff Charles "Charley" Zimmerman, a thirty-six-year-old Republican who was known for stealing headlines in capturing "rum runners" or "bootleggers". During the thirteen years of Prohibition, Indiana was a state mostly known for its strict laws against the sale, possession, or consumption of alcohol. In Indiana, the Volstead Act was popular and county sheriffs and local police were expected to strictly enforce it.

Zimmerman had been kept busy in capturing liquor scofflaws. Steuben County's strategic location along U.S. 20 at the confluence of three states—Indiana, Michigan and Ohio—meant a lot of illegal booze made its way through the county from Detroit, Chicago, Indianapolis, and Toledo, and back again.

Either by plan or a poor case of happenstance, Zimmerman was missing from Steuben County on the day Burke's body was found. He had told family and friends he was traveling to visit his brother in Jay County. His trip to see his brother was a lie, one that would complicate his life for years to come. Confounding matters was the discovery of Burke's Hudson automobile locked up inside Sheriff Zimmerman's garage in downtown Angola, complete with blood stains on the seats, and one of Zimmerman's revolvers inside.

Amidst initial suspicions about the unidentified body found in the ashes of the burned barn at Ray (north of Fremont and Clear Lake) were those of Sheriff Zimmerman. His return to the city coincided with the return of his twenty-four-year old divorcee clerk, Miss Nellie Coleman. Coleman had told family she was going to Chicago for the wedding of a friend, but her Chicago friends reported she did not attend the festivities.

The lies told by Zimmerman and Coleman about their whereabouts quickly where exposed and the married Sheriff had a lot of explaining to do about his clandestine getaway with the attractive young woman from his office. Zimmerman's Republican allies at the county courthouse were quick to abandon him, with Circuit Court Judge C.E. Carlin leading the charge that Zimmerman resign immediately—prompting Zimmerman to submit his resignation to the county commissioners and then withdraw it four days later.

The publicity was too much for Coleman who quit her job in the sheriff's office and left town. It was later learned Zimmerman, though he remained married, continued to support Coleman as she moved from Angola to Pennsylvania, and eventually back to South Bend. Zimmerman told reporters he had decided against quitting his job, or leaving town "because his wife had forgiven him for his journey with the pretty female deputy."[1]

Zimmerman jumped back into his job and took the lead in investigating Burke's murder along with the County Coroner Frank B. Humphreys and state police detectives. A multitude of leads were exhausted—two young men arrested near Twin Falls, Idaho driving a car carrying stolen license plates from Angola were initially considered suspects in the murder, and then cleared.

Rumors began circulating that either Zimmerman himself had committed the murder in some sort of incredible crime tale straight from the movie screens, or was being framed by illegal liquor runners in the region who had grown weary of his enforcement techniques. Zimmerman had experienced a run of difficulties—his Crooked Lake cottage had been burned in an arson fire, and he had lost a case in which he had attempted to seize the vehicle of liquor runners, only to be told by the court to return it.

In the midst of the mystery surrounding the death and subsequent activities, a rejuvenated Sheriff Zimmerman made headlines again on August 30, just a day after he withdrew his resignation. *The Angola Herald* reported that Zimmerman had kept his pledge to "come back and make good" as Sheriff by seizing a truckload of Canadian whisky and beer, valued at about $36,000, and arresting the truck's driver, J. P. Hiller.

Zimmerman told reporters he came upon Hiller's truck parked alongside a Steuben County highway as he returned from the murder scene near Ray. A mechanic was working on the truck at the time Zimmerman said, "I asked the driver what he was hauling and he told me general freight."[1]

Unsatisfied with that answer, Zimmerman searched the truck and found several kegs of beer, and 300 cases of bottled beer hidden behind a row of boxes containing 100 cases of Canadian whisky.

Aware of the bad news that had swirled around him, Zimmerman was happy to wait until the next morning to formally unload the truck and its contents outside the Steuben County Jail with a reported several hundred curious onlookers watching. He also was eager to tell reporters that he had just learned he had earned certification from the federal Civil Service Commission to be a federal prohibition officer.

Two weeks later on September 13, Zimmerman again summoned reporters after seizing a cargo of 424 cases of Black Label beer, valued at more than $5,000, from a truck he stopped along U.S. 20 west of Angola. "Sheriff Zimmerman's suspicions were first aroused when he observed the [truck] trailer without carrying a license," the *Garrett Clipper* account noted. "The men driving the truck, which was en route from Detroit to Chicago, readily admitted the nature of their business when questioned and submitted to arrest without resistance."[2]

During the subsequent months, little progress was made by Zimmerman in making an arrest for Burke's murder and as 1928 came to a close, Zimmerman was not a candidate for a third term as Sheriff, his political and personal lives eclipsed by the swirl of rumors that continued to circulate.

Once out of office, it didn't take long for his successor to settle on Zimmerman as the prime suspect in Burke's murder. The former Sheriff surrendered on an indictment of murder on February 7, 1929, just one month after he had left office.

A spectacular trial followed in April in which attorneys for Zimmerman argued that he was the victim of a vast and clumsy conspiracy by underworld figures who wanted him out of the way of their liquor running through northern Indiana. Attorneys for the state disagreed and argued that the evidence confirmed "the sad spectacle of a good sheriff gone wrong" who had brought shame to the name of Steuben County.[3]

Zimmerman's defense rested on the embarrassing disclosure that he and Miss Coleman had, in fact, slipped away for an amorous trip to a Michigan lake cottage. Zimmerman's attorneys urged jurors not to judge the former lawman on the basis of his personal life, but on the evidence related to Burke's murder. Buttressing his defense was testimony by Coleman confirming Zimmerman's version of events.

Defense attorney Howard Mountz said Zimmerman's decision to engage in an extra-marital affair was "a grievous error, and for which we make no excuse. He has paid bitterly for that error."[4]

Zimmerman was acquitted on the charge of murder against Burke, but the prohibition aspects of the evidence in the case prompted federal authorities to continue to look into Sheriff Zimmerman and the activities of the Steuben County Sheriff's Department. Similar ongoing investigations in nearby Allen County had already netted the arrest of several prominent political and law enforcement officials in Fort Wayne, some of whom likely were squealing or lying about Zimmerman in plea deals with federal prosecutors.[5]

On June 29, 1929, the *Angola Herald* and newspapers across the Midwest carried the news that Zimmerman was once again under arrest. This time Zimmerman was joined in jail by one of his former deputies, Russell Eckert, as both men surrendered to federal authorities after being indicted for conspiracy to violate the federal Prohibition Act.

"The two indictments were found by the late grand jury at South Bend against Zimmerman for complicity in a conspiracy in which more than a score of Allen County people was included and for participating in a conspiracy in Steuben County," the *Angola Herald* attempted to explain to its readers.[6]

The indictments were based on allegations against Zimmerman and Eckert stretching back into 1927, a year before the murder-mystery that enthralled local residents. Federal informants alleged that Zimmerman and Eckert had assisted in transporting 20 cases of whisky through Steuben County and ran a regular "pick up" operation for rum-runners near the Powers School in York Township along U.S. 20, east of Angola. The indictment also suggested Zimmerman worked to procure illegal whisky for a local Republican state legislator.

Trial for Zimmerman and Eckert was set for the federal court scheduled to convene in Fort Wayne in December 1929. The two Angola lawmen were among 151 people facing Prohibition-related charges.[7] The cases were eventually delayed until April and May 1930 because of the long list of defendants the court had to deal with.

During the trial, Zimmerman took to the witness stand to counter allegations raised by six witnesses for the government. Zimmerman denied that he and his deputy had hijacked liquor from suspects in April 1927 and then knowingly allowed it to be stolen from the county jail by other rum runners friendly to the Sheriff.

Frank Walsh and Byron Bond, both of Edon, Ohio, said they had purchased the whiskey in Detroit for $900 and were later extorted for money and a few of the bottles by Zimmerman and Eckert.

Zimmerman confirmed that he and his deputy had gone to York Township on a report of a fire. "As we got to the Powers school house, our lights flashed on a car standing alongside the school," he said. "We saw another car headed north. We approached the one headed east and started after it. It would not stop so I fired in the air a few times. I had had information that the school house was used as a point for transferring liquor. After I fired, the car stopped and we searched it and found nothing. It went on. When we returned to the school house . . . in the vestibule of the school house we found five cases of liquor wrapped in brown packages."[8]

In closing arguments, Zimmerman's local attorneys argued that he was an upstanding citizen and had often angered "rum runners" because of his aggressive enforcement of Prohibition in Steuben County. Assistant federal attorney William Duff disagreed saying "I believe Zimmerman is guilty. I wish he weren't. I thought he was a fine man when I knew him first."[9]

Zimmerman said the liquor was confiscated and destroyed. Character witnesses testifying for him included Thomas French, former Steuben County prosecutor, a former mayor of Angola, and a local bank president. As the *Indianapolis Star* reported, Zimmerman had been hailed in the past "as a martyr to the cause of Prohibition" which had resulted in his "frame up" for the mysterious murder. "Prior to the current exposures," the *Star* noted, "Zimmerman was undoubtedly the most popular sheriff Steuben County ever had. He was termed the 'fearless sheriff' when county residents discussed his capture of bootleggers. He received threatening letters, he claimed, which has caused him to be raised up another notch as a hero."[10]

The defense was successful as on May 10, 1930, jurors acquitted both Zimmerman and Eckert on all charges.[11]

After all the dust had settled on the riotous reign of Sheriff Zimmerman, the *Angola Herald* offered its readers an epilogue of sorts on January 15, 1930, when it reported in a small item on page 1 that "Former Sheriff Charles Zimmerman, associated with one of his brothers, has engaged in the restaurant business at Greenville, Ohio, buying out a place there last week. An Angola person who saw him there last week said that he is in sound and good health, despite the various rumors to the contrary which have been floating about this community of late."[12]

Endnotes

1. *Angola Herald,* April 26, 1929
2. *Garrett Clipper,* Aug. 30, 1928
3. *Angola Herald,* April 12, 1929
4. Ibid.
5. *Angola Herald,* June 29, 1929
6. Ibid.
7. *Garrett Clipper,* Dec. 2, 1929; *Indianapolis News,* Dec. 16, 1929
8. *Angola Herald,* June 29, 1929
9. Ibid.
10. *Indianapolis Star,* July 27, 1929
11. Associated Press, May 10, 1930; *Garrett Clipper,* May 12, 1930
12. *Angola Herald,* Jan. 15, 1930

SULLIVAN COUNTY

VICTIM(S):
Donald L. Clayton, 38

PERPETRATOR(S):
Jerry Wayne Cliver, 31

DATE OF DEATH(S):
March 23, 1984

A SMART COP MAKES A SMART FUGITIVE

On the cold night of January 31, 1984, firefighters were called to a fire at the two-story log cabin home of Indiana State Trooper Jerry Wayne Cliver of Sullivan County.

Fire officials said the fire was reported at 1:55 a.m. as Cliver arrived home and discovered a fire on the bottom floor of the cabin home. Firefighters extinguished a fire in the living room, although damage was extensive. Firefighters left a short time later but were called back at 3:45 a.m. when Cliver reported the house was burning again, this time on the second floor.

On the second run, twelve firefighters fought the blaze for almost three hours but could not save any of the home this time. A third fire erupted around 7:20 a.m. and had to be watered down. Efforts to save the home were hampered by a lack of fire hydrants in the unincorporated area just southeast of the Sullivan city limits.[1]

A state fire marshal's investigator was dispatched to the scene and joined with investigators from the Sullivan County Sheriff's Department to look into what they now suspected may have been arson. Prosecutors were so convinced that someone had set the house on fire they scheduled a Sullivan County grand jury to hear evidence about the fire beginning March 28, 1984.

Among the twenty-five witnesses receiving subpoenas was Trooper Cliver.[2]

The grand jury would never hear testimony from Cliver. Events in Trooper Cliver's life would interrupt those proceedings and supersede any arson investigation.

At about 10:30 p.m. on Friday, March 23, 1984, for reasons that are still mostly inexplicable, Trooper Cliver went to the Dugger, Indiana, home of his ex-wife, thirty-year-old Jerri Lynn Cliver, and summarily shot her and her new boyfriend, thirty-eight-year-old Donald L. Clayton. Jerri Lynn was critically injured, and Donald was killed instantly.

Trooper Cliver, who had been remarried less than a month before to another woman on February 16, 1984, came home to his new wife, Amy Noble Cliver, and she instantly knew something was terribly wrong.

"He stood at the door for a minute," Amy Cliver said. "He was kind of shaking. I noticed as soon as he walked in, something was wrong. I could tell by the look on his face."[3]

Amy said her new husband, Jerry, said, "You won't believe what I've done," and then admitted he had shot his ex-wife, Jerri Lynn, and her boyfriend.

Amy's comments came during a hearing in Sullivan County Circuit Court on Monday morning, March 24, 1984, as prosecutors sought an arrest warrant for the now-unaccounted-for state trooper. Judge George E. Taylor issued warrants for murder and attempted murder for Cliver.

Amy told the court her husband was at their Sullivan home from about 4 to 9 p.m. Friday night, and "he was perfectly all right—in a good mood," she said. He abruptly got up from a chair at 9 p.m. and announced he was going out to "get a couple of drinks," although he left their home in his marked Indiana State Police patrol unit.[4]

From there, police are unsure where Cliver went, but they do know he phoned Jerri Lynn's home at about 9:30 p.m. on the pretense of making arrangements to pick up the couple's two children, five-year-old Carly and two-year-old Caleb, the following day.

Jerri Lynn's mother, Mary Jo Delph, told the court that she listened in to the first few moments of the conversation between Cliver and her daughter on an extension phone and noted no real hostilities. Amy told the court, however, that Cliver was upset because he had heard Clayton's voice in the background when he called his ex-wife.

At about 10:30 p.m., after she had retired for the evening, Delph, who lived in another house on the same rural Sullivan County lot her daughter's trailer was on, said she heard "a horrible sound." She said she looked out the window in time to see Cliver entering the front door of her daughter's home after having kicked in the door.

As Delph woke her husband, she said she heard gunshots ring out. Seconds later, she said, Cliver came running out of the house and ran into a nearby woods.

"He acted like he had no knowledge of my screams," Mrs. Delph said.[5]

Mrs. Delph entered her daughter's home to find her two grandchildren seated on the floor in the living room still watching TV. One was crying, she said, but both were unharmed.

In the kitchen, Mrs. Delph found her daughter bloody and moaning. She had gunshot wounds to her hand, chest, and abdomen, Mrs. Delph said. The Sullivan County coroner later determined she had suffered wounds from two bullets.

Police found the body of Donald Clayton, a Linton, Indiana, resident, slumped nude over a hobby horse toy in the children's bedroom. Coroner William Tennis said he had been shot three times and died instantly.[6]

Tennis told reporters the bullets used on both Jerri Lynn and Clayton were "high caliber, copper clad, hollow-point shells."[7]

Detectives were able to get a brief statement from Jerri Lynn before she was taken to the intensive care unit at Terre Haute Regional Hospital for treatment of her wounds. Her statement confirmed it was her ex-husband, Jerry Cliver, who had attacked her and her boyfriend.

Sullivan County Prosecutor John S. Elmore said Jerri Lynn's statement was key. A search was underway to find Cliver. Elmore warned residents that Cliver should be considered "extremely dangerous." Guards were placed on Jerri Lynn's hospital room to ensure that Cliver had no chance to finish his deed.[8]

Cliver's new wife, Amy, told detectives that her husband had returned to their home in his state police car but left almost immediately driving her 1974 Chevy Malibu.

Jerri Lynn's mother, Mrs. Delph, said the entire incident baffled her. She said Cliver made it clear he did not want to be married to Jerri Lynn anymore, "but he didn't want anyone else to have her," she said.[9]

Detectives assigned to the case quickly began to put together the fractured pieces of Cliver's life. By 1984, he was undergoing major changes. With the final realization that his marriage to Jerri Lynn was over, he decided almost immediately to marry Amy.

Added to the mix was the suspicious fire that destroyed his log-cabin home.

If his personal life was in flux, so was his professional life. Superiors at the Indiana State Police had grown weary of Cliver. He was assigned to the Terre Haute post and patrolled Sullivan County, something Cliver was not happy about. He had requested transfers back to the Jasper post, requests that had been denied.

"I denied his transfer," said state police supervisor Robert McClure. "I will not transfer a poor quality performer. His performance was not meeting my expectations."[10]

Despite such an assessment, Coroner Tennis who had worked with Cliver on many cases said, "He's highly skilled in technical maneuvers. He's always been considered by his peers to be very intelligent and very skilled in police training."[11]

A native of Dugger, Indiana, Cliver had been a state trooper for ten years in 1984 when his world began to crumble. Just before the shootings at his ex-wife's house, for example, he reported his service revolver had been stolen (a suspicious and significant foul-up for a police officer), and he was issued a new one.[12]

Three days after the shootings, and with few clues to go on regarding Cliver's whereabouts, state and local officials called on the FBI to help locate the wanted state trooper. In Indianapolis, embarrassed Indiana State Police officials moved quickly to fire Cliver on March 31, 1984, based on the charges leveled against him.

Prosecutor Elmore won an order from the Sullivan Circuit Court to seal the grand jury's findings in its review of the earlier fire at Cliver's home. Elmore said the case would remain sealed as Cliver was still at large.[13]

On April 1, 1984, a railroad employee turned in a gun he found along a rail line running parallel to U.S. 41 near Evansville. Indiana State Police investigators confirmed it was the replacement weapon issued to Cliver a few weeks before the shootings and was likely the one used in the attacks.[14]

From that point on, state, federal, and local investigators were stumped and simply could not locate Cliver. That was until more than a year later on Tuesday, April 23, 1985, when the front page of the *Sullivan Daily Times* declared the news, "Cliver captured in Florida."[15]

Cliver's thirteen months on the run had come to an end that day just before 8 a.m. as he reported for work at a construction site in Fort Lauderdale, Florida. FBI agents swooped in and arrested Cliver without incident.

The FBI said Cliver was using the alias of "James George Zoller," and they had tracked him to Fort Lauderdale after a man using that name was arrested by police in nearby Sunrise, Florida, on February 8, 1985, for using a stolen license plate on his car.

Cliver had successfully avoided detection while under arrest as "Zoller," posted a $2,500 bond, and was set free until nabbed by the FBI. Routine fingerprint checks on the suspect "Zoller" weren't conducted, however, until after he was released and the FBI confirmed it was in fact Cliver.

The arrest of Cliver was not only good news back in Indiana, but good news for FBI officials who had placed the wayward cop on their "Top 20 Most-Wanted Fugitives List" for 1984.[16]

As more of Cliver's run from the law became known, Prosecutor Elmore and Sullivan attorney Douglas S. Followell acknowledged to reporters that each had received telephone calls from Cliver during the thirteen months he was at large. The calls to Elmore and Followell followed known calls Cliver made to his new wife, Amy Cliver.

Elmore said the call from Cliver covered general topics. "It was the first of what I hoped would be a series of communications that would lead to him turning himself in. He did tell me that he'd thought about turning himself in a thousand times."[17]

Although Cliver would not disclose where he was, he told Elmore he had recently been in and out of jail (the result of the arrest at Sunrise, Florida).

Followell was circumspect about his conversations with a man he considered his client but said, "I don't think he was trying to avoid capture to any great extent. He was probably very apathetic to the situation."[18]

Cliver's arrival in Sullivan County via an Indiana State Police airplane on Monday, May 6, 1985, was big news across Indiana. Cliver was now sporting a full beard and large eyeglasses. State police ensured heavy security was in place for his arrival at the Sullivan County airport after death threats were received against him.[19]

At the courthouse in Sullivan, Judge Taylor entered the standard not guilty pleas for Cliver and ordered him held without bond at the Sullivan County Jail. Because of his past as a state trooper, jail authorities would have to make special arrangements to keep their murder suspect away from other inmates.[20]

"It was my idea [to isolate him] and he agreed to it," said Sullivan County Sheriff Joe Fitch. "I don't anticipate any problem with Jerry. He's promised me he'll be no problem. But we still must treat him as a prisoner."[21]

It was a promise, Sheriff Fitch would learn, that Jerry Cliver had no intention of keeping.

At 1:55 a.m. on Saturday, October 12, 1985, just sixteen days before the scheduled start of his trial, Cliver escaped from the Sullivan County Jail prompting another massive search similar to the unsuccessful one more than two years ago when he was first sought.

County Prosecutor Elmore said human error appeared to be at fault in allowing Cliver to slip away. "I know the natural reaction will be that faulty [jail] design aided his escape," Elmore said. "But what I've found so far in my investigation is that it is human error and mistakes that were responsible for Cliver's escape."[22]

Sheriff's Department officials did cite jail design problems as the reason for the escape. Deputy Sheriff Ray King told the *Sullivan Daily Times* that the section of the jail where Cliver was held, normally a women's dorm, did not lock down at night.

"It's a design flaw in the jail, but that area cannot be locked down electronically like the other areas in the jail," King said.[23]

King explained that Cliver had slipped out of a crank-style window in the jail that opens the window about ten inches. Although covered by a metal mesh netting on the outside, "some of them are so loose you can open them with your fingers," King said.[24]

Elmore was incensed. "You don't keep your most serious offenders in the least secure place in the jail," he said.[25]

The man on the spot, besides Cliver, was Sheriff Fitch—although Fitch was out of town on vacation at the time of the escape and his family was struggling to reach him to notify him of what had transpired back home.[26]

State police immediately joined local officials in the search for Cliver, bringing in helicopters and hound dogs to try and track his path. Guards were again placed on Jerri Lynn Cliver, who was at home but still recovering from her gunshot wounds.

Cliver's attorney Followell said he was stunned by Cliver's escape and said he thought they were developing a good case in his defense for his upcoming trial.[27]

Once again, the FBI stepped in to help find Cliver as state police investigators acknowledged that he was likely "long gone" from Indiana.[28]

Also like last time, Cliver would remain free about a year, finally being captured in dramatic fashion following a shootout and a four-hour chase with Florida Highway Patrol (FHP) officers on Thursday, October 9, 1986, between Gainesville and Orlando, Florida.

The capture began at about 4 a.m. that day as a Florida Highway Patrol officer attempted to pull Cliver over for a burned-out taillight. After he stopped, Cliver jumped from his car and fired one shot from a .22-caliber pistol at the trooper who was still seated in his vehicle.

It was a sickening scene. Cliver, once a state police officer himself, had struck Trooper Harry Dennard, Jr., in the chest with a bullet. A bullet-proof vest, however, saved the officer from death.

Seriously wounded, the Florida trooper returned fire striking Cliver in the legs. Despite his injuries, the desperate Cliver commandeered an *Orlando Sentinel* newspaper delivery truck that had stopped in traffic. In doing so, Cliver kidnapped the driver and fled toward Gainesville.

As the bullet wounds in his legs weakened him, Cliver ordered the newspaper truck driver to take over the wheel. Eventually, "the driver slammed on the brake, stopped the vehicle, jumped out and fled," said Lieutenant Robert McClure of the Florida Highway Patrol.[29]

From there, Cliver was able to drive another twenty-three miles before finally surrendering without further incident, McClure said.

The violent incidents in Florida would greatly impact the pending case against Cliver back in Sullivan County. Orange County, Florida, prosecutors were insistent that they try Cliver on various charges there before returning him to Indiana for prosecution.

During the latest year he was at large, Cliver had fled at first to California, authorities learned. He was arrested on a handgun charge in Laguna Beach, California, on November 11, 1985, using the name of "Wayne Manuel"—just a few weeks after escaping the Sullivan County Jail. Police there fingerprinted him, booked him, and then released him on the charge. Again, a fingerprint check with the FBI was not made until Cliver was released and was again at large.[30]

On March 30, 1987, Cliver was sentenced on four separate charges in Orange County, Florida, including attempted murder, attempted negligent homicide, kidnapping, and carrying a concealed firearm. He received a sentence of forty-six years and is housed at the Avon Park Correctional Institution in Florida.

In June 1988, Cliver was returned to Indiana to face charges for the murder of Donald Clayton and the attempted murder of his ex-wife, Jerri Lynn. In court testimony, Cliver said he did not remember the shooting but did recall that he and his wife had talked calmly on the phone earlier in the evening and did not argue.[31]

He decided to plead guilty to the Indiana charges in an agreement with prosecutors that his Indiana sentence of forty-years run concurrently with the Florida sentence. Indiana officials have reserved the right to force Cliver to serve the remainder of his Indiana sentence should he ever gain an early release in Florida.

Cliver was released from prison in Florida in 2009 and returned to Indiana a free man. Because his sentences in Florida ran concurrently with his Indiana charges, the twenty-two years served in a Florida penitentiary fulfilled the sentencing terms in both states. Florida, like Indiana, grants "good time" or "gain time" release for prisoners who serve without incident during their incarceration. Cliver, now in his sixties, has maintained a low profile since returning to Sullivan County and reportedly lives a quiet life in a secluded, rural area of the county.[32]

Endnotes

1. *Sullivan Daily Times*, Jan. 31, 1984.
2. *Sullivan Daily Times*, March 26, 1984.
3. Ibid.
4. Ibid.
5. Ibid.
6. Ibid.
7. Ibid.
8. Ibid.
9. *Terre Haute Tribune-Star*, March 25, 1984.
10. *Sullivan Daily Times*, March 26, 1984.
11. Ibid.
12. *Sullivan Daily Times*, March 27, 1984.
13. *Sullivan Daily Times*, March 30, 1984.
14. *Sullivan Daily Times*, April 2, 1984.
15. *Sullivan Daily Times*, April 23, 1985.
16. Ibid.
17. *Sullivan Daily Times*, April 29, 1985.
18. Ibid.
19. *Sullivan Daily Times*, May 6, 1985.
20. Ibid.
21. Ibid.
22. *Sullivan Daily Times*, Oct. 14, 1985.
23. Ibid.
24. Ibid.
25. Ibid.
26. Ibid.
27. *Terre Haute Tribune-Star*, Oct. 13, 1985.
28. *Terre Haute Tribune-Star*, Oct. 14, 1985.
29. *Sullivan Daily Times*, Oct. 10, 1986.
30. *Terre Haute Tribune-Star*, Oct. 11, 1986.
31. *Terre Haute Tribune-Star*, March 20, 1994.
32. *Greene County Daily World*, Sept. 1, 2009.

SWITZERLAND COUNTY

VICTIM(S):
Unidentified runaway slave

PERPETRATOR(S):
Samuel Mead

DATE OF DEATH(S):
June 24, 1857

NO JUSTICE FOR A KENTUCKY KILLER

On Wednesday, June 24, 1857, Samuel Mead of Switzerland County appointed himself as the one responsible to locate three runaway slaves from Kentucky. Some Hoosiers believe Mead did so because "he is one of that class of men who reside on the borders of Indiana and Kentucky who take the place of dogs trained to hunt down Negroes in the more Southern States," as the *Madison Dollar Weekly Courier* put it.[1]

By all accounts, however, Mead got a little carried away—even his fellow "Negro catchers" said that Mead "fired too soon," striking one of three runaways in the stomach and killing him.

Officially, in 1857 in the years leading up to the U.S. Civil War, Kentucky was no longer a slave-holding state. Congress prohibited the importation of slaves in 1808, and Kentucky prohibited the importation of slaves for sale in 1833. "However, because of the lucrative nature of the slave trade, slaves continued to be bought and sold, despite legal restrictions," historian James Klotter reports.[2]

"In order to gain maximum benefit from their slaves, Kentucky slaveholders also frequently hired out skilled slaves as carpenters, blacksmiths, brick masons, coopers, herders, stevedores, waiters, and factory workers," Klotter wrote.[3]

Klotter adds that in the era when Mead shot the Kentucky slave on Indiana soil, "roughly one-quarter of Louisville's enslaved were hired out. The hiring-out system provided masters with considerable flexibility in using slave labor and afforded the enslaved a sense of freedom and perhaps a small measure of independence not experienced on larger plantations in the Deep South."[4]

Regardless of the legal or actual practices in Kentucky, Switzerland County, Indiana authorities were not willing to let the murder go unpunished. The Switzerland County coroner held an inquest and "the coroner's jury found a verdict in accordance with the facts" and a requisition was prepared ordering Kentucky officials to apprehend and return Mead to Indiana on a charge of "willful murder."[5]

A Switzerland County grand jury similarly found against Mead, indicting him for murder in the November 1857 term—although he remained at large.

The *Madison Dollar Weekly Courier* said the problems started when Mead surprised the runaways, and vice versa near Vevay, Indiana, in Switzerland County. Vevay, the county seat, is located directly across the Ohio River from Ghent, Kentucky, and about seventy miles northeast and upriver from Louisville, Kentucky.

"The pursuers came upon the Negroes suddenly, both parties surprised and startled; Mead instantly fired and killed one of the Negroes, one of the two left made no resistance—it is probable they intended to make none; the third one fled, shouting, 'Don't kill me! Don't kill me!' with Mead in pursuit," the account in the *Courier* relayed.

Mead caught up with the third fleeing slave, but also with two white men from Vevay, who ordered Mead not to kill the "fugitive."

The tone of the *Madison Dollar Weekly Courier's* report on the incident reflected the growing abolitionist views among many Hoosiers. "Mead immediately turned to his friends, and retreated precipitately with the live Negro to Kentucky, where it is probable he will be presented with gold-headed canes, silver-mounted pistols, and silver pitchers for his gallantry," the *Courier* bitterly reported.[6]

To be certain, not all Hoosiers, just like not all Kentuckians, were of one mind on the slavery issue. While Indiana was not a slave-holding state, life was not good for early African Americans in pre-Civil War years here.

As Indiana rewrote its constitution in 1850-51, Article 13 was introduced by some of the constitutional delegates to ban further Negro migration into the state and to promote the colonization of blacks. In statewide voting on the constitution, an overwhelming majority favored the "Negro exclusion article" that carried a majority in all Indiana counties except Elkhart, LaGrange, Randolph, and Steuben.[7]

Just a few years later in 1863, federal officials seeking men to draft for the army to fight for the Union were met with gunfire by unwilling civilians in Rush County, Indiana.[8]

William Sandford of Carrollton, Kentucky, reported to Louisville, Kentucky, four days after the shooting near Vevay to claim the captured "boys" Mead and his men had returned to Kentucky.[9]

The *Louisville Daily Democrat* took up the issue of the killed slave, saying, "It was only a Negro shot—why would a jury of Hoosiers bother themselves about it? To be sure, twelve men selected from the intensest American community in Switzerland County, after hearing the facts, upon their solemn oaths, found a verdict of 'willful murder.'"[10]

The *Daily Democrat* seemed to find a contradiction in the verdict and existing Indiana law. "These [jurors] don't know that it is not murder to kill a [Negro]" in Indiana, and that the Indiana legislature had yet to act "to make it unlawful to kill Negroes in the running season. Deer and quails are protected by game laws—why not [Negroes]?"[11]

By July 1, 1857, it appeared likely that Kentucky officials were not going to cooperate with returning Mead to Indiana, and editorials in newspapers there began to ridicule the indictment from Switzerland County, calling it a "singular proceeding" not worthy of further consideration.

The editors of *Madison Dollar Weekly Courier* had apparently had enough of the delaying in apprehending Mead and in a front page editorial offered their opinion: "Murder is a crime, recognized as such in the criminal codes of all the States. Killing a Negro willfully, with malice aforethought, is murder in any slave state as well as in Indiana."[12]

"A Negro has been killed in Indiana, and that even an inquest should be held to inquire into the circumstances of the killing is deemed by our Kentucky neighbors 'a singular proceeding!'" the *Courier's* editors wrote.[13]

The newspaper and many on the Indiana side of the river were not only incensed that Mead was seemingly getting away with murder but were angered that Kentucky officials were thumbing their nose at an Indiana court.

"To send Mead to Indiana for trial is certainly not more obnoxious to the feelings and prejudices of Kentuckians than the enforcement of the fugitive slave laws to the Indianians," the *Courier* declared.[14]

Mead would receive "a fair trial" under what news reports indicated were "milder" criminal codes in Indiana than in Kentucky.

"The South says the Union is valueless unless their rights are respected," the editorial continued. "And that their rights will not be respected unless they can make Negro catching hounds of the people of free States. Now, what is the Union worth in the North if men are allowed to come from the slave States and shoot down men in the free States with impunity?"[15]

Mead was never apprehended or tried for killing the slave, and the matter faded into the past as news of the impending "war between the states" began to take over the daily agenda of Hoosiers, and all Americans.

The debate over slavery, however, continued on both sides of the river and was especially intense for Kentucky, a Union border state in the war. The debate was equally intense on the Hoosier side of the river, as many citizens helped form critical links of the nation's Underground Railroad that stretched across parts of Indiana offering freedom for enslaved blacks.

"The conflicting pulls of economic gain, westward expansion, and fundamental support for slavery caused Kentuckians to be morally divided over the issue of slavery before, during, and immediately after the Civil War," Klotter explains. "Though loyal to the Union, the Kentucky majority never intended to end slavery or reject notions of white supremacy."[16]

Endnotes

1. *Madison Dollar Weekly Courier*, June 26, 1857.
2. Klotter, James. "Slave Life in Kentucky," *Our Kentucky: A Study of the Bluegrass State* (1992), The University Press of Kentucky, Lexington, KY, pages 108-109.
3. Ibid., pages 108-109.
4. Ibid., pages 108-109.
5. *Madison Dollar Weekly Courier*, June 26, 1857; *Madison Dollar Weekly Courier*, June 30, 1857.
6. *Madison Dollar Weekly Courier*, June 26, 1857.
7. Crenshaw, Gwendolyn. "Bury Me In A Free Land," *The Abolitionist Movement in Indiana, 1816-1865* (1993) Indiana Historical Bureau, Indianapolis, IN, page 7.
8. *New York Times*, June 12, 1863.
9. *Madison Dollar Weekly Courier*, June 30, 1857.
10. *Louisville* (Ky.) *Democrat*, June 28, 1857.
11. Ibid.
12. *Madison Dollar Weekly Courier*, July 1, 1857.
13. Ibid.
14. Ibid.
15. Ibid.
16. Klotter, page 103.

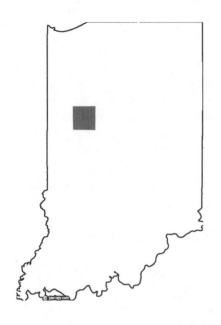

TIPPECANOE COUNTY

VICTIM(S):
John P. Grove, 57;
Wallace "Bill" McClure, 55

PERPETRATOR(S):
Samuel Baxter, 20;
John Burns, 19

DATE OF DEATH(S):
Feb. 7, 1928

A MYSTERY COMES TO A SAD END

During the first weeks of February 1928, the unprecedented criminal trial of an Indiana governor was expected to dominate the headlines of most every Hoosier newspaper.

That was true, except in north central Indiana where two Tippecanoe County sheriff's deputies had gone missing, along with their two prisoners on what was considered a routine transfer of prisoners from the county jail to the Pendleton Reformatory in Madison County.

The group was last seen at 6 a.m., Tuesday, February 7, 1928, as the two prisoners, Samuel Baxter and John Burns, were handcuffed together and placed in the back seat of a black 1920 Studebaker touring car. The car, driven by its owner, Deputy Sheriff John P. Grove, also carried Deputy Wallace "Bill" McClure—two men accustomed to transferring inmates from county to state custody.

Baxter and Burns were convicted a week prior in their second trial on charges of having robbed a restaurant at West Point, Indiana, of $65. Both men were sentenced to five to twenty-one years at the Pendleton Reformatory.

Tippecanoe County Sheriff C.M. Johnston told reporters that deputies Grove and McClure were expected back from Pendleton no later than 9:30 a.m. that day. By noon, they wondered whether they had experienced car trouble. By 3 p.m., when they still had not returned, the sheriff's department became suspicious.

Sheriff Johnston called the Pendleton Reformatory only to learn the men had never arrived with their prisoners. Something was wrong. The eighty-three-mile trip should have taken about two hours. A second check by telephone at 7 p.m. confirmed that the men had not arrived as expected.

The *Lafayette Journal & Courier* reported, "There is much speculation as to what might have happened. Burns and Baxter, facing at least five years' imprisonment, might have decided to resort to desperate measures."[1]

Local men formed a posse, including men from American Legion Post No. 11, and a search commenced. State police joined the search immediately, as did county and city police departments from surrounding areas.

Most of the attention of the search was focused on the roads between Lafayette east to Pendleton.

They also searched rivers and creeks near bridges for fear the deputies' car had left the roadway. Other searches stretched south toward Lebanon, Noblesville, and Indianapolis. Even a stone quarry at Kokomo was searched after a letter claimed the deputies' bodies were dumped there. Still, nothing turned up.

The search continued for days, with the *Journal & Courier* noting, "The case is developing into a mystery surpassing the wildest dreams of a romancer. The officers and their prisoners have vanished as completely as though wiped off of the earth by a hand from the sky."[2]

Sheriff Johnston told reporters that the officers may have been "trussed up in some woods or farm building" or slain and asked area farmers to report any suspicious activity on their lands.

Reporters also focused on the background of the two prisoners.

Burns, just nineteen years old, was said to have been raised by "destitute parents" who "did everything in their power to mold him into a useful, respectful young man." He had served a previous term at a Pontiac, Illinois, reformatory on a robbery charge. Reports said he had only gone as far as the eighth grade before dropping out.[3]

Twenty-year-old Baxter was said to be a good student but got into trouble while still at West Lafayette High School for theft. Paroled in November 1926, he completed his high school diploma before being arrested again for the West Point, Indiana, restaurant robbery.

The third day into the mystery, a big break came in the form of a phone call from police at Danville, Illinois. They notified the Tippecanoe County sheriff that Burns and Baxter had been there, sixty-six miles *west* of Lafayette, between 9 a.m. and noon on Tuesday, the day the mystery began.

The men apparently had attempted to stay in the home of Burns's uncle, Otto Smith. Mr. Smith reported the young men were driving a dark-colored Studebaker, and he ordered them to leave his home, calling his nephew a "bad boy" and saying he was suspicious of their activities, even though he was unaware they were fugitives.

Even more troubling, Mr. Smith reported the young men were traveling alone. There was no sign of Deputies Grove and McClure.

On February 11, Grove's Studebaker was found abandoned in Decatur, Illinois. Investigators found evidence of a fierce battle inside the car, including a bullet hole in the windshield. The same day, Grove's bullet-pierced hat was found near Maple Point in Tippecanoe County.

Unknown to Indiana investigators, February 11 was also the day Burns and Baxter were being detained and arrested at a town called Atoka in southern Oklahoma, more than 800 miles away from Lafayette. Burns and Baxter used fake names when being arrested for carrying firearms without a license and were sentenced to thirty-six days in the Atoka County Jail.

It wouldn't be until February 16, however, nine days into the search, that the bodies of the two deputies would be found. Outside of the original search area, the deputies' bodies were found accidentally by men preparing to install a new fence in a woods about three miles west of Covington, Indiana, in Warren County, just inside the Indiana border.

The bodies were found face up and reported to be in "good shape" despite several days of heavy rain. Grove's right arm was extended at his side, and McClure had been placed on top of his arm. Both were lying on top of a small blanket from Grove's car and were partially covered with brush.

Lying within sight of a gravel road that connected the two Warren County towns of Foster and Gessie, the two bodies "were close together. Both men were fully dressed. There were four branches about two inches in diameter on top of the corpses, the portion of the auto robe over Grove's face being helped by the dead boughs. The heads were side by side as if care had been taken to place them in that position."[4]

Authorities transferred the bodies to Williamsport, Indiana, for autopsies. The examinations showed Grove was shot twice through the back with a .38-caliber pistol and suffered head wounds. The bullets pierced Grove's back and neck, indicating he was attacked from behind while still driving. McClure was also shot twice, with both shots piercing his body and passing all the way through. McClure also suffered severe head wounds, believed to be from the manner in which they were overtaken and disarmed. The weapon was likely an engine crank left in the car.

Initially, it was unclear what weapon was used to kill the men, as Grove's .38 was found in his pocket and had not been fired. The deputies' two smaller caliber weapons were missing, however.

The investigation revealed the two deputies were overpowered by their prisoners shortly after they left Lafayette, near the town of Maple Point, a settlement east of the city.

The trail soon grew very cold, although some investigators believed both men would eventually return to their hometown. By May 1928, the theory proved true as a tip came in to Lafayette Police that Burns was holed up in his aunt's home in West Lafayette. A 1:30 a.m. raid of the home early on Monday, May 21, yielded Burns hiding behind a davenport in the living room of his aunt's home.

He was described as having "aged remarkably since the day he became a fugitive charged with double murder … Then he was a boy, now he looks like a man of 35 or 40, his face haggard and drawn, his body emaciated and a black moustache adorning his upper lip. His face is tanned dark brown, making him look like a Negro."[5]

Under ten hours of questioning, Burns told an unbelievable story that the car driven by Deputy Grove had been overcome by three other Chicago-area bandits who sought to help free Burns and Baxter. He placed blame for their murder on the other men, admitting to only helping place the dead officers' bodies in the field in Warren County.

His story did not match evidence, as bullets entered both of the victim's backs—not a likely occurrence in the type of shootout that Burns described. Further, bullet holes from inside the car made his story seem farfetched. Burns was not deterred and went to trial with his claim.

Before trial, he told authorities about how he and Baxter were arrested in Oklahoma and how they had decided, upon release from there, to go their separate ways to avoid further detection. Burns said he then hitched rides to Texas, back to Missouri, and then to Monroe, Louisiana, where he found work as a laborer.

"I wanted to come back to Lafayette many times," Burns told investigators, "and stayed away as long as I could."[6]

He continually denied having anything to do with the officers' cold-blooded murders but felt such guilt it prevented him from eating or working.

"I am glad it is over," he said. "You don't know what I have gone through. It has been torture for months … Even in the daytime if I would be walking along the street or road, I'd imagine arms were stretched out to get me. Many times I thought an arm was reaching for me and I would turn around and shudder as I realized it was only a delusion."[7]

Burns' trial for the murder of the two officers began in early June 1928. He kept his story up about the other Chicago men who had killed the officers while trying to free him and Baxter.

State witnesses, including several former inmates at the Tippecanoe County Jail, testified that Burns and Baxter were brash young men, gloating they did not intend to remain incarcerated. Their fellow inmates offered testimony that Burns and Baxter even showed off two guns they somehow had obtained at the jail in the days before they were to be transferred to the Pendleton Reformatory.

Burns testified in his own defense, apparently not impressing the jury, who delivered a guilty verdict late on Friday evening, June 8, 1928, at the close of a four-day trial. On Saturday, June 9, 1928, Tippecanoe County Circuit Court Judge Homer W. Hennegar sentenced Burns to life in prison.

His accomplice, Samuel Baxter, would prove more elusive, but he, too, would eventually be made to answer for his actions. He remained a fugitive for three years until police arrested him on August 27, 1931, in Albuquerque, New Mexico, where he worked under the assumed name of "Al Casey" as a foreman on a water tower construction project. His three years of freedom had not only produced a new name for Baxter but also a wife and a one-year-old daughter.

The FBI had helped distribute 1,500 flyers bearing Baxter's picture and fingerprints to police agencies across the United States. A tip based on one of those flyers led police to Baxter, who struggled briefly with police. They then shot him once in the leg as he tried to flee.

Baxter attempted to fight extradition to Indiana but failed. As soon as his leg healed, he was returned to Tippecanoe County to face trial. He was found guilty of second-degree murder Friday, January 8, 1932, in Lafayette, after seven hours of deliberation. The verdict surprised Baxter and his new family (Texas natives) who thought a manslaughter conviction was possible. He was sentenced to life in prison at the Indiana State Prison at Michigan City, where Burns was also housed.

Endnotes

1. *Lafayette Journal & Courier*, Feb. 8, 1928.
2. *Lafayette Journal & Courier*, Feb. 9, 1928.
3. *Lafayette Journal & Courier*, Feb. 10, 1928.
4. *Attica Ledger & Tribune*, Feb. 17, 1928.
5. *Lafayette Journal & Courier*, May 21, 1928.
6. *Lafayette Journal & Courier*, May 22, 1928.
7. Ibid.

TIPTON COUNTY

VICTIM(S):
Nestor Rios Vargas, 36

PERPETRATOR(S):
None convicted

DATE OF DEATH(S):
September 2, 1942

A FRIDAY NIGHT FIGHT LEADS TO MURDER

In the last weeks of August 1942, the United States Employment Service put out a call for men and women to come to Tipton and Madison counties to help pick and can that year's abundant tomato crop.

Among those who have traditionally come to Indiana to harvest the tomato crops have been migrant farm workers from Mexico. Carrying on generations of tradition, many of them moved across the country finding work in harvests as the growing seasons came to an end.

One of those workers was Nestor Rios Vargas, thirty-five, listed in reports as a "Mexican farm worker" but also listed as having a residence in Eagle Pass, Texas. Police reported Vargas was seriously injured during a "brawl" on Friday night, August 28, 1942, near the corner of Jefferson and Independence streets in downtown Tipton.[1]

Arrested was Gerald Glen Grose, twenty-five, a Tipton County resident, who police said was implicated in beating Vargas. Also held was Leonidas Ruis, thirty-eight, a brother-in-law to Vargas, who was arrested for carrying a "stove shaker" in his pocket.

Vargas was in Tipton County working as a tomato picker at the Herbert Werner Farm just east of Tipton at Hobbs, Indiana. He spent Friday evening relaxing and drinking with Ruis and some of his brothers at a Tipton bar.[2]

Grose apparently was unwinding in the same way, in the same downtown tavern, when the fight ensued.

420

No statement could be taken from Vargas, who remained unconscious after his head struck an iron grate in the sidewalk after being struck by Grose. Vargas suffered a deep cut on the left side of his skull and face, police said.[3]

On September 2, 1942, Vargas died of his injuries after suffering the effects of pneumonia for several days and never regaining consciousness.

"When admitted to the hospital, Vargas was bleeding from the ears and nose and his chances of pulling through appeared very slight," the *Tipton Daily Tribune* reported.[4]

Grose, meanwhile, already held on an assault and battery charge at the Tipton County Jail, had his charges increased to manslaughter.[5]

Tipton County Prosecutor Horace Holmes said his office and police were rounding up witnesses to the argument between the two men in order to prove their charge against Grose. Holmes admitted, however, that his office was struggling to find cooperative witnesses and that many "don't seem to care about talking about it."[6]

Grose, Holmes said, refused to talk to police about the brawl and remained silent about his role in it.

Upon Vargas's death, a disagreement erupted as to whether he was a legal U.S. citizen. Born in Mexico, some of his family and friends reported he gained U.S. citizenship in 1913 and was widowed. He was survived by two brothers (who were also in Tipton County working) and two sisters back in Texas.[7] Other relatives, however, said he was not a U.S. citizen and was only in the country on a work-related visa.

The *Tipton Daily Tribune* relayed that "Vargas came to this county about three weeks ago ... they have picked tomatoes in this county for a number of years, coming down from Michigan's fruit packing season."[8]

As Holmes continued his investigation, members of the Vargas family contacted the Mexican Consulate's Office in Chicago to ask for their help in investigating the circumstances of Vargas's death. As they did, Vargas's family chose to bury him at St. Joseph's Cemetery in Tipton.

"He was never naturalized [as a citizen] although he was registered with the selective service system," an unnamed family spokesman (described as "young and well educated") told the *Tipton Daily Tribune*.[9]

"We are not angry with the people of this community," the young Mexican spokesman told the *Tribune*. "We realize there are all kinds of people, both good and bad, here just as they are everywhere else. All we want is full justice and we feel this can best be done through the Mexican Consulate in Chicago."[10]

A few days later, Prosecutor Holmes reported he had secured two witness statements, including one that indicated Vargas had attempted to leave the bar unmolested when the argument began, but that Grose followed him outside onto the sidewalk.

"When the two men reached the Diana Theatre, Grose seized the Mexican from behind and either shoved him or struck him in such a manner that his body bounced back from the theatre wall," the witness statement released by Holmes said. "As Vargas bounced back, Grose dealt him a single blow and the Mexican crumpled to the sidewalk, his head striking the pavement with a thud. Grose then turned around and walked back into the tavern."[11]

Despite the witness statements, the case against Grose lingered for months. During that time, he remained free on bond. Grose's attorney, Floyd Harper, said his client admitted striking Vargas but did so only in self-defense.[12]

In February 1943, more than six months after the original assault, it was announced Grose's Tipton County trial would be delayed. His attorneys were seeking to move the case to Howard County in order to ensure an impartial jury.[13]

Tipton County Circuit Court Judge Frank B. Russell granted Grose's request to move the case to Howard County, delaying the start of the trial further.

In May 1943, Grose said he would plead guilty to a lesser charge to avoid trial, although the state refused to accept the plea agreement.[14]

His trial finally opened on May 10, 1943, at the Howard County Courthouse in Kokomo. One eyewitness to the fight, Kenneth Addison of Tipton, told the jury that he saw Grose strike Vargas as he walked in front of him, and watched the man fall to the cement sidewalk. Gilbert Goodnight, another witness, offered essentially the same scenario.[15]

The tavern's operators, Mr. and Mrs. Everett Stout, testified that they were aware of no problems between the two men before the argument took place outside the bar. Two other bar patrons, Mildred Mock and Lucille Mullins, testified that "the Mexicans were not causing any trouble in the bar."[16]

George Preston, seated at the bar with Grose, said Grose believed Vargas had muttered a derogatory remark at him as he exited the bar.[17]

Prosecutor Holmes argued that Vargas's friends had told detectives that it was impossible for the man to have insulted Grose as he did not know how to speak English. His efforts were hampered considerably, however, when the Mexican Consulate was unable to produce any of the fellow Mexicans drinking with Vargas that night.[18]

Grose testified in his own behalf, admitting he had two prior arrests for assault and battery, and one arrest for a traffic law violation. He stuck to his story that he feared Vargas was armed and would hurt him.[19]

Ten minutes after the jury room door was closed on May 13, 1943, the jury foreman emerged to inform the court bailiff that they had reached a verdict.

As the *Tipton Daily Tribune* put it, "In less time than it takes the average jury to organize and elect its foreman, the group of 10 men and two women decided the case and set Grose free."[20]

Prosecutor Holmes said he was "surprised" at the verdict and the speed at which it was reached. Grose and his mother, who sat at the defense table with him, were overjoyed and returned to Tipton, free of the charges.[21]

Endnotes

1. *Tipton Daily Tribune*, Aug. 29, 1942.
2. Ibid.
3. Ibid.
4. *Tipton Daily Tribune*, Sept. 2, 1942.
5. *Tipton Daily Tribune*, Sept. 3, 1942.
6. Ibid.
7. Ibid.
8. Ibid.
9. *Tipton Daily Tribune*, Sept. 4, 1942.
10. Ibid.
11. *Tipton Daily Tribune*, Sept. 5, 1942.
12. *Tipton Daily Tribune*, April 5, 1943.
13. *Tipton Daily Tribune*, Feb. 27, 1943.
14. *Tipton Daily Tribune*, May 4, 1943.
15. *Tipton Daily Tribune*, May 11, 1943.
16. Ibid.
17. Ibid.
18. *Tipton Daily Tribune*, May 13, 1943; May 14, 1943.
19. *Tipton Daily Tribune*, May 13, 1943.
20. *Tipton Daily Tribune*, May 14, 1943.
21. Ibid.

UNION COUNTY

VICTIM(S):
Eliza Beth (McCollum) Heller;
John Wesley Heller;
Sarah Heller;
Mary Heller, infant;
Catherine Mackelroy, 9

PERPETRATOR(S):
Isaac Young Heller, 27

DATE OF DEATH(S):
Unknown date 1831 and
February 27, 1836

A KILLER IN THE NAME OF GOD

Isaac Young was a troubled man and a dangerous man—one who felt God was speaking to him and had visions of the devil that tormented him throughout his adolescent years.

Despite being obviously mentally ill, at the time, little to no treatment existed for mental illness, particularly the paranoid delusions suffered by Isaac. He continued to see visions, hear voices, and become convinced the devil was taking many forms around him in order to destroy him.

Born in Dauphin County in central Pennsylvania on May 2, 1809, he was one of nine children born to John and Sarah (Heller) Young. The family of nine children was left alone, however, when their parents died.

Isaac was only thirteen at the time of his parents' deaths, and it seemed to send him into the abyss.

An older brother, Emanuel, took him in. Emanuel and his wife were devoted members of the Dunkard, or United Brethren, Church.

Overwhelmed with nearly constant voices that spoke to him about "end times theology" and a heavy reader of the book of Revelations, Isaac later wrote that "during the whole time … I was the slave of those harassing fears at night, believing that I was continually pursued and watched by the Devil, so terrified was my imagination that sometimes I would become frightened at my own shadow in the broad light of day."[1]

Though tormented for years by visions and voices, Isaac said, "I universally concealed my fears of the devil from my brothers and the church, less they would doubt the reality of my religion."[2]

During one of his torments, Isaac set out to "walk around the world" and spread the gospel but only made it as far as his brother Benjamin's home. Benjamin and his wife, devout Lutherans, took Isaac in even though the young couple had also offered shelter to Catherine Mackelroy, a nine-year-old girl who had previously been orphaned.

It was at Benjamin's house, however, in the summer of about 1831, that Isaac committed an unthinkable crime.

Still tormented by voices and violent dreams, he awoke one night convinced that a beast "with several heads and ten horns" appeared to him in his sleeping room, "and I was compelled to fight with and conquer it."[3]

During his panic, Isaac said, "It appeared to me that I was forcibly impelled to a bed in my room, where a little orphan girl, which belonged to my brother's family, was sleeping. I immediately fell to beating the little unoffending creature on the head with my fists."[4]

The noise of the attack, and the little girl's shrieks, woke his brother Benjamin and his wife who hid the small girl under a bed elsewhere in the house and began fleeing Isaac's growing rage themselves. The family eventually escaped through an open window in a bedroom but were unable to get to the orphaned girl who was originally attacked.

"When I found out my brother and his wife were gone, I searched the cradle for their infant, intending to kill it," Isaac said. "While thus engaged, I heard a moan from under the bed. It was the unfortunate little girl I had beaten upstairs. I got on my knees and commenced to beating it with my club. It still moaned—I went upstairs and got my pantaloons; came down with them in my hand; took my knife out of my pocket, and dragged the child from under the bed and cut off its head."[5]

Isaac then fled back to his brother Emanuel's house and confessed to him what he had done at Benjamin's house. By daylight, the sheriff had been summoned, and Isaac was arrested without incident.

At trial, Isaac remained violent, attacking the sheriff and other jailers and was chained down during the entire proceeding. Quickly convicted of the horrible crime, Isaac was taken to a jail cell in Harrisburg, Pennsylvania, the state capitol.

While in jail, Isaac remained chained to the floor of his cell for much of his incarceration but was offered more and more freedom as his mood calmed.

After what appears to be less than a year in jail, Emanuel paid a $275 bill to the jailer, and Isaac was set free. The superintendent of the prison gave Isaac the advice to change his last name from Young to Heller (using his mother's maiden name) and supported his move to Indiana.

In April 1831, Isaac arrived in Cincinnati, Ohio, with his new name, Isaac Heller, intending to make a fresh start. He worked there as a laborer until he heard of work in a grocery store in Union County, Indiana, near the town of Liberty. By August of 1831, he had met Eliza Beth McCollam, and the two were quickly married. (She was apparently unaware of Isaac's violent past.)

A highly religious woman, Eliza came from a family of devout Methodists, but the young couple joined the Dunkard, or United Brethren, Church. Two years into his marriage, however, Isaac's struggles began to resurface.

"I became strongly impressed with the belief that it was my duty to preach the gospel, and consequently, frequently spoke in public," Isaac said.[6]

In addition to spontaneous public preaching, Isaac again gravitated toward the book of Revelations and its visions of "end time" theology. His work continued to suffer, and he and his family fell deep into debt. It was at this time, Isaac again thought he could travel at least the entire state spreading the gospel, starting out in the night "less my creditors arrest me, and by that means, I should be thwarted my design."[7]

Finding few audiences to listen to his ramblings, Isaac returned home. "When I went out to chop some wood, [I] felt myself again endowed with the spirit of prophecy—though I clearly saw my wife should shortly die—and went directly to the house and told her. She appeared to believe me and was deeply affected."[8]

Isaac's wife apparently believed trouble was at hand, because on at least one occasion, she asked her husband to take her and the children to a neighbor's house when she found him sharpening his razor for hours on end. He even took to stripping himself naked in the Indiana winter "as I thought myself becoming purified."[9]

Temptations to kill people around him continued to grow, although he resisted strong urges, by his own count, on at least six different occasions. It made little difference.

"About two weeks before I killed my family, some of my neighbors told me that unless I provided for my family better than I had, I would be taken to the poor house. This troubled me very much," Isaac wrote. "I conversed with my wife on the subject, who endeavored much to appease my grief, told me if I would keep calm and use some exertions to provide for the family, I had nothing to fear, and she said she would do all in her power to help me."[10]

By this time, however, Isaac's mental illness was zapping him of any energy to keep the family alive. "My energies were unaroused, and although it seemed to me that my family was dear to me, and that I could not bear to be separated from them, yet, strange and unaccountable as it may seem, I determined to kill them."[11]

Isaac meditated and prayed heavily on the evening of February 26, 1836, but still determined to kill his family. Upon waking on February 27, 1836, he saw his wife nursing their infant daughter, Mary, near the fireplace. "That morning, before breakfast, my wife handed me the babe. I was tempted to throw it in the fire, but my heart failed me," he said.

"After breakfast my wife was sitting by the fire with her sun bonnet on, suckling her infant, the other two children were under the bed getting apples. I got up with feelings I cannot describe, observed that I must go and chop some wood, I took my ax from under the bed, walked up by the side of my unsuspecting and unoffending wife. I struck the fatal blow, she fell, she shrieked, but she never spoke, she fell forward, and I struck her twice more and then left her."

His son, John Wesley, was standing next to the bed with tears running from his eyes from what he had just witnessed. "He implored me to spare him, [but] I struck him on the head and he fell, and I cut it off."

He called out to his daughter, Sarah, who was still under the bed and "dragged his little daughter out from under the bed, placed his foot upon her chest, she raised her hands for protection, and at the first blow he cut off the fingers of one hand, and then nearly took off her head [with the ax]."[12]

"I called her, the little victim came at my command, and shared the same fate as her mother and brother," he wrote.[13]

Infant Mary was still alive after falling from her dead mother's arms and was partially trapped beneath her mother's corpse. Isaac took the ax and cut her head off as well.

His wife Eliza Beth's ten-year-old sister, who was staying with the family at the time, successfully escaped the home unharmed.

Isaac fled his home but was captured about six miles south and offered no resistance. He quickly confessed his crimes and wrote a detailed confession of not only the murder of his family but also of the orphaned girl in Pennsylvania years before.

Found guilty and sentenced to die by hanging at the jail in Liberty, Isaac still had some roadside preacher left in him. Newspaper reports claim he spoke to the assembled crowd gathered to witness his execution about his religious beliefs for about twenty-five minutes before he was hanged just after 3 p.m. on April 29, 1836.[14]

The *Brookville American* reported, "Perhaps the deed for which he suffered stands unparalleled in the annals of crime. Yet he has now atoned for his offence, justice is satisfied, and will not his fellow beings be also."[15]

For his part, Isaac concluded, "To give a reason for the enormous crimes I have committed is more than I can do. I do believe, however, that I have been led on my indulging in cruel thoughts and temptations without taking the proper measures to restrain them ..."[16]

Endnotes

1. Written confession of Isaac Young Keller, Collection of the Indiana State Library, Indiana Division, page 4.
2. Heller confession, page 5.
3. Heller confession, page 6.
4. Heller confession, page 7.
5. Heller confession, pages 7-8.
6. Heller confession, page 11.
7. Ibid.
8. Heller confession, page 12.
9. Heller confession, page 13.
10. Ibid.
11. Ibid.
12. Heller confession, page 19.
13. Heller confession, page 14.
14. *Liberty Star*, April 30, 1936.
15. *Brookville American*, May 6, 1836.
16. Heller confession, page 14.

VANDERBURGH COUNTY

VICTIM(S):
Mary Holland, 33;
Wesley Kerr, 29;
Wilhelmina Sailer, 47;
Raymond Duncan, 29;
Goebel Duncan, 51;
Elizabeth Duncan, 20

PERPETRATOR(S):
Leslie "Mad Dog" Irvin, 30

DATE OF DEATH(S):
December 1954 - March 1955

A LANDMARK RULING IN THE CASE OF LESLIE 'MAD DOG' IRVIN

During the four months between December 2, 1954, and March 28, 1955, residents of Vanderburgh County and all of the southeast corner of Indiana lived in terror as an unknown killer continued to strike, seemingly at will.

In all, six men and women would be killed in Evansville and Mount Vernon, Indiana, and across the Ohio River in Henderson, Kentucky. Police eventually nabbed thirty-year-old ex-con Leslie "Mad Dog" Irvin and charged him in the killings.

Irvin's 1955 case, because of the way it was handled by police and prosecutors, would become a landmark case that law school students wishing to enter criminal law study to this day.

The cases started simply enough, with police initially thinking they had a random botched liquor store robbery on their hands. Just after 11 p.m. on Thursday, December 2, 1954, Evansville Police responded to a report of a woman shot at the Bellemeade Liquor Store at 1656 Bellemeade Avenue, just a few blocks south of the University of Evansville campus.

There, they found the body of thirty-three-year-old Mary Holland dead and stuffed between a toilet and the wall at the back of the liquor store. Mary's husband, A.C. "Doc" Holland, had found the body when he returned to the store that he and his wife operated.

Police said Mrs. Holland, who was three months pregnant at the time of her death, was shot with a .38-caliber pistol and had no other visible marks on her body other than the bullet wound and a small scrape on her face believed to be the result of her fall next to the toilet. The bullet had struck Mrs. Holland in the right temple and exited her head into the bathroom wall. Powder burns on her head indicated she had been shot at close range.[1]

Police were without any solid leads.

Vanderburgh County Coroner H.T. Combs, MD, said based on his examination of Mrs. Holland's body and the level of rigor mortis that had set in, he estimated she had been shot at least an hour before being found at 11:10 p.m.

Mr. Holland said he had just left his job as assistant yard master at the Union Depot rail yard to go to the store. "I always go home and help her close up, and I drove straight out there."[2]

Mr. Holland said he found it odd that his wife was not in the front of the store where she usually was. "I went back to the store room. It was dark and I couldn't see her. Then I looked down by the toilet and she was there—all bloody," he said.[3]

Police pieced together that a would-be customer had robbed Mrs. Holland. A fifth of whiskey had been placed on the counter, taken down from the shelf behind the register, likely upon the request of a customer. The cash register was open after the one-cent button had been pushed. All the cash except some pennies and nickels had been removed. Mrs. Holland's purse was found, its billfold and all cash missing as well.

Hopes for fingerprints on the liquor bottle on the counter were dashed. The only ones found on the bottle belonged to Mrs. Holland.

Investigators questioned bus drivers and cab drivers in the area, but none of them reported seeing anything. Likewise, neighbors close to the store said they had not heard any shot. Neighbors grieved over Mrs. Holland's death. She and her husband were active in the community, Mrs. Holland having been elected a Democratic precinct committeewoman. She was also active in her parish, St. Paul's Episcopal Church, where her funeral was conducted.

As detectives continued to search for clues in Mrs. Holland's death, a second robbery-murder popped up just before Christmas on December 23, 1954. Just after 1:30 a.m. that morning, twenty-nine-year-old father,

Wesley Kerr, working the overnight shift at the Standard Oil Station at the junction of U.S. 41 and Franklin Street in Evansville, was shot and killed in a robbery.

By this time, local officials were very worried—the *Evansville Courier* teamed up with local merchants to offer a $3,500 reward leading to the arrest and conviction of the killer or killers of Mrs. Holland and Mr. Kerr. Evansville police chief Kirby Stevens promptly canceled all requested days off for officers, saying his department was devoting its full effort to solving the crimes.

Chief Stevens said, "We are no further right now than we were the nights the murders were committed. They are two of the worst crimes I've seen in the more than 30 years I've been a policeman."[4]

He added, "One was the work of a homicidal maniac—Kerr's death—and the other may have well been."[5]

Stevens said Kerr had been forced at gunpoint to kneel in front of a toilet inside the gas station and was shot in the back of the head with a .38-caliber weapon. The restroom was only accessible from outside the gas station, so the killer had time to lead him away from the cash register. Before leaving, the killer once again cleaned out the cash register and left few clues.

A Christmas Day report in the *Courier* noted that there was no apparent struggle in either case and theorized that "an ordinary bandit doesn't go into a robbery with the intention of killing ... But such a deliberately placed shot in the head, a spot nearly always fatal, points to a different kind of criminal. If he's a killer-by-compulsion, he probably isn't a member of the criminal underworld or he would have shown his tendencies before."[6]

As in the case of Mrs. Holland, few new clues surfaced, despite the help of the FBI, the Indiana State Police, and the Vanderburgh County Sheriff's Department.

The case fell cold until March 1955 when four quick murders occurred in succession in Mount Vernon, Indiana, and Henderson, Kentucky.

On March 21, 1955, forty-seven-year-old housewife Wilhelmina Sailer was found shot to death inside her farmhouse near Mount Vernon, Indiana. Her seven-year-old son, John Ray Sailer, found his mother dead as he stepped off the school bus that afternoon. Mrs. Sailer had been bound with a cord behind her back and was shot at point-blank range in the head. The home was burglarized as well.

As Posey County officials conferred with state and Vanderburgh County authorities, Kentucky officials began a probe into the shocking March 28, 1955, killings of three family members, fifty-one-year-old Goebel Duncan; his twenty-nine-year-old son, Raymond Duncan; and Raymond's new wife, twenty-year-old Elizabeth Duncan. A suspect's name finally popped up.

Leslie Irvin, an ex-con from Indiana who traveled frequently between Evansville and Northern Kentucky, was held for questioning after a witness reported seeing his black 1947 Chevrolet sedan (bearing Indiana plates) at the Duncan home shortly before the murders occurred. He was picked up from his place of employment at the F. Bayard Culley Power Plant on the Ohio River near Yankeetown, Indiana, but his name was not released for days as police questioned him about not only the Duncan murders, but also the three unsolved Indiana cases.[7]

A fifth victim, Goebel's forty-nine-year-old wife, Mrs. Mamie Duncan, was shot but survived her wounds, although she remained unconscious for months afterward and was forever blind because of the damage the bullet caused. Elizabeth's two-year-old daughter was left unharmed. All four of the murder victims had been killed with a .32-caliber weapon, police said. Elizabeth and Mamie were shot in their home, while Goebel and Raymond had been abducted, bound with rope, and found shot to death, dumped in a ditch three miles from their home.

Tightlipped police told reporters they were taking their still publicly unnamed suspect to Indianapolis for a polygraph examination but said questioning so far had elicited a confession from him to more than two dozen burglaries and robberies throughout Vanderburgh and Posey counties in Indiana and in Henderson County, Kentucky.[8]

On April 12, 1955, Irvin's name was first published in news reports as he was formally charged with the Duncan murders, along with a photograph of him being led from the State Police Headquarters in Indianapolis (following his polygraph exam) with his suit jacket pulled over his face. Detectives said Irvin was "boiling mad" that his picture had been put in the paper and threatened to punch any reporters he could reach.[9]

Investigators acknowledged they had seized not only Irvin's shoes, clothing, and automobile for processing, but they had also found several weapons, including a .32- and a .38-caliber weapon that were similar to the ones used in the killings. Police noted that some of the loot stolen from the Duncan home had also been recovered from Irvin.

Irvin's police record was released, showing he had been sentenced in January 1945 to ten to twenty years in prison for armed robbery in Indianapolis but was released after only nine years and moved to Evansville in May 1954.

Henderson County, Kentucky, authorities were not eager to let loose of Irvin, whom they held in the Duncan family slayings. That did not stop Indiana authorities, however, with proceeding with charges against him in the Kerr, Holland, and Sailer murders. The two states' authorities finally struck a deal to allow Irvin to be tried first for Kerr's killing, and the case was moved one county north to Gibson County, Indiana, on a change of venue.

During Irvin's initial appearances in Gibson County Circuit Court, jail officers escorted the suspect into the courtroom handcuffed and held on a long, dog-leash-style chain that linked him to Gibson County Sheriff Earl Hollen, who was seated next to him. Reporters quickly picked up on the spectacle at the courthouse in Princeton, and Irvin thereafter was referred to in most reports as Leslie "Mad Dog" Irvin.

A five-week trial in the Kerr case opened with testimony in a rare Saturday session, on December 10, 1955. The first "witness" was the bullet-damaged cap that Kerr had worn the night he was slain.

Prosecutors worked vigorously to get entered into evidence the alleged confession Irvin made on not only the Kerr case but also the Holland and Sailer cases. Police Chief Stevens said, outside the jury's presence, that Irvin had led them to the site where a gun believed to have been used in the slayings was found in Vanderburgh County. Irvin's defense attorneys argued their client had been coerced into confessing and had been held in a room at the Evansville City Jail known as the "hot box" in order to obtain the statement.

A new twist was added when the judge demanded to hear, again outside the jury's presence, a clandestine tape recording of Irvin's statement given to police. Police had lodged a microphone into the wall of a detective's office at the police station and attempted to record Irvin speaking without his knowledge. The recording "was so muffled and so low-pitch that full audibility was impossible … traffic noises and the ringing of telephones in another room when the recording was made provided 'static' to blotch the purported confession."[10]

Although mostly inaudible, the thirty-minute tape recording came complete with a transcript Evansville Police detectives said they were able to make after listening to the tape over and over again.

A reporter for the *Courier* wrote that he could make out at least some of the tape as it played, including Irvin saying to Detective Hudson, "I don't know what's wrong with me. There's something wrong somewhere."[11]

Gibson County Circuit Court Judge A. Dale Eby finally ruled that the jurors could hear the alleged taped confession and read the transcript police had prepared from it. Judge Eby said, "I don't think there's any evidence there were any threats made …" to Irvin to obtain the confession. He noted, "Perhaps he didn't have the best bed in town to sleep on," but said police had not coerced the statement.[12]

The *Courier* noted, "The increased tension of the trial Friday exacted its toll from Irvin, whose spirit seemed to have been broken by defense reversals of recent days. At times he sat with his eyes closed during the courtroom proceedings, and his face was deeply flushed."[13]

"As an added precautionary measure," the *Courier* report said, "a leash-like restraining chain is attached to [Irvin's] handcuffs and held by Sheriff Earl Hollen as the prisoner is being taken to and from the courthouse."[14]

A new "reversal" would terribly hurt Irvin's chances. Judge Eby allowed A.C. "Doc" Holland, husband of the slain Mary Holland, to testify in the case even though Irvin was on trial for Kerr's murder, not Mrs. Holland's.

In his closing argument, Prosecutor Howard Sandusky referred to Irvin as a "mad dog" and said, "This is not a crime that was done in passion. It is a crime where a man, just to steal some money, killed a human being. He killed just to save his own skin. This killer, Leslie Irvin, deserves no mercy."[15]

Jurors got the case on December 20, 1955, and deliberated only ninety minutes before returning a guilty verdict and recommending he be sent to the electric chair. Irvin, described as "an emotionless man with a stony-calm face," had little reaction beyond "a slight clenching of his large hands" when the verdict was read.[16]

The *Courier* published a large front-page photograph of Irvin, his attorneys, and his mother, Alice Irvin, listening to final arguments in the courtroom—a rarity since cameras have long since been banned from Indiana courtrooms. Irvin lunged at photographers moments later as they continued to take his picture and that of his weeping mother. He was unable to reach them because of the leash Sheriff Hollen continued to hold on him.

While the Irvin case had dominated the news in Southern Indiana for weeks and months, more shocking news was to follow. On Friday morning, January 20, 1956, the Evansville newspapers carried the startling news that Irvin had slipped out of the "escape-proof" Gibson County Jail at Princeton, Indiana, as he awaited his scheduled June 12, 1956, execution date.

"The horrifying news that Leslie Irvin ... had escaped struck Evansville with a greater impact than any case in history," the *Courier* reported. "The first reaction was disbelief that a man as infamous as Irvin could walk away from his Princeton cell in the night. Then the dull fear that he would return to Evansville to make good on his boasts of revenge."[17]

The investigation showed that Irvin had spent his time in jail fashioning at least fifty different types of keys using the paperback covers of "dime novels" he was allowed to have and wrapping them in tin foil and glue. Other inmates, intimidated by the now-famous Irvin, assisted by keeping quiet about Irvin's long-held escape plans.

Despite reports in the *Courier* that said the city's "... fear is reflected in its empty streets," local residents did not need to fear. Irvin had made a quick escape west, first to Las Vegas, Nevada, then to Los Angeles, California. He finally "settled" in San Francisco, California, where he remained until February 9, 1956, when he was arrested in a pawn shop there as he tried to sell two diamond rings he had stolen in an earlier burglary in a wealthy Los Angeles neighborhood.

"I'm Leslie Irvin, and I'm wanted in Indiana for six murders," he reportedly told San Francisco police officers. "I've been convicted of one and I'm not guilty of any."[18]

During his return trip to Indiana, Irvin reportedly talked freely about his escape, saying he used three separate keys from the book covers in order to escape and that he had gained at least fifteen rides as he hitchhiked west to Las Vegas from Indiana. Also during the return trip, Gibson County's Sheriff Hollen returned to his practice of holding Irvin on the end of a chain resembling a dog leash.

In August 1956, the Indiana Supreme Court entered a stay of execution for Irvin to allow his attorneys to pursue their appeal that their client had been convicted in an atmosphere of bias. On July 9, 1957, the U.S. Court of Appeals granted Irvin an indefinite stay of his execution, just hours before he was to be executed, so the court could consider whether the guilty verdict against him had been obtained while violating his Sixth Amendment rights.

The Sixth Amendment to the U.S. Constitution says that "… in all criminal prosecutions, the accused shall enjoy the right to a speedy trial by an impartial jury."

On November 9, 1960, the U.S. Supreme Court heard oral arguments in Washington DC regarding Irvin's claims that his Sixth Amendment rights had been violated. The nation's highest court overruled Irvin's conviction for the Kerr murder on June 5, 1961—the first time it had ever overturned a murder conviction based on pretrial publicity surrounding a case.[19]

Supreme Court Justice Tom Clark wrote, "With his life at stake, it is not requiring too much that [Irvin] be tried in an atmosphere undisturbed by so huge a wave of public passion and by a jury in which two-thirds of the members admit, before hearing any testimony, to possessing a belief in his guilt."[20]

Irvin was tried again, this time further away in Sullivan County, Indiana, and was convicted of Kerr's murder on June 13, 1962. He received a life sentence to be served at the Indiana State Prison in Michigan City, where he remained until his death from lung cancer on November 9, 1983.

Endnotes

1. *Evansville Courier*, Dec. 2, 1954.
2. *Evansville Courier*, Dec. 3, 1954.
3. Ibid
4. *Evansville Courier*, Dec. 25, 1954.

5. Ibid.
6. Ibid.
7. *Evansville Sunday Courier & Press*, April 10, 1955.
8. *Evansville Courier*, April 11, 1955.
9. *Evansville Courier*, April 12, 1955.
10. *Evansville Courier*, Dec. 16, 1955.
11. Ibid.
12. *Evansville Courier*, Dec. 17, 1955.
13. Ibid.
14. Ibid.
15. *Evansville Courier*, Dec. 21, 1955.
16. Ibid.
17. *Evansville Courier*, Jan. 20, 1956.
18. *Evansville Courier*, Feb. 10, 1956.
19. *Irvin vs. Dowd*, U.S. Supreme Court Ruling, June 5, 1961.
20. Ibid.

VERMILLION COUNTY

VICTIM(S):
Mary Ann Alderson, 69;
Leualla A. Hopkins, 89;
Margaret A. Rolando Hornick, 79;
Dorthea L. Hixon, 80;
Cecil I. Smith, 75;
Freddie Dale Wilson, 56;
Derek H. Maxwell, Sr., age unknown.

PERPETRATOR(S):
Orville Lynn Majors, 38

DATE OF DEATH(S):
Various dates between January 8, 1994
and February 16, 1995

THE ANGEL OF DEATH

In early 1995, the editors of the mortality and morbidity newsletter published by the Centers for Disease Control and Prevention (CDC) in Atlanta, Georgia, began to notice an unusual trend in Vermillion County, Indiana.

Although in recent years, Vermillion County had slipped into a rare group of Indiana counties with a death rate that exceeded its birth rate, a suspicious trend began to show up in death rates emanating from the tiny western Indiana county located on the border with the state of Illinois.

On March 7, 1995, hospital administrators at Vermillion County Hospital received reports from nursing staff at the hospital who were concerned about the growing number of people dying at the facility. Nursing supervisor Dawn Stirek expressed particular concern about one nurse, Orville Lynn Majors, noting the death rate soared while he was on duty.[1]

437

Hospital administrator John Ling, who had his own worries about the growing number of "code blues" he heard being called in the hospital, notified police on March 8, 1995. On March 9, 1995, Ling suspended Majors with pay based on Stirek's suspicions.[2]

Unsatisfied with the hospital's response, a person at the hospital sent an anonymous letter to the Indiana State Department of Health (ISDH), the agency responsible for licensing the small county hospital, alleging at least twenty-three suspicious deaths at the hospital and implicating Majors.[3]

ISDH and CDC officials quickly recognized that something was terribly, terribly wrong at the hospital in Clinton, Indiana. State Health Commissioner John C. Bailey, MD, would later describe the hospital as suffering from "a complete system breakdown."

Ling told ISDH investigators that he had developed "a gut feeling" as early as November 1994 that something was wrong at the hospital, court records would later show.[4]

A review found that the hospital's mortality review committee—a committee of doctors and other clinicians who review the charts of all patients who die at the facility—had not met for months on end.

The Indiana State Police stepped in. A statistical analysis was conducted that indicated a patient in the hospital had a 43 percent greater chance of dying when one factor was in place: Orville Lynn Majors was on duty.

In fact, in the twenty-two months Majors had been employed as a licensed practical nurse (LPN) at the hospital, 147 patients had died—most while he was on duty. Those 147 deaths represented a huge jump over the average of only twenty-six deaths per year at the fifty-six-bed facility. In 1994, the number of deaths jumped to 101, sixty-seven of them in the last six months of the year and sixty-three of them while Majors was on duty.[5]

By the second half of 1994, Majors had been hired on full-time at the hospital and assigned to work in the intensive care unit (ICU), which treated some of the facility's sickest patients.[6]

He had worked on and off at the hospital since 1989 and had previously worked as a respiratory therapist at Daviess County Hospital in Washington, Indiana, and at Greene County General Hospital in his hometown of Linton, Indiana. The Daviess County Hospital job came to an abrupt end, however, on September 5, 1984, when the hospital fired him for producing falsified records in an attempt to cover the fact that he was not certified as a respiratory therapist.[7]

Five years later in 1989, Majors applied for and received a license as a practical nurse from the State of Indiana. He lied on his application about not having any prior criminal record. He failed to disclose a public intoxication misdemeanor conviction from Vigo County.[8]

In August 1989, Vermillion County Hospital hired Majors as a part-time LPN. Personnel records show he was falling out of favor as early as October 1990 for excessive use of sick leave, a problem that resulted in a written reprimand for him in April 1991.[9]

By May 1991, Majors' hours had been greatly reduced, and he was listed only as an "as-needed" employee. Hospital administrators classified him as not eligible for rehire. However, all of that was apparently forgotten in February 1993 when the hospital rehired him. By September 1994, he had been made a full-time employee when a nursing supervisor went on maternity leave.

Majors, although being an LPN, gained a reputation was as "take-charge" person and reportedly was often domineering of some of his nursing colleagues, most of whom were RNs, women, and older than he was. One nurse would later tell reporters that when Majors did not get his way, he would throw fits and cry and scream at colleagues in the ICU.

As the full scope of the problems at the hospital became known, State Health Commissioner Bailey announced a total of eight licensing violations at Vermillion County Hospital and said the state would impose an $80,000 fine. Among the problems cited at the hospital, Dr. Bailey said, were lax security for the hospital's controlled substances and missing vials of potassium chloride and other drugs.[10]

Meanwhile, the Indiana State Police were stepping up their involvement by adding additional investigators to what would turn out to be an investigation stretching over thirty-three months.[11]

Majors himself went before state and national reporters on April 26, 1995, to declare he was not a killer.

"I'm appalled. I'm shocked. I'm dumbfounded because I love nursing and I love taking care of people," Majors told reporters from the office of his attorney, I. Marshall Pinkus. "And I think I'm an excellent nurse; I think my [hospital] evaluations reflect that."[12]

To support his client's claims, Pinkus produced 1993 and 1994 personnel evaluations from the hospital that showed his work "exceeded expectations" and included letters of support sent in to the hospital from former patients and their families.[13]

Pinkus told reporters that he was assisting Majors only because he might have been libeled or slandered in the ongoing matter, not because Majors had any involvement in any criminal act. Pinkus said, "He has not killed anybody … He doesn't believe that any care that he ever provided was of a negligent fashion that could kill anyone."[14]

Majors, while acknowledging a large number of deaths in the ICU, said the fact that he worked so much overtime was the only reason he was present for more of those deaths than any other nurse. He also told reporters that he had worked for years without a problem as a home health nurse.

"If he was a killer, some madman killer, he certainly had a great opportunity to kill," Pinkus said of Majors' time as a home health nurse. "None of these people have died under his care."[15]

Majors said, "Right now, I feel like a scapegoat, but who wouldn't after they've had their name dragged through the mud. I don't know by who, and I don't know why. I don't know if it's revenge or not."[16]

Despite his claims of innocence, the next day, the Indiana State Board of Nursing placed Majors' license on a ninety-day emergency suspension, saying he presented "a clear and present danger to the public."[17]

As the criminal investigation wore on, Indiana State Police officials set up a satellite office in downtown Clinton and applied for a $330,000 federal grant to help fund the investigation (a grant they would later win). In June 1995, twenty-six families of patients who had died at Vermillion County Hospital filed a tort claim notifying the facility that they intended to sue for wrongful death.

On August 28, 1995, the Indiana Attorney General's Office filed a five-count civil complaint against Majors and asked the state nursing board to revoke his license for his possible involvement in at least twenty-six deaths.[18]

In September, Majors and his attorney fired back, filing notice that they planned to sue the hospital and others for his suspension and for defaming his character. That same month, court-ordered exhumations began in and around Vermillion County as the Indiana State Police stepped up its investigation of Majors and the hospital deaths.

On September 20, 1995, the state nursing board voted five to two to uphold the emergency suspension of Majors' nursing license. Days later, the hospital administrator with the "gut feeling," John Ling, resigned from his post.

In December 1995, the nursing board finalized its suspension of Majors' license. Testimony at the hearings for Majors included a report by nursing experts that revealed Majors frequently and widely acted outside the scope of his LPN license. The hospital was finally able to fire Majors on May 6, 1996.

Detectives for the state police reported in September 1996 that they had now conducted more than 500 interviews and reviewed 165 patient files, in addition to the seven autopsies performed on exhumed bodies.

One big break in the tedious investigation came out of the blue in November 1996 when Majors' former lover, twenty-eight-year-old Kenny Hoffeditz, implicated Majors in a scheme to use checks stolen from a Bloomfield, Indiana, residence. In a telephone call monitored by police, Majors talked to Hoffeditz (who was incarcerated at the Greene County Jail at the time of the call) about the stolen checks and about obtaining some methamphetamine.[19]

Detectives were jubilant. Because of the allegations of stolen checks and possible drug activity, they successfully sought a search warrant for Majors' home which they served on January 31, 1997.[20]

Indiana State Police sergeant Maurice "Bud" Allcorn reported that while searching Majors' home for the stolen checks and drugs, he noticed several other items, including what appeared to be drug vials stolen from Vermillion County Hospital. Among the items seized by Allcorn and other detectives were notebooks written by Majors, vials (including one labeled "epinephrine"), and letters from Hoffeditz to Majors.[21]

Detectives also got a break during an April 9, 1997, interview with Majors' nineteen-year-old nephew, Jason Crynes. Crynes told detectives that Majors had supplied him with illegal drugs in the past and that both of them had used illegal drugs together.

Crynes also told detectives he believed his uncle killed patients at the hospital based on derogatory remarks he would make, particularly about elderly patients. He also told them about a bag of medical supplies Majors kept close to him in his van.

A search warrant was quickly obtained for Majors' van. Among the items recovered was an empty plastic vial that showed trace amounts of potassium chloride.

Eight more exhumations and autopsies were performed between April 29 and July 14, 1997, as police continued to probe deeper into Majors' life.

Thirty-three months of investigating (costing the state and federal governments more than $1.5 million) reached a climax on December 29, 1997, as police and Vermillion County Prosecutor Mark Greenwell announced they were charging Majors with six separate counts of murder.

Greenwell was silent on the charges, but Majors' attorney Pinkus was not.

"It's kind of like a shotgun effect," Pinkus said. "You shoot a shotgun, and you hope that it hits something. By having six shots, they're hoping they can convince a jury of just one of them."[22]

The sixty-three-page probable cause affidavit against Majors included charts and statistics police had put together during their lengthy investigation. They said their analysis proved the six patients in question did not die natural deaths.

Majors was officially charged with killing these Vermillion County Hospital patients:

- Mary Ann Alderson, 69, of Rosedale, Indiana, who died on March 7, 1994.

- Luella A. Hopkins, 89, of Cayuga, Indiana, who died on January 8, 1994.
- Margaret A. Rolando Hornick, 79, of Universal, Indiana, who died on November 25, 1994.
- Dorthea L. Hixon, 80, of Clinton, Indiana, who died on April 23, 1994.
- Cecil I. Smith, 75, of Rockville, Indiana, who died on April 3, 1994.
- Freddie Dale Wilson, 56, of Clinton, Indiana, who died on February 16, 1995.

Majors was led into the Vermillion County Courthouse to face the charges in handcuffs and leg shackles, escorted by police. His sweater-shirt was bulked up by a bulletproof vest officers had put on him before leading him into the courthouse.

The brief, ten-minute hearing allowed Majors to hear Special Judge Ernest E. Yelton of Clay County read the documents charging him and informing him that he faced a maximum penalty of sixty-five years in prison on each of the six charges if convicted.

Greenwell broke his silence after the initial hearing, saying that it had been difficult to determine which deaths of the many investigators reviewed to charge Majors with.

"It became our job to determine if it was a strong enough case to take it to trial," Greenwell told reporters. "I don't mean to say there are only six homicides."[23]

Over the following months, Pinkus won a motion to move the trial from Vermillion County to Clay County, and prosecutors added a seventh murder charge, alleging Majors also killed patient Derek Maxwell, Sr., who died at the hospital on November 18, 1994.

Prosecutors suffered a setback as the case prepared to go to trial when Judge Yelton banned the statistical and epidemiological studies that showed Majors was present at least eighty-three times when an unexpected death happened at the hospital between 1993 and 1995. The judge said the studies would prove too prejudicial for jurors. Yelton did, however, allow materials gathered during searches of Majors' home and van.[24]

In July 1999, hundreds of Miami County residents reported to the courthouse hundreds of miles away in Peru, Indiana, as the case to be heard in Clay County was going to require an "imported jury" to help ensure impartiality. In spite of these precautions, many Miami County residents had already heard of the case, which was widely profiled on national television, including an hour-long edition of NBC's *Dateline*.

Majors' six-week trial produced a long parade of circumstantial evidence against him. Among the seventy-nine witnesses who testified was Donald

Miller of Linton, who said he met Majors through his nephew and overheard him talking about the hospital patients who had died.

"He said that he done it," Miller said.

Miller also said that Majors discussed the drug potassium chloride. "He more or less said it induced a heart attack."[25]

Miller testified that everyone was "joking and laughing" that evening, a fact Majors' attorneys used in an attempt to show that Majors was just kidding and did not mean what he said.[26]

Others testified they had witnessed Majors standing over the beds of patients holding injection needles, in some instances, just before cardiac arrest set in.[27]

On Sunday, October 17, 1999, jurors returned their verdict of guilty on six of the seven counts against Majors. Majors was found guilty of murdering Alderson, Hixon, Hopkins, Hornick, Wilson, and Maxwell. The jury deadlocked on the case of Cecil I. Smith, and he was acquitted of that charge.

As the verdict was read, Majors' elderly mother, Anna Bell Majors, an oxygen tank at her side and tears falling from her face, "... dropped her head into her hands and said to herself, in a whimpering voice, 'Oh, God,'" the *Terre Haute Tribune-Star* reported.[28]

Majors' sister, Debbie McClelland of Linton, reacted angrily, yelling to the horde of reporters in the hallway outside the courtroom, "He didn't kill nobody! They're wrong! They're making a liar out of God," she said, shaking her arms.[29]

Pinkus told reporters, "We feel like the jury made a big mistake, and we hope that they and the prosecutors can live with their consciences."[30]

Majors' outspoken attorney said the most damning evidence presented against his client was the fact that police had found empty or nearly empty vials of potassium chloride at a home where Majors once lived and in the van he drove.

Prosecutors Nina Alexander and Greg Carter presented toxicological evidence showing that the patients had died from overdoses of potassium chloride and epinephrine.

Pinkus and his co-counsel, Carolyn Rader, argued repeatedly that no homicides had actually ever occurred and that all of the hospital deaths were due to natural causes. They seemingly had no choice, some said, because to acknowledge the cases were murders would leave Majors with few options other than an insanity defense or trying to implicate someone else.

On November 15, 1999, Judge Yelton sentenced Majors to 360 years in prison for killing the six patients, calling him "the worst of criminals."

"When a nurse does wrong, he is the worst of criminals," Yelton said, adding that he felt Majors was "a paragon of evil at its most wicked."[31]

"He was entrusted with these people's care," the judge said. "In response, he committed diabolical acts that extinguished the frail lives of six people."[32]

Majors did not speak during the sentencing and left the courthouse without making any comment. Family members of the six victims he was charged with killing (and other family members of patients who died) expressed relief that the matter was now over.

Majors was not finished, however, and in September 1998, filed a direct appeal of his conviction to the Indiana Supreme Court, citing juror misconduct and other errors in the trial. The court took its time reviewing the lengthy appeal and upheld Majors' convictions in the six cases on August 14, 2002.

Of the more than eighty wrongful death suits brought against the tiny hospital from families of patients who died there, about sixty were settled with payments through Indiana's Patient Compensation Fund by 2002. The respected Terre Haute Regional Hospital later took over management of Vermillion County Hospital, preserving a hospital in the rural community and helping restore a level of trust there.

Endnotes

1. *Terre Haute Tribune-Star*, Dec. 30, 1997.
2. Ibid.
3. Ibid.
4. Ibid.
5. CourtTV Web site.
6. *Terre Haute Tribune-Star*, Dec. 30, 1997.
7. Ibid.
8. Ibid.
9. Ibid.
10. *Terre Haute Tribune-Star*, April 22, 1995; *Indianapolis Star*, April 22, 1995.
11. *Terre Haute Tribune-Star*, Dec. 30, 1997.
12. *Terre Haute Tribune-Star*, April 27, 1995.
13. Ibid.
14. Ibid.
15. Ibid.
16. Ibid.
17. *Terre Haute Tribune-Star*, April 28, 1997.
18. *Terre Haute Tribune-Star*, Dec. 30, 1997.
19. Ibid.

20. Ibid.
21. Ibid.
22. *Terre Haute Tribune-Star*, Dec. 30, 1997.
23. *Terre Haute Tribune-Star*, Dec. 31, 1997.
24. Associated Press, Aug. 29, 1999.
25. *Terre Haute Tribune-Star*, Oct. 9, 1999.
26. Ibid.
27. CourtTV Web site.
28. *Terre Haute Tribune-Star*, Oct. 18, 1999.
29. Ibid.
30. Ibid.
31. *Terre Haute Tribune-Star*, Nov. 16, 1999.
32. Ibid.

VIGO COUNTY

VICTIMS:
21 young men found dead in Indiana and Illinois between 1982 and 1984.

PERPETRATOR(S):
Larry Eyler, 41

THE BLOOD LUST OF LARRY EYLER

On August 4, 1978, the *Terre Haute Tribune-Star* ran a four-paragraph brief in their "Statistics" column, just after the listings of recent births and marriage license filings, that would quietly foretell the beginning of the career of Indiana's most evil serial killer, ever.

On that day, the *Tribune Star* reported that a then twenty-five-year-old Larry Eyler was arrested for "stabbing another man during a fight Thursday morning south of the city." The arrest was recorded at 3:30 a.m. that day following the "fight" near 26th Street and Springhill Road.[1]

The story indicated nineteen-year-old Craig Long of Terre Haute had suffered a stab wound in the chest and was listed in serious condition at Regional Hospital in Terre Haute.

Observers may have thought it only a fight, but it was one of the first known attacks carried out by Eyler who eventually would admit to killing twenty-one young men across Indiana and Illinois in a blood lust unknown in state history.

The "fight" was actually a sadistic sexual assault that included Eyler plunging a knife deep into Long's chest after tying him and attempting to sexually molest him. Long, an ex-Marine, had escaped Eyler's grasp, played dead, and eventually found help at a nearby trailer park.

Before the case went to trial, however, Long was told by his attorney that a private individual wanted to pay him $25,000 for his medical bills and lost

446

work, and the case fell apart. On November 13, 1978, Eyler was able to plead guilty to a lesser charge of aggravated battery, paid a $43 fine and court costs, and walked free.[2]

Eyler's destructive drive would not end until August 21, 1984, however, when Chicago Police arrested him for the last time. Now thirty-one-years-old, Eyler was held for suspicion of murder. And unlike at least two other times before, he would not elude responsibility.

Police picked up Eyler after Joe Balla, a janitor for the four-story apartment building at 1640 W. Sherwin Ave. in Uptown Chicago, followed his agitated dog at about 6:30 a.m. on Tuesday, August 21, 1984, to a dumpster behind the apartment building. As Balla removed the six heavy gray garbage bags from the dumpster (believing they did not come from a tenant of the building and angry that the dumpster was being filled up by non-residents), one of the gray bags, although double-bagged, burst open and revealed a portion of the dismembered body of a young man. He immediately called police.

As police questioned Balla about his find and taped off the alley from onlookers, another resident of an adjacent building, 1628 W. Sherwin Ave., approached officers and said they had seen Eyler placing the bags in the dumpster at about 4 p.m. the afternoon before. The witness said Eyler appeared to be struggling with the heavy weight of the bags and quoted Eyler as saying he was "getting rid of some shit from his apartment."[3]

Inside the bags was the body of a young man cut into eight parts, distinguished by tattoos between some of his fingers. The coroner reassembled the body parts and photographed the victim's face. He showed it to family members, who quickly identified the victim as fifteen-year-old Danny Bridges, a local runaway who spent a lot of time on the streets of Chicago.

"Detectives said the body had been dismembered either by somebody who had been a butcher, or who had medical experience because the cuts were clean," the *Chicago Sun-Times* reported. "The head was severed from the chest, as were both arms and legs. The legs had been cut into two pieces, Cook County Medical Examiner Robert J. Stein said."[4]

Police went to Eyler's first-floor apartment next door and immediately detained him. The native Hoosier had only lived in the apartment in the heart of the city's uptown gay community for about two months. Regardless, he was a familiar figure to Illinois investigators—by this point, many in law enforcement already believed him to be a serial killer of at least nineteen men in Indiana and Illinois.

Forensic investigators tore apart Eyler's freshly painted apartment, using luminol spray and black lights to reveal a massive amount of blood that had been cleaned up in the apartment. The blood spatters covered the floors, walls, and ceiling of the bedroom, and revealed a blood trail where detectives knew

Danny's body had been dragged to the bathtub. Blood stains all over the tub and evidence of human tissue in drains were also found. Pieces of the wood floor pried up by police revealed even more blood that was not cleaned up.

This evidence was added to a fingerprint of Eyler's found on one of the trash bags containing Danny's body and evidence of newly purchased hacksaw blades and trash bags matching those holding the remains.

Unlike Eyler's previous murders, outside elements had not destroyed evidence, and Eyler could not escape the fact that he had been seen dumping the bags that contained Danny's body.

At last, his killing spree was over.

Eyler was indicted for Danny's murder just two days later on August 23, 1984. A probable cause affidavit said Eyler had picked up Danny for the purpose of sex on Sunday evening, August 19, 1984, at Washington Square Park in Chicago. Eyler was held without bond. Police and state's attorneys in Illinois worked closely together to avoid any legal pitfalls that could possibly compromise their case—or worse yet, set Eyler free again.

It was a legitimate concern. Eyler had been in custody once before—in Lake County, Illinois, when he was arrested and charged on October 28, 1983, for the murder of twenty-eight-year-old Ralph Calise, a Lake Forrest, Illinois, man. Calise's body had been found August 31, 1983, in a field near Illinois Route 60, just off the Tri-State Tollway. Calise had suffered nineteen stab wounds.

At the time of the October 1983 arrest, police said evidence collected at the scene linked Eyler to the murder. Other evidence Illinois authorities were counting on had been gathered by their Indiana counterparts back on September 30, 1983, when an Indiana State Trooper stopped Eyler's pickup truck on Interstate 65 near Lowell, Indiana. (Ironically, the traffic stop occurred very near where four bodies would be unearthed on an abandoned farm in Newton County, Indiana, just one month later.)

Indiana troopers had confiscated a pair of handcuffs, a bloodstained hunting knife, rope, duct tape, a pair of bloodstained boots, and rubber gloves from the truck. They did not yet have enough evidence, however, to detain Eyler for a specific crime.

Law enforcement agencies across Indiana and Illinois had begun to coordinate their efforts. Eyler complained police were harassing him. He filed a suit against police in U.S. District Court claiming they were violating his civil rights and sought $250,000 in damages.

Eyler told the *Sun-Times* that his life had been "hell every day" since the Indiana police stopped him in September. He said he was confused as to why police would think he was "a cold-blooded murderer," as he said one detective put it.

"If I was a murderer," he said, "they would have had the evidence by now. They've swept out my truck, swept my place in Terre Haute, they've taken their shots at questioning and scared me to death."[5]

He added, "Financially, it's almost destroyed me. I can't work without my truck. I know my mother stays up nights and cries about this. Everybody asks my friends. This is going to be with me the rest of my life."[6]

Of all his statements, the last one was most true. Eyler's acts *would* stay with him the rest of his life.

But that would have to come later. In February 1984, just six months before Danny Bridges' chopped-up body was found in the dumpster, Eyler was released from jail. His mother, Shirley DeKoff of Terre Haute, paid a reduced bail of $10,000, and he walked out of the Lake County Jail in Waukegan, Illinois.

Lake County (Illinois) Judge William Block had earlier reduced his bond from $1 million to the $10,000 figure, saying there was no reason to hold Eyler on such a large bond. A week before, Judge Block had thrown out the evidence Indiana authorities had collected and said it could not be used against him in the investigation of Calise's death because police had improperly detained Eyler without arresting him or without probable cause of a crime.

Prosecutors lost appeals sent all the way to the U.S. Supreme Court in an attempt to keep the evidence collected from Eyler's truck in use while attempting to prosecute Calise's murder.

Now, however, Eyler was behind bars for good. He stood trial for Danny Bridges' murder in Chicago in July 1986. The trial was only possible because a janitor was upset about the number of bags Eyler had placed in a dumpster. Otherwise, "Danny Bridges' body would be buried in some landfill," said Assistant Cook County, Illinois, state's attorney Mark Rakoczy.[7]

Grisly testimony followed, and Eyler was convicted on July 10, 1986. He was sentenced to death by Cook County (Illinois) Criminal Court Judge Joseph Urso on October 3, 1986. Judge Urso told Eyler he had committed a "barbaric crime" and said, "Mr. Eyler, I pray to God that he will have mercy on your soul."[8]

Eyler's time on Illinois's death row would eventually motivate him to offer to help Indiana and Illinois authorities in wrapping up more than a dozen unsolved murders of men in both states. Before it was over, he implicated himself in the deaths of twenty-one young men, including Steven Crockett, nineteen; John R. Johnson, twenty-five; Steven Agan, twenty-three; John L. Roach, twenty-one; Edgard Underkoffer, twenty-seven; Gustavo Herrara, twenty-eight; Ervin Dwayne Gibson, sixteen; Jimmy T. Roberts, eighteen; Daniel Scott McNieve, twenty-one; Ralph Calise, twenty-eight; Michael Bauer, twenty-two; John Bartlett, nineteen; Richard E. Bruce, Jr., twenty-five; David M. Block, twenty-two; Richard Wayne, twenty-one; Danny Bridges, fifteen; and the bodies of five other men who were never identified by authorities.

By November 1990, Eyler began talking to Indiana authorities formally about one specific case, the murder of twenty-three-year-old Steven Agan of Terre Haute whose mutilated and tortured body was found in Vermillion County, Indiana, on December 28, 1982.

Eyler's new cooperativeness coincided with the release of a bombshell book, *Freed to Kill,* by former Chicago reporter Gera-Lind Kolarik that linked Eyler to as many as twenty-three murders.

On December 14, 1990, Eyler was rushed into the Vermillion County Courthouse at Newport, Indiana, where he offered an eighteen-minute confession to Judge Don Darnell, implicating not only himself in Agan's murder, but also his long-time friend and benefactor, fifty-three-year-old Dr. Robert David Little, the library sciences department chair and professor at Indiana State University.

Although long-suspected of either actual involvement in Eyler's crimes, or at least assisting him after the fact, the rumpled, gray-haired Dr. Little was never before directly implicated. A week later, Vermillion County authorities arrested Dr. Little and charged him, along with Eyler, with the slaying of Agan.

Eyler told the court that he and Dr. Little had picked up Agan from his job at a car wash in Terre Haute on December 19, 1982, and that Dr. Little wanted to engage in a "scene" with Agan. Eyler said Agan had agreed to take part in some sexual activity with the men. Prosecutors attempted to get Eyler to admit he had used a prescription drug to subdue Agan (and other victims), but he took the Fifth Amendment and refused to answer such questions.

Eyler was willing to say he and Dr. Little first took Agan to the professor's tidy Terre Haute townhouse to pick up duct tape, a knife, and a camera and then drove Agan to a vacant farm along Indiana 63 just outside Newport, Indiana.

Once in a shed on the farm property around 2 a.m., Agan's hands were tied above him to a beam, an ace bandage was placed over his eyes, and Dr. Little photographed the scene and instructed Eyler to pull down Agan's pants. Two flashlights were used, Eyler said, to illuminate the "scene" taking place.

"I told Agan to make peace with God, and I waited a few moments. Then Dave [Dr. Little] said 'kill the motherfucker.' I stabbed Mr. Agan maybe three times. David came over and he stabbed Mr. Agan a few times ... the rage in me built up again, and I hit Mr. Agan with a board" although he knew the man was already dead.[9]

Eyler claimed that Dr. Little then masturbated over the dead man's body and complained that the "scene" had gone too fast.

Eyler told the court that a 1983 search of Dr. Little's town home, where Eyler had lived on and off over the years, did not reveal the photos because police only searched his room. He said had they searched Dr. Little's room, they would have found the photos of Agan's torture and murder.

The mutilation of Agan's body, however, did not stop just because he was dead.

Eyler said Dr. Little ordered him to cut Agan's dead body down from the beam and to take him outside and finish him off (although he was already dead).

"I was in such a, you know, high state, you know, excitement at the time … I wasn't really paying any attention. So then I took him back and while Mr. Little took a picture of it, I took a knife and I just cut Mr. Agan open," Eyler told the court.[10]

Grisly photos of Agan's body would show wounds so severe his internal organs were exposed.

Eyler said that as he gutted Agan's body, he got a considerable amount of blood on himself and Dr. Little.

Dr. John E. Pless, the forensic pathologist who examined Agan's body after it was discovered, said, "I've seen several bodies that have been cut up … this is the worst that I've seen without the body being cut into pieces."[11]

Dr. Pless concluded that many of the gaping, gutting wounds on Agan's body were inflicted after the man was dead. Deep cuts and stabs to Agan's genitals, however, had been done while he was alive, the pathologist said.

Eyler offered his damning testimony against Dr. Little with no agreement in place back in Illinois to remove him from death row. His attorney, noted Chicago defense lawyer Kathleen Zellner, said Eyler had "nothing to gain." He knew that what he had done to Agan was horrible and agreed to plead guilty not just for the purpose of implicating Dr. Little, but because "he just wanted to clear his conscience."[12]

For his confession, Judge Darnell sentenced Eyler to sixty years in prison, although the sentence was meaningless because he was already on death row in Illinois. Eyler continued to deny, however, that he killed Danny Bridges (for which he was sentenced to death) and instead said Dr. Little had killed the boy. Dr. Little was never charged in connection with Bridges' death, however.

Dr. Little's own murder trial for the Agan slaying opened in April 1991 in Vermillion County Circuit Court. As he had in December 1990, Eyler returned to Newport and implicated Dr. Little in Agan's torture and death.

Evidence included horrible photos of Agan's mutilated body, his bloody clothing, and a section of the bloody cross beam from the shed where Agan's body had been hung for the torture "scene." Most revealing, however, was a key found under Agan's body that unlocked a door where Eyler had once worked—linking him directly to the crime scene.

Prosecutors also presented financial records to prove that the elder Little had often given money to Eyler. Two other men testified that Dr. Little had paid them money in the past to pose nude for him and that he enjoyed creating photographic "scenes" with nude men in his townhouse.

Dr. Little's defense team attempted to show he was not in Indiana at the time of Agan's disappearance and murder but was visiting his elderly parents in Florida for the Christmas holiday. Dr. Little's elderly mother testified via videotape that her son always visited them at Christmas in Florida. Prosecutors countered, however, that no plane ticket or financial transactions could be found proving that Dr. Little had made the trip in 1982. Prosecutors also produced car repair records from 1982 that showed Dr. Little could have been in Indiana around Christmas 1982.

Dr. Little did not testify himself. Defense attorneys worried that his bookish appearance and slight speaking voice, combined with knowledge of his homosexuality, would not sit well with a small-town Indiana jury.

In his closing arguments, Dr. Little's attorney Dennis Zahn told jurors, "Eyler is manipulating the court system to save his life. God forbid you let him."[13]

On April 17, 1991, jurors concluded seven hours of deliberations by acquitting Dr. Little of Agan's murder. The professor sighed and smiled as the verdict was read.

Moments later in a news conference with his attorneys, Dr. Little read a prepared statement where he thanked his attorneys "for the magnificent job of providing the information that proved I was innocent."[14]

He added, "I'm sorry that the Agan family had to be put through this awful ordeal. I know it's been difficult on them. It's difficult enough without something like this happening. My sympathy goes out to them. Obviously, I'm very happy it's over."[15]

Dr. Little said he was eager to return to his teaching position for the summer session at Indiana State. The university had suspended him pending the outcome of his trial and during his incarceration awaiting trial. By 1992, the university had eliminated the master's degree program in library science and combined the program with the social sciences department. In 1996, the university closed the program.

In 1995, Dr. Little settled a civil lawsuit brought against him by Agan's parents, Robert and Barbara Agan of Terre Haute, for an undisclosed amount.

The case never went to trial. Also in 1995, another wrongful death suit brought against Dr. Little for Danny Bridges' murder was dismissed by a Cook County judge because it was filed after the statute of limitations had run its course.

Eyler returned to death row in Illinois, his attorney Zellner promising that he could help solve other murders in exchange for being removed from his death sentence. Cook County state's attorney Jack O'Malley was having none of that. He said death row was "exactly where he belongs."[16]

In 1992, Eyler's appeal for the murder of Danny Bridges went forward, with a new witness emerging implicating Dr. Little in the murder and claiming that Dr. Little had also attacked him with a knife at a Chicago hotel in 1984.

Eyler's appellate attorneys also revealed Dr. Little had paid the rent, signed the lease for and furnished Eyler's uptown Chicago apartment where Bridges was slain, and paid as much as $20,000 toward Eyler's defense for the Bridges' murder. This involvement in Eyler's life, they claimed, supported the theory that Dr. Little used Eyler to procure younger, attractive men to engage in sexual scenes.

Cook County judge Urso refused to overturn Eyler's conviction in the Bridges' case and returned him to death row in November 1992. He would not live to see the appeal of Urso's ruling to the Illinois Supreme Court.

At 12:30 p.m. on Sunday, March 6, 1994, Eyler died in the infirmary at the Pontiac Correctional Facility in Illinois from complications due to AIDS. He was forty-one years old. His attorney, Kathleen Zellner, said he had been seriously ill for about ten days. She said he knew he had contracted the HIV virus as early as 1984.

"He knew when he testified at David Little's trial in the Steven Agan murder that he was dying," Zellner said. "I believe Larry was truthful. Larry had no incentive to lie to anyone."[17]

Zellner told reporters Eyler had begun compiling the list of his victims in 1990, and it reached twenty-one victims, including those found on the startling "killing field" on a vacant farm in Newton County, Indiana, in October 1983 where four men had been buried side by side in a ritualistic fashion.

Eyler's outspoken attorney maintained the claim that he was "selected and prepared for his mission to kill during those two years. He was encouraged, he was aided, he was abetted, he was supported in his killing spree in every possible way that you could support somebody."[18]

Zellner said Eyler's need for a father figure and his self-loathing over his homosexuality caused him to act out a deep hatred for men. She said this left Eyler open to an "accomplice" who "wielded sufficient power to command a killing spree" from him. She added, "This accomplice was very much the mastermind and very much in control of Larry Eyler. Larry Eyler was someone that if he cared about you, it was not that difficult to get control of him."[19]

Eyler's mother, Shirley DeKoff, spoke to Patricia Pastore, a reporter with the *Terre Haute Tribune-Star,* about two months after her son died.

She said she was with her son the day before he died in prison. She said his illness had reduced his voice to a whisper. "Just before I left, he touched my cheek and said, 'What happened to the person who wanted to be so good, Mom? What happened to that little boy?'"[20]

Larry was the youngest of DeKoff's four children. Her other three children have all enjoyed law-abiding adult lives, one as a college professor, one as a junior high school teacher, and another as a probation officer. "It's been terrible for my children and their families," she said. "Each of the other children worked their way through college and are good, upstanding citizens. You can't say anything bad about the rest of them."[21]

DeKoff said she was shocked when Larry confessed to the Agan murder. "That was more pain than I thought I could bear," she said.[22]

She added, "I was a working mother who made many mistakes, but who did the best she could with what she had at the time. The memory of the sweet and good Larry I knew will always be with me. I never knew the other Larry."[23]

Endnotes

1. *Terre Haute Tribune-Star,* Aug. 4, 1978.
2. Kolarik, Gera-Lind. *Freed to Kill: The True Story of Serial Murderer Larry Eyler.* New York: Avon Books, HarperCollins Publishers, 1992, page 6.
3. Kolarik, page 291.
4. *Chicago Sun-Times,* Aug. 21, 1984.
5. *Chicago Sun-Times,* Oct. 23, 1983.
6. Ibid.
7. *Chicago Tribune,* July 2, 1986.
8. *Chicago Tribune,* October 4, 1986.
9. *Indianapolis Star,* December 14, 1990.
10. Kolarik, page 398.
11. *Terre Haute Tribune-Star,* April 16, 1991.
12. *Terre Haute Tribune-Star,* Dec. 14, 1990.
13. *Terre Haute Tribune-Star,* April 18, 1991.
14. Ibid.
15. Ibid.

16. *Indianapolis Star,* April 19, 1991.
17. *Terre Haute Tribune-Star,* March 7, 1994.
18. *Terre Haute Tribune-Star,* May 1, 1994.
19. Ibid.
20. *Terre Haute Tribune-Star,* May 3, 1994.
21. Ibid.
22. Ibid.
23. Ibid.

WABASH COUNTY

VICTIM(S):
Edward Boyle, between 45-50;
Aaron French, 55;
Sarah French, 35;
John French, 13;
Sarah French, 11;
Louisa French, 8;
Tillman French, 6;
Baby daughter of
French family, 15 months

PERPETRATOR(S):
John Hubbard and Sarah Hubbard, ages unknown.

DATE OF DEATH(S):
Oct. 7, 1854 and December 1855

A JAILHOUSE VISIT REVEALS A HORRIBLE SECRET

Sarah Hubbard went to the Wabash County Jail to visit her husband, John, early on the morning of Sunday, April 6, 1855. Just days before, John had been arrested and charged with the murder of canal laborer, Edward Boyle of Wabash.

It was what Mrs. Hubbard said to her husband that day, whispered in the corners of the jailhouse, that would reveal an even more sickening crime.

Boyle's death had been bad enough. His body was found in mid-March 1855 after water was drained from a canal near the Hubbard's home. Police believed he was actually killed sometime in December 1854 shortly after coming into about $500. Boyle had been a boarder in the home of John Hubbard.

Hubbard was arrested for Boyle's murder on March 27, 1855, and was awaiting trial at the time of his wife's visit.

Mrs. Hubbard would not be allowed to leave that day. Their conversation was overheard, revealing that both of them were suspects in an even more gruesome killing, one that took the lives of seven members of the French family of rural Wabash County.

On April 7 and 8, police searched the home occupied by the Hubbards and removed floorboards in the home. They "discovered the earth peculiarly piled up on one place. They ran an ax helve through the earth a short distance until it struck something soft, that made it rebound. They then inserted a pick which passed through the dirt and into the breast of a child. When the pick was withdrawn, it brought the body of the child with it."[1]

As the grisly excavation moved forward, police found the bodies of fifty-five-year-old Aaron French and his thirty-five-year-old wife Sarah at the bottom of a pile of rotting corpses. Above them were the bodies of their five children: thirteen-year-old John, eleven-year-old Sarah, eight-year-old Louisa, six-year-old Tillman, and a fifteen-month-old female child whose name was not disclosed.

All had suffered several blows to the head from an ax. Mrs. French also suffered a broken neck and arm. Police believed they had been killed many months before in October 1854.

"All were buried in their clothes except Mrs. French, who was naked. The dress that Mrs. French usually wore has been recognized on the person of Mrs. Hubbard."[2]

Police learned that John and Sarah Hubbard and their son, Richard (described by reporters as an "idiot"), had joined the French family in late September 1854. It is believed that Mr. French, although often bedfast with illness and barely making enough to feed his large family, had mercy on the destitute Hubbards and invited them to stay.

By October 1854, however, the French family was out of sight, and the Hubbards were telling anyone who asked that the family had moved away with family members to Iowa. Despite the fact that the Frenches had lived there for about four years, it appears no one seriously questioned the Hubbards' story about their abrupt "departure."

Weeks of work resulted in the August 2, 1855, indictment of John and Sarah Hubbard for the murders of the French family. They were to be tried separately.

John Hubbard's case went forward first—after prosecutors and the defense went through the names of more than 100 Wabash County residents before settling on a jury. The trial opened in Wabash on September 3, 1855. Hubbard's defense consisted mostly of character witnesses testifying to his good will and nature.

Jurors were unimpressed. They returned a verdict of guilty on the multiple murder charges during the early morning hours of September 8, 1855.

At a later sentencing hearing, John Hubbard told Judge John M. Wallace of Wabash Circuit Court that he had "had difficulties with certain Irish Catholics in the neighborhood of his cabin and surmised that revenge might have led them to concert a deep-laid plot for his ruin."[3]

He added in a written statement read to the court, "My presumed guilt is wholly without a motive, and inconsistent with my past character. But Providence, careful of right and revengeful of wrong, remains to me now my only, but a confident hope of deliverance."[4]

Judge Wallace told Hubbard the French family had "fallen victim to your unnatural thirst for blood. It appears also, that this unfortunate victim of your cruelty, confiding in your honesty, integrity and humanity, kindly received you and your wife into his own house, humble though that home was, and to some extent in your poverty-stricken condition, shared with you his condition of life. This was your condition in his house too, at a time, without apparent cause (indeed, what cause could there be for it), you ruthlessly murdered every member of his family, not even sparing those infant children, whose sweet smiles of innocence should have awakened your own personal feeling and deferred you from the accomplishment of the bloody purpose of your heart …"[5]

Judge Wallace sentenced Hubbard to be put to death by hanging in Wabash on December 13, 1855. "And may God, in His infinite goodness, have mercy on your soul," the judge said.

John Hubbard appealed his case unsuccessfully to the Indiana Supreme Court and sought a reprieve from the governor, which also was unsuccessful.

Hubbard requested Elder Townsend, a Baptist minister working in Wabash at the time, to be his spiritual adviser as he prepared for death (despite Townsend's opposition to the death penalty). A diary kept by Elder Townsend was obtained many years later by the Wabash County Historical Society. It revealed detailed accounts of his time with Hubbard.

"I think the time given him to prepare to meet his God was about one month. I soon visited him in the jail and found him altogether callous, trusting in Universalism. I endeavored to drive him from that false rest, and entreated him to pray to almighty God to pardon his sins," Townsend wrote.[6]

Townsend said Hubbard refused to forgive those he considered his enemies and responsible for his being charged with murder. "My efforts failed to bring him to anything like a sense of his guilt," Townsend wrote.[7]

Thursday, December 13 arrived as a cold, misty, rainy morning in Wabash. Townsend wrote that he dreaded the proceedings but went forward and met Hubbard in his cell. Hubbard was dressed in a suit purchased for him by the county. "I had lost all hope of fixing his mind on the Lord Jesus

Christ, so I delivered a faithless prayer, and the best advice I could give him," Townsend said.[8]

Outside the jail, a crowd estimated between 3,000 and 5,000 residents crowded in to get a look at the execution about to occur. Townsend called them "raving maniacs" in his diary and said a chant of "Bring out Hubbard!" continued for a long time.

Townsend said the sheriff decided to proceed with the hanging immediately, as a false rumor had spread among the crowd that Hubbard had won a last-minute reprieve. Authorities believed the assembled would never have accepted that and would have overrun the jail to lynch Hubbard themselves.

Townsend wrote that Hubbard was smoking his pipe and put it down and said, "Come Mr. Townsend and lead me to the gallows, for I am prepared to go. My mother had me baptized on the high sea."[9]

Hubbard climbed the stairs of the gallows with Townsend and another pastor, Elder Skinner, with him. He had Townsend tell the crowd that he still proclaimed his innocence. Townsend, instead, grew faint and had to be assisted. Elder Skinner told the crowd of Hubbard's continued claim of innocence.

Townsend said he regained his composure enough to witness "the rope was passed around his neck and he was made to stand on the trap door, and the cap was drawn over his face. I then stepped up to him, gave him my hand and asked him if he knew me. He said he did. I told him to look to Jesus. I stepped to one side, the trigger was sprung, and Hubbard was swung below by the neck, until the doctors pronounced him dead."[10]

He added, "I had seen mad cattle in a panic, but never thought that rationale human beings in a Christian land could ever be induced to act so. As soon as Hubbard was taken away, the number of men that were pressing forward to obtain a small portion of the rope to carry in their pocket to drive away witches or to cure tooth ache or something else, impelled me to wonder if I were not dreaming. That night when I got home, if I would look out into the dark, I could see Hubbard swinging before me."[11]

Hubbard's body would not remain in the grave long but instead, became the grand prize in a macabre contest between medical students and doctors in Wabash and some from Huntington and Fort Wayne, who sought to seize the body for medical tests and anatomy studies. The Wabash doctors succeeded by digging up Hubbard's body during the early morning hours of December 14, 1855.

The body was taken to a building along Canal Street in Wabash. "Here the body was put into a condition for dissecting, but the doctors were not permitted to hold forth there very long, as some young men who occupied apartments adjoining the dissecting room became aware of what was being done and raised such a racket that what remained of the murderer was packed into a sack and toted across the street in open daylight to a room where prying eyes and keen ears would not intrude."[12]

Hubbard's skeleton was reconstructed by a Dr. Dicken from LaFontaine, Indiana, and was placed on display in a biology classroom at the LaFontaine High School.

All of this occurred before Mrs. Sarah Hubbard's trial finally opened in April 1856 at the Grant County Courthouse in Marion on a change of venue. The testimony of her trial mirrored that offered in her husband's unsuccessful attempt to avoid conviction.

The jury found her guilty as charged and sentenced her to a sentence of hard labor in the state prison for the rest of her natural life. Her sentence, in fact, was an impetus for state officials to begin exploring the need for a separate Indiana Women's Prison (which was eventually opened in Indianapolis). Sarah Hubbard died at the new women's prison on January 13, 1887, having served thirty-one years.

Endnotes

1. *Wabash Plain Dealer*, Nov. 17, 1955.
2. *Wabash Plain Dealer*, Nov. 17, 1955.
3. *History of Wabash County, Indiana*. Chicago: John Morris Printer, 1884.
4. Ibid.
5. Ibid.
6. *Wabash Plain Dealer*, Nov. 19, 1955.
7. Ibid.
8. Ibid.
9. Ibid.
10. Ibid.
11. Ibid.
12. *Wabash Plain Dealer*, Nov. 20, 1955.

WARREN COUNTY

VICTIM(S):
Avis Madison Dutcher, 41

PERPETRATOR(S):
Claire Ratliff, 27

DATE OF DEATH(S):
September 18, 1926

A SMALL-TIME CRIMINAL LEARNS TO BECOME A KILLER

It is said that sometimes, when a young man goes to prison all he learns is to become a more violent criminal.

Twenty-seven-year-old Claire Ratliff of Williamsport, Indiana, was about to prove that theory right late on Saturday evening, September 18, 1926, in downtown Williamsport.

The county seat town was mostly deserted by 11:30 p.m. that evening, except for a few remaining folks holding on to the last of the weekend. Ratliff, who had been in trouble with the law before but was never known to be violent, was among them.

When Warren County Sheriff Avis M. Dutcher and Williamsport Town Marshal Lee Briar spotted Ratliff standing along Main Street, they approached him to serve a routine warrant for reckless driving.

It wasn't the first time Sheriff Dutcher and Ratliff had had an encounter— the sheriff had arrested the young man two years earlier, to the day, on a bootlegging charge when Ratliff was found at the Warren County Fair with beer. That was the charge that had sent Ratliff away for eighteen months.

On this night, Ratliff stood on Main Street. His presence there had "aroused considerable excitement in anticipation of his [possible] arrest," the *Williamsport Review Republican* reported.[1]

Sheriff Dutcher walked up to Ratliff, informed him of the warrant, and asked him to come with him to the jail. Ratliff at first resisted and asked to go see his lawyer, Ned McCabe, whose office was adjacent to the grocery store.

For some reason, the sheriff and town marshal obliged and walked with Ratliff a few steps toward McCabe's office.

"Sheriff Dutcher was known as an extremely daring but also exceptionally cautious officer, and the desperate chances he took, which cost his life, are not thoroughly understood by his friends," the *Lafayette Journal & Courier* reported.[2]

In fact, Dutcher had heard rumors that Ratliff had vowed to "get" the sheriff for the bootlegging charge that resulted in him being sent to the Pendleton Reformatory for eighteen months. Ratliff didn't come from a good family, reporters noted. A native of Attica, Indiana, he had been known for shooting off his mouth and having a temper.

His brother, Oak Ratliff, committed suicide by taking poison in the summer of 1915 as the sheriff approached to arrest him for stealing and reselling another farmer's team of mules.

Claire's resentment toward the police was real and only got nastier in his eighteen months behind bars.

On this night, despite not believing Ratliff to be a dangerous man, Marshal Briar told investigators that he had searched him briefly when they first encountered him on the street. "Ratliff was walking a step or two ahead of us, and when he came to the stairs leading to McCabe's [office], Ratliff went on. Dutcher said, 'Here, where are you going? This is the stairs.' Ratliff whirled around and pointed the pistol we did not know he had and said, 'I'm not going up there and you're not going to turn a key on me.'"[3]

Briar said he and Dutcher talked the young man out of shooting them— even though he had the "jump" on them as the two officers' guns were still in their holsters. Dutcher convinced Ratliff to go back to his Ford Roadster. which was parked in front of the Spear Grocery Store, so they could go to Attorney McCabe's home.

"[Ratliff] sat behind the steering wheel, Dutcher then got in and I climbed in after them," Marshal Briar recalled. "Dutcher had no more got in when he grabbed Ratliff's right hand with his left hand and grabbed at Ratliff's throat with his right hand. I grabbed at Ratliff's left hand [as well]."[4]

Ratliff broke free of the sheriff's grasp, and the two men scuffled on the front car seat for a few moments. Ratliff fell out of the still-parked car with the sheriff on top of him.

As they fell to the street, Briar said the sheriff's gun fell from his pocket and "quick as lightning, Ratliff pulled his own pistol and shot the sheriff."[5]

Briar was able to strike Ratliff at least twice on the head with his billy club, the second blow causing the wood implement to break in half.

"Sheriff Dutcher swooned to the street as he got out of the automobile," the *Journal & Courier* reported. "He called to Marshal Briar, 'He got me twice,' … he died before medical aid could be summoned."[6]

The *Williamsport Review Republican* noted that Mr. and Mrs. Luther Spear, owners of the grocery store who were closing their store for the night, brought a seat cushion out for Dutcher to be placed on. He died on the spot.

Other witnesses reported Ratliff shot at the sheriff three times in the scuffle; another said they heard four shots. All agreed that immediately after the shots, Ratliff fled quickly on foot. As he did, Marshal Briar fired at least two shots at him, with Ratliff returning fire. Briar was uninjured and was unsure if any of his bullets had struck Ratliff.

Two deadly shots struck Sheriff Dutcher, one through his left shoulder, lodging in the chest, and a second shot into his stomach near his navel. Warren County Coroner Van Hamilton ruled it was the second shot that caused his death.

"Never in history has citizenry in such magnitude turned out in a manhunt in this section of Indiana," the *Journal & Courier* declared. "Before daylight, more than a thousand men and boys were patrolling the highways in every section of Warren and Fountain counties."[7]

Indiana State Police immediately joined the search, enlisting the aid of hound dogs from Illinois to try and track Ratliff's trail from the downtown shooting. Governor Ed Jackson also ordered Company F of the Indiana National Guard to assist in the search for the "desperado."

"Avis Dutcher was popular with the people of his county, and his friends were out to avenge his death," one report noted. "Although they knew the man who had slain the sheriff was a desperate character, the spirit of fear did not enter into a single man or boy who took part in the hunt."[8]

The posse, though intense, was unsuccessful, and the community turned its attention to honoring Sheriff Dutcher with a large funeral at the Methodist Episcopal Church. Attendance was estimated at more than 2,000.

Dutcher's wife, Dora, a nurse at Home Hospital in Lafayette, had raced to her husband's side on Saturday night when informed he had been shot. His body had remained at their home until the time of the funeral. The Dutchers had a full and busy home as the parents of two of their own children (the youngest just nineteen months old) and three from Dutcher's first marriage that ended when his wife died.

Early on Thursday morning, September 23, Ralph Robinson, the night telegraph operator at the Wabash railroad station in Williamsport, was ending his shift of duty and caught the distinctive odor of decaying flesh. Upon investigation, he found the badly decomposed body of a man lying hidden on a steep hill behind the railroad station. An autopsy confirmed the body was that of Ratliff.

The coroner declared the death a suicide after finding Ratliff's .15-caliber handgun lying next to his body. Three bullet holes were found in the body, however, suggesting at least two of Marshal Briar's shots in the downtown shootout had hit their mark. One shot through the heart, from a .15-caliber weapon, was the fatal one.

Endnotes
1. *Williamsport Review Republican*, September 23, 1926.
2. *Lafayette Journal & Courier*, Sept. 20, 1926.
3. Ibid.
4. Ibid.
5. Ibid.
6. Ibid.
7. Ibid.
8. Ibid.

WARRICK COUNTY

VICTIM(S):
Brandy R. Southard, 21;
Kathy Tyler, 29;
John Jay Tyler, Jr., 29

PERPETRATOR(S):
John M. Stephenson, 33

DATE OF DEATH(S):
March 28, 1996

A RECORD-SETTING TRIAL FOR A TRIPLE MURDERER

Prosecutors never revealed a specific a motive for the crime behind the longest and most expensive trial in Indiana history, but it didn't matter.

After 140 total trial days stretching from opening statements on September 24, 1996 to sentencing on June 17, 1997, jurors took only three hours to return a verdict of guilty against thirty-three-year-old John Matthew Stephenson of Rockport, Indiana, for the ambush murders of three Warrick County residents.

Taxpayers shelled out more than a half million dollars to convict Stephenson in a trial that produced a bound transcript of 132 volumes, each volume 250 pages in length.[1]

Prosecutors took 122 days presenting testimony from eighty-five separate witnesses. Defense attorneys took thirteen days to call fifty witnesses.

Attorneys for both the state and Stephenson's defense made no apologies.

"It's taken longer than we anticipated to get to this point," Warrick County Prosecutor Todd Corne told jurors in a tremendous understatement as he began his closing argument.[2]

Defense attorney Anthony Long thanked jurors for "tolerating" him over the many months of the trial. He continued, "When you believe in a case [and] believe in what you do, you do it with a passion."[3]

Jurors made quicker work of their tasks. After just three hours of deliberation, they convicted Stephenson of three counts of murder and later recommended the death penalty.

At his sentencing, reporters described Stephenson as entering with a smile, seemingly confident of an acquittal on charges that were never attached to a specific motive. As the verdicts were read, his head fell and he stared at the floor.

Family members of victims Kathy and John Tyler, both twenty-nine years old, and twenty-one-year-old Brandy Southard wept as the verdicts were read. This portion of their long nightmare had concluded. It was an especially important ending for Brande Tyler, who was just ten years old when both of her parents were gunned down.

All three victims died during a violent ambush sometime either late on Thursday, March 28, 1996, or during the early morning hours of Friday, March 29, 1996. The exact time of death, never pinpointed by either side at trial, was a key bone of contention as Stephenson attempted to offer an alibi for the time prosecutors believe the murders occurred.

Witnesses called against Stephenson provided damning testimony.

Two of them, Brian Mossberger and Dale Funk, placed the thirty-round SKS assault rifle and knife used to kill the three victims in Stephenson's hands.

Funk testified he was with Stephenson when the fatal shots were fired near the intersection of two gravel roads, Eble and Youngblood, near Yankeetown, Indiana, in southeastern Warrick County.

Mossberger told the jury Stephenson and Funk visited him on the night of the shootings and that the two men left to chase a pickup truck driven by John Tyler. He said they later returned asking him to hide the assault rifle. They washed off a bloody knife and said, "Jay, Kathy, and Brandy are no more."[4]

Jurors also heard portions of a taped interview Stephenson gave to two Indiana State Police detectives.

Other witnesses provided a direct trail for the Chinese-made SKS assault rifle used to kill the three victims. Prosecution witnesses included the gun dealer who sold the weapon when it was new in 1993, a variety store owner who resold the gun in 1995, and a Newtonville, Indiana, man who testified that Stephenson purchased the gun from him at his yard sale for $100 just weeks before the March 28, 1996, shooting.

Defense attorneys pointed to a lack of physical evidence linking Stephenson to the crime. Forensic experts testified that Stephenson's Buick Regal contained no blood or other evidence, although Indiana State Police sergeant David Lee Anderson told the court "it was very unusual to me that we found nothing in the vehicle" and suggested it had been cleaned up before being nabbed by police.[5]

Stephenson's defense attorneys focused most of their effort on attempts to bring before the jury multiple other theories and suspects for the killings. They even presented a civil engineer to provide estimates of driving times between various locations where Stephenson was seen the night of the attack in an attempt to create doubt that he could have been present when the shooting occurred.

The valiant defense effort continued even during the sentencing phase, when defense attorneys called Sister Helen Prejean, best-selling author of the novel *Dead Men Walking*, to testify about her beliefs that the death penalty was a cruel and inappropriate sentence.

Regardless, Warrick County Superior Court Judge Edward Campbell sentenced Stephenson on June 17, 1997, to die by lethal injection as punishment for his crimes.

The crimes were discovered at 7 a.m. on that Friday morning by passersby who saw the Tylers' 1980 Datsun pickup truck in a ditch along the side of the road and all three passengers dead on the truck's only seat.

The investigation revealed the Tylers had given Brandy Southard a ride home from her job in Evansville at 10 p.m. Thursday night. The murder scene was just a mile from her home. Southard had suffered a seizure in the weeks before and had stopped driving her own car until doctors could determine what was wrong with her.

Family members of all of the victims were dumbfounded about why the attack had occurred, although Southard's family reported she had received menacing phone calls in the last few weeks from a man threatening to burn down her mobile home.

The pickup truck was riddled with bullets, Warrick County Sheriff Bruce Hargrave said, estimating the truck was struck between ten and thirty times. The shots were all believed to have been fired from behind the truck.

One of the truck's rear wheels was found burned to the rim. John Tyler's foot rested on the accelerator at the time he died, indicating the trio was attempting to flee the barrage when the crash occurred.

Investigators focused their probe on Stephenson, and an arrest warrant was issued for him. He turned himself in to police in Owensboro, Kentucky, on April 6, 1996.

Before his trial would even start, defense attorney Long would try and focus attention on other possible suspects. A separate drug trial involving Herschel Seifert of Boonville, Indiana, brought a dramatic twist.

Long asked Seifert on the stand whether he had ordered Stephenson to murder the Tylers and Southard.

"Based on my rights under the Fifth Amendment, I respectfully refuse to answer," he said.[6]

Seifert was facing charges related to more than a pound of "crank" found at his Posey County home.

Prosecutor Corne was unimpressed. He acknowledged that Seifert's trial may have revealed possible motives, such as grudges held by area drug dealers for alleged unpaid "crank" or methamphetamine debts by the Tylers or alleged snitching to police about drug activity by Southard. But he said none of that exonerated Stephenson.

"If there was some conspiracy … I don't have any reason to dispute or disagree with that," Corne said. "But at this point, I don't see how that absolves John Stephenson of committing this offense."[7]

Corne said Seifert's trial could indicate others may also need to be charged, "but I don't see anything in that that would show me that Mr. Stephenson shouldn't be sitting where he is."[8]

Stephenson appealed his conviction to the Indiana Supreme Court in January 1999, claiming that two key state witnesses should not have been allowed to testify, alleging one of them lied to police investigators.

Although appealing his sentence, Stephenson said in a 1997 interview that he may actually prefer being executed to life in prison.

"What's life in prison?" Stephenson asked. "What kind of life do I have to look forward to. I think [being executed] would be a blessing. No suffering man, no suffering."[9]

The state's highest court rejected Stephenson's direct appeal in January 2001, but he filed an additional post-conviction relief appeal a year later. In it, he argued that the use of a stun belt under his clothes at the trial prejudiced jurors against him.

If Stephenson had misbehaved during the trial, sheriff's deputies could have delivered a painful electric shock to him with a remote control but never had to. The appeal noted that at least four of the jurors knew he was wearing the belt.

Indiana State Police detective Marvin Heilman, the lead investigator on the case, was not swayed. "The facts were that [Stephenson] committed the crime and there was no evidence to show anyone else did… The witnesses we had … were easy to attack because of their lifestyle," Heilman said. "But most murder victims don't get killed on their way to church. Most people, by their lifestyle, take chances and maybe they shouldn't."[10]

Stephenson's post-conviction appeal was stymied by the Indiana Supreme Court which voted unanimously in April 2007 to reject it. Chief Justice Randall Shepard took particular issue with Stephenson's claims that he lacked proper defense counsel at trial. Shepard noted that the trial was the longest and most expensive in state history—and that he had been afforded a defense "well beyond any notion of what the Sixth Amendment guarantees."[11]

Stephenson may still file federal appeals to his conviction.

Endnotes

1. *Evansville Courier*, July 14, 1998; *Indianapolis Star*, Feb. 7, 1999.
2. *Evansville Courier*, May 9, 1997.
3. Ibid.
4. Ibid.
5. *Evansville Courier*, March 25, 1997.
6. *Evansville Courier*, May 7, 1997.
7. Ibid.
8. Ibid.
9. *Evansville Courier*, Sept. 27, 1999.
10. *Evansville Courier*, January 25, 1999.
11. *Evansville Courier & Press*, April 27, 2007.

WASHINGTON COUNTY

VICTIM(S):

Patton Gibson, 70;
Otis "Odie" Gibson, 21;
William Gibson, 45

PERPETRATOR(S):

Pleas Spurlock, 31 (slaying of Patton Gibson);
John Spurlock, 36 (slaying of Patton Gibson);
Arch Bishop, 47 (slaying of William Gibson)

DATE OF DEATH(S):

December 14, 1930 (Patton Gibson slaying);
December 27, 1930 (Otis "Odie" Gibson slaying);
October 31, 1940 (William Gibson slaying)

A DEADLY FAMILY FEUD

Feuds have been at the center of American folklore and mythology for generations. Almost everyone has heard of the Hatfields and the McCoys simply on the basis of their long-held family feuds. Comic strips, books, movies, songs, and even a TV game show—*"Family Feud"*—are built around the old trope that violent feuds between rival families can stretch out across generations.

Salem, Indiana was the site of an infamous family feud where scores were settled at the end of a gun. On the snowy night of December 27, 1930, Otis, Gifford, Daniel, and Alonzo Gibson, all brothers, stormed the Washington County Jail in downtown Salem in an attempt to exact revenge on the two men accused of killing their seventy-year-old father, Patton Gibson. The Gibson boys, apparently convinced that courthouse justice was not to be found and accustomed to another form of justice brought with them to Indiana from their East Tennessee homes, were intent on revenge. In the end, Otis Gibson would be dead and the other three Gibson boys became short-lived fugitives later rounded up by local sheriff's posse.

The Gibson-Spurlock feud, at the base of the violence that struck Salem, was a long-simmering one that the families brought with them to Indiana from Tennessee. As the Great Depression settled in, life in many Appalachian regions of the nation grew desperate. Many families moved west; the Gibson's and the Spurlock's settled, at least temporarily, in Indiana.

Feuds are detailed in American history as far back as the eighteenth century, but gain their notorious reputation particularly from the first half of the twentieth century. "(Feuds) have become an entrenched part of mythology and folklore that many Americans are surprised to discover actually happened and that the feudists were real people," historian Altina L. Waller posits in her book, *Feud: Hatfields, McCoys, and Social Change in Appalachia, 1860-1900.1* The mythology surrounding feuds, however, has obscured thinking about the feud as a historic event, and it has become readily subject to exaggeration and legend. Waller links the existence of feuds to southern and isolated rural areas of the United States as a result of broader isolation from any diversity and a lack of formal education (both attributable to the bypassing of mountainous regions of West Virginia, Tennessee, and Kentucky for more fertile and more easily harnessed flat lands of Indiana, Ohio and Illinois). Alcohol abuse, homemade alcohol, government efforts to restrict its production and consumption, the growing monetary value of booze as government restrictions were applied, and familial traditions based on honor above all else have created volatile moments born out of a lack of restraint and self-control.

The Gibson brothers knew all about violence in the preservation of honor. As they stormed the county jail that cold night, they were seemingly intent on hurting anyone who got in their way. The Spurlock brothers apparently lived by a similar standard—local authorities said the initial murder of the elderly Patton Gibson had been fueled by boasts the old man and his sons had made of allegedly killing some of their Spurlock rivals during a recent visit back to West Virginia and Tennessee.

A first-person account of the attack at the jail was offered in the days following by Ida Trinkle, wife of Washington County Sheriff Milton Trinkle. She said, "My husband and I were alone [at the sheriff's living quarters inside the jail] when the Gibson boys came. We didn't suspect they would cause serious trouble. We refused to give them the keys and they started pushing us back toward the door of the jail."[2]

Mrs. Trinkle said her husband attempted to trick the Gibson boys by giving them a key that only opened an outer door inside the jail, not the cell doors holding the Spurlock brothers. An alert merchant across the street from the jail sounded the alarm of trouble at the jail and the Salem town marshal was summoned. "My husband tried to talk to the boys, but they wouldn't listen," she said.[3]

Sheriff Trinkle's "trick," however, proved a bad idea as it locked him, his wife, and the Gibson boys in a small space where they began firing their guns. Both the Sheriff and Mrs. Trinkle suffered non-life threatening wounds and were about to relent and let them have the Spurlock boys when the Gibson brothers' look-out, Otis, engaged in a gun battle on the front porch of the jail with the Salem marshal, Elmer Gerald. Though shot first, Gerald got the better of the melee, fatally wounding Otis with a shot in the chest. Gerald would later recover from his wounds.

When the Gibson boys inside the jail called out for Otis to let them out of the room where the Sheriff had taken them, they heard the shots outside and attempted to bolt. However, the exit door had also been locked. With Otis dead outside there was no escape until Mrs. Trinkle's elderly friend, who stayed with the family in their living quarters, slipped in and released the lock. Gifford, Daniel, and Alonzo Gibson fled the scene, racing past their dead brother Otis without their expected catch, the Spurlock brothers.

"The three Gibson boys fled and Mr. Trinkle and myself got out the best we could the way we were shot up," Mrs. Trinkle reported. "Neither of us [was] seriously wounded. I got several shots in the leg from the shotgun, and it's pretty painful. I have been taking care of the telephone calls here (at the jail) because there's nobody else to do it." Mrs. Trinkle seemed to take it all in stride, however, telling reporters that "it sure was a busy place around here for a while, and a mighty exciting time."[4]

Since Sheriff Trinkle also injured, local merchants and residents joined a former sheriff and about two hundred volunteers to scour the county looking for the Gibson brothers. Meanwhile, state police officials were called in to relocate the Spurlock brothers to the more secure Clark County Jail at Jeffersonville. The Associated Press reported on its national wire, "Salem tonight took on a military appearance, with a constant movement of men carrying rifles and shotguns, either joining the posse or returning for a rest. Members of the American Legion tramped through the swirling snow, and drifts covered places where the posse had hoped it might be possible to track the objects of their search."[5]

Gifford Gibson (whose name was sometimes reported as "Gilford") was the first brother found—at his home in rural Washington County. He declared to the posse, "I'll come peaceful so long as you ain't got no Spurlocks with you."[6] He was initially held at the Floyd County Jail in New Albany for safe-keeping, but was eventually released after posting bond on an odd charge of "burglary" for having attempted to help remove the Spurlock brothers from the Salem jail. The other three Gibson brothers were never apprehended.[7]

The fact that the Gibson brothers remained at large prompted heavy security for the Spurlock brothers' trial that went underway months later in October 1931 at the Jackson County Courthouse in nearby Brownstown. Jackson County Sheriff Meredith Stewart confirmed he had received reports that the Gibson boys might once again try to exact revenge, but he vowed no such thing would happen. "I am going to do my best to thwart any feud killings in my county," Stewart said. "I will carry a high-powered rifle when I escort the Spurlock's back and forth between the jail and the courthouse. If anybody tries to pot my prisoners, I'll shoot to kill." The sheriff also ordered all members of the Spurlock family attending the trial to be searched for weapons before entering the courthouse.[8]

The Jackson County jury deliberated for twelve hours before rendering a guilty verdict for manslaughter in October 1931 for both Pleas and John Spurlock in the death of Patton Gibson. They were later sentenced to a term of two to twenty-one years in prison. Both were released on parole on the same day five years later in October 1936 and ordered to "stay out of Indiana and Tennessee" as a term of their probation. Both men relocated to Virginia; Pleas took work as a miner, and John worked in farming.[9]

By this time, the long-simmering Gibson-Spurlock feud had resulted in twelve reported deaths over a period of three decades.[10] This was not the last time, however, that the Gibson family would make headlines for wanton violence. On Halloween Day, 1940, William Gibson, then forty-five years old and the younger brother of the fugitive Gibson brothers who had stormed the jail nine years earlier, was shot and killed in a corridor of the Washington County Courthouse in Salem as he emerged from a grand jury room.

William Gibson was being questioned by members of the grand jury about a shooting days earlier at a Millport tavern in which he was accused of firing a gun into a moving vehicle. Washington County Sheriff Charles W. Moore witnessed the shooting of Gibson in the courthouse and immediately disarmed and arrested Arch Bishop, an angry forty-seven-year-old father of one of the boys that William Gibson had allegedly menaced with a firearm. Bishop, a local farmer, had already testified before the grand jury but waited outside for Gibson to emerge before shooting him.[11] Bishop was later housed in the same cells that held Pleas and John Spurlock less than ten years earlier for the murder of another Gibson family member.

A Washington County jury found Bishop guilty on a charge of manslaughter and he was sentenced to a term of two to twenty-one years. He served just under two years, winning parole in December 1943 with a caveat that he never again possess a weapon of any kind.[12]

Endnotes

1. Waller, Altina L. (1988). *Feud: Hatfields, McCoys, and Social Change in Appalachia, 1860-1900.* Chapel Hill, NC: University of North Carolina Press.
2. Associated Press, Dec. 28, 1930
3. Associated Press, Dec. 28, 1930
4. Associated Press, Dec. 28, 1930
5. Associated Press, Dec. 30, 1930
6. United Press, Dec. 29, 1930
7. INS News Service, Oct. 6, 1931
8. INS News Service, Oct. 6, 1931

9. Indiana State Archives, Indiana Commission on Public Records
10. *New York Times*, Dec. 28, 1930
11. Associated Press, Oct. 31, 1940
12. Indiana State Archives, Indiana Commission on Public Records

WAYNE COUNTY

VICTIM(S):
Mary Kathleen "Katina" Phillips, 11

PERPETRATOR(S):
Earl E. Sauerheber, 15

DATE OF DEATH(S):
Sometime after June 15, 1986

TWO YOUNG LIVES INTERSECT IN MURDER

Earl Sauerheber and Katina Phillips were two young people experiencing the understandable restlessness of living in a small town, being young, and wanting to do more than their ages would allow.

Katina was only eleven years old. Her mother was appropriately cautious about what her daughter did and where she went. In fact, the last time Katina's mother, Mary Phillips, ever saw her was when she arrived home from work on June 15, 1986. That evening, Katina chose to leave the house without permission.

Sauerheber, just fifteen-years-old in 1986, had already established a record as a teenager who could find trouble. That year, he was transferred to the Wernle Children's Home in Katina's working-class neighborhood in Richmond, Indiana. Sauerheber had been sent to the Wernle Home, about 180 miles from his home in New Albany, after being involved in two assaults.

Sauerheber was housed at the Wernle Karner House facility near Katina's home at 107 S. 13th St. in Richmond. Katina had come to know several of the boys who lived there, including a few she liked so much she had written their names or initials along the edges of her tennis shoes.

When Katina left home without permission, Mary Phillips kept up her search for her during all the hours she wasn't at work. She heard from one neighbor that Katina had been seen at the Richmond Rose Festival that summer. As July gave way to August, she still had not been home, and Mary was heartsick with worry.

"She hasn't been back here to the house. All her clothes are still there," Mary said. "She's very mature for her age. She likes to go places and do things. It makes no sense to me, unless she just wants to be her own boss."[1]

Three days later on Saturday morning, August 10, 1986, news would work its way through the neighborhood that the badly decomposed body of a young child had been found inside a home at 105 S. 12th St., just a block from Mary Phillips' home. The landlord of the vacant house was cutting grass and doing yard work and decided to check on the interior of the house.

Inside, police and Wayne County Coroner Paul Patterson found a child's body. A front window on the vacant home was broken, apparently allowing someone to gain entry.

The news shook Mary Phillips, but she held out hope.

"It's really cruel," Mary told a reporter from the *Richmond Palladium-Item*. "People keep shoving articles in your face about somebody finding a little girl dead. God!"[2]

Mary's hope was resting on a report that a girl fitting Katina's description was seen on the previous Saturday at a free clothing shop. "I just keep telling myself that she was seen last Saturday," Mary said.[3]

Coroner Patterson said the state of decomposition made it next to impossible to accurately estimate the age or gender of the child. Patterson did believe the child had likely been dead about eight weeks.

By the next morning, Mary's hopes were dashed.

"There's no doubt," Patterson told reporters. The body was that of Katina. Dental records compared with the corpse confirmed the worst. Mary also identified jewelry and clothing found with the body as belonging to Katina.

Her body was found naked except for a shirt found tied around her neck. Her remaining clothing was piled in another room. Underneath her clothing, police found a light bulb from which they obtained a latent fingerprint.

Police and the coroner would not immediately reveal the cause of death. A few days later, however, a death certificate for Katina listed her cause of death as ligature strangulation.

When her body was placed in the vacant home, or the exact day she was killed, would remain a mystery for now. Police records indicated a run to the vacant house on June 16, 1986, and no body was found that day.

Katina's father, Jack Phillips, said his daughter had never run away before and described her as a happy child. Teachers and classmates at her school, Vaile Elementary School, described her as a good student, a sweet child. In her recently completed fourth-grade school year, she'd been named "Most Improved Student of the Year" for her class.

Police immediately turned their focus on the Wernle facility, Karner House, on South 13th Street, situated a one to two block walk from Katina's house and the vacant house where her body was found. Tips to police indicated that one or more of the boys housed there may know something about Katina's death. And neighbors reported some of the boys were known to enter the vacant house where Katina had been found.

Further pointing toward the Karner House were the names of boys who lived there that Katina had written on her tennis shoes. Katina's mother, Mary Phillips, said her daughter often visited the group home.

Search warrants were issued for the Karner House at 59 S. 13th St. to look for items belonging to Katina. The search warrant specified police could look for tennis shoes belonging to two boys living at the home and take finger- and palm prints from the two boys. Police reportedly gathered three pairs of shoes and other items.[4]

Just as police seemed to be narrowing their search for Katina's killer, the clues began to disappear. Difficulties in questioning the juvenile boys housed at the Karner House also contributed to problems investigating the case, police said (although Wernle officials later strongly denied claims they kept the boys from being questioned by police). Unable to question the boys and blocked in their efforts to gain saliva and pubic hair samples and additional fingerprints from other boys, by 1992, Richmond Police declared the case inactive.

But in August 1995, Richmond Police received a tip that proved promising. A former resident of the Karner House told police he believed Sauerheber was involved with Katina and may have been responsible for her death. Detectives immediately interviewed their source, now an inmate at the Wayne County Jail, who told them Karner House officials had "told us all to be quiet" about the case (again, a charge Wernle officials denied).[5]

Detectives then went to the Lawrence County Jail at Bedford where Sauerheber was being held on a separate assault charge. Now a twenty-five-year-old man, Sauerheber faced a mountain of evidence police were piling up.

Police had confirmed Sauerheber was AWOL from Karner House from June 14-16, 1986. They also matched his fingerprints from when he was booked at the jail with the print found on the light bulb under Katina's discarded clothing.

Sauerheber denied knowing Katina or having any involvement in her death. A warrant was issued on August 21, 1995, allowing police to collect samples of his hair, saliva, and blood.

Four days later, Sauerheber was transferred to the Wayne County Jail in Richmond and subjected to more questioning.

Under questioning, he admitted that he had strangled Katina during a sexual encounter that went wrong and after she bit his finger in the tussle. Sauerheber said Katina had agreed to some mutual touching and kissing and had removed her clothes at his request. However, when he attempted copulation, Katina resisted and asked him to stop. It was during this time she bit Sauerheber while trying to defend herself.

Sauerheber was arrested August 28, 1995, and charged with Katina's murder. Although he was fifteen years old at the time of the crime, a juvenile under Indiana law, juvenile jurisdiction over his case was eventually waived, and he was tried for murder, felony murder, and attempted rape as an adult.

Police were relieved to have solved the case but still angry they were thwarted in their efforts to reach Sauerheber earlier.

A jury convicted Sauerheber of murder and one count of attempted rape. On October 3, 1996, Wayne County Superior Court Judge Robert Reinke sentenced Sauerheber to sixty years for his crimes. Judge Reinke said the maximum sentence was required, given Sauerheber's violent history, which included an additional charge brought against him for the alleged strangling of a thirty-two-year-old Floyd County woman in 1992.

"There is every indication that the defendant values no one's life, with the exception of his own," Judge Reinke said.

In September 1998, the Indiana Supreme Court affirmed Sauerheber's sentence on an appeal he filed, based mostly around his claims that the statement he gave police implicating himself was improperly gained. The court disagreed.

In 2007, Sauerheber was incarcerated at the Wabash Valley Correctional Facility in Carlisle, Indiana. From there, he placed a personal ad on the Web site, friendsbehindthewall.com, in which he asked for correspondence from a "special lady."

He wrote, "I hope that after you have read my ad, you will take it into your heart to let me hear from you. I'm looking for someone special who will give me the opportunity to prove my sincereness."[6]

Calling himself a "laid back, open-minded" guy—he said his goals were to prepare for the future and outlined completing associate's and bachelor's degrees from Indiana State University while in prison.

"Please feel free to touch me with your kind words," he wrote. "I look forward to hearing from you."[7]

Endnotes
1. *Richmond Palladium-Item*, Aug. 7, 1986.
2. *Richmond Palladium-Item*, Aug. 11, 1986.

3. Ibid.
4. *Richmond Palladium-Item*, Aug. 15, 1986.
5. *Richmond Palladium-Item*, Aug. 29, 1995.
6. From www.friendsbehindthewall.com
7. Ibid.

WELLS COUNTY

VICTIM(S):
Bruce Moser, 20;
Maragret "Meg" Moser, 22

PERPETRATOR(S):
None ever charged.

DATE OF DEATH(S):
January 6, 1978

A YOUNG FAMILY IN LOVE DESTROYED

The pastor who eulogized Bruce and Margaret "Meg" Moser at their funeral remarked: "Margaret and Bruce had joy and happiness in their little mobile home. Now God has called them to a better home. This home never can be destroyed."[1]

It was a reminder to those who gathered to mourn the murdered young couple that life is short, but even in a short life, love and joy can be shared with one another. Love and joy were what brought the two together as students at Portland High School in nearby Jay County, and kept them as husband and wife. It also guided their new roles as parents to their young daughter in the trailer home they rented along Indiana State Road 3, just north of the Wells-Blackford county line, near Montpelier, Indiana. It was an isolated area, the nearest neighbors more than a mile away, but it was convenient to Bruce's job as a meat cutter at Bob's IGA Supermarket in Huntington, and Meg's just-completed studies at Ball State University in Muncie.

Love and joy, however, were tragically missing from Bruce and Meg's last day, January 6, 1978, as both were shot execution style in their home. The whole story of their horror would not be known until January 8, however, when the Wells County sheriff answered a call to check on the couple's welfare after Bruce failed to report to work for two days.

Bruce, just twenty years old and a few short years removed from a noteworthy basketball career for the Portland High School Panthers and a

480

few semesters at Ball State University, was found still wearing his winter coat, his hands and feet tied with the laces from his boots. He lay face-down on the living room floor, shot at least twice in the back of the head. Meg, twenty-two, was found lying face-up in her bed, naked from the waist down with indications she had been tied up previously. She had been shot at least twice in the head. Tests later confirmed she likely was sexually assaulted.

The couple's seventeen-month-old daughter, Kerri Allyn, was found blood-soaked and crying on the bed next to her mother. Other than suffering from dehydration from being alone for at least two days, the child suffered no injuries. Kerri Allyn was taken from the home to a local hospital for treatment, and released later to her grandparents.[2]

Investigators know that Bruce asked to leave work early on Wednesday, January 6, to take his wife to a doctor's appointment. Meg never made the appointment, fueling speculation that Bruce may have surprised an intruder who was already in his home when he returned home from work early that day. A .22-caliber rifle belonging to Bruce was found in the home along with shell casings, believed to be the murder weapon.

Wells County Sheriff Paul Gerwig was first on the scene and was shocked by what he found. He spotted Bruce's lifeless body through a door window at the trailer and called for back-up, and then he used a box to step on to see into a bedroom window where he saw Meg lying dead on her bed and the eyes of little Kerri Allyn staring back at him.

"The sheriff said his initial thought was a heart-gripping one that the child was dead in that fixed-gaze pose," the *Bluffton News-Banner* reported. "But the eyes seemed to widen even more ... quickly detectives summoned by the sheriff were on the scene and with the sheriff they kicked in the locked front door, entering the midst of the gruesome tragedy setting."[3]

Sheriff Gerwig was "deeply moved and grieved" and reporters noted, "tough lawman that he may be, [he] simply cannot shake off the emotion of that moment, amid his dedication toward helping solve the crime and day-night toil since the discovery."[4]

Multiple theories began to emerge: Was the massacre the result of a botched home invasion and/or rape attempt on Meg? Had Meg met someone while completing her bachelor's degree in criminal justice at Ball State University who had developed an unnatural interest in her? Had Bruce made someone angry who sought revenge? Or was it just a random, cruel act by a thief or drug-crazed soul?

The questions outnumbered the answers for a long time.

Police even pursued the idea that the murders were somehow connected to an earlier murder case where Bruce had been a witness for the prosecution. Bruce had testified at trial about his discovery of the body of Ronald Parks, twenty-seven, of Union City, Ohio, along a Jay County road on March 2, 1974. Bruce had been returning from a late-night date with Meg when he spotted the body dumped along a rural county road.

Three Union City, Indiana, men were implicated in the case, one being convicted of first-degree murder, but court records showed Bruce's testimony had been limited only to his discovery of the body. He had not provided material evidence to convict any of the men, police said, meaning revenge against him seemed unlikely.[5]

Local business leaders posted a $1,000 reward for information on the case, and police diligently pursued every possible lead for years to come. Despite their best efforts, three decades later, the case remains officially unsolved. A suspect, a local trucker and industrial worker from Fort Wayne known to travel in the area, was questioned but never charged or tried for the murders. Most investigators believed he was the man responsible but lacked evidence to arrest him.

Endnotes

1. *Bluffton News-Banner*, Jan. 10, 1978.
2. *Bluffton News-Banner*, Jan. 9, 1978.
3. Ibid.
4. Ibid.
5. *Portland Commercial Review*, Jan. 7, 1978.

WHITE COUNTY

VICTIM(S):
Gregory W. Debish, II, 3;
John Michael Shanklin, 2;
Christopher M. Shanklin, six months

PERPETRATOR:
Elizabeth K. Shanklin, 60

DATE OF DEATH(S):
Gregory – May 10, 1995;
Christopher – June 29, 1974;
John – September. 26, 1974

AN EVIL HISTORY REPEATS

When Elizabeth Shanklin's two sons died within about ninety days of each other in 1974, many, many questions were raised about the two children: John Michael aged five-years, and Christopher only six months old.

In 1974, both boys' deaths were investigated by local police and child welfare officials, but no criminal charges were ever brought. The infant Christopher had died first – on June 29, 1974 – and the cause of death was ruled Sudden Infant Death Syndrome. Sympathy poured in for Elizabeth and her husband Michael and her young daughter Melissa and her other son John.

Unbelievably, death struck the Shanklin home for a second time just three months later on September 26, 1974 when two-year-old John was found dead. The investigation into his death resulted in a ruling that he had died of acute bronchitis.[1]

It would take nearly three decades, but eventually Elizabeth began to tell the real truth of what had happened to her sons, but not before a third boy in her care was dead. Sadly, on May 10, 1995, Shanklin's five-year-old grandson, Gregory Debish II, was dead. Gregory, the son of Elizabeth's daughter Melissa and her estranged husband, Gregory Debish I, had been placed in Elizabeth's care after both of the boy's parents were jailed. Melissa was awaiting hearings for allegedly setting her husband's home on fire, and Gregory was later jailed

483

on a child neglect charge for going to work and leaving his child unattended at home.

Because no investigation back in 1974 had revealed anything was wrong with Elizabeth's two sons dying suddenly in one three-month period, as the grandmother to Gregory II, she was allowed to care for the boy. Surprising to anyone but perhaps Elizabeth herself, an ambulance was summoned to her home on May 10, 1995 as Gregory II was not breathing and later died as a result of asphyxiation.

A neighbor, Sandy Scott, sixty-four, told police that Shanklin had come to her home and asked to use the telephone to call for medical help for the boy. Scott said she offered to rush the boy to the nearest hospital ten miles away. "It was a nightmare I tried to forget," Scott said. "She came and got me. I saw the little guy. His lips were just so blue."[2]

In the months that followed a White County grand jury indicted Elizabeth for her grandson's death, a charge to which she plead guilty in May 1996. Prosecutors had wanted to include charges for the deaths of the other two boys in 1974, but lacked a lot of evidence to make their case, and settled for a guilty plea from Elizabeth to Gregory's death.

In 2003, while she was serving her sentence for Gregory's death, Elizabeth began talking to correctional staff about a series of bad dreams she was having. Elizabeth told a counselor that her dreams kept showing her the faces of her two dead sons, Christopher and John.

Shanklin originally approached a staff psychiatrist at the Rockville Correctional Center about her concerns, but was advised that any incriminating statements she may make would not be held in confidence and would be reported to authorities. Frustrated and still wanting to unburden herself, Shanklin then approach the prison's female chaplain, Beverly Roddy, and began to confide in her. She also later confided in another prison counselor and agreed to tell her story to police.

In January and February 2003, detectives from the White County Sheriff's Department and the Indiana State Police interviewed Shanklin. It was then she confessed that she had, in fact, smothered both John and Christopher back in 1974.

White County Prosecutor Robert Guy told reporters that Shanklin said she killed her sons "because she was selfish and didn't want them to have the attention . . . that she could not get from other people." He added that Shanklin provided "new information [that] confirmed all our beliefs that these were not mere family tragedies—they were intentional events."[3]

Everyone wanted to know, why had Shanklin done it—killed her two sons, and later her grandson. Investigators pieced together through their interviews with her that Christopher was killed out of frustration with his crying. John and Gregory were later killed, it seems, because Shanklin enjoyed the sympathy and attention the deaths had given her from family and friends.

In October 2005, Shanklin agreed to plead guilty to two counts of second degree murder under the laws that were in place in 1974 when she murdered her sons. The plea agreement called for twenty year sentences for each death, to be served consecutively, a sentence finalized in November 2005. John Million, a Monticello attorney who represented Shanklin in the cases involving her sons, argued unsuccessfully that Shanklin's admissions to police and correctional officials about the deaths should be withheld from the court. He argued that the statements were obtained inappropriately, but the court found Shanklin had waived her right to an attorney at the time stating a desire to clear her conscience.[4]

Shanklin only served eleven years of the new sentences. The Indiana Department of Correction reported Shanklin died at the Rockville Correctional Center on October 26, 2016, at the age of sixty-nine, of natural causes.

Endnotes

1 *Indianapolis Star*, April 6, 2005
2 *Indianapolis Star*, April 6, 2005
3 *Indianapolis Star*, April 6, 2005
4 Associated Press, Oct. 23, 2005

WHITLEY COUNTY

VICTIM(S):
Harry Zumbrun, 21

PERPETRATOR(S):
Clarence E. Thomas, 31

DATE OF DEATH(S):
July 3, 1936

GOING BACK TO FINISH THE JOB

Clarence Thomas had made a clean getaway from his last-minute robbery of the Dug Out filling station in northern Whitley County on a sunny Friday morning in 1936, but he went back to "finish the job," fearing he would be identified by the wounded but not dead victim. By doing so, he quickly escalated his previously petty career as a thief and robber to that of a cold-blooded killer.

In "finishing the job," Thomas brutally ended the life of the young filling station operator, Harry Zumbrun, twenty-one, "for the sordid blood money gain of a trifling sum of $32 to replenish losses sustained in an all-night poker game at Fort Wayne Thursday night."[1]

Thomas, thirty-one, a South Bend native, had just rented a cottage a month before the July 3, 1936, incident at nearby Round Lake, near the settlement of Tri-Lakes. Part of his ritual that summer included hanging out in the filling station. He later would tell police that the idea to rob Zumbrun was simply an impulse after catching a glimpse of the cash drawer when it was opened for a customer buying candy.

On that Friday morning, Walter Gaskill, a bakery truck driver for the Holsum Bakery Company of Fort Wayne, stopped by to make a delivery at the Dug Out around 10:40 a.m. He reported Thomas and Zumbrun talking casually when he visited the store. He overheard Thomas talk about wanting to buy the cottage he was renting at Round Lake, and how he enjoyed the quiet Whitley County area over his previous home in the more populous South Bend.

He had reason to enjoy being away from the South Bend area. There he had been sentenced to twenty years of probation for his role in an Elkhart County robbery. He'd also served one year of a one- to ten-year sentence for robbery in Gary.[2]

Shortly after Gaskill left to finish his deliveries, the last person to see Zumbrun alive was Jay Phail of Churubusco, Indiana. Phail purchased gasoline at the station at 11 a.m. and noticed Thomas was still present. Statements from Gaskill and Phail helped police locate and apprehend Thomas the next day as he celebrated Independence Day. As he emerged from his cottage drinking a bottle of beer, he greeted officers politely, and offered no resistance as they placed him under arrest.

His face seemed familiar to investigators—it should have.

Thomas and his wife, Theresa, had visited the crime scene at the Dug Out during the afternoon hours of July 3, along with many other curious area residents, and were ordered from the area by police (before police knew he was a suspect). After leaving the station with his unsuspecting wife, Thomas worked his regular shift at the International Harvester plant in Fort Wayne and returned home early the next day.

Once in custody on Saturday, July 4, intense questioning was undertaken by the Whitley County sheriff and detectives from the Indiana State Police (which included a lie detector test given on Saturday evening by an examiner who drove to Whitley County from Indianapolis to administer it; Thomas failed the test). Eventually, Thomas calmly and matter-of-factly admitted slaying Zumbrun. Newspaper reports credited ISP Detective Al Teusch of the Ligonier Post with breaking Thomas's resolve by showing him grisly photographs taken of Zumbrun's lifeless body splayed out on the gas station floor.

"You hit him in the head, didn't you?" Teusch reportedly jabbed at Thomas, bringing the surprisingly calm response, "Yes, I did it."[3]

Thomas walked officers through the tragic scene, a robbery he repeatedly admitted he did not plan to commit.

"Thomas coolly told us how he committed the crime," said Sergeant Harry Sutherlin of the Indiana State Police. "He first picked up a hammer, which was lying on a counter, and struck Zumbrun on the head with the wooden handle of the hammer, telling him it was a hold-up."[4]

Detectives described Zumbrun as being five foot nine inches tall and of a stocky build of almost 180 pounds—"very strong and capable of putting up a good fight against ordinary odds," Sgt. Sutherlin said. Zumbrun did resist, causing a scuffle between the two men with Thomas striking him in the head a second time, this time with the steel end of the hammer and knocking him unconscious.[5]

Thomas told investigators he made a clean getaway and headed south down State Road 102 toward Tri-Lakes. "I then decided that maybe Zumbrun was not dead and was in misery, and I did not want him to suffer, so I came back, parked my car on the outside of the station by the pumps … went back into the kitchen of the station, found a butcher knife and slashed the unconscious man's throat and fled," Thomas told investigators.[6]

As Thomas left the station for a second time, he was seen driving away by a trucker, Carl Sheets of Decatur, Indiana, who noticed the car and Thomas and moments later discovered Zumbrun's body.

Thomas's motive was simple enough—he had been paid at his International Harvester job on Thursday night his regular $37.50 weekly salary, and subsequently lost it all in a poker game that evening. Afraid to tell his wife he had lost his earnings, Thomas spotted Zumbrun's cash and decided to rob him.

An autopsy showed Zumbrun suffered a brutal attack. Beyond the massive blow to his head just above the left ear that cracked his skull and drove bone fragments into his brain, the victim's throat was slit twice from below the left ear to the right ear, severing the jugular vein. He never had a chance.

The only saving grace was that Zumbrun's young wife, Mary, and their son, Ken Adair, sixteen months old, were away from the small apartment at the back of the filling station visiting relatives.

Zumbrun had leased the station just ten months before the attack, and had suffered one previous hold-up. He graduated from Churubusco High School in 1933, where he was a member of the debate team and band. He and Mrs. Zumbrun were active members of the Blue River Church of the Brethren in nearby Merriam, Indiana. Reports described him as "highly respected and well-liked by all who knew him. For that reason, his untimely end by such a brutal slaying aroused great indignation throughout Churubusco and all of Whitley County," the *Columbia City Post* reported.[7]

Newspaper reports said more than 1,000 people attended Zumbrun's funeral at the Blue River Church, most standing silently outside the church, which quickly was filled to capacity. Zumbrun was laid to rest a short time later at the Christian Chapel Cemetery at Merriam.

Thomas's fate was sealed quickly, with Whitley County grand jury members returning an indictment for the murder and robbery of Zumbrun. Thomas resisted none of the efforts, immediately entering guilty pleas, and had to be convinced by the judge to accept the assistance of a local attorney who happened to be in the courtroom to witness the proceedings. He told officers he preferred death to a life sentence in prison.

"Thomas was very calm when Judge [Rob R.] McNagny informed him that he could see no excuse for the crime and that Thomas must be sentenced to death," the *Columbia City Post* reported.[8]

Final justice also came quickly, with Thomas electrocuted in the state's electric chair at the state prison in Michigan City just after midnight on October 19, 1936. United Press International reported that Thomas "left his death row cell in the state prison three minutes after Midnight and walked to the chair without assistance. The first shock was delivered at 12:04 a.m. Eight minutes later he was removed from the chair ... and pronounced dead. The current was sent through his body for one minute."[9]

United Press's report said that "the slayer weakened only once in his last hours. That was when his wife, Theresa, visited him Sunday afternoon. Both wept but Thomas recovered his composure in a few minutes."[10]

After his wife departed the prison, he enjoyed a last meal reportedly consisting of food he requested—fried chicken, mashed potatoes, biscuits, creamed peas, apple pie, coffee, and cigarettes.

Finally strapped into the electric chair, Thomas made no statement (although he recanted his confession several times in the months leading up to his execution). His wife, Theresa, had made a last-minute appeal to save his life earlier, but no clemency was granted. He was buried in a pauper's grave on the grounds of the state prison at Michigan City.

Endnotes

1. *Columbia City Post*, July 6, 1936.
2. Ibid.
3. Ibid.
4. Ibid.
5. Ibid.
6. Ibid.
7. Ibid.
8. *Columbia City Post*, July 7, 1936.
9. *Columbia City Post*, Oct. 19, 1936.
10. Ibid.